Creo Manufacturing 13 Black Book

By
Gaurav Verma
Matt Weber
(CADCAMCAE Works)

Edited by
Kristen

ISBN # 978-1-77459-226-7

DEDICATION

To teachers, who make it possible to disseminate knowledge
to enlighten the young and curious minds
of our future generations

To students, who are the future of the world

THANKS

To my friends and colleagues

To my family for their love and support

Training and Consultant Services

At CADCAMCAE Works, we provide effective and affordable one to one online training on various software packages in Computer Aided Design(CAD), Computer Aided Manufacturing(CAM), Computer Aided Engineering (CAE), Computer programming languages(C/C++, Java, .NET, Android, JavaScript, HTML and so on). The training is delivered through remote access to your system and voice chat via Internet at any time, any place, and at any pace to individuals, groups, students of colleges/universities, and CAD/CAM/CAE training centers. The main features of this program are:

Training as per your need

Highly experienced Engineers and Technician conduct the classes on the software applications used in the industries. The methodology adopted to teach the software is totally practical based, so that the learner can adapt to the design and development industries in almost no time. The efforts are to make the training process cost effective and time saving while you have the comfort of your time and place, thereby relieving you from the hassles of traveling to training centers or rearranging your time table.

Software Packages on which we provide basic and advanced training are:

CAD/CAM/CAE: CATIA, Creo Parametric, Creo Direct, SolidWorks, Autodesk Inventor, Solid Edge, UG NX, AutoCAD, AutoCAD LT, EdgeCAM, MasterCAM, SolidCAM, DelCAM, BOBCAM, UG NX Manufacturing, UG Mold Wizard, UG Progressive Die, UG Die Design, SolidWorks Mold, Creo Manufacturing, Creo Expert Machinist, NX Nastran, Hypermesh, SolidWorks Simulation, Autodesk Simulation Mechanical, Creo Simulate, Gambit, ANSYS and many others.

Computer Programming Languages: C++, VB.NET, HTML, Android, Javascript and so on.

Game Designing: Unity.

Civil Engineering: AutoCAD MEP, Revit Structure, Revit Architecture, AutoCAD Map 3D and so on.

We also provide consultant services for Design and development on the above mentioned software packages

For more information you can mail us at:
cadcamcaeworks@gmail.com

Table of Contents

Chapter 1 : Starting with Manufacturing

Chapter 2 : Starting with Expert Machinist

Chapter 3 : Tool Setting

Chapter 4 : Machine Setting

Chapter 5 : Operations and Cutting Strategies

Chapter 6 : Creating Toolpaths and Output

Chapter 7 : Introduction to CMM and Managing Post Processor

Chapter 8 : Project

Chapter 9 : Starting with NC Assembly

Chapter 10 : Machine Setup

Chapter 11 : Milling Operations

Chapter 12 : Multi-Axis Milling Operations

Preface

Creo Manufacturing is the group of apps in Creo Elements/Pro package that are used to assist in various streams of Computer Aided Manufacturing like NC Assembly, Expert Machinist, CMM, Sheetmetal, Cast Cavity, Mold Cavity, Harness, and Process Plan. This book covers the applications of Expert Machinist, NC Assembly, and CMM apps. Using the Expert Machinist app, you can create NC programs for machining some of the most difficult machining jobs. This app gives you the capability to generate NC programs suitable for 3-axes, 4-axes, or 5-axes milling machines.

The **Creo Manufacturing 13 Black Book** is 6th edition of book on Creo Manufacturing updated on Creo 13.4 version of software. The book is written to help professionals as well as students in creating NC programs for very complex jobs that are machined in the Machine shop. The book covers almost all the information required by a learner to master the Expert Machinist, NC Assembly, and CMM modules of Creo. It covers basic as well as advanced topics like NC machines, milling tools with their uses, tool setting, machine setting, cutting strategies, 4 axis milling, 5 axis milling, NC Features, creation of output for a specific machine, CMM, and so on. Some of the salient features of this book are :

In-Depth explanation of concepts

Every new topic of this book starts with the explanation of the basic concepts. In this way, the user becomes capable of relating the things with real world.

Topics Covered

Every chapter starts with a list of topics being covered in that chapter. In this way, the user can easily find the topic of his/her interest easily.

Instruction through illustration

The instructions to perform any action are provided by maximum number of illustrations so that the user can perform the actions discussed in the book easily and effectively. There are about 850 small and large illustrations that make the learning process effective.

Tutorial point of view

At the end of concept's explanation, the tutorial make the understanding of users firm and long lasting. Almost each chapter of the book has tutorials that are real world projects. Moreover, most of the tools in this book are discussed in the form of tutorials.

For Faculty

If you are a faculty member, then you can ask for video tutorials on any of the topic, exercise, tutorial, or concept. As faculty, you can register on our website to get electronic desk copies of our latest books, self-assessment, and solution of practical. Faculty resources are available in the **Faculty Member** page of our website (**www.cadcamcaeworks.com**) once you login. Note that faculty registration approval is manual and it may take two days for approval before you can access the faculty website.

Formatting Conventions Used in the Text

All the key terms like name of button, tool, drop-down, and so on have been kept bold.

Free Resources

Link to the resources used in this book are provided to the users via email. To get the resources, mail us at ***cadcamcaeworks@gmail.com*** with your contact information. With your contact record with us, you will be provided latest updates and informations regarding various technologies. The format to write us mail for resources is as follows:

Subject of E-mail as ***Application for resources of .... book***.
Also, given your information like
Name:
Course pursuing/Profession:
Contact Address:
E-mail ID:

Note: We respect your privacy and value it. If you do not want to give your personal informations then you can ask for resources without giving your information.

About Authors

The author of this book, Matt Weber, has authored many books on CAD/CAM/CAE available already in market. **Mastercam Black Books** are one of the most selling books in Mastercam field. The author has hands on experience on almost all the CAD/CAM/CAE packages. If you have any query/doubt in any CAD/CAM/CAE package, then you can contact the author by writing at cadcamcaeworks@gmail.com

The author of this book, Gaurav Verma, has written and assisted in more than 16 titles in CAD/CAM/CAE which are already available in market. He has authored **AutoCAD Electrical Black Books** which are available in both **English** and **Russian** language. He has also authored books on vocational courses like Automotive Service Technician and Machinist. He has provided consultant services to many industries in US, Greece, Canada, and UK.

For Any query or suggestion

If you have any query or suggestion, please let us know by mailing us on ***cadcamcaeworks@gmail.com***. Your valuable constructive suggestions will be incorporated in our books and your name will be addressed in special thanks area of our books on your confirmation.

Chapter 1

Starting with Manufacturing

Topics Covered

The major topics covered in this chapter are:

- ***Introduction to Manufacturing.***
- ***Types of Machines.***
- ***NC Machines.***
- ***Applications of CAM.***
- ***Starting Creo Parametric Manufacturing.***
- ***Creo Parametric Manufacturing User Interface.***
- ***Common Operations like Save, Close, Send, and so on.***
- ***Advantages and Disadvantages of CAM.***

INTRODUCTION TO MANUFACTURING

Manufacturing is the process of creating a useful product by using a machine, a process, or both. For manufacturing a product, there are some steps to be followed:

- Generating model of final product.
- Deciding Workpiece; selection of raw material and shape/size of workpiece depends on the application of the product.
- Forging, Casting, or any other pre machining method for creating layout for final shape.
- Roughing processes.
- Finishing Processes.
- Quality Control.

These processes are the main topics of this book. An introduction of these processes is given next.

As the "Generating Layout of final product" is above all the steps, it is the most important step. One should be very clear about the final product because all the other steps are totally dependent on the first step. The layout of final product can be a drawing or a model created by using any modeling software like SolidWorks, Inventor, Solid Edge, and so on. You can also use the Design environment of Mastercam software to create the model.

The next step is "Selection of Raw material/Workpiece". This step is solely dependent on the first step. Our final product defines what should be the raw material and the workpiece shape. Here, workpiece is the piece of raw material of desired shape to be used for the next step or process.

The next step is "Forging, Casting, or any other process for creating outline of the final shape". The outline created for the final shape is also called Blank in industries. In this step, various machines like Press, Cutter, or Moulding machines are used for creating the blank. In some cases of Casting, there is no requirement of machining processes. For example, in case of Investment casting, most of the time there is no requirement of machining process. Machining processes can be divided further into two processes:

- Roughing Processes
- Finishing Processes

These processes are the main discussion area of this book. An introduction to these processes is given next.

Roughing Process

Roughing process is the first step of machining process. Generally, roughing process is the removal of large amount of stock material in comparison to finishing process. In a roughing process, the quantity of material removed from the workpiece is more important than the quality of the machining. There are no close tolerances for roughing process, so the main areas of concern are maximum limit of material that can be removed without harming the cutting tool life. So, these processes are relatively cheaper than the finishing process.

In manufacturing industries, there are three principle machining processes called Turning, Milling, and Drilling. In case of roughing process, there can be turning, milling, drilling, combination of any two, or all the processes. Along with these machining processes, there are various other processes like shaping, planing, broaching, reaming, and so on. But these processes are used in special cases.

Finishing Process

Finishing process can include all the machining processes discussed in case of roughing processes but in close tolerances. Also, the quality of machining at required accuracy level is very important for finishing. Along with the above discussed machining processes, there are a few more machining processes like Electric Discharge Machining(EDM), Laser Beam Machining, Electrochemical Machining, and so on. These processes are called unconventional machining processes because of their cutting method. In unconventional machining processes, the cutting is not performed by mechanical pull/push of tool in the workpiece. In these machining processes, electrical discharge, chemical reaction, laser beams, and other sources are used for cutting. Some of the common machines used for machining processes are discussed next.

TYPES OF MACHINES

There are various types of machines for different type of machining process. For example- for turning process, there are machines like conventional lathe and CNC Turner. Similarly for milling process, there are machines called Milling machine, VMC or HMC. Some of the machines are discussed next with details of their functioning.

Turning Machines

Turning machine is a category of machines used for turning process. In this machine, the workpiece is held in a chuck (collect in case of small workpieces). This chuck revolves at a defined rotational speed. Note that the workpiece can revolve in either CW(Clockwise) or CCW(Counter-Clockwise) direction but cannot translate in any direction. The cutting tool used for removing material can translate in X and Y directions. The most basic type of turning machine is a lathe. But now a days, lathes are being replaced by CNC Turning machines, which are faster and more accurate than the traditional lathes. The CNC Turning machines are controlled by numeric codes. These codes are interpreted by machine controller attached in the machine and then the controller commands various sections of the machine to do a specific job like asking the motor of cutting tool to rotate in clockwise direction by 10 degree. The basic operations that can be done on turning machines are:

- Taper turning
- Spherical generation
- Facing
- Grooving
- Parting (in few cases)
- Drilling
- Boring
- Reaming
- Threading

Milling Machines

Milling machine is a category of machines used for removing material by using a perpendicular tool relative to the workpiece. In this type of machine, workpiece is held on a bed with the help of fixtures. The tool rotates at a defined speed. This tool can move in X, Y, and Z directions. In some machines, the bed can also translate and rotate like in Turret milling machines, 5-axis machines, and so on. Milling machines are of two types; horizontal milling machine and vertical milling machine. In Horizontal milling machine, the tool is aligned with the horizontal axis (X-axis). In Vertical milling machine, the tool is aligned with the vertical axis (Y-axis). The Vertical milling machine is generally used for complex cutting processes like contouring, engraving, embossing, and so on. The Horizontal milling machines are used for cutting slots, grooves, gear teeth, and so on. In some Horizontal milling machines, table can move up-down by motor mechanism or power system. By using the synchronization of table movement with the rotation of rotary fixture, we can also create spiral features. The tools used in both type milling machine have cutting edge on the sides as well as at the tip.

Drilling Machines

Drilling machine is a category of machines used for creating holes in the workpiece. In Drilling machine, the tool (drill bit) is fixed in a tool holder and the tool can move up-down. The workpiece is fixed on the bed. The tool goes down, by motor or by hand, penetrating through the workpiece. There are various types of Drilling machine available like drill presses, cordless drills, pistol grip drills, and so on.

Shaper

Shaper is a category of machines, which is used to cut material in a linear motion. Shaper has a single point cutting tool, which goes back-forth to create linear cut in the workpiece. This type of machine is used to create flat surface of the workpiece. You can create dovetail slot, splines, key slot, and so on by using this machine. In some operation, this machine can be an alternative for EDM.

Planer

Planer is a category of machines similar to Shaper. The only difference is that, in case of Planer machine, the workpiece reciprocates and the tool is fixed.

There are various other special purpose machines (SPMs), which are used for some uncommon requirements. The machines discussed above are conventional machines. The unconventional machines are discussed next.

Electric Discharge Machine

Electric Discharge Machine is a category of machines used for creating desired shapes on the workpiece with the help of electric discharges. In this type of machines, the tool and the workpiece act as electrodes and a dielectric fluid is passed between them. The workpiece is fixed in the bed and tool can move in X, Y, and Z direction. During the machining process, the tool is brought near to the workpiece. Due to this, a spark is generated between them. This spark causes the material on the workpiece to melt and get separated from the workpiece. This separated material is drained with the help of dielectric fluid. There are two types of EDMs which are listed next.

Wire-cut EDM

In this type of EDM, a brass wire is commonly used to cut the material from the workpiece. This wire is held in upper and lower diamond shaped guides. It is constantly fed from a bundle. In this machine, the material is removed by generating sparks between tool and workpiece. A Wire-cut EDM can be used to cut a plate having thickness up to 300 mm.

Sinker EDM

In this type of EDM, a metal electrode is used to cut the material from the workpiece. The tool and the workpiece are submerged in the dielectric fluid. Power supply is connected to both the tool and the workpiece. When tool is brought near the workpiece, sparks are generated randomly on their surfaces. Such sparks gradually create impression of tool on the workpiece.

Electro Chemical Machine

Electro Chemical Machine is a category of machines used for creating desired shape by using the chemical electrolyte. This machining works on the principles of chemical reactions.

Laser Beam Machine

Laser Beam Machine is a category of machines that uses a beam, a highly coherent light. This type of light is called laser. A laser can output a power of up to 100MW in an area of 1 square mm. A laser beam machine can be used to create accurate holes or shapes on a material like silicon, graphite, diamond, and so on.

The machines discussed till now are the major machines used in industries. Some of these machines can be controlled by numeric codes and are called NC machines. NC Machines and their working are discussed next.

NC MACHINES

An NC Machine is a manufacturing tool that removes material by following a predefined command set. An NC Machine can be a milling machine or it can be a turning center. NC stands for Numerical Control so, these machines are controlled by numeric codes. These codes are dependent on the controller installed in the machines. There are various controllers available in the market like Fanuc controller, Siemens controller, Heidenhain controller, and so on. The numeric codes change according to the controller used in the machine. These numeric codes are compiled in the form of a program, which is fed in the machine controller via a storage media. The numeric codes are generally in the form of G-codes and M-codes. For understanding purpose, some of the G-codes and M-codes are discussed next with their functions for a Fanuc controller.

Code		Function
G00	-	Rapid movement of tool.
G01	-	Linear movement while creating cut.
G02	-	Clockwise circular cut.
G03	-	Counter-clockwise circular cut.
G20	-	Starts inch mode.
G21	-	Starts mm mode.
G96	-	Provides constant surface speed.
G97	-	Constant RPM.
G98	-	Feed per minute
G99	-	Feed per revolution
M00	-	Program stop
M02	-	End of program
M03	-	Spindle rotation Clockwise.
M04	-	Spindle rotation Counter Clockwise.
M05	-	Spindle stop
M08	-	Coolant on
M09	-	Coolant off
M98	-	Subprogram call
M99	-	Subprogram exit

These codes as well as the other codes will be discussed in the subsequent chapters according to their applications.

As there is a long list of codes which are required in NC programs to make machine cut workpiece in the desired size and shape, it becomes a tedious job to create programs manually for each operation. Moreover, it take much time to create a program for small operations on a milling machine. To solve this problem and to reduce the human error, Computer Aided Manufacturing (CAM) comes in light. Various applications of CAM are discussed next.

APPLICATIONS OF COMPUTER AIDED MANUFACTURING

Computer Aided Manufacturing (CAM) is a technology which can be used to enhance the manufacturing process. In this technology, the machines are controlled by a workstation. This workstation can serve more than one machines at a time. Using CAM, you can create and manage the programs being fed in the workstation. Some of the applications of CAM are discussed next.

1. CAM with the combination of CAD can be used to create complex shapes by machining in a small time.
2. CAM can be used to manage more than one machines at the same time with less human power.
3. CAM is used to automate the manufacturing process.
4. CAM is used to generate NC programs for various types of NC machines.
5. 5-Axis Machining

CAM is generally the next step after CAD (Computer Aided Designing). Sometimes CAE (Computer Aided Engineering) is also required before CAM. There are various software companies that provide the CAM software solutions. CNC Software is one of those companies which publishes Mastercam software. Mastercam is one of the most popular software for CAM programming.

MANUFACTURING APPS IN CREO PARAMETRIC

There are various apps that can work seamlessly with Creo Parametric. The list of available apps can be found in the **New** dialog box of Creo Parametric. To select any manufacturing app, start Creo Parametric and click on the **New** button available in the **Data** panel of the **Ribbon**. The **New** dialog box will be displayed; refer to Figure-1.

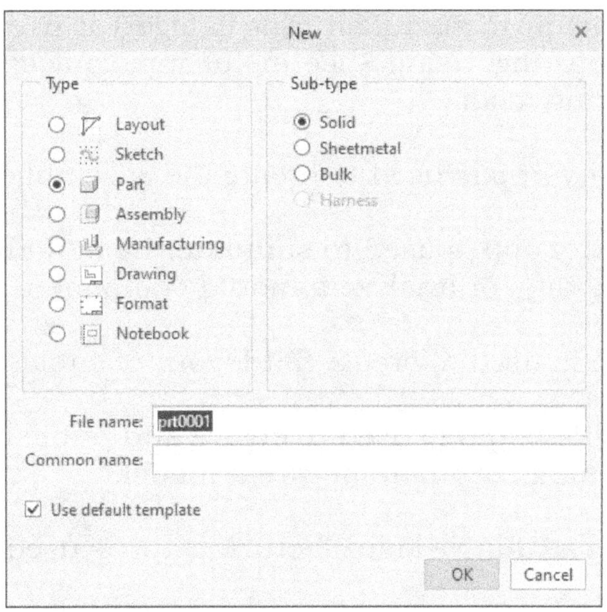

Figure-1. New dialog box

Select the **Manufacturing** radio button from the **Type** area in the dialog box. The options in the **Sub-type** area will change according to manufacturing category; refer to Figure-2. The options available in Creo Parametric for manufacturing with their short description are given next.

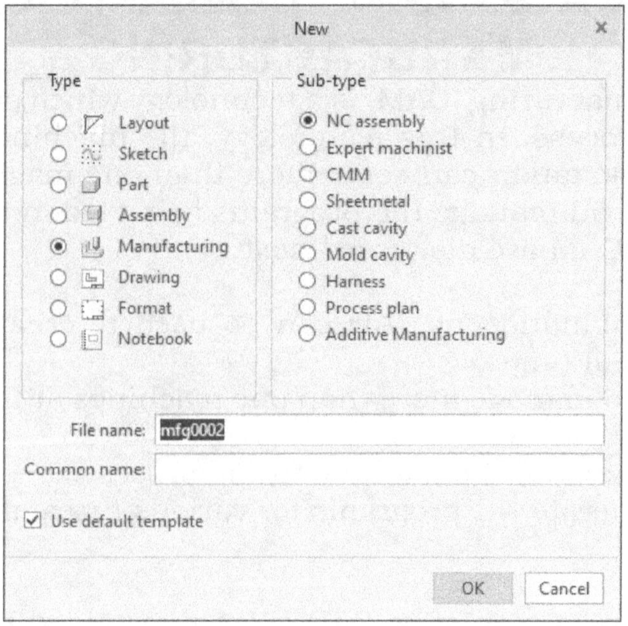

Figure-2. New dialog box with manufacturing options

NC Assembly - NC Assembly app is used to create an NC program using an assembly created in Creo Parametric or any other modeling software. You can also create an assembly by using the tools available in this apps.

Expert Machinist - Expert Machinist app is used to create an NC program by using a reference model.

CMM - CMM app is used to create a sequence measurement in reference to the model created in Creo Parametric.

Sheetmetal - Sheetmetal app in manufacturing category is used to create NC sequence for sheetmetal manufacturing. Using Sheetmetal app, you can create various designs in a single manufacturing model.

Cast Cavity - Cast Cavity app is used to create die assemblies and castings.

Mold Cavity - Mold Cavity app is used to simulate the moulding process. Using this app, you can create, modify, or analyze a mould component.

Harness - Harness app is used to create flat layout of cables on a nail board.

Process Plan - Process Plan app is used to create and publish the documentation of process to create, assemble, or manufacture a model.

Additive Manufacturing - Additive Manufacturing app is used to perform 3D printing using a 3D model.

In this book, we will start with Expert Machinist to create NC programs. The method to start Expert Machinist app is discussed next.

STARTING EXPERT MACHINIST

To start Expert Machinist app, start Creo Parametric. The interface of Creo Parametric will be displayed; refer to Figure-3. Click on the **New** tool from the **Data** panel in the **Ribbon**. The **New** dialog box will be displayed.

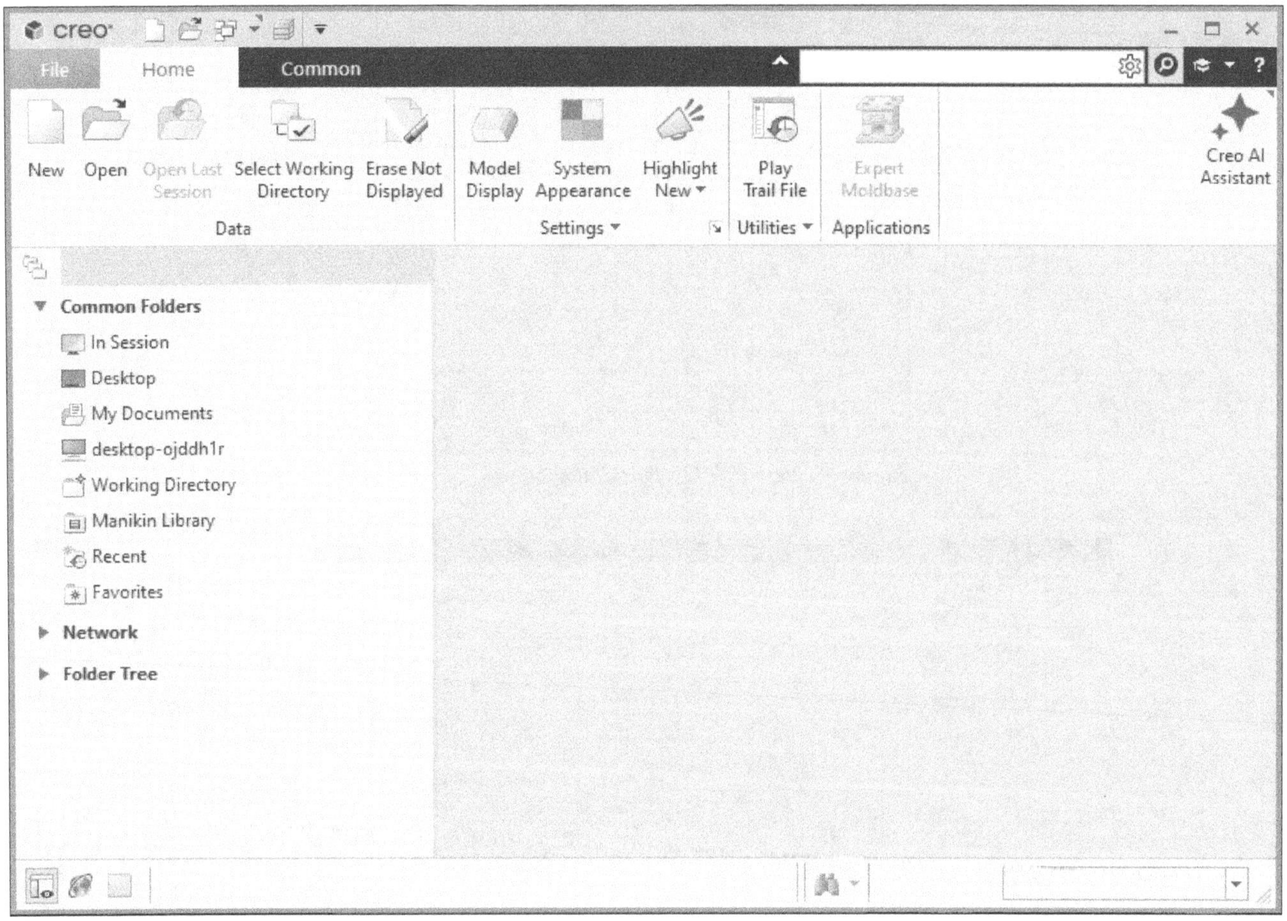

Figure-3. Interface of Creo Parametric

Select the **Manufacturing** radio button from the **Type** area. The options related to manufacturing will be displayed in the **Sub-type** area; refer to Figure-2. Select the **Expert machinist** radio button from the **Sub-type** area and specify desired name of file in the **Name** edit box. By default, the **Use default template** check box is selected in this dialog box. So, the units and other settings used are default one. Clear this check box to select a different template. If you click on the **OK** button after clearing the check box, the **New File Options** dialog box will be displayed; refer to Figure-4. Select desired template and then click on the **OK** button from the dialog box. The Expert Machinist interface of Creo Parametric will be displayed; refer to Figure-5.

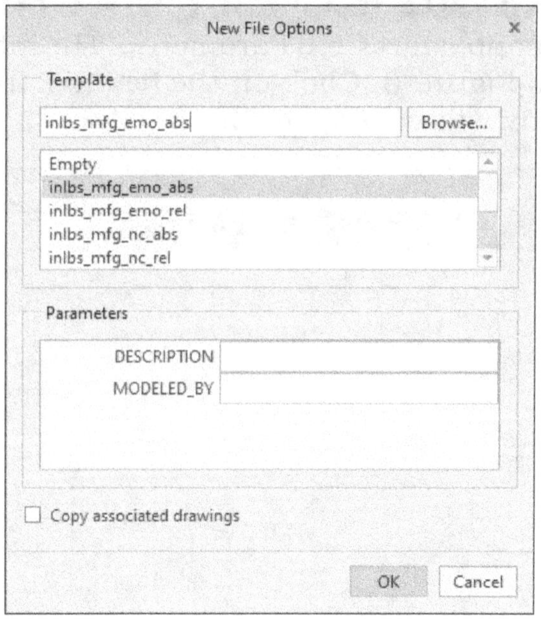

Figure-4. New File Options dialog box

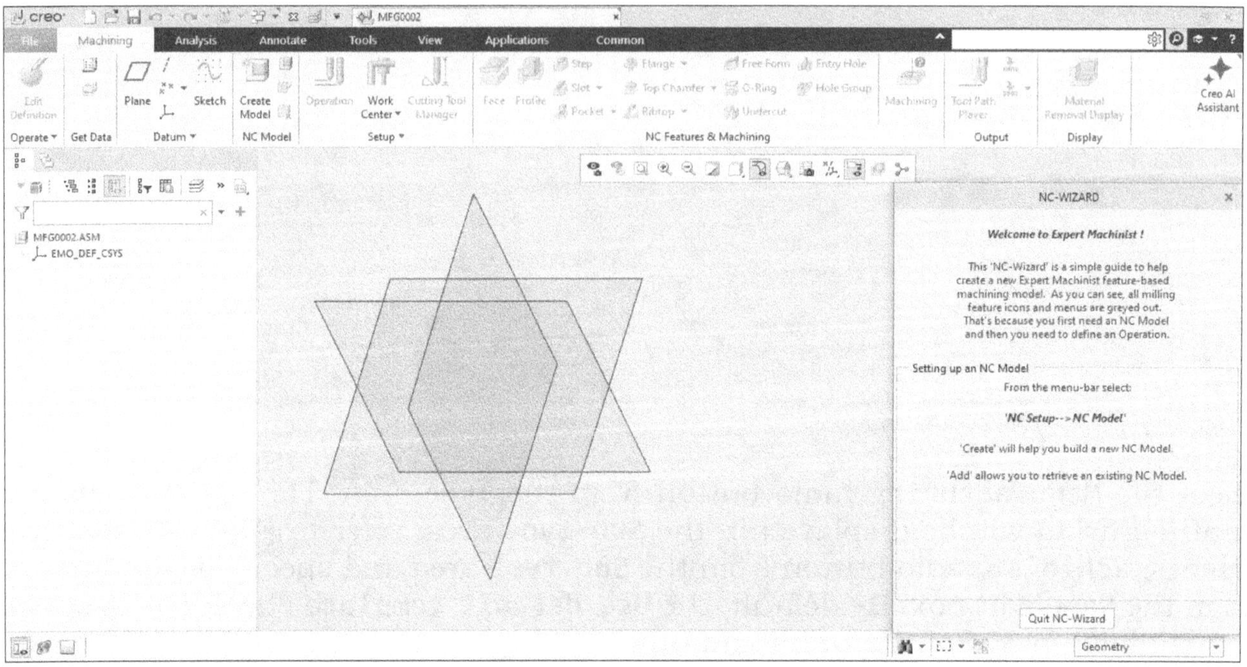

Figure-5. Interface of Expert Machinist

With the Expert Machinist, the **NC-WIZARD** dialog box will be displayed; refer to Figure-6. The **NC-WIZARD** dialog box provides a step by step guide for creating an Expert Machinist model. If you do not want to display this dialog box, click on the **Quit NC-Wizard** button.

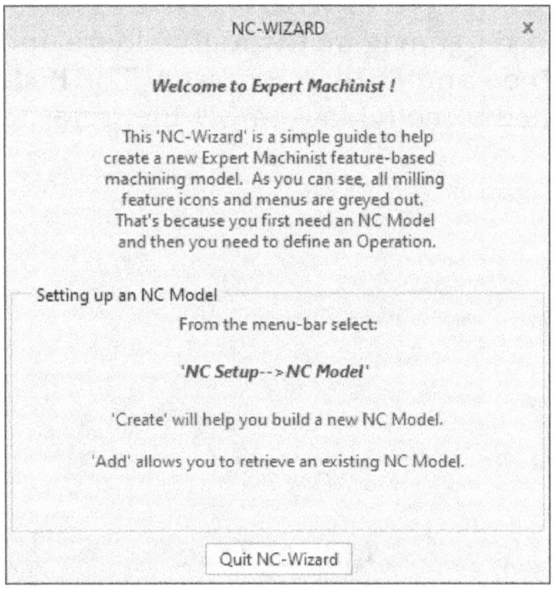

Figure-6. The NC Wizard dialog box

The other options available in the UI (User Interface) of Creo Expert Machinist are discussed next.

CREO PARAMETRIC INTERFACE

The interface of Creo Parametric comprises of various elements like Navigator panel, Browser, Ribbon, File menu, and so on; refer to Figure-7. These elements are discussed next.

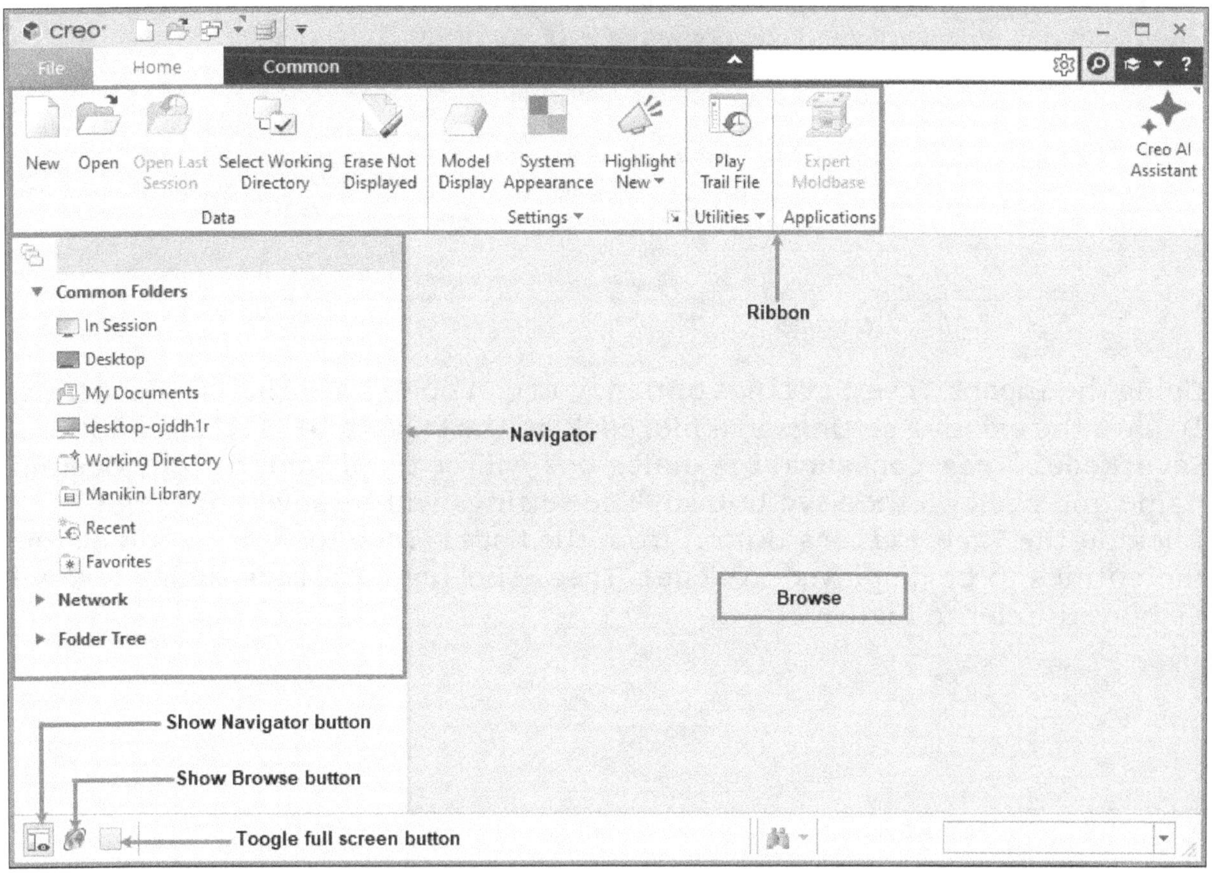

Figure-7. Creo Parametric interface

Navigator panel

The **Navigator** panel is used to navigate through folders and features. This panel has two tabs named: **Model Tree** and **Folder Browser**. The **Model Tree** tab will be active only when you have opened a model/assembly file; refer to Figure-8.

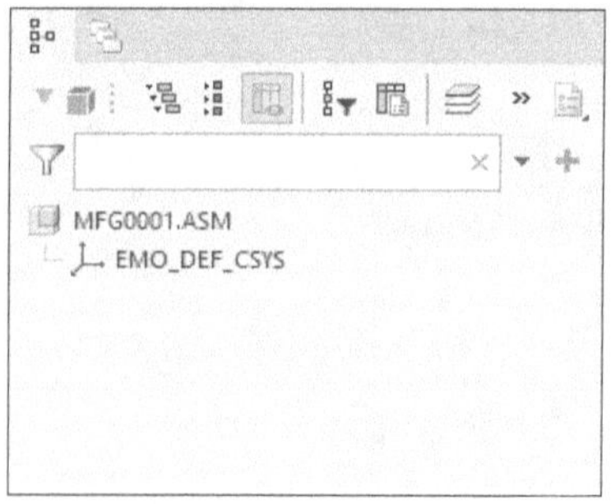

Figure-8. Model Tree

Model Tree

- The **Model Tree** contains all the features that are created automatically or manually while creating model or assembly.
- The green line in the **Model Tree** represents the position where the next feature will be inserted. You can drag this line up or down to create or suppress features.
- Click on the **Settings** button to display the menu related to settings; refer to Figure-9.

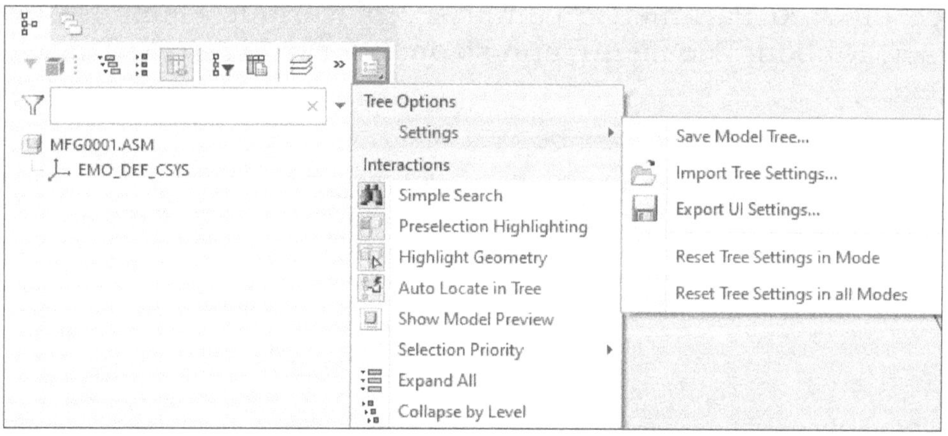

Figure-9. Model Tree settings

- Using the **Import Tree Settings** option, you can open an earlier saved setting file.
- To save the existing settings in a file, click on the **Export UI Settings** option. The **Save Model Tree Configuration** dialog box will be displayed. Specify desired file name and click on the **Save** button. The settings will be saved in **.cfg** file.
- Click on the **Tree Filters** button from the **Model Tree** toolbar to add or remove the entities to be displayed in **Model Tree**. The **Tree Filters** dialog box will be displayed; refer to Figure-10.

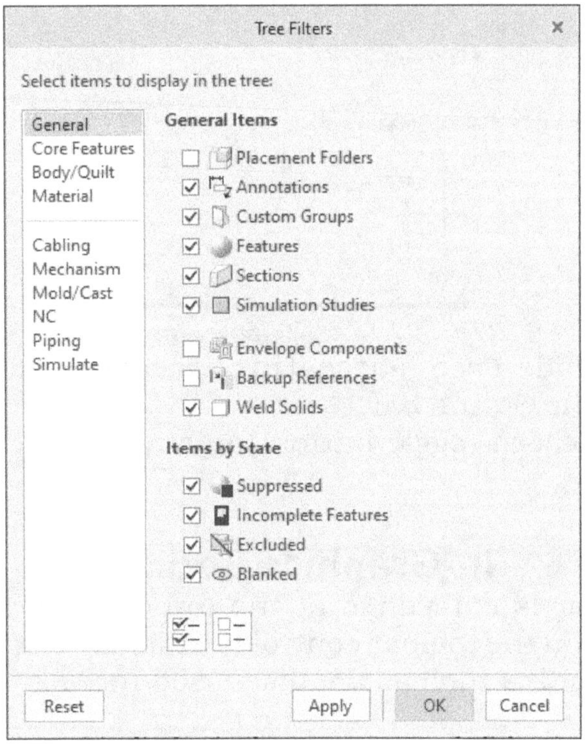

Figure-10. Tree Filters dialog box

- Select the check boxes that you want to display in the **Model Tree** and click on the **OK** button from the dialog box.

Folder Browser

- Click on the **Folder Browser** button to display the **Folder Browser**; refer to Figure-11.

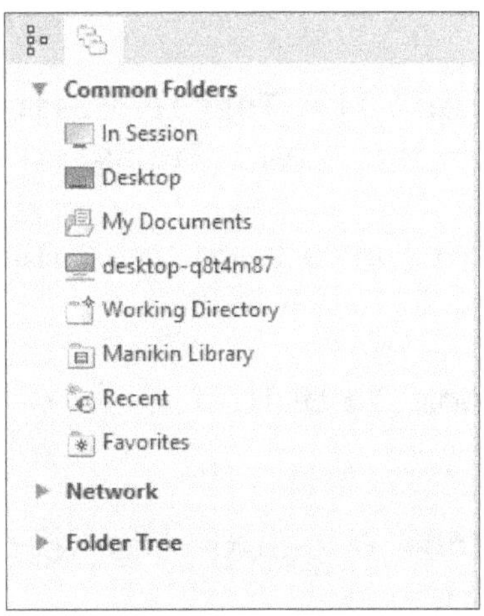

Figure-11. Folder Browser

- Using the **Folder Browser**, you can quickly browse through the folders to get desired files.
- To display or hide the **Navigation** panel, click on the **Show Navigator** toggle button in the Status bar; refer to Figure-12.

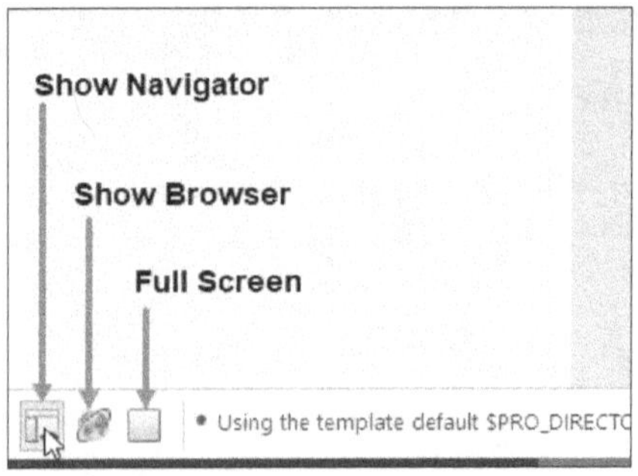

Figure-12. Show Navigator button

- Similarly, to show/hide **Creo Parametric browser** click on the **Show Browser** toggle button from the Status bar.
- Click on the **Full Screen** toggle button to activate/deactivate full screen mode of software.

In-Graphics Toolbar

The **In-Graphics** toolbar is embedded at the top of the graphics window; refer to Figure-13. The buttons on the toolbar control the display of graphics. Various options available in the **In-Graphics** toolbar are discussed next.

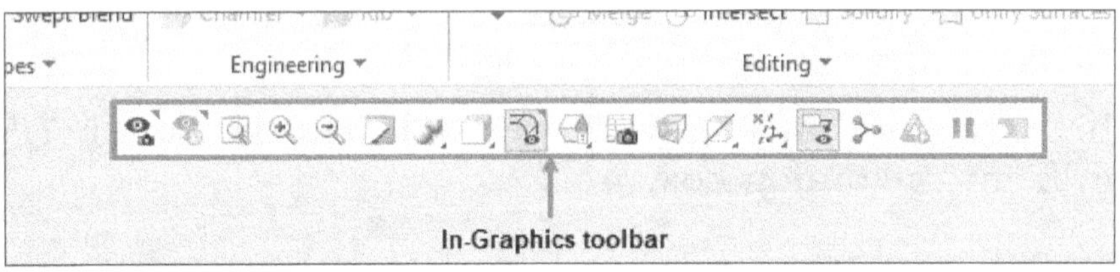

Figure-13. In Graphics toolbar

- **Capture Visibility** button : The **Capture Visibility** button is used to save currently visible state of objects as a temporary view so that you can use it again later.

- **Toggle Visibility** button : The **Toggle Visibility** button is used to switch between the currently visible state and the saved view state of objects.

- **Refit** button : The **Refit** button is used to adjust the zoom level to fully display the object on the screen.

- **Zoom In** button : The **Zoom In** button is used to zoom in the target geometry to view in greater detail.

- **Zoom Out** button : The **Zoom Out** button is used to gain a wider perspective of the geometrical context.

- **Repaint** button : The **Repaint** button is used to redraw the current view.

- **Rendering Options** button : Click on the **Rendering Options** button to toggle the ambient occlusion effect and scene background on or off.

- **Display Style** button : Click on the **Display Style** button to set desired display style for the model.

- **Tangent Edges** button : The **Tangent Edges** button is used to toggle the display of edges between tangent surfaces.
- **Saved Orientations** button : The **Saved Orientations** button is used to set desired orientation for the model.
- **View Manager** button : The **View Manager** button is used to set the orientations, appearances, representations, sections, and layers of the model.
- **Perspective View** button : The **Perspective View** button is used to toggle the perspective view.
- **Transparency Control** button : The **Transparency Control** button is used to set transparency for bodies, quilts, and tessellated geometry in the model.
- **Datum Display Filters** button : The **Datum Display Filters** button is used to define desired datum display filters for the model.
- **Annotation Display** button : The **Annotation Display** button is used to turn on or off 3D annotations and annotation elements.
- **Spin Center** button : The **Spin Center** button is used to show the spin center and use it in the default location, or hide the spin center to use the pointer location as the spin center.
- **Simulate** button : Click on the **Simulate** button to toggle the simulation on or off.
- **Pause Simulation** button : Click on the **Pause Simulation** button to pause or resume the simulation.
- **Animation Options** button : The **Animation Options** button is used to display the animated deformation result and toggle the color bands/color band animation in the deformation display.

RIBBON

Ribbon is the area of the application window that holds all the tools for designing and editing; refer to Figure-14.

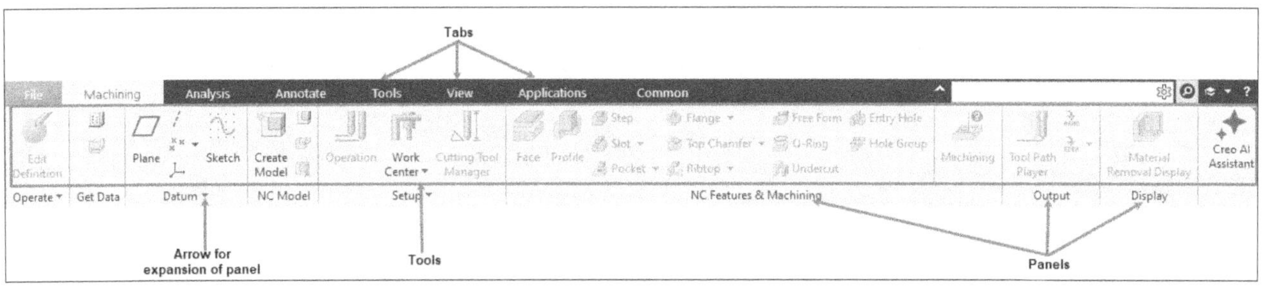

Figure-14. Ribbon

The tools in the **Ribbon** will be discussed later in the book as per their need in designing.

FILE MENU

The options in the **File** menu are used to perform operations related to files; refer to Figure-15.

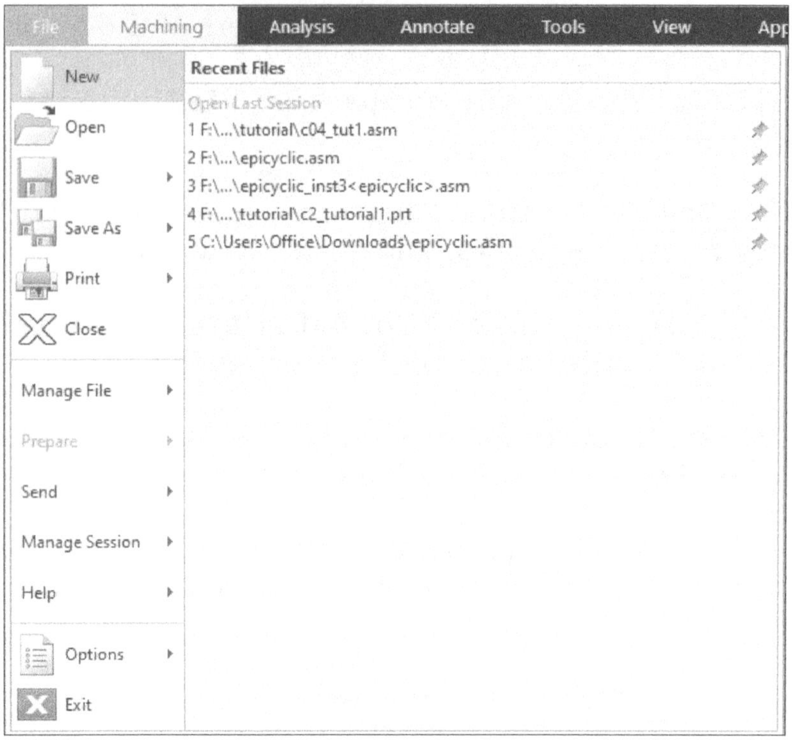

Figure-15. File menu

Customizing the Ribbon

- To customize the **Ribbon**, click on the **Options** tool from **Options** cascading menu in the **File** menu. The **Creo Parametric Options** dialog box will be displayed.
- Select the **Ribbon** from **Customize** node from the left area of the dialog box. The updated dialog box will be displayed; refer to Figure-16.

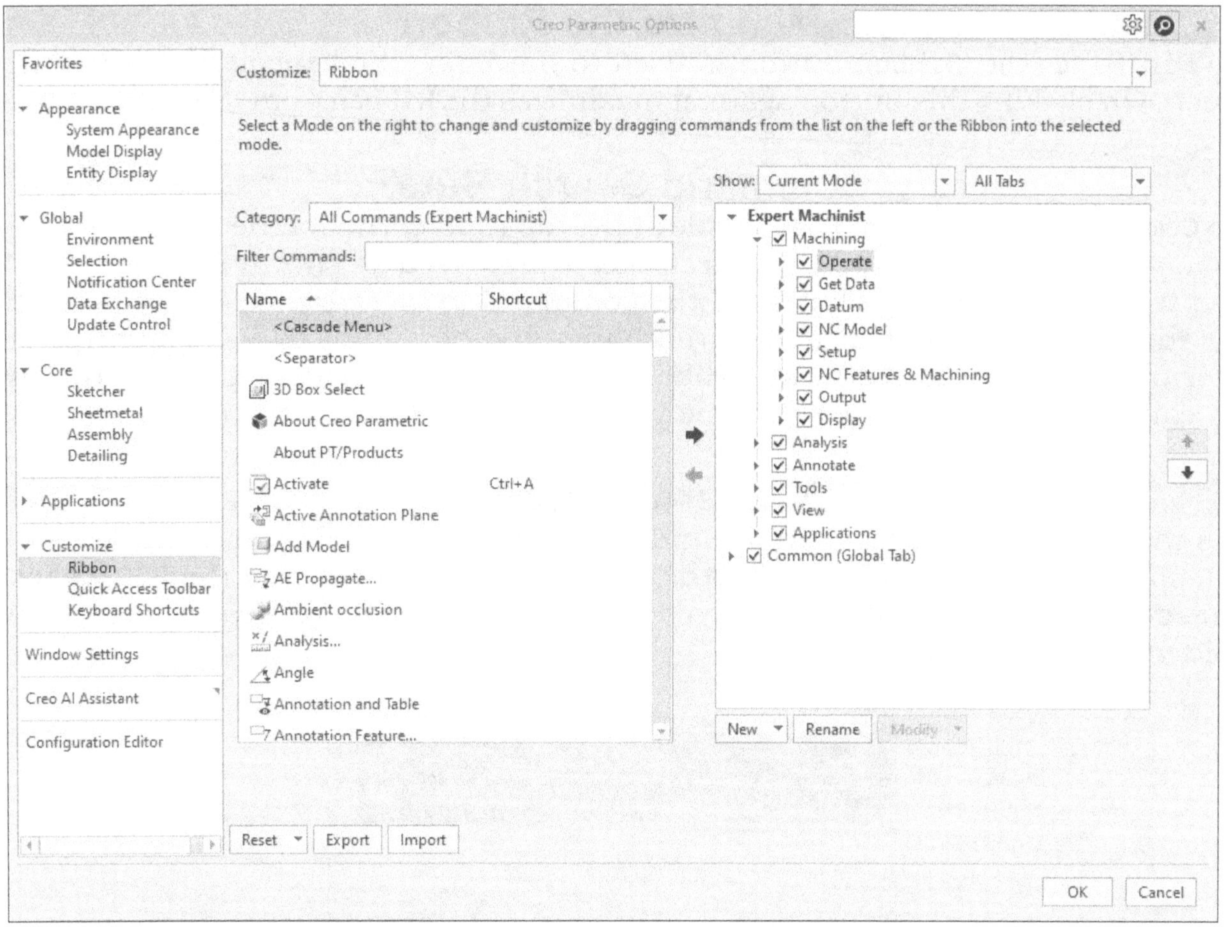

Figure-16. Creo Parametric Options dialog box

- Now, select the specific command from left area of the dialog box. Select the panel from right area of the dialog box on which you want to add that command and click on **Adds selected item to the Ribbon**.
- Select the **New Group** or **New Tab** button from **New** drop-down in the right area of the dialog box to create any new group or tab depending on the requirement. The new group or tab will be added.
- Similarly, you can add the command for **Quick Access Toolbar** and buttons for **Keyboard Shortcuts** from **Customize** node.

Search Bar

There are various tools in the help bar which are used to understand the Creo Parametric software; refer to Figure-17. The tools of this bar are discussed next.

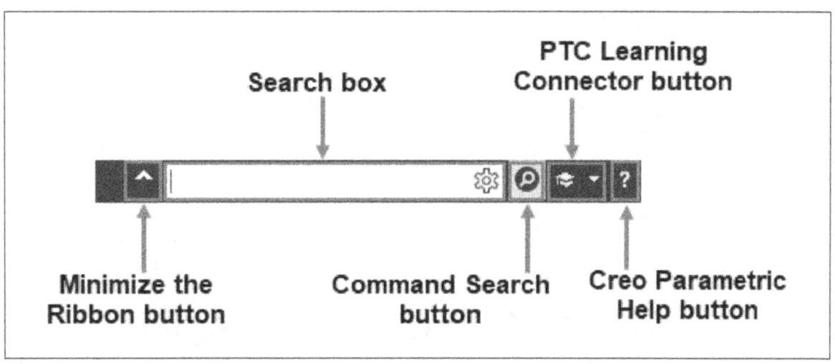

Figure-17. Help Bar

Minimize the Ribbon

The **Minimize the Ribbon** button is used to minimize the **Ribbon** from the current screen. On clicking this button again, it maximizes the **Ribbon** from the current screen.

Command Search Button

The **Command Search** button is available at the top right corner of the program window. When you click this button, the search box is displayed as shown in Figure-17. You need to enter the first few letters of the command to be searched in the box. When you enter the first letter in the search box, a list of commands starting from that letter will be displayed. You can invoke any command by selecting it from the list or you can enter the next letter to refine your search.

PTC Learning Connector

This tool is used to learn the tools and commands of Creo Parametric. To use this tool, click on **PTC Learning Connector** button from Help bar and the **PTC Learning Connector** dialog box will be displayed; refer to Figure-18. You can search desired topic from the Search bar.

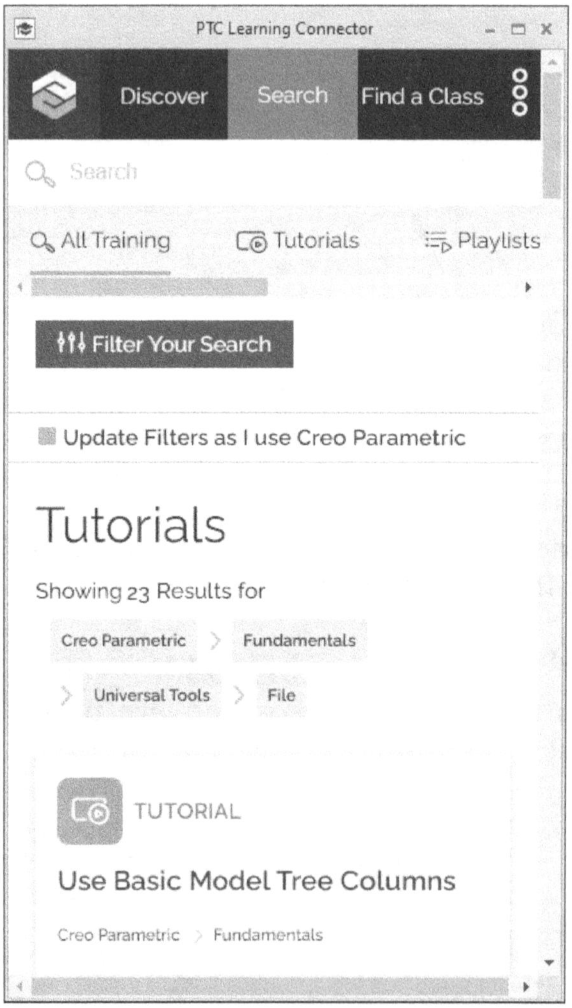

Figure-18. PTC Learning Connector dialog box

Creo Parametric Help

Click on the **Creo Parametric Help** button from the Help bar. The PTC Creo parametric Help website will be displayed.

Tip: If you want to change the predefined unit system, click on **File > Prepare > Model Properties** from the menu bar to display the **Model Properties** dialog box. In this dialog box, click on the **change** link button on the right of the **Units** option under the **Materials** head. The **Units Manager** dialog box will be displayed with the **System of Units** tab selected. Next, select desired unit system from the list box and then click on the **Set** button. The **Changing Model Units** message box will be displayed. Click on the **OK** button from the message box. The new unit system will be set and displayed with the red arrow on the left.

CREO AI ASSISTANT

Creo AI Assistant is CAD embedded AI assistant model to help you during designing process with customized help topics, tips, and good design practices. Since the model is trained on help and other official data from PTC, there are fewer chances of error in response but still it is your call in the end as a design engineer.

If you are running Creo Parametric 13 and **Creo AI Assistant** tool is not available in the **Ribbon** by default, then select the **Enable Creo AI Assistant** check box from **Creo AI Assistant** page **Creo Parametric Options** dialog box; refer to Figure-19. The procedure to use this assistant is given next.

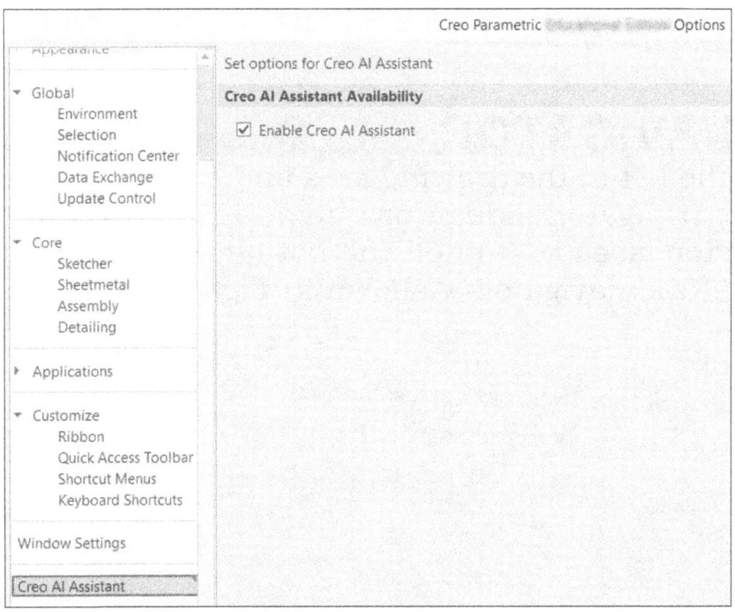

Figure-19. Creo AI Assistant page

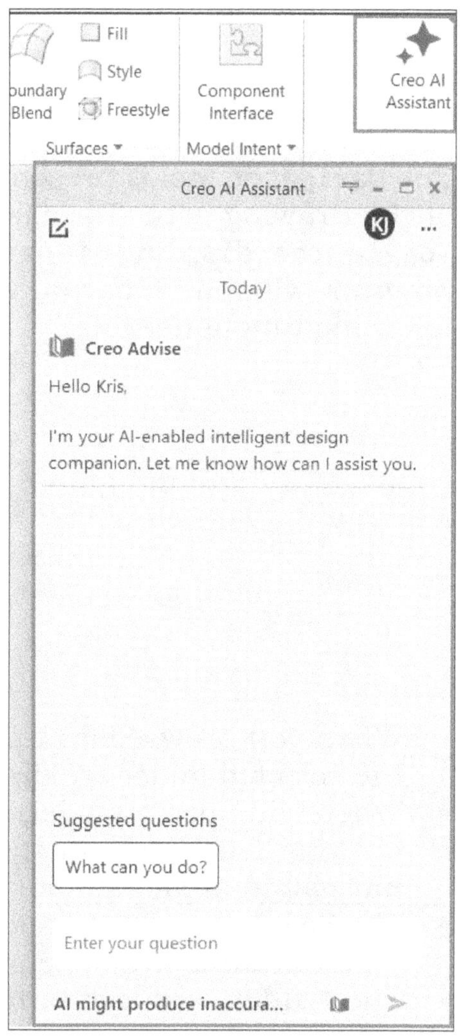

Figure-20. Creo AI Assistant window

- Click on the **Creo AI Assistant** tool from right in the **Ribbon**. The Creo AI Assistant window will be displayed; refer to Figure-20. Note that you might need to create separate account to login into Creo AI Assistant even if you have already login into PTC account.
- After login, Type your query in the edit box and click on the **Send message** button. After processing for a moment depending on internet connection and complexity of your query, Creo AI Assistant will provide advice on query.

Note that by default, **Creo Advice** option is active in the **Assistant** which provides general tools related help and tip but if you are a commercial version user then you can also use Creo Assist mode of the AI assistant by selecting the **Creo Assist** option from **New Chat** flyout; refer to Figure-21. In Creo Assist mode, the AI assistant will be aware of your current design in graphics area and give you relevant help. This mode might not be available in educational version of software.

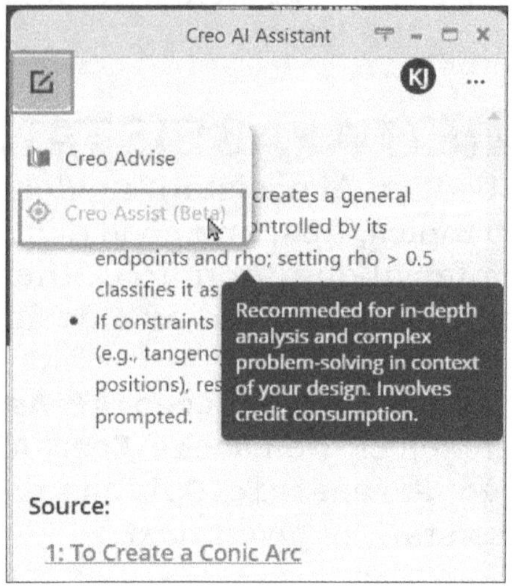

Figure-21. Creo Assist option

NAVIGATOR

The **Navigator** tool is present on the left in the drawing area and can slide in or out of the drawing area. To make the navigator slide in or out, you need to select the **Toggle the display of navigation area** button on the bottom left corner of the program window. A partial view of the navigator is shown in Figure-22. It has the following functions:

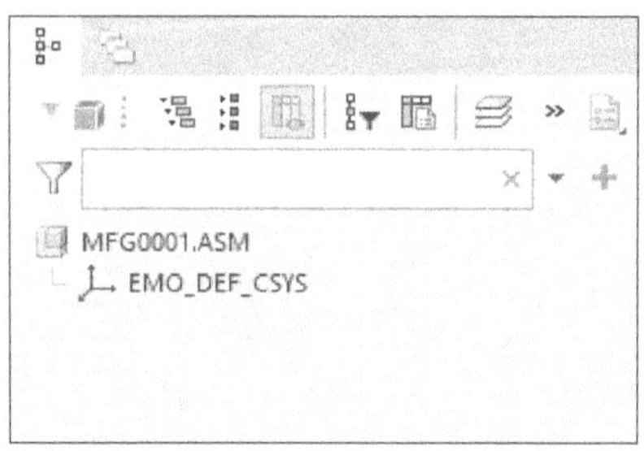

Figure-22. Partial view of the Navigator

- When you browse files using the navigator, the browser expands and the files in the selected folder are displayed in the browser.
- When you open a model, the **Model Tree** is displayed in the navigation area. The buttons on the top of the navigator are used to display different items in the navigation area.
- The **Model Tree** button is used to display the **Model Tree** in the navigation area. This button is available only when a model is opened.
- The **Folder Browser** button is used to display the folders that are in the local system.
- Any other location, if available on your system, can also be accessed by using the navigator.

SELF ASSESSMENT

Q1. What is the first and most important step in the manufacturing process?

A. Finishing Process
B. Quality Control
C. Generating model of final product
D. Selection of raw material

Q2. What defines the selection of raw material and shape/size of the workpiece?

A. Finishing process
B. Final product
C. Machine availability
D. Quality control

Q3. What is the industrial term for the outline created for the final shape?

A. Stock
B. Layout
C. Blank
D. Core

Q4. Which process focuses more on quantity of material removed than quality?

A. Finishing process
B. Forging
C. Casting
D. Roughing process

Q5. Which of the following is NOT a principle machining process?

A. Turning
B. Drilling
C. Milling
D. Welding

Q6. What is the function of a turning machine?

A. Holding the tool stationary and rotating the bed
B. Rotating the workpiece and translating the cutting tool
C. Translating both tool and workpiece simultaneously
D. Only drilling holes

Q7. In vertical milling machines, the tool is aligned along which axis?

A. X-axis
B. Z-axis
C. Y-axis
D. XY plane

Q8. What is the purpose of a drilling machine?

A. To rotate the bed
B. To create flat surfaces
C. To create holes
D. To perform taper turning

Q9. Which machine cuts in linear motion using a single-point tool?

A. Planer
B. Shaper
C. Lathe
D. EDM

Q10. In a planer machine, which part moves during cutting?

A. Tool
B. Chuck
C. Workpiece
D. Collet

Q11. What is used as a dielectric fluid medium in EDM processes?

A. Water
B. Oil
C. Acid
D. Not mentioned

Q12. Which EDM type uses a continuously fed wire for cutting?

A. Sinker EDM
B. Wire-cut EDM
C. CNC EDM
D. Chemical EDM

Q13. What machining technique uses chemical reactions to shape material?

A. EDM
B. Laser machining
C. Electro Chemical Machining
D. Milling

Q14. What type of light is used in Laser Beam Machining?

A. Incandescent
B. Fluorescent
C. Coherent
D. Ultraviolet

Q15. What is NC in NC machines?

A. Numeric Code
B. Numerical Control
C. Network Control
D. Navigation Command

Q16. What is the function of G01 in NC code?

A. Clockwise circular cut
B. Linear movement while cutting
C. Tool stop
D. Program end

Q17. Which M-code is used to start spindle rotation clockwise?

A. M00
B. M03
C. M08
D. M99

Q18. What is the role of CAM in manufacturing?

A. Generate 3D models
B. Control manual tools
C. Automate NC program generation
D. Generate raw materials

Q19. What software is commonly used for CAM programming?

A. AutoCAD
B. SolidWorks
C. Mastercam
D. Creo View

Q20. Which Creo app is used to simulate the molding process?

A. Cast Cavity
B. Expert Machinist
C. Mold Cavity
D. Process Plan

Q21. Which machining process uses a high-velocity stream of abrasive particles?

A. Ultrasonic Machining
B. Water Jet Machining
C. Abrasive Jet Machining
D. Plasma Arc Machining

Q22. In NC programming, which code specifies rapid positioning movement?

A. G00
B. G01
C. G02
D. G03

Q23. Which non-traditional machining process works best for hard and brittle materials using ultrasonic waves?

A. EDM
B. Laser Beam Machining
C. Ultrasonic Machining
D. Chemical Machining

Q24. What is the main advantage of CNC over NC?

A. Lower cost
B. Manual programming
C. Re-programmable and automated
D. Limited to 2D shapes

Q25. Which axis is typically considered the vertical axis in a 3-axis CNC milling machine?

A. X-axis
B. Y-axis
C. Z-axis
D. A-axis

Q26. What does the M08 code in CNC machining indicate?

A. Spindle on
B. Coolant on
C. Program end
D. Stop tool

Q27. Which process uses photochemical reactions to remove material?

A. Electrochemical Machining
B. Photochemical Machining
C. EDM
D. Plasma Arc Cutting

Q28. Which file type is commonly used to export NC code from CAM software?
A. .DXF
B. .NC
C. .STEP
D. .DWG

Q29. What is backlash in machine tools?

A. Forward acceleration of tool
B. Backward movement of workpiece
C. Lost motion in gears due to clearance
D. Tool deflection during machining

Q30. Which of the following processes is best suited for machining intricate internal cavities in hardened materials?

A. Milling
B. Wire EDM
C. Turning
D. Drilling

FOR STUDENT NOTES

FOR STUDENT NOTES

Chapter 2

Starting with Expert Machinist

Topics Covered

The major topics covered in this chapter are:

- ***Manufacturing Processes in Expert Machinist.***
- ***Logical sequence used for creating an NC manufacturing model.***
- ***Importing Model for manufacturing.***
- ***Creating NC Model for manufacturing.***
- ***Retrieving stock from a model.***
- ***Configuring Units for the NC Model.***

MANUFACTURING SEQUENCE IN EXPERT MACHINIST

The Expert Machinist app incorporates various manufacturing processes in a predefined order. The sequence of operations performed in Expert Machinist to create NC model is given in the flowchart (Figure-1) given next.

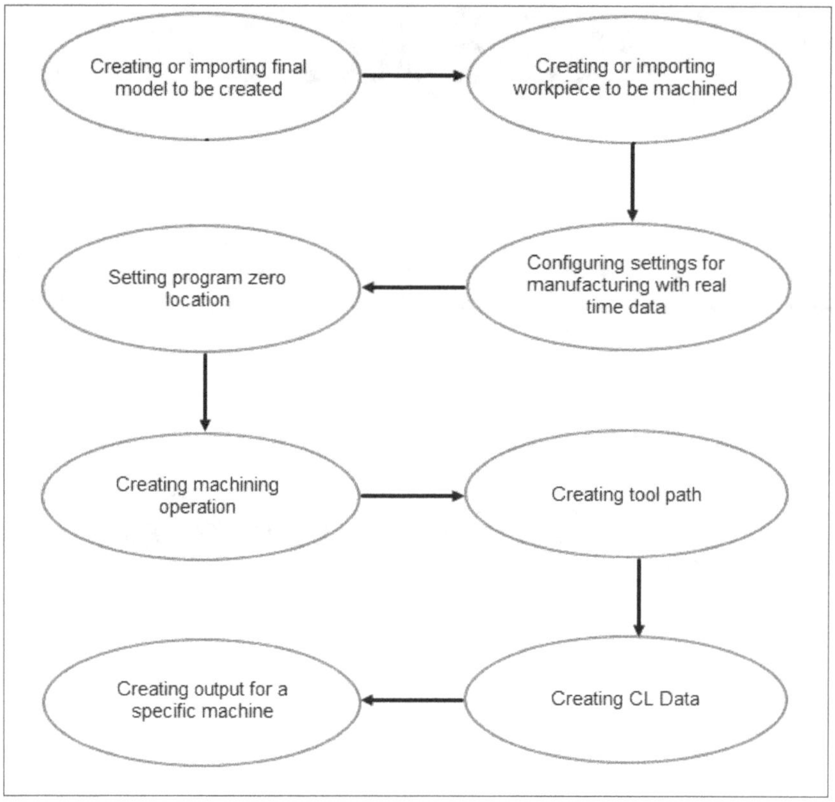

Figure-1. Flowchart for creating manufacturing model

As you can see from the flowchart; the first step for creating a manufacturing sequence is either importing a model of final product or creating model of the final product required after manufacturing. General practice for a CAM engineer is importing the model. The procedure to import a model for manufacturing is given next.

CREATING NC MODEL

NC model is the detailed manufacturable model used by Creo Manufacturing module to create machining codes. The NC model contains data like base model, stock design, manufacturing parameters, and so on. The procedure to create an NC model is given next.

- Click on the **Create Model** button from **NC Model** panel of the **Machining** tab in the **Ribbon**. You will be prompted to specify the name of the model to be created.
- Enter the name of the NC model in the input box displayed and click on the ✓ button. The **Open** dialog box will be displayed; refer to Figure-2.
- Select an assembly or a part to be used as reference part for workpiece. This assembly/part represents the final output that you want to achieve after machining. After selecting part/assembly, click on the **Open** button. If the selected entity has more than one instances then the **Select Instances** dialog box will be displayed; refer to Figure-3. Otherwise, the reference model will be displayed in the modeling area and **NC Model Menu Manager** will be displayed.

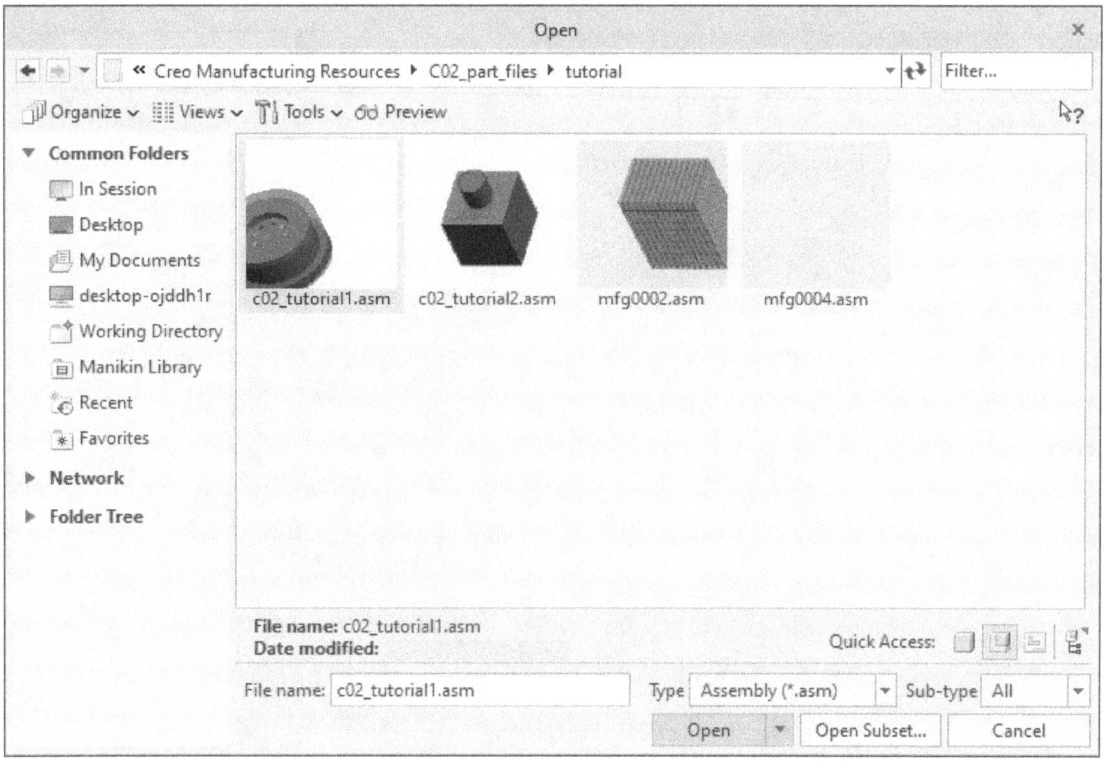

Figure-2. Open dialog box

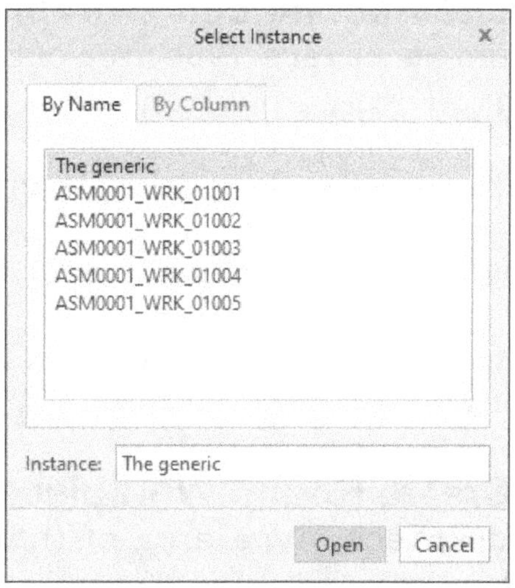

Figure-3. Select Instance dialog box

- Now, using the options in the **Menu Manager**, you can create stock on the model that represents actual stock to be machined. The procedure to create stock on the model is given next.

Creating Stock

- Click on the **Create Stock** option from the **NC Model Menu Manager**. The **Auto Workpiece Creation** contextual tab will be displayed; refer to Figure-4. The options in the **Ribbon** are given next.

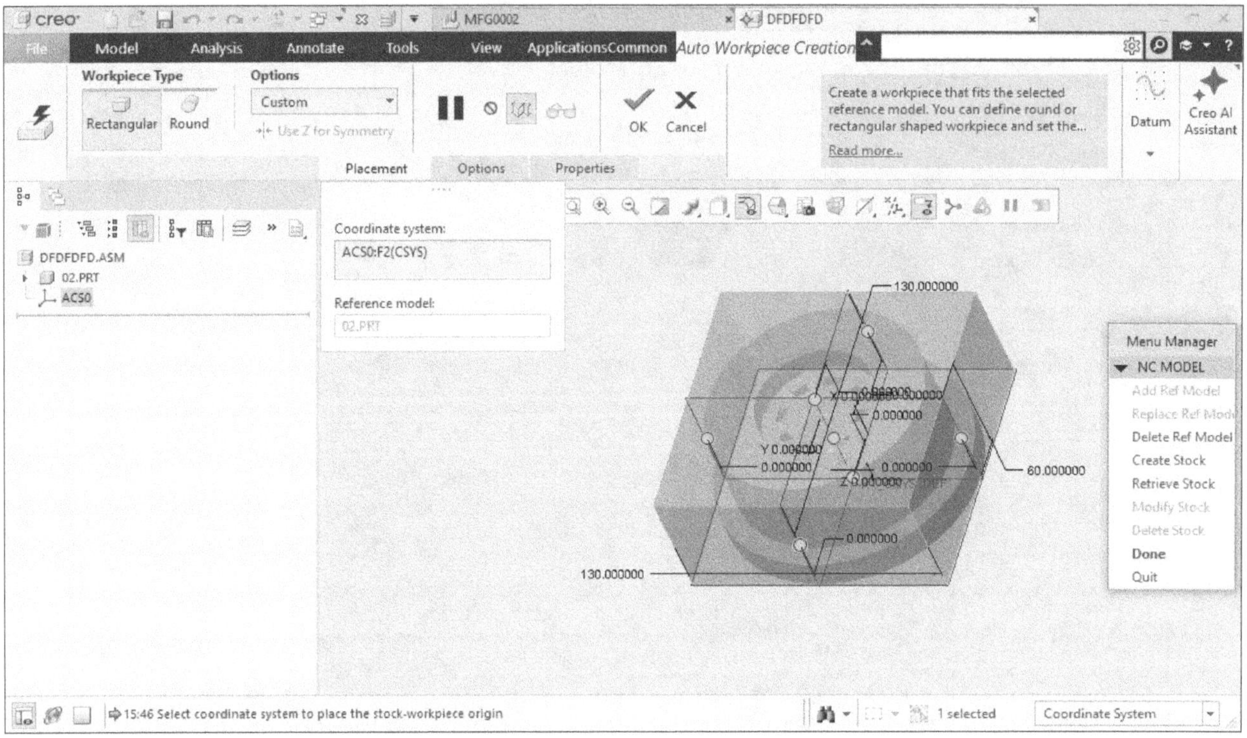

Figure-4. Auto Workpiece Creation contextual tab

Create Rectangular Workpiece

Select **Rectangular** option from **Workpiece Type** area of the **Auto Workpiece Creation** contextual tab in the **Ribbon**.

- On selecting this option, a rectangular jacket is created around the reference model; refer to Figure-4.
- Using the handles displayed on the workpiece, you can add or remove the stock in the specific direction.
- You can also add the material by using the edit box displayed on double clicking on the value corresponding to the selected handle.

Create Round Workpiece

Select **Round** option from **Workpiece Type** area of the **Auto Workpiece Creation** contextual tab in the **Ribbon**.

- On selecting this option, a round jacket is created around the reference model; refer to Figure-5.

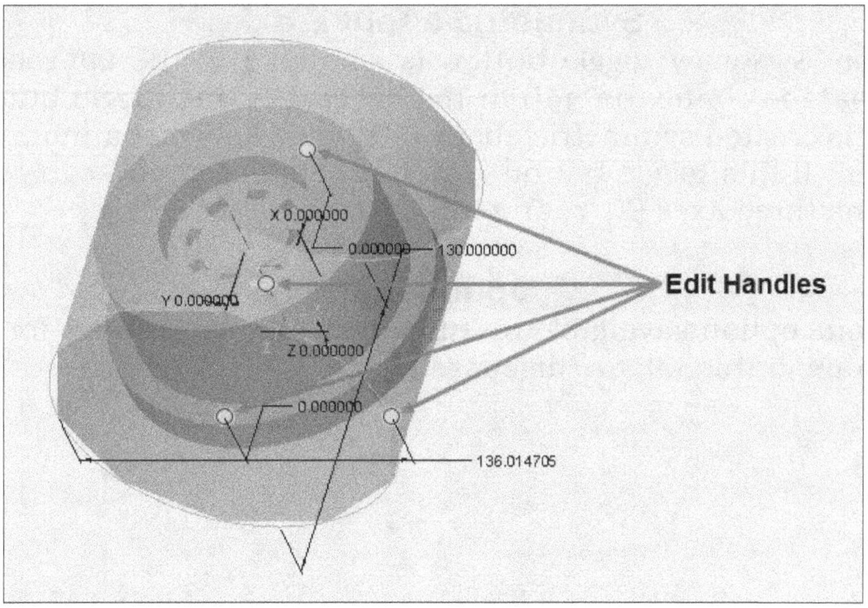

Figure-5. Stock created after selecting the Round option

- You can change the value of stock in different directions using the edit handles in the similar way as done for rectangular stock.

Stock-workpiece's sub-shape

The **Stock-workpiece's sub-shape** drop-down is available in the **Options** area of **Auto Workpiece Creation** contextual tab in the **Ribbon**; refer to Figure-4.

- Options in this drop-down are used to change the shape of stock created around the workpiece.
- There are two options available in this drop-down, **Custom** and **Envelope**.
- The **Custom** option is used to create a customized workpiece i.e. you can change the size of workpiece by using the edit boxes or edit handles. The **Envelope** option is used to create an envelope around the reference model. Figure-6 shows the stock creation using **Custom** and **Envelope** option.

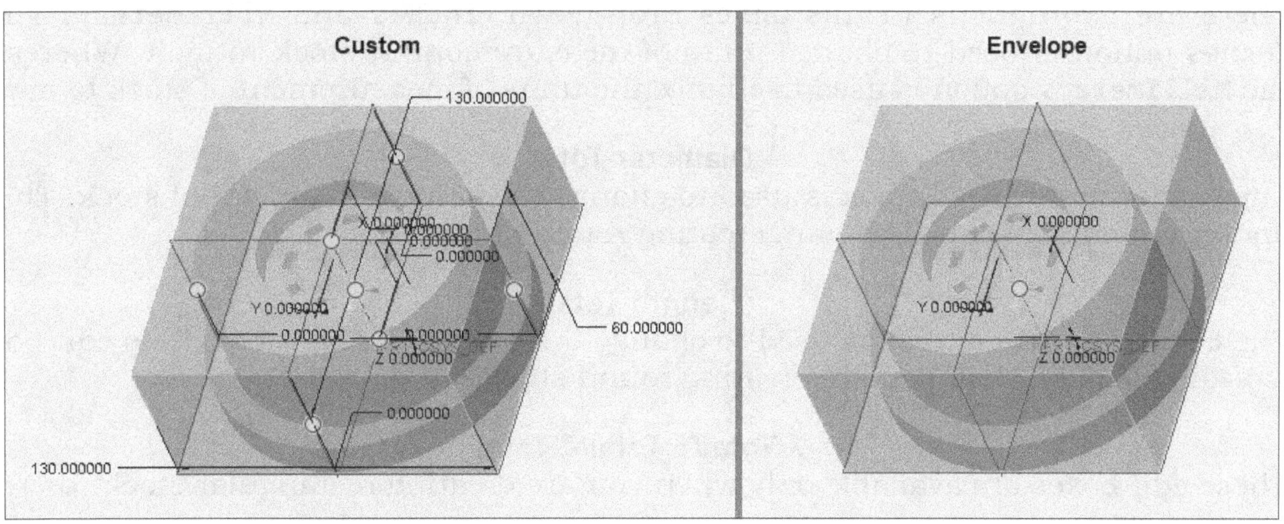

Figure-6. Stock created using Custom and Envelope option

Symmetric about Z axis

The **Use Z for Symmetry** toggle button is available in the **Options** area of **Auto Workpiece Creation** contextual tab in the **Ribbon**. If this toggle button is selected then the stock is created symmetric about the Z axis i.e. you cannot rotate the stock in any direction. If this toggle button is not selected then you can rotate the stock about any of the three axes (X, Y, and Z).

Options tab

There are various options available in this tab to change settings for stock; refer to Figure-7. Options in this tab are discussed next.

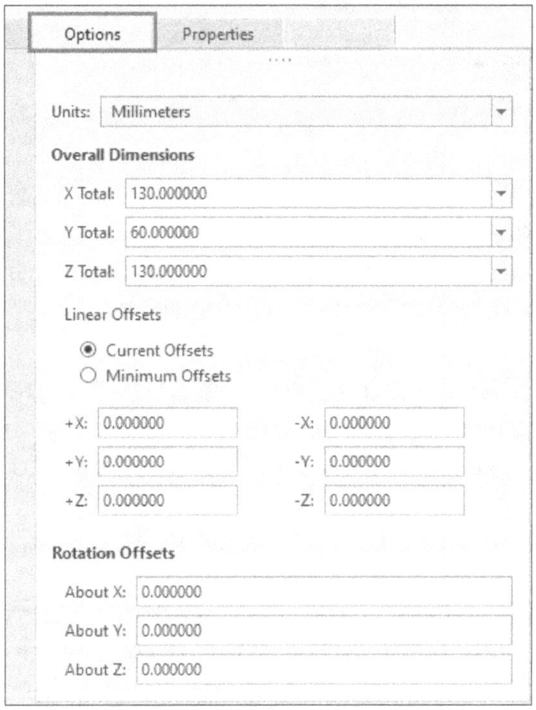

Figure-7. Options tab

Units

There are two options in this **Units** drop-down; **Inches** and **Millimeters**. The **Inches** option is used to change units of measurement of stock to inch. Whereas the **Millimeters** option is used to change the units of measurement of stock to mm.

Diameter Total

The **Diameter Total** edit box is used to change the value of diameter of stock. This option is available only if you are creating round stock.

Length Total

The **Length Total** edit box is used to change the total length of stock. This edit box is available only when you are creating round stock.

X Total/Y Total/Z Total

These edit boxes are available only when you are creating rectangular stock.

- The **X Total** edit box is used to specify the thickness of stock in X direction.
- The **Y Total** edit box is used to specify the thickness of stock in Y direction.
- The **Z Total** edit box is used to specify the thickness of stock in Z direction.

Linear Offsets

There are two radio buttons in this area; **Current Offsets** and **Minimum Offsets**.

- On selecting the **Current Offsets** radio button, you can specify the thickness of stock around the reference model.
- If the **Minimum Offsets** radio button is selected then you can specify the minimum thickness of stock around the reference model.
- If you are creating rectangular stock then six edit boxes will be available in the **Linear Offsets** area to specify the thickness in X, Y, and Z direction.
- If you are creating round stock then three edit boxes will be available in the **Linear Offsets** area to specify stock in diameter and length.

Rotation Offsets

There are three edit boxes available in this area; **About X**, **About Y**, and **About Z**. These edit boxes are used to specify rotation value of stock about X, Y, and Z axes.

- After creating desired stock, click on the **OK** button from **Auto Workpiece Creation** contextual tab and then click on the **Done** button from the **NC Model Menu Manager**. The assembly environment of Creo Parametric will be displayed; refer to Figure-8.

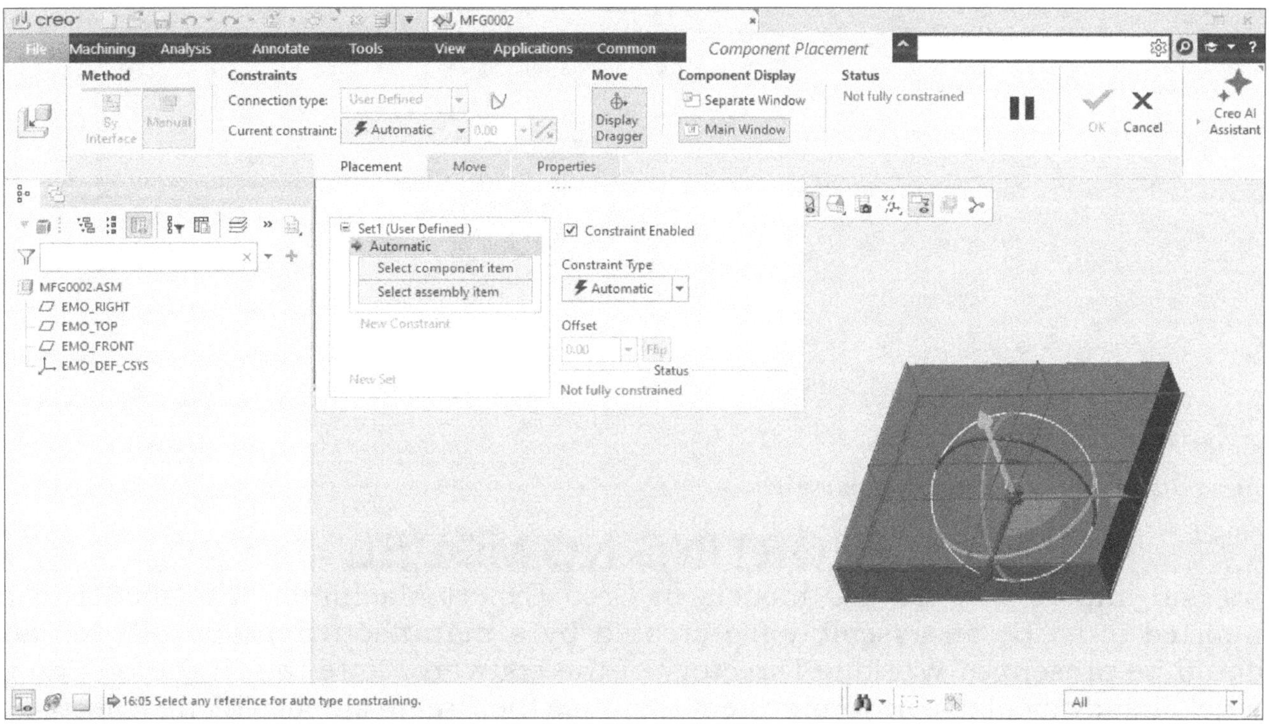

Figure-8. The assembly environment of Creo Parametric

- Also, you will be prompted to constrain the workpiece by proper constraints. In this case, select the **Default** option from the **Current constraint** drop-down in **Constraints** area of **Component Placement** contextual tab in the **Ribbon**; refer to Figure-9 and click on the **OK** button. The workpiece will be placed at origin.

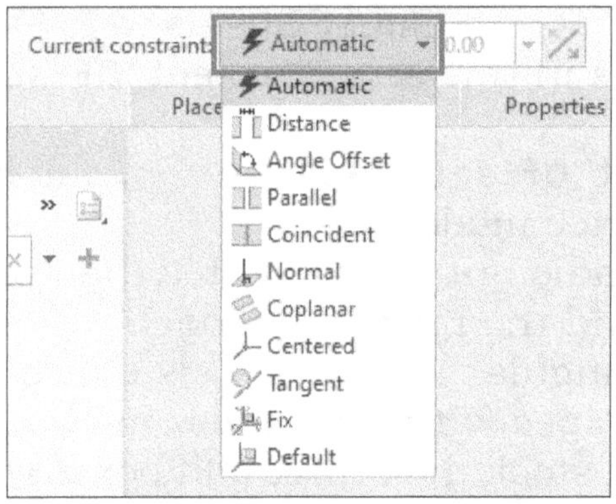

Figure-9. Current constraint drop down

After assembling the workpiece, the model will be displayed as shown in Figure-10.

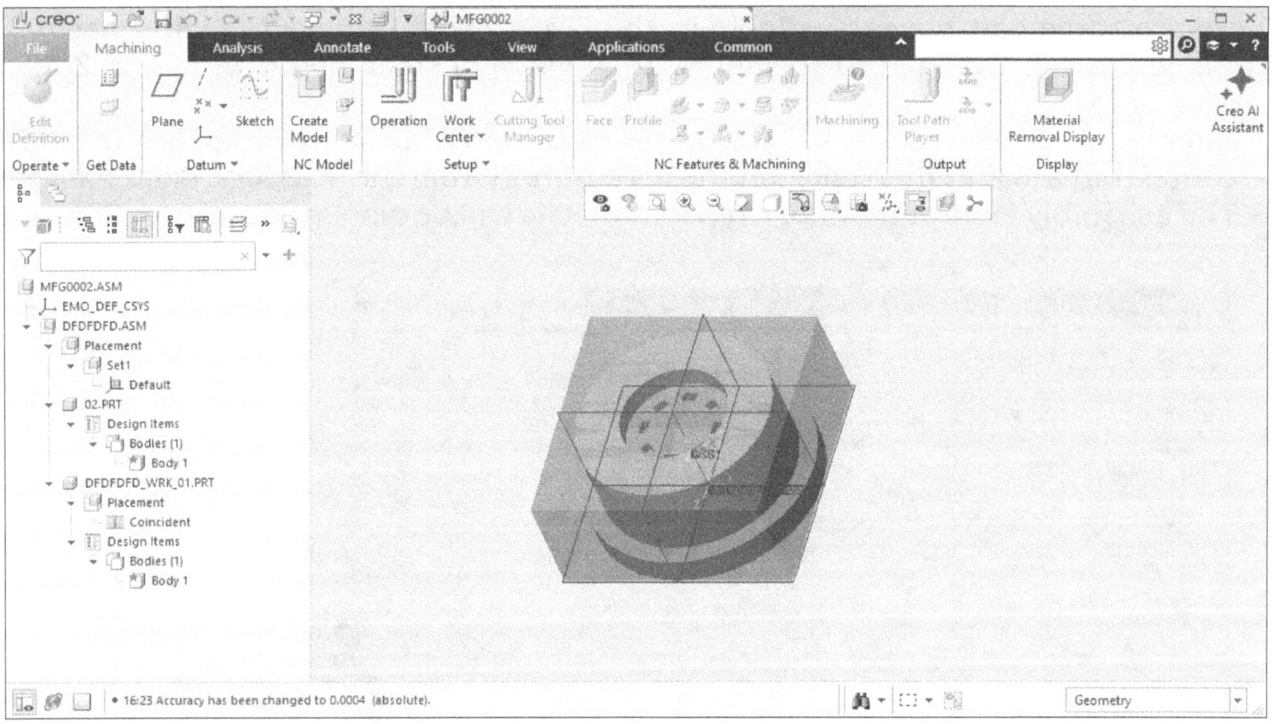

Figure-10. The model after assembling the workpiece

IMPORTING NC MODEL

You can import only the NC models in Creo Expert Machinist. The model to be imported must be an assembly file created by a manufacturing app of Creo and should be present in Working Directory of the software. Note that if there is no nc model already available in your system then use the Create Model which is discussed earlier. The procedure to import the assembly file is given next.

- Click on the **Add Model** button from the **NC Model** panel of the **Machining** tab in the **Ribbon**; refer to Figure-11. The **Choose NC Model** dialog box will be displayed; refer to Figure-12.

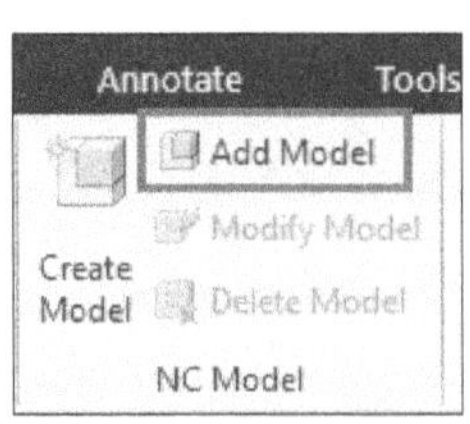

Figure-11. Add Model button

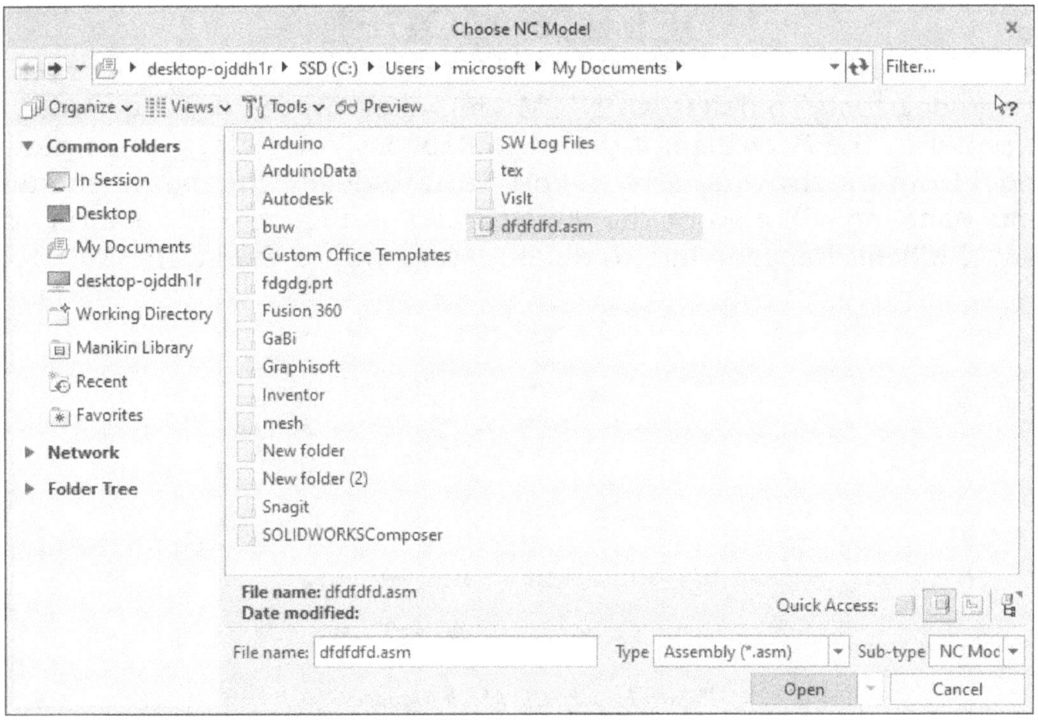

Figure-12. Choose NC Model dialog box

- Browse to desired file using this dialog box and select the model file to be imported. Now, click on the **OK** button from the dialog box; a new window of Creo Parametric will be displayed along with **NC Model Menu Manager**; refer to Figure-13.

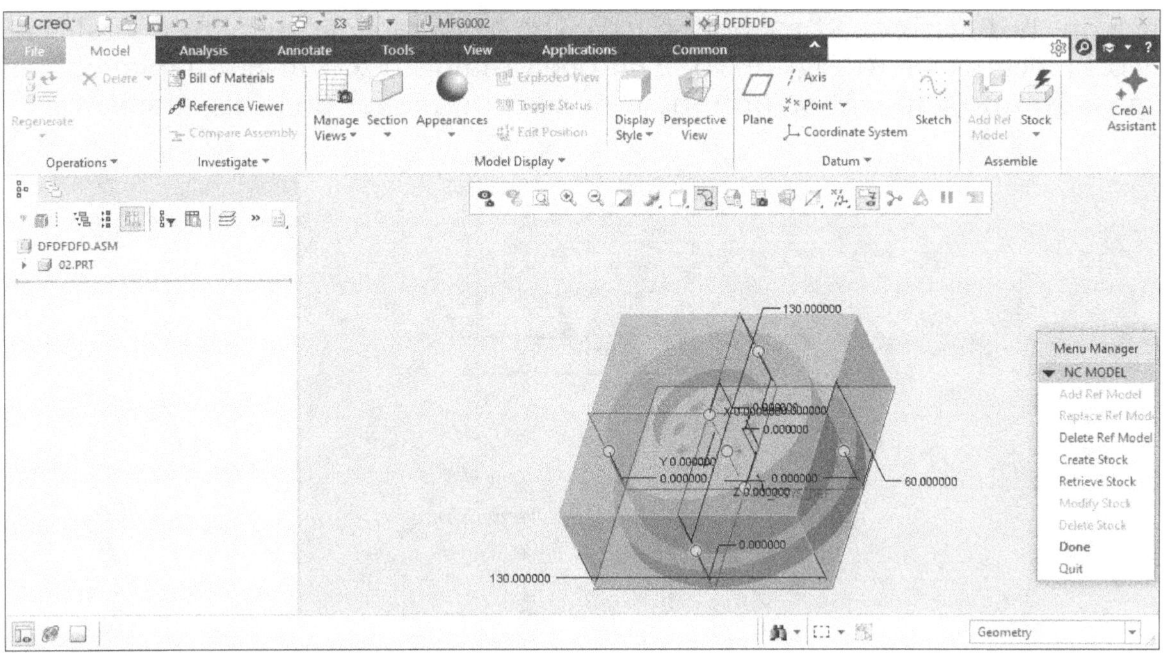

Figure-13. Creo Parametric window with Menu Manager

MODIFY MODEL

You can modify the NC Model present in the drawing area depending on your requirement by using the **Modify Model** tool. To modify the model, click on the **Modify Model** tool from the **NC Model** panel of the **Machining** tab in the **Ribbon**. You will be prompted to select an NC Model and **NC Model Menu Manager** will be displayed. Select the **Modify Stock** option from the **Menu Manager**, the **Auto Workpiece Creation** contextual tab will be displayed. Options in this tab have already been discussed.

DELETE MODEL

You can delete one or more of the NC Model present in the drawing area by using the **Delete Model** tool. To delete an NC Model, click on the **Delete Model** tool from **NC Model** panel in the **Machining** tab of the **Ribbon**. You will be prompted to select an NC Model from the drawing area. If you want to delete the parent model then the **Child Menu Manager** will also be displayed; refer to Figure-14. Various options are available in the **Menu Manager** like to delete, suspend, or freeze the NC Model.

Figure-14. CHILD Menu Manager

RETRIEVING STOCK

You can add an assembly or a model as a stock by using the **Retrieve Stock** option. The procedure to use this tool is discussed next.

- Click on the **Retrieve Stock** option from the **Menu Manager** displayed while creating a workpiece; refer to Figure-15. The **Open** dialog box will be displayed; refer to Figure-16 and you will be prompted to select a file for creating stock.

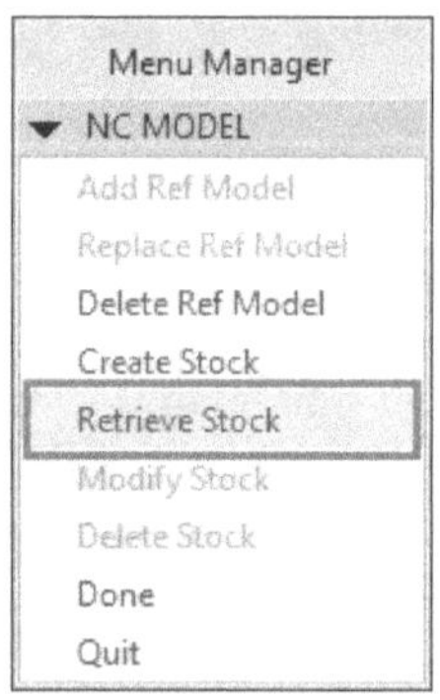

Figure-15. NC MODEL Menu Manager

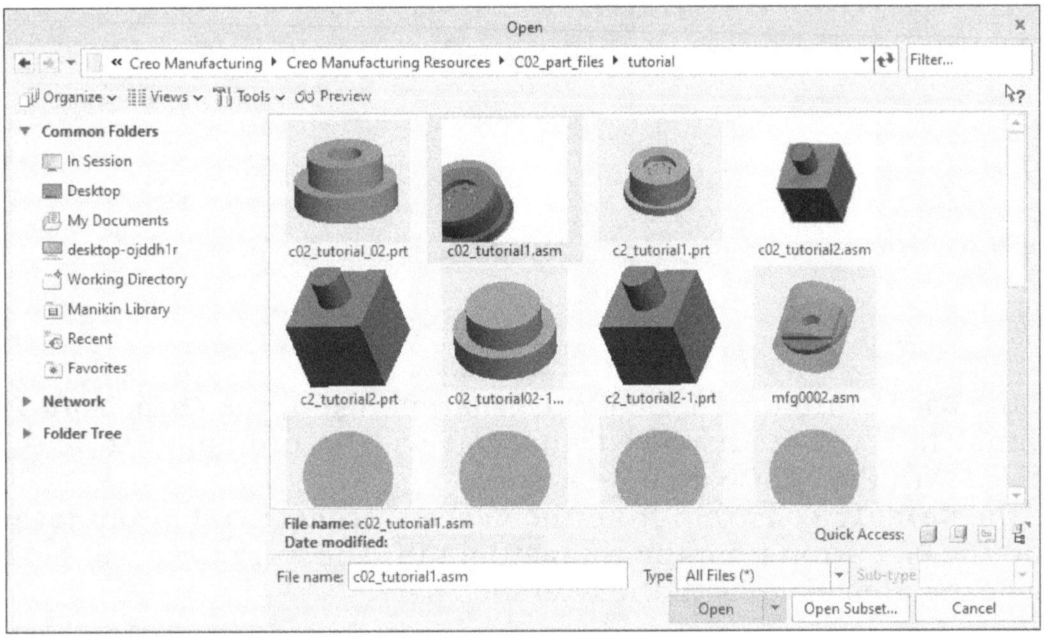

Figure-16. Open dialog box

- Select desired stock file and click on **Open** button from the dialog box. The **Component Placement** contextual tab will be activated and you will be prompted to assemble the stock with the reference part; refer to Figure-17.

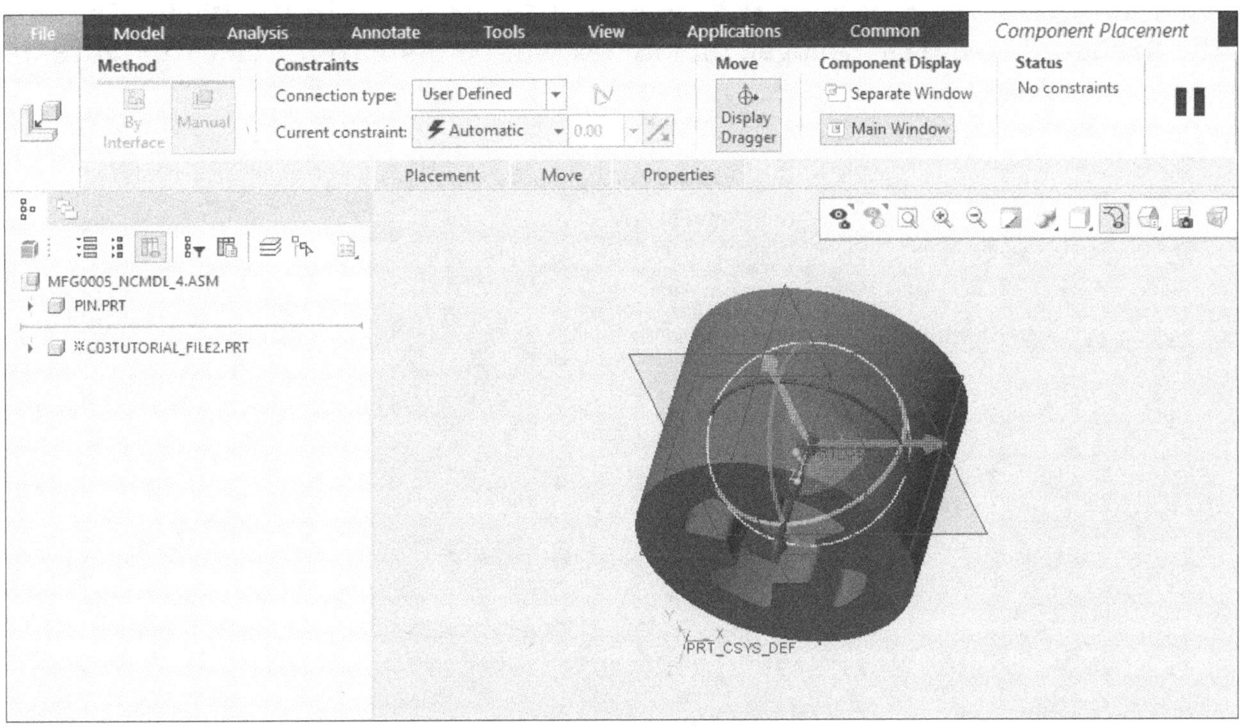

Figure-17. The application window with the Component Placement tab activated

- Assemble the stock with the reference part using proper constraints and then click on the **OK** button from the contextual tab. The **NC MODEL Menu Manager** will be displayed as shown in Figure-18.

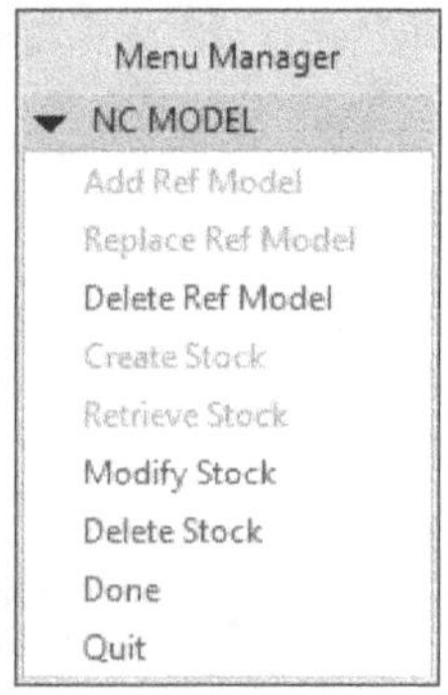

Figure-18. NC MODEL Menu Manager

- Select the **Done** button from the **Menu Manager**. Again, the **Component Placement** contextual tab will be displayed and you will be prompted to assemble the workpiece with the NC Coordinate system.
- Select the **Default** constrain from the **Current constraint** drop-down list and click on the **OK** button from the contextual tab. The workpiece will be created in the modeling area along with the reference part.

Setting Units for the NC Model

While working in the **Expert Machinist** environment, you can change the units of model any time. The procedure to use this tool is discussed next.

- Click on the **Units** tool from the expanded **Setup** panel in the **Machining** tab of the **Ribbon**. The **Units Manager** dialog box will be displayed; refer to Figure-19.

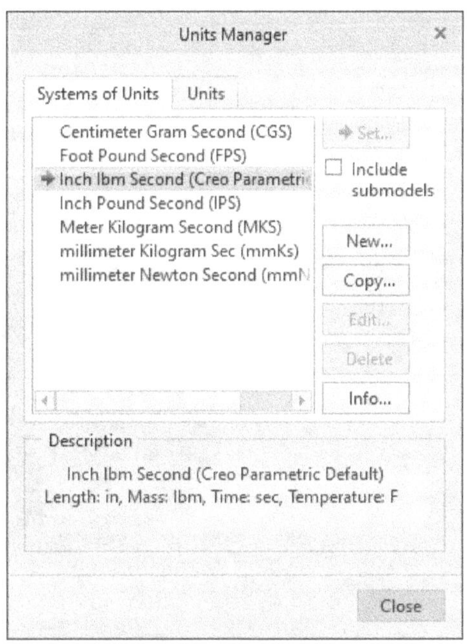

Figure-19. Units Manager dialog box

- There are two tabs available in this dialog box; **Systems of Units** and **Units**. Options available in these tabs are discussed next.

System of Units

Options of this tab are displayed as shown in Figure-19. These options are discussed next.

Set

A red arrow is displayed adjacent to the unit system selected by the current template. In this case, **Inch lbm Second** is selected. So, a red arrow is displayed adjacent to the unit system.

- To set any other unit system, select desired unit system from the list and click on the **Set** option from the right. The **Changing Model Units** dialog box will be displayed; refer to Figure-20.

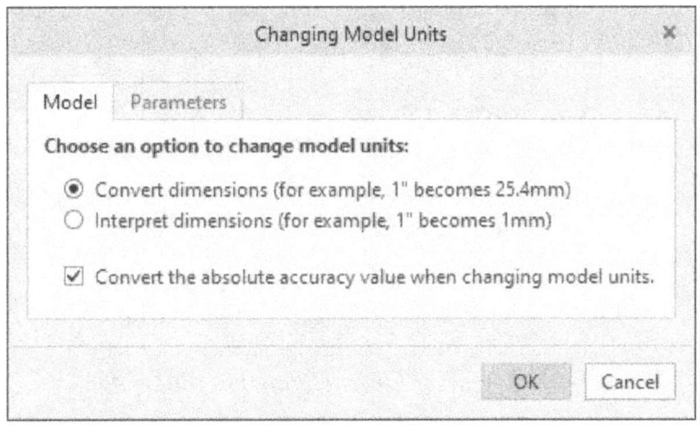

Figure-20. Changing Model Units dialog box

- Select the **Convert dimensions** radio button if you want to convert the values of previous unit in current unit. This option is useful when a model was created in inches and you want to convert it to mm. Select the **Interpret dimensions** radio button if you have earlier selected inches as unit by mistake but want to create the model in mm. Select the required option from **Changing Model Units** dialog box and click on **OK** button.
- The red arrow will shift to that selected unit system and the unit system will be set.

New

The **New** option is used to create a user defined unit system. The procedure to use this tool is discussed next.

- Click on the **New** button from **Units Manager** dialog box. The **System of Units Definition** dialog box will be displayed; refer to Figure-21.

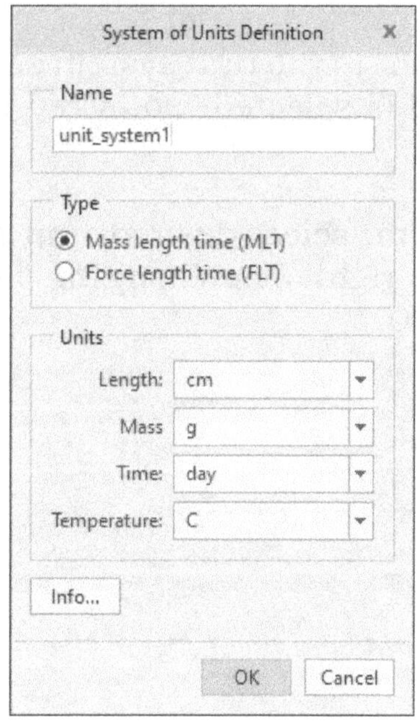

Figure-21. System of Units Definition dialog box

- Specify desired name in the **Name** edit box.
- Select desired type of unit system from the **Type** area, the options available in the **Units** area will modify accordingly.
- Select desired option from the **Length**, **Mass/Force**, **Time**, and **Temperature** drop-downs.
- Click on the **Info** button to check the derived units. The **INFORMATION WINDOW** will be displayed; refer to Figure-22. All the derived units from the current unit system are displayed in this window.
- After checking the derived units, click on the **Close** button from the window and then click on the **OK** button from the **System of Units Definition** dialog box. A new unit system will be displayed in the unit system list in the **Systems of Units** tab.

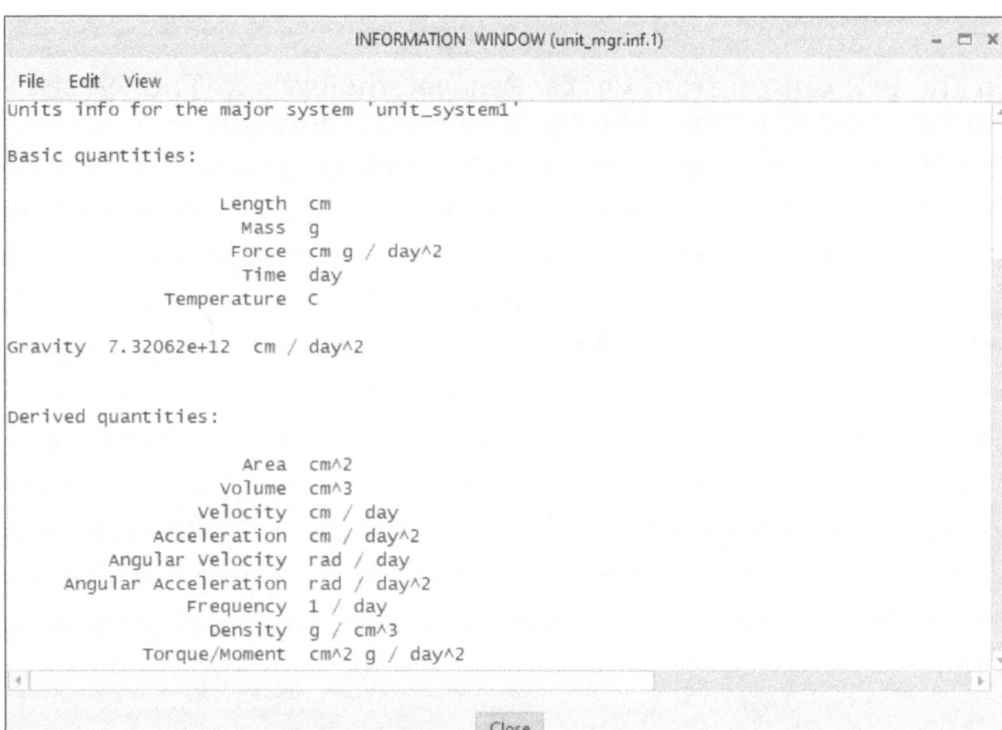

Figure-22. INFORMATION WINDOW

Copy

The **Copy** option is used to create a copy of the already created unit system.

- Click on the **Copy** button from the **Units Manager** dialog box. The **Copy System of Units** dialog box will be displayed; refer to Figure-23.

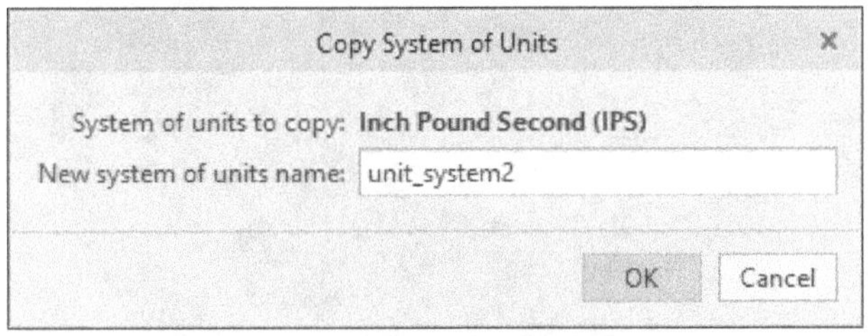

Figure-23. Copy System of Units dialog box

- Specify desired name of unit system in the **New system of units name** edit box.
- After specifying the parameters, click on the **OK** button to create a copy of the currently set unit system.

Edit

The **Edit** option is used to edit an already created unit system. Click on the **Edit** button, the **System of Units Definition** dialog box is displayed. This dialog box is similar to the one displayed on clicking on the **New** option.

Delete

The **Delete** option is used to delete an already created unit system. By using this option, you can delete only the custom created unit system. To delete a custom unit system, click on the **Delete** option from the dialog box. A confirmation dialog box will be displayed. Click on the **Confirm** button from the dialog box. The unit system will be deleted.

Info

The **Info** option is used to display information about the selected unit system.

- Click on the **Info** button, the **INFORMATION WINDOW** is displayed. Options in this window have already been discussed.

TUTORIAL 1

In this tutorial, you will import a reference model as shown in Figure-24 and you will create a workpiece having uniform thickness of 2 over the reference model. The model file for reference model is available in the Resources kit.

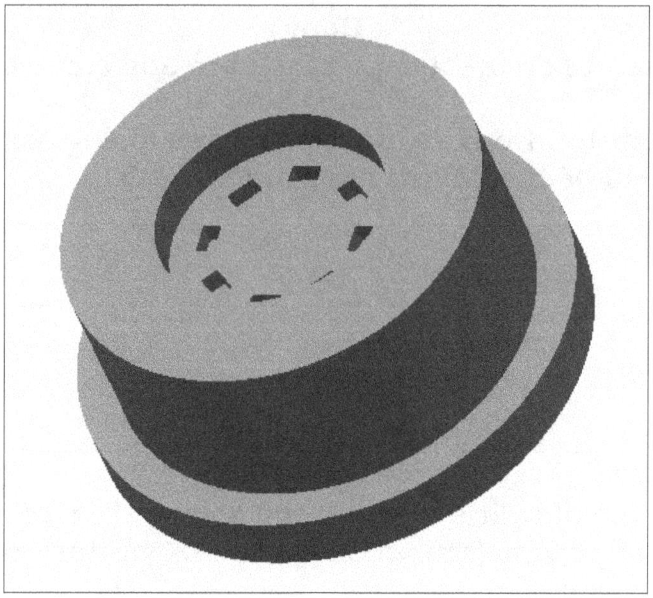

Figure-24. A reference model to be imported

Steps required to complete the tutorial:

1. Copy the model from the resource kit in your local drive.
2. Open the **Expert Machinist** application window by using the metric template.
3. Create a new workpiece using the reference model copied from the resource kit.

Copying the reference model

- Extract the resources kit folder provided with the book at desired location.
- Set the folder as working directory.

Tip: To set a folder as working directory, select **Folder Browser** option from the **Navigator** area and expand the **Folder Tree** node. Select desired folder from the **Folder Tree** and right click on it, a shortcut menu is displayed. Click on the **Set Working Directory** option from the shortcut menu, the folder will become the current working directory.

Starting Expert Machinist

- Open the Creo Parametric application by double-clicking on the Creo Parametric icon on the desktop.
- Click on the **New** button from the **Data** panel in the **Home** tab of the **Ribbon**. The **New** dialog box will be displayed; refer to Figure-25.

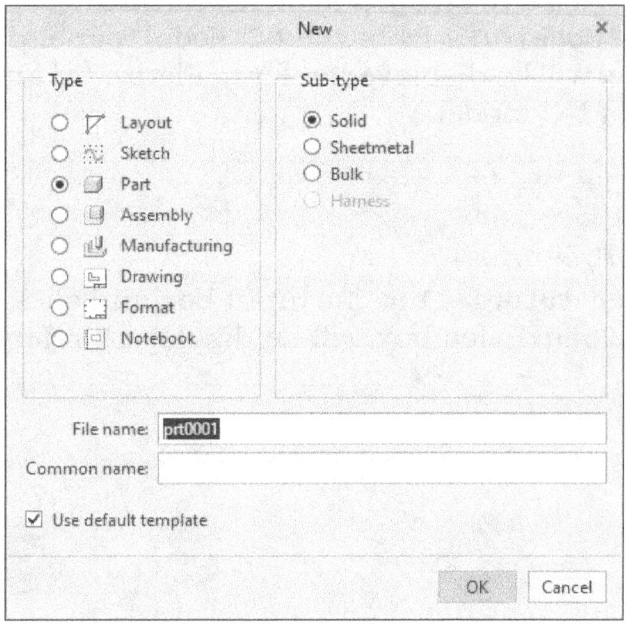

Figure-25. New dialog box

- Select the **Manufacturing** radio button from the **Type** area and **Expert Machinist** from the **Sub-type** area.
- Specify the name as **c02tutorial1** in the **Name** edit box and clear the **Use default template** check box from the dialog box.
- Click on the **OK** button from the dialog box. The **New File Options** dialog box is displayed; refer to Figure-26.

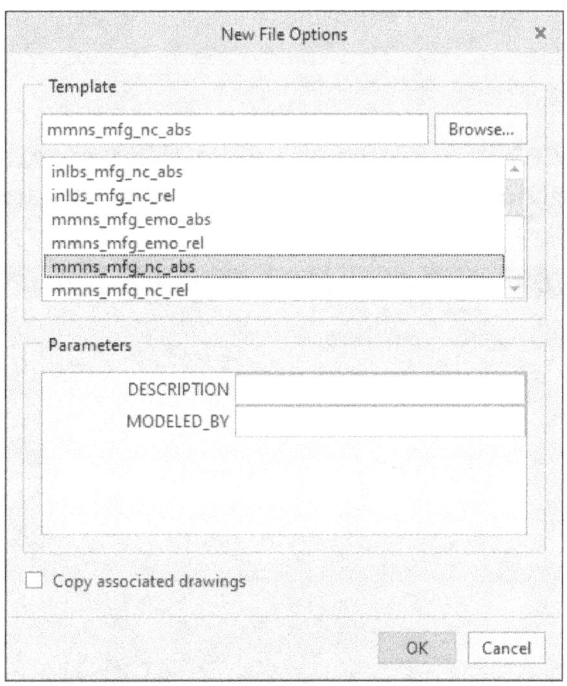

Figure-26. New File Options dialog box

- Select the **mmns mfg nc abs** option from the list of templates displayed and click on the **OK** button from the dialog box. The **Expert Machinist** environment of the Creo Parametric will be displayed with metric units selected.

Creating a new NC Model

- Choose the **Create Model** tool from the **NC Model** panel of **Machining** tab in the **Ribbon**. An input box will be displayed; refer to Figure-27 and you will be prompted to enter the name of NC model.

Figure-27. An input box

- Enter the name as **nc tutorial1** in the input box and click on the button from the input box. The **Open** dialog box will be displayed; refer to Figure-28.

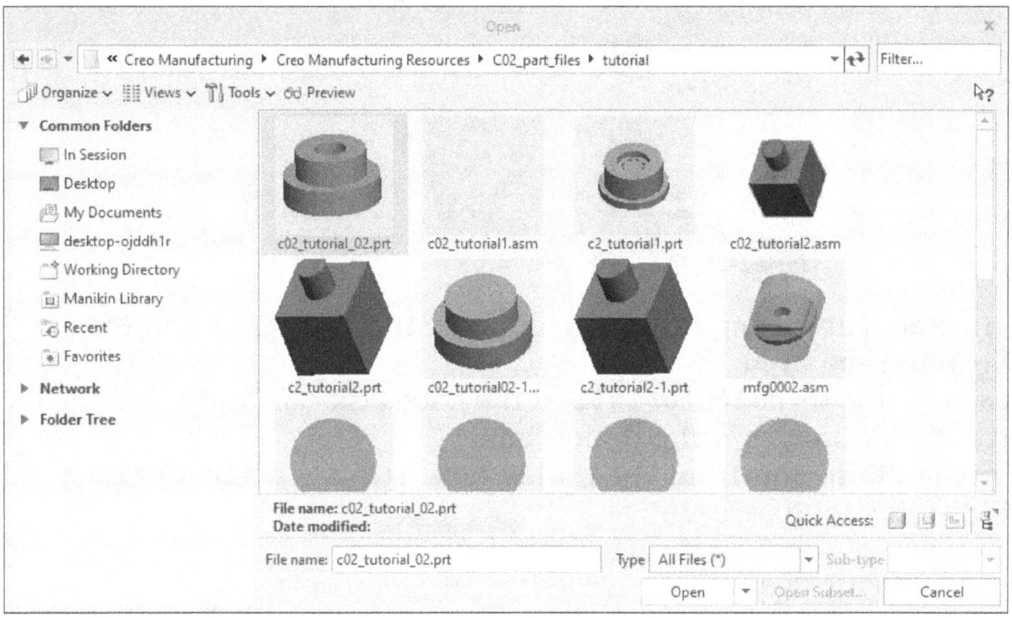

Figure-28. Open dialog box

- Browse to the folder **C02** in resources, select the **tutorial1.prt** file and click on the **Open** button from the dialog box. The application window will be displayed as shown in Figure-29.

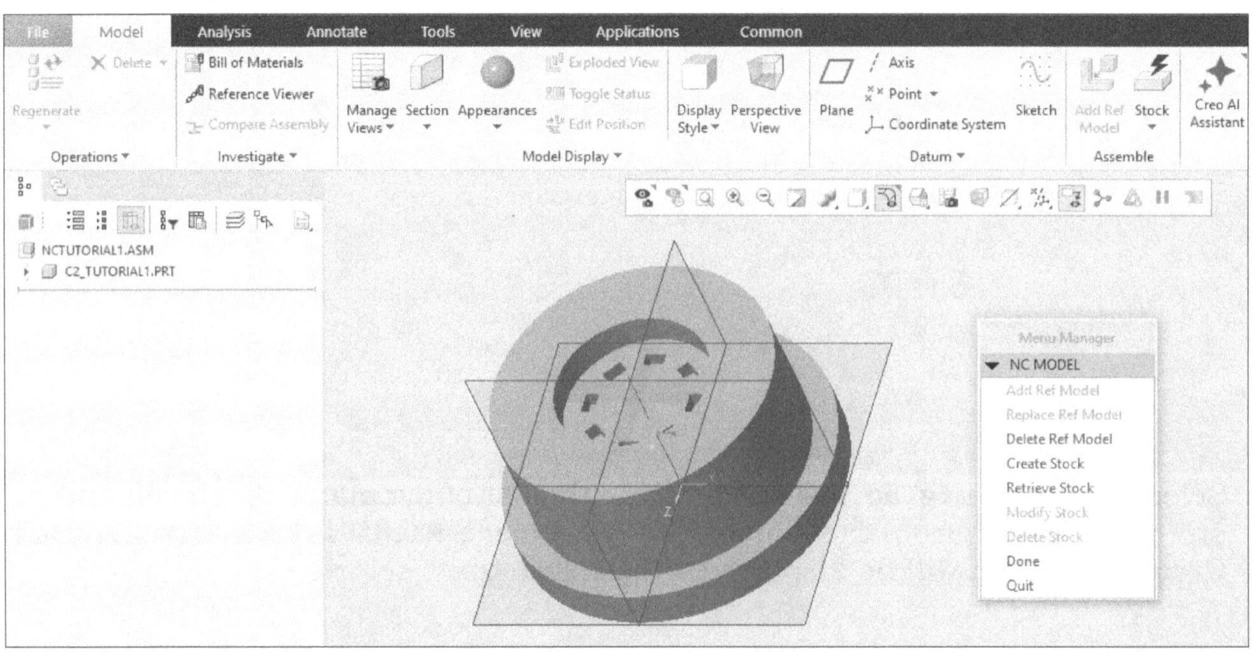

Figure-29. The application window after selecting the file

- Click on **Create Stock** option from the **NC MODEL Menu Manager**. A rectangular stock is created around the reference model; refer to Figure-30.

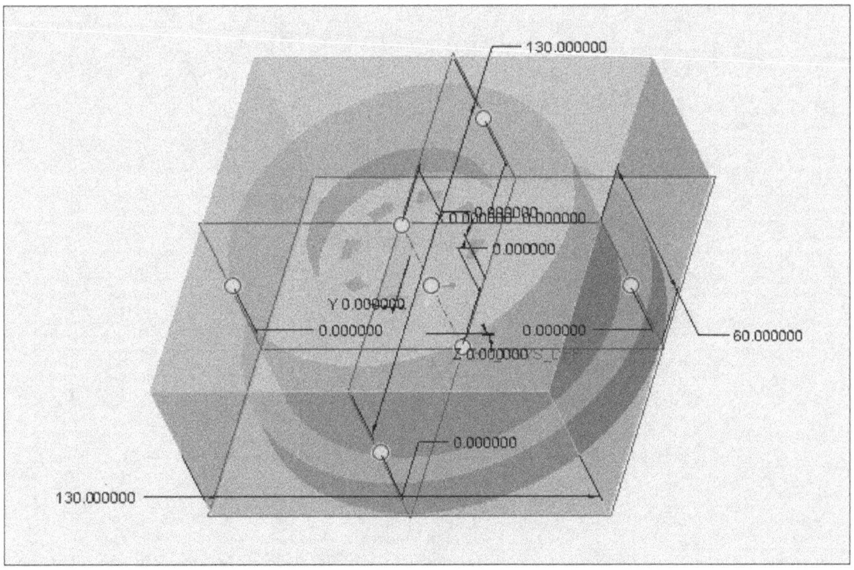

Figure-30. A rectangular block created around the reference model

- Click on the **Round** button from **Workpiece Type** area of the **Auto Workpiece Creation** contextual tab. The model will be displayed as shown in Figure-31.

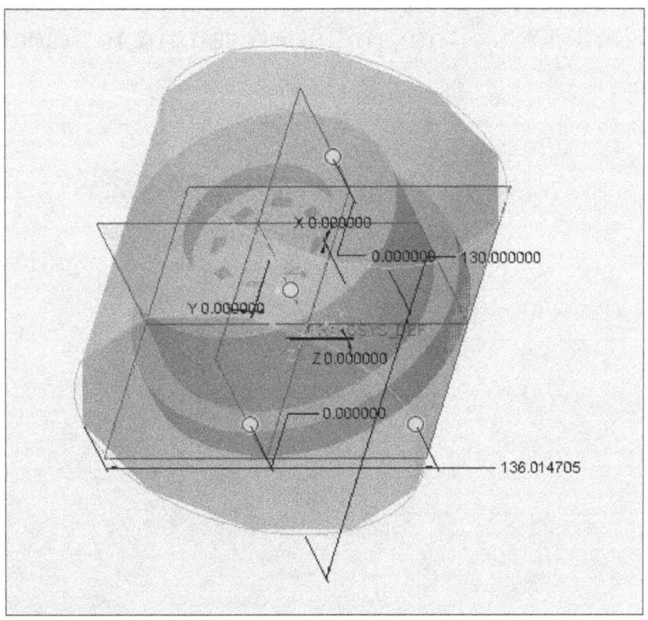

Figure-31. The model after selecting the Round button

- Click on the **Options** tab, a flyout is displayed. Enter **90** in the **About X** edit box available in the **Rotation Offsets** area of the flyout, the model will be displayed as shown in Figure-32.

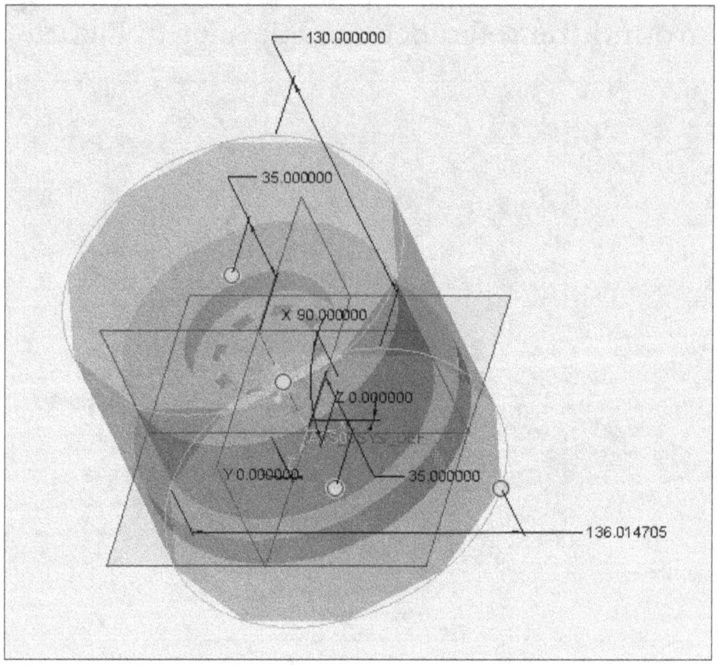

Figure-32. The model after specifying 90 in the About X edit box

- Specify the value of diameter and length offsets as **2** in the **Diameter**, **Length(+)** and **Length(-)** edit boxes, respectively in **Linear Offsets** area of **Options** tab; refer to Figure-33. Make sure that millimeters unit is selected in the **Units** drop-down list.

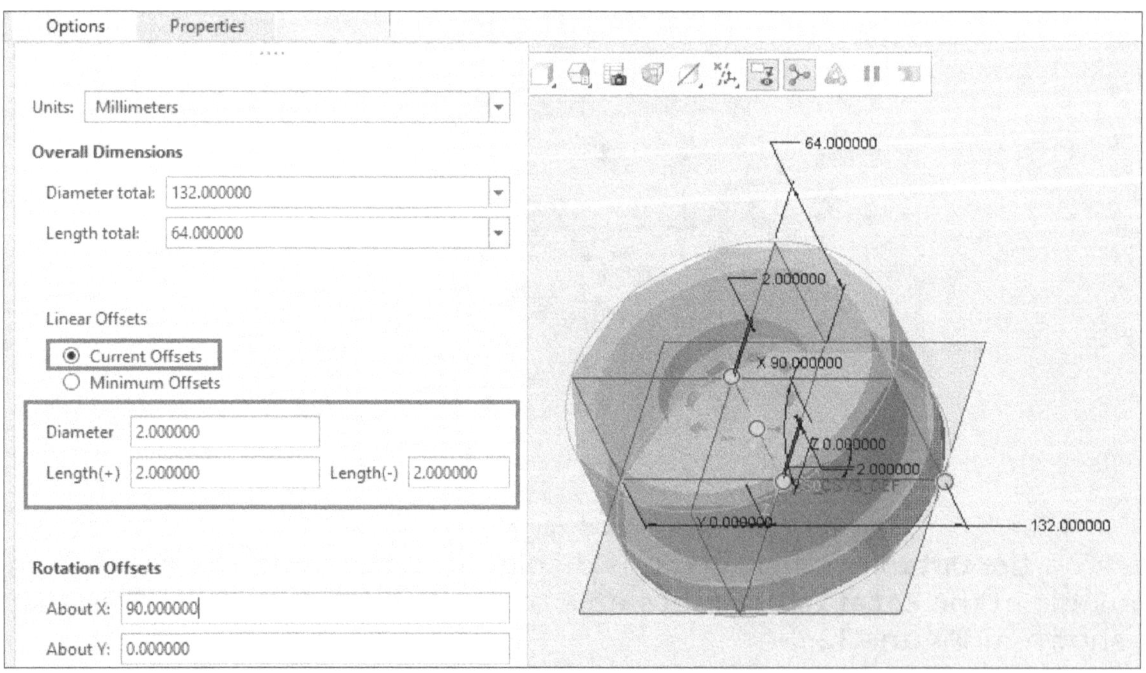

Figure-33. Offsets for stock

- Click on the **OK** button from the **Ribbon** to create the workpiece. The workpiece will be displayed as a green transparent round block; refer to Figure-34.

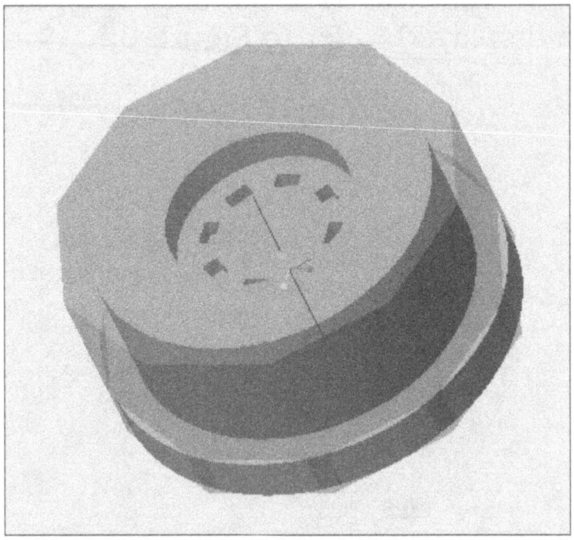

Figure-34. The workpiece with the reference model

- Click on the **Done** option from the **NC MODEL Menu Manager**, the Expert Machinist environment will be displayed along with the **Component Placement** contextual tab selected. You are now prompted to place the workpiece with reference part in Machine coordinate system.
- Click on the **Default** option from the **Current constraint** drop-down list in the **Ribbon** and click on the **OK** button.

TUTORIAL 2

In this tutorial, you will import a reference model provided in the resources as **c02 tutorial2** and you will create a workpiece by using a retrieved model provided in resources as **c2 tutorial2-1.prt**. The model file for reference model and retrieving model are available in the Resources kit.

Steps required to complete the tutorial:
1. Copy the model from the resource kit in your local drive.
2. Open the **Expert Machinist** application window by using the metric template.
3. Retrieving the model provided for creating workpiece.

Copying the reference model

- Extract the resources kit folder provided with the book at desired location.
- Browse to the location **\resources\chapter2\data** and copy the file in the **Creo Manufacturing\Chapter2\tutorial** folder in your local drive.
- Set Creo Manufacturing folder as a working directory.

Tip

To set a folder as working directory, select **Folder Browser** option from the **Navigator** area and expand the **Folder Tree** node. Select desired folder from the **Folder Tree** and right click on it, a shortcut menu is displayed. Select the **Set Working Directory** option from the shortcut menu, the folder will become the current working directory.

Starting Expert Machinist

- Open the Creo Parametric application by double clicking on the Creo Parametric icon on the desktop.

- Click on the **New** button from the **Data** panel in the **Home** tab of the **Ribbon**. The **New** dialog box will be displayed; refer to Figure-35.

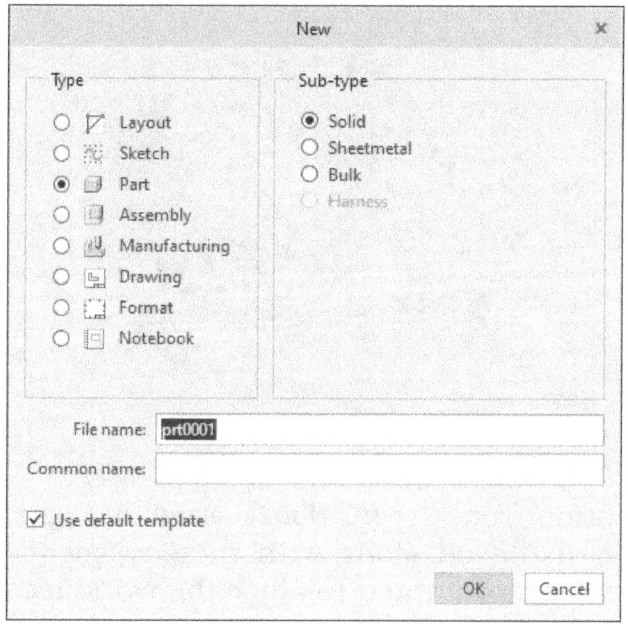

Figure-35. New dialog box

- Select **Manufacturing** radio button from the **Type** area and **Expert Machinist** from the **Sub-type** area.
- Specify the name as **c02 tutorial2** in the **Name** edit box and clear the **Use default template** check box from the dialog box.
- Click on the **OK** button from the dialog box. The **New File Options** dialog box is displayed; refer to Figure-36.

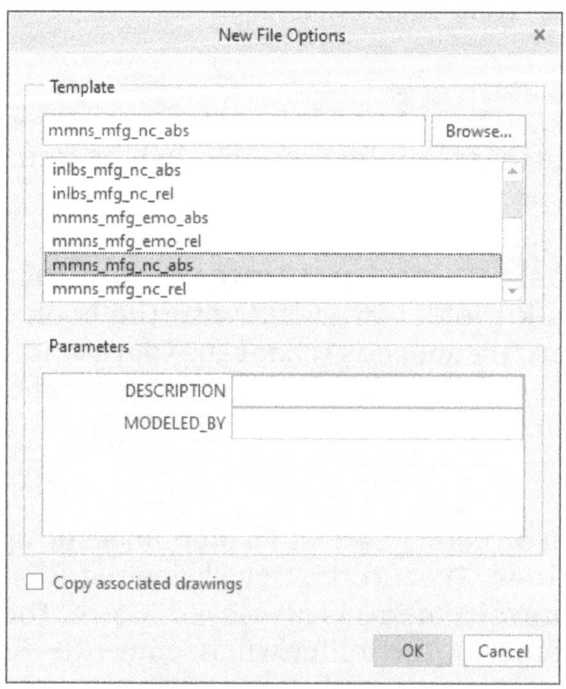

Figure-36. New File Options dialog box

- Select the **mmns mfg nc abs** option from the list of templates displayed and click on the **OK** button from the dialog box. The Expert Machinist environment of the Creo Parametric will be displayed with metric units selected.

Creating a new NC Model

- Click on the **Create Model** tool from the **NC Model** panel of **Machining** tab in the **Ribbon**. An input box will be displayed; refer to Figure-37 and you will be prompted to enter the name of NC model.

Figure-37. An input box

- Enter the name as **nc tutorial2** in the input box and click on the ✓ button from the input box. The **Open** dialog box will be displayed along with **NC MODEL Menu Manager**; refer to Figure-38.

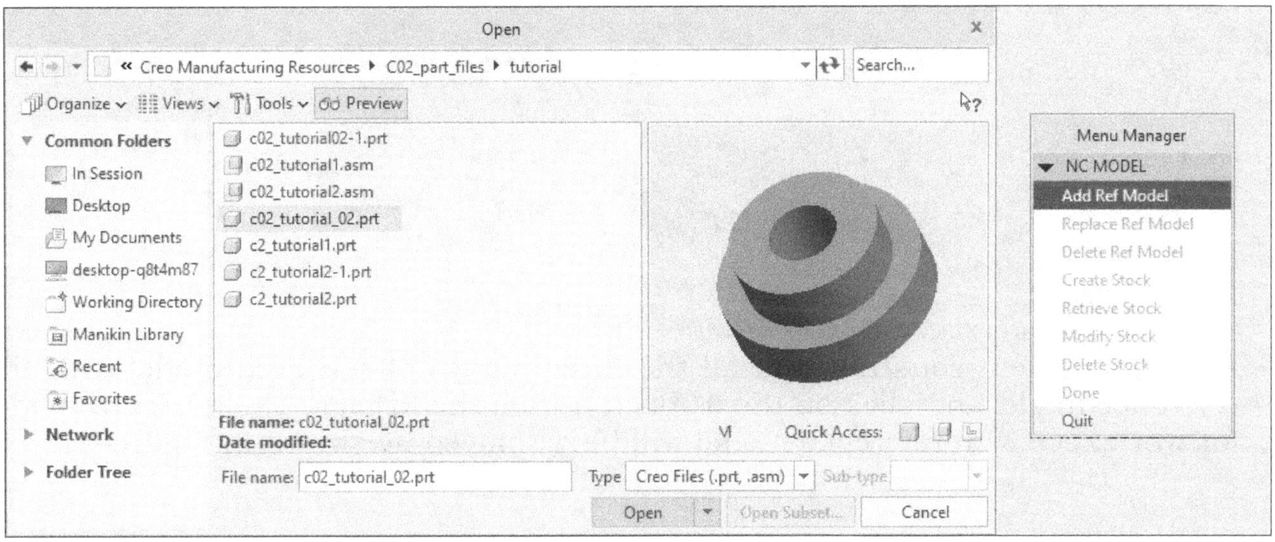

Figure-38. Open dialog box along with NC MODEL menu manager

- Browse to the location **Creo Manufacturing\Chapter 2\tutorial**, select the **C2 tutorial2.prt** file, and click on the **Open** button from the dialog box. The application window will be displayed; refer to Figure-39.

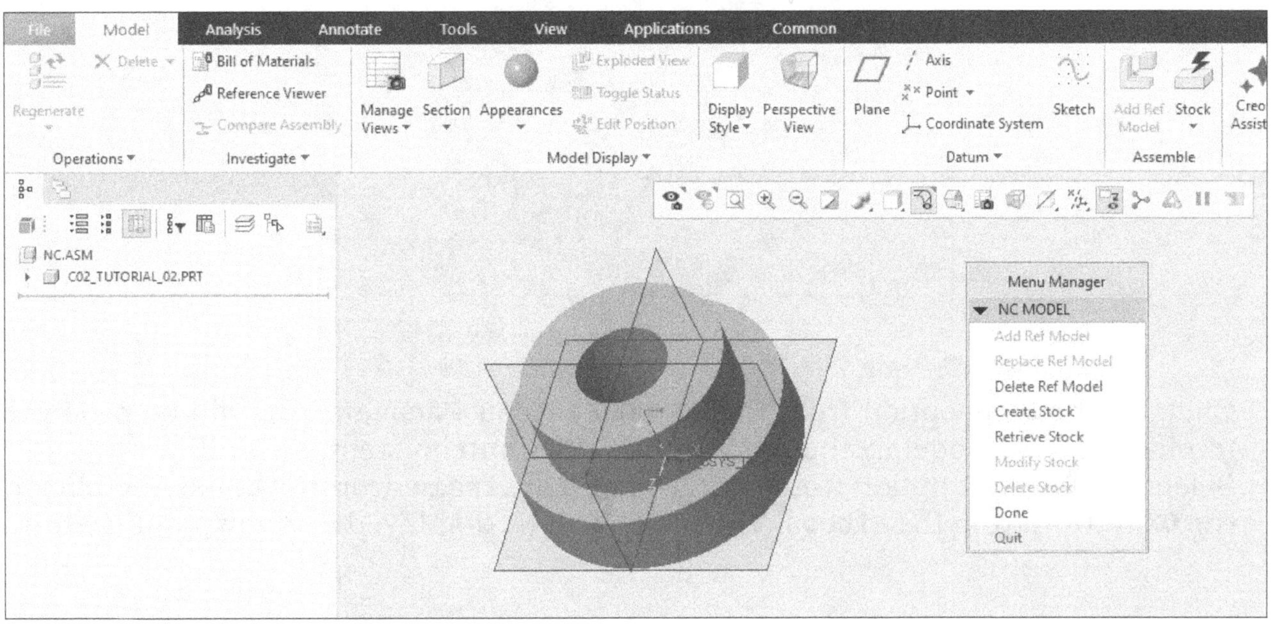

Figure-39. The application window after selecting the file

- Click on the **Retrieve Stock** option from the **NC MODEL Menu Manager**. The **Open** dialog box will be displayed.

- Browse to the location **Creo Manufacturing\Chapter 2\tutorial**, select the **C02 tutorial2-1.prt** file, and click on the **Open** button from the dialog box. The application window will be displayed as shown in Figure-40.

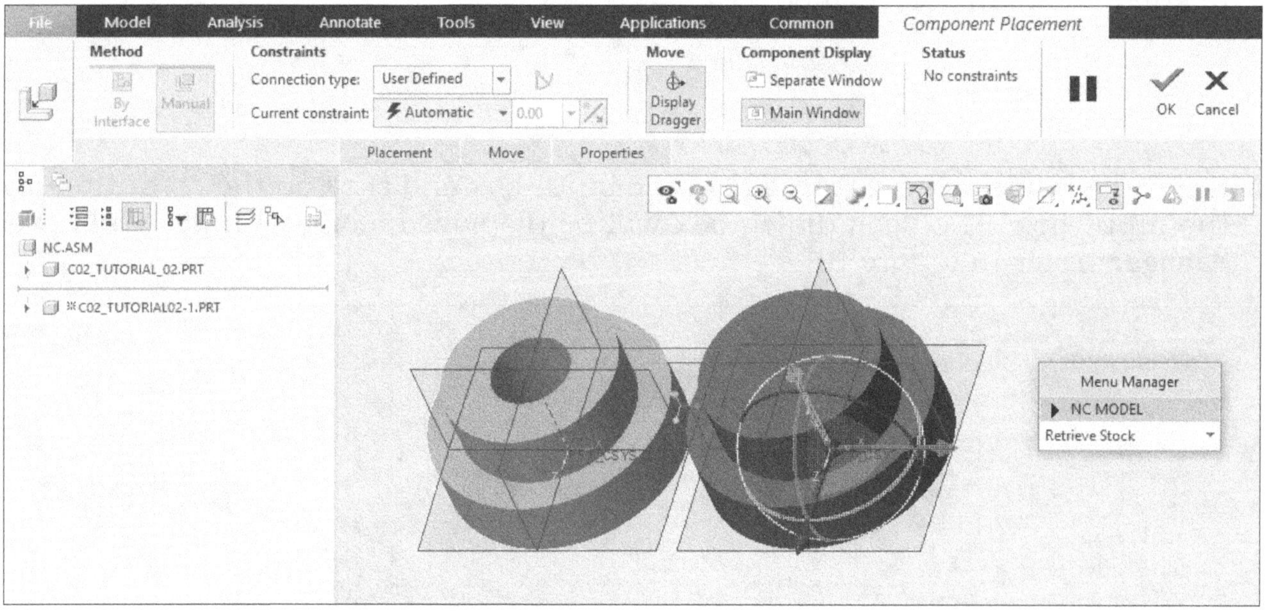

Figure-40. The application window after inserting the file

- Apply coincident constraint on all the three planes of retrieved model with the reference model and click on the **OK** button from the **Ribbon**. The retrieved model for workpiece with reference model will be displayed as shown in Figure-41.

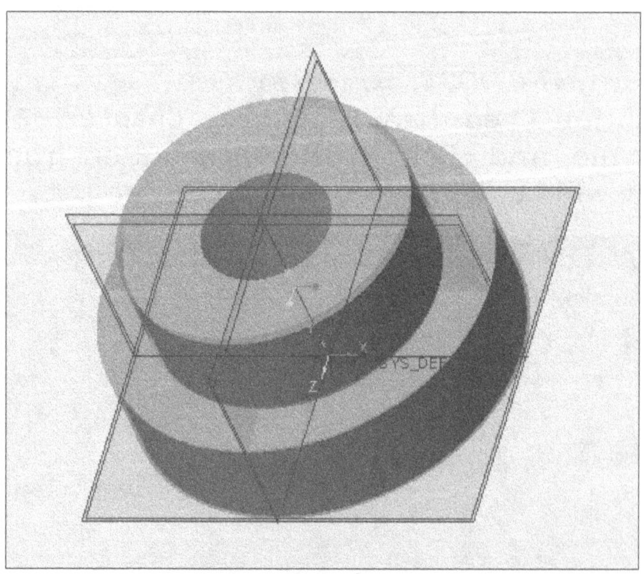

Figure-41. The model after retrieving the model of workpiece

- Click on the **Done** option from the **NC MODEL Menu Manager**. You will be prompted to place the nc model in the machining coordinate system.
- Select the **Default** option from the **Current constrain** drop-down list and click on the **OK** button from the **Ribbon**. The model will be displayed as shown in Figure-42.

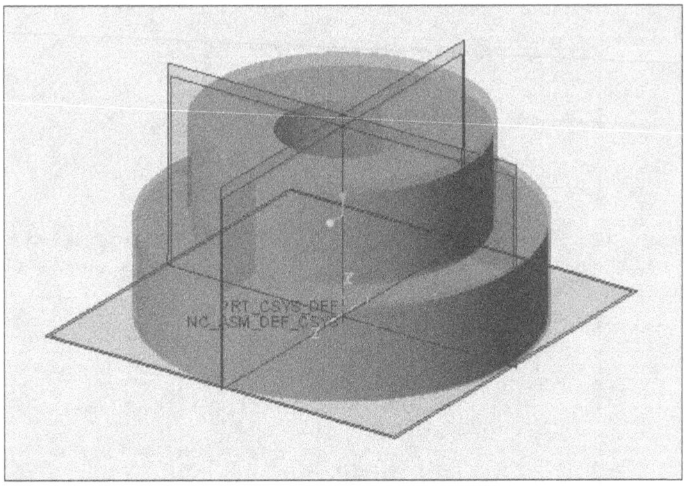

Figure-42. The reference model with workpiece

PRACTICE 1

Create a workpiece for the model given in Figure-43. Dimensions of the model are given in Figure-44. You can also find this model in the exercise area of the resources kit.

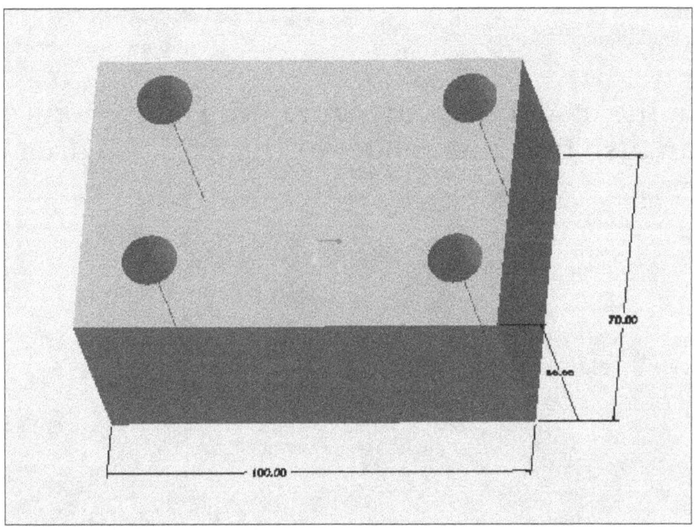

Figure-43. Practice 1

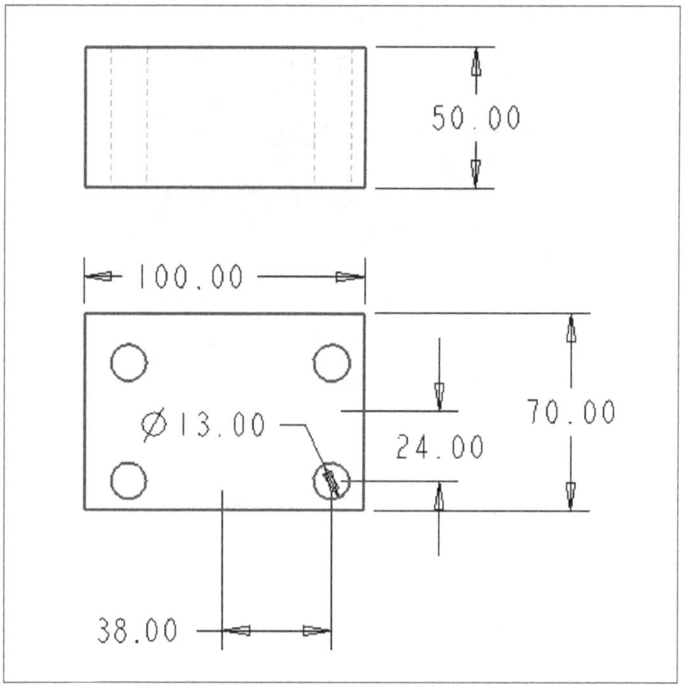

Figure-44. Dimension for Practice 1

PRACTICE 2

Create a workpiece for the model given in Figure-45. Dimensions of the model are given in Figure-46. You can also find this model in the exercise area of the resources kit.

Figure-45. Practice 2

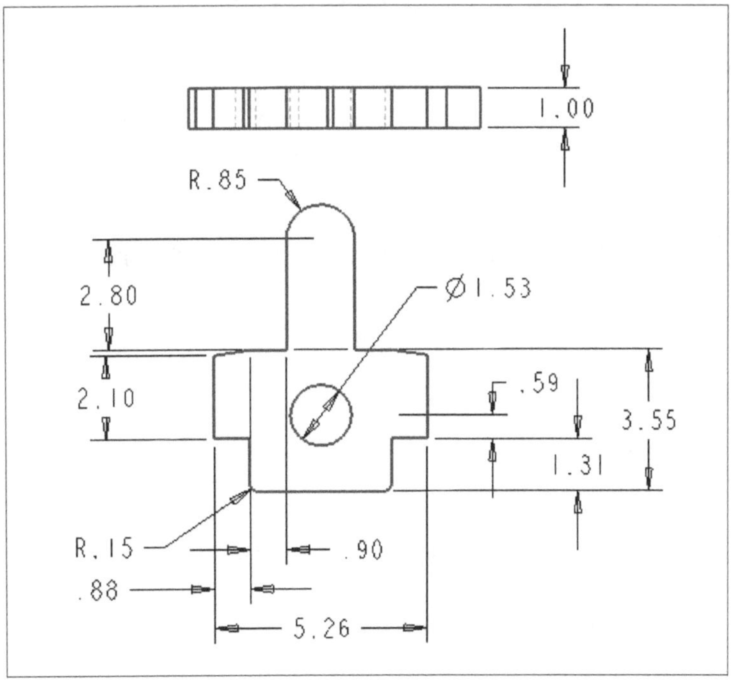

Figure-46. Dimension for Practice 2

SELF-ASSESSMENT

Q1. What type of file can be imported in Creo Expert Machinist?

A. Part files only
B. Drawing files only
C. NC assembly files created by manufacturing apps of Creo
D. Any CAD file

Q2. What is the purpose of the 'Create Stock' option in NC Model Menu Manager?

A. To assemble parts
B. To convert units
C. To define material to be machined
D. To export models

Q3. What shape does the Rectangular option create around the reference model?

A. Spherical
B. Elliptical
C. Rectangular jacket
D. Triangular prism

Q4. In which area is the 'Workpiece Type' located?

A. Units tab
B. Options tab
C. NC Model Menu Manager
D. Auto Workpiece Creation contextual tab in the Ribbon

Q5. Which of the following allows for symmetric stock creation about the Z axis?

A. Default constraint
B. Use Z for Symmetry toggle
C. Units drop-down
D. Info button

Q6. Which drop-down in the Options tab is used to define stock shape as Custom or Envelope?

A. Workpiece Type
B. Linear Offsets
C. Stock-workpiece's sub-shape
D. Component Placement

Q7. What does the Diameter Total edit box control?

A. Thickness of rectangular stock in Y direction
B. Length of rectangular stock
C. Diameter of round stock
D. Z offset of the model

Q8. What does selecting the Interpret dimensions radio button in the Changing Model Units dialog box do?

A. Converts dimension values
B. Ignores all dimensions
C. Retains unit but adjusts modeling units
D. Interprets inches as millimeters without conversion

Q9. How many rotation offset directions are available while creating stock?

A. One
B. Two
C. Three
D. Four

Q10. Which of the following tools is used to delete an NC Model?

A. Create Stock
B. Modify Model
C. Delete Model
D. Remove Part

Q11. What option allows retrieval of an existing assembly or model as stock?

A. Import Part
B. Retrieve Stock
C. Replace Stock
D. Insert Stock

Q12. What unit options are available in the Units drop-down in the Options tab?

A. Inches and Feet
B. Millimeters and Meters
C. Inches and Millimeters
D. Inches and Centimeters

Q13. What happens when the Envelope option is selected in stock sub-shape?

A. Rotated jacket is formed
B. User defines size manually
C. Automatic envelope is formed around model
D. No changes occur

Q14. Which option allows the creation of a user-defined unit system?

A. New
B. Copy
C. Delete
D. Edit

Q15. Which step follows clicking Done in the NC Model Menu Manager during stock creation?

A. Creating constraints
B. Opening new model
C. Saving workspace
D. Launching simulation

Q16. What happens when you double-click on a handle of the stock during creation?

A. The stock is deleted
B. The handle is locked
C. An edit box appears to input a value
D. The handle changes direction

Q17. Which edit boxes are used to define rectangular stock thickness in all directions?

A. Diameter Total and Length Total
B. X Total, Y Total, Z Total
C. About X, About Y, About Z
D. Units and Custom

Q18. When creating a round workpiece, which options are available for Linear Offsets?

A. Six edit boxes for X, Y, Z directions
B. Two for diameter only
C. Three for diameter and length
D. None

Q19. What does the Modify Model tool allow you to do?

A. Convert the model into part file
B. Export the NC model
C. Modify the existing stock of the NC model
D. Change the color of the model

Q20. What must you do after retrieving a stock file and assembling it?

A. Delete the previous version
B. Use the Edit command
C. Constrain it with the reference part
D. Reboot Creo

Q21. What does the Info button show in the System of Units Definition dialog box?

A. Model errors
B. Active constraints
C. Derived units of the current unit system
D. Stock thickness values

Q22. What action does the 'Set' button perform in the Units Manager dialog box?

A. Copies the current unit system
B. Deletes the selected unit system
C. Assigns the selected unit system as current
D. Changes the temperature units only

Q23. Which file type is selected in the Open dialog box while importing a model for NC?

A. .dwg
B. .asm or .prt
C. .obj
D. .igs

Q24. In the Expert Machinist template selection, which option enables working in millimeters?

A. inch lbm sec
B. mmns mfg nc abs
C. imperial template
D. default manufacturing

Chapter 3

Tool Setting

Topics Covered

The major topics covered in this chapter are:

- ***Foundation of Tooling.***
- ***Various tools available for milling and parameters.***
- ***Creating a tool setup.***
- ***Saving a tool setup.***
- ***Importing a tool setup.***
- ***Creating a user defined tool.***
- ***Checking for minimum radius.***
- ***Checking for shortest edge.***

TOOLING OF A MACHINE

Tool is the main cutting member of machine. All the output of a machine depends on the type of tool selected. The tool selection in return depends on two main factors: Machine to be used and type of machining. Like, for lathe machines generally HSS bar is used, for CNC turning machine tungsten coated bits are used.

TOOLS AVAILABLE FOR MACHINING IN EXPERT MACHINIST

Expert Machinist is mainly used for creating programs for milling machines. Various tools that are generally used in a milling machine are discussed next.

End Mill

End Mill is a type of milling cutter used for removing material in axial as well as other directions. A few end mill can not cut material in axial direction which means they can not be used for drilling purpose. In a milling machine, End Mill cutter is used for operations like profiling, facing, plunging, and tracing. Parameters required to define an end mill cutter in Expert Machinist are displayed in Figure-1. Along with the dimensions shown in Figure-1, you need to specify number of flutes, dimension units, and the material of tool in Expert Machinist.

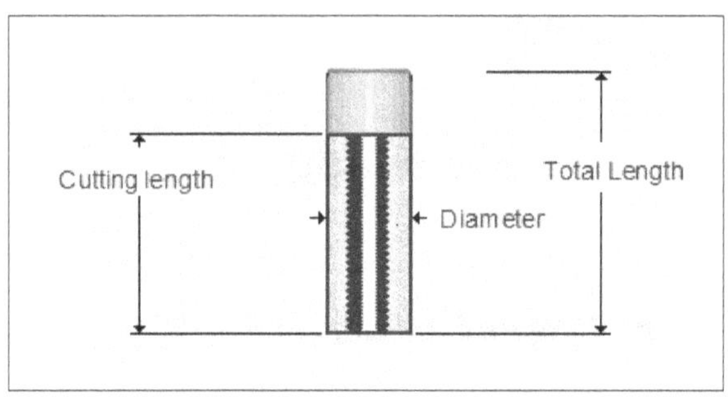

Figure-1. An End Mill with parameters

Ball Mill

Ball Mill, also called Ball Nose mill, is a type of milling cutter which is hemispherical at the bottom. These type of cutters are used to create 3D contour shapes in workpiece. These type of cutters are used in machining moulds and dies having 3D curves. Figure-2 shows the shape of a Ball Mill cutter and parameters required in Expert Machinist.

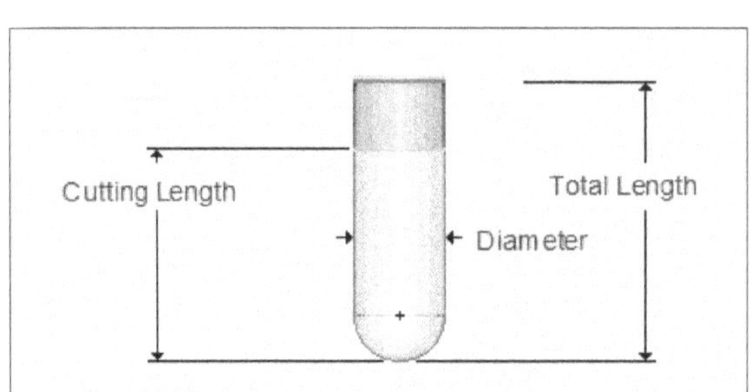

Figure-2. A Ball Mill with parameters

Bull Mill

Bull Mill, also called Bull Nose mill, is a type of milling cutter having fillet of specified value at the corner edges. This type of cutter is used for creating filleted corners in the workpiece. Generally, dies and moulds having internal fillets are machined by using this type of cutters. Figure-3 shows a Bull mill with the parameters required in Expert Machinist.

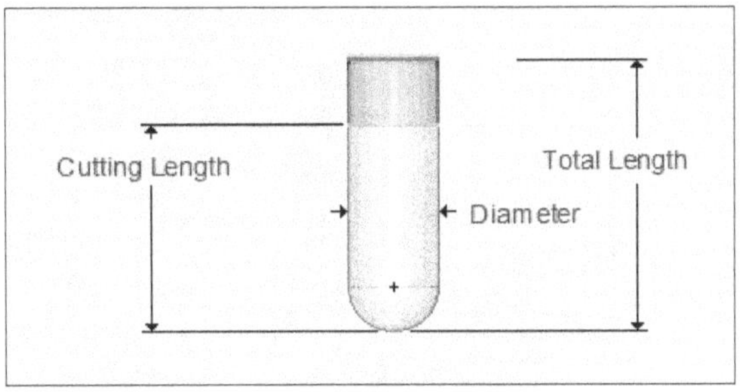

Figure-3. A Ball Mill with parameters

Taper Mill

Taper Mill is a type of milling cutter having radius at corner edges and taper at the cutting length. It is similar to the Bull Mill having the only difference that it has taper at the cutting length. This type of cutter is used for creating profiles having taper at the walls as well as fillet at the bottom. Figure-4 shows a Taper mill with the parameters required in Expert Machinist.

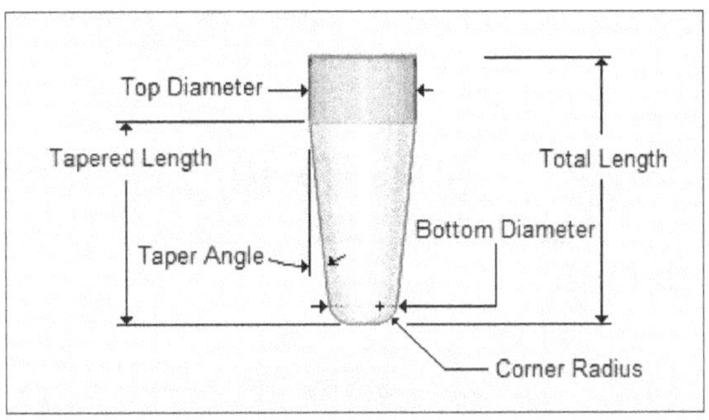

Figure-4. A Taper Mill with parameters

Taper Ball Mill

Taper Ball Mill is a type of milling cutter having curvature of a ball at the end. It is similar to a ball mill with the only difference that it has tapers cutting edges. This type of cutter is used for creating profiles having taper at the walls as well as fillet at the bottom. Figure-5 shows a Taper mill with the parameters required in Expert Machinist.

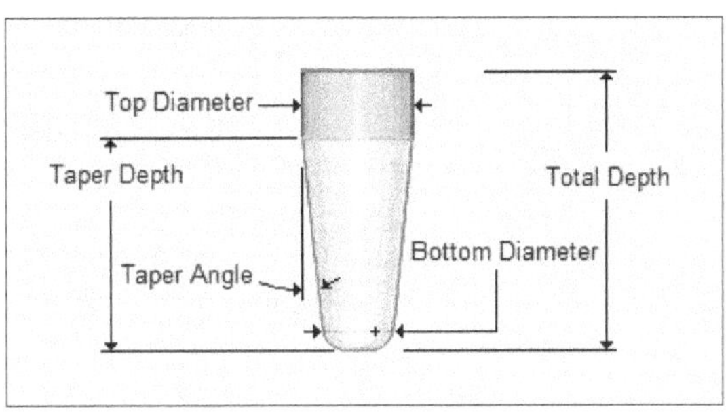

Figure-5. A Taper Ball Mill with parameters

Drill

Drill is a type of milling tool used to create holes in a workpiece. A drill can not be used for creating profile on the workpiece. Moreover, a drill can cut along the perpendicular axis because the bottom edges are the cutting edges. You should not use the side edges of a drill for cutting purpose. Figure-6 shows a drill with the parameters required in Expert Machinist.

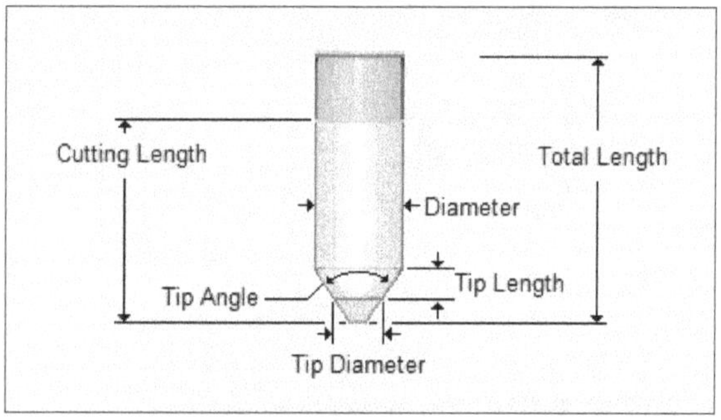

Figure-6. A Drill with parameters

Basic Drill

A basic drill is similar to the drill discussed earlier. The only difference is that it does not have tip. So, you do not need to specify the tip length and tip diameter.

Countersink

A countersink is a type of drill used to create countersunk holes in the workpiece. It is similar to the drill discussed earlier. The only difference is that its tip angle is 90 degree by default.

Spot Drill

A Spot drill is similar to basic drill discussed earlier. The only difference is that its tip angle is 90 degree by default.

Tap

Tap is a type of milling cutter used to create threads in a hole. Figure-7 shows a Tap with the parameters required in Expert Machinist.

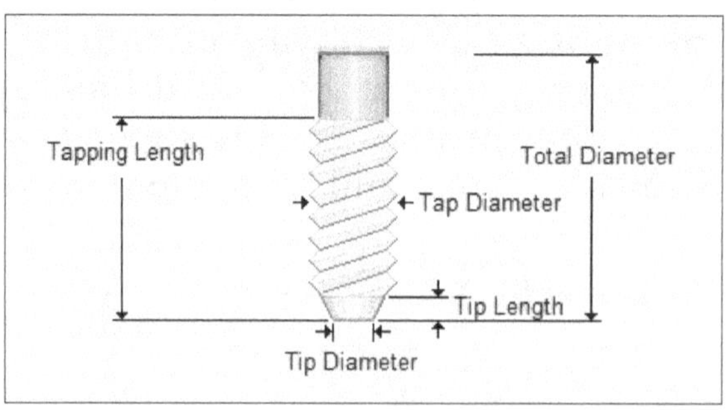

Figure-7. A Tap with parameters

Reamer

Reamer is a type of milling cutter used to increase the diameter of a hole. The total increase in diameter is less than 5% of the diameter of the hole. Also, the tolerance of the hole diameter created by reaming is less than 0.1 mm. So, a reamer is used to create accurate holes. Figure-8 shows a Reamer with the parameters required in Expert Machinist.

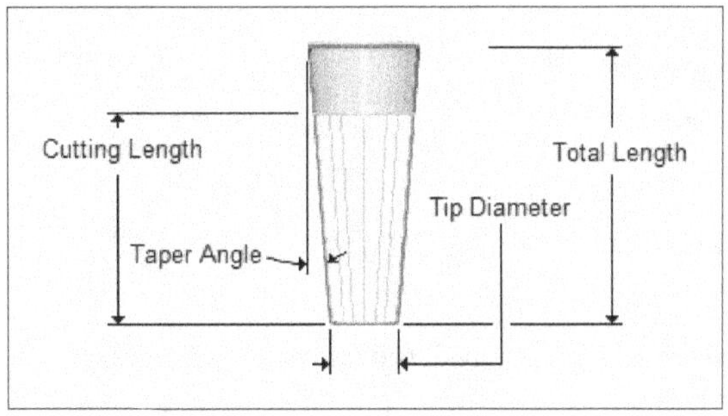

Figure-8. A Reamer with parameters

Boring Bar

Boring Bar is a type of milling cutter used to increase the diameter of a hole. Figure-9 shows a Boring Bar with the parameters required in Expert Machinist.

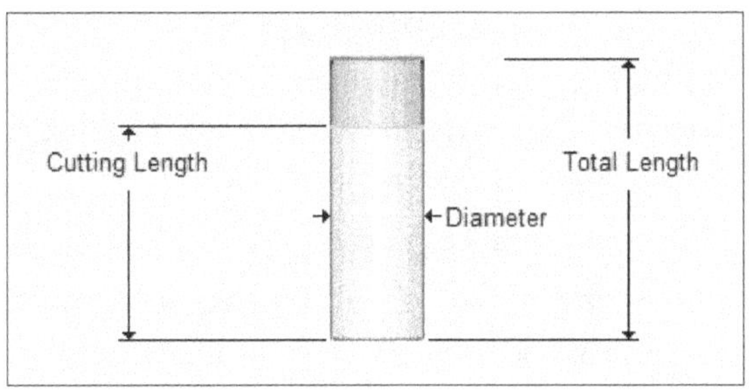

Figure-9. A Boring Bar with parameters

Center Drill

Center drill is a type of milling cutter used to make center holes. Mainly, it is used to provide starting hole for a larger diameter hole.

Back Spotting

Spot drill is used to provide a starting point for a common drill. The process of drilling such a point is called back spotting. Figure-10 shows a Spot drill with the parameters required in Expert Machinist.

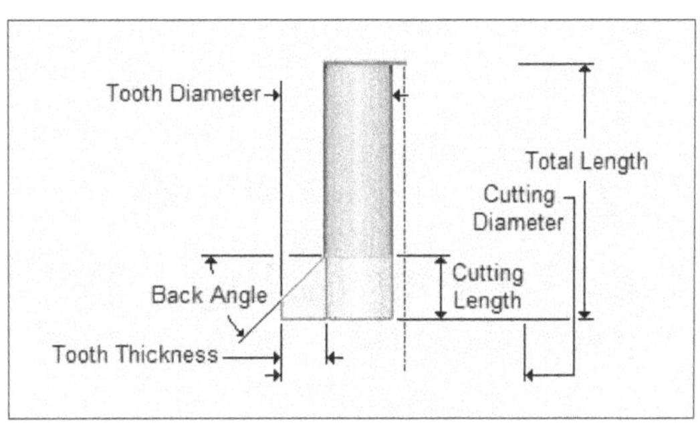

Figure-10. A Spot drill with parameters

Side Milling

Side Milling tool is a type of milling cutter used to remove material of large area from face and walls of the workpiece. Figure-11 shows a Side Milling tool with the parameters required in Expert Machinist.

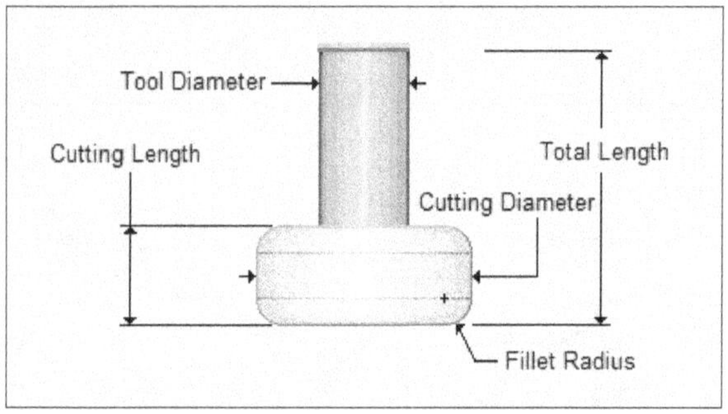

Figure-11. A Side Milling tool with parameters

Key Cutter

Key Cutter is a type of milling cutter used to cut slots for key in a workpiece. Shape of this tool is similar to the Side Milling tool but the Cutting length of this tool is less and diameter is more.

Lollipop

Lollipop is a type of milling cutter used to create undercut in a workpiece. This tool can also be used for machining curvatures on a workpiece.

Grooving

Grooving tool is a type of milling cutter used to create undercut in a workpiece. This tool is also used to create deep grooves in the workpiece.

Corner Rounding

As the name suggests, this type of milling tools is used to create rounds at the corners of the workpiece. Shape of the tool is displayed as shown in Figure-12.

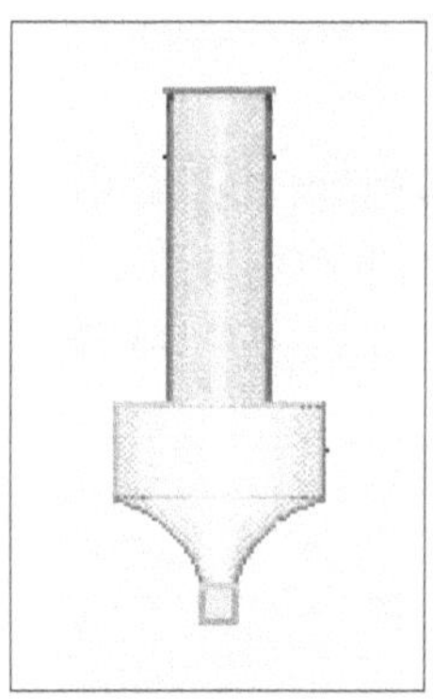

Figure-12. A Corner Rounding tool

Chamfering

As the name suggests, this type of milling tools is used to create chamfers at the edges of the workpiece.

Thread Mill

Thread Mill is a type of milling tools is used to create threads in a hole created earlier in the workpiece.

Plunge Mill

Plunge Mill is a type of milling tools used for heavy plunging operations where tool will force its way vertically downward in stock. The Material Removal Rate of this tool generally high.

Multi Tip

This is a user specified tool created in Expert Machinist. This tool has a geometry specified by the user. Also, it has cutting edges specified by the user.

CREATING A TOOL SETUP

A tool setup is the arrangement of tools required for an operation on a specific machine. So, before creating a tool setup, you must have an operation and a machine already created in Creo Expert Machinist. The procedure of creating a tool setup is discussed next.

- To create a machine, click on the **Machine Tool Manager** tool from the **Work Center** drop-down in the **Setup** group of the **Machining** tab of the **Ribbon**. The **Milling Work Center** dialog box will be displayed; refer to Figure-13.

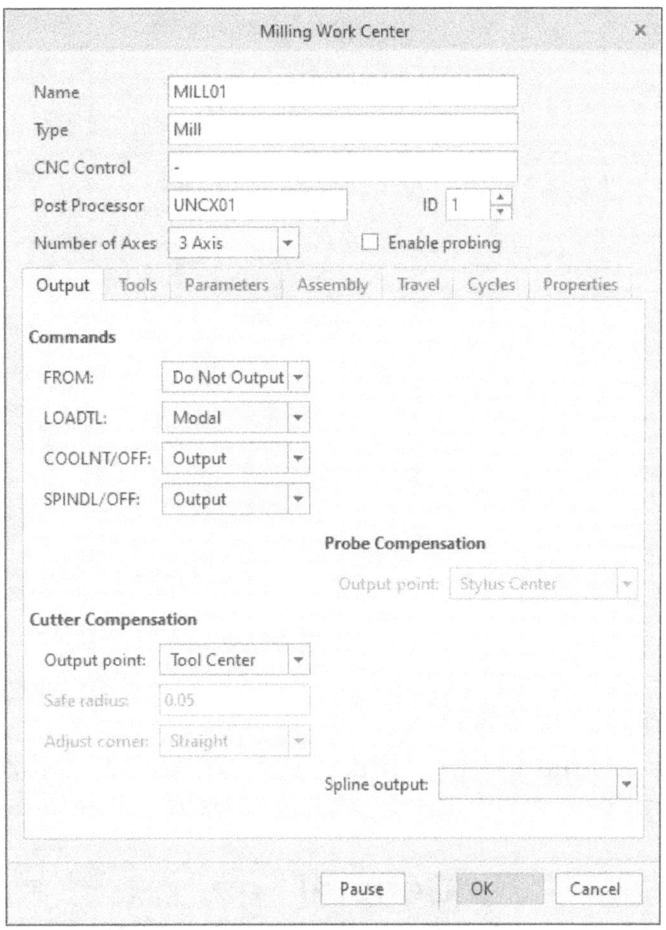

Figure-13. Milling Work Center dialog box

- Click on the **OK** button from the dialog box to create the machine. (You will learn more about machines later in this book.)
- Click on the **Operation** tool from **Setup** group in the **Machining** tab of the **Ribbon**. The **Operation** contextual tab will be displayed in the **Ribbon**; refer to Figure-14.

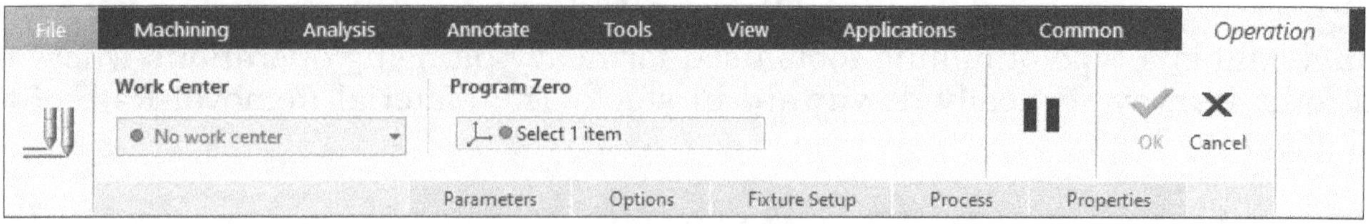

Figure-14. Operation contextual tab

- Click on the drop-down button in the **Work Center** area of the **Ribbon** and select the **MILL01** from the list. You will be prompted to select a coordinate system.
- Select the default coordinate system from graphics area and click on the **OK** button from the **Ribbon**.
- Now, the **Cutting Tool Manager** tool will become activate in **Ribbon**. Click on the **Cutting Tool Manager** tool from the **Setup** group in the **Machining** tab of the **Ribbon**. The **Tools Setup** dialog box will be displayed as shown in Figure-15.

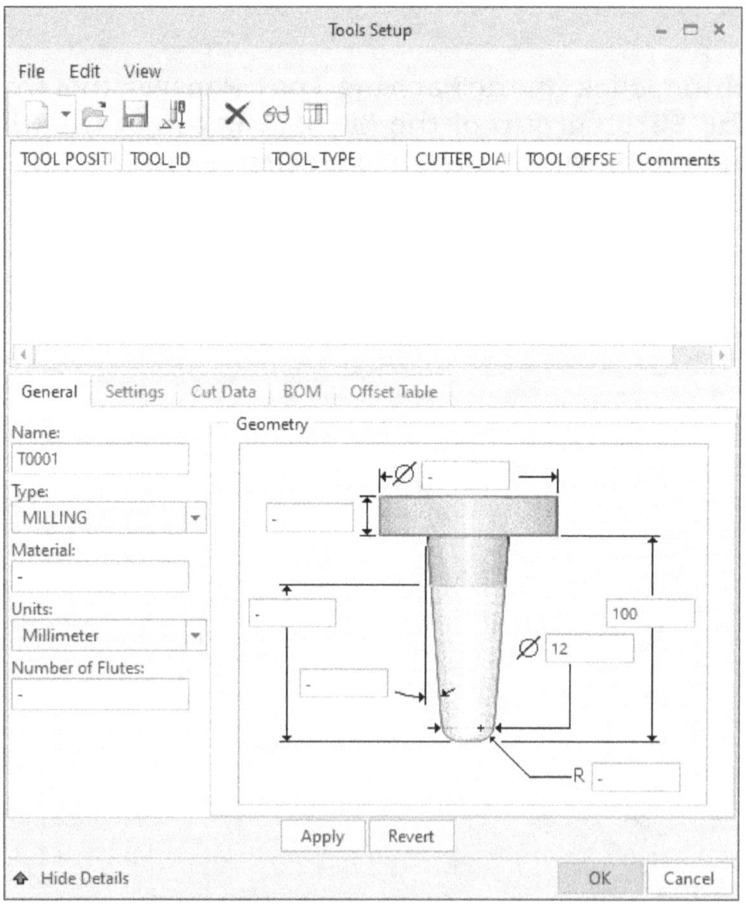

Figure-15. Tools Setup dialog box

There are five tabs available in this dialog box; **General**, **Settings**, **Cut Data**, **BOM**, and **Offset Table**. Options available in these tabs are discussed next.

General Tab

The options in the **General** tab are used to specify general information about the tool. The options available in this tab are discussed next.

Name

The **Name** edit box is used to specify the name of the tool.

Type

Options in the **Type** drop-down list are used to specify the type of tool. Tools in this drop-down list are available according to the machine selected for the Work center. The type of tools available in this drop-down list have already been discussed.

Units

The options in the **Units** drop-down list are used to specify the unit of measurement for the tool. There are five options available in this drop-down list; **INCH**, **Foot**, **Millimeter**, **Centimeter**, and **Meter**.

Number of Flutes

The **Number of Flutes** edit box is used to specify the number of flutes of the tool.

After specifying the above settings, click on the **Apply** button to create the tool. On clicking the **Apply** button, the tool will be added to the tool list displayed above in the dialog box.

Settings Tab

The options in the **Settings** tab are used to specify settings for tool number, offset number, gauge length, and so on; refer to Figure-16. Various options available in this tab are discussed next.

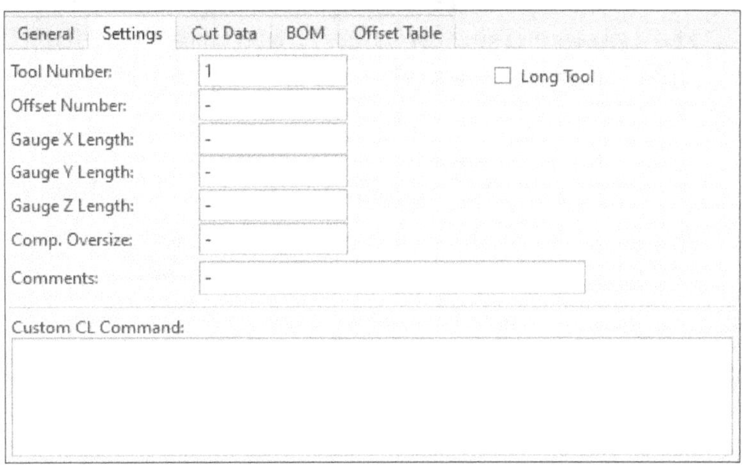

Figure-16. Settings tab

Tool Number

The **Tool Number** edit box is used to specify the number of the tool. This tool number is used by the machine while machining.

Offset Number

The **Offset Number** edit box is used to specify the offset number for the current tool. If you have earlier worked on the NC machine then it would be easy for you to understand this number.

Tip: Offset number is the number specified in the Offset table of the tool compensation in the NC machine. Offset table consists of offset values for the respective offset number. Offset is a value specified in the machine for wear compensation. When tool starts machining the component due to friction and heat, the edge of tool starts wearing hence it cuts lesser material than it was assumed to cut. So, to compensate the tool wear, this offset value is specified.

Gauge X Length

The **Gauge X Length** edit box is used to specify the gauge length of the tool tip along the X axis.

Gauge Z Length

The **Gauge Z Length** edit box is used to specify the gauge length of the tool tip along the Z axis.

Comp. Oversize

The **Comp. Oversize** edit box is used to specify difference between the actual maximum tool diameter and the cutting diameter specified in the programming. This value is used for gauge checking.

Comments

The **Comments** edit box is used to write comments about the tool and is using techniques.

Cut Data Tab

The options in **Cut Data** tab are used to specify cutting data for the tool. On clicking this tab, the options are displayed as shown in Figure-17. The options in this tab are discussed next.

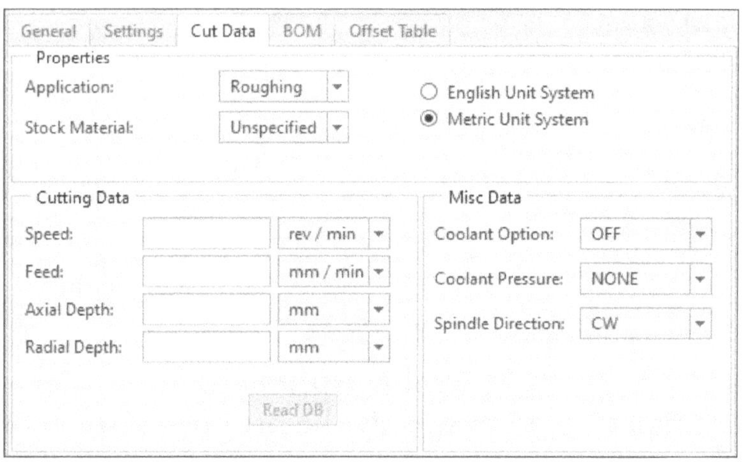

Figure-17. Cut Data tab

Application

The **Application** drop-down is used to specify the purpose for which the tool is being created. There are two options available in this drop-down i.e. Roughing and Finishing.

Stock Material

The **Stock Material** option is used to specify the material to be used for the stock. Click on **Stock Material** drop-down, a list of material available is displayed. This list depends on the parameters specified in the mfg wp material list.xml file in the program directory.

English Unit System / Metric Unit System

These radio buttons are used to set unit system in which the parameters of the tool will be specified.

- Select the **English Unit System** radio button if you want to specify the required parameters for the tool in Inches.
- Select the **Metric Unit System** radio button if you want to specify the required parameters for the tool in Millimeters.

Speed

The **Speed** option is available in the **Cutting Data** area of the **Tools Setup** dialog box. This option is used to specify the rotational speed at which the tool will perform cutting. You can specify the rotational value in two ways, revolution per minute or meters/feet per minute.

Feed

The **Feed** option is available in the **Cutting Data** area of the **Tools Setup** dialog box. This option is used to specify the feed rate at which the tool will cut through the workpiece. You can specify value for feed rate in two ways, mm/inch per minute or mm/inch per tooth.

Axial Depth

The **Axial Depth** option is available in the **Cutting Data** area of the **Tools Setup** dialog box. This option is used to specify the depth along axis of tool in the workpiece at which the cutting operation will be performed.

Radial Depth

The **Radial Depth** option is available in the **Cutting Data** area of the **Tools Setup** dialog box. This option is used to specify the depth along the radial direction of tool in the workpiece at which the cutting operation will be performed.

Coolant Option

The **Coolant Option** drop-down is available in the **Misc Data** area of the **Tools Setup** dialog box. The options in the **Coolant Option** drop-down are used to specify the condition of coolant during machining process. There are six options available in this drop-down; **Flood**, **Mist**, **OFF**, **ON**, **TAP**, and **THRU**.

- If you select the **Flood** option, the coolant will start flowing through all the passages available in the machine along the tool.
- **Mist** option is used if you require a mist of coolant at the workpiece.
- **OFF** option is used when you do not require coolant while cutting the material.
- **ON** option is used to make the flow of coolant at standard settings.
- **TAP** option is used to make the flow of coolant like a tap, i.e. natural flow.

- **THRU** option is used to make the flow of coolant through the tool holder as well as through the vents available for the workpiece.
- Similarly, select the **THRU SPNDL**, **THRU TOOL**, and **FROM RAIL** option to make the coolant flow through spindle, tool, and rail, respectively.

Coolant Pressure

The **Coolant Pressure** drop-down is available in the **Misc Data** area of the **Tools Setup** dialog box. The options in this drop-down list are used to specify the pressure at which the coolant will flow while cutting operation is performed. There are four options available in this drop-down; **NONE**, **LOW**, **MEDIUM**, and **HIGH**.

Spindle Direction

The **Spindle Direction** drop-down is also available in the **Misc Data** area of the **Tools Setup** dialog box. The options in this drop-down list are used to specify the direction in which the spindle will rotate while cutting.

BOM Tab

The options in **BOM** tab are used to specify the bill of material for the tool. A bill of material for tools provide the information like tool type, quantity available, and so on. This information helps in managing process design.

Offset Table Tab

The options in the **Offset Table** tab are used to set a table of offset values respective to the offset numbers; refer to Figure-18. This offset number is used by the tool for specifying the tool wear compensation. You can add as much offset numbers as required.

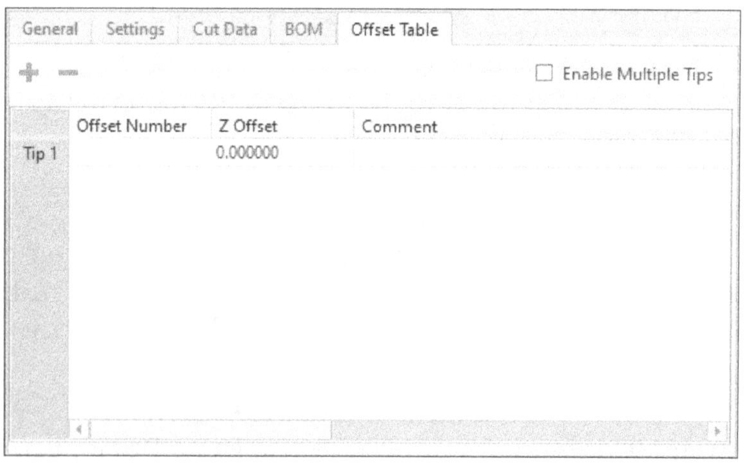

Figure-18. Offset Table tab

- To add more than one offset numbers, select the **Enable Multiple Tips** check box. The plus button adjacent to the check box will get activated.
- Click on the plus button to add more offset numbers in the table.

Save tool parameters to a file

This tool is used to save the parameters specified for the selected tool in the form of an **xml** file. The procedure to save tool parameters to a file is discussed next.

- Click on the **Save tool parameters to a file** tool from the toolbar available at the top of the **Tools Setup** dialog box.
- The tool will be saved in the form of an xml file in the default directory. The tool will be saved with the file name specified in the **Name** edit box of the **General** tab in the dialog box.

New drop-down

The tools in the **New** drop-down are used to create new tool setup based on the templates available in this drop-down. Figure-19 shows the tools available in this drop-down. Select any of the tool available in this drop-down. The template will be loaded on the basis of the selected tool.

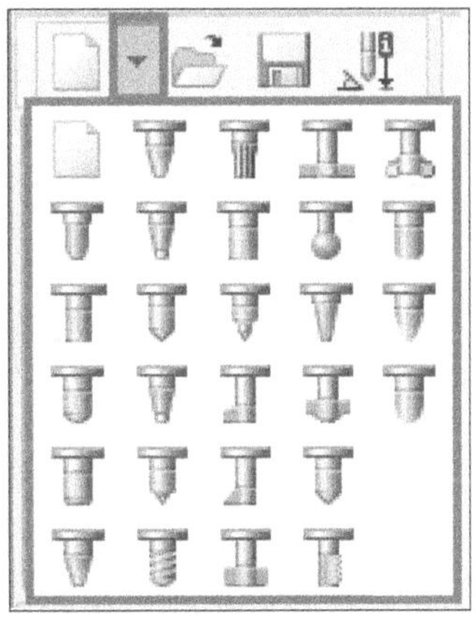

Figure-19. New drop down

Retrieve tool from disk

The **Retrieve tool from disk** tool is used to add a tool in the system from a file. The description about the tool is saved in the form of an xml file. The procedure to retrieve the tool from disk is given next.

- Click on the **Retrieve tool from disk** tool from the tools available below the menu bar in the dialog box. The **Open** dialog box will be displayed; refer to Figure-20.

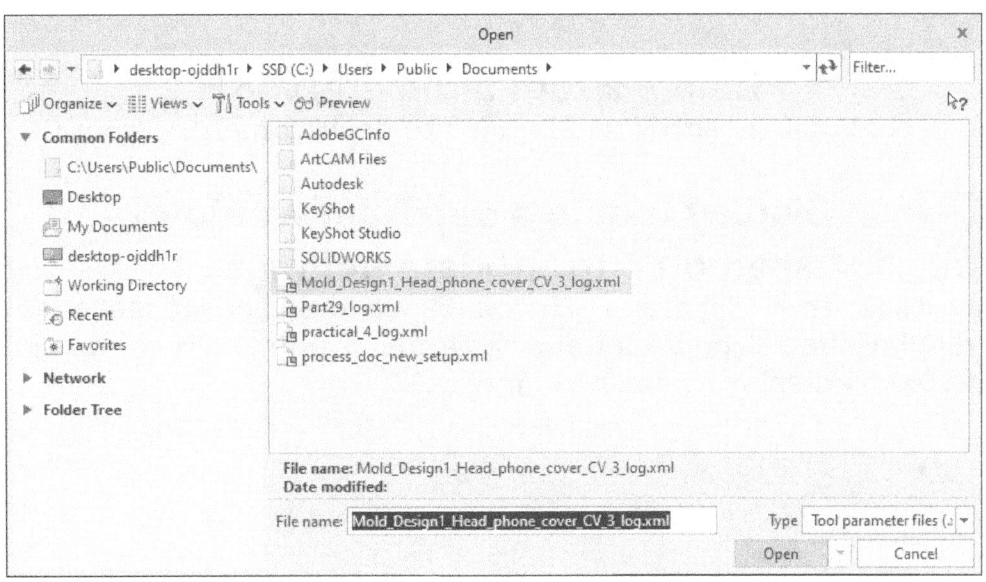

Figure-20. Open dialog box

- Browse to desired file and then click on **Open** button from the dialog box. The tool description in the selected file will be added in the tool list.

Showing Tool Info

The **Show tool info** tool is used to display parameters of selected tool in PTC Browser; refer to Figure-21.

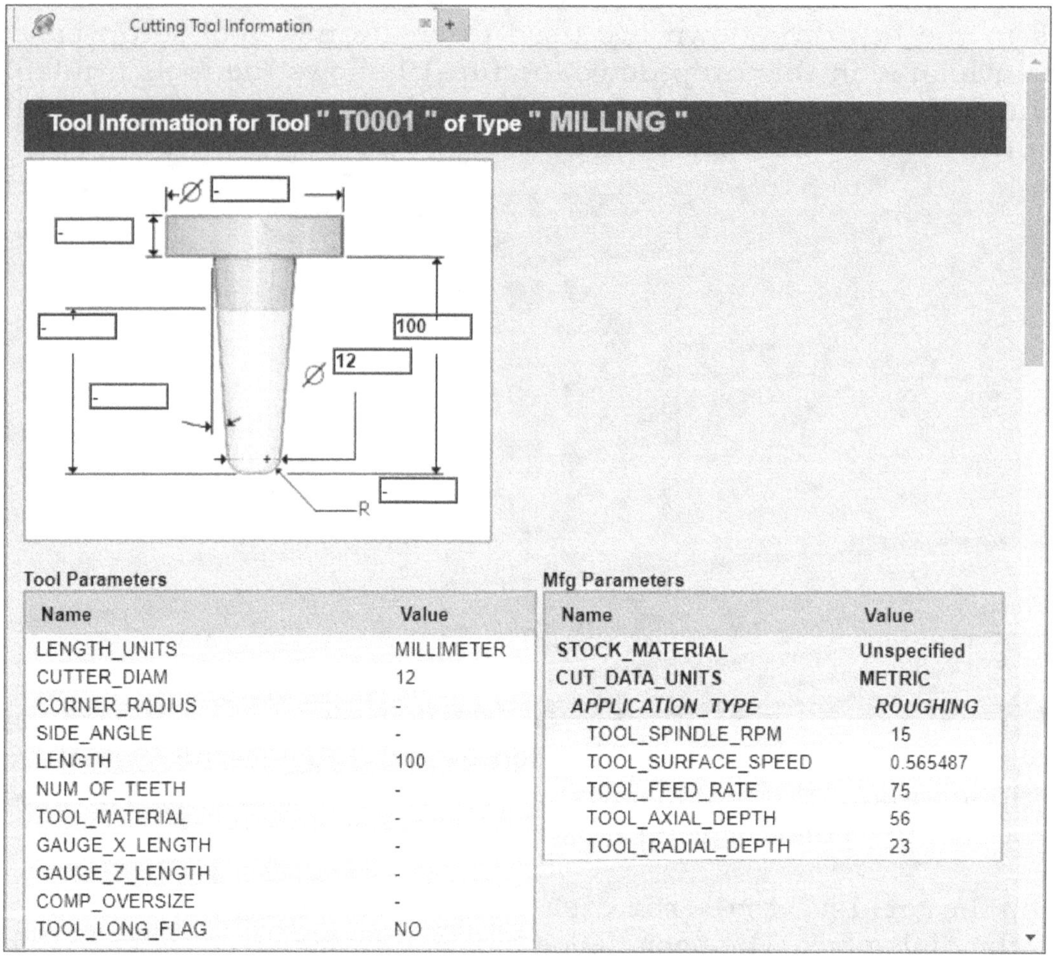

Figure-21. Cutting Tool Information window

Delete a tool table entry

The **Delete a tool table entry** tool is used to delete an entry from the table.

Display tool in a separate window based on current data settings

The **Display tool in a separate window based on current data settings** tool is used to display the selected tool in a separate window. On choosing this tool, a separate window is displayed; refer to Figure-22.

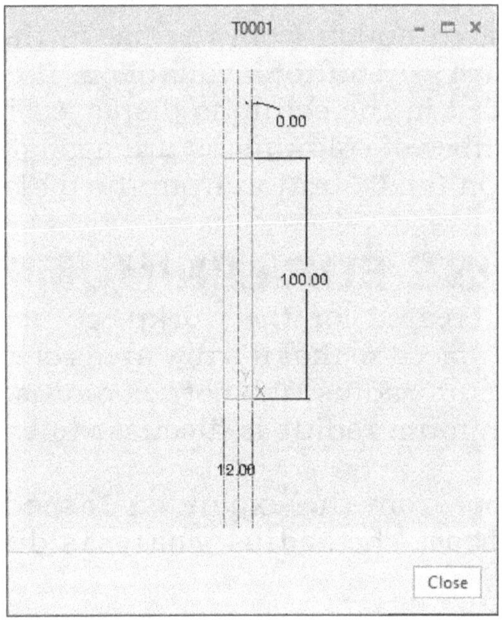

Figure-22. Tool window

The tool in this window is displayed with the parameters specified in the edit boxes of **Geometry** area in the **General** tab. Click on the **Close** button from the dialog box to exit.

Customize Tool Parameter Columns

The **Customize Tool Parameter Columns** tool is used to customize the columns in the tool table of the **Tool Setup** dialog box.

- Click on the **Customize Tool Parameter Columns** tool. The **Column Setup Builder** dialog box will be displayed, as shown in Figure-23.

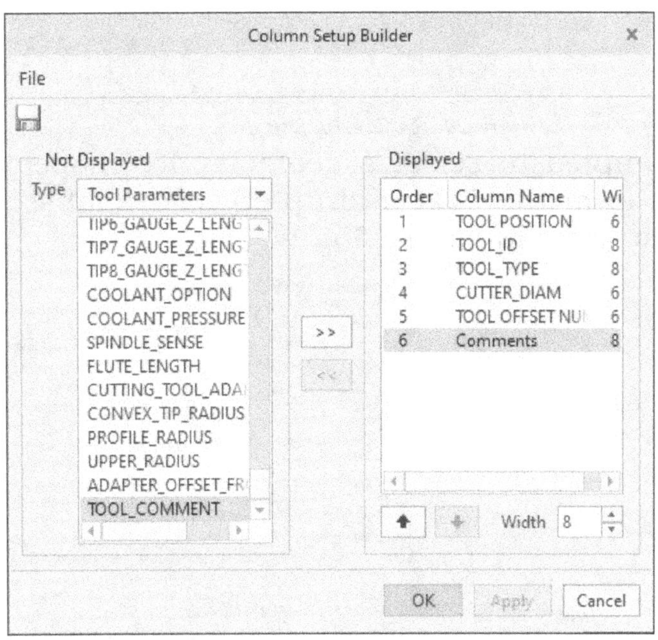

Figure-23. Column Setup Builder dialog box

There are two areas in the **Column Setup Builder** dialog box, i.e. **Not Displayed** and **Displayed**. Select desired option from the list in the **Not Displayed** area and then click on the **Add column** >> button available in the middle of both areas. The selected option will be added in the columns displayed in **Tools Setup** dialog box. You can add as many number of columns as are available in the list. After setting desired parameters, click on the **OK** button from the dialog box.

CHECKING FOR MINIMUM RADIUS

Whenever a tool setup is created for the workpiece, it is important to check for minimum radius in the workpiece so that narrow areas of workpiece can be machined. On the basis of this minimum radius, the corner radius of the tool is decided. The procedure to check for minimum radius is discussed next.

- Click on the **Radius** tool from the expanded **Inspect Geometry** group in the **Analysis** tab of the **Ribbon**. The **Radius Analysis** dialog box will be displayed; refer to Figure-24.

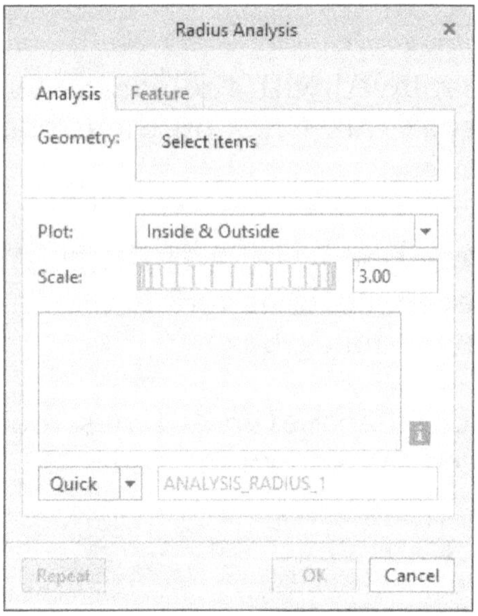

Figure-24. Radius Analysis dialog box

- Also, you are prompted to select a geometry for inspection. Now, select the **Component** option from the **Filter** drop-down available at the bottom of the application window, refer to Figure-25.

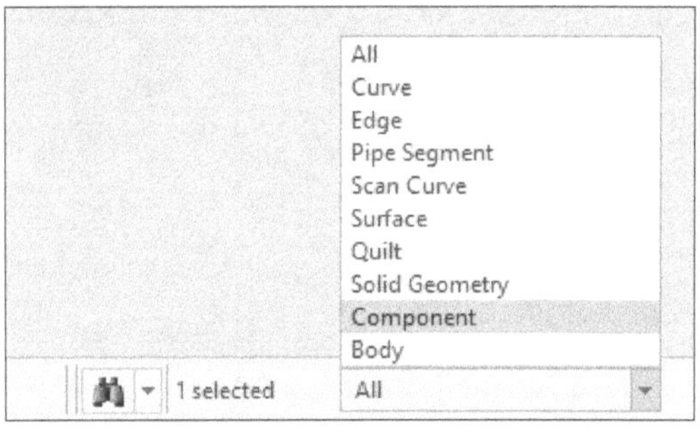

Figure-25. Component option in Filter drop down

- Select the component from the **Model Tree** (in the left of the application window) for which you want to check the minimum radius.

- Figure-26 shows a model with its minimum radius displayed both from inside and outside. Figure-27 shows the respective dialog box.

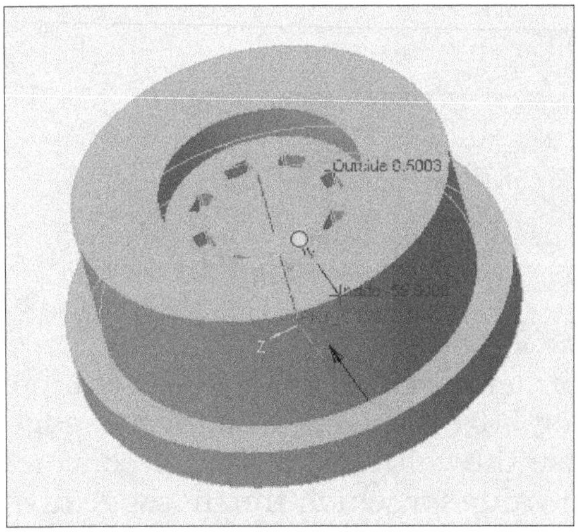

Figure-26. Model with minimum radius curve selected

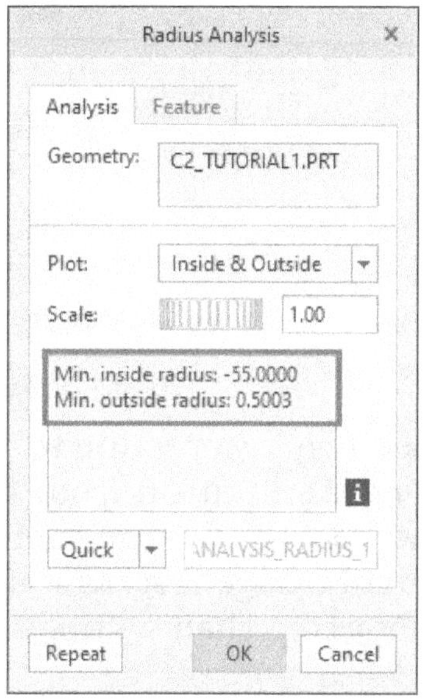

Figure-27. Radius Analysis dialog box

- You can display the Inside radius only or the Outside radius only by using the respective option from the **Plot** drop-down in the **Radius Analysis** dialog box. Minimum radii of the curve are highlighted in the dialog box in an ellipse.
- After checking parameters, click on the **OK** button from the dialog box.

CHECKING FOR SHORTEST EDGE

Whenever a tool setup is created for the workpiece, it is also important to check for shortest edge in the workpiece. The procedure to check the shortest edge is given next.

- Click on the **Short Edge** tool from the **Model Report** group in the **Analysis** tab of the **Ribbon**. The **Short Edge** dialog box will be displayed; refer to Figure-28. Also, you are prompted to select a part for which you want to check the shortest edge.

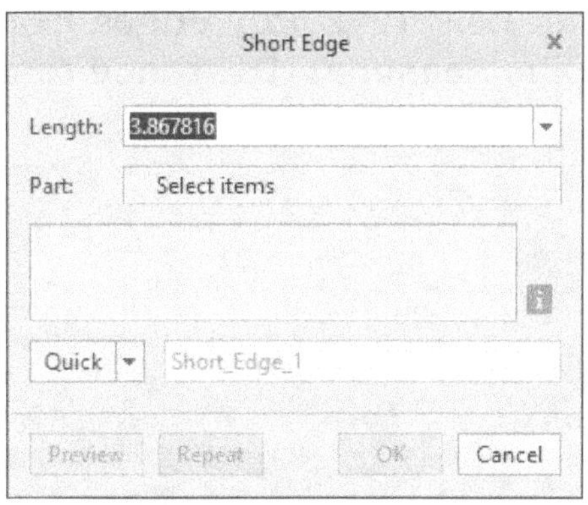

Figure-28. Short Edge dialog box

- Select a part from the **Model Tree**. The result will be displayed with respect to the length value specified in the **Length** edit box in the dialog box; refer to Figure-29.

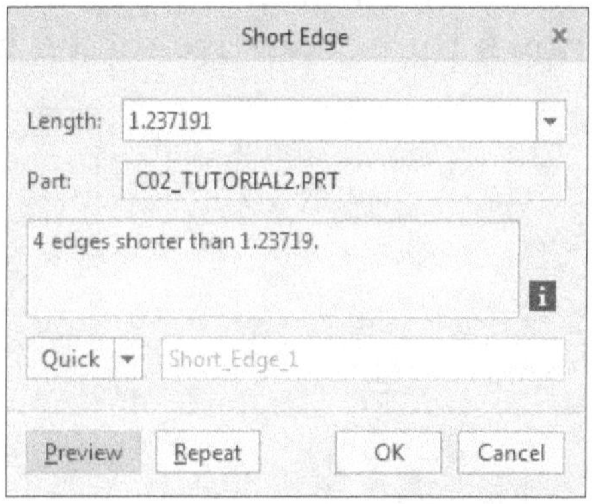

Figure-29. Short Edge dialog box after selecting part

- Now, specify a lower value than the earlier specified value in the edit box and click on the **Preview** button from the dialog box. If the result shows **0 edges shorter than the** specified value then increase the value by desired precision till you get the same message. The last specified value for which the message displayed is, **0 edges shorter than** value, will be the shortest edge.

CHECKING FOR MAXIMUM DEPTH OF CUT IN THE WORKPIECE

Whenever a tool setup is created for the workpiece, it is also important to check for the maximum depth of cut that is to be achieved. On the basis of this depth, you can decide the total length of the tool and cutting length of the tool to avoid any accident in the machine.

- To check for the maximum depth of cut, click on the **Distance** tool from the **Measure** drop-down in the **Measure** panel of the **Analysis** tab in the **Ribbon**. You will be asked to select entities to be measured.
- Hold the **CTRL** key and select the edge of bottom face and the corresponding edge of top face of the cavity that are maximum vertical distance apart. The distance will be displayed in a box in the Modeling area; refer to Figure-30. Note that you can use selection filters for selecting only edges from the model. After checking the distance value, close the **Measure: Distance** toolbox.

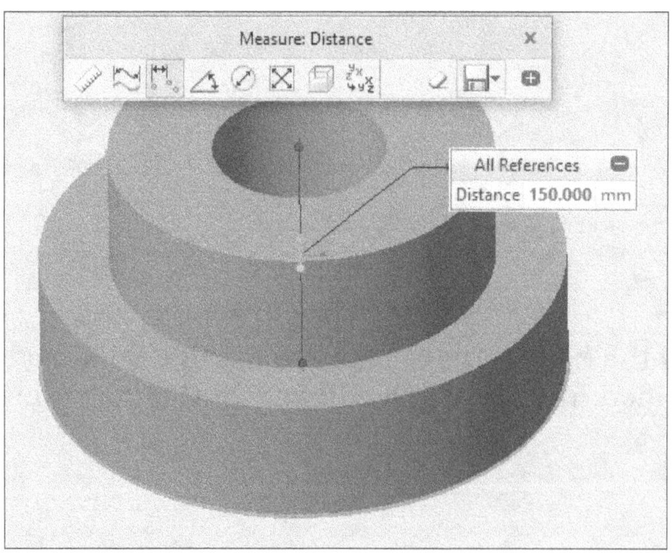

Figure-30. Measuring distance

TUTORIAL 1

In this tutorial, you will import a reference model, as shown in Figure-31 and you will import the workpiece reference model. Then you will create a tool setup for various operations on the workpiece. The model file for reference model is available in the Resources kit.

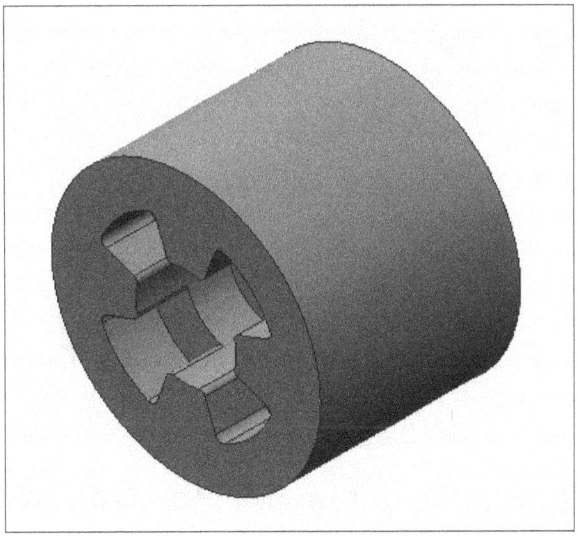

Figure-31. Reference model for tutorial 1

Steps:

- Copy the model from the resource kit in your local drive.
- Open the Expert Machinist application window by using the metric template.
- Create a new workpiece using the reference model provided.
- Find out various operations to be performed on the workpiece.
- Create a tool setup for various operations

Copying the reference model

- Extract the resources kit folder provided with the book at desired location.
- Browse to the location **\resources\chapter3\data** and copy the files in the **Creo Manufacturing\Chapter3\tutorial** folder in your local drive.
- Set the Creo Manufacturing folder as a working directory.

Starting Expert Machinist

- Open the Creo Parametric application by double clicking on the Creo Parametric icon on the desktop.
- Click on the **New** button from the **Data** panel in the **Home** tab of the **Ribbon**. The **New** dialog box will be displayed; refer to Figure-32.

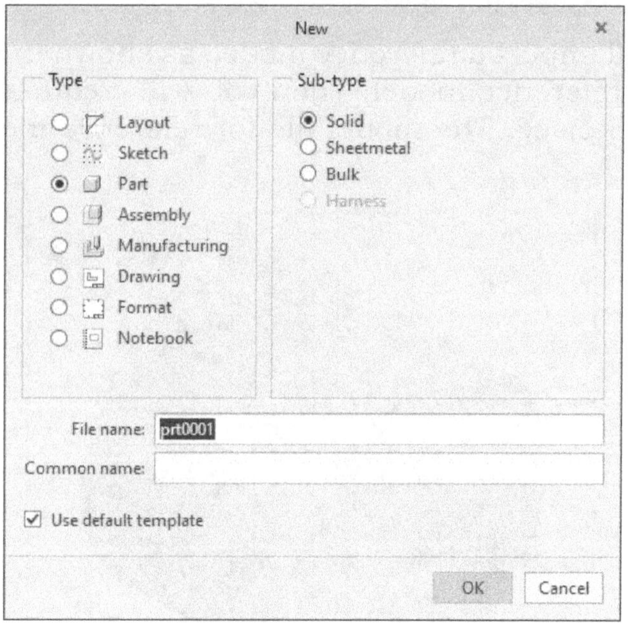

Figure-32. New dialog box

- Select the **Manufacturing** radio button from the **Type** area and **Expert Machinist** from the **Sub-type** area.
- Specify the name as **C03 tutorial1** in the **File name** edit box and clear the **Use default template** check box from the dialog box.
- Click on the **OK** button from the dialog box. The **New File Options** dialog box is displayed; refer to Figure-33.

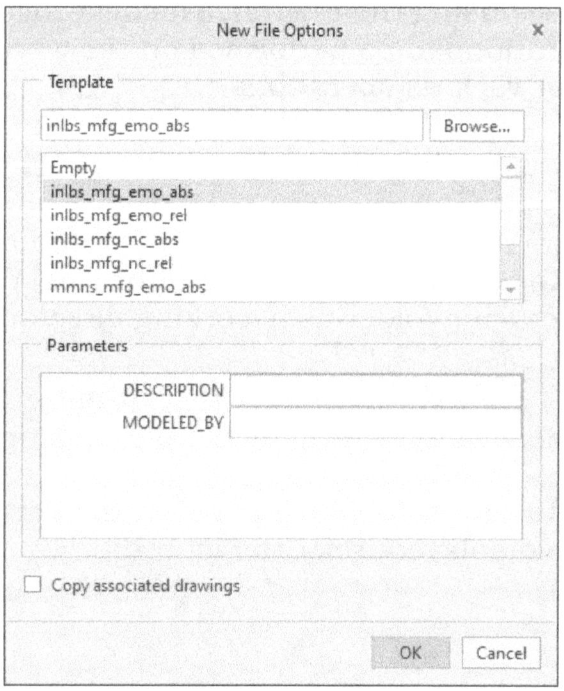

Figure-33. New File Options dialog box

- Select the **mmns mfg nc abs** option from the list of templates displayed and click on the **OK** button from the dialog box. The Expert Machinist environment of the Creo Parametric will be displayed with metric units selected.

Creating a new NC Model

- Click on the **Create Model** tool from the **NC Model** panel of **Machining** tab in the **Ribbon**. An input box will be displayed; refer to Figure-34 and you will be prompted to enter the name of NC model.

Figure-34. Input box

- Enter the name as **nc tutorial1** in the input box and click on the button from the input box. The **Open** dialog box will be displayed along with **NC MODEL Menu Manager**.
- Browse to the location **Creo Manufacturing\Chapter 3\tutorial**, select the **C03 tutorial1.prt** file and click on the **Open** button from the dialog box. The application window will be displayed; refer to Figure-35.

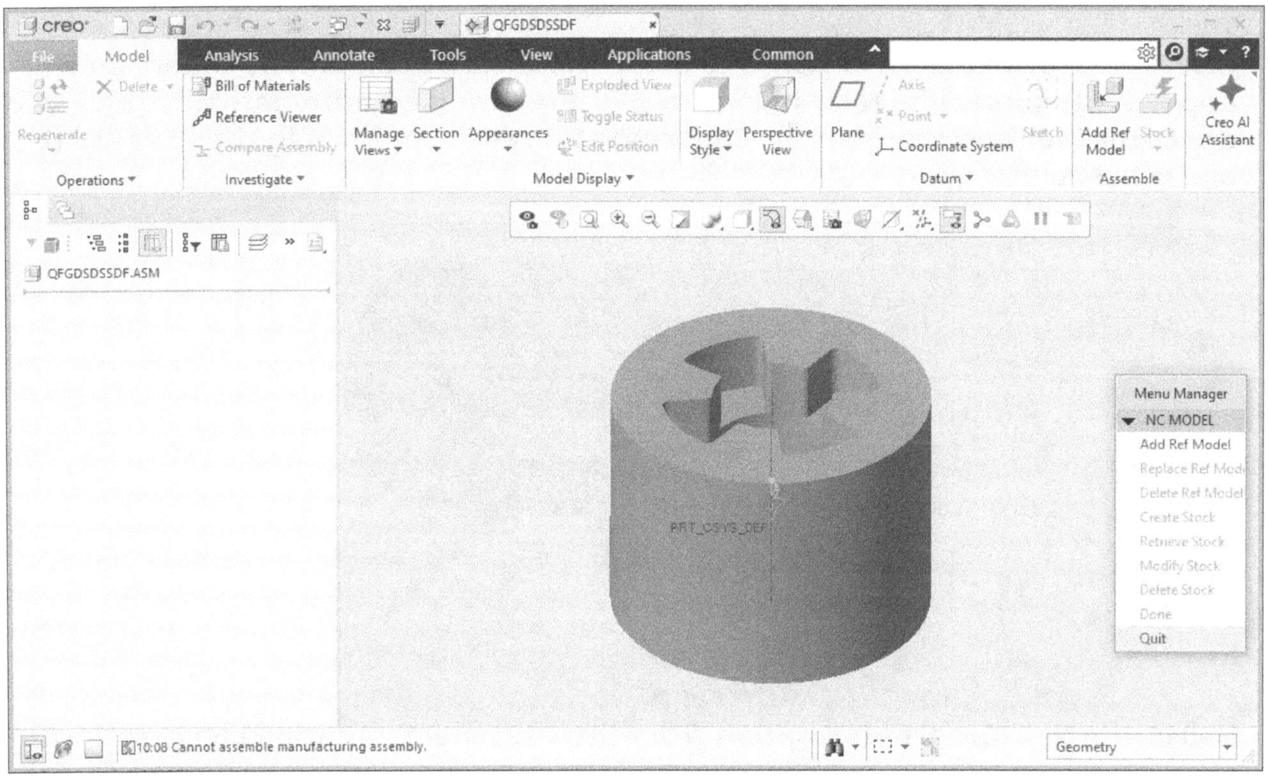

Figure-35. Application window after selecting the file

- Click on the **Retrieve Stock** option from the **NC MODEL Menu Manager**. The **Open** dialog box will be displayed again.
- Select the **C03 tutorial file2.prt** from the **Creo Manufacturing\Chapter 4\tutorial** location and click on the **OK** button from the dialog box. The workpiece and reference model will be displayed as shown in Figure-36.

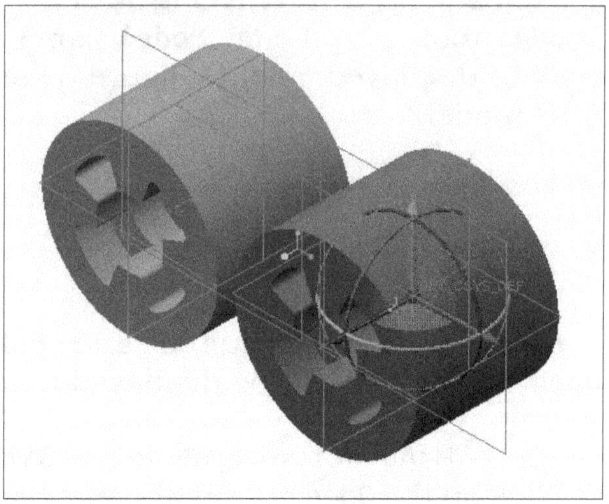

Figure-36. Workpiece with the reference model

Now, we will constrain the workpiece with the reference model.

- Select the bottom faces of both the components. The coincident constrain will be applied automatically; refer to Figure-37. If not applied automatically then select the **Coincident** option from the **Constraint Type** drop-down in the **Placement** tab of the **Ribbon**.

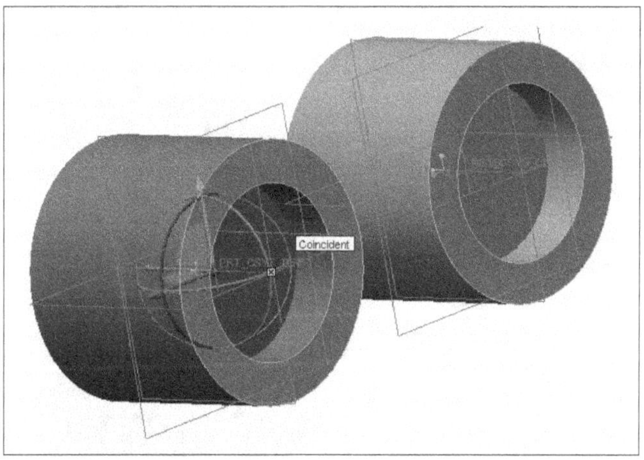

Figure-37. Faces to be selected

- Select the **New Constraint** option from the **Placement** tab in **Ribbon**. You will be prompted to select a reference.
- Select the center axes of both the components and click on the **Coincident** option from the **Constraint Type** drop-down in the **Placement** tab. The components will be displayed as shown in Figure-38.

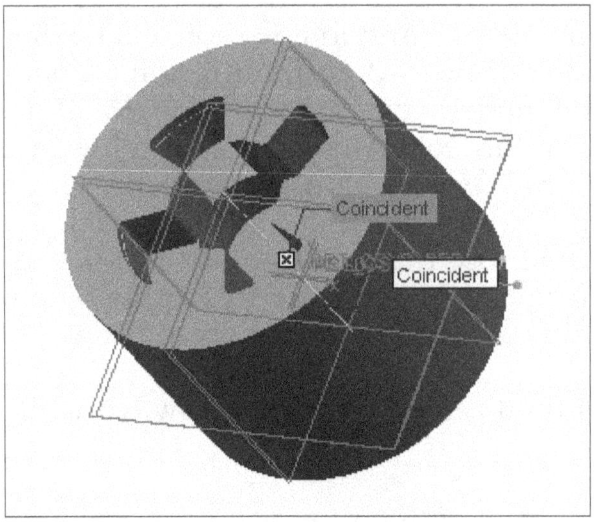

Figure-38. Workpiece assembled with the reference model

- Click on the **OK** button from the **Ribbon** and click on the **Done** option from the **NC MODEL Menu Manager**. The Expert Machinist environment will be displayed along with the **Component Placement** contextual tab selected. You are now prompted to place the workpiece with reference part in Machine coordinate system.
- Select the **Default** option from **Current constraint** drop-down in the **Component Placement** contextual tab of the **Ribbon** and click on the **OK** button.

Analyzing for tool setup

Now, before we start creating a tool setup, it is important to check a few parameters of the workpiece like minimum radius, shortest edge of the workpiece, total depth of cut, material of the workpiece, and so on.

Checking for minimum radius

- To check for minimum radius, click on the **Radius** tool from **Measure** drop-down in the **Measure** group of **Analysis** tab in the **Ribbon**. The **Radius Analysis** dialog box will be displayed; refer to Figure-39.

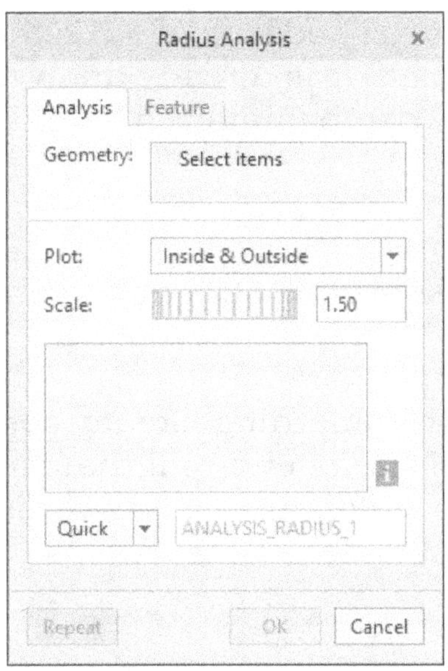

Figure-39. Radius Analysis dialog box

- Select the **C03TUTORIAL FILE.PRT** from the **Model Tree** in the left of the application window. The minimum outside and inside radii will be displayed in the dialog box. Here, Minimum Inside radius = -3 and Minimum Outside radius = 4.
- On a close look at the model, you can see two type of arrows in the model. One type of arrows are green in color and other are blue in color. The green arrows represent the outside radius and blue arrows represent the inside radius.
- All the radii are displayed on the walls of the model. The walls are cut by side edges of the milling tool. So, there is no need of fillet at the bottom of the tool. Now, moving back to the tools available in Expert Machinist, you can find that **End Mill** is best for this machining as it does not have fillet at bottom.

Till this step, the tool is finalized as End Mill. Now, you will check for the diameter of the tool.

Checking for shortest edge

- To check for the shortest edge, click on the **Short Edge** tool from **Model Report** group in the **Analysis** tab of the **Ribbon**. The **Short Edge** dialog box will be displayed; refer to Figure-40.

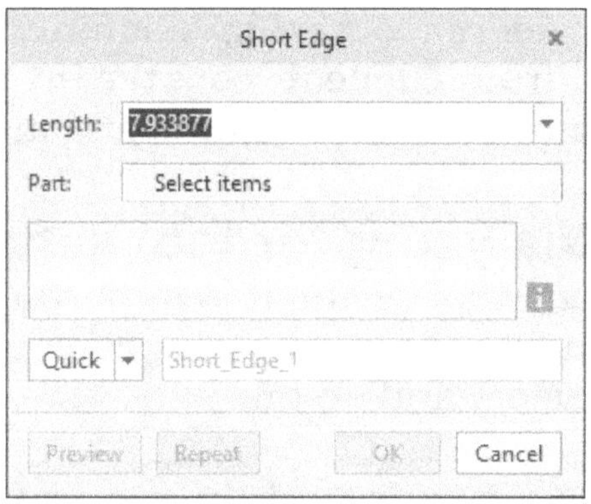

Figure-40. Short Edge dialog box

- Select the **C03TUTORIAL FILE.PRT** from the Model Tree in the left of the application window. A message will be displayed in the dialog box as **16 edges shorter than 5.12250**.
- As per the analysis, the shortest edge is of **5.1225** mm. So, the only criteria here is radius in the reference part. It is already analyzed that minimum radius is 3. So, the diameter of the tool can be finalized as 6.

Indepth

The above analysis made for short edge might be confusing to some of my friends. Let's solve this mystery.

- Figure-41 shows a part with something like my company name engraved on it. If you are asked to define the size of end mill that can make those engraving cuts, what should be the criteria for diameter. Answer is; the shortest distance in the two edges of the engraving.

Figure-41. A part with engraving

- Now, this is a time to try new tool i.e. **Distance**. Click on the **Distance** tool from the **Measure** drop-down in the **Measure** group of the **Analysis** tab in the **Ribbon**. You will be prompted to select a reference. Select the two points while holding the **CTRL** key; refer to Figure-42. The distance value will be displayed in a box as **1.48952**.

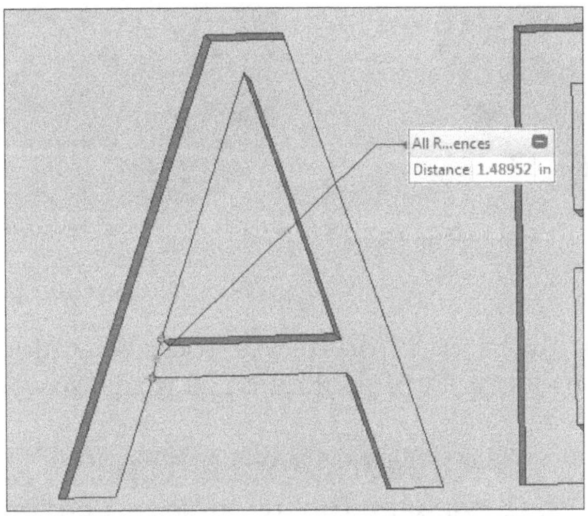

Figure-42. Minimum distance value in A

Similarly, select the points and edges in **M and O**; refer to Figure-43.

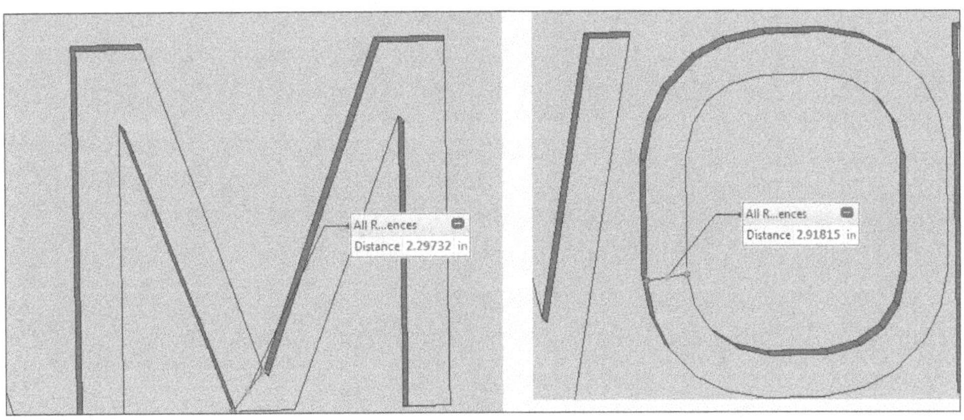

Figure-43. Minimum distance value in M and O

Checking for Maximum depth in workpiece

Getting back to our tutorial, we need to check the maximum depth of cut from the top face so that we can avoid any accident caused by tool holder colliding with the workpiece. For example, if we take a drill having less length than the cutting depth required then the tool holder will collide with the face in which the drilling is being done. You can check the maximum depth of cut by using the **Distance** tool.

- Click on the **Distance** tool from the **Measure** drop-down in the **Measure** group of the **Analysis** tab in the **Ribbon**. The **Measure: Distance** toolbar will be displayed and you will be prompted to select two references to find out the distance.
- Select the two references to be selected; refer to Figure-44. The distance between the two edges will be displayed; refer to Figure-45.

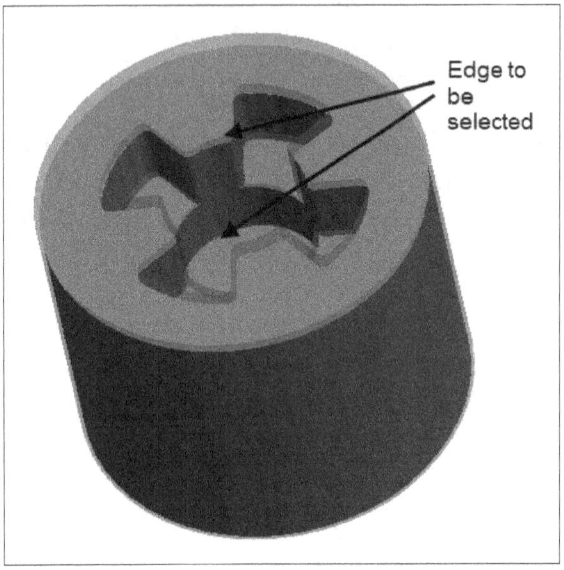

Figure-44. References to be selected

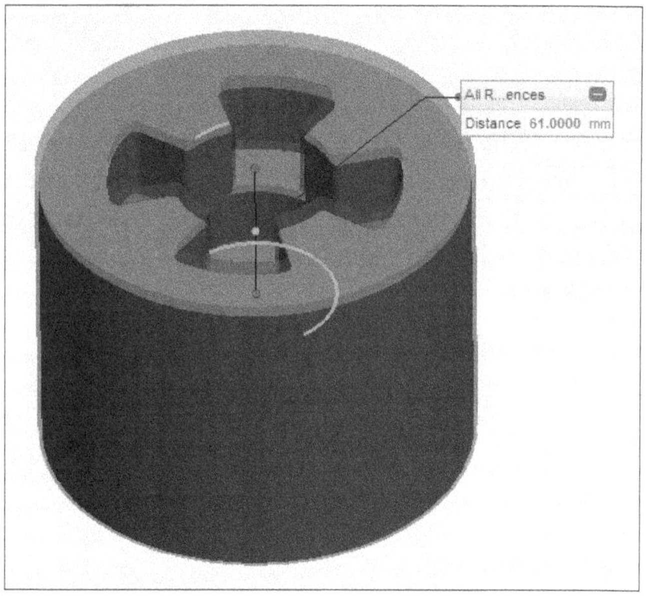

Figure-45. Distance value displayed between the edges

Till this step, we have finalized end mill as our tool. We calculated the total diameter of tool as **6.0** mm and total length of tool as **61.0** mm. Now, we will create tool setup for our desired tool.

Creating tool setup

- Click on the **Machine Tool Manager** tool from **Work Center** drop-down in the **Setup** group of **Machining** tab in the **Ribbon**. The **Milling Work Center** dialog box will be displayed; refer to Figure-46.

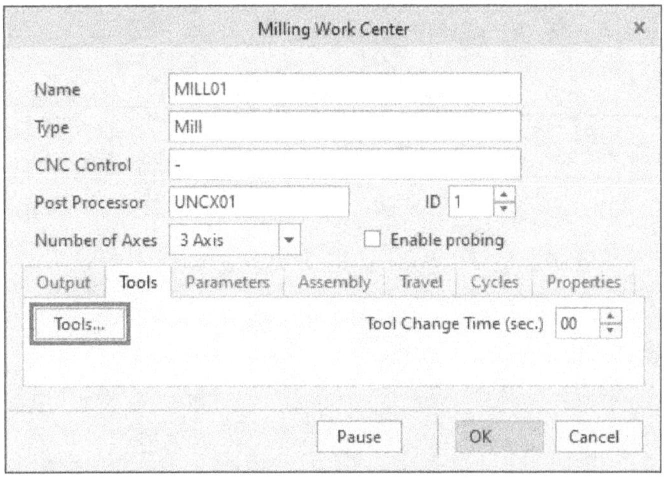

Figure-46. Milling Work Center dialog box with Tools tab selected

- Click on the **Tools** button from the **Tools** tab in the dialog box. The **Tools Setup** dialog box will be displayed; refer to Figure-47.

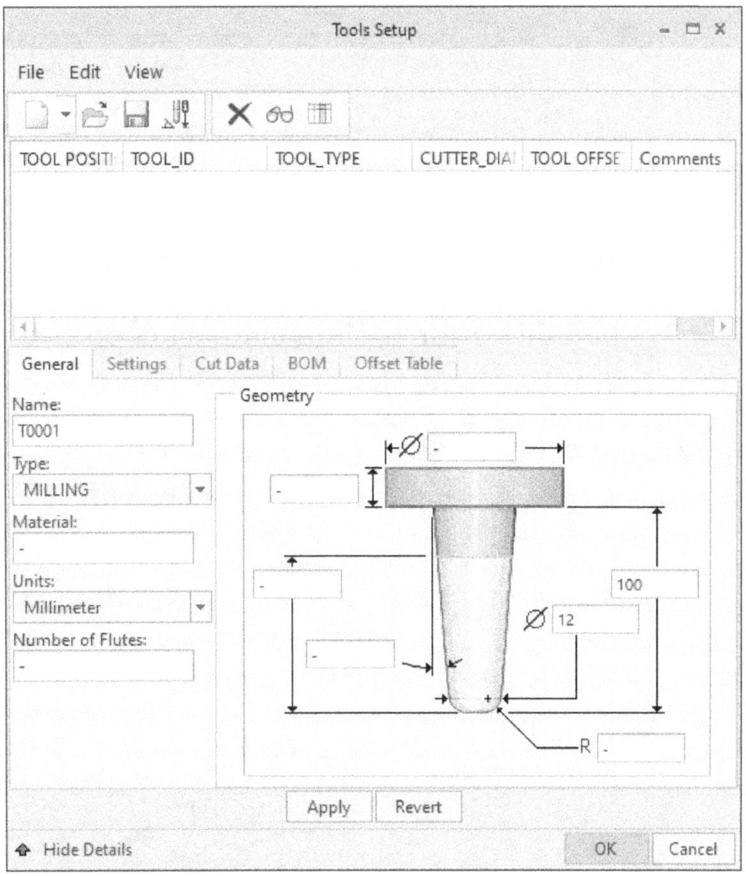

Figure-47. Tools Setup dialog box

- Specify the name as **End mill rough** in the **Name** edit box of **General** tab in the dialog box.
- Select the **End Mill** option from the **Type** drop-down. The dialog box will be displayed as shown in Figure-48.

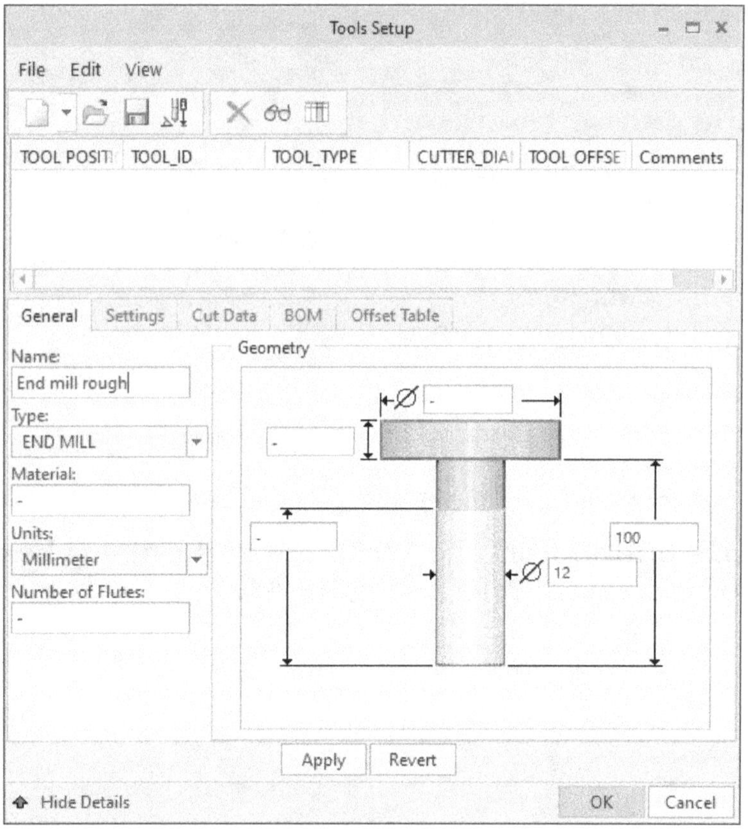

Figure-48. Modified Tools Setup dialog box

- Select the unit as **Millimeter** from the **Units** drop-down.

Now, we need to specify the values for tool geometry according to the value found by the analyses.

- Specify the values of geometry as shown in Figure-49.

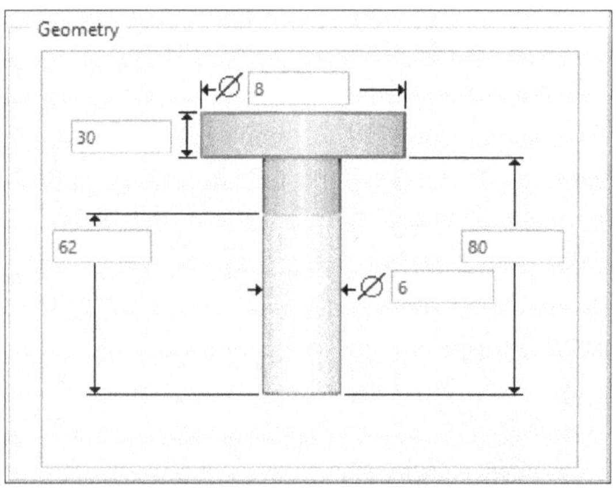

Figure-49. Tool geometry with required values

Now, we will specify other parameters of the tool.

- Click on the **Settings** tab and specify the **Offset Number** as **01**.
- Click on the **Cut Data** tab and select the **Roughing** option from the **Application** drop-down list.
- Select the **Metric Unit System** radio button from the **Properties** area.

- Specify the **2500 rev/min**, **15 mm/min**, **1 mm**, and **1 mm** in the **Speed**, **Feed**, **Axial Depth**, and **Radial Depth** edit boxes in the **Cutting Data** area of the dialog box.
- Select the **ON**, **MEDIUM**, and **CW** options from the **Coolant Option**, **Coolant Pressure**, and **Spindle Direction** drop-down lists, respectively.
- Click on the **Apply** button. The tool will be displayed in the tool list of the dialog box.

Similarly, create a tool setup having following parameters:-

- Tool Name : End Mill Finish
- Tool Type : END MILL
- Tool Number : 2
- Offset Number : 02
- Application : Finishing
- Speed : 2000 rev/min
- Feed : 12 mm/min
- Axial Depth : 0.4 mm
- Radial Depth : 0.4 mm
- Coolant conditions same as above.

- Save the file by clicking on the **Save tool parameters to a file** tool from the toolbar in the **Tools Setup** dialog box.
- Click on the **OK** button from the dialog box to exit.
- Click on the **OK** button from the **Milling Work Center** dialog box to exit.

PROBLEM 1

In this problem, you will import a reference model as shown in Figure-50 and you will create a workpiece having uniform thickness of 2 over the reference model. Then you will create a tool setup for various operations on the workpiece. The model file for reference model is available in the Resources kit.

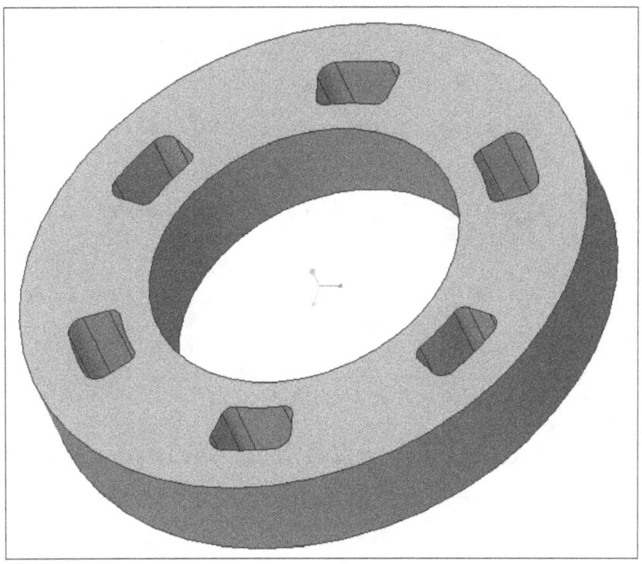

Figure-50. Reference model for Problem 1

PROBLEM 2

In this problem, you will import a reference model as shown in Figure-51 and Figure-52. Then you will create a tool setup for various operations on the workpiece. The model file for reference model is available in the Resources kit.

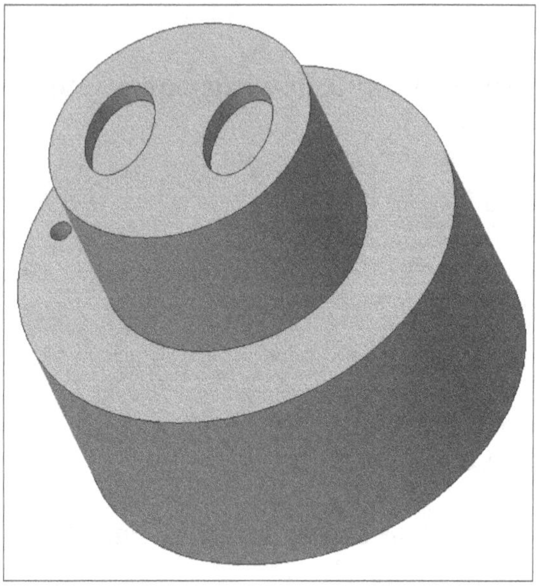

Figure-51. Reference model for Problem 2 (Isometric view)

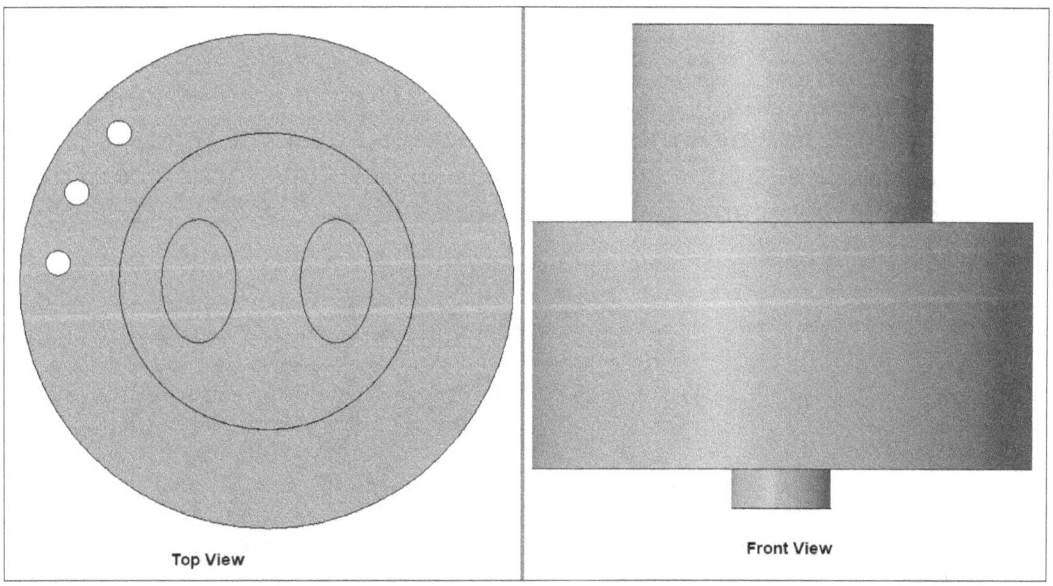

Figure-52. Reference model for Problem 2

SELF-ASSESSMENT

Q1. Which tool is primarily used for profiling, facing, and plunging operations in Expert Machinist?

A. Ball Mill
B. End Mill
C. Bull Mill
D. Drill

Q2. What is the main distinguishing feature of a Ball Mill?

A. Tapered sides
B. Flat cutting edge
C. Hemispherical bottom
D. Sharp point

Q3. Which tool is used to create internal fillets in dies and moulds?

A. Bull Mill
B. End Mill
C. Taper Ball Mill
D. Lollipop

Q4. What differentiates a Taper Mill from a Bull Mill?

A. Flute count
B. Material
C. Taper at cutting length
D. Overall length

Q5. Which tool is used to create threads in a hole?

A. Reamer
B. Tap
C. Drill
D. Taper Ball Mill

Q6. Which tool is used to increase hole diameter with high accuracy?

A. Drill
B. Tap
C. Boring Bar
D. Reamer

Q7. Which tab in the Tools Setup dialog box allows you to define tool name, type, and number of flutes?

A. Settings
B. BOM
C. General
D. Offset Table

Q8. What does the "Offset Number" in the Settings tab help to specify?

A. Cutting depth
B. Tool compensation
C. Tool material
D. Coolant pressure

Q9. Which cutting tool is designed specifically for undercut machining?

A. Lollipop
B. Chamfering
C. Taper Mill
D. Countersink

Q10. Which tool is used to save tool parameters in XML format?

A. Retrieve tool from disk
B. Display tool in separate window
C. Save tool parameters to a file
D. Delete a tool table entry

Q11. Which of the following is a user-defined custom geometry tool in Expert Machinist?

A. Key Cutter
B. Taper Ball Mill
C. Multi Tip
D. Side Milling

Q12. What is the purpose of the "Gauge Z Length" in the Settings tab?

A. Set flute count
B. Specify rotational speed
C. Define tool tip length in Z-axis
D. Set coolant pressure

Q13. What is the role of a Spot Drill?

A. Create holes with threading
B. Mill profiles
C. Start point for drilling
D. Cut undercuts

Q14. What tool in Expert Machinist is best suited for slot cutting in a workpiece?

A. Reamer
B. Key Cutter
C. Chamfer Tool
D. Bull Mill

Q15. What is displayed when using the "Show tool info" option?

A. CAD drawing
B. BOM
C. Tool parameters in PTC browser
D. Offset table

Q16. What happens when the "Enable Multiple Tips" checkbox is selected in Offset Table tab?

A. Allows coolant control
B. Allows adding offset values
C. Saves tool in XML
D. Changes units to Metric

Q17. Which of these tools is used to create deep grooves or undercuts?

A. Lollipop
B. Grooving
C. Chamfering
D. Plunge Mill

Q18. What is the cutting characteristic of a Plunge Mill?

A. Horizontal cutting
B. Taper edge finishing
C. Vertical heavy material removal
D. Hole threading

Q19. What is the main function of the "Customize Tool Parameter Columns" tool?

A. Save tool parameters to a file
B. Create a new tool setup
C. Customize columns in the tool table
D. Display tool shape in 3D

Q20. In the Column Setup Builder dialog box, which two areas are available?

A. Previewed and Active
B. Displayed and Hidden
C. Not Displayed and Displayed
D. Default and Custom

Q21. Which button adds a selected column from "Not Displayed" to "Displayed"?

A. Insert
B. OK
C. Add column
D. Apply

Q22. Which tool is used to determine the narrowest regions of a workpiece?
A. Distance

B. Radius
C. Edge Check
D. Column Setup

Q23. From which group is the Radius tool accessed?

A. Model Report
B. Measure
C. Inspect Geometry
D. Setup

Q24. What does the Filter drop-down in the Radius Analysis dialog box allow you to select?

A. Units
B. Component
C. Depth
D. Tool type

Q25. What type of radii can be selected in the Radius Analysis tool?

A. Top and bottom
B. Inside and Outside
C. Full and Partial
D. Curved and Flat

Q26. How are minimum radii represented in the Radius Analysis dialog box?

A. Dashed lines
B. Arrows
C. Ellipses
D. Dots

Q27. Which tool is used to find the shortest edge in a workpiece?

A. Distance
B. Radius
C. Short Edge
D. Offset Table

Q28. What does the Length edit box in the Short Edge dialog box specify?

A. Cutting speed
B. Feed rate
C. Maximum radius
D. Value to compare edge lengths

Q29. How do you determine the shortest edge length using the Short Edge tool?

A. Decrease length until 0 edges are found
B. Increase radius until error appears
C. Use filter and select smallest dimension
D. Change tool parameters and preview

Chapter 4

Machine Setting

Topics Covered

The major topics covered in this chapter are:

- ***Basics of Machine.***
- ***Use of 3 Axes, 4 Axes, and 5 Axes machines.***
- ***Machines in Creo Manufacturing.***
- ***Setting Milling Work Center.***

MILLING MACHINE

Machine is a component of manufacturing process that enables any cutting operation on the workpiece with the help of a tool. The types of machines have already been discussed. In Expert Machinist, there are three type of machines available, i.e. 3-Axis, 4-Axis, and 5-Axis. In this chapter, you will learn about the applications and the settings of these machines.

3-AXIS MACHINE

In a 3-Axis machine, cutting operation can be performed in three directions: along X-axis, along Y-axis, and along Z-axis. Figure-1 illustrates a model of 3-Axis machine. There can be other types of 3-Axis milling machines having different directions. The arrows in the figure show the direction in which the cutting operation can be performed. In NC programming, three parameters will be required to specify the position of the tool while cutting.

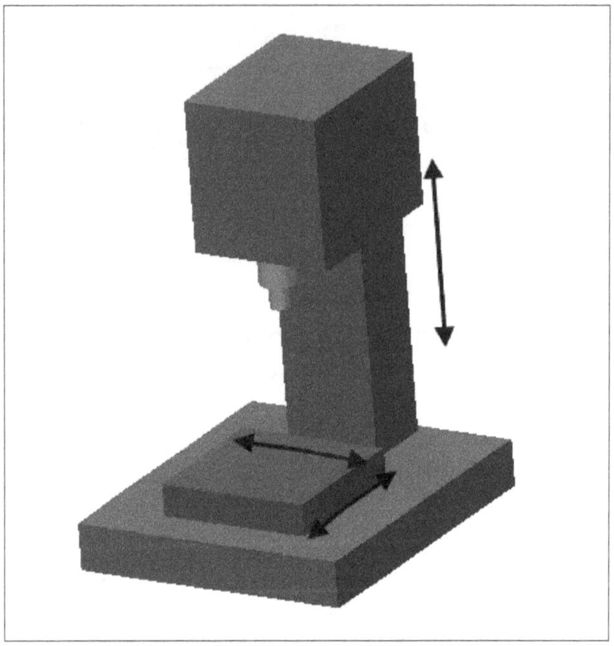

Figure-1. Model of a 3 Axis milling machine

4-AXIS MACHINE

In a 4-Axis machine, cutting operation can be performed in three translational directions and one rotational direction. Figure-2 illustrates a model of 4-Axis machine. There can be other type of 4-Axis milling machines having different directions. The arrows in the figure show the direction in which the cutting operation can be performed. In NC programming, four parameters will be required to specify the position of the tool while cutting.

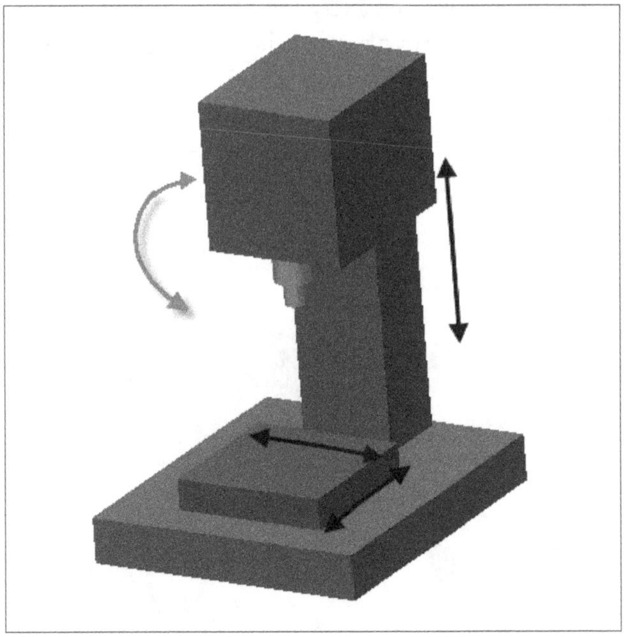

Figure-2. Model of a 4 Axis milling machine

5-AXIS MACHINE

In a 5-Axis machine, cutting operation can be performed in three translational directions and two rotational directions. Figure-3 illustrates a model of 5-Axis machine. The arrows in the figure show the direction in which the cutting operation can be performed. In NC programming, five parameters will be required to specify the position of the tool while cutting.

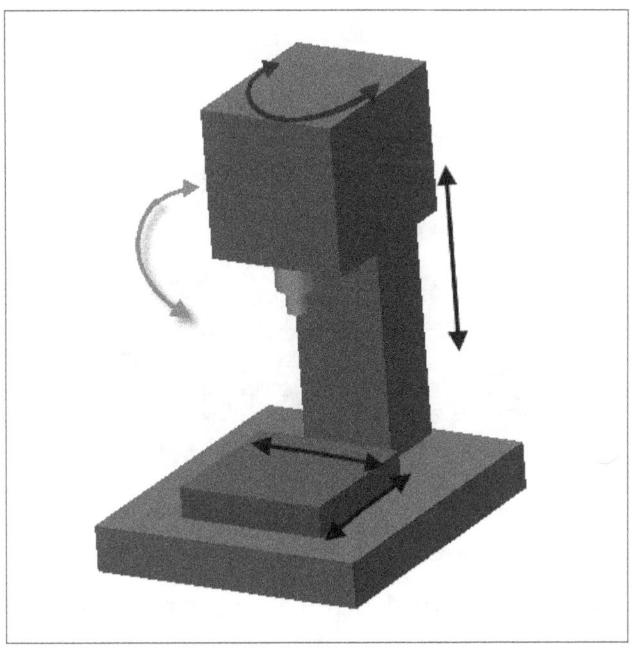

Figure-3. Model of a 5 Axis milling machine

USE OF 3-AXES, 4-AXES, AND 5-AXES MACHINES

Uses of different type of milling machines is mainly dependent on the part to be machined. If machining is to be done perpendicular to the workpiece then 3-Axes machine can do the job. For example, the model given in Problem 1 of Chapter 3 can be machined easily by using the 3-Axes machine; refer to Figure-4. If the part to be machined has some inclined pockets; refer to Figure-5 then you need to use the 4-Axes machine.

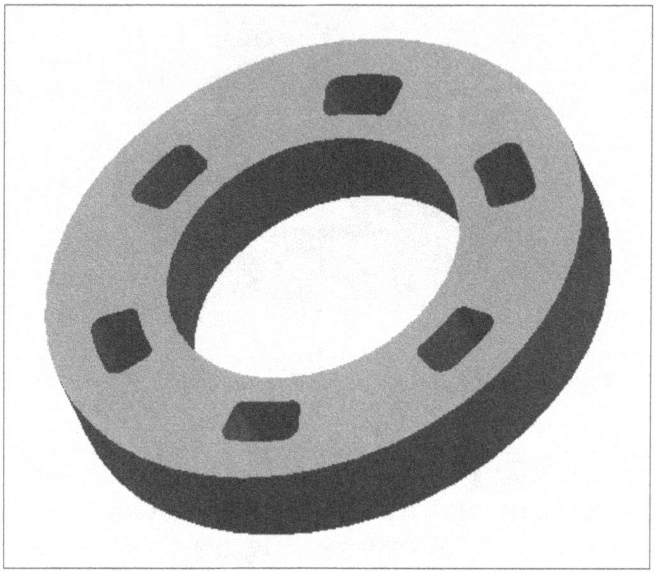

Figure-4. Model that can be machined by 3 axes machine

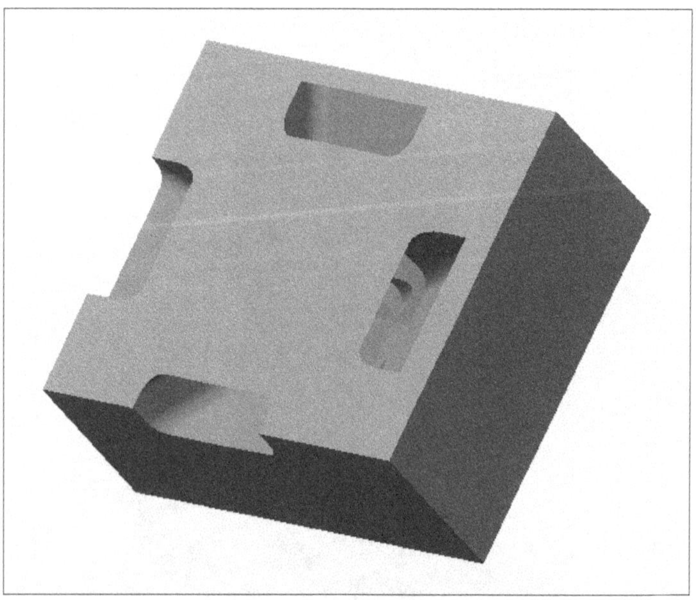

Figure-5. Model that can be machined by 4 axes machine

Similarly, if the part has an inclined cut in two or more directions then it can be machined by 5-Axes machine; refer to Figure-6.

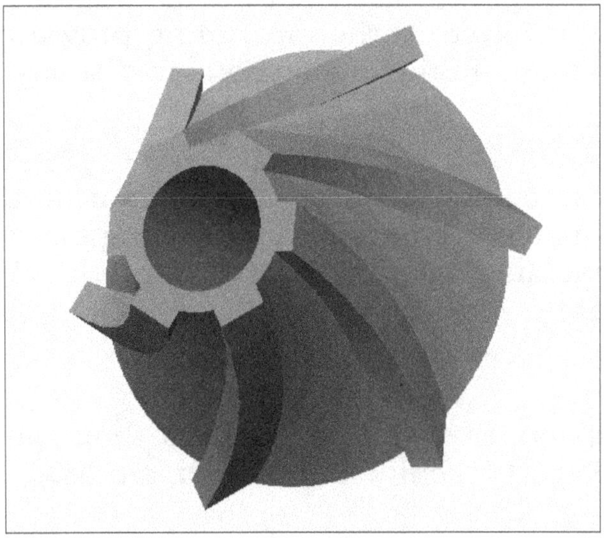

Figure-6. Model that can be machined by 5 axes machine

MACHINES IN CREO MANUFACTURING

In Creo Manufacturing application, you can generate the program codes for all the three types of milling machines discussed earlier. The procedure to add machine in Expert Machinist is discussed next.

- Click on the **Machine Tool Manager** from the **Work Center** drop-down in the **Setup** panel of the **Machining** tab in the **Ribbon**. The **Milling Work Center** dialog box will be displayed; refer to Figure-7.

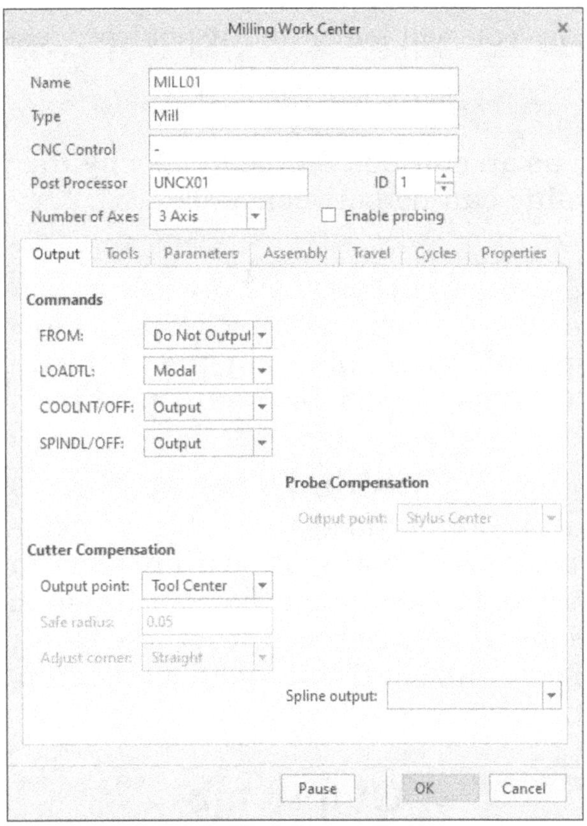

Figure-7. Milling Work Center dialog box

In this dialog box, you can specify all the parameters related to your machine. These parameters are directly involved in the machining program being created by this software. Various parameters in this dialog box are discussed next.

Name

The **Name** edit box is used to specify a user defined name of the machine. This name is used to identify the machine when we are creating operation sequence and are prompted to select a machine. Also, the information related to machine is saved in **machinename.cel** format.

Type

The **Type** edit box displays the type of machine that you are using to perform operations. In case of Expert Machinist, it will remain **Mill**.

CNC Control

The **CNC Control** edit box is used to specify the name of CNC Controller, you are using in your machine, like Fanuc, Haas, Mazak, Siemens, and so on. This field is optional to specify. But its good to specify full information because it will be reflected in the documentation of the program.

Post Processor

In **Post Processor** edit box, you can specify the name of post processor to be used for this machine. There is long list of post processor available with Creo. Post Processor is a kind of small program developed to create NC codes for the specific type of Machine. For example, Fanuc 15MA has a different post processor and HaasVF8 has a different post processor. You will learn about post processors later.

ID

This is a spinner as well as an edit box. You can specify the post processor id in this spinner/edit box. The value can be between 1-99.

Number of Axes

This option is a kind of drop-down. In this drop-down, there are three options available. Using these options, you can specify the number of axes available in your machine. You can select 3 Axis, 4 Axis, or 5 Axis machine.

Enable Probing

The **Enable probing** check box is used to enable probing. Probing is the system that is used to find the position of workpiece with respect to tool position. If you are familiar with CMM then you can assume it as coordinate measuring system. Apart from these common options, there are some other important options available in the tabs in the dialog box. These tabs and the practical meaning of the options in these tabs are discussed next.

Output tab

The options in the **Output tab** are used to specify data related to the machine that is added in the output file.

FROM drop-down

The options in the **FROM** drop-down are used to specify whether the starting position of the tool before doing any cutting operation will be added in the output file or not. There are three options available in this drop-down list; **Do Not Output**, **Only at Start**, and **At Every Sequence**.

- Select the **Do Not Output** option if you do not want to display the starting position of the tool in the output file.
- Select the **Only at Start** option if you want to display the starting position of the tool at the beginning in the output file.
- Select the **At Every Sequence** option if you want to display the starting position of the tool for every operation sequence in the output file.

LOADTL drop-down

The options of **LOADTL** drop-down are used to specify how the LOADTL command will work for the selected machine. LOADTL command is used to load tool from the Turret. There are three options in this drop-down; **Modal**, **Not Modal**, and **Not Modal on Position Moves**.

- If the **Modal** option is selected then the LOADTL command will be added in the output file at only those locations where tool is being changed for a different operation.
- If the **Not Modal** option is selected then the LOADTL command will be added before every tool path sequence.
- If the **Not Modal on Position Moves** is selected then Tool position will be created for each tool path sequence at starting as well as the end position of the tool path sequence.

COOLNT/OFF drop-down

The options of **COOLNT/OFF** drop-down are used to specify whether the commands related to coolant will be reflected in the output file or the coolant operation will be controlled manually by machine panel.

- If you select the **Output** option then the **COOLNT/OFF** command will be added in the output file for each tool path sequence.
- If you select the **Do Not Output** option then the **COOLNT/OFF** command will be added only at the end of output file.

SPINDL/OFF drop-down

The options in the **SPINDL/OFF** drop-down are used in the same way as for **COOLNT/OFF**.

Output Point

The options in **Output Print** drop-down are used to define the point that is considered as cutting point of the tool for machining. There are two options available in this drop-down, i.e. **Tool Center** and **Tool Edge**.

- If you select the **Tool Center** option from this drop-down, then the tool path will be created with reference to the tool center and will be reflected in the same way in the output file.

- If you select the **Tool Edge** option then the tool path and codes in the output file will be generated according to the edge of tool.

Safe Radius

The **Safe Radius** edit box is available only when the **Tool Edge** option is selected in the **Output Point** drop-down. This edit box is used to specify safe radius value that can be created by the selected tool on a concave corner. This value is dependent on the type of tool you are using for machining. You can find the safe radius value for your selected tool in the Tooling Catalogue of the opted company.

Adjust Corner

There are three options available in the **Adjust Corner** drop-down list. These options are used to specify the shape of workpiece at convex corners after the cutting operation is performed.

- If the **Straight** option is selected then at the convex corners, the tool paths will be extended automatically until they intersect each other.
- If the **Fillet** option is selected then fillet is automatically created at the convex corners in the tool path.
- The **Automatic** option is used when you want system to automatically use the **Straight** or **Fillet** option based on geometry of corners.

Probe Compensation Output Point

The **Output Point** drop-down is active only when the **Enable Probing** check box is selected. The options in this drop-down are used to specify the point to be considered for generating the probing output file. There are two options available in this drop-down; **Stylus Center** and **Contact Point**.

- If you select the **Stylus Center** option then the output of probing will be generated according to the position of center of probe ball.
- If you select the **Contact Point** option then the output of probing will be generated according to the position of contact point.

Rotation Area

The options of the **Rotation Area** are available only if the **4 Axis** is selected in the **Number of Axes** drop-down list. The options in this area are discussed next.

Rotation Mode

The options in the **Rotation Mode** drop-down are used to specify whether the value for rotation is according to MCS (Machine Coordinate System) or its incremental, i.e. from the previous position of the tool.

Rotation Direction

The options in **Rotation Direction** drop-down are used to specify the direction of the tool rotation. By default, the **Shortest** option is selected in this drop-down. Hence, the machine will use the shortest method to reach the specified angle, it can be CLW or CCLW. The other two options in this drop-down are used to specify the rotation method as clockwise (CLW) and counter clockwise (CCLW) as per their names.

Rotation Axis

The **Rotation Axis** drop-down list is used to specify whether to use the A axis of the machine or B axis of the machine for rotating cutting tool.

Tools tab

The options in **Tools** tab are used to specify the data related to tooling. There are two buttons and one spinner in this tab. The **Tools** button and its function have already been discussed. The other options are discussed next.

Tool Change Time (.sec)

This spinner is used to specify the time delay that is required by the machine to change the tool. If there are four tools in the turret named T1, T2, T3, and, T4; and you want to use the fourth tool after using the first tool. Let the tool change time is 2.5 seconds. Then the total time required to change from T1 to T4 will be :

Total Time = Time required for (T1->T2 + T2->T3 + T3->T4)
= 2.5 + 2.5 + 2.5 = 7.5 seconds.

Probes

The **Probes** button is active only when you select the **Enable Probing** check box in the **Milling Work Center** dialog box. This button is used to specify the setting related to probe for CMM validation.

- Click on **Probes** button from the **Tools** tab. The **Probe Setup** dialog box will be displayed as shown in Figure-8.

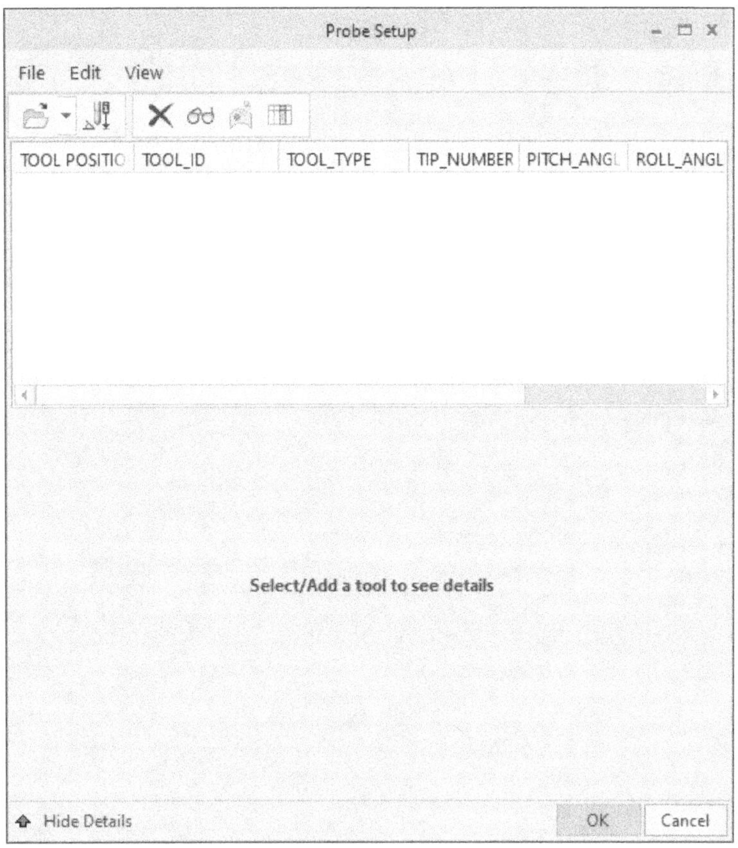

Figure-8. Probe Setup dialog box

- There are two options to add probes in the setup using this dialog box. Either you can select from the Default Probes or you can use your own created probe.
- To use a default probe, click on the **File** button and select the **Default Probes** option from the flyout. The **Open** dialog box will be displayed; refer to Figure-9.

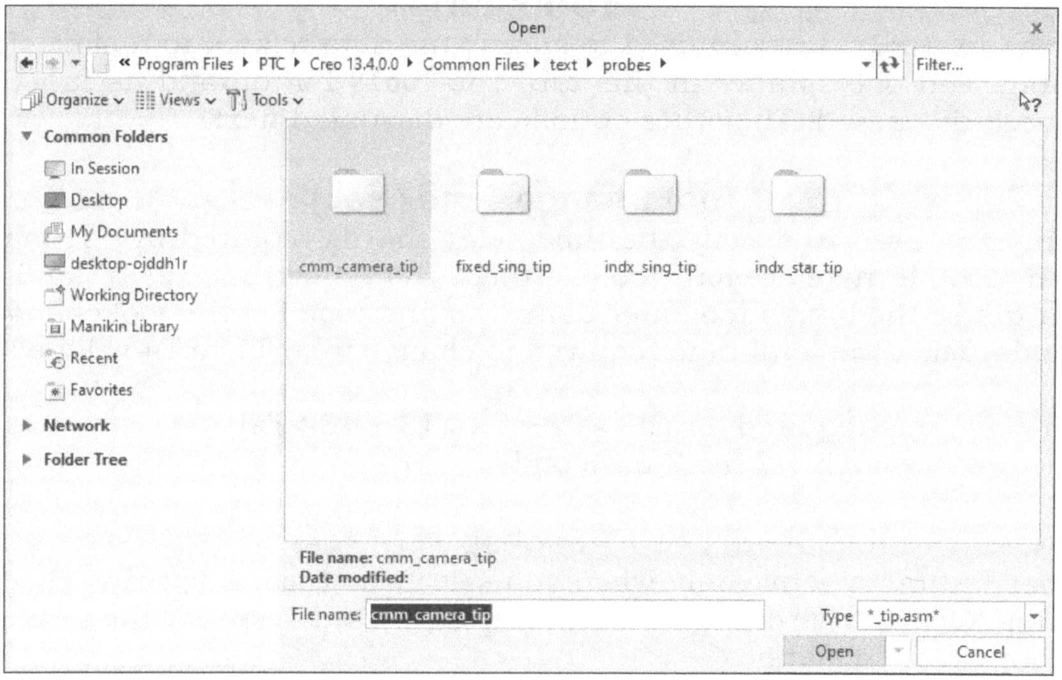

Figure-9. Open dialog box displayed on selecting Default Probes option

- Select one of the default probe, the options related to selected probe will be displayed; refer to Figure-10.

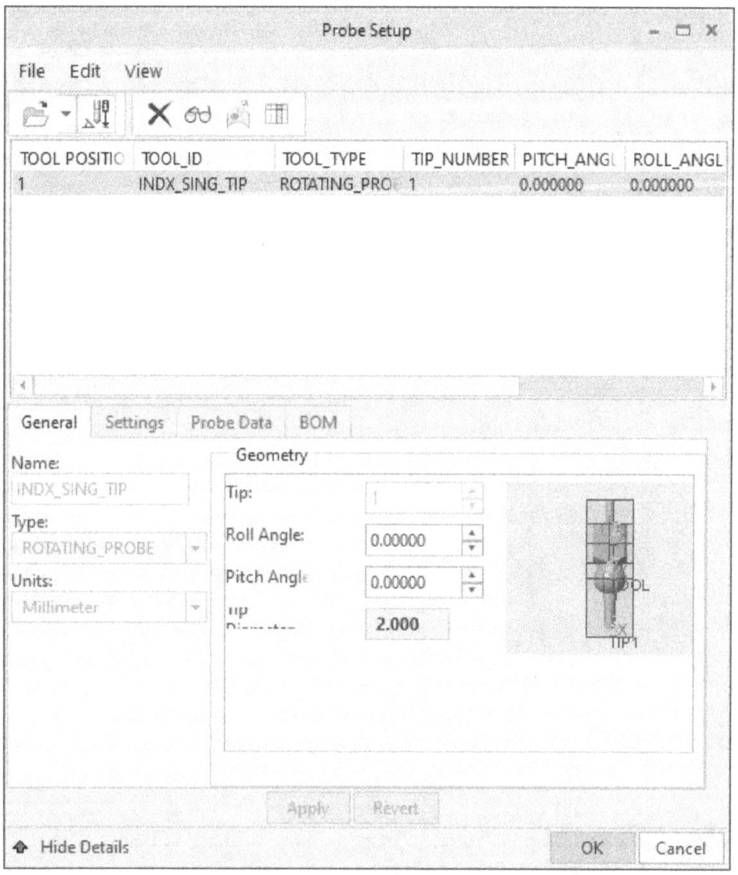

Figure-10. Probe Setup dialog box after selecting default Probe

The tabs and their options displayed in this dialog box are discussed next.

General Tab

The options in **General** tab are used to specify general settings related to the probe. The options in this tab are dependent on the probe selected. Main parameters that can be specified by using these options are: number of tips of probe, roll angle, pitch angle, and diameter of tip.

Settings Tab

The options in **Settings** tab are used to specify the probe number, register number, and comments related to the probe. Scanning check box in this tab is used to enable scanning of surface or segments that are generated automatically by measure points specified.

Probe Data Tab

The options in **Probe Data** tab are used to specify the feed rate at which the measurement will be done by the probe. You can specify measure feed in metric unit system as well as imperial unit system.

BOM Tab

The options in the **BOM** tab are used to specify Bill of Material of the selected probe.

You will learn about Probes in more details in Chapter related to CMM.

Parameters Tab

The options in the **Parameters** tab are used to specify parameters related to power of machine and rotational speed of the spindle. The options of this tab are discussed next.

Maximum Speed (RPM)

The **Maximum speed(RPM)** edit box is used to specify the maximum rotational speed of the spindle attainable for manufacturing. The value specified in this edit box can not be negative. Also, the value specified will be in rounds per minute.

Horsepower

The **Horsepower** edit box is used to specify the power of main motor in HP unit.

Rapid Traverse

The options in **Rapid Traverse** drop-down are used to specify the unit to be used to specify rapid traverse/feed rate.

Rapid Feed Rate

The **Rapid Feed Rate** edit box is used to specify feed rate at which the tool will move in a non-cutting step.

Defaults

The **Default** button is used to invoke the **SELECT SITE Menu Manager**; refer to Figure-11. The options in this **Menu Manager** are used to specify the location of SITE file(*.sit) for the machine. This file contains the parameters related to CMM which will be discussed later in this book.

- To link a SITE file with the Machine, click on **Current Dir** option from the **Menu Manager**. The **SITE TYPE** section will be displayed in **Menu Manager**; refer to Figure-12.

Figure-11. SELECT SITE Menu Manager

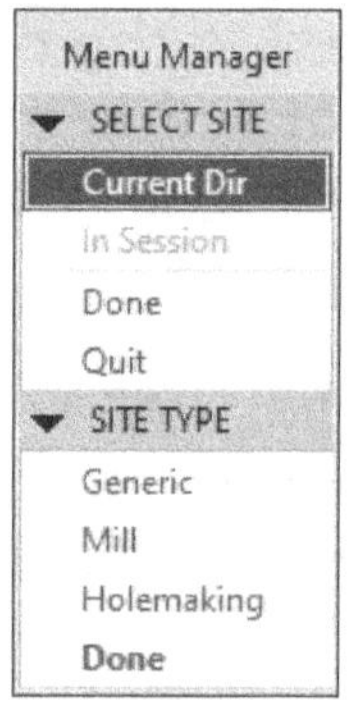

Figure-12. SITE TYPE section

- Select desired type from the **SITE TYPE** section. The **Open** dialog box will be displayed as shown in Figure-13.

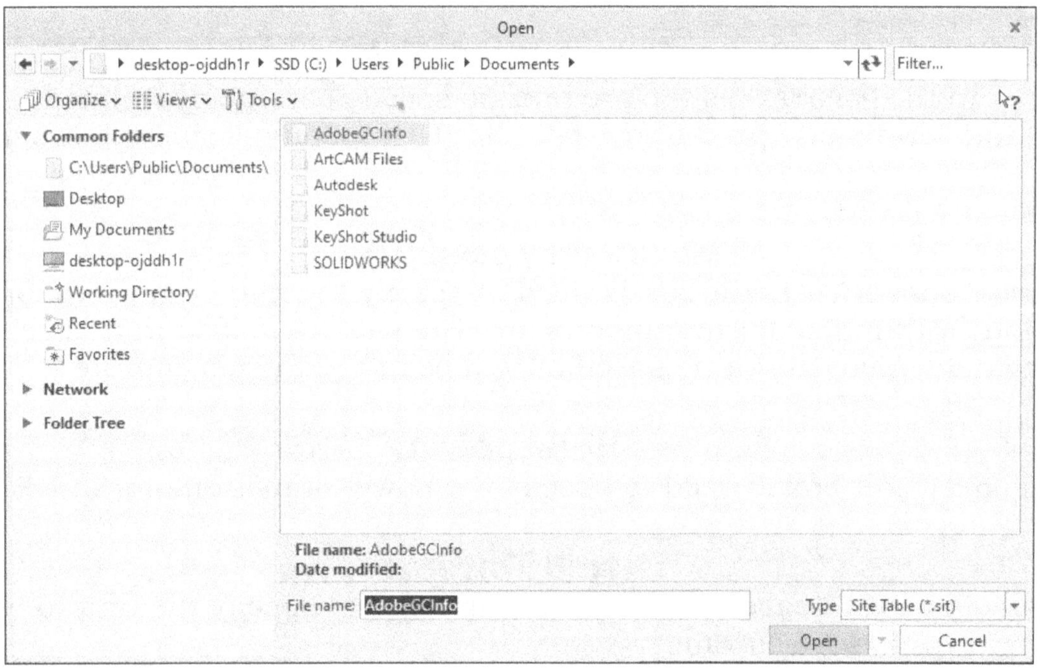

Figure-13. The Open dialog box

- Select desired file by using the options in dialog box and then choose the **Open** button. A message will be displayed at the information bar available at the bottom of the application window informing that the file has been successfully read; refer to Figure-14.

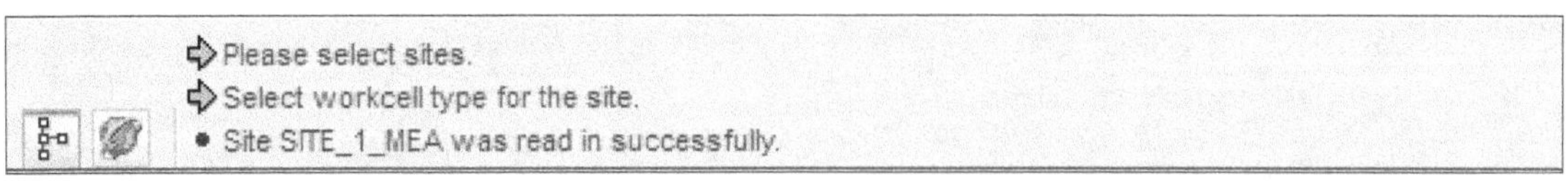

Figure-14. Message displayed in the information bar at the bottom of the application window

This message informs that the file has been linked successfully. Now, choose the **Resume** button in the **Milling Work Center** dialog box to activate the dialog box again.

PPRINT

The **PPRINT** button is used to invoke the **PPRINT Menu Manager** as shown in Figure-15. The options in this **Menu Manager** are used to specify data that you want to include in the Cutter Location Data file(CL Data file).

Figure-15. PPRINT Menu Manager

- To specify the data to be included, click on the **Create** button from the **Menu Manager**. The **Activate PPRINT** dialog box will be displayed; refer to Figure-16.

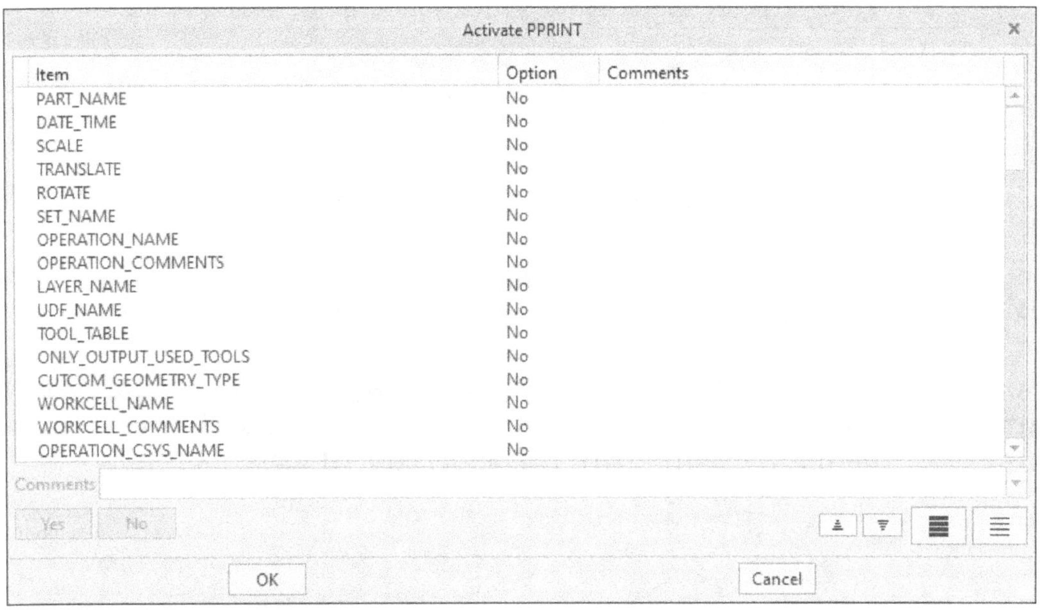

Figure-16. Activate PPRINT dialog box

- In this dialog box, various parameters are displayed in the **Item** column.
- In the **Option** column adjacent to desired parameter, you can specify the **Yes** or **No** option. The **Yes** option means the parameter will be included in the CL Data file. If you select the **No** option then the adjacent parameter will not be included in CL Data file.
- You can select multiple parameters at a time. After selecting the parameters, select the **Yes** button at the bottom of the dialog box.
- The selected parameters will be included in the CL Data file. You can select and deselect all the parameters by using the and the buttons, respectively.
- After specifying the parameters, click on the **OK** button from the dialog box. The **Modify**, **Save**, and **Show** buttons will become active in the **Menu Manager**.

These options are discussed next.

Modify

If you select the **Modify** option, the active PPRINT file will be displayed in the **Activate PPRINT** dialog box. You can modify the values in the file by using the option in the dialog box.

Save

The **Save** option is used to save the PPRINT file. The procedure to save the file is discussed next.

- Click on the **Save** option. An input box will be displayed at the top of the modeling area of the application window and you will be prompted to specify the name of the file. Specify the name of the PPRINT file; refer to Figure-17.

Figure-17. PPRINT file name input box

- After specifying the name, click on the ✓ button. The file will be saved at the location displayed at the bottom of the information bar; refer to Figure-18.

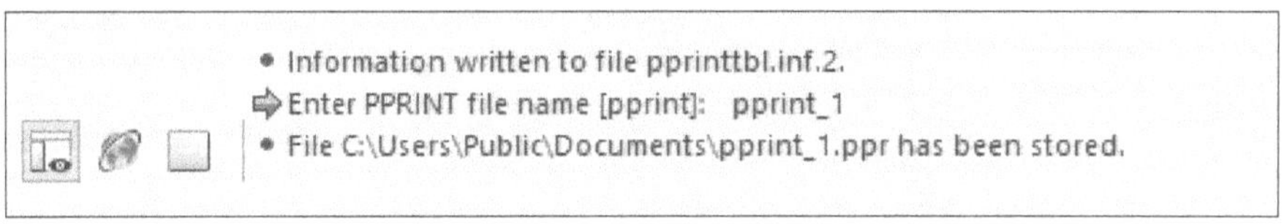

Figure-18. Message displayed at the bottom after saving the file

Show

The **Show** option is used to display the content of active PPRINT file.

- Click on the **Show** option from the **Menu Manager**. The **INFORMATION WINDOW (pprinttbl.inf)** will be displayed; refer to Figure-19. Note that you cannot modify the content of the file by using this **INFORMATION WINDOW**.

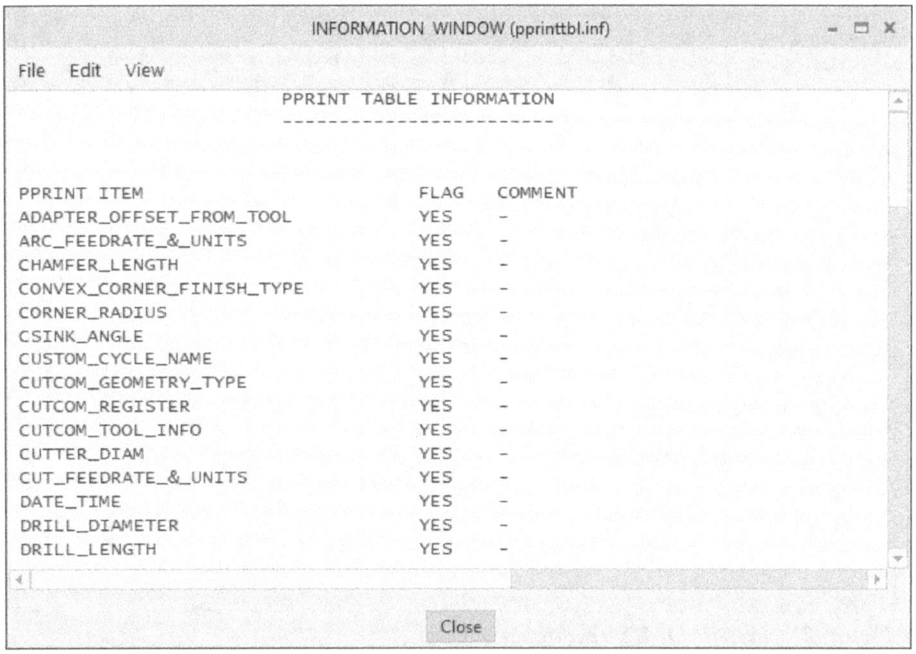

Figure-19. INFORMATION WINDOW (pprinttbl.inf)

Retrieve

The **Retrieve** option is used to link an already saved PPRINT file with the current machine.

- On selecting the **Retrieve** option, the **Open** dialog box will be displayed.
- Select desired file and click on **Open** button. The confirmation message will be displayed at the bottom in Information bar.

Click on the **Done/Return** option from **Menu Manager** to exit the tool.

DMIS Text

The **DMIS** button is used to define Dimensional Measuring Interface Standard (DMIS) text data. This data is used by dimension measuring equipment for analysis, collection, and archiving. DMIS acts as a bridge between CNC machining and CMM coordinate measuring operation. The procedure to use this option is discussed next.

- Click on the **DMIS** button from **Parameters** tab in the **Milling Work Center** dialog box. The **DMIS TEXT Menu Manager** will be displayed; refer to Figure-20.

Figure-20. DMIS TEXT Menu Manager

- Click on the **Create** option from the **Menu Manager**. The **Activate DMIS Text** dialog box will be displayed; refer to Figure-21.

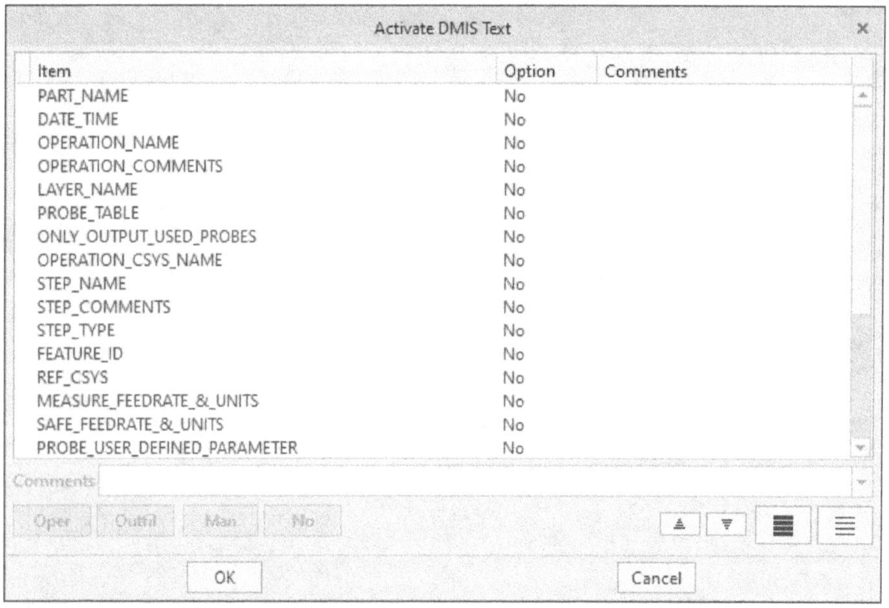

Figure-21. Activate DMIS Text dialog box

- Set the parameters in the dialog box as discussed earlier and click on the **OK** button.

The other options of **DMIS TEXT Menu Manager** are same as discussed earlier. Click on the **Done/Return** option from **Menu Manager** to exit.

Assembly Tab

The options in the **Assembly** tab are used to add and link an already created machine assembly; refer to Figure-22. This assembly will also be used for the simulation purpose. The options in this tab are discussed next.

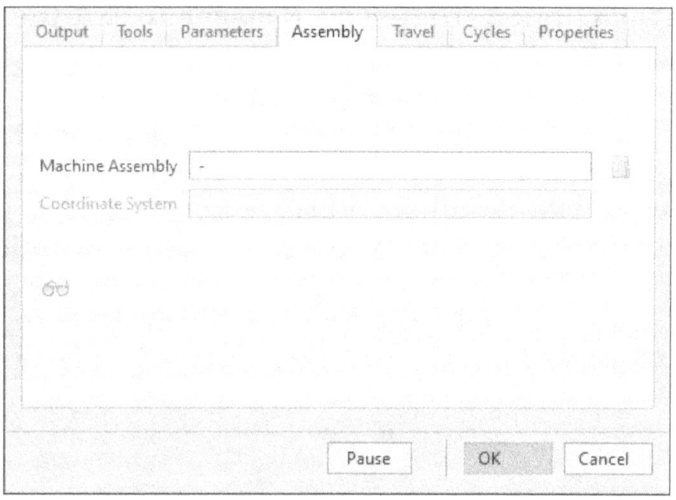

Figure-22. Assembly tab in the Milling Work Center dialog box

Machine Assembly

The **Machine Assembly** option is a type of information collector. This option displays the path of machine assembly to be added in the system.

- To add an assembly file, click on the **Open** button adjacent to the collector. The **Open** dialog box will be displayed; refer to Figure-23.

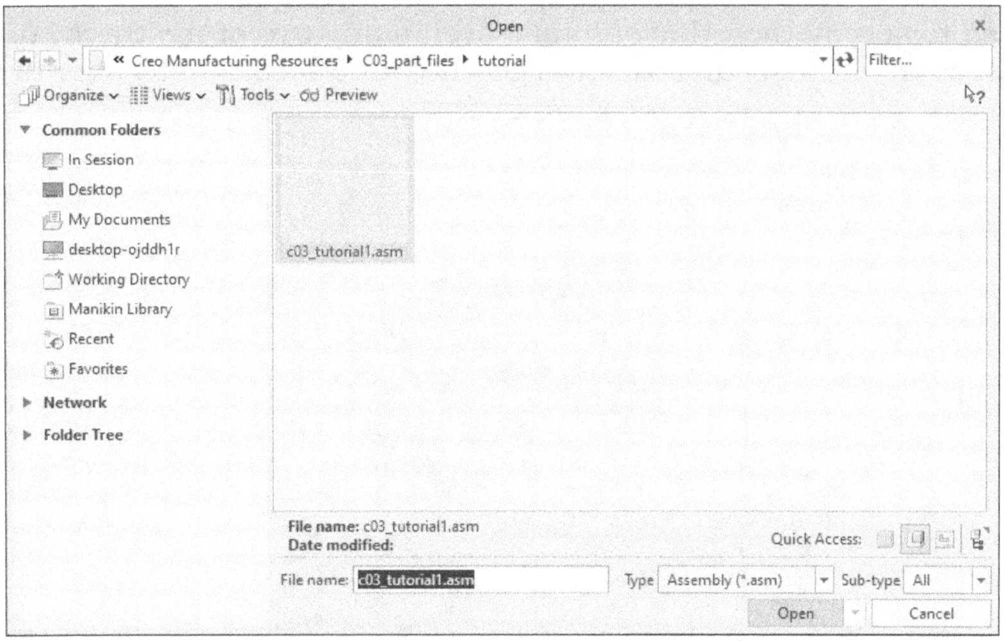

Figure-23. Open dialog box for inserting assembly file

Select the machine assembly file and click on the **Open** button from the dialog box. The assembly file name will be displayed in the **Machine Assembly** collector.

Coordinate System

The **Coordinate System** collector is active only after you have selected the machine assembly file. This collector is used to store the coordinate system according to which the machine assembly is to be placed. The coordinate system selected is directly matched with the coordinate system of the machine assembly while placing.

You can see the preview of the machine assembly by using the preview button.

Travel

The options of **Travel** tab are used to specify the total travel of tool that is available for the selected machine. After clicking on this tab, the **Milling Work Center** dialog box is displayed as shown in Figure-24.

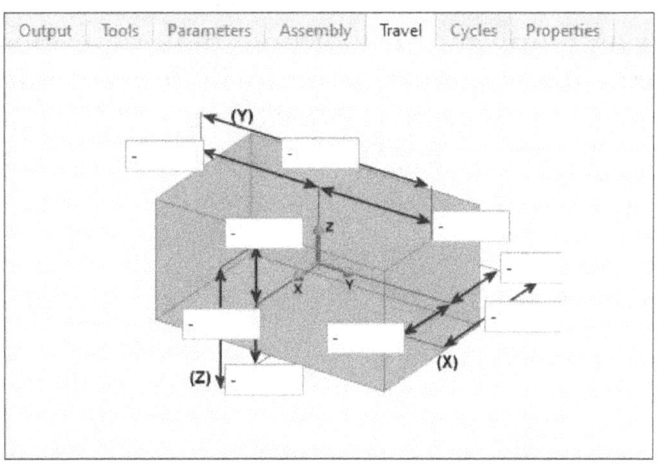

Figure-24. Travel tab in the Milling Work Center dialog box

- As you can see from the above figure, there are three edit boxes for each direction. You need to specify the value of total travel in any two of the three edit boxes for each direction, the last edit boxes will get the value accordingly; refer to Figure-25.

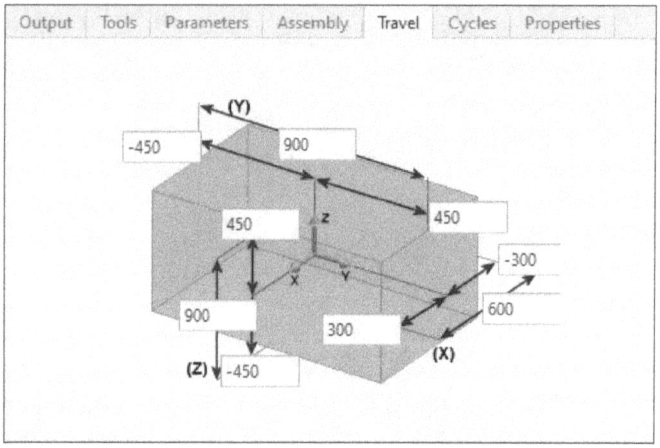

Figure-25. Travel tab after specifying the values

Cycles

The options in the **Cycles** tab are used to configure hole making cycles for the machine. The **Milling Work Center** dialog box after clicking on this tab is displayed as shown in Figure-26.

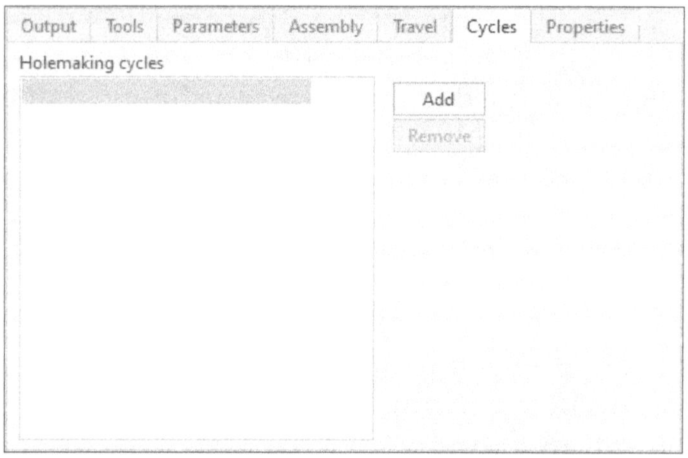

Figure-26. Cycles tab in the Milling Work Center dialog box

- Here, you can add as many number of hole making cycles as you want. These cycles will be stored with the machine and will be used later while machining.
- To add a hole making cycle, click on the **Add** tool from the dialog box. The **Customize Cycle** dialog box will be displayed; refer to Figure-27.

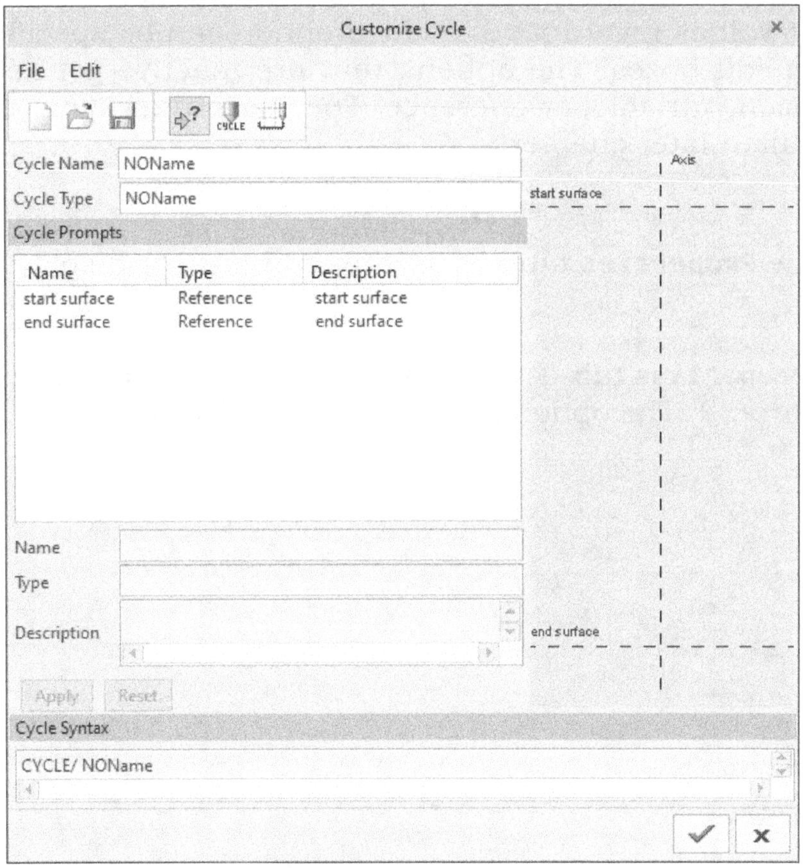

Figure-27. Customize Cycle dialog box

The options in this dialog box are discussed next.

Cycle Name

The **Cycle Name** edit box is used to specify the name of the hole making cycle.

Cycle Type

The **Cycle Type** edit box is used to specify a keyword for the current cycle.

Cycle Prompts

This area stores the information regarding the starting surface and ending surface of the cycle. Preview of the starting surface and end surface is displayed in the right of this area. If you right click on empty space in this area, a shortcut menu is displayed as shown in Figure-28.

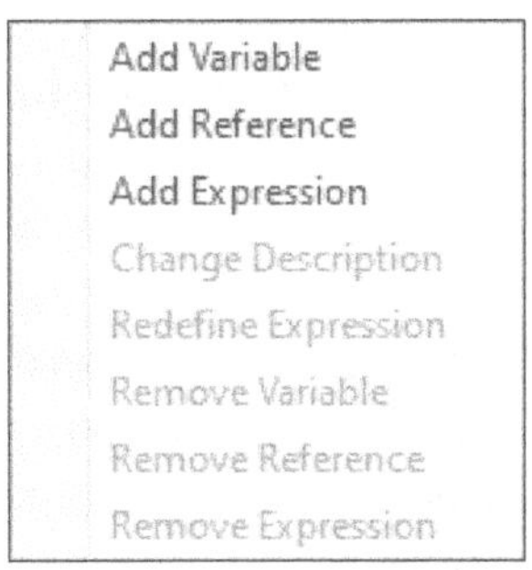

Figure-28. Shortcut menu

Using this shortcut menu, you can add options like variable, reference, or expression for the cycle. The values regarding the added option can be specified in **Name**, **Type**, and **Description** edit boxes. The options that are inactive get activated after you select an expression, variable, or reference. The **Customize Cycle** dialog box will be discussed in detail in later chapters.

Properties

The options in the **Properties** tab are used to edit and/or display properties of the created machine.

- Click on the **Properties** tab. The **Milling Work Center** dialog box is displayed as shown in Figure-29. The options in this tab are discussed next.

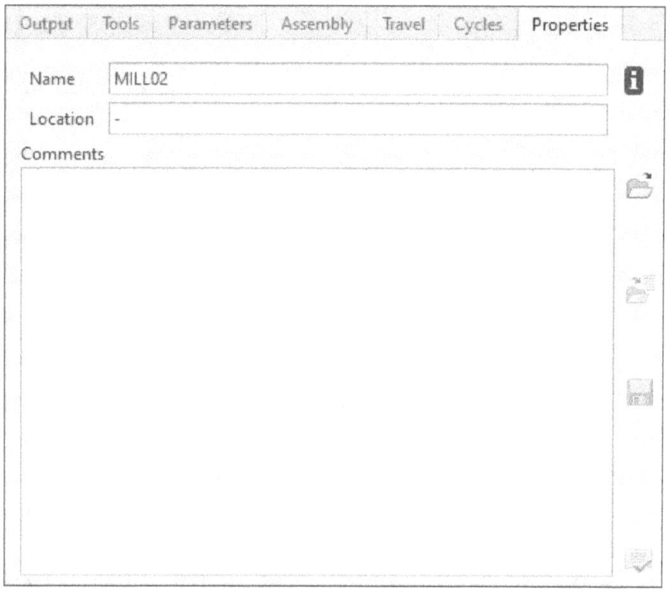

Figure-29. Properties tab in the Milling Work Center dialog box

Name

The **Name** edit box is used to specify name of the machine to be created. The information button adjacent to this edit box is used to display the complete information of the machine.

Location

The **Location** edit box is used to specify location of machine files.

Comments

The **Comments** edit box is used to specify comments about the selected machine.

- You can also load comments from text files by using the **Open** button displayed adjacent to the edit box.
- Using the **Insert** button, you can insert more text in the file.
- Using the **Save** button, you can save the loaded comment.
- The **Insert** and the **Save** buttons will be active only after specifying at least one character in the **Comments** edit box.

PRACTICAL 1

In this tutorial, you will create a machine with following parameters:

- Name of machine is **Fanuc milling center01** with post processor UNCX03 and number of axes = **3**. CNC Control is Fanuc 18i.
- Coolant added in the output file
- From location to be added for each tool movement in the output file
- Tool corner to be filleted, radius for safe corner should be 0.8 mm from the tool edge.
- 3 tools with the specifications as shown in Figure-30 and changing time for tool should be 4 second.

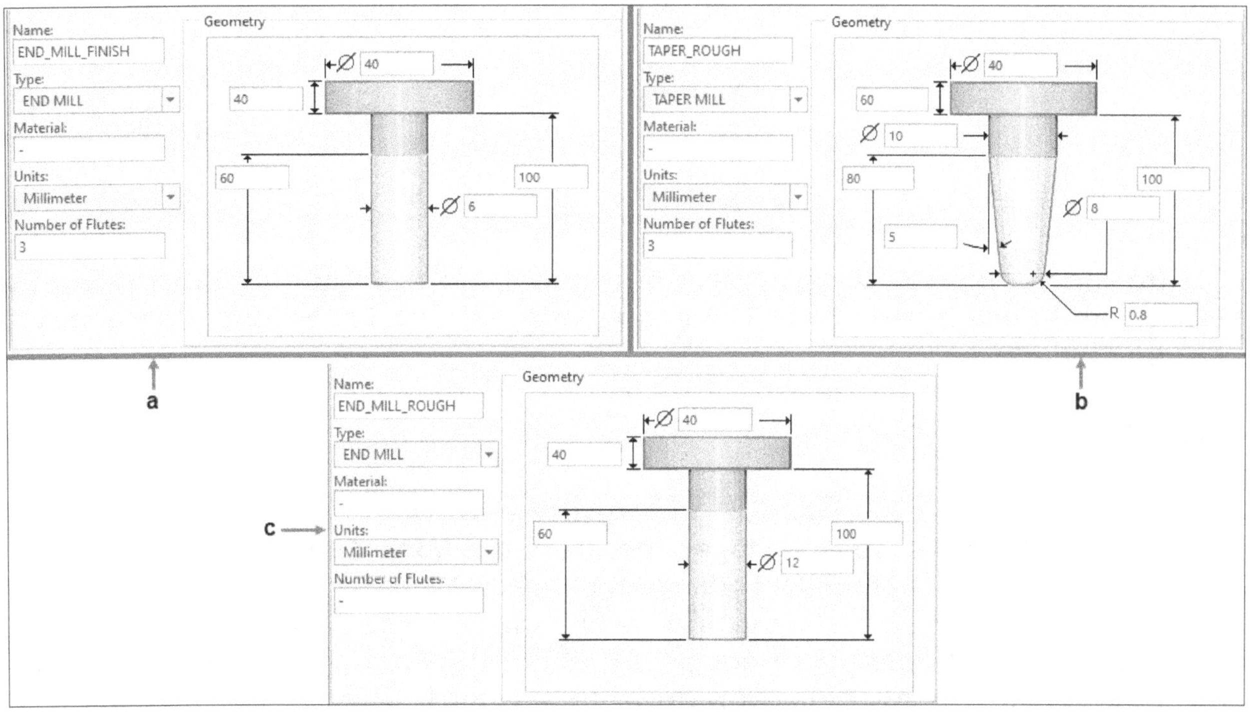

Figure-30. Specifications for the tools

- Maximum RPM of machine spindle is 7500 and rapid feed rate is 25 mm per minute.
- Total travel of machine is 900 mm in each direction.

Starting Creo Expert Machinist

- Start Creo Parametric and click on the **New** button from the **Ribbon**.
- Select **Manufacturing** radio button from the **Type** area and **Expert Machinist** radio button from the **Sub-type** area of the dialog box.
- Specify the name of the file as **C04 tut1** and clear the **Use default template** check box.
- Now, click on the **OK** button from the dialog box. The **New File Options** dialog box will be displayed. Select the **mmns mfg nc abs** template and then click on the **OK** button.

Adding an NC model in the system

- Click on the **Create Model** tool from **NC Model** panel in the **Ribbon**. An input box will be displayed to define the name of the nc model.

- Click on the **Accept value** button from the prompt. The default name will be accepted and you will be prompted to select a part file as reference model.
- Select the file **C2 tutorial1** by using the options in the dialog box and then click on the **Open** button.
- Click on the **Create Stock** option from the **NC MODEL Menu Manager** displayed; refer to Figure-31. The **Auto Workpiece Creation** contextual tab will be added in the **Ribbon** and the related options will be displayed.

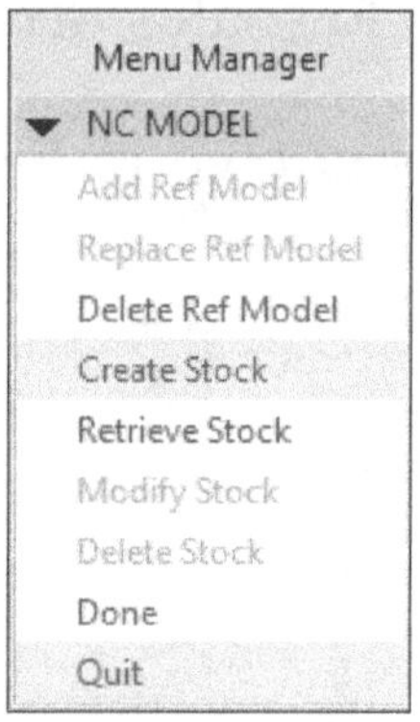

Figure-31. NC MODEL Menu Manager

- Create the workpiece as per your requirement and click the **OK** button from the **Ribbon** and **Done** button from the **Menu Manager**. The **Component Placement** tab will be displayed.
- Place the workpiece at the default position and click on the **OK** button from the **Ribbon**.

Creating Machine Setup

- Click on the **Machine Tool Manager** tool from the **Work Center** drop-down in the **Setup** panel. The **Milling Work Center** dialog box will be displayed. Click in the **Name** edit box displayed at the top and specify the name as **Fanuc milling center01**.
- Enter the name of Post processor as **UNCX03** in the **Post Processor** edit box. Set the value of **Number of Axes** drop-down to **3** if not set by default.
- Enter **Fanuc 18i** in the **CNC Control** edit box.
- Click in the **COOLNT/OFF** drop-down and select **Output** option, if not selected.
- Select the **At Every Sequence** option from the **FROM** drop-down.
- Select the **Tool Edge** option from the **Output point** drop-down. The options below the drop-down become active.
- Click in the **Safe radius** edit box and specify the value as **0.8** mm. Also, select the **Fillet** option from the **Adjust corner** drop-down.
- Click on the **Tools** tab and then click on the **Tools** button. The **Tools Setup** dialog box will be displayed.
- Specify the parameters as displayed in Figure-30 (**a**) and then click on the **Apply** button displayed at the bottom. The tool will be added in the setup; refer to Figure-32.

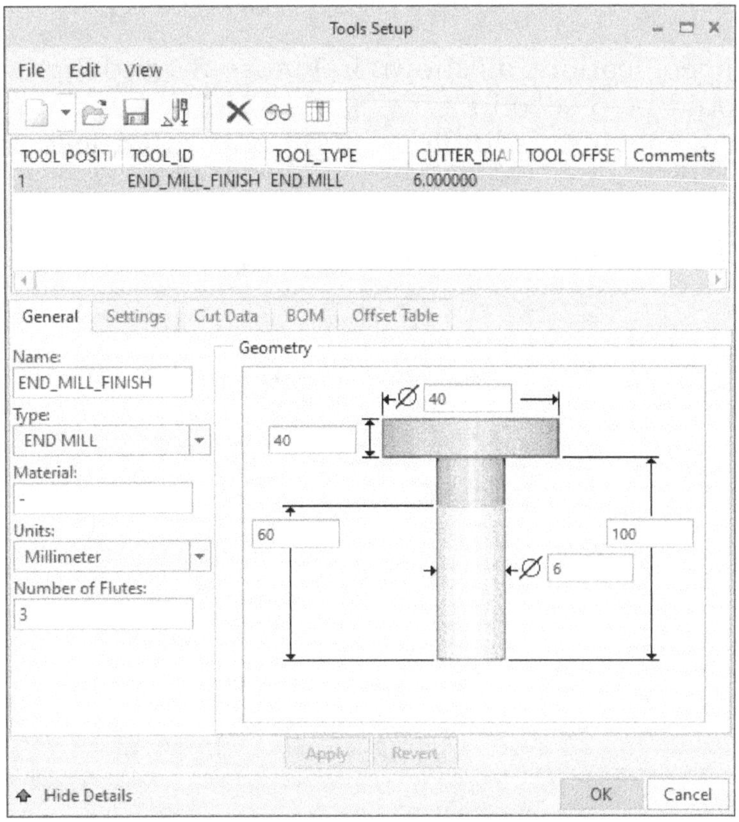

Figure-32. Tools Setup dialog box after adding a tool

- To add more tool, click on the **New** button displayed in the toolbar at the top and specify the parameters in the same way as in step 9.

Tip
You can also save the tools if you want to used them later.

- Click on the **OK** button after adding all the required tools. The **Milling Work Center** dialog box will be displayed again.
- Set the value **04** in the **Tool Change Time (sec.)** spinner.
- Click on the **Parameters** tab in **Milling Work Center** dialog box and enter **7500** in the **Maximum Speed (RPM)** edit box.
- Select **MMPM** in the **Rapid Traverse** drop-down, if not selected.
- Enter the value as **25** in the **Rapid Feed Rate** edit box.
- Click on the **Travel** tab and specify the value of total travel 900 each direction i.e. 450 in positive and 450 in negative of each direction.
- Now, click on the **OK** button from the dialog box to create the machine.

PROBLEM 1

In this problem, you will create a machine with following parameters:

1. Name of machine is **Haas Milling Center01** with post processor UNCX01 and number of axes = **4**. CNC Control is Haas.
2. From position of tool should be displayed only at the start of operation.
3. Coolant added in the output file.

4. Tool corner to be filleted, radius for safe corner should be 0.8 mm from the tool edge.
5. 2 tools with the specifications as shown in Figure-33 and Figure-34, and changing time for tool should be 6 second.
6. Maximum RPM of machine spindle is 9000 and rapid feed rate is 250 mm per minute.

Total travel of machine is 900 mm in X direction, 600 in Z direction, and 500 in Y direction.

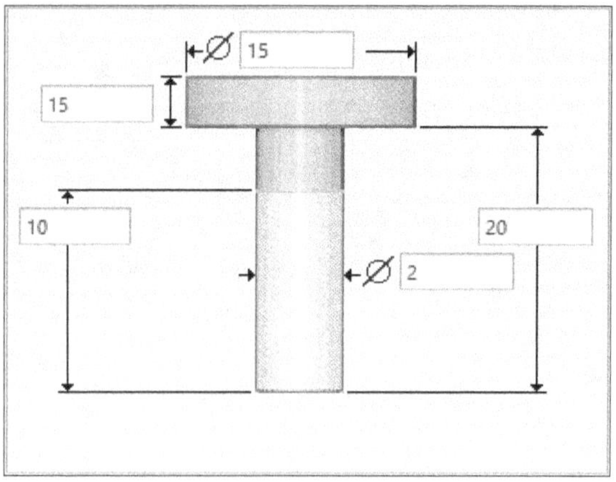

Figure-33. Specification of first tool

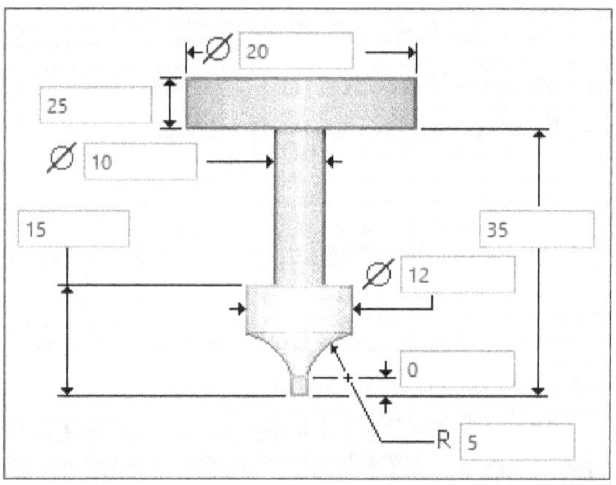

Figure-34. Specification of second tool

SELF-ASSESSMENT

Q1. What is the purpose of the "Machine Tool Manager" in Creo Manufacturing?

A. To create custom tool paths
B. To edit design sketches
C. To specify machine parameters for operations
D. To simulate G-code

Q2. Which field in the Milling Work Center dialog box specifies the user-defined name of the machine?

A. Type
B. ID
C. CNC Control
D. Name

Q3. What is the range of valid values for the post processor ID?

A. 1–100
B. 0–100
C. 1–99
D. 0–99

Q4. What does the “Enable Probing” check box do?

A. Enables simulation of tool motion
B. Enables probe-based workpiece alignment
C. Displays probe size
D. Sets probe color

Q5. What is the role of the "FROM" drop-down in the Output tab?

A. Set coolant on/off
B. Control spindle speed
C. Specify starting position output
D. Load tool information

Q6. Which option adds LOADTL command only where a tool is changed?

A. Not Modal
B. Modal
C. At Every Sequence
D. Do Not Output

Q7. What does the "Tool Edge" option in Output Point define?

A. Center of the machine
B. Depth of tool cut
C. Tool path based on tool edge
D. Rotation speed of tool

Q8. Which edit box appears only when "Tool Edge" is selected in Output Point?

A. Horsepower
B. Safe Radius
C. Rapid Feed Rate
D. Spindle Speed

Q9. What does the “Adjust Corner” drop-down NOT include?

A. Fillet
B. Straight
C. Blend
D. Automatic

Q10. In probing, which option reflects output as per contact location?

A. Stylus Center
B. Contact Point
C. Probe Angle
D. Tip Offset

Q11. What does the "Rotation Mode" drop-down define in 4-Axis setup?

A. Feed rate
B. Spindle angle
C. Tool change speed
D. Whether rotation is MCS-based or incremental

Q12. What does the Tool Change Time (.sec) spinner define?

A. Tool load duration
B. Spindle on time
C. Time to change between tools
D. Tool tip speed

Q13. Which tab in Probe Setup is used to define roll and pitch angle?

A. Settings
B. General
C. Probe Data
D. BOM

Q14. What is the function of the "Rapid Feed Rate" edit box?

A. To control coolant flow
B. To set spindle RPM
C. To define feed rate for non-cutting tool motion
D. To control probe speed

Q15. What does the "Defaults" button in the Parameters tab open?

A. Cycle prompt dialog
B. General settings
C. SELECT SITE Menu Manager
D. Load tool window

Q16. Which button is used to specify data to be included in the CL Data file?

A. DMIS
B. Retrieve
C. Modify
D. PPRINT

Q17. What does the Save option in PPRINT Menu Manager do?

A. Save comments only
B. Save tool settings
C. Save selected CL Data parameters
D. Save model geometry

Q18. What is the use of the "Retrieve" option in PPRINT Menu Manager?

A. Open probe
B. Link saved PPRINT file
C. Reset all options
D. Select measurement unit

Q19. What is DMIS used for?

A. Generating CAM file
B. Connecting Creo with CAD
C. Interfacing CNC and CMM
D. Generating STL for 3D printing

Q20. What does the “Machine Assembly” option in Assembly tab collect?

A. Machine comments
B. Machine file path
C. Probe types
D. Tool settings

Q21. What must be selected before using Coordinate System collector?

A. Post Processor
B. Travel Limit
C. Machine Assembly File
D. Probing Tool

Q22. What is defined using the Travel tab?

A. Spindle size
B. Feed rate
C. Tool diameter
D. Total movement range of tool

Q23. Which tool is used to define hole-making sequences?

A. Drill Tool
B. Add Tool in Cycles tab
C. Machine Tool Manager
D. CNC Control

Q24. Which tab is used to define probe number, register, and comments?

A. Settings
B. Parameters
C. BOM
D. Cycle Prompts

Q25. What is stored in the BOM tab of Probe Setup?

A. Bill of Materials of the probe
B. Tool RPM
C. Probe angle
D. Feed rate settings

Q26. What does the “Horsepower” field specify?

A. Speed of tool
B. Power of spindle motor
C. Power of probe
D. Feed rate unit

Q27. What does the "Show" option in PPRINT do?

A. Allows modifying parameters
B. Displays active file content
C. Starts probe setup
D. Launches simulation

Chapter 5

Operations and Cutting Strategies

Topics Covered

The major topics covered in this chapter are:

- ***Machining Operations.***
- ***Operations in Creo Manufacturing.***
- ***Various cutting strategies for machining in Creo Manufacturing.***
- ***Setting Milling Work Center.***

OPERATIONS

In any kind of machining, operations are the cutting steps to get the required shape and size from the workpiece. One operation can cut only a small portion of the workpiece and one operation can cut almost all the workpiece to get desired parameters in one go. Area of cut and depth of cut depends upon the type of operation to be performed. The function of operations in Creo Manufacturing is discussed next.

OPERATIONS IN CREO MANUFACTURING

In Creo Manufacturing, operation is a process that cuts material from the workpiece. An operation is composed of various cutting strategies. The operation can have more than one tools involved in the process. The process is discussed next.

- Click on the **Operation** tool from **Setup** panel in the **Machining** tab of the **Ribbon**. The **Operation** tab will displayed in the **Ribbon**; refer to Figure-1.

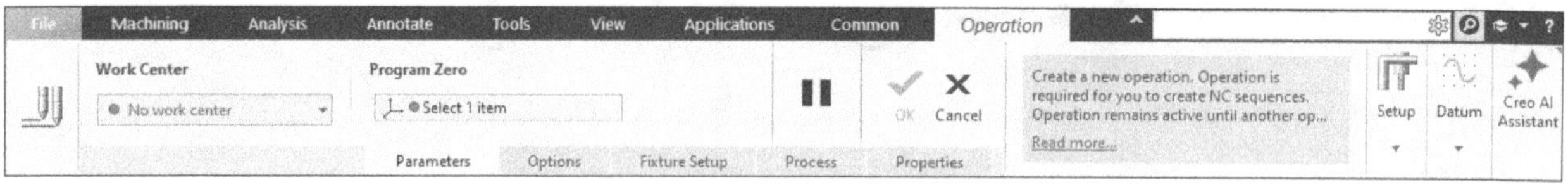

Figure-1. Operation tab in the Ribbon

The options of this tab are discussed next.

Work Center

The options of **Work Center** drop-down are used to specify a machine for the selected operation. The machines created in the current session are displayed in this drop-down list.

Program Zero

This is a type of value collector. This option stores the coordinate system that is defined as the zero position for the current operation. To define a program zero position, click in this option and then select the coordinate system that you want to specify as the program zero position.

Parameters Tab

The options in the **Parameters** tab are used to specify basic parameters regarding the cutter location(CL) file of current operation; refer to Figure-2. The options in this tab are discussed next.

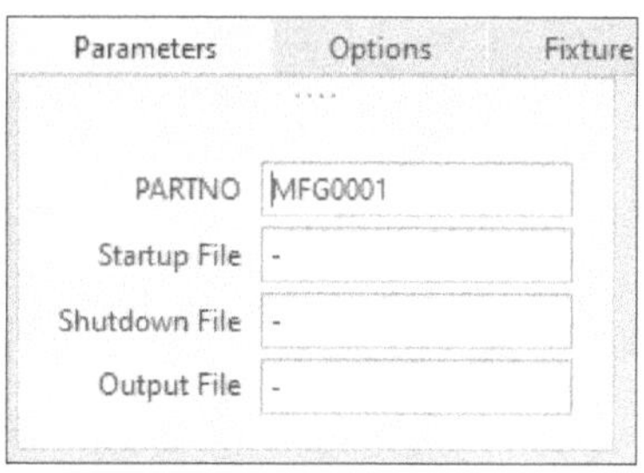

Figure-2. Parameters tab

PARTNO

The **PARTNO** edit box is used to specify the part name or number. This name/number is displayed at the top of the nc program to be generated. This name/number is used to identify the nc programs later.

Startup File

The **Startup File** edit box is used to specify the name of the CL file that is to be included at the starting of nc program. These codes are added in the file after Part number, machine, and unit codes in the nc program. To add a startup file, copy the required file in the current working directory and then specify the name of the file in the **Startup File** edit box.

Shutdown File

The **Shutdown File** edit box is used to specify the name of the CL file that is to be included at the end of the nc program. This edit box works in the same way as **Startup File** edit box.

Output File

The **Output File** edit box is used to specify the name of the output file to be created for the current operation. To specify the names of the files in all the edit boxes, you should use alphanumeric keys only.

Options Tab

The options in the **Options** tab are used to specify the stock material for the current operation. If you have selected a 4 axes milling machine then the options related to rotation of tool will also be displayed in this tab; refer to Figure-3. The options in this tab are discussed next.

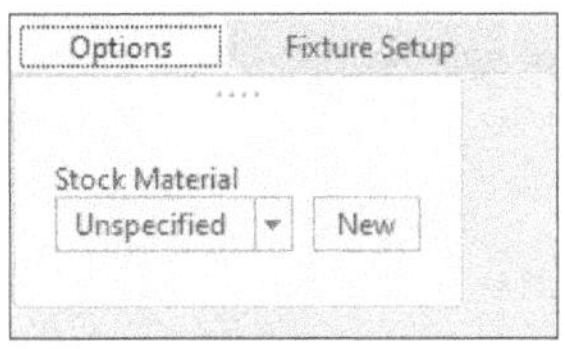

Figure-3. Options tab

Stock Material

The options in the **Stock Material** drop-down list are used to specify the conditions of the stock material. The specified stock material name is saved in the mfg wp material list file in the default directory.

Use Rotary Clearance

The **Use Rotary Clearance** check box is used to enable safe clearance distance for the rotary bed of the 4 Axes machine. On selecting this check box, the options below this check box become active.

Clearance

The **Clearance** edit box is used to specify the clearance value for the tool when the table rotates. For example, the value is specified in this edit box as 5. Then the tool will move to such a position that it is away from table rotation range by 5 mm. Note that this rotation range also counts the fixtures and other assemblies attached to the table.

Safe Point

There are three edit boxes available under this head. Specify the safe values in X, Y, and Z directions for the tool at which the tool will retract when table rotate.

Fixture Setup

The options in the **Fixture Setup** tab are used to set a fixture for workpiece in the current operation. The process to add the fixture is given next.

- Click on the **Add a fixture component** button from the tab. The **Open** dialog box will be displayed and you are prompted to select an assembly or a part for the fixture; refer to Figure-4.

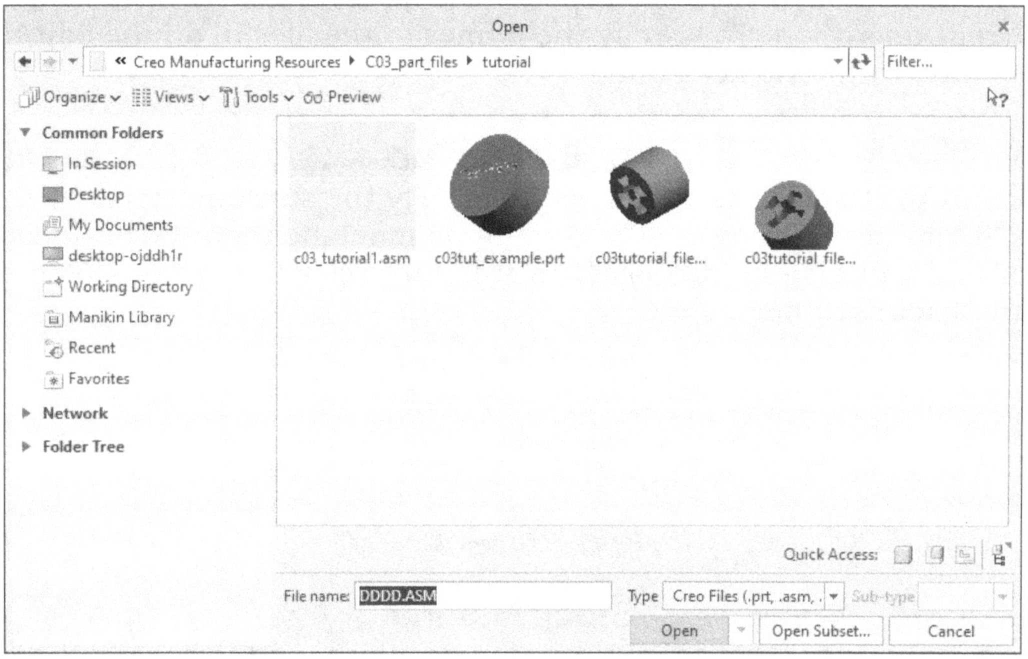

Figure-4. Open dialog box on clicking Add a fixture component button

- Click on the **Type** drop-down if you want to select a file of other format.
- After selecting desired format, browse and select the file that you want to use as a fixture and then click on the **Open** button. The **Component Placement** tab will be displayed in the **Ribbon** and the selected fixture part will be displayed in the modeling area; refer to Figure-5.

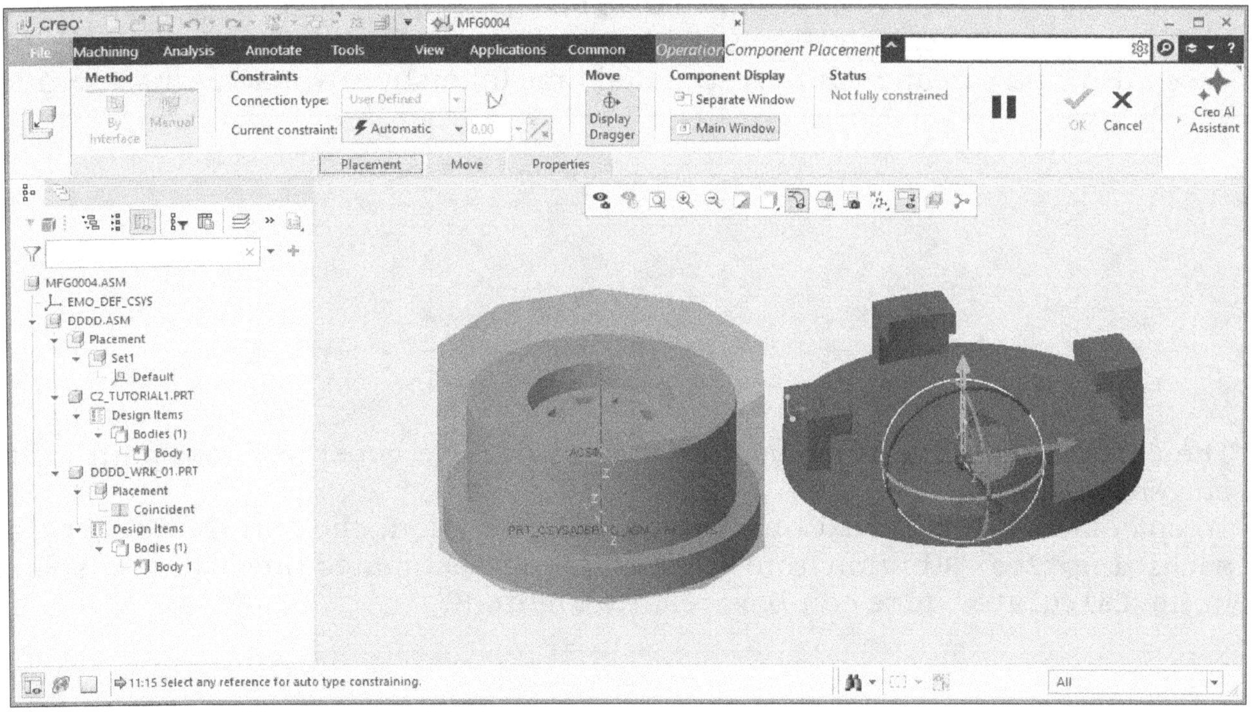

Figure-5. Component Placement tab and the fixture part

- Assemble the fixture and the workpiece as desired.
- Click on **OK** button from the **Ribbon**. The workpiece and the fixture will get assembled and displayed in the modeling area along with the **Fixture Setup** tab; refer to Figure-6.

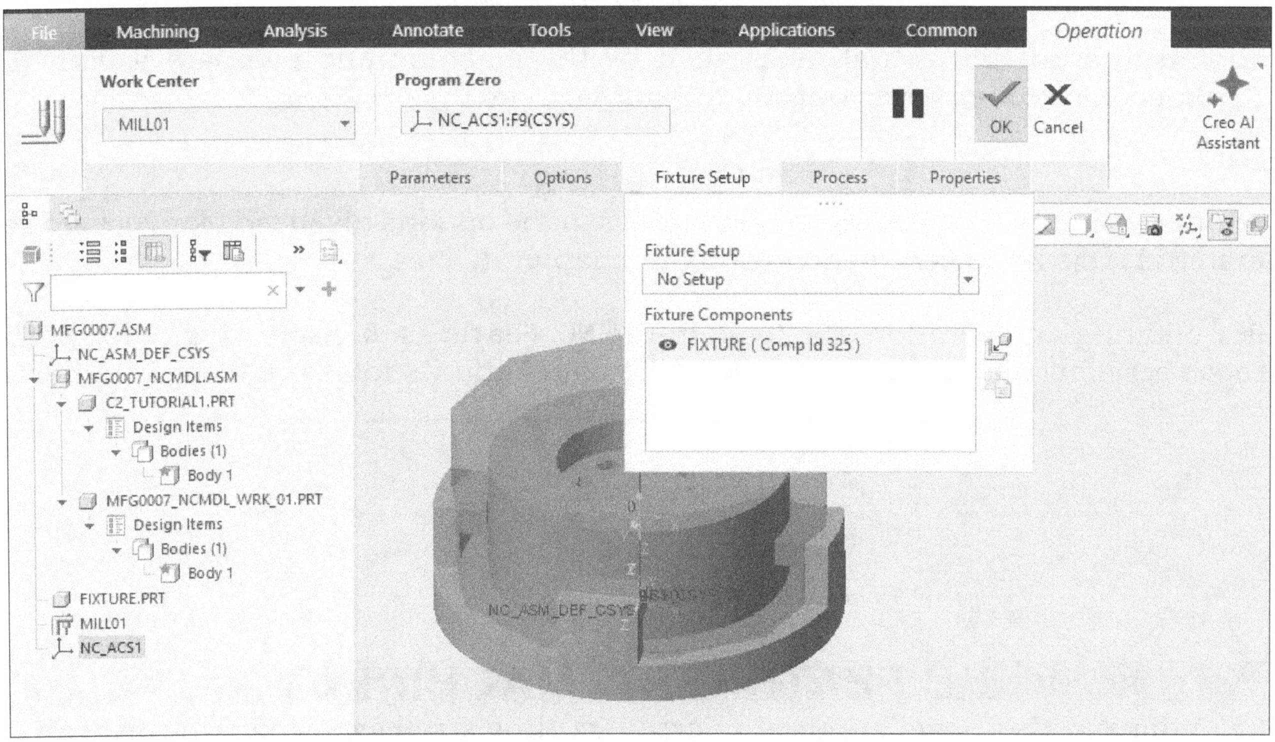

Figure-6. Modified Operation tab and the assembled workpiece

Process

The options in the **Process** tab are used to specify actual time taken by a machining process. Also, you can find out the estimated time taken by any machining operation; refer to Figure-7.

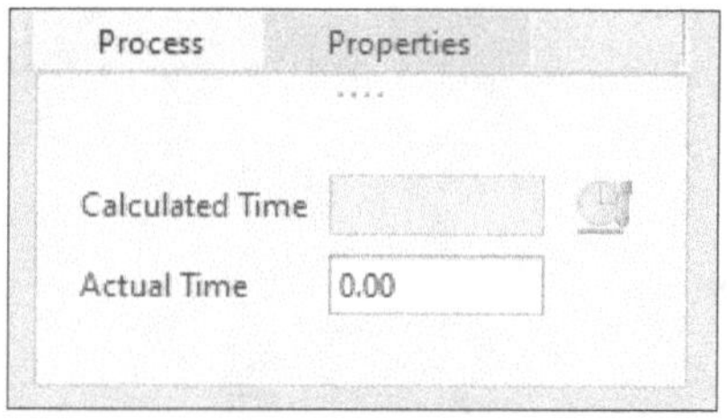

Figure-7. Process tab

- The **Calculated Time** is active only when you have generated tool path for the current operation.
- To calculate the estimated time for current operation, click on the **Recalculate machining time** button from **Process** tab. The estimated time will be displayed in the **Calculated Time** edit box; refer to Figure-8.

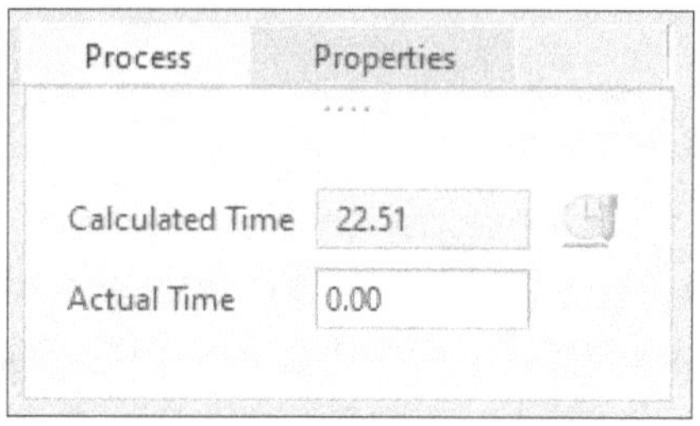

Figure-8. Process tab with calculated values

You can find out the actual time taken by the machine and compare it with the calculated time to improve your machining process.

Properties

The options in the **Properties** tab are similar to the options discussed for **Properties** tab in **Milling Work Center** dialog box in chapter 4.

After creating an operation, the tools in the **NC Features & Machining** panel of the **Ribbon** get activated; refer to Figure-9. The panel and its tools are discussed next.

Figure-9. Panel for creating cutting strategies

NC FEATURES & MACHINING

The options in this panel are used to create cutting strategies which in turn can be used to create tool paths. These options and their patterns of creating tool paths are discussed next.

Face

As the name suggests, this option is used to perform facing operation. A facing operation is used to remove material from the top face of workpiece to create flat face. The procedure to use this tool is discussed next.

- Click on the **Face** tool from the **NC Features & Machining** panel. The **Face Feature** dialog box along with the **SELECT SRFS Menu Manager** will be displayed; refer to Figure-10.

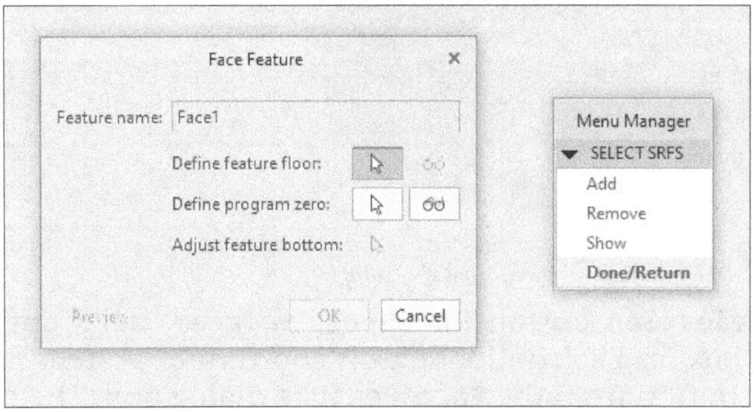

Figure-10. Face Feature dialog box with SELECT SRFS Menu Manager

- By default, the **Define feature floor** button is selected so you are prompted to select the feature floor. Boundaries of the selected feature floor will become boundaries of the face milling area.
- Figure-11 shows a workpiece assembled with the reference model and the face to be selected for face milling. Figure-12 shows the area that will be machined by face milling feature.

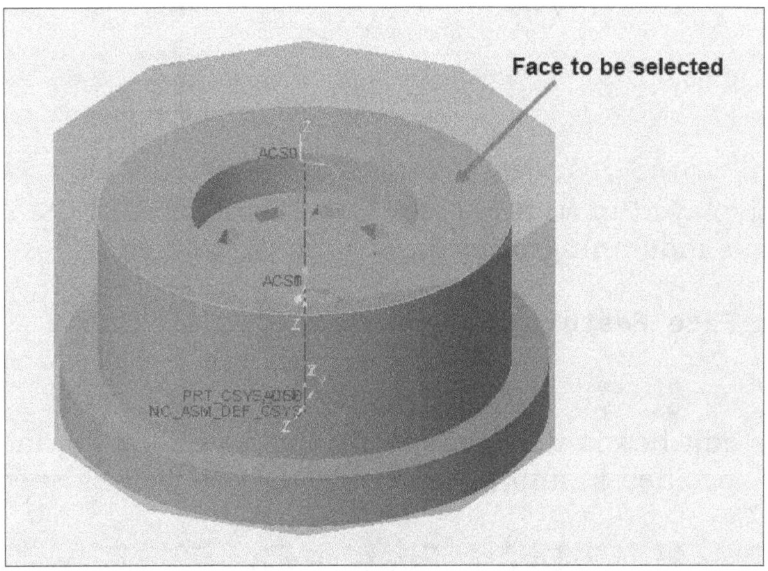

Figure-11. Workpiece and reference model assembled together

- After selecting the face, click on the **Done/Return** option from the **Menu Manager**. The volume to be machined will be highlighted; refer to Figure-12.

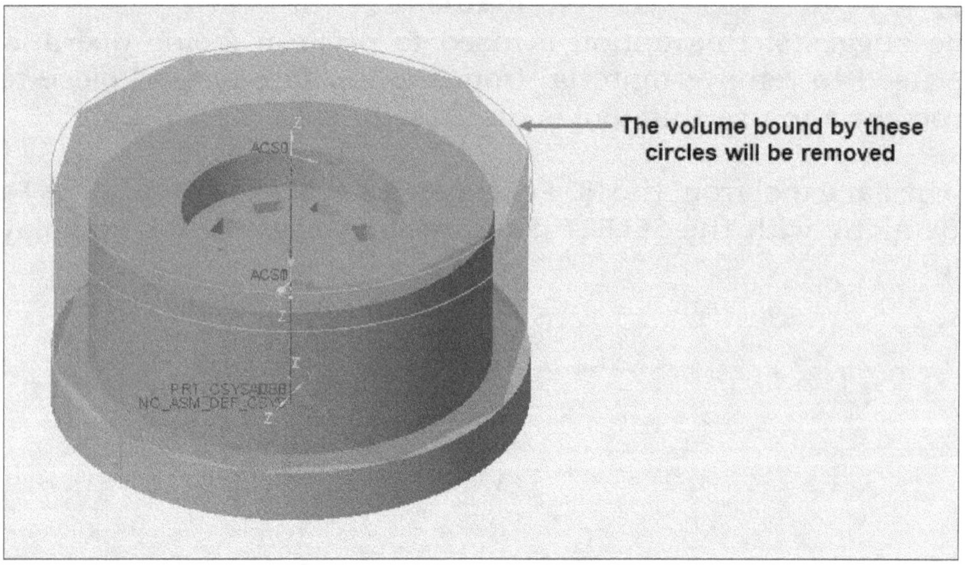

Figure-12. Material to be removed from the workpiece

- Click on the **Selection** button for **Define program zero** option from the **Face Feature** dialog box and select the default coordinate system from **Model Tree**.
- Click on the **OK** button from the **Face Feature** dialog box. The face milling feature will be created and displayed in the **Model Tree** at the left of the application window; refer to Figure-13.

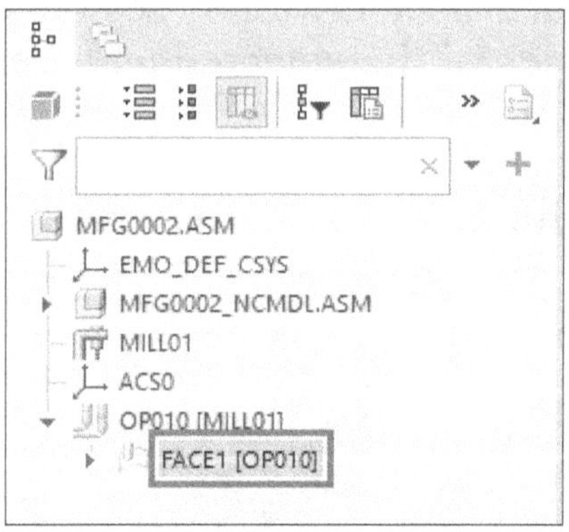

Figure-13. Face milling feature added

- In the name displayed in **Model Tree**, OP010 represents the operation number under which this machining process is to be performed.

The options in the **Face Feature** dialog box are discussed next.

Feature Name

The **Feature name** edit box is used to specify the name for the face milling feature. The name can be specified in alphanumeric letters as well as special letters.

Define Feature Floor

The **Define feature floor** option is used to select the feature face that is to be machined.

- To select the feature face, click on the button adjacent to this option, the **SELECT SRFS Menu Manager** will be displayed. If you have already select the feature face then the **Warning** message box will be displayed; refer to Figure-14.

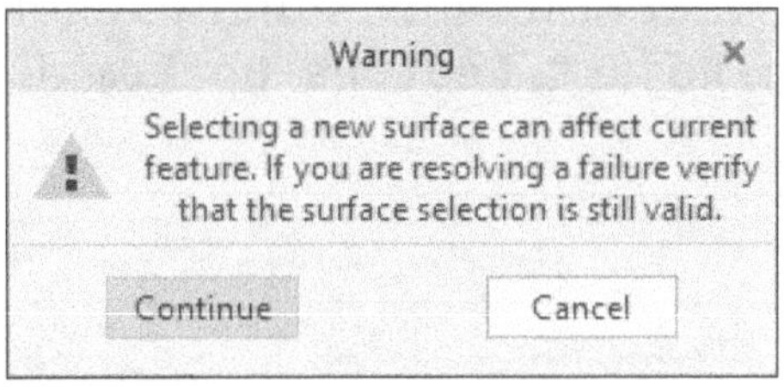

Figure-14. Warning message box

- It warns that the new selection can affect the current selections.
- Click on the **Continue** button in such case. The **SELECT SRFS Menu Manager** will be displayed. The options in the **Menu Manager** are as follows:

Add

Select the **Add** option from the **Menu Manager** if you want to add more faces for face milling and then click on the surfaces that you want to add.

Remove

Select the **Remove** option if you want to remove a surface from the current selection and then select the surfaces that you want to remove from the selection. This option is active only when you already have some selected faces.

Show

The **Show** option is used to highlight the faces that are selected for the face milling process.

Done/Return

The **Done/Return** option is used to accept the selections and return to the **Face Feature** dialog box.

Define Program Zero

The **Define program zero** option is used to define the zero position of the program. The procedure to use this option is discussed next.

- Click on the button adjacent to this option. The **WIND CSYS Menu Manager** will be displayed; refer to Figure-15. You are prompted to select a coordinate system.

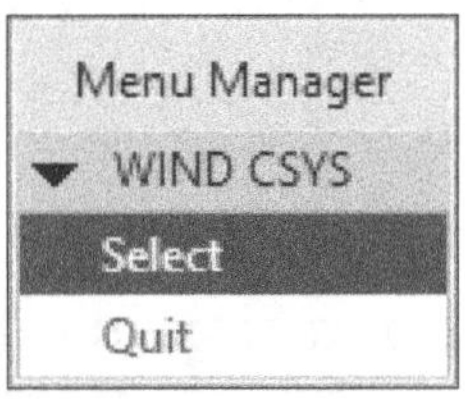

Figure-15. WIND CSYS Menu Manager

- Select the coordinate system where you want to define the program zero position. The **Menu Manager** will disappear automatically.

The button is used to display the preview for the adjacent option.

Adjust Feature Bottom

The **Adjust feature bottom** option is used to change the depth of face milling. The procedure is discussed next.

- To change the total depth of cut for face milling, click on the [select] button adjacent to this option. The **Define/Adjust Feature Bottom** dialog box will be displayed as shown in Figure-16.

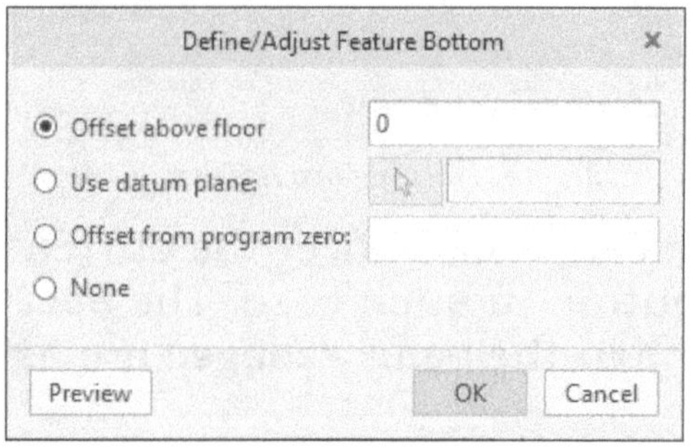

Figure-16. Define Adjust Feature Bottom dialog box

The options in this dialog box are discussed next.

Offset Above floor

Select this radio button if you want to specify maximum depth of cut above the current selected face. Specify the distance value in the edit box adjacent to this radio button by which you want to shift the cutting depth. A negative value in this edit box will move the maximum depth of cut to below the current selected face.

Use Datum Plane

Select this radio button if you want to select an already existing datum plane as the maximum depth of cut. Click on the arrow button and select desired datum plane.

Offset from Program Zero

Select this radio button if you want to specify the maximum depth of cut above or below the program zero by a specified value. Specify the distance value in the edit box adjacent to this edit box.

None

The **None** option is used to remove any override applied on the maximum depth of cut.

Click on the **OK** button from the dialog box to apply the changes.

In short, the Face operation is used to remove material from the face of the workpiece.

Profile

As the name suggests, this milling operation is used to cut material as per the profile selected. Note that the profile can only be selected on side walls of the workpiece. The procedure to use this tool is discussed next.

- Click on the **Profile** tool from the **NC Features & Machining** panel of the **Machining** tab in the **Ribbon**. The **Profile Feature** dialog box is displayed along with **SELECT SRFS Menu Manager** and **Select** dialog box; refer to Figure-17.

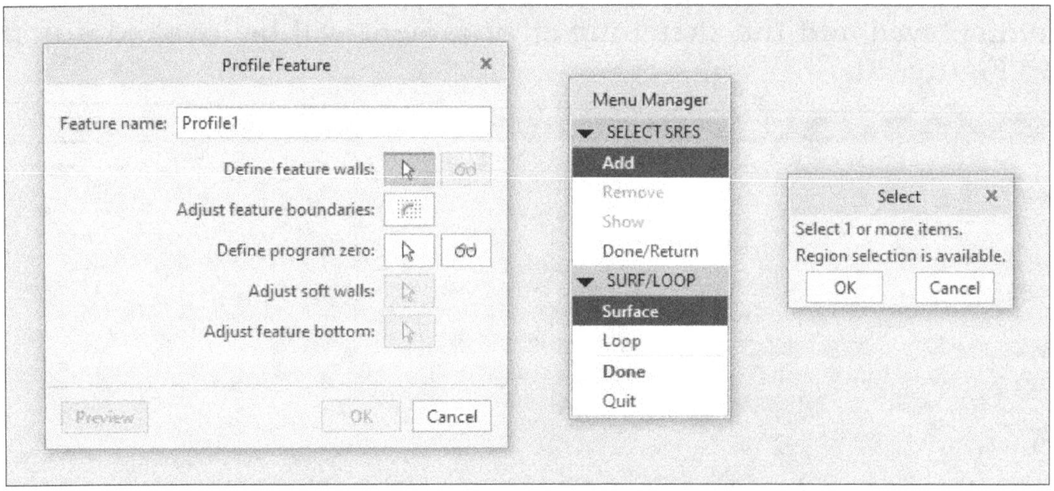

Figure-17. Profile Feature dialog box with SELECT SRFS Menu Manager and Select dialog box

- Also, you are prompted to select a surface (check the Information Bar displayed at bottom by dragging the splitting line upwards).
- Select the side walls of the reference model to remove the material from sides of the workpiece as per the selected surface; refer to Figure-18.

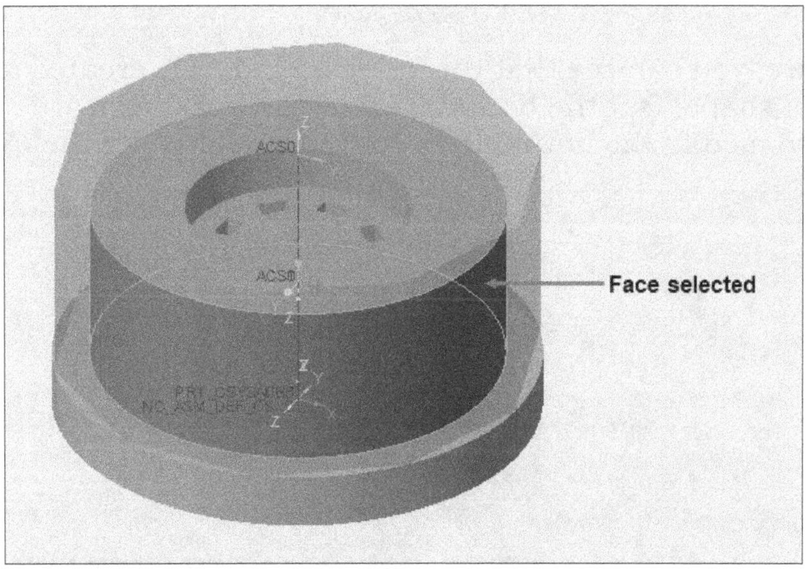

Figure-18. Face selected for profile milling

- Click on the **Done/Return** button from the **Menu Manager**. In some cases, after clicking on the **Done/Return** button, you may get the **Mill Feature Error** message box; refer to Figure-19.

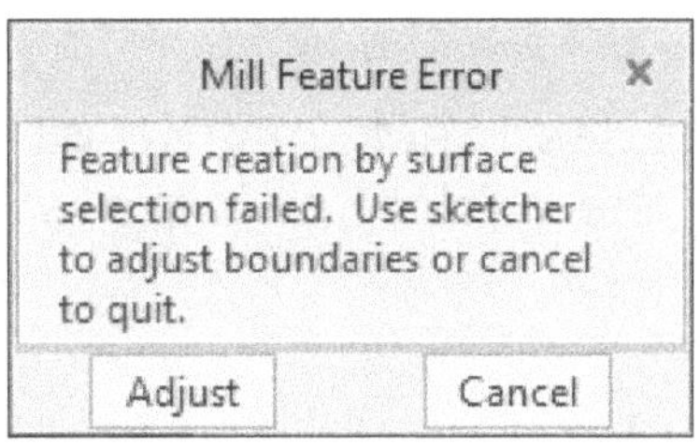

Figure-19. Mill Feature Error message box

- In such cases, you are prompted to adjust the boundaries of the milling area that is created after selecting the feature.

- Click on the **Adjust** button from the dialog box. The top view of the selected surfaces will be displayed and the sketching environment will be invoked automatically; refer to Figure-20.

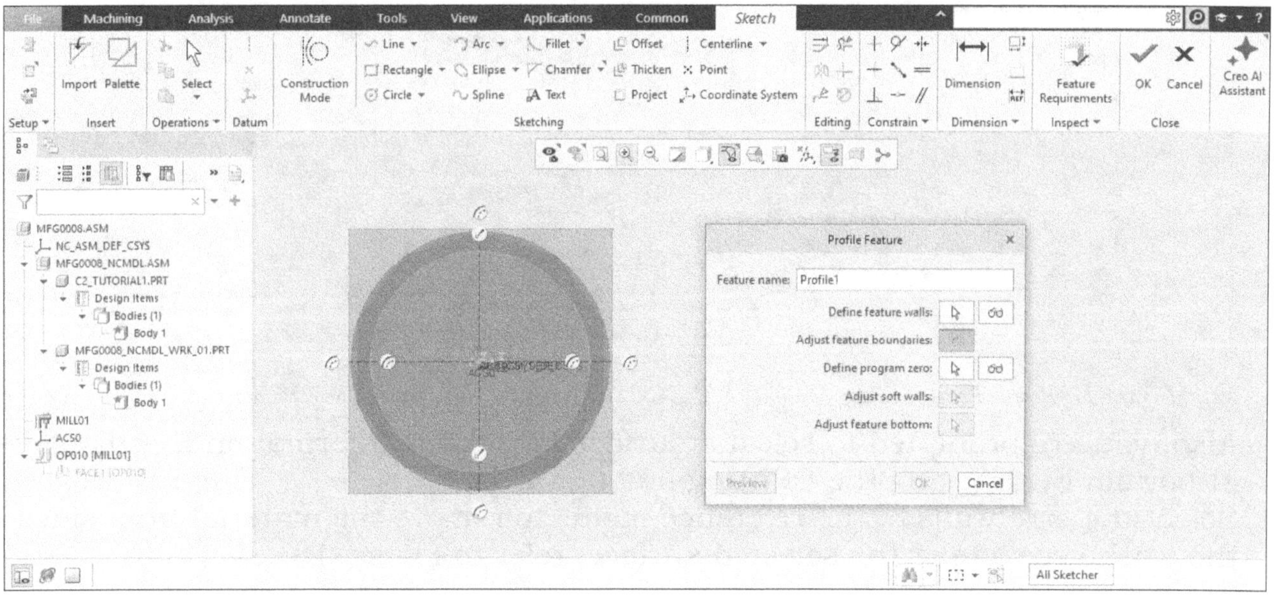

Figure-20. Sketching environment with the top view of selected surface

- From the figure, you can see that the outer boundaries created automatically are rectangular in shape. But the boundaries of our workpiece are circular in shape. So, we need to modify the boundaries so that it looks like the Figure-21.

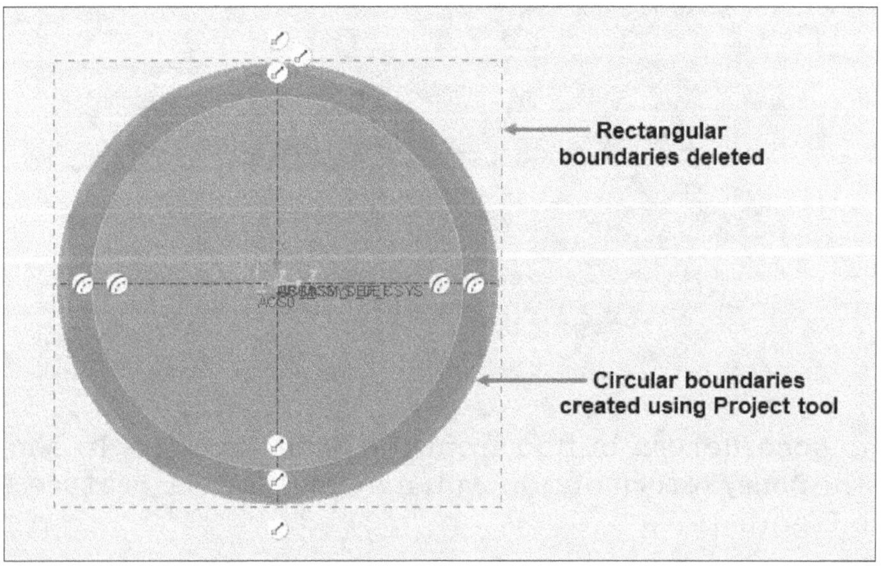

Figure-21. Selected surface after modifications

- After modifying the boundaries, click on the **OK** button from the **Ribbon**. The preview of workpiece with the milling volume will be displayed automatically; refer to Figure-22.

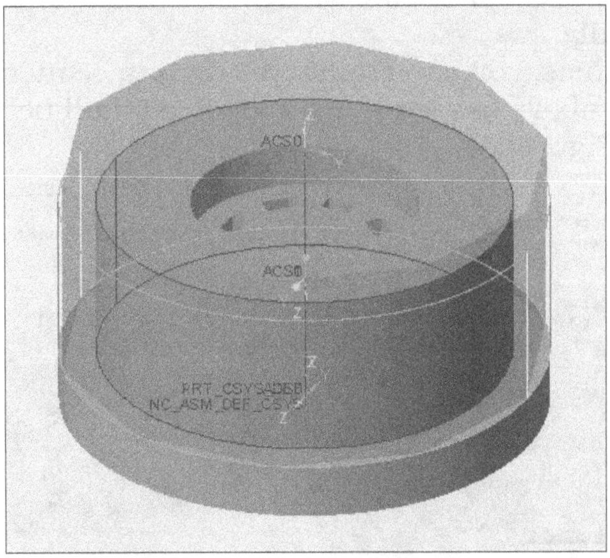

Figure-22. Preview of the workpiece

- Click on the **OK** button from the **Profile Feature** dialog box to create the operation.

The options displayed in the **Profile Feature** dialog box are discussed next.

Define Feature Walls

The **Define feature walls** option is used to select the walls on which the profile milling is to be performed. Figure-23 shows a workpiece with reference model having curves on the walls.

- To machine these walls, click on the selection button adjacent to **Define feature walls** option. The **SELECT SRFS Menu Manager** will be displayed and you will be prompted to select the wall surfaces for profile milling.

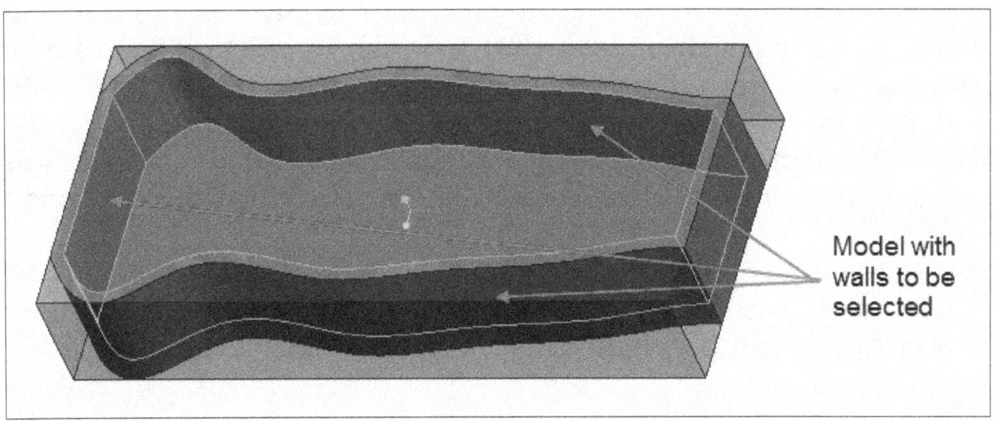

Figure-23. Walls to be selected for profile milling

- Select the wall faces; refer to Figure-23 and then click on the **Done/Return** option from the **Menu Manager**. Note that the selected surfaces must be consecutive. If your selection is right then all the buttons in the **Profile Feature** dialog box will become active.

Adjust Feature Boundaries

The **Adjust feature boundaries** option is used to adjust the boundaries for the milling area. The procedure to use this tool is discussed next.

- Click on the **Adjust feature boundaries** option, the sketcher environment is invoked automatically.
- Using the sketcher tools, you can modify the area to be machined by the operation. For example, in the above case, we can specify a small belt as milling area for the operation; refer to Figure-24.

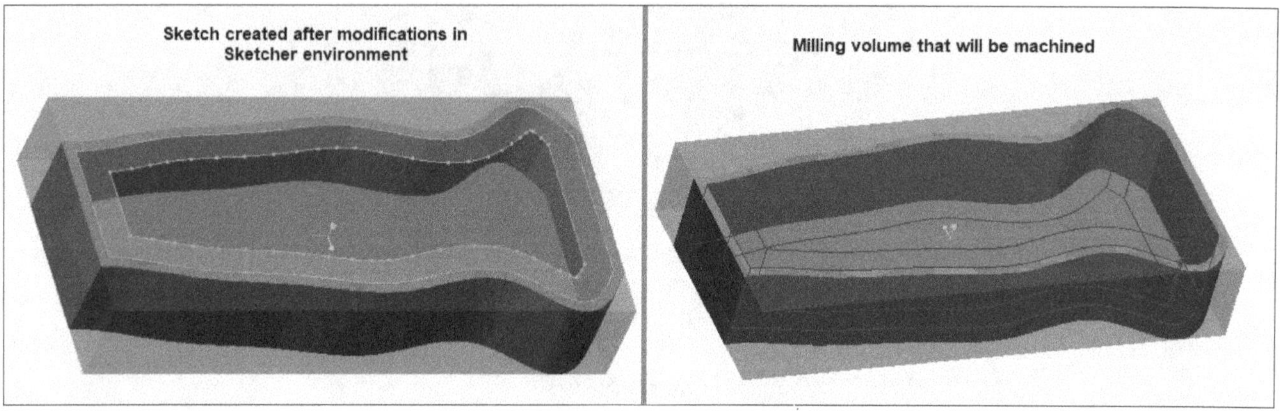

Figure-24. Adjusting feature boundaries

- Figure also shows the output that will be generated after making such changes. After modifications in the sketch, click on the **OK** button from the **Ribbon**. The output volume will be displayed. If you have created a wrong sketch then some of the buttons in the **Profile Feature** dialog box will become inactive and you need to modify the sketch again.

Define Program Zero

The **Define program zero** button has the same function for each of the milling operations. This option has been discussed earlier in **Face** milling topic in this chapter.

Adjust Soft Wall

The **Adjust soft walls** option is used to convert the Hard Walls into Soft Walls. In Creo Manufacturing, any wall or face that belongs to workpiece is termed as Soft. Whereas any wall or face that belongs to the reference model is termed as Hard. So, using this option, you can transfer any face to soft wall. Hard walls define the boundaries of the output model so the tool path around the hard walls are more accurate and dense with respect to the soft walls. The procedure to use this option is discussed next.

- To add a hard wall to soft wall, click on the **Adjust soft walls** option. The walls of selected surfaces will be highlighted in violet color; refer to Figure-25.

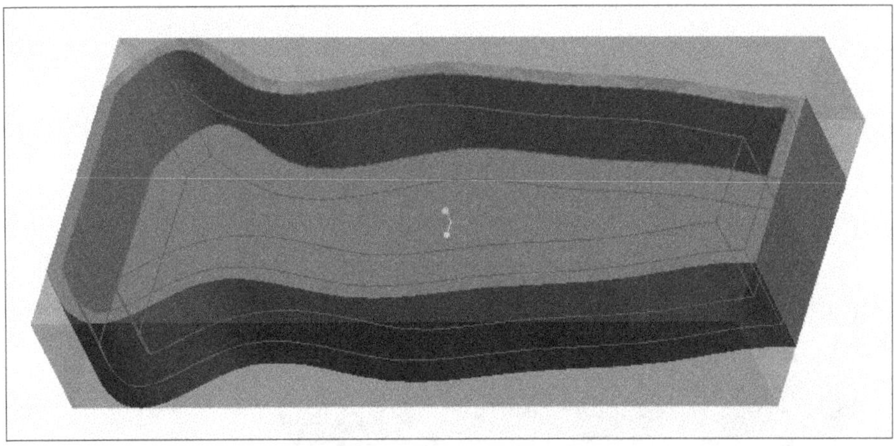

Figure-25. Walls higlighted in violet color

- Also, the **SELECT SRFS Menu Manager** will be displayed. Select the surfaces that you want to add in the soft walls; refer to Figure-26.

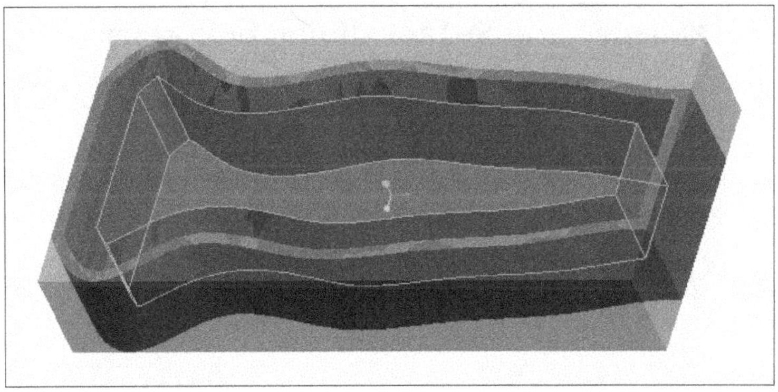

Figure-26. Highlighted faces to be transferred to soft walls

- After selecting the walls, click on the **Done/Return** button from **SELECT SRFS Menu Manager**. The soft walls will be created.
- Note that when you click on the **Preview** button from the **Profile Feature** dialog box. The soft walls are displayed in CYAN color and hard walls are displayed in RED color.

Adjust Feature Bottom

The **Adjust feature bottom** option has been discussed earlier in **Face** topic of this chapter.

After defining all the options, click on the **OK** button from the dialog box to create the feature.

Step

The **Step** tool is used to create steps in the milling process. The step milling feature is used when you want to create pins or other boss features on the workpiece; refer to Figure-27. The procedure to use this tool is discussed next.

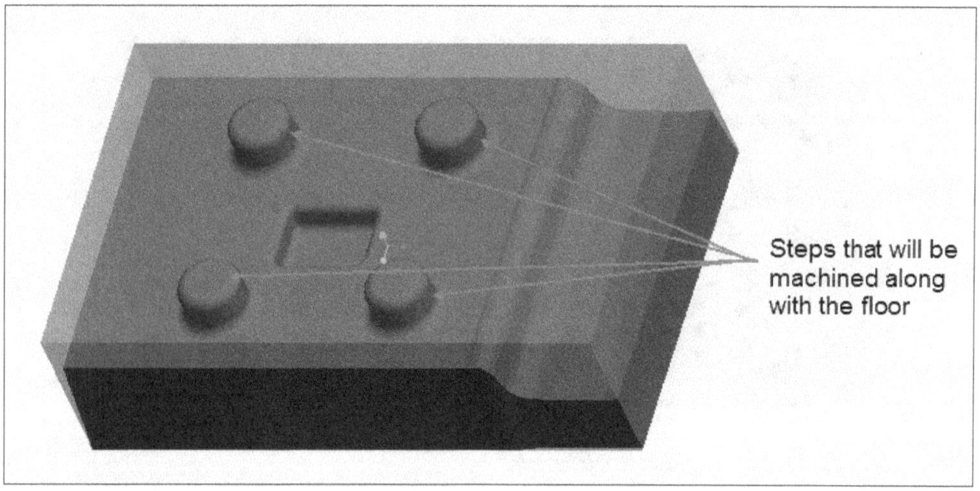

Figure-27. Workpiece with steps to be machined

- Click on the **Step** tool from the **NC Features & Machining** panel of the **Machining** tab in the **Ribbon**. The **Step Feature** dialog box will be displayed along with the **SELECT SRFS Menu Manager** and **Select** dialog box; refer to Figure-28.

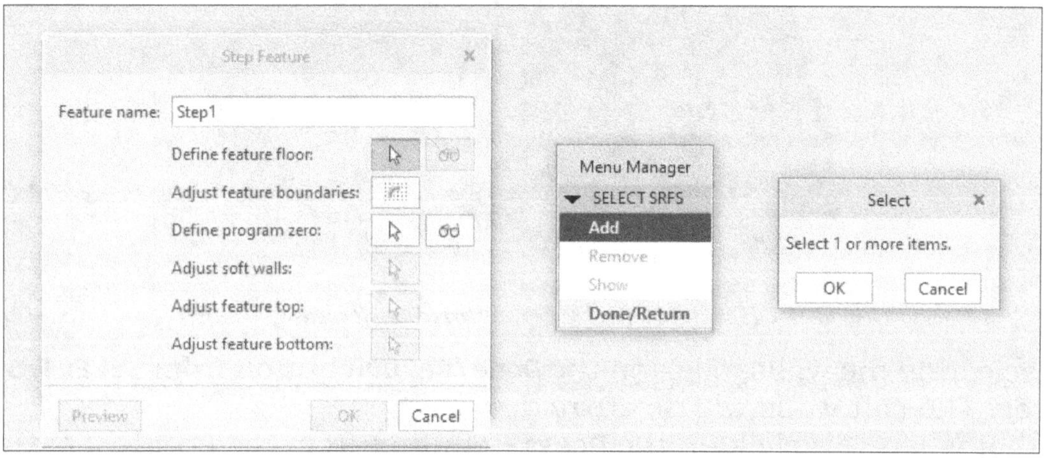

Figure-28. Step Feature dialog box with SELECT SRFS Menu Manager and Select dialog box

- You are prompted to select surface to define base of the step feature. Select the surface as shown in Figure-29.

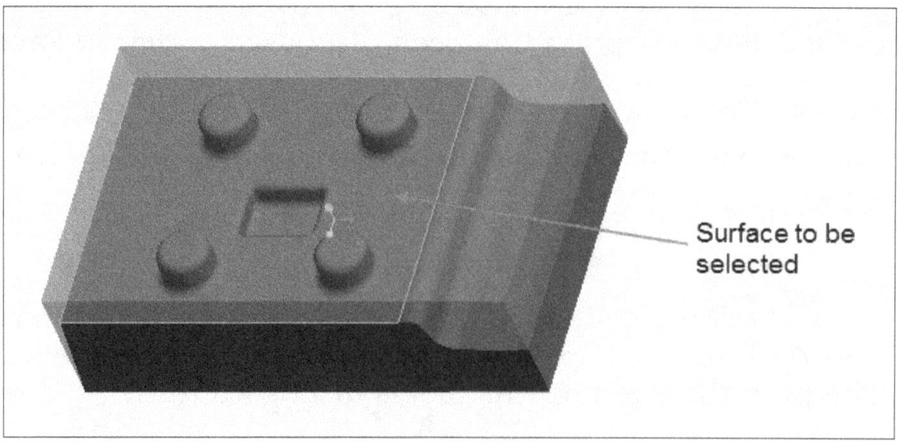

Figure-29. Surface to be selected for the step feature

- Click on the **Done/Return** option from the **Menu Manager**. If the selection is correct, preview of the feature will be displayed automatically; refer to Figure-30.

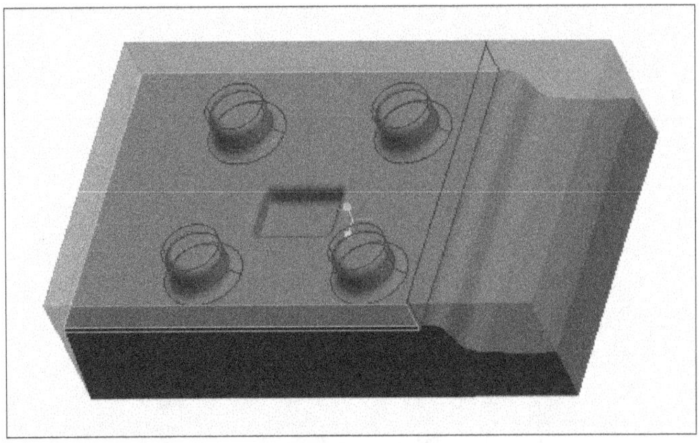

Figure-30. Preview of the Step feature

- In this figure, the red boundaries show the hard walls and cyan boundaries show the soft walls. Click on the **Adjust soft walls** option if you want to add any wall to soft walls. Like in this case, a wall is desired to be in soft side; refer to Figure-31.

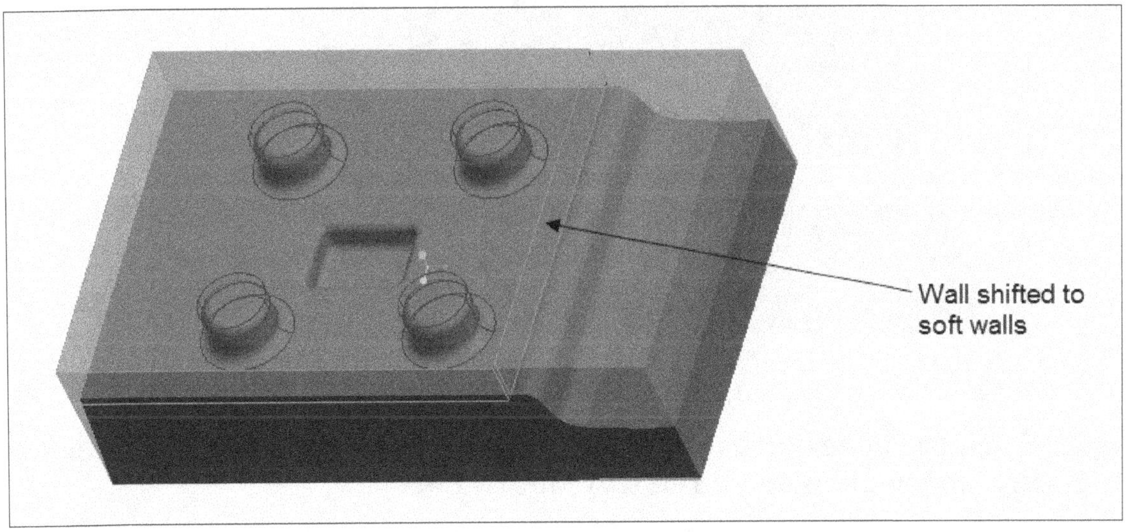

Figure-31. Walls after shifting

- Click on the **OK** button from the dialog box to create the feature. The options in this dialog box have already been discussed.

Slot

As the name suggests, the **Slot** tool is used to create slots in the workpiece. The procedure to use this tool is discussed next.

- Click on the down arrow displayed adjacent to **Slot** in the **NC Features & Machining** panel of the **Ribbon**. A list of tools will be displayed.
- Now, click on the **Slot** tool from the list displayed. The **Slot Feature** dialog box is displayed along with the **SELECT SRFS Menu Manager** and **Select** dialog box; refer to Figure-32.

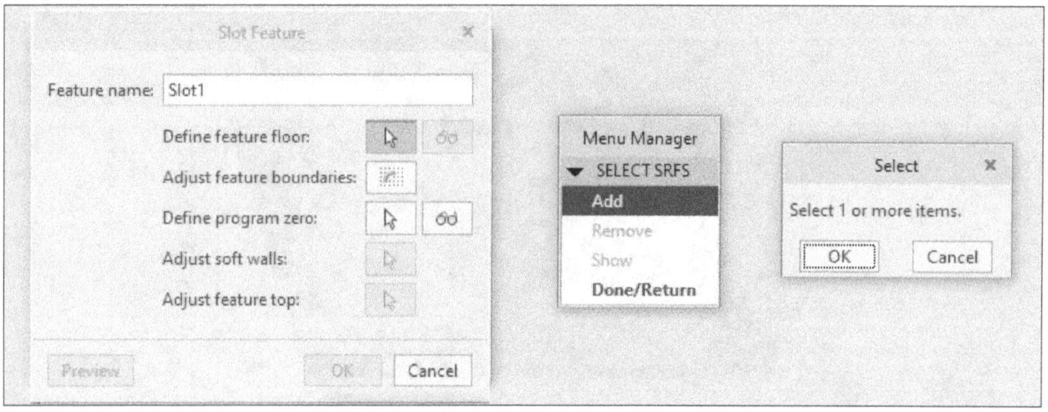

Figure-32. Slot Feature dialog box with SELECT SRFS Menu Manager and Select dialog box

- Select the surfaces that you want to include for the slot feature; refer to Figure-33.

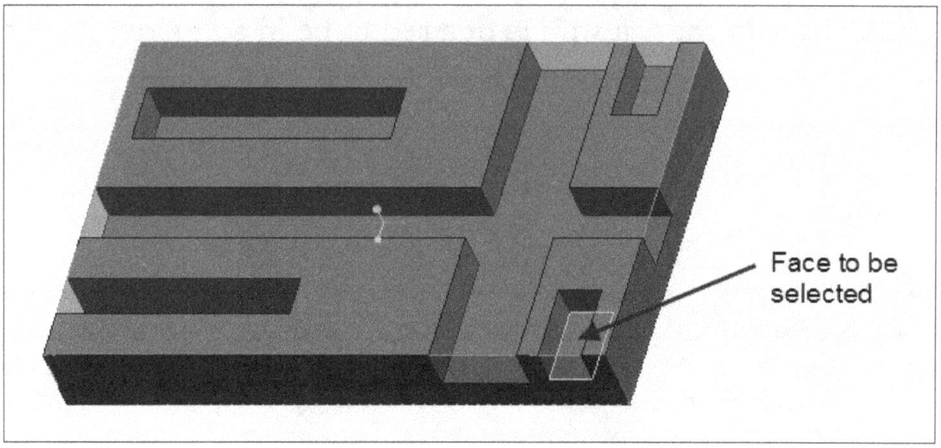

Figure-33. Face to be selected for slot feature

- Now, click on the **Done/Return** button from the **Menu Manager**. The preview of the slot feature will be displayed; refer to Figure-34.

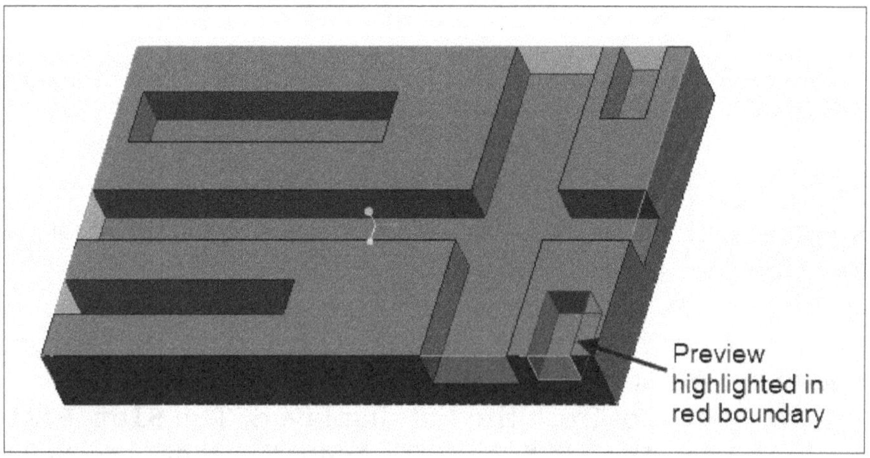

Figure-34. Preview of slot feature

- Click on the **OK** button from the **Slot Feature** dialog box to create the feature.

The options in this dialog box have already been discussed in this chapter.

Through Slot

As the name suggests, this tool is used to create through slots in the workpiece. The procedure to use this tool is discussed next.

- Click on the down arrow displayed adjacent to **Slot** in the **NC Features & Machining** panel of the **Ribbon**. A list of tools will be displayed.
- Now, click on **Through Slot** tool in this list to activate the tool. On clicking this tool, the **Through Slot Feature** dialog box is displayed along with the **SELECT SRFS Menu Manager** and **Select** dialog box; refer to Figure-35.

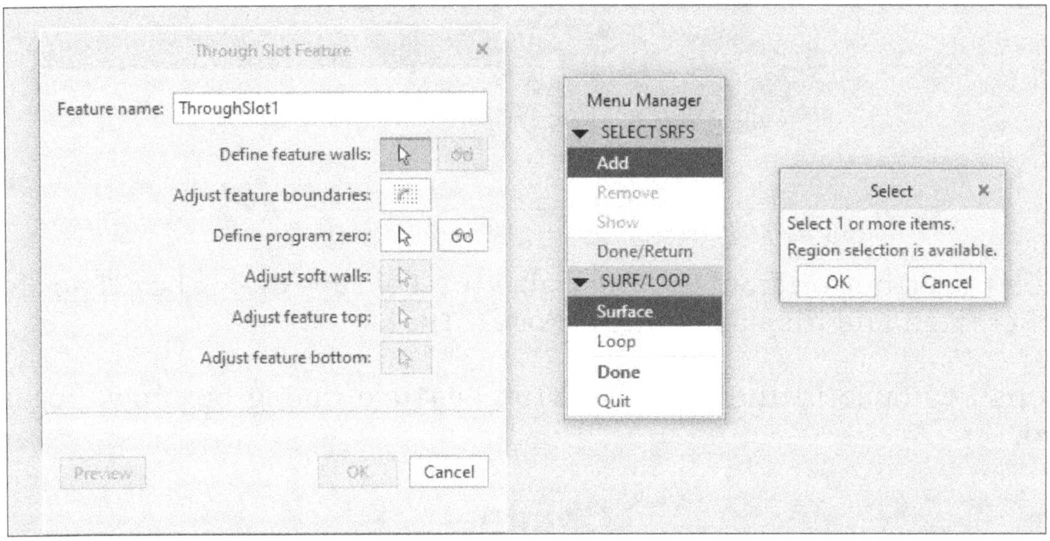

Figure-35. Through Slot Feature dialog box with SELECT SRFS Menu Manager and Select dialog box

- Also, you are prompted to select walls of the reference model where you want to create a through slot feature.
- Select the walls of the reference model; refer to Figure-36 and click on the **Done/Return** button from the **Menu Manager**. The preview of the feature will be displayed; refer to Figure-37.

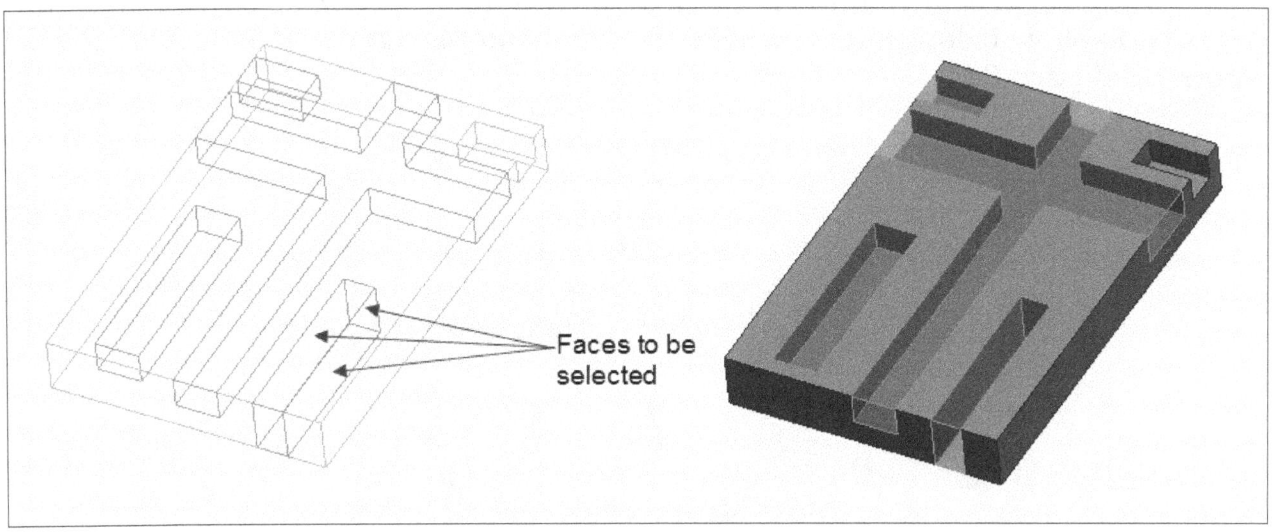

Figure-36. Model in wireframe and shading style with the faces to be deleted

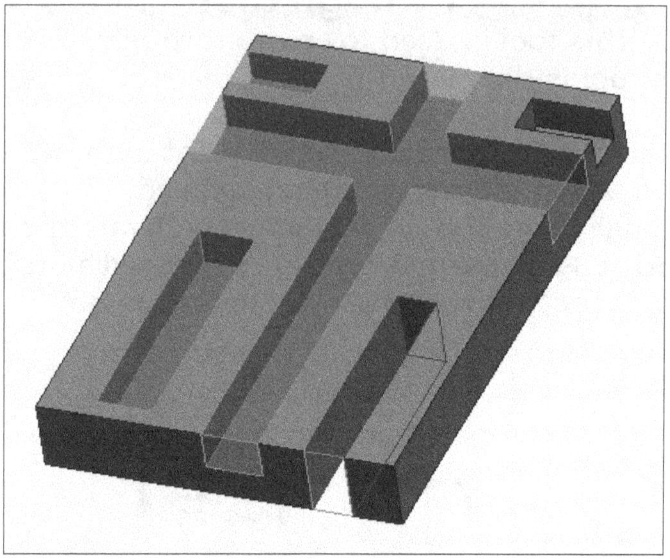

Figure-37. Preview of the through slot feature

- Click on the **OK** button from the **Through Slot Feature** dialog box. The slot feature will be created and displayed in the **Model Tree**.

The options available in the **Through Slot Feature** dialog box have already been discussed.

Channel

As the name suggests, the **Channel** tool is used to create channel of two or more slots intersecting each other in the workpiece. The procedure to use this tool is discussed next.

- Click on the down arrow displayed adjacent to **Slot** in the **NC Features & Machining** panel of the **Ribbon**. A list of tools will be displayed.
- Now, click on **Channel** in this list to activate the tool. The **Channel Feature** dialog box is displayed along with the **SELECT SRFS Menu Manager** and **Select** dialog box; refer to Figure-38.

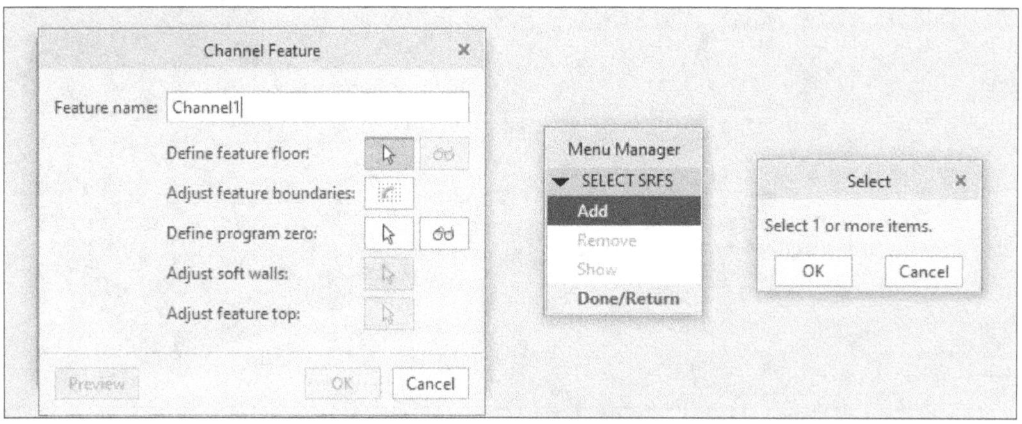

Figure-38. Channel Feature dialog box with SELECT SRFS Menu Manager and Select dialog box

- Also, you are prompted to select floor of the reference model where you want to create the channel feature.
- Select the surface; refer to Figure-39 and click on the **Done/Return** option from the **Menu Manager**. Preview of the channel feature will be displayed; refer to Figure-40.

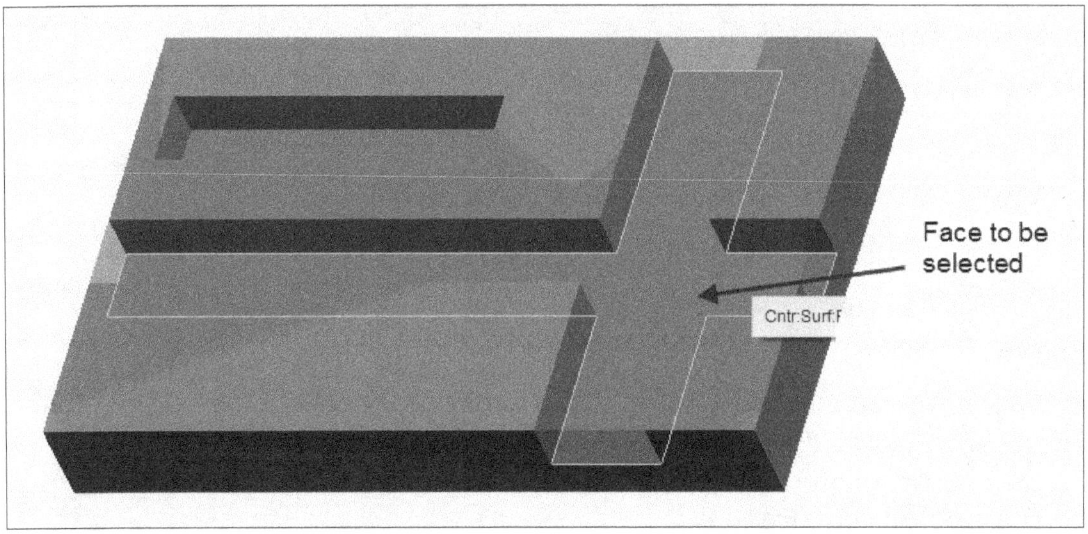

Figure-39. Model with the face to be selected for slot feature

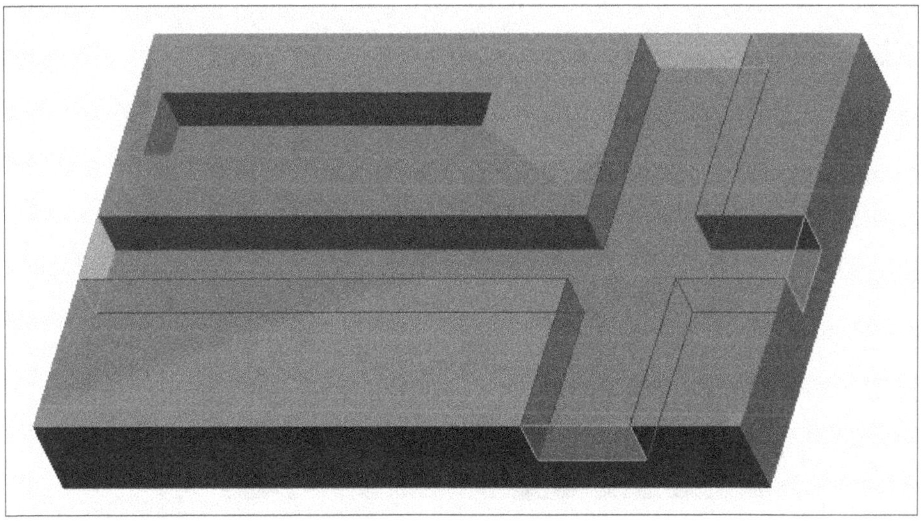

Figure-40. Preview of the slot feature

- Click on the **OK** button from the dialog box to create the feature. The options in the **Channel** dialog box are same as discussed earlier.

Pocket

As the name suggests, the **Pocket** tool is used to remove material from the workpiece in the form of a pocket. This tool is used when you have the slot bound by hard walls. The procedure to use this tool is discussed next.

- Click on the down arrow displayed adjacent to **Pocket** in the **NC Features & Machining** panel of the **Ribbon**. A list of tools will be displayed.
- Now, click on **Pocket** in this list to activate the tool. The **Pocket Feature** dialog box is displayed along with the **SELECT SRFS Menu Manager** and **Select** dialog box; refer to Figure-41.

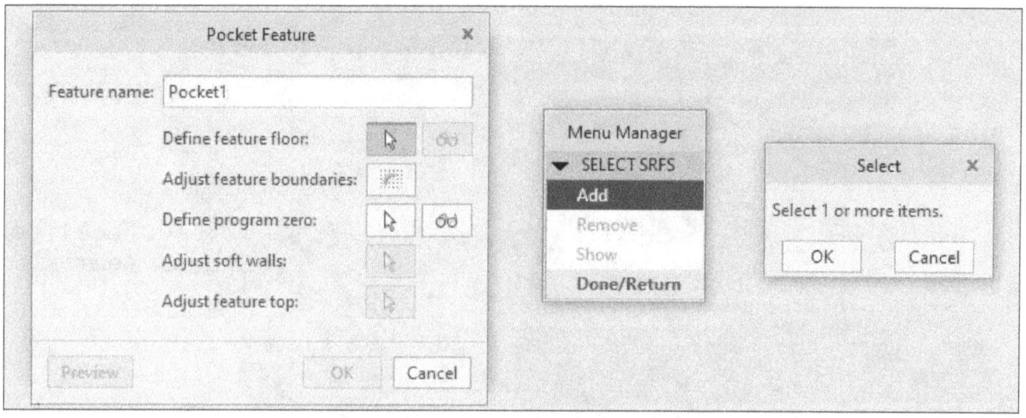

Figure-41. Pocket Feature dialog box with SELECT SRFS Menu Manager and Select dialog box

- Also, you are prompted to select floor of the reference model where you want to create the pocket feature.
- Select the floor surface; refer to Figure-42 and click on the **Done/Return** option from the **Menu Manager**. The preview of the pocket feature will be displayed; refer to Figure-43.

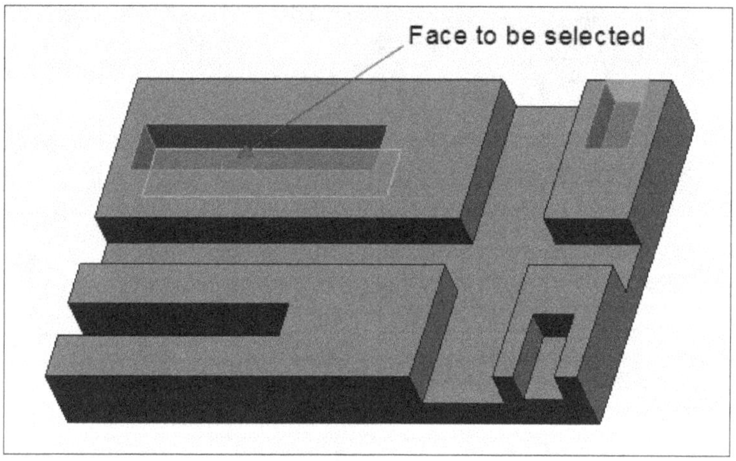

Figure-42. Face to be selected for pocket feature

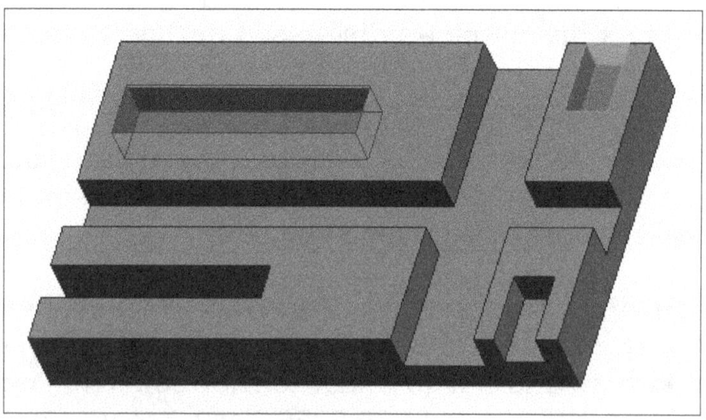

Figure-43. Preview of the pocket feature

- Click on the **OK** button from the **Pocket Feature** dialog box to create the pocket feature. The options of the **Pocket Feature** dialog box are same as discussed earlier.

Through Pocket

The **Through Pocket** tool works in the same way as **Pocket** tool does with the only difference that there is no floor. This tool is used when we have a through slot bound by hard walls. The procedure to use this tool is discussed next.

- Click on the down arrow displayed adjacent to **Pocket** in the **NC Features & Machining** panel of the **Ribbon**. A list of tools will be displayed.
- Now, click on the **Through Pocket** tool in this list to activate the tool. The **Through Pocket Feature** dialog box is displayed along with the **SELECT SRFS Menu Manager** and **Select** dialog box; refer to Figure-44.

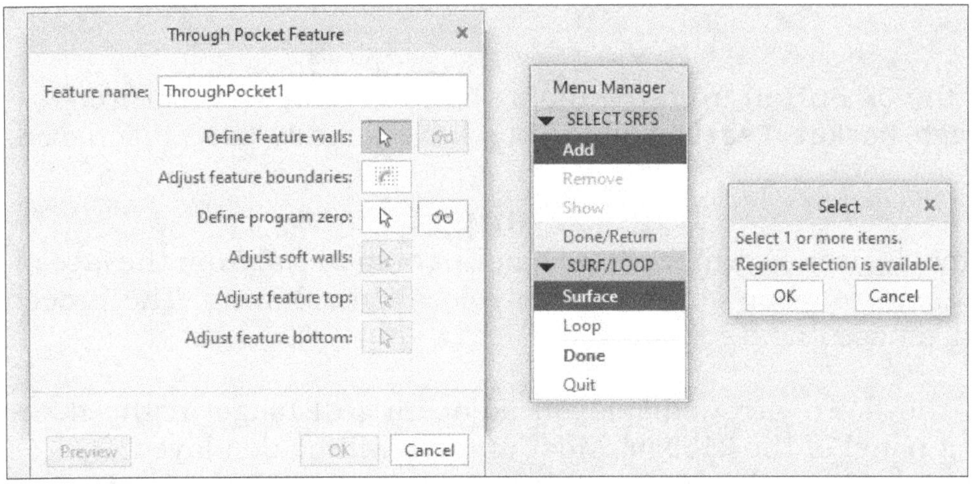

Figure-44. Through Pocket Feature dialog box with SELECT SRFS Menu Manager and Select dialog box

- Also, you are prompted to select walls of the reference model which you want to create through pocket feature.
- Select the wall surfaces; refer to Figure-45 and click on the **Done/Return** button from the **Menu Manager**. The preview of the through pocket feature will be displayed; refer to Figure-46.

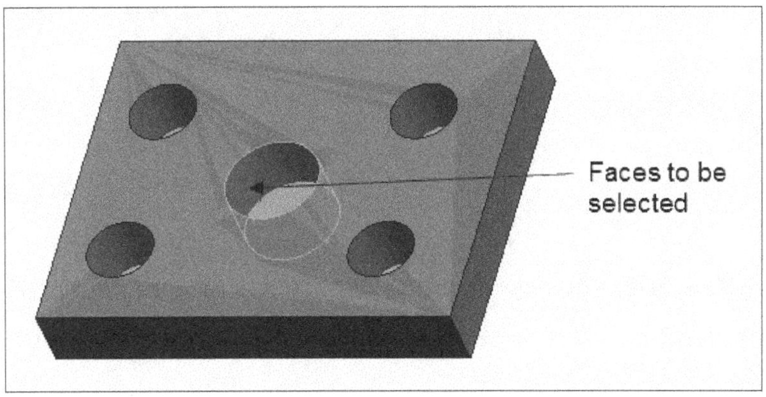

Figure-45. Walls to be selected for through pocket feature

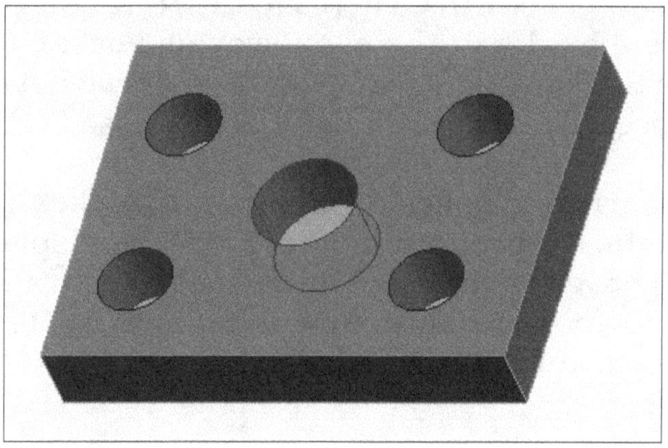

Figure-46. Preview of the through pocket feature

- Click on the **OK** button from the dialog box to create the feature. The options in the **Through Pocket Feature** dialog box have already been discussed.

Flange

The **Flange** tool is used to remove large amount of material from the face of workpiece. Use this NC feature when you want to avoid air machining. The procedure to use this tool is discussed next.

- Click on the down arrow displayed adjacent to **Flange** in the **NC Features & Machining** panel of the **Ribbon**. A list of tools will be displayed.
- Now, click on **Flange** in this list to activate the tool. The **Flange Feature** dialog box is displayed along with the **SELECT SRFS Menu Manager** and **Select** dialog box; refer to Figure-47.

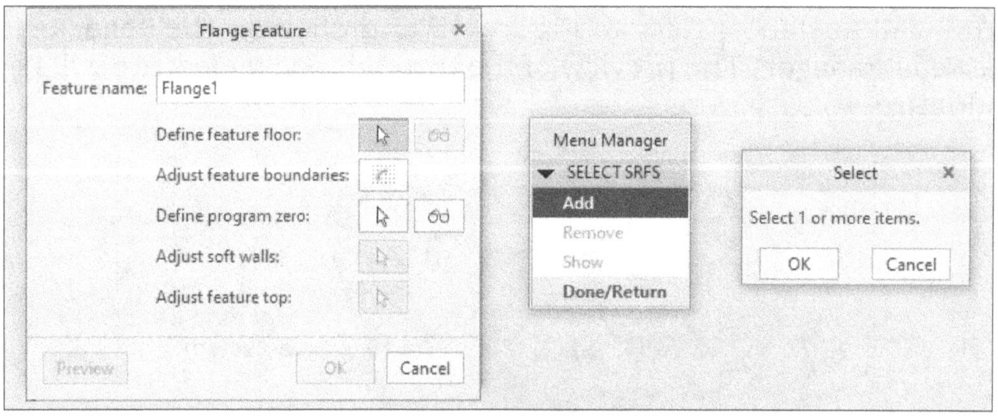

Figure-47. Flange Feature dialog box with SELECT SRFS Menu Manager and Select dialog box

- Also, you are prompted to select floor of the reference model where you want to create the flange feature.
- Select the face of the reference model; refer to Figure-48 and then click on the **Done/ Return** button. Preview of the flange feature will be displayed; refer to Figure-49.

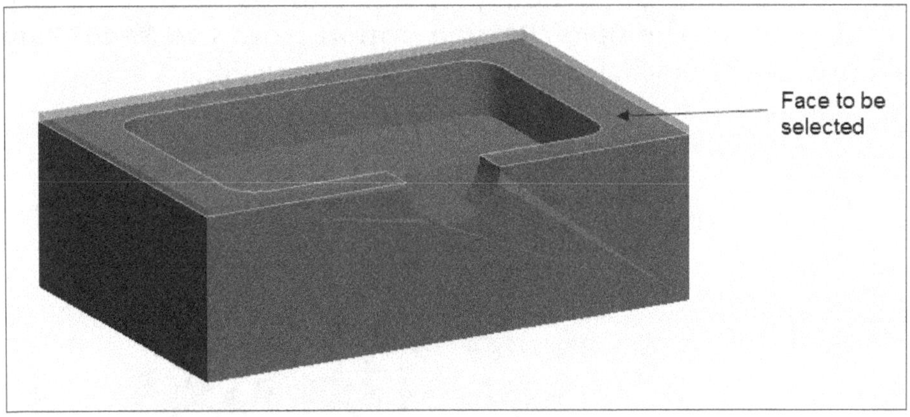

Figure-48. Face to be selected for flange feature

Figure-49. Preview of the flange feature

Slab

The **Slab** tool is used to remove large amount of material from the face of workpiece. The procedure to use this tool is discussed next.

- Click on the down arrow displayed adjacent to **Flange** in the **NC Features & Machining** panel of the **Ribbon**. A list of tools will be displayed.
- Now, click on the **Slab** tool in this list to activate the tool. The **Slab Feature** dialog box is displayed along with the **SELECT SRFS Menu Manager** and **Select** dialog box; refer to Figure-50. Also, you are prompted to select floor of the reference model where you want to create the slab feature.

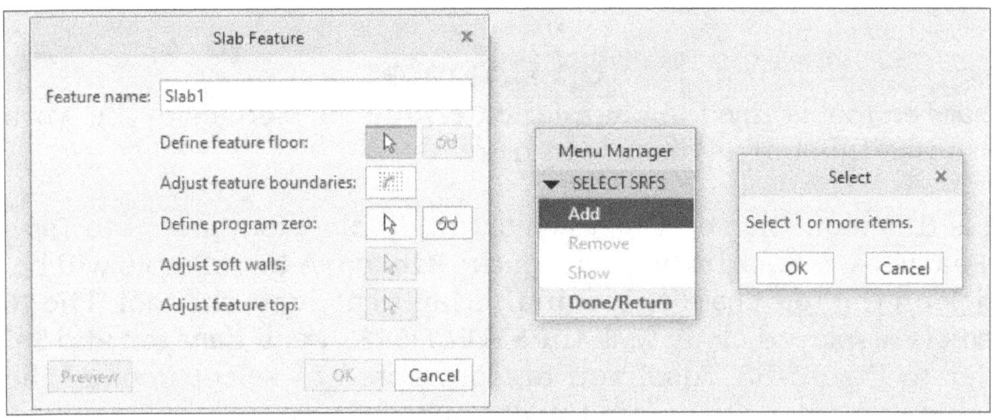

Figure-50. Slab Feature dialog box with SELECT SRFS Menu Manager and Select dialog box

- Select face of the model on which you want to perform slab milling; refer to Figure-51 and click on the **Done/Return** option from the **Menu Manager**. Preview of the slab feature will be displayed; refer to Figure-52.

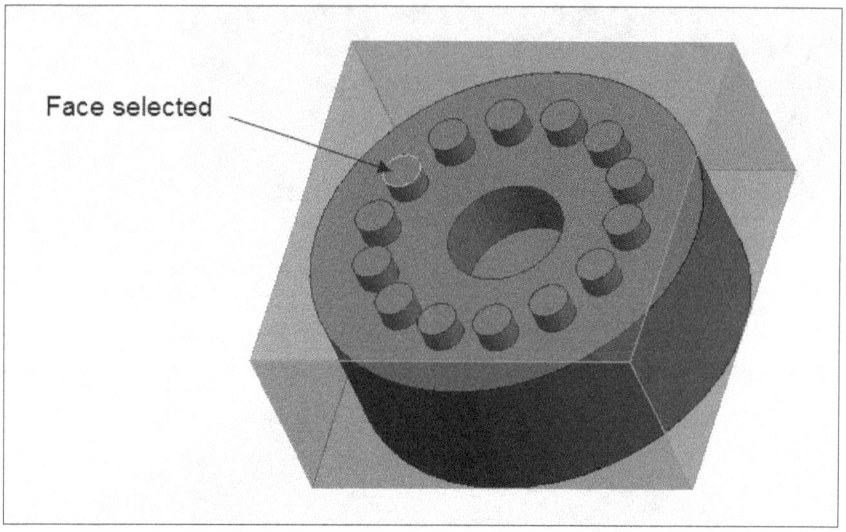

Figure-51. Face selected for slab milling

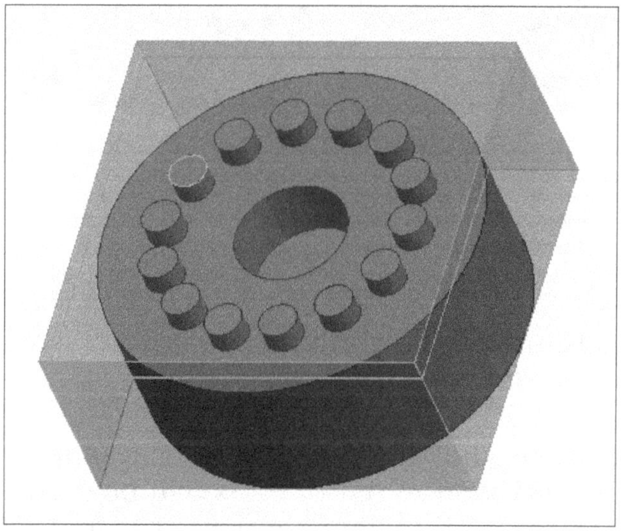

Figure-52. Preview of the slab feature

Note that in the preview, the faces coplanar to the selected face will be machined automatically. The options in the **Slab Feature** dialog box are same as discussed earlier.

Top Chamfer

The **Top Chamfer** tool is used to chamfer external sharp edges of the workpiece. The procedure to use this tool is discussed next.

- To access this tool, click on the down arrow displayed adjacent to **Top Chamfer** in the **NC Features & Machining** panel of the **Ribbon**. A list of tools will be displayed.
- Now, click on the **Top Chamfer** tool in this list to activate the tool. The **TOP CHAMFER** dialog box is displayed along with the **SELECT SRFS Menu Manager** and **Select** dialog box; refer to Figure-53. Also, you are prompted to select floor of the reference model where you want to create the chamfer feature.

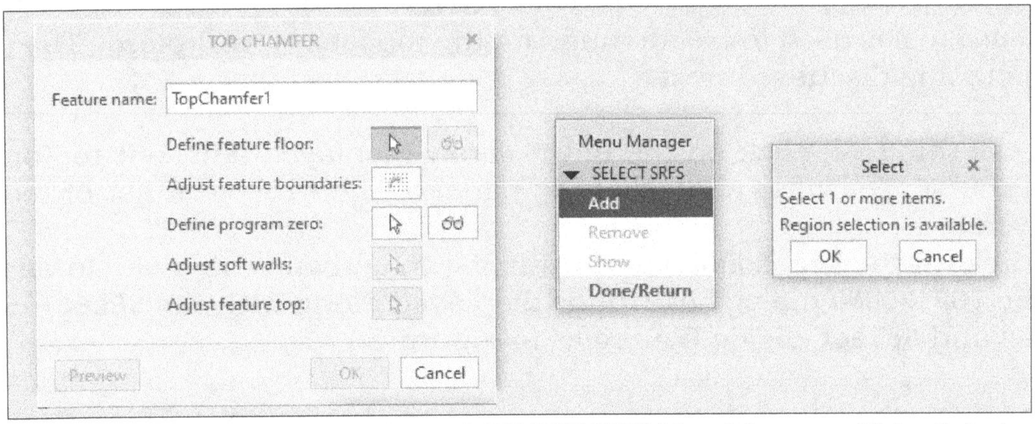

Figure-53. TOP CHAMFER dialog box with SELECT SRFS Menu Manager and Select dialog box

- Select the chamfered face as shown in Figure-54 and click on the **Done/Return** button from the **Menu Manager**. Preview of the chamfer feature will be displayed as shown in Figure-55.

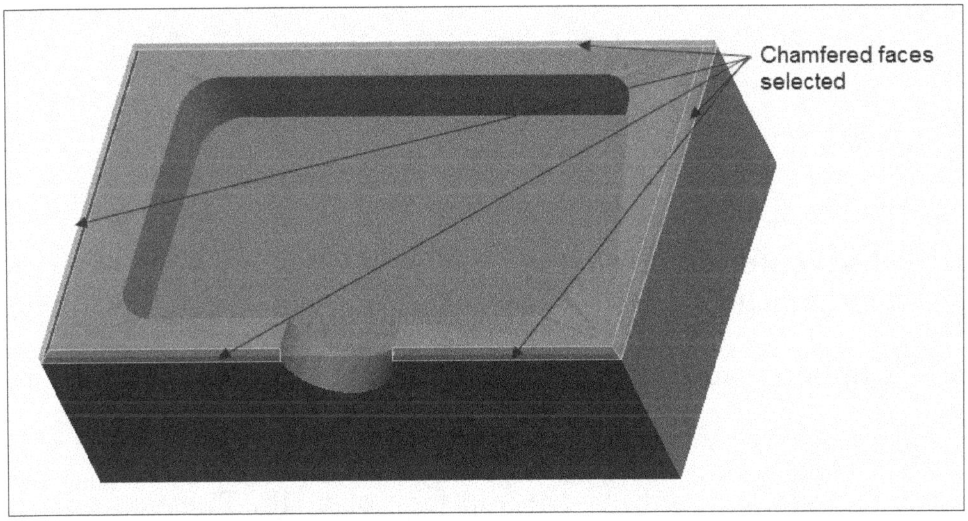

Figure-54. Chamfered faces to be selected

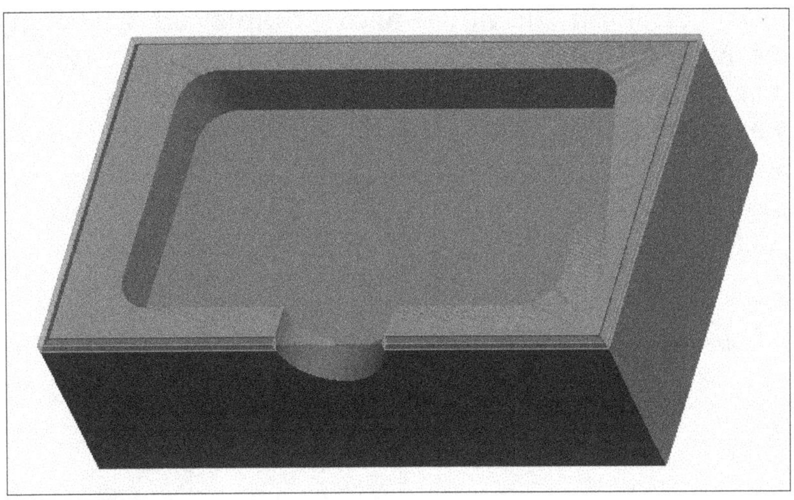

Figure-55. Preview of chamfer feature

- Click on the **OK** button from the dialog box to create the feature.

Top Round

The **Top Round** tool is used to create round on the top face of workpiece. The procedure to use this tool is discussed next.

- To access this tool, click on the down arrow displayed adjacent to **Top Chamfer** tool in the **NC Features & Machining** panel of the **Ribbon**. A list of tools will be displayed.
- Now, click on the **Top Round** tool in this list to activate the tool. On clicking this tool, the **TOP ROUND** dialog box will be displayed along with the **SELECT SRFS Menu Manager** and **Select** dialog box; refer to Figure-56.

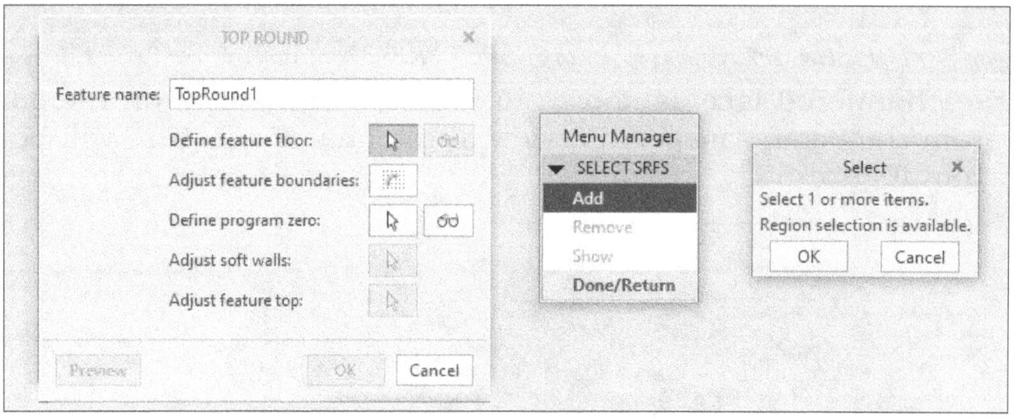

Figure-56. TOP ROUND dialog box with SELECT SRFS Menu Manager and Select dialog box

- Also, you are prompted to select floor of the reference model where you want to create the round feature.

This tool and its options work in similar way as the **Top Chamfer** tool do.

Ribtop

The **Ribtop** tool is used to machine the top face of a rib. The procedure to use this tool is discussed next.

- To access this tool, click on the down arrow displayed adjacent to **Ribtop** tool in the **NC Features & Machining** panel of the **Ribbon**. A list of tools will be displayed.
- Now, click on the **Ribtop** tool in this list to activate the tool. On clicking this tool, the **Rib Top Feature** dialog box is displayed along with the **SELECT SRFS Menu Manager** and **Select** dialog box; refer to Figure-57.

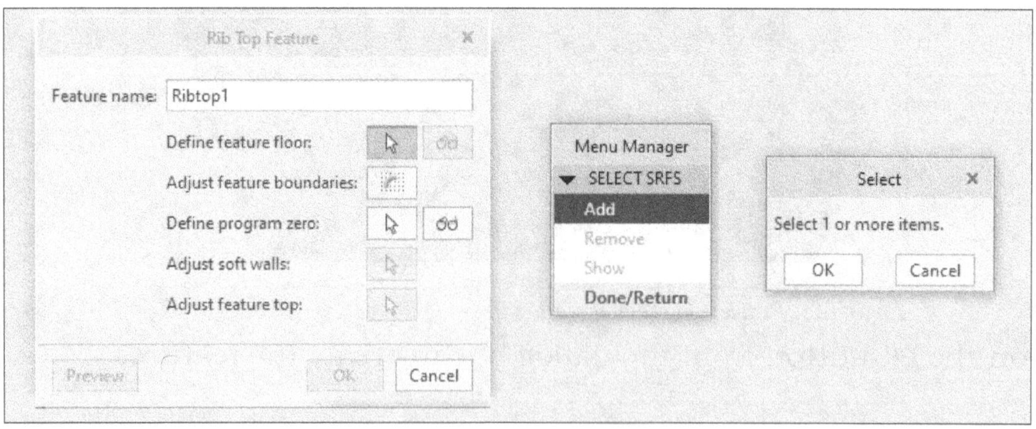

Figure-57. Rib Top Feature dialog box with SELECT SRFS Menu Manager and Select dialog box

- Also, you are prompted to select floor of the reference model where you want to create the rib top feature. Note that rib feature is generally created after pocket milling or slot milling.
- Figure-58 shows an nc model with the material left on rib after pocket milling. Highlighted face is selected for rib top milling.

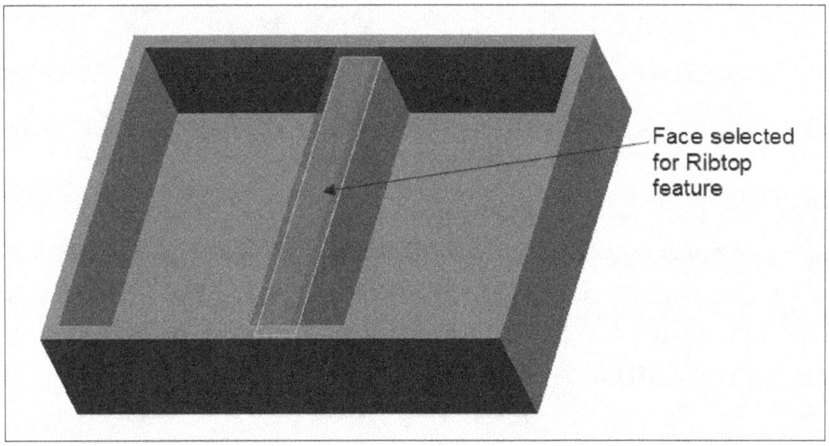

Figure-58. NC MODEL with the face to be selected for ribtop feature

- Figure-59 shows the preview of the rib top feature to be created. Click on **OK** button from the dialog box to create the feature. The options of the dialog box have already been discussed.

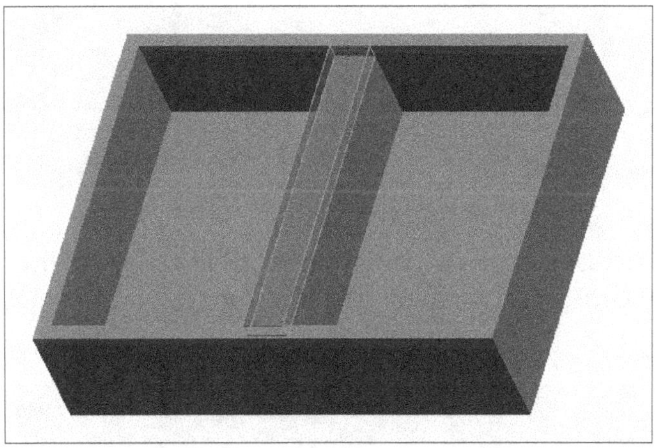

Figure-59. Preview of the ribtop feature

Bosstop

The **Bosstop** tool is used to machine the top face of the boss feature. The procedure to use this tool is discussed next.

- To access this tool, click on the down arrow displayed adjacent to **Ribtop** in the **NC Features & Machining** panel of the **Ribbon**. A list of tools will be displayed.
- Now, click on the **Bosstop** in this list to activate the tool. On clicking this tool, the **Boss Top Feature** dialog box will be displayed along with the **SELECT SRFS Menu Manager** and **Select** dialog box; refer to Figure-60.

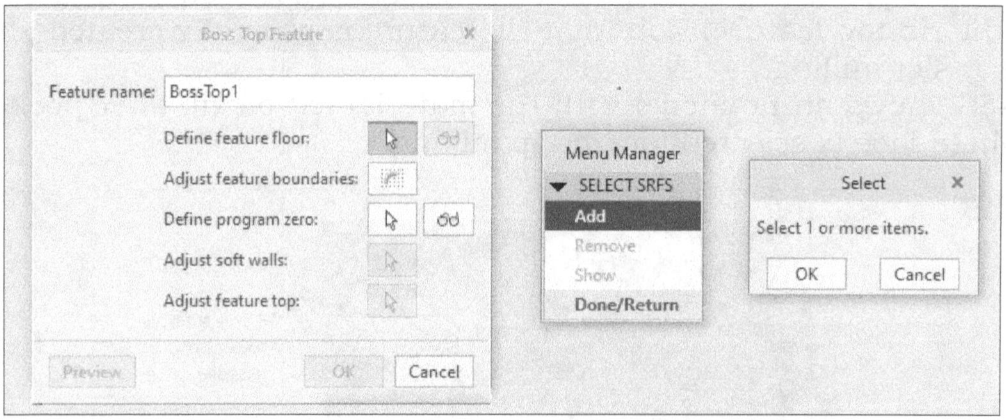

Figure-60. Boss Top Feature dialog box with SELECT SRFS Menu Manager and Select dialog box

- Also, you are prompted to select floor of the reference model where you want to create the boss top feature. Note that boss top feature is generally created after step milling or slot milling.
- Figure-61 shows an nc model with the material left on top face of a boss after step milling. Highlighted face is selected for boss top milling.

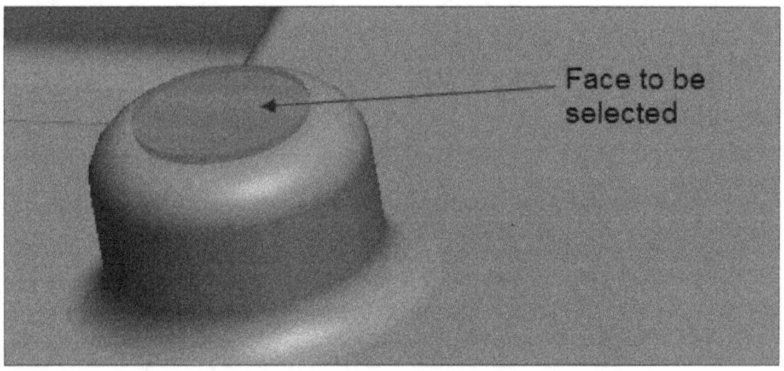

Figure-61. Face of the boss to be selected for the boss feature

- Figure-62 shows the preview of the boss top feature to be created. Click on the **OK** button from the dialog box to create the feature. The options in the dialog box have already been discussed.

Figure-62. Preview of the boss top feature

Free Form

The **Free Form** tool is used to machine at a specified path. The procedure to use this tool is discussed next.

- Click on the **Freeform** tool from the **NC Features & Machining** panel in the **Machining** tab of the **Ribbon**. On clicking this tool, the **Freeform Milling** dialog box is displayed; refer to Figure-63.

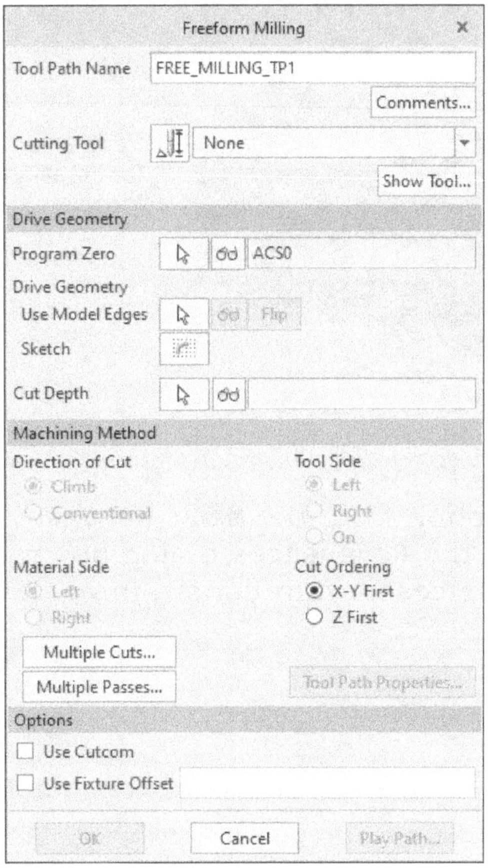

Figure-63. Freeform Milling dialog box

- Select desired tool from the **Cutting Tool** drop-down by clicking in the down arrow adjacent to **None** option. Now, we need to specify the custom path on which the tool will move.
- To create the tool path, click on the **Create or Redefine sketch** button adjacent to **Sketch** in the dialog box. On doing so, the **SETUP SK PLN Menu Manager** (short form of Setup sketching plane) will be displayed; refer to Figure-64.

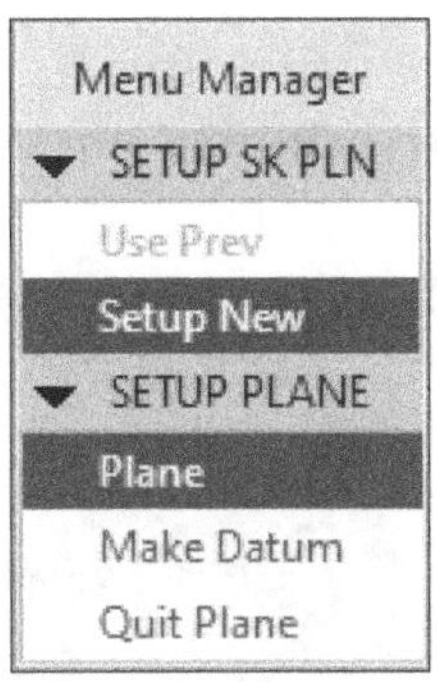

Figure-64. SETUP SK PLN Menu Manager

- Select the face or plane on which you want to create the tool path; refer to Figure-65. You will be prompted to specify the orientation plane by using the options in the **SKET VIEW Menu Manager**; refer to Figure-66.

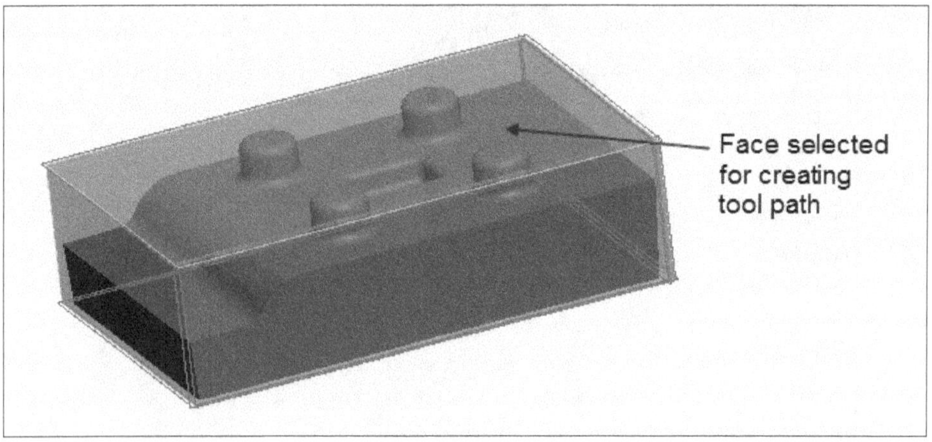

Figure-65. Face selected for creating freeform milling

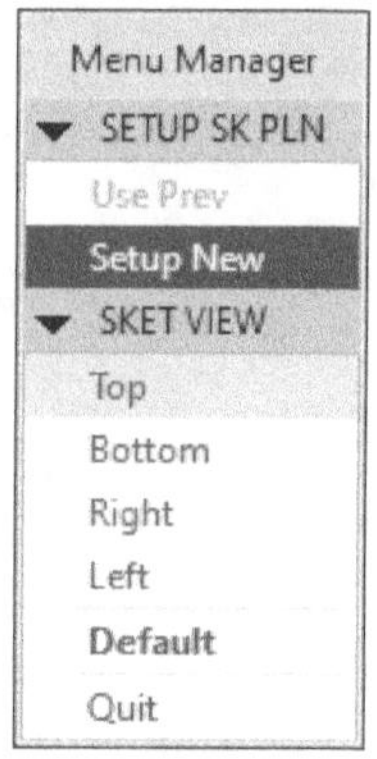

Figure-66. SKET VIEW Menu Manager

- Click on the **Default** option from the **Menu Manager**. The sketcher environment will become active and the **References** dialog box will be displayed, prompting you to select three references for fully constraining the sketch; refer to Figure-67.

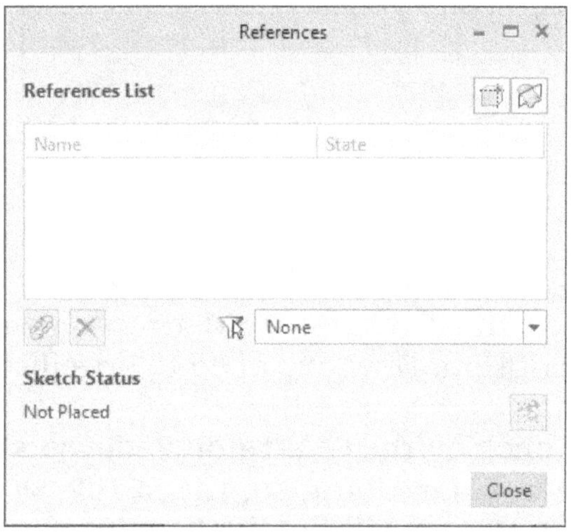

Figure-67. References dialog box

- Select two planes which are perpendicular to each other and a corner point then click on the **Solve** button from the **References** dialog box and then click on the **Close** button.
- Now, create sketch of the tool path; refer to Figure-68 and click on the **OK** button from the **Ribbon**. The **Freeform Milling** dialog box will become active again.

Figure-68. Sketch creating for tool path

- Specify the depth of cut by clicking on the button adjacent to **Cut depth** in the dialog box.
- On clicking this button, the **HEIGHT Menu Manager** is displayed; refer to Figure-69. By default, the **Specify Plane** option is selected in the **Menu Manager**. So, you can select a plane up to which you want to create the cut.

Figure-69. HEIGHT Menu Manager

You can also specify the depth value from the plane on which you sketched the tool path. To do so, select the **Z Depth** option from the **Menu Manager** and specify the depth value in the message box displayed in the middle of the screen. After specifying the value, click on the **Done/Return** option from the **Menu Manager** displayed and click on the **OK** button from the dialog box to create the tool path.

Note
Specify the value of depth of cut in negative otherwise the tool will move in positive Z direction i.e. above the workpiece.

The options of the Freeform Milling dialog box will be discussed in next chapter.

O-Ring

The **O-Ring** tool is used to machine grooves in the top face of the workpiece. The procedure to use this tool is discussed next.

- Click on the **O-Ring** tool from the **NC Features & Machining** panel of the **Machining** tab in the **Ribbon**. The **O-Ring Feature** dialog box is displayed along with the **SELECT SRFS Menu Manager** and **Select** dialog box; refer to Figure-70.

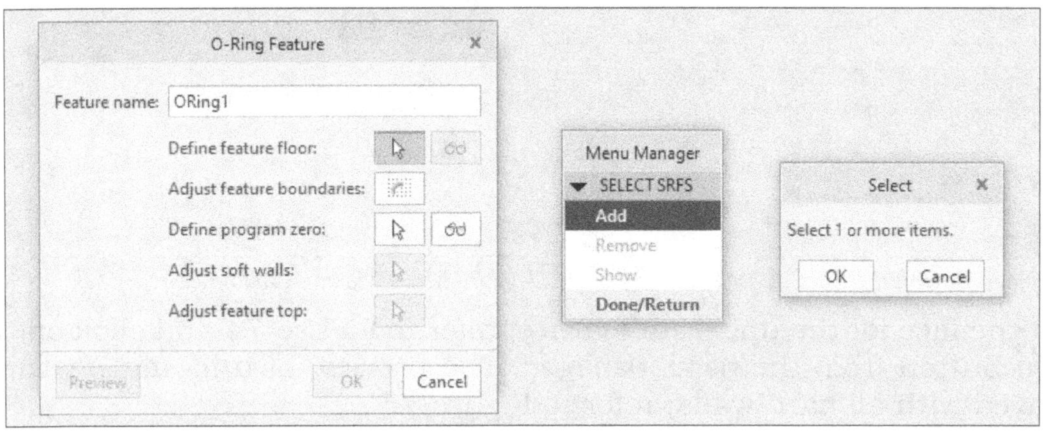

Figure-70. O Ring Feature dialog box with SELECT SRFS Menu Manager and Select dialog box

- You are prompted to select floor of the reference model where you want to create the O-ring feature. Select the face for the O-ring feature; refer to Figure-71 and click on the **Done/Return** button from the **Menu Manager**. Figure-72 shows the preview of the O-ring feature displayed on clicking on the **Done/Return** button.

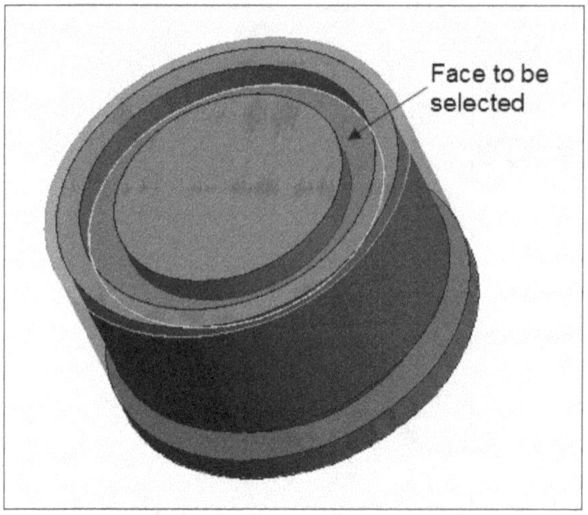

Figure-71. Face to be selected for O ring feature

Figure-72. Preview of the O ring feature

- Click on the **OK** button from the dialog box to create the feature. The options in the dialog box have already been discussed.

Undercut

The **Undercut** tool is used to machine undercuts in the workpiece. The procedure to use this tool is discussed next.

- Click on the **Undercut** tool from the **NC Features & Machining** panel of the **Machining** tab in the **Ribbon**. The **UNDERCUT** dialog box is displayed along with the **SELECT SRFS Menu Manager** and **Select** dialog box; refer to Figure-73. You are prompted to select ceiling of the reference model where you want to create the undercut feature.

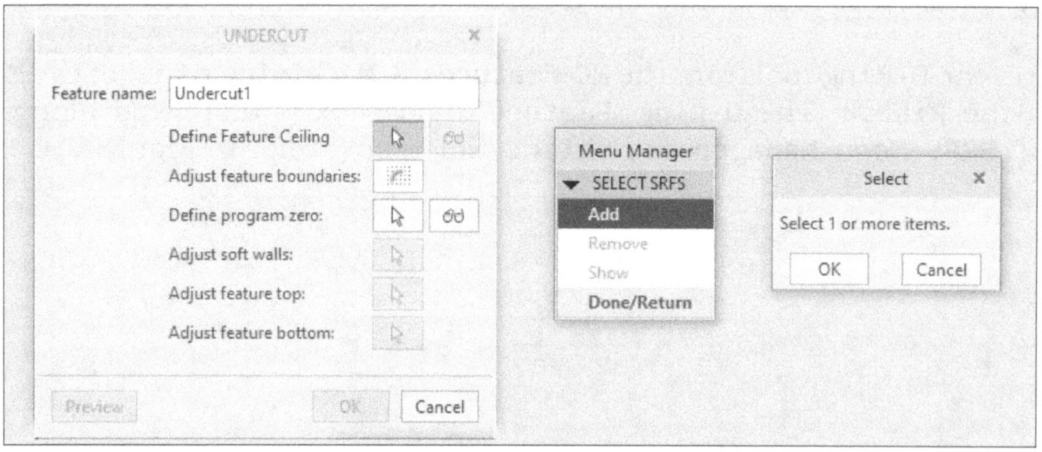

Figure-73. UNDERCUT dialog box with SELECT SRFS Menu Manager and Select dialog box

- Select the face for the undercut feature; refer to Figure-74 and click on the **Done/Return** button from the **Menu Manager**. The preview of undercut feature will be displayed with all hard walls; refer to Figure-75.

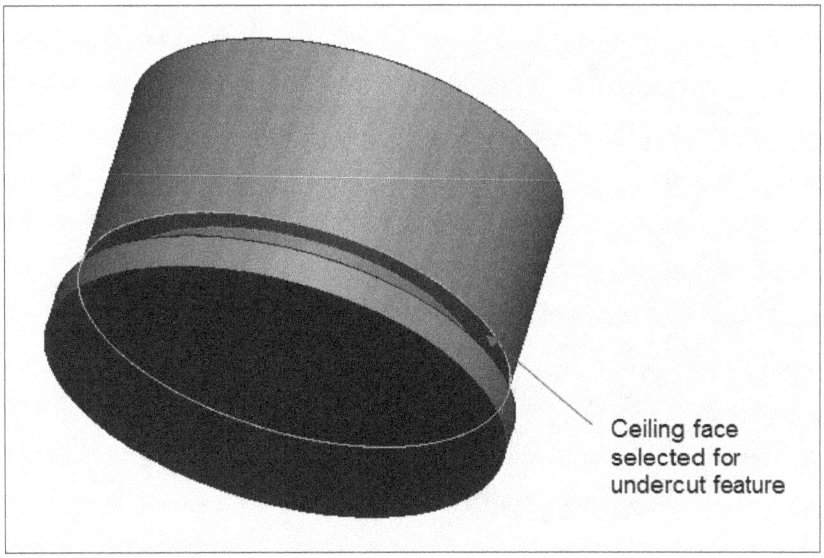

Figure-74. Face to be selected for creating undercut

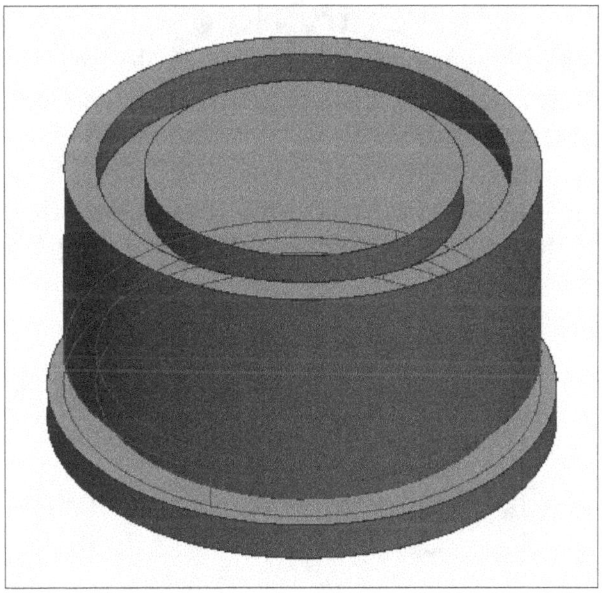

Figure-75. Preview of the undercut feature with all hard walls

- We need to make outer walls as soft walls to create the feature. To do so, click on the **Adjust soft walls** button from the **UNDERCUT** dialog box. You will be prompted to select the walls to be converted to soft walls.
- Select the outer two walls and click on the **Done/Return** button from the **Menu Manager** displayed. Preview of the undercut feature will be displayed; refer to Figure-76.
- Click on the **OK** button from the dialog box to create the feature. The options in the dialog box have already been discussed.

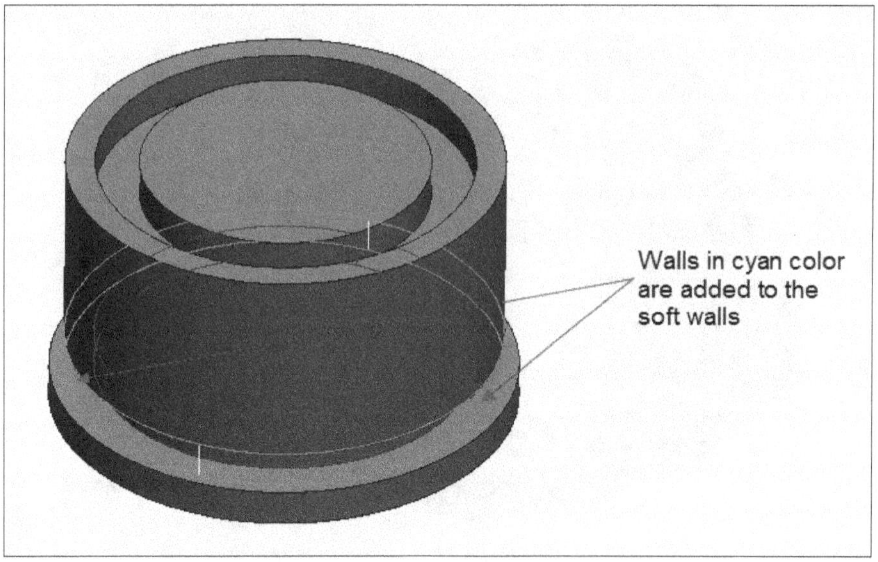

Figure-76. Preview of the undercut feature with the walls added recently in soft walls

Entry Hole

The **Entry Hole** tool is used to machine an entry hole for closed features like pocket feature, through pocket feature, O-ring feature, and so on. The procedure to use this tool is discussed next.

- Click on the **Entry Hole** tool from the **NC Features & Machining** panel of the **Machining** tab in the **Ribbon**. The **Entry Hole** dialog box is displayed; refer to Figure-77.

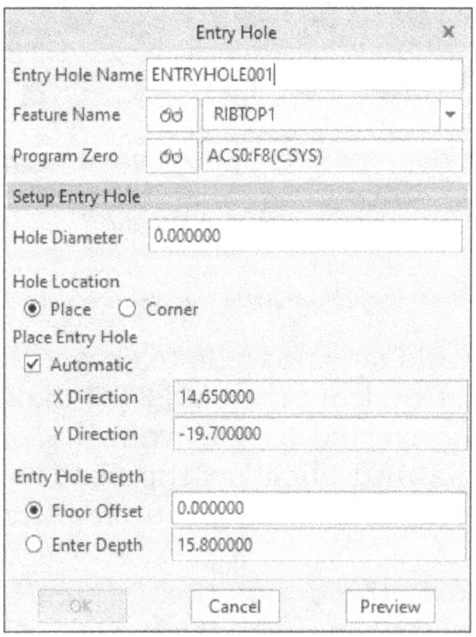

Figure-77. Entry Hole dialog box

- By default, a closed nc feature is selected in the **Feature Name** drop-down of the dialog box. Specify the hole diameter in the **Hole Diameter** edit box and press **ENTER**.
- Select the reference model from drawing area. The **OK** button will be activated. Click on the **OK** button from the dialog box to create the entry hole.

Hole Group

The **Hole Group** tool is used to machine a group of drill holes in the workpiece. The procedure to use this tool is discussed next.

- To create a hole group, choose the **Hole Group** tool from the **NC Features & Machining** panel of the **Machining** tab in the **Ribbon**. The **Drill Group** dialog box is displayed; refer to Figure-78.

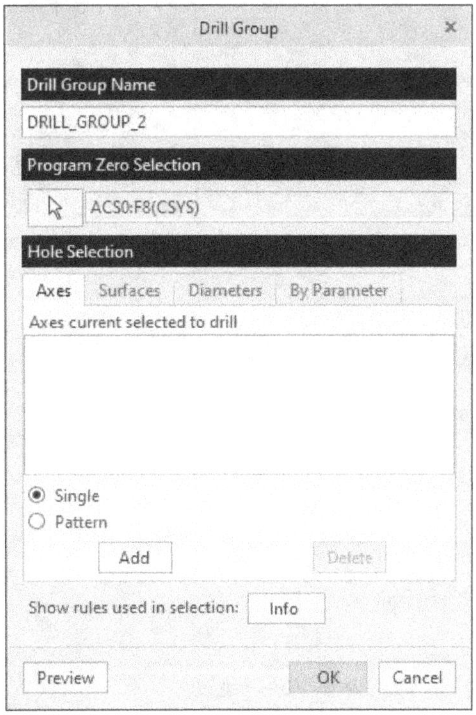

Figure-78. Drill Group dialog box

- By default, **Axes** tab is selected in the dialog box. So, we need to select the axes of holes that we want to create.
- Axes can be selected in two ways; either one by one using the **Single** radio button in the dialog box or by using the pattern of the holes by selecting the **Pattern** radio button. Select desired radio button.
- In our case, the **Pattern** radio button is used. Select the **Pattern** radio button and then click on the **Add** button from the dialog box. The system prompts to select a hole.
- Select one of the holes in the pattern; refer to Figure-79 and press the middle button of mouse. The axes of all the holes will be displayed in the **Axes** current selected to drill area; refer to Figure-80.

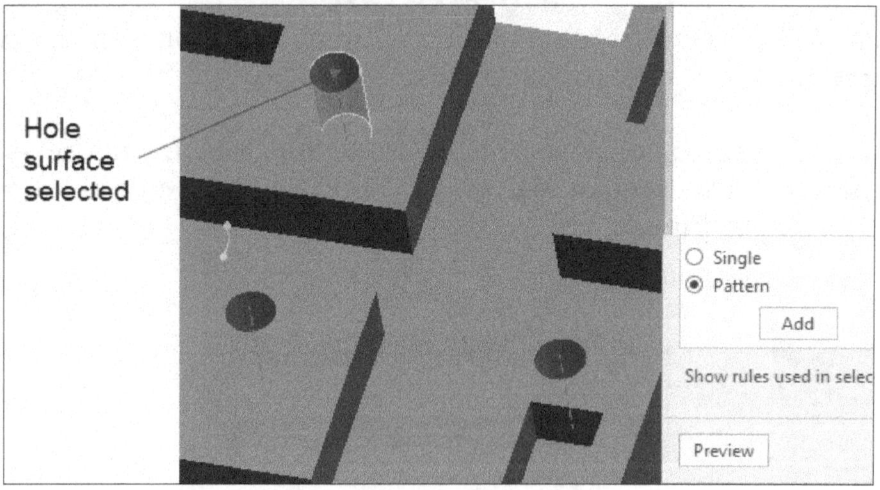

Figure-79. Pattern radio button selected and the hole surface selected

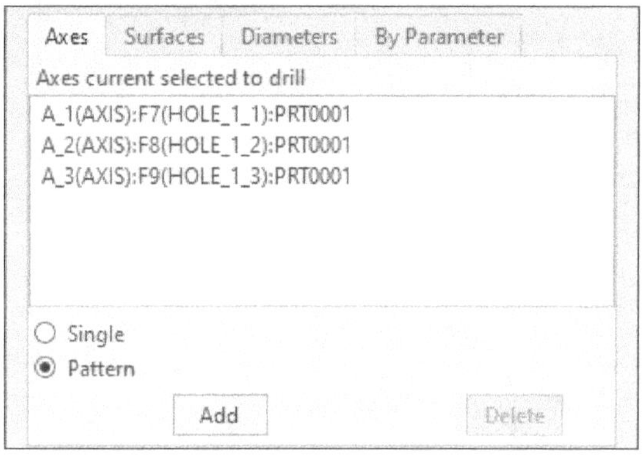

Figure-80. Axes of holes added

- Click on the **OK** button from the **Drill Group** dialog box to create the drill group feature. The options in the **Drill Group** dialog box are discussed next.

Drill Group Name

The **Drill Group Name** edit box is used to specify a user defined name for the drill group.

Program Zero Selection

The **Program Zero Selection** option is a kind of data collector. Click on the arrow adjacent to the box of this data collector, the system prompts to select a coordinate system. Select desired coordinate system; the selected coordinate system will be used as program zero and its name is displayed in the box of the collector.

Hole Selection

It is an area having four tabs; Axes, Surfaces, Diameters, and By Parameters. The options in **Axes** tab have been discussed while creating this feature. Rest of the options are discussed next.

Surfaces

The options in the **Surfaces** tab work in the same way as in **Axes** tab.

- Click on this tab and click on the **Add** button from the dialog box. You will be asked to select surfaces of the holes.

- Select surface of the hole. If you want to add multiple holes then press and hold the **CTRL** key and click on the surfaces of the holes.
- Press the middle mouse button and the selected surfaces will be added in the **Surface(s) for gathering holes to drill** area of the dialog box.

Diameters

The options in the **Diameters** tab are used to select the holes for the drill group feature according to their diameters.

- To add the diameters, select the **Diameters** tab and then click on the **Add** button from the dialog box. The **Select Hole Diameter** dialog box is displayed; refer to Figure-81.

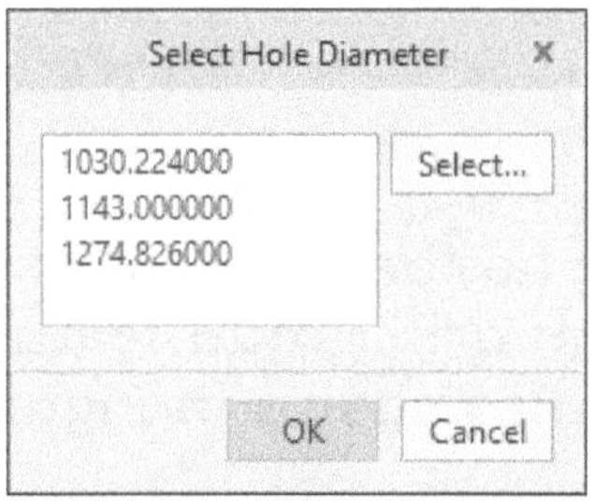

Figure-81. Select Hole Diameter dialog box

- Select a diameter from the dialog box and then click on the **OK** button from the dialog box. The holes of selected diameter will be automatically added in the list and the diameter will be displayed in the **Diameter(s) of holes selected to drill** area; refer to Figure-82.

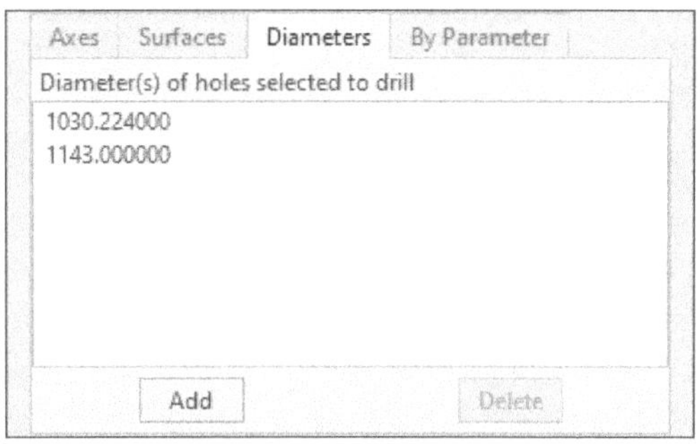

Figure-82. Diameter of selected holes

By Parameters

The options in the **By Parameters** tab are displayed as shown in Figure-83.

- Select desired parameter from the **Feature Parameter** list box and select the value from the **Value** drop-down displayed below the list.
- By default, the = operator is selected in the **Operator** drop-down. For example, select the **DRILL DEPTH** parameter from the list; the values of the holes available in the modeling area are displayed in the **Value** drop-down.
- Select one of the values from the drop-down and click on the **Add** button. All the holes satisfying the conditions will be added in the drill group at the bottom in the dialog box.

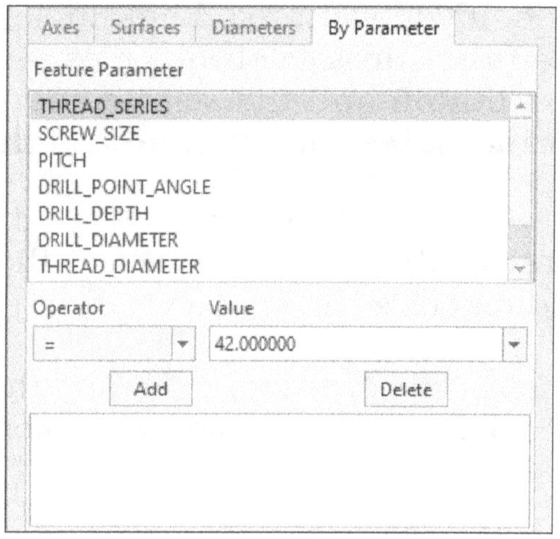

Figure-83. By Parameter tab and its options

Info

The **Info** tool is available at the bottom of the dialog box and is used to summarize about the holes selected for the drill group feature. On clicking this button, the information window is displayed as shown in Figure-84.

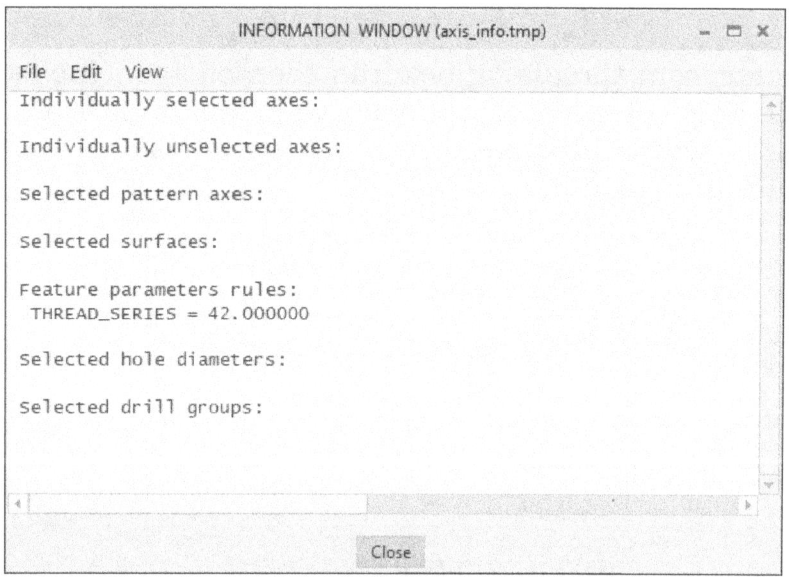

Figure-84. INFORMATION WINDOW

TUTORIAL 1

In this tutorial, you will create the NC features for the model displayed in Figure-85. From back side, the model is displayed as shown in Figure-86. *You can request the resource kit of this book at cadcamcaeworks@gmail.com.*

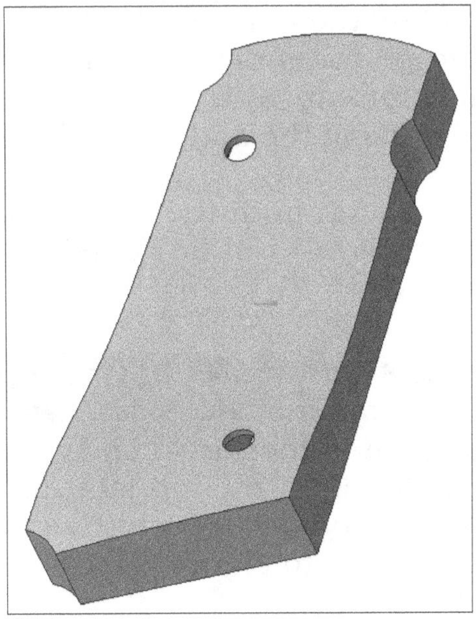

Figure-85. Model for Tutorial 1

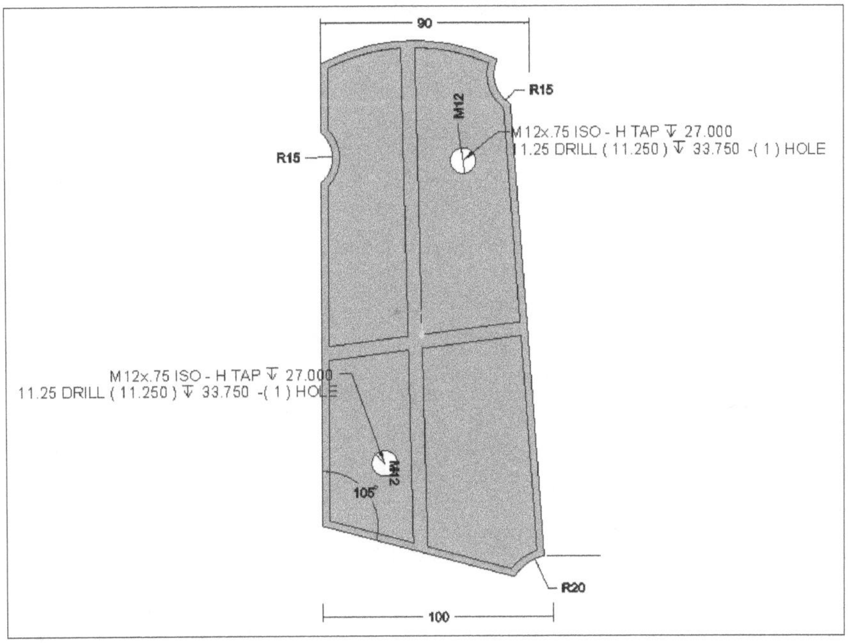

Figure-86. Back side of the model

Starting Creo Expert Machinist

- Start Creo Parametric and click on the **New** button from the **Ribbon**.
- Select the **Manufacturing** radio button from the **Type** area and **Expert Machinist** radio button from the **Sub-type** area of the dialog box.
- Specify the name of the file as **C05 tut1** and clear the **Use default template** check box.

- Click on the **OK** button from the dialog box. The **New File Options** dialog box will be displayed. Select the **mmns mfg nc abs** template and then click on the **OK** button.

Adding an NC model in the system

- Click on the **Create Model** button from the **NC Model** panel in the **Ribbon**. An input box will be displayed to define the name of the NC model.
- Click on the **Accept value** button from the input box. The default name will be accepted and you will be prompted to select a part file as reference model.
- Select the file **c5 model1** by using the options in the dialog box and then click on the **Open** button.
- Click on the **Create Stock** option from the **Menu Manager** displayed in the right. The **Auto Workpiece Creation** tab will be added in the **Ribbon** and the related options will be displayed.

Creating stock material (Workpiece)

- Click on the **Create Stock** button from **NC Model Menu Manager** displayed in right. Also, drag handles and various values are displayed on the workpiece.
- Now, we will add 3 mm material on the top face and 3 mm material on bottom face of the workpiece. For that, type 3 in both the **+Y** and **-Y** edit boxes displayed on clicking the **Options** tab; refer to Figure-87.

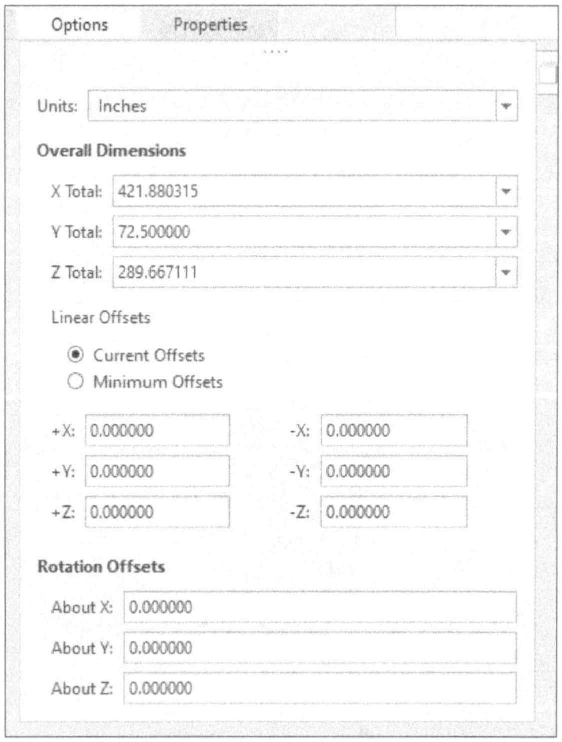

Figure-87. Options tab with the values to be specified

- Click on **OK** button from the **Ribbon** and click on the **Done** button from the **Menu Manager**. The assembly environment will be displayed.
- Select the **Default** option from the **Current constraint** drop-down and click on the **OK** button from the **Ribbon**; refer to Figure-88.

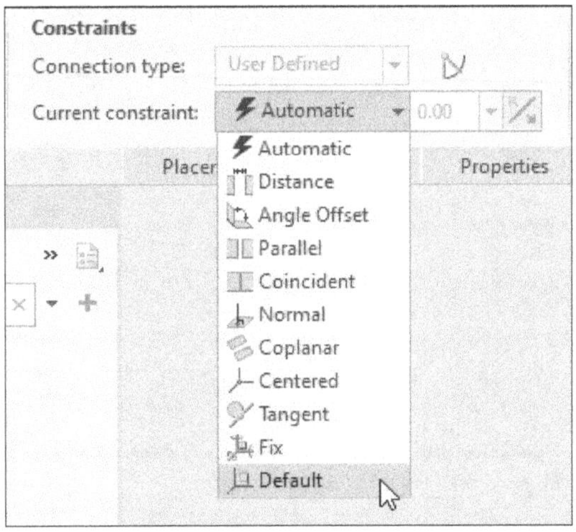

Figure-88. Default constraint in the Current constraint drop-down

Creating Machine Setup

- After specifying the above parameters, the workpiece and the reference model will be placed at the default position i.e. coincident with the assembly coordinate system. Click on the down arrow displayed below **Work Center** in the **Setup** panel of the **Machining** tab in the **Ribbon**; a drop-down will be displayed. Click on the **Machine Tool Manager** tool from the drop-down. The **Milling Work Center** dialog box will be displayed.
- Click on the **Tools** tab at the top in the dialog box. The **Milling Work Center** dialog box will be displayed; refer to Figure-89.

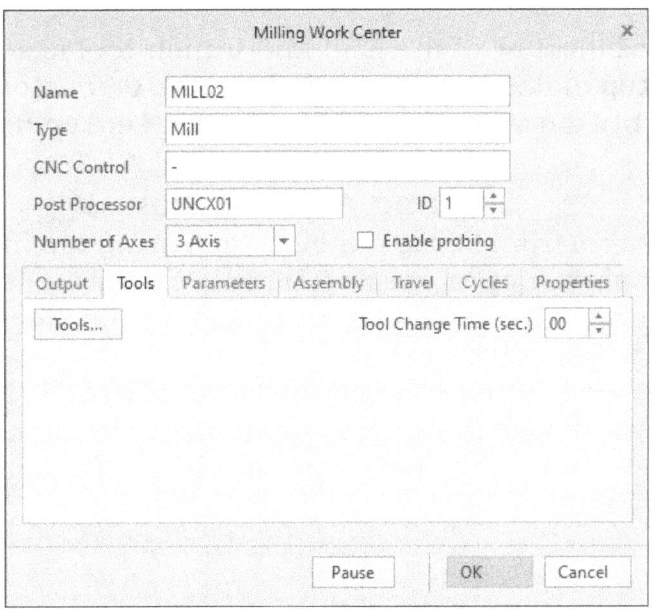

Figure-89. Milling Work Center dialog box

- Click on the **Tools** tool from the dialog box. The **Tool Setup** dialog box will be displayed.
- Create the tools with the parameters as shown in Figure-90 and Figure-91.

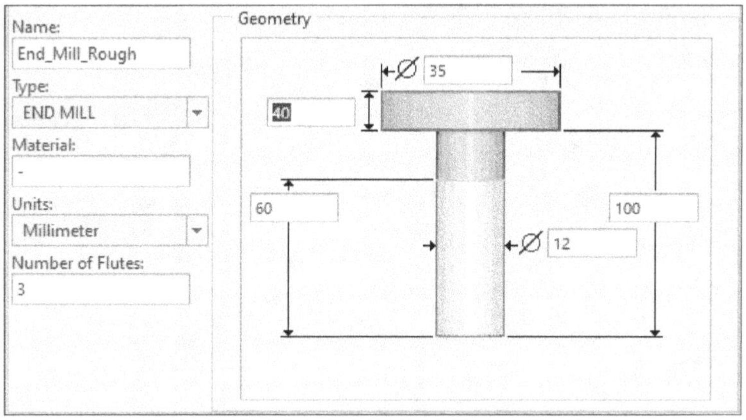

Figure-90. Parameters for End Mill Rough

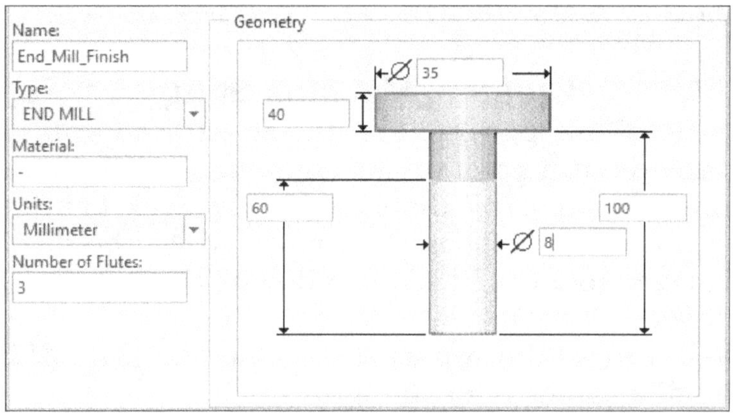

Figure-91. Parameters for End Mill Finish

- Make sure that **Tool Number** of the End Mill Finish tool is set to 2 in the **Settings** tab of the **Tool Setup** dialog box. Now, click on the **OK** button from the **Tool Setup** dialog box and **OK** button from the **Milling Work Center** dialog box.

Creating an Operation

- Click on **Operation** tool from **Setup** panel of **Machining** tab in the **Ribbon**. On doing so, the **Operation** tab will open in the **Ribbon**.
- Click on the drop-down displaying **No Work Center** (i.e. **Work Center** drop-down), a list of machines will be displayed.
- Select the machine earlier created from the list i.e. MILL01. Now you need to select a coordinate system to specify the zero position of the machine.
- Click on the **Datum** button at the extreme right in the **Ribbon**. A drop-down will be displayed; refer to Figure-92.

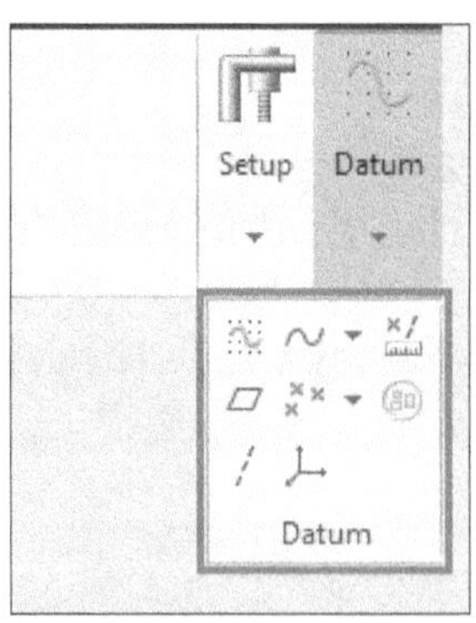

Figure-92. Drop down displayed on clicking the Datum button

- Click on the **Coordinate System** tool in the drop-down. The **Coordinate System** dialog box will be displayed; refer to Figure-93.

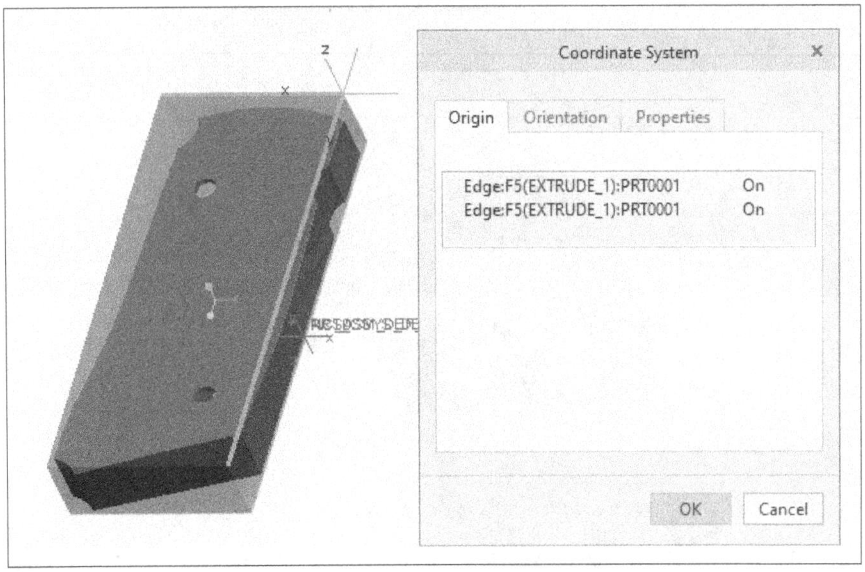

Figure-93. NC Model with coordinate system and the Coordinate System dialog box

- Select the edges in such a way that the coordinate system is displayed as shown in Figure-93 (in Isometric view).
- Click on **OK** button from the dialog box, the coordinate system is created.
- Click on **Resume** ▶ button from the **Ribbon**. Now, you are allowed to select the coordinate system.
- Select the coordinate system created recently and click on the **OK** button from the **Ribbon**. An operation will be created and added in the **Model Tree** at the left.

Creating NC Features to remove material

NC features are used to decide the pattern in which the material will be removed. Selection of NC features depend on shape of model.

Profile Feature

- Click on **Profile** tool from the **NC Features & Machining** panel in the **Ribbon**. The **Profile Feature** dialog box will be displayed along with the **SELECT SRFS Menu Manager** and **Select** dialog box.
- Select the side walls of the reference model while holding the **CTRL** key; refer to Figure-94.

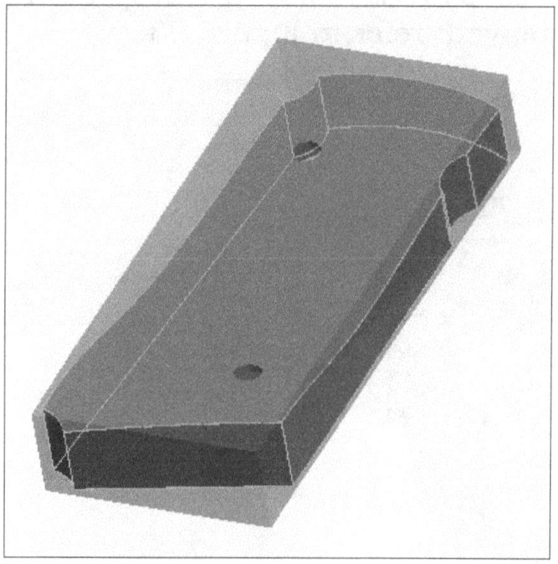

Figure-94. Side walls to be selected

- After selecting the highlighted walls, click on **Done** button from the **SURF/LOOP Menu Manager** and then click on the **Done/Return** button from the **SELECT SRFS Menu Manager**. Preview of the feature will be displayed.
- Click on the **OK** button from the **Profile Feature** dialog box to create the feature. The feature will be created and added below OP010 [MILL01] as PROFILE1 [OP010].

Slot Feature

- Click on the **Slot** tool from the **NC Features & Machining** panel in the **Ribbon**. The **Slot Feature** dialog box will be displayed along with the **SELECT SRFS Menu Manager** and **Select** dialog box.
- Select the top face of the reference model while holding the **CTRL** key; refer to Figure-95.

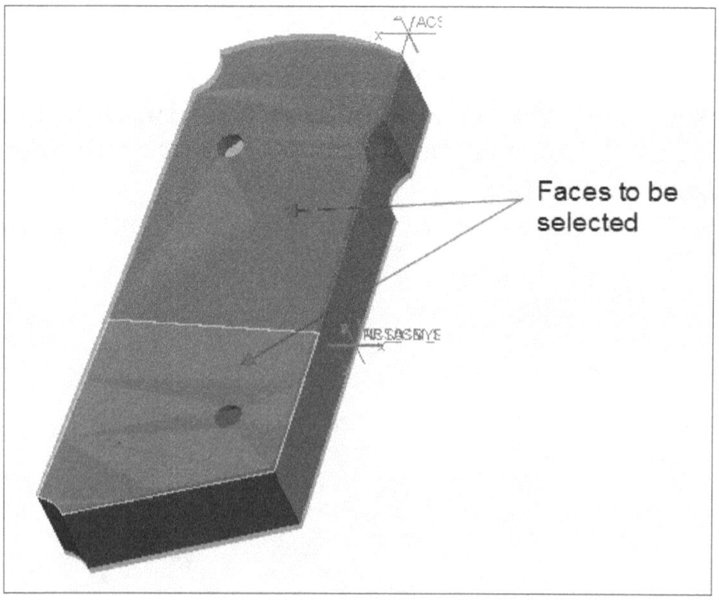

Figure-95. Faces to be selected for step milling

- After selecting the faces, press the middle mouse button twice. The preview of the feature will be displayed.
- Click on the **OK** button from **Slot Feature** dialog box. The feature will be created.

Creating operation to machine from other side

Now, we need to machine the part from other side. So, we need to place the part in reverse manner i.e. upside-down on the machine. Same, we need to do in Expert Machinist. This can be done by creating a new operation sequence. In this step, we will create a new Operation sequence.

- Rotate the part in such a way that the bottom face is displayed; refer to Figure-96.

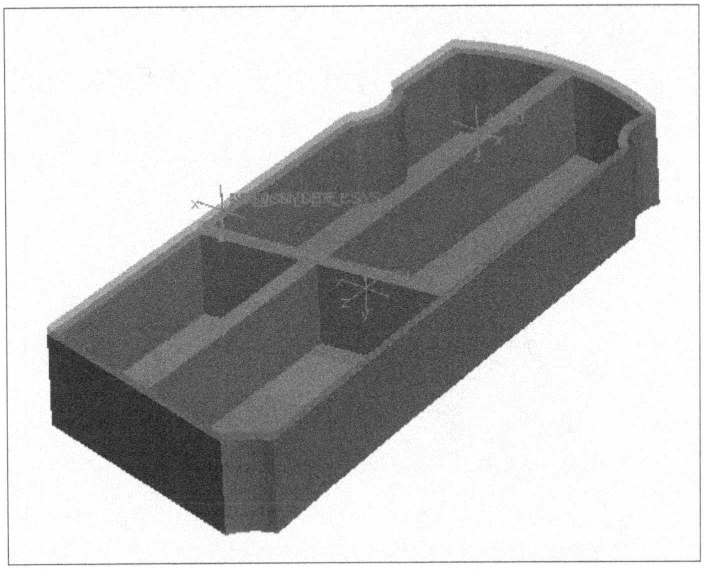

Figure-96. Reverse side of the reference part

- Click on the **Operation** tool from the **Setup** panel in the **Machining** tab of the **Ribbon**. The **Operation** tab will open in the **Ribbon**.
- Select the **MILL01** option from the **Work Center** drop-down in the **Ribbon**.
- Click on the **Datum** button at the extreme right of the **Ribbon**. A drop-down will be displayed.
- Click on the **Coordinate System** tool from the drop-down. The **Coordinate System** dialog box will be displayed.
- Select the edges in such a way that the coordinate system is placed as shown in Figure-97.

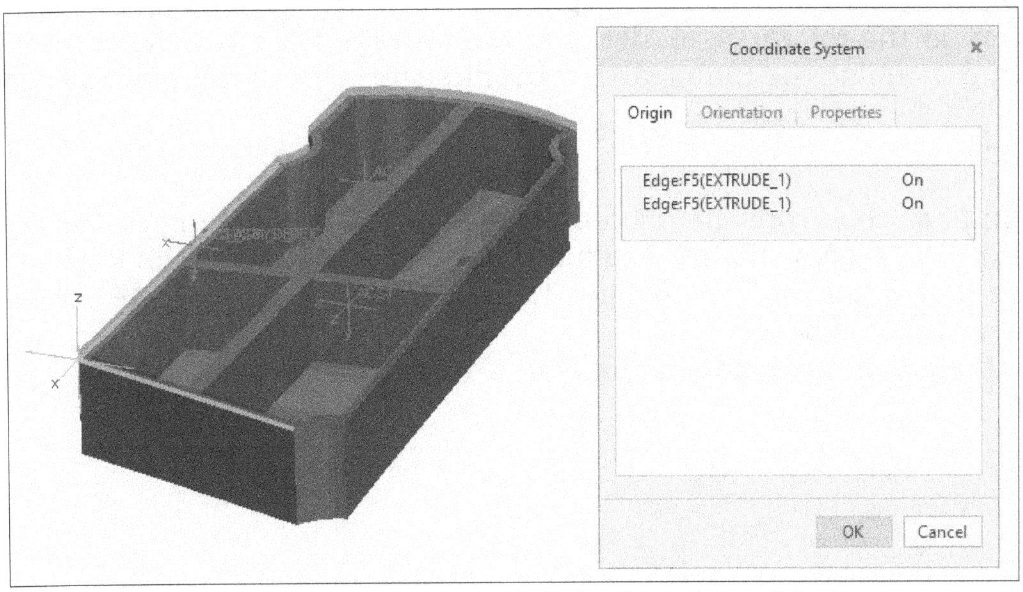

Figure-97. The coordinate system to be created with the Coordinate System dialog box

- Click on the **OK** button from the dialog box and **Resume** button from the **Ribbon**.
- Now, select the recently created coordinate system and click on the **OK** button from the **Ribbon**. A new operation OP020 [MILL01] will be added in the **Model Tree**.

Creating NC Features to remove material

Pocket Feature

- Click on **Pocket** tool from the **NC Features & Machining** tab of the **Ribbon**. The **Pocket Feature** dialog box will be displayed along with the **SELECT SRFS Menu Manager** and **Select** dialog box.
- Select the face of the reference model as shown in Figure-98 to remove material in the form of a pocket.

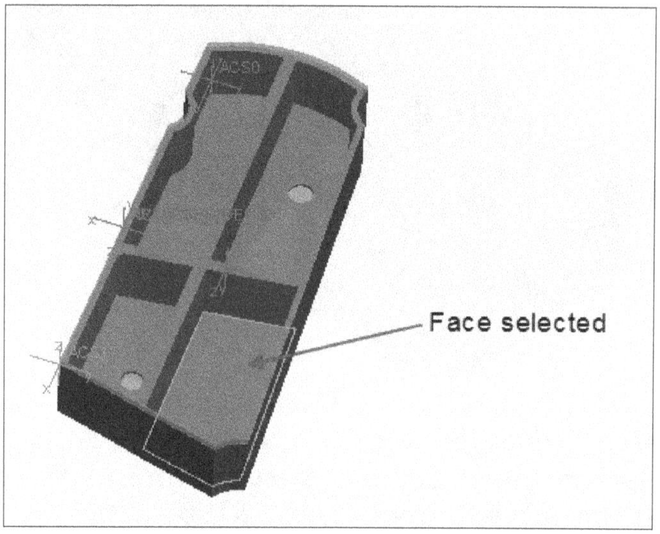

Figure-98. Face to be selected to create a pocket feature

- Press the middle mouse button twice. Preview of the pocket feature will be displayed.
- Click on **OK** button from the dialog box to create the feature.

Similarly, create the other pocket features one by one by selecting the corresponding faces. The model should be displayed as Figure-99 after selecting the **Material Removal Display** button from the **Display** panel of the **Machining** tab. Now, the only material left on the reference model is at the faces of the ribs. Here, we will remove this material by using the Slab feature, because it removes the material from a large area and with same tolerance.

Slab Feature

- Click on **Slab** tool from the drop-down displayed on clicking at the down arrow adjacent to **Flange** in the **NC Features & Machining** tab of the **Ribbon**. The **Slab Feature** dialog box will be displayed along with the **SELECT SRFS Menu Manager** and **Select** dialog box.
- Select the face of the model as shown in Figure-99.

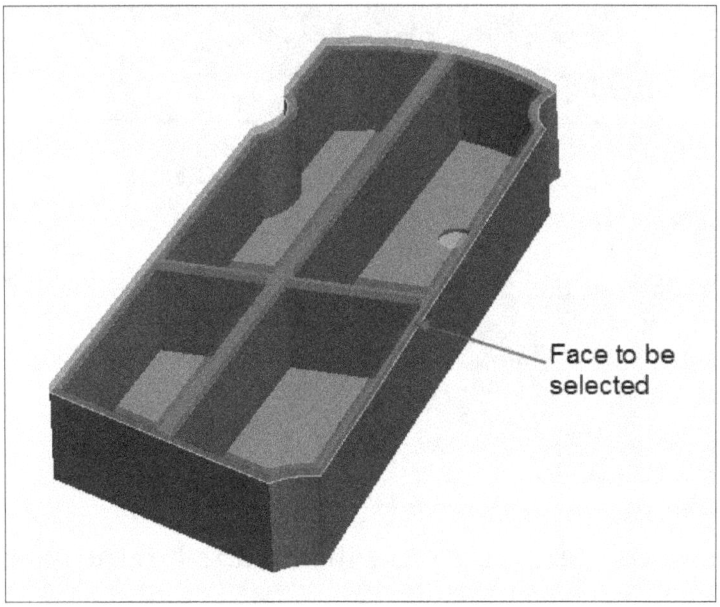

Figure-99. Face to be selected for the slab feature

- Press the middle mouse button twice. Preview of the slab feature will be displayed as shown in Figure-100.

Figure-100. Preview of the slab feature

- Click on the **OK** button from the dialog box to create the feature.

Hole Group

- Click on the **Hole Group** tool from the **NC Features & Machining** tab of the **Ribbon**. The **Drill Group** dialog box will be displayed.
- Click on **Add** button from the dialog box. You will be allowed to select the faces to add their corresponding axes in the list.
- Press and hold the **CTRL** key and select faces of the holes; refer to Figure-101.

Figure-101. Faces to be selected for creating holes

- Press the middle mouse button. Axes will be added in the **Axes current selected to drill** list box.
- Click on the **OK** button from the dialog box. The feature will be created and the material would be removed.

Press **CTRL+S** to save the nc model.

TUTORIAL 2

In this tutorial, you will create the nc feature for the model in Figure-102. You can request the resources kit of this book at cadcamcaeworks@gmail.com

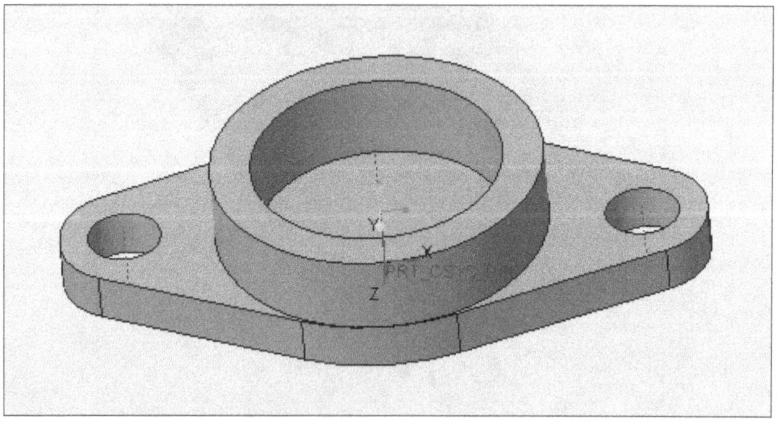

Figure-102. Model for Tutorial 2

Starting Creo Expert Machinist

- Start Creo Parametric and click on the **New** button from the **Ribbon**.
- Select **Manufacturing** radio button from the **Type** area and **Expert Machinist** radio button from the **Sub-type** area of the dialog box.
- Specify the name of the file as **C05 TUT2** and clear the **Use default template** check box.
- Now, click on the **OK** button from the dialog box. The **New File Options** dialog box will be displayed. Select the **mmns mfg nc abs** template and then click on the **OK** button.

Adding an NC model in the system

- Click on the **Create Model** button from **NC Model** panel in the **Ribbon**. A prompt will be displayed to define the name of the NC model.
- Click on the **Accept value** ✓ button from the prompt. The default name will be accepted and you will be prompted to select a part file as reference model.
- Select the file **C05 TUT2** by using the options in the dialog box and then click on the **Open** button.
- Click on the **Create Stock** option from the **Menu Manager** displayed in the right side of the screen. The **Auto Workpiece Creation** tab will be added in the **Ribbon** and the related options will be displayed.

Creating stock material

- Click on the **Create Stock** button from the **NC Model Menu Manager** displayed. The drag handles and various values are displayed from the workpiece.
- Now, we will add 3 mm material on the top face and all other faces except bottom face of the workpiece. For that, type 3 in **+Y**, **+X**, **-X**, **+Z**, and **-Z** edit boxes from **Options** tab; refer to Figure-103.

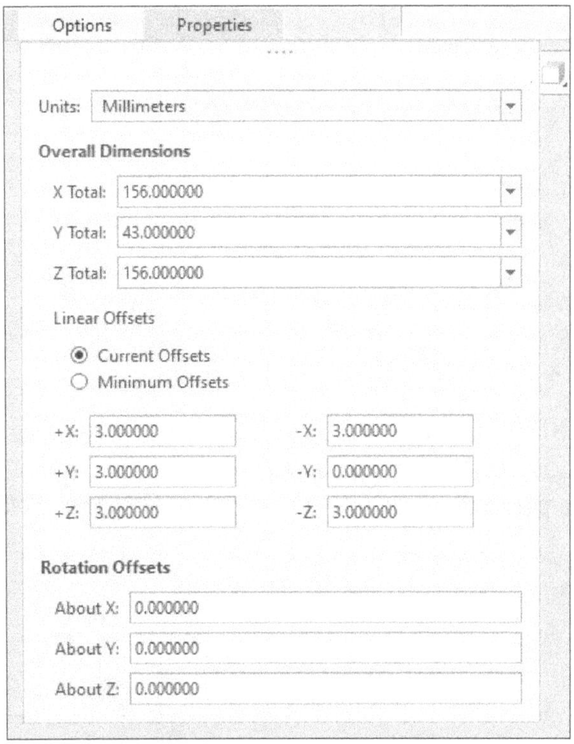

Figure-103. Options tab on specifing the values

- Click on the **OK** button from the **Ribbon** and click on the **Done** button from the **Menu Manager**. The assembly environment will be displayed.
- Select the **Default** option from the **Current constraint** drop-down and click on the **OK** button from the **Ribbon**.

Creating Machine Setup

- After specifying various parameters, the workpiece and the reference model will be placed at the default position i.e. coincident with the assembly coordinate system. Click on the down arrow displayed below **Work Center** from the **Setup** panel of the **Machining** tab in the **Ribbon**. A drop-down will be displayed.

- Click on the **Machine Tool Manager** tool from the drop-down. The **Milling Work Center** dialog box will be displayed; refer to Figure-104.

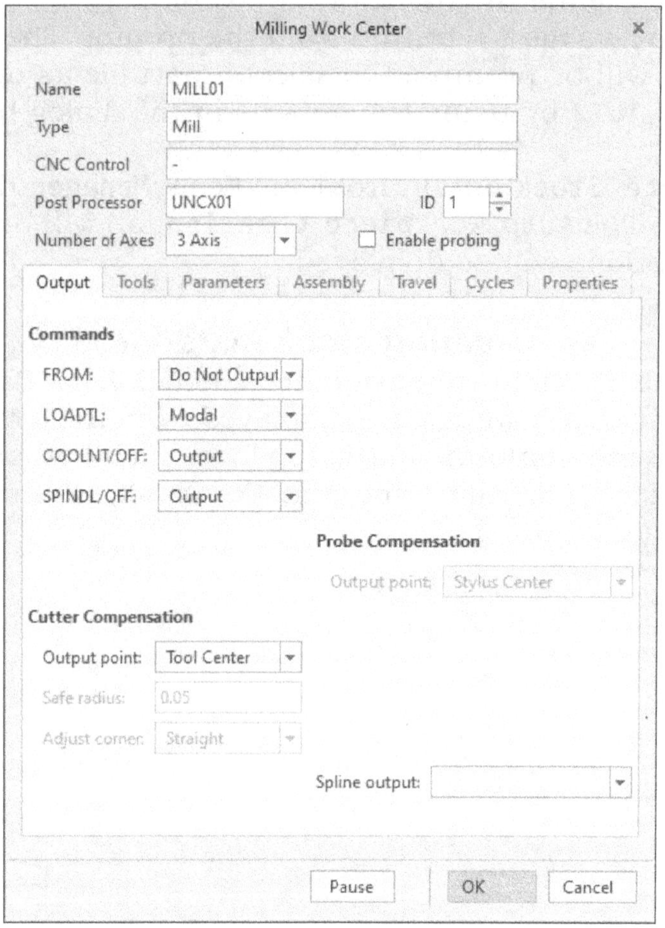

Figure-104. Milling Work Center dialog box

- Click on the **Tools** tab from the dialog box and click on the **Tools** button. The **Tools Setup** dialog box will be displayed.
- Create the tools with parameters as shown in Figure-105 and Figure-106.

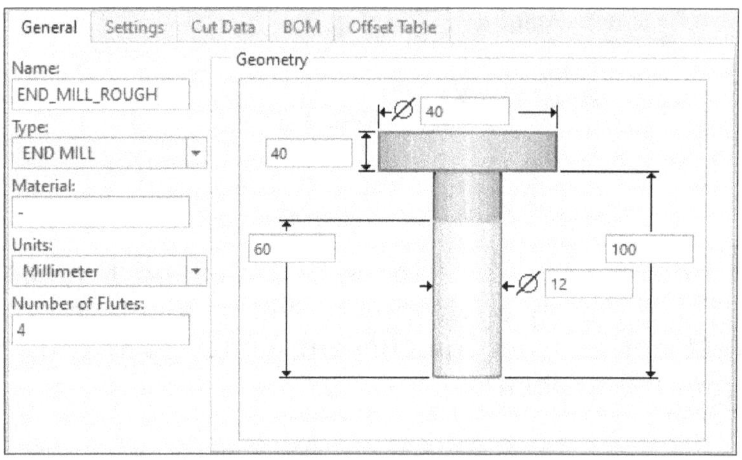

Figure-105. Parameters for End Mill Rough

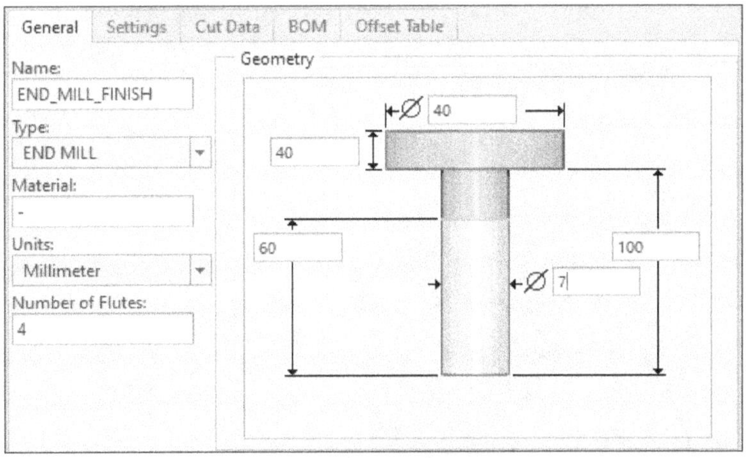

Figure-106. Parameters of End Mill Finish

- Make sure that **Tool Number** of the End Mill Finish tool is set to 2 in the **Settings** tab of the **Tools Setup** dialog box. Now, click on the **OK** button from the **Tools Setup** dialog box and then click on the **OK** button from the **Milling Work Center** dialog box.

Creating an Operation

- Click on **Operation** tool from **Setup** panel of **Machining** tab in the **Ribbon**. On doing so, the **Operation** contextual tab will open in the **Ribbon**.
- Click on the **Work Center** drop-down. A list of machines will be displayed.
- Select the machine earlier created from the list i.e. MILL01. Now, you need to select a coordinate system to specify zero position of the machine.
- Click on the **Datum** drop-down at the extreme right in the **Ribbon**. The options will be displayed; refer to Figure-107.

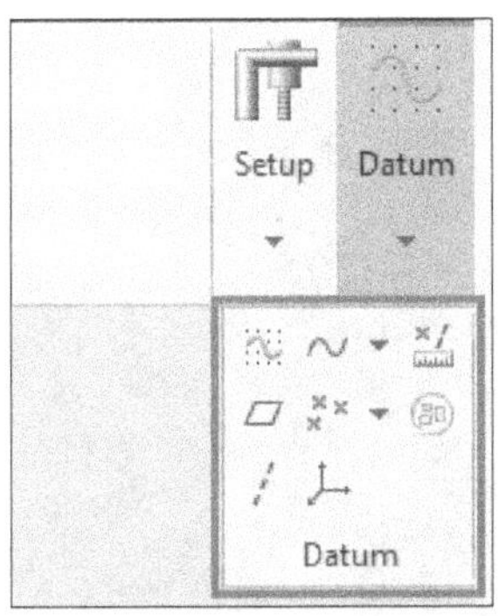

Figure-107. Datum drop down options

- Click on the **Coordinate System** tool from the drop-down. The **Coordinate System** dialog box will be displayed; refer to Figure-108.
- Select the Top face of the Stock and adjust the coordinate system as displayed in above figure.
- Click on the **OK** button from the dialog box. The coordinate system is created.
- Click on **Resume** ▶ button from the **Ribbon**. Now, you are allowed to select the coordinate system.
- Select the coordinate system created recently and click on the **OK** button from the **Ribbon**. An operation will be created and added in the **Model Tree** at the left.

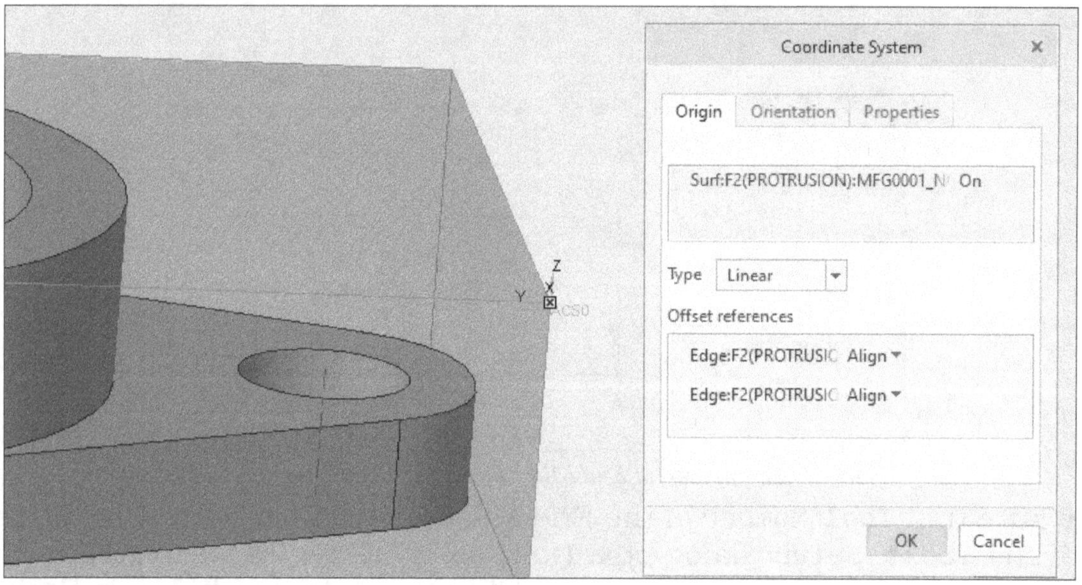

Figure-108. NC Model with Coordinate System dialog box

Creating NC Features to remove material

Profile Feature

- Click on the **Profile** tool from **NC Features & Machining** panel in **Ribbon**. The **Profile Feature** dialog box will be displayed along with the **SELECT SRFS Menu Manager** and **Select** dialog box.
- Select the side walls of the reference model while holding the **CTRL** key; refer to Figure-109.

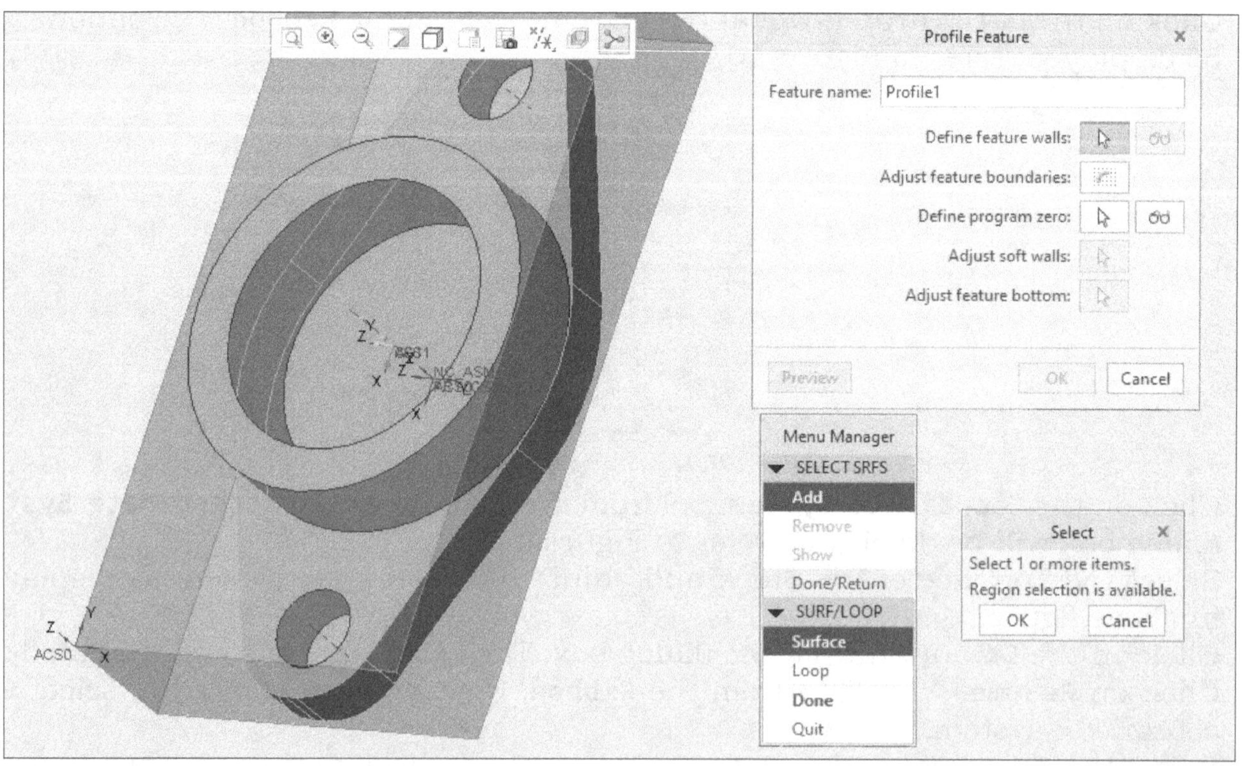

Figure-109. Side walls to be selected for Profile option

- After selecting the highlighted walls, click on **Done** button from the **SURF/LOOP Menu Manager** and then click on the **Done/Return** button from the **SELECT SRFS Menu Manager**. Preview of the feature will be displayed.

- Click on the **OK** button from the **Profile Feature** dialog box to create the feature. The feature will be created and added below OP010 [MILL01] as PROFILE1 [OP010].

Flange Feature

- Click on the **Flange** tool from the **NC Features & Machining** panel in the **Ribbon**. The **Flange Feature** dialog box will be displayed along with the **SELECT SRFS Menu Manager** and **Select** dialog box.
- Select the face of the reference model as shown in Figure-110.

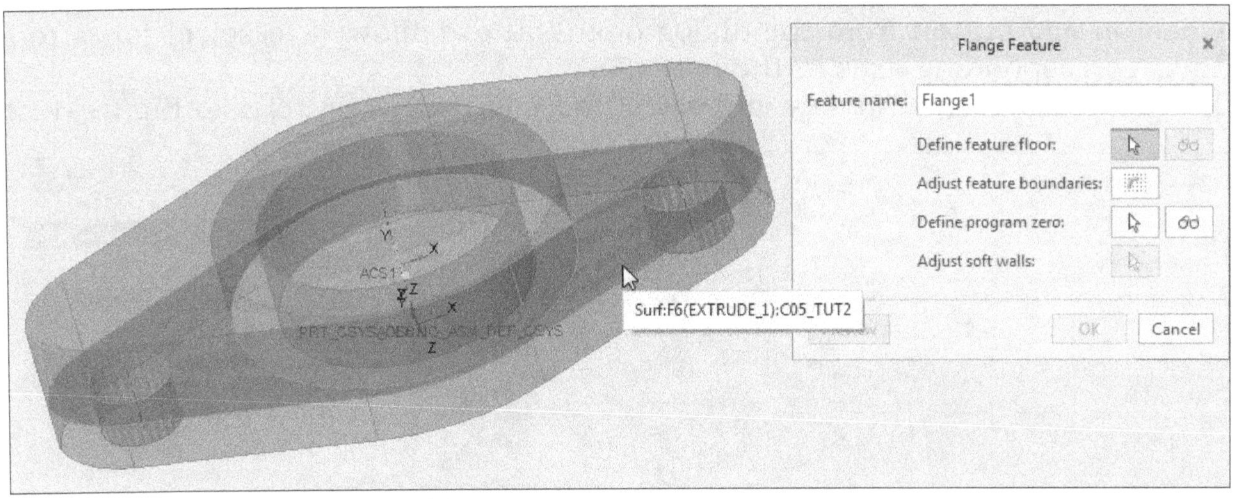

Figure-110. Selection of face for Flange feature

- After selecting the highlighted face, click on the **Done** button from the **SELECT SRFS Menu Manager**. Preview of the feature will be displayed.
- Click on the **OK** button from the **Flange Feature** dialog box to create the feature. The feature will be created and added below FLANGE1 (OPO10).

Pocket Feature

- Click on the **Pocket Feature** tool from the **NC Features & Machining** tab of the **Ribbon**. The **Pocket Feature** dialog box will be displayed along with the **SELECT SRFS Menu Manager** and **Select** dialog box.
- Select the face of the reference model as shown in Figure-111 to remove material in the form of a pocket.

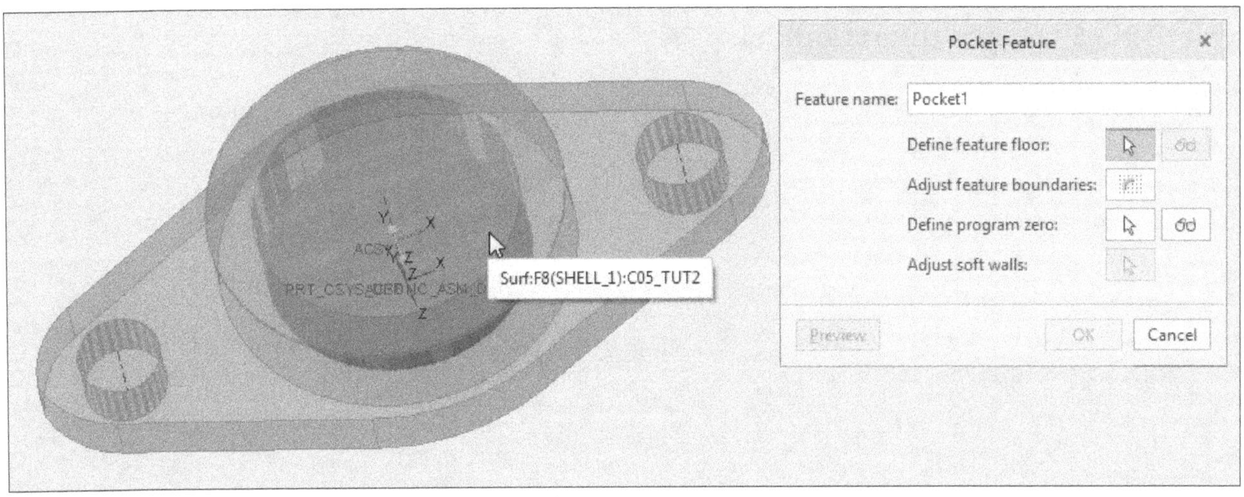

Figure-111. Selection of face for pocket feature

- Press the middle mouse button twice. Preview of the pocket feature will be displayed.
- Click on the **OK** button from the dialog box to create the feature.
- Click on the **Material Removal Display** button from **Ribbon** to check current preview of the specific feature.

Hole Group

- Click on **Hole Group** tool from the **NC Features & Machining** tab of the **Ribbon**. The **Drill Group** dialog box will be displayed.
- Click on **Add** button from the dialog box. You are allowed to select faces to add their corresponding axes in the list.
- Press and hold the **CTRL** key and select faces of the holes; refer to Figure-112.

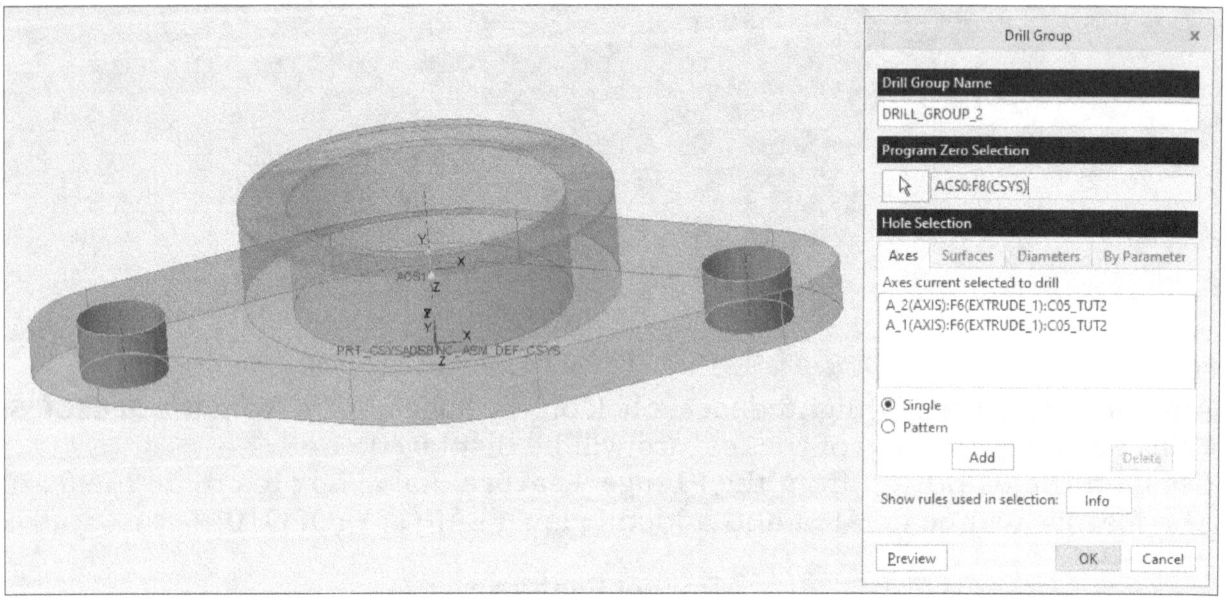

Figure-112. Selection for Hole Group feature

- Press the middle mouse button, axes will be added in the **Axes current selected to drill** list box.
- Click on the **OK** button from the dialog box. The feature will be created and the material would be removed.

Press **CTRL+S** to save the nc model.

PROBLEM 1

In this problem, you will import a reference model as shown in Figure-113 & Figure-114 and you will create a workpiece having uniform thickness of 2 over the reference model. Then you will create a machine setup including the required tools for various operations on the workpiece. Then you will create all the required nc features. The model file for reference model is available in the Resources kit.

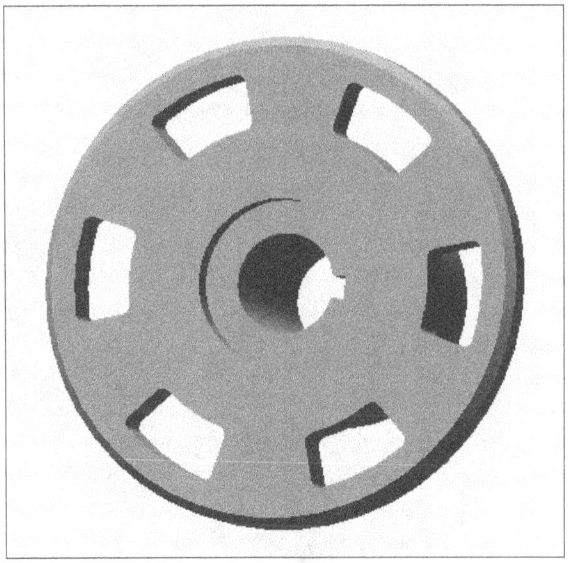

Figure-113. Isometric view of the model

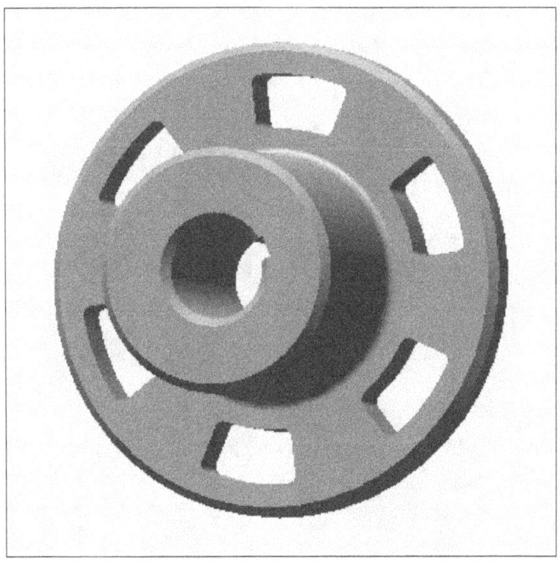

Figure-114. Reverse side view of the model

Problem 2

In this problem, you will import a reference model as shown in Figure-115 & Figure-116. Then you will create a machine setup including the required tools for various operations on the workpiece. Then you will create all the required nc features. The model file for reference model is available in the Resources kit.

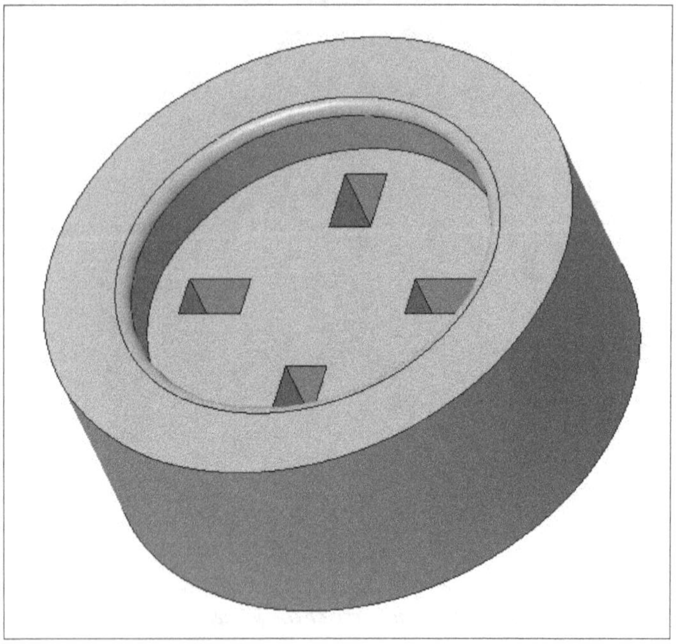

Figure-115. First view of Problem 2

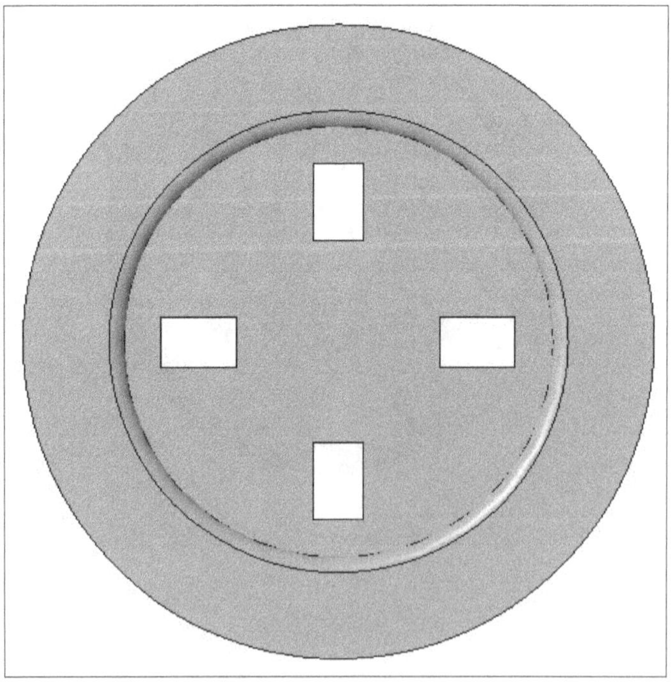

Figure-116. Second view of Problem 2

SELF-ASSESSMENT

Q1. What does the Operation tool in Creo Manufacturing allow you to create?

A. Surface Finishes
B. Toolpath Animations
C. Material Removal Process
D. Sketch Features

Q2. Which drop-down is used to specify the machine used for an operation?

A. Parameters
B. Work Center
C. Tool Setup
D. NC Features

Q3. What is stored using the Program Zero option in an operation?

A. Tool angle
B. Stock material
C. Output file path
D. Coordinate system zero position

Q4. What is the use of the Startup File in the Parameters tab?

A. To generate tool diameter
B. To launch interface
C. To include a CL file at the start of NC program
D. To define feature depth

Q5. What does the Use Rotary Clearance option enable in a 4-axis milling machine?

A. Reduced material waste
B. Safer clearance during table rotation
C. Faster tool movement
D. Automatic face selection

Q6. In the Fixture Setup tab, what must you select to add a fixture component?

A. Machining axis
B. Curve path
C. Assembly or part file
D. Toolpath animation

Q7. What button is used to calculate the estimated machining time in the Process tab?

A. Generate CL
B. Tool Simulation
C. Recalculate machining time
D. Activate NC

Q8. What does the Face operation primarily do?

A. Cuts holes
B. Drills bosses
C. Removes material from top surface
D. Adds finishing texture

Q9. Which option in the Face Feature dialog box is used to select the machining face?

A. Define feature floor
B. Adjust soft walls
C. Profile depth
D. Define toolpath curve

Q10. What does the Adjust Feature Bottom option allow you to change?

A. Face radius
B. Tool sharpness
C. Depth of cut
D. NC Sequence type

Q11. What is the primary function of the Step tool in Creo Manufacturing?

A. To create holes in the model
B. To create pins or boss features
C. To define soft walls
D. To machine a through slot

Q12. Which color represents hard walls in the Step Feature preview?

A. Green
B. Blue
C. Red
D. Cyan

Q13. What is the purpose of the Slot tool in NC Features & Machining panel?

A. To create through holes
B. To create flat faces
C. To create slots in the workpiece
D. To define NC sequences

Q14. What is the key difference between Slot and Through Slot features?

A. Slot is only for faces; Through Slot is for walls
B. Through Slot requires external CAM
C. Through Slot creates partial slots
D. Slot supports rib features

Q15. Which tool is used to create two or more intersecting slots?

A. Pocket
B. Flange
C. Channel
D. Ribtop

Q16. Which feature removes material to create a recessed shape bounded by hard walls?

A. Through Pocket
B. Ribtop
C. Step
D. Pocket

Q17. What distinguishes the Through Pocket tool from the Pocket tool?

A. Pocket is automatic; Through Pocket is manual
B. Through Pocket does not have a floor
C. Through Pocket is used for rib creation
D. Pocket only works with Channel tool

Q18. Which tool is best used to remove large areas of material from the face and avoid air machining?

A. Flange
B. Slot
C. Pocket
D. Bosstop

Q19. Which tool is designed to chamfer external sharp edges of the workpiece?

A. Ribtop
B. Top Round
C. Top Chamfer
D. Channel

Q20. The Bosstop tool is typically used after which of the following operations?

A. Channel and Ribtop
B. Pocket or Slab
C. Step or Slot
D. Chamfer or Round

Q21. What is the Bosstop tool used for in Creo Manufacturing?

A. To create holes in the model
B. To chamfer sharp edges
C. To machine the top face of a boss feature
D. To sketch a toolpath manually

Q22. After which operations is the Bosstop tool typically used?

A. Flange and Slab
B. Step Milling or Slot Milling
C. Face Milling or Pocket Milling
D. Ribtop or Freeform Milling

Q23. What does the Freeform tool in Creo allow you to do?

A. Drill at predefined coordinates
B. Create a cut along a custom sketched path
C. Engrave text
D. Create hard wall pockets

Q24. In Freeform Milling, how do you specify the cutting depth?

A. Only through the Sketch
B. From the Feature Manager
C. By selecting Z Depth or Plane
D. By entering values in Property Editor

Q25. What should the depth of cut value be to cut into the workpiece in Freeform?

A. Zero
B. Positive
C. Neutral
D. Negative

Q26. What is the primary function of the O-Ring tool?

A. To define rib walls
B. To machine circular grooves on the top face
C. To sketch a chamfer manually
D. To create through holes

Q27. What is the purpose of the Undercut tool?

A. Machine top edges
B. Chamfer sharp edges
C. Machine recessed areas with soft outer walls
D. Create internal ribs

Q28. Why is it necessary to convert outer walls to soft walls in Undercut?

A. To disable the tool path
B. To activate sketch mode
C. To allow tool access for undercut geometry
D. To convert hard walls into geometry

Chapter 6

Creating Toolpaths and Output

Topics Covered

The major topics covered in this chapter are:

- ***Generating Tool paths.***
- ***Various analysis that are performed on tool paths.***
- ***Checking for possible gouges.***
- ***Checking for tool clearances.***
- ***Mimicking a tool path.***
- ***Creating output file.***

TOOL PATHS

Tool path is an imitation of the path at which tool moves while cutting material from the workpiece. While doing a cutting operation, the tool does not move at random paths. Rather, it follows a specific path. In Creo Expert Machinist, there are various patterns (tool paths) that a tool follows while doing a specific operation. These patterns are applied by using the dialog boxes that are displayed while creating tool paths for various operations. For example, when you have created a face milling feature on the workpiece; then you are required to create a tool path for that feature. And, while creating a tool path for face milling feature; the options related to face milling are displayed in the related dialog box. In the previous chapter, we have created face milling feature and other such nc features. Here, we will generate tool paths for these features one by one.

Tool path for a Milling

Select a milling feature (like; **PROFILE1 [OP010]**) from the **Model Tree** displayed at the right in the modeling area and right-click on it. A shortcut menu will be displayed; refer to Figure-1.

- Click on the **Create Toolpath** option from the shortcut menu. The **Profile Milling** dialog box will be displayed as shown in Figure-2.

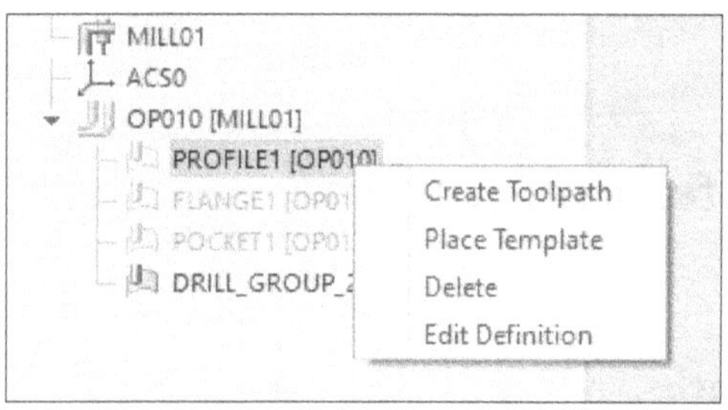

Figure-1. Shortcut menu for creating toolpath

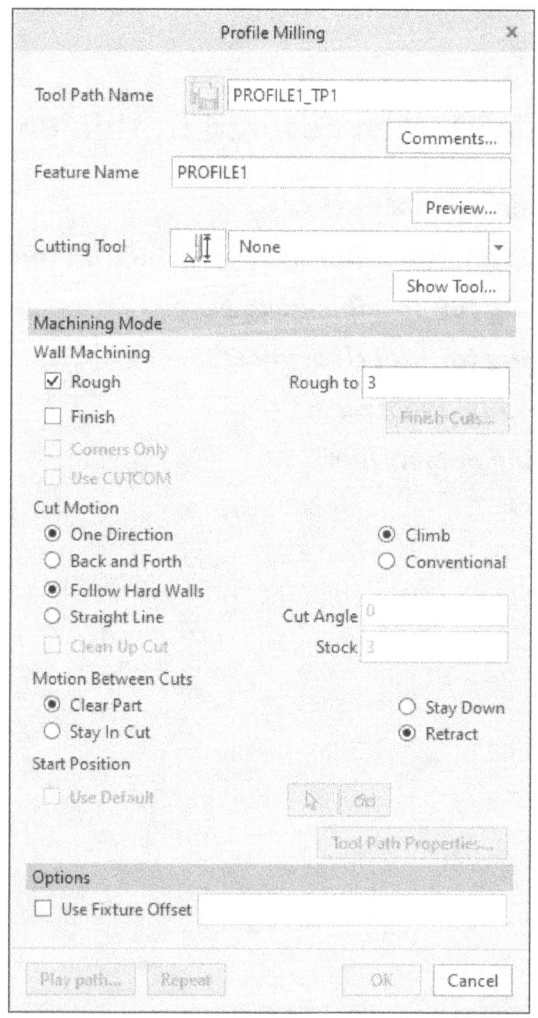

Figure-2. Profile Milling dialog box

Note

You can also generate tool path of an NC feature by using **Machining** *tool available at the right-most in the* **NC Features & Machining** *panel of the* **Machining** *tab in the* **Ribbon**. *On clicking this tool, the* **Select Feature** *list box is displayed. Select a feature from the list box and click on the* **OK** *button available below this list box. The related tool path generation dialog box will be displayed.*

- Click on the down arrow displayed adjacent to the **Cutting Tool** in the dialog box. The list of the tools created earlier will be displayed.
- Select an appropriate tool from the list and click on the **OK** button from the dialog box. The toolpath will be created with the name **feature name TPnumber** and will be listed below its NC feature in the **Model Tree**.
- Here, **feature name** is the name of feature for which you will be creating the tool path. **number** is the sequence number of the toolpath for current feature.

Note

The list displayed on clicking the down arrow of Cutting Tools is sorted and filters automatically depending on the feature for which you are creating the tool path. For example if you are creating tool path for creating undercut then the tools that are capable of under cutting will only be displayed in the list.

Figure-3 shows a tool path created and added below the Face NC feature.

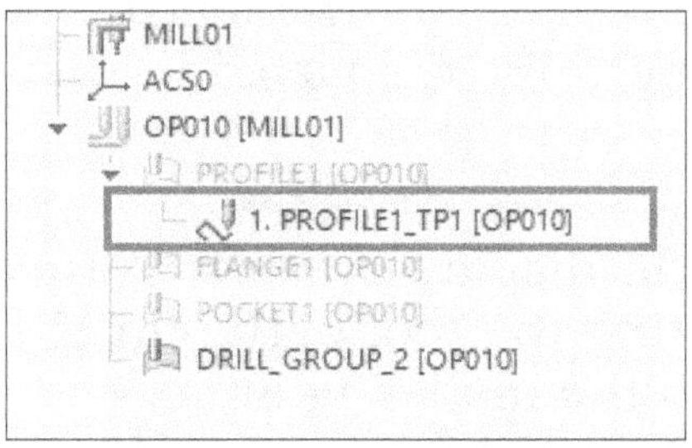

Figure-3. Toolpath created for Profile NC feature

Various options available in the **Profile Milling** dialog box and their effects are discussed next.

Tool Path Name

The **Tool Path Name** is an edit box used to specify name of the tool path by which it will be listed in the **Model Tree** and its output will be generated. The default pattern of the naming in this edit box is feature **name TPsequence number [Operation Number]**. You can specify any desired name in the edit box. But the maximum number of characters that can be specified are 32.

Comments

The **Comments** button is used to display a window in which you can write the comments related to the current cutting strategy (tool path). On clicking this button, the **Machine Strategy Comments** window will be displayed as shown in Figure-4.

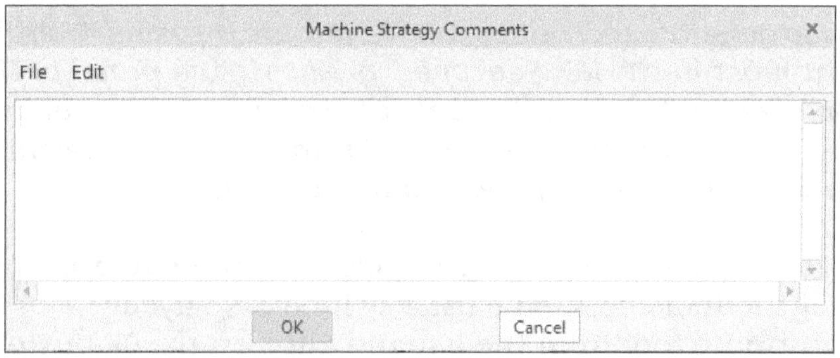

Figure-4. Machine Strategy Comments dialog box

- Write the comments related to the tool path in the text box of this window.
- You can open an already existing text file by using the **Open** button available in the **File** menu of this window.
- After writing the text, you can save it as a text file by using the **Save** or **SaveAs** button available in the **File** menu.
- Also, you can insert matter written in a text file by using the **Insert** button available in the **Edit** menu.
- After specifying the comments, click on the **OK** button available at the bottom of the window to apply the comment.

Feature Name

The **Feature Name** box displays name of the feature for which you are creating the tool path. You can not edit the value displayed in this box.

Preview

The **Preview** button is used to display preview of the NC feature (in the modeling area) for which you are creating the tool path. On clicking this button, the feature is highlighted in blue color in the modeling area.

Cutting Tool

This is an area having a button named **Access Tool Manager** and a drop-down having list of tools available in the machine setup.

- On clicking the **Access Tool Manager** button, the **Tools Setup** dialog box is displayed. This dialog box and its options have already been discussed in Chapter 3 (Tool Setting).
- You can either create new tool by using the options in the **Tools Setup** dialog box or you can select from the already existing tool available in the **Cutting Tool** drop-down of **Profile Milling** dialog box.

Show Tool

The **Show Tool** button is used to display preview of the tool selected from the list. On clicking this tool, a preview window is displayed having name of the tool as the title of the window; refer to Figure-5. You can zoom in/out and pan in this window by using the mouse gestures.

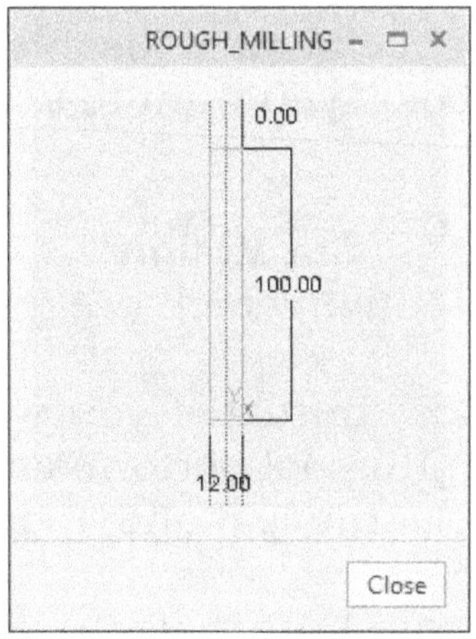

Figure-5. Preview window of tool

Machining Mode

There are four section available in this area. These options are used to specify the machining process. The sections available in this area are; **Wall machining**, **Cut Motion**, **Motion Between Cuts**, **Options**, and **Start Position**. Note that options in this area can change depending on the toolpath being created. These sections are discussed next.

Wall Machining

There are five options are available in this area which are discussed next.

- Select the **Rough** check box if you want to do roughing operation of the workpiece. The **Rough to** edit box becomes available. Enter the amount of stock to remain on the hard walls after roughing in the edit box. This edit box is discussed next.
- Select the **Finish** check box, if you want to do the finishing process on the workpiece. This is the cutting pass in which accuracy of the machine is achieved.
- Click on the **Finish Cuts** button if you want to specify the multiple cuts at multiple offsets from the hard walls. On clicking this button, the **Finish Cuts** dialog box will be displayed; refer to Figure-6. This dialog box is used to specify the number of passes that will be required to do finishing on the workpiece. You can also set depth for each cutting pass on walls as well as floors. After setting desired parameters, click on the **OK** button from the dialog box.

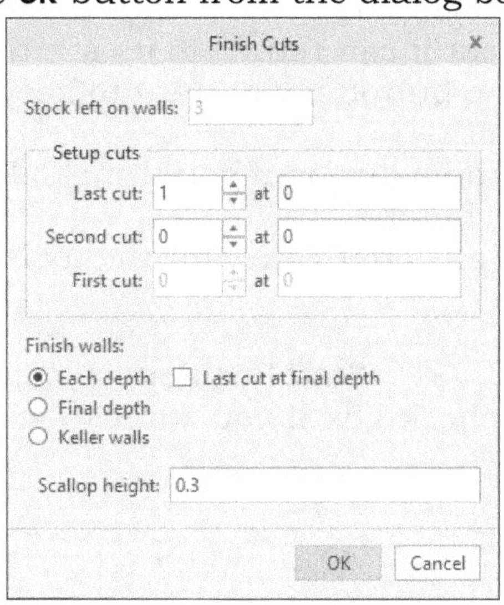

Figure-6. Finish Cuts dialog box

- Select the **Corners only** check box to remove the material only from the corners of a model. In our case, this check box is disabled.
- Select the **Use CUTCOM** check box if you want to use cutter diameter compensation for this tool path.

Cut Motion

There are many options in this section which are discussed next.

- Select the **One Direction** radio button if you want to cut the material in only one direction. Note that when the tool performs a cutting operation then the tool moves upward i.e. up to the clearance plane; moves to the starting line and then again does the next cutting pass.
- Select the **Back and Forth** radio button if you want to cut the material in both the motions of tool i.e. Forward motion as well as the reverting back of tool to its starting line.
- Select the **Climb** radio button if you want to cut the material using the climb cutting motion. The tool rotates in Counter Clockwise direction with respect to stock material. This radio button is active when **One Direction** check box is selected.
- Select the **Conventional** check box if you want to cut the material in the conventional manner i.e. the tool rotates clockwise with respect to the stock material. This radio button is active when **One Direction** check box is selected.
- Select the **Follow Hard Walls** check box if you want that each cut will follow the contour of the hard walls of the feature.
- Select the **Straight Line** check box if you want to cut the model in straight line cuts.
- Click in the **Cut Angle** edit box and specify the value of cut.
- Select the **Clean Up Cut** check box if you want to clean the scallops using the straight line cuts.
- Click in the **Stock** edit box and specify additional value to clean up the cuts around scallops.

Motion Between cuts

There are four options in this section which are discussed next.

- Select the **Clear Part** radio button if you want to move the tool upwards in a non-cutting pass. Selecting this radio button makes the tool away from the workpiece in upward direction so that it can return to its starting line at rapid speed.
- Select the **Stay Down** radio button if you want to keep the tool at cut depth while connecting to the cut depth.
- Select the **Stay In Cut** radio button if you want to keep the tool engaged in the material at the end of each cut.
- Select the **Retract** radio button if you want the tool to retract before connecting to the next cut.

Start Position

- Select the **Use Default** check box if you want to start the cutting from default zero position.

Tool Path Properties

The **Tool Path Properties** button is used to specify various properties related to the tool path. On clicking this button, the **Tool Path Properties** dialog box will be displayed as shown in Figure-7. The dialog box with its options will be discussed later in this chapter.

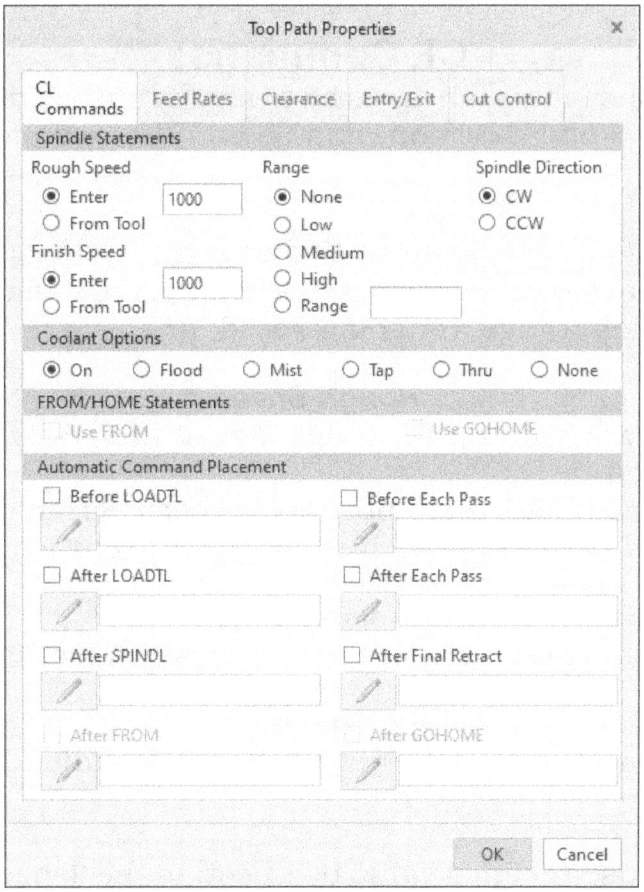

Figure-7. Tool Path Properties dialog box

Options

- Select the **Use Fixture Offset** check box if you want to add offset to the original tool path because of a fixture installed on the machine. This fixture can be used for workpiece as well as for the tool.

After specifying various parameters, click on the **OK** button from the dialog box to create the tool path and add it to its NC feature in the **Model Tree**.

- Click on the **Cancel** button to cancel the operation. You can create tool path of the feature similar to the current feature in the **Model Tree** by choosing the **Next** button.
- The **Play Path** button is used to display simulation of tool and workpiece while tool moves on the tool path being created. This button will be discussed later in this chapter.

TOOL PATH PROPERTIES

The **Tool Path Properties** dialog box is displayed on clicking the **Tool Path Properties** button from the Face Milling, Profile Milling, or any other toolpath generation dialog box. There are five tabs in this dialog box; **CL Commands**, **Feed Rates**, **Clearance**, **Entry/Exit**, and **Cut Control**. These tabs and their options are discussed next.

CL Commands

The **CL Commands** options in this tab are used to modify entries related to CL commands like spindle speed, rotation direction, and so on. The options in this tab and their effects are discussed next.

Spindle Statements

The **Spindle Statements** section is used to set values of variables related to spindle like direction of rotation, range, roughing speed, and so on.

Rough Speed

- Select the **Enter** radio button for **Rough Speed** to specify the value in RPM for rough cutting speed.
- If you select the **From Tool** radio button for **Rough Speed** then the cutting speed will be assumed as the speed specified for the current tool.

Finish Speed

The options for **Finish Speed** work in the same way as for **Rough Speed**.

Range

There are five radio buttons available to specify the spindle RPM range in which the spindle speed can vary.

- You can specify a user defined value by selecting the **Range** radio button. An edit box adjacent to the radio button will become active where you can specify the value of range.

Spindle Direction

There are two radio buttons to specify direction in which the spindle will rotate.

- You can rotate the spindle either clockwise direction **(CW)** or in counter clockwise direction **(CCW)** by selecting the respective radio button.

Coolant Options

There are six radio buttons available in this section which are discussed next.

- Select the **ON** radio button if you want the coolant to flow in the normal mode i.e. through the pipes aimed at the workpiece directly.
- Select the **Flood** radio button if you want the coolant to flow at high speed through all the vents made for coolant in the working area.
- Select the **Mist** radio button if you want to create the mist of coolant in working area.
- Select the **Tap** radio button if you want the coolant to flow through the tool vents. This radio button is selected while doing a tapping cycle.

- Select the **Thru** radio button if you want the coolant to pass through the tool as well as through the coolant pipes.
- Select the **None** radio button if you do not want the coolant to flow on the workpiece.

FROM/HOME Statements

There are two check boxes in this section which are discussed below.

- Select the **Use FROM** check box if you want to manually add some CL commands with the **FROM** statement in the output.
- Select the **Use GOHOME** check box if you want to manually add some CL commands with **GOHOME** statement.

On selecting the check boxes, the respective options in the **Automatic Command Placement** area will become active.

Automatic Command Placement

The options in this section are used to customize CL output automatically.

- Select any of the check box in this area and then you can specify the user-defined CL commands before or after the command corresponding to the selected check box. For example, if you want to stop the coolant before loading a tool then select the **Before LOADTL** check box and then specify the command in the corresponding edit box.
- If you do not remember to the command then select the edit  button. The **CL Command** dialog box will be displayed; refer to Figure-8.

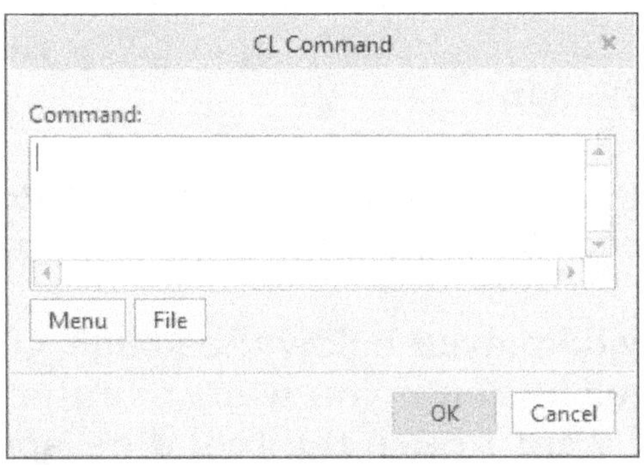

Figure-8. CL Command dialog box

- Now, either you can use an already existing CL file by using the **File** button in the dialog box or you can use the menu containing all the CL codes. Click on the **Menu** button to display the **cmd edit Menu Manager**; refer to Figure-9.

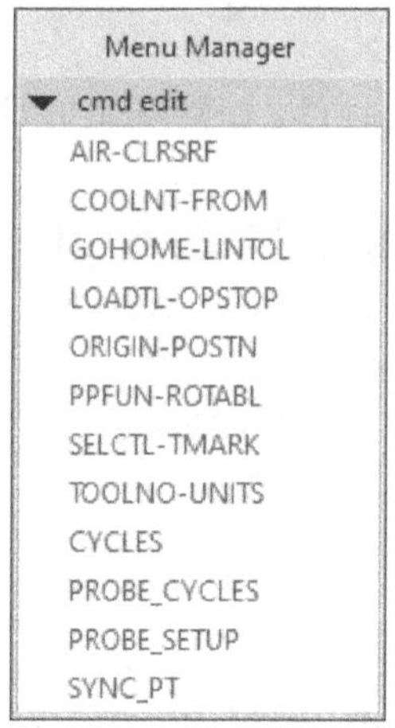

Figure-9. cmd edit Menu Manager

- Click on the **COOLNT-FROM** option then **COOLNT** option and then **OFF** option from the **Menu Manager**. The command will be added in the **CL Command** dialog box.
- Click on the **OK** button from the dialog box. The command will be added before **LOADTL** command in the CL output.

Feed Rates

The options in the **Feed Rates** tab are used to specify feed rates for various operations being performed on the workpiece like positioning, retract, rough cutting, side entry, and so on. Some of the options will not be available because of the operation selected. For example, for Facing operation, the positioning options will not be available. You can set the value of feed rate for operation by using the two methods; either by specifying the value in edit box or by using the data specified for the current tool. The method of setting feed rate for Roughing is given next. The method for setting feed rate for other will be the same.

- Select the unit in which you want to specify the feed rate by selecting corresponding radio button from the **Feed Units** section of the tab. In this case, we will use **MMPM** radio button.
- Click on the down arrow displayed below the **Rough Cutting**. A list of options will be displayed. Select **Enter** option if you want to enter a value manually or select **From Tool** option if you want to use the tool data specified for the current tool. In our case, we will select the **Enter** option.
- On selecting the **Enter** option, the edit box adjacent to the drop-down will be active. Specify desired value of feed in the edit box.

Clearance

The options in the **Clearance** tab are used to specify clearance distance between the workpiece and the tool while doing specific cutting passes displayed in this tab. You can specify the clearance distance for following cutting passes in the dialog box:

- **Initial Approach**
- **Final Withdrawal**
- **Between Cuts**
- **Between Passes**

There are five ways for specifying clearance distance for each of the above cutting pass. These ways are discussed next.

Along Z-Axis

Select the **Along Z-Axis** radio button if you want to specify the clearance distance for the selected cutting pass along the Z-axis. On selecting this radio button, the edit box adjacent to the selected radio button will become active. Now, specify desired value in the edit box. The distance specified will be calculated from the Coordinate System selected for the Operation.

Clear Workpiece

Select the **Clear Workpiece** radio button if you want to specify clearance from the outermost face layer of the workpiece. The clearance distance specified in the adjacent edit box will be calculated along the Z direction from the top face of the workpiece.

Clear Feature

Select the **Clear Feature** radio button if you want to specify the clearance from the reference model. Note that in this case also, the direction will be along the Z direction.

Go Delta

Select the **Go Delta** radio button if you want to specify the distance value from the last cut tool path. The direction here will also be along the Z direction.

None

Select the **None** radio button if you do not want to specify the clearance distance. Note that this radio button is not available for the clearance specified for **Between Cuts**. For **Between Cuts**, you must have to specify the clearance value.

Indepth

The values specified for clearance play very important role in the machine output. The wrong values specified in these edit boxes can restrict the tool path creation by this software and you might get the error as **Check Setup** in the information bar displayed below in the application window. In some cases, it may cause an accident in the real time machining if the user ignores these values. So, this is recommended that you take extra care when specifying values in the edit boxes of the **Clearance** tab.

Entry/Exit

The options in the **Entry/Exit** tab are used to specify the options related to entry and exit of the tool for each cutting step. There are three areas in this dialog box; Setup Landing/Lift, Finish Cuts, and Side clearance. The options of these areas are discussed next.

Setup Landing/Lift

There are two categories available in this section i.e. **Soft Landing** and **Soft Lift**.

- Select desired radio buttons for the **Soft Landing** and **Soft Lift**.
- There are three radio buttons for each of the categories in the dialog box; **Automatic**, **Always**, and **Never**.

- If you select the **Automatic** radio button then the soft lift and landing will automatically be applied on the tool path.
- Select the **Always** radio button if you want to specify the value for landing and lift distance manually for the tool path. On selecting this radio button, the corresponding edit box will become active automatically. The specified value will be according to the unit system selected.
- Select the **Never** radio button if you do not want to specify the landing/lift in the tool path.

Finish Cuts

There are two categories available in this section; Arc Entry and Arc Exit to define movement of cutting tool for finishing passes at the entry of tool at arc and exit of tool at the end of arc.

- Select the **All Finish Passes** radio button if you want to apply arc entry/exit parameters for finish cutting passes.
- Select the **Net Finish Passes** radio button if you want to apply arc entry/exit parameters for final finish cutting passes.
- Select the **Do not use** radio button if you do not want to apply circular entries to finish passes.
- If you have selected the **All Finish Passes** radio button and **Net Finish Passes** radio button then options to define arc swing, radius, and blend overlap will be displayed. The value selected in **Arc Swing** drop-down defines the length of arc in degrees. The value specified in **Radius** edit box defines radius of arc. The value specified in **Blend Overlap** edit box defines extra length of arc to be added at the start/end of circular finishing passes.

Side clearance

There is one edit box available in this area. Specify the value of side clearance (distance from hard walls) in the edit box.

Cut Control

The options in the **Cut Control** tab are used to specify parameters for the cut. The options in this tab are discussed next.

Maximum Cut

The options in this section are used to specify depth of cut or step over limit for the cuts. There are two options in this area; **Depth of Cut** and **Stepover**. You can specify the depth of cut for each cutting pass by using the **Depth of Cut** options. This is the vertical distance between one cutting pass and its successive cutting pass. The **Stepover** option is used to specify horizontal distance between one cutting pass and its successive cutting pass.

Indepth

The step over value is used at the same cutting plane and the depth of cut is the vertical distance between such two cutting planes; refer to Figure-10.

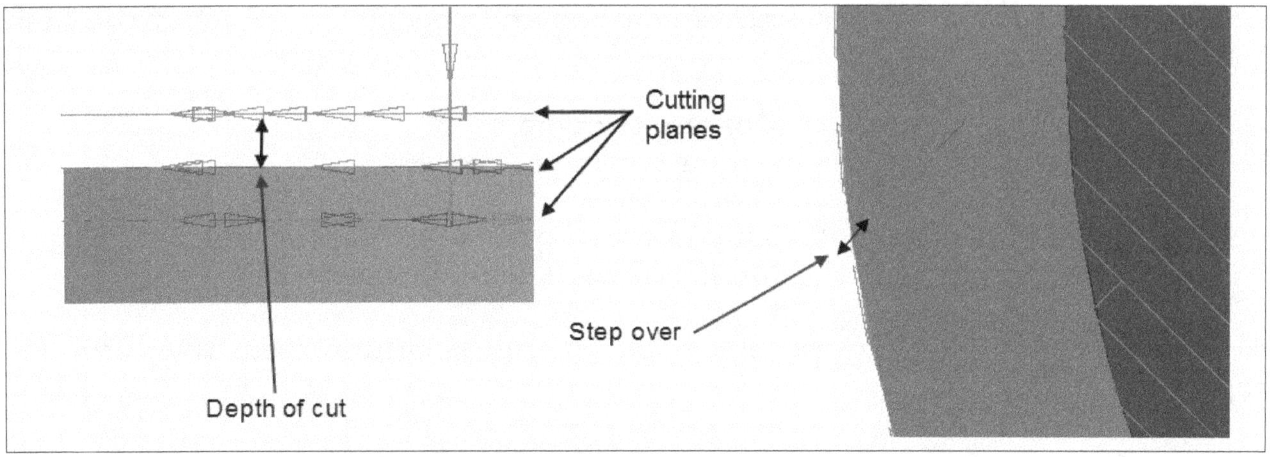

Figure-10. Stepover value and Depth of Cut value

CUTCOM Control

The options of **CUTCOM Control** section is active when **Use CUTCOM** check box is selected in the **Profile Milling** dialog box.

- Click in the **Register** edit box and enter the number of machine offset register to be used for tool path.
- Click on the **On/Off Move** edit box and enter the length of linear move during which **CUTCOM** will be invoked and cancel for this tool path.
- Select the **Perpendicular** radio button if you want the linear move to be perpendicular to the following move of the tool path.
- Select the **Tangent** radio button if you want the linear move to be tangent to the following move of the tool path.
- Select the **Allow Z Moves** check box to allow straight vertical moves in the toolpath.

Options

There are various options in this section which are discussed next.

- Click in the **Tolerance** edit box and specify the value for tolerance.

Stay in Cut

The options in this area are used to specify the extent up to which the tool will remain engaged with the material while cutting.

- Select the **On** option from the **Tool Center** drop-down if you want to move the tool away from the workpiece when the center of the tool is exactly on the edge of soft wall.
- Select the **To** option from the drop-down if you want to move the tool away from the edge to specified distance value from the edge of soft wall. The distance value can be specified in the edit box available below this drop-down.
- If you select the **Past** option from the drop-down list then tool will cross specified distance from the edge of soft wall and then will move away.

Circle Moves

- Select the **Points Only** radio button if you do not want to use CL file output in circular interpolation. It uses the points only for output.
- Select the **Arc Only** radio button if you want to use output circle statement and number of points for arc in CL data.

- Click in the **Number of Arc Points** edit box and specify the value for the points of arc.

Corners condition

The options of this section are used for cutting in corners.

- Select the **Fillet** radio button if you want to make corners round.
- Select the **Straight** radio button if you want to make corners straight.

After specifying various parameters, click on the **OK** button from the **Tool Path Properties** dialog box.

TOOL PATH PLAYER

The **Tool Path Player** tool is available in the **Output** panel in **Ribbon**. This tool is used to simulate the cutter running on the tool path. This tool is active only when you select an operation or a tool path from the **Model Tree**. The procedure to use this tool is discussed next.

- Click on the **Tool Path Player** tool from the **Ribbon**. The system will process all the information provided by you in various relevant dialog boxes and after the completion of process, the **PLAY PATH** dialog box will be displayed with the preview of tool in the Modeling area; refer to Figure-11.

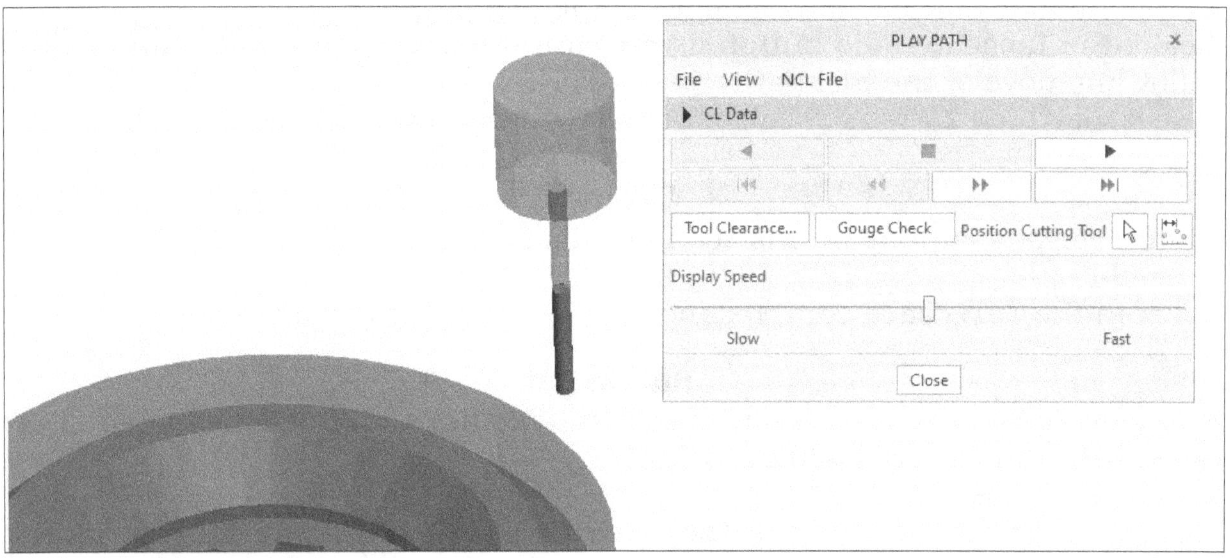

Figure-11. PLAY PATH dialog box with the preview of tool

- Click on the **Play Forward**  button from the dialog box to play the simulation of the tool. The system will start simulation of tool path.

The options available in this dialog box are discussed next.

File Menu

The options in the **File** menu are related to file handling i.e. opening file, saving file, and so on. Using the **Save as MCD** option from this menu, you can save the CL (Cutter Location) file as MCD (Machine Control Data) file. An MCD file includes the data related to Post Processor and various checks that can be performed on the CL file.

View Menu

The options in **View** menu are more related to analysis of tool path. Various options available in this menu are discussed next.

Wireframe

The **Wireframe** option is selected by default. As a result, the tool path is displayed in the form of wireframe i.e. in red colored lines in this case. This option is inactive in the menu as you cannot deselect this option until you select any alternate option.

NC Check

The **NC Check** option is selected when the tool path is to be simulated on a machine. To activate it, click on the **NC Check** option from the **View** menu.

Show Remaining Material

The **Show Remaining Material** option is used to perform material analysis. In some cases, a specific type of tool is not able to cut material from the workpiece. This option generally available when performing turning process. Note that this process is not available for Expert Machinist.

Display Tool

The **Display Tool** option is selected when you want to display the tool.

Display Tool Tip

The **Display Tool Tip** option is selected when you want to display the trajectory of the tool tip while removing material for the current operation.

Display Tool Kerf

The **Display Tool Kerf** option is selected when you want to display the impression of perimeter of tool while removing material from the workpiece.

Display Cycles

The **Display Cycles** option is active only for holemaking NC sequences and Thread Turning. This option is selected when you want to include all the tool motions of the CYCLE command or thread cycle in the simulation.

Shaded Tool

The **Shaded Tool** option is selected when you want to display the tool in shaded style. If you deselect this option then the tool will be displayed as wireframe model.

Collision Checking

The **Collision Checking** option is available for the complete assembly of machine and fixtures. If you have selected this option then the volume that is interfering with the machine or fixture setup will be displayed in red color. Note that the collision between tool and workpiece can not be displayed using this option.

Stop at Collision

The **Stop at Collision** option if selected, will force the tool to stop while simulating tool path as soon as the tool collides with interfering objects.

NCL File Menu

The options in the **NCL File** menu are used to operate and edit Numeric Cutter Location (NCL) file. Using the options in this menu, you can control the path of tool simulation by following the CL file. You can insert a user defined command in the current CL file and check its simulation.

CL Data

This node is selected when you want to check the CL file while simulating the tool path. To display the CL data, click on the **CL Data** node displayed below the menu bar. On selecting this node, the node expands and the CL Data file is displayed; refer to Figure-12.

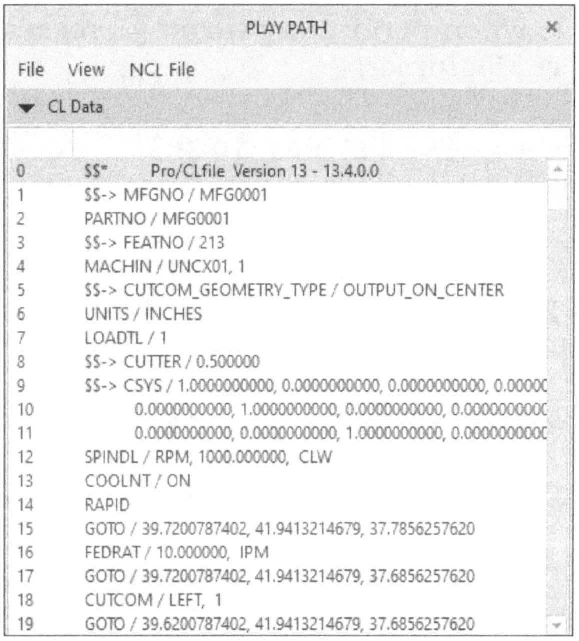

Figure-12. PLAY PATH dialog box with expanded CL Data node

Below the **CL Data** area, there are various buttons to perform the operations like starting, stopping, forwarding, and so on. These buttons are standard options to play simulations. The slider displayed below the buttons is used to increase or decrease the speed of slider. Other buttons and options are discussed next.

Tool Clearance

The **Tool Clearance** button is used to check the tool clearance while the tool follows the tool path. On selecting this button, the **MEASURE Menu Manager** is displayed; refer to Figure-13.

Figure-13. MEASURE Menu Manager

The options in this **Menu Manager** are similar to the tools available in the **Measure** drop-down of **Measure** panel in the **Analysis** tab of the **Ribbon**. The result of measurement will be displayed in the **Information Bar** available below the modeling area.

Gouge Check

The **Gouge Check** button is used to check clearance and other parameters of tool path by using the gouge.

- Click on the **Gouge Check** button from the **PLAY PATH** dialog box. The **MFG CHECK Menu Manager** will be displayed.
- Select the surface for which you want to perform gouge check. Press the middle mouse button three times to exit the selection process.
- On doing so, the **GOUGE CHECK Menu Manager** is displayed; refer to Figure-14.

Figure-14. GOUGE CHECK Menu Manager

- Select desired options to specify related parameters for the gouge check and then click on the **Run** option from the **Menu Manager** to perform the check. Make sure that you have already setup a probe for gouge check.

Position Cutting Tool

This option is available at the right of the **Gouge Check** button. By selecting this option, you can position the tool at any specific point on the tool path. The procedure to use this tool is discussed next.

- Click on this option and then click on the position where you want to place the tool. On doing so, the tool will be placed at the specified point and the cutting step corresponding to the selected point will be highlighted in the CL Data.

Similarly, you can use the **Measure Distance** button in the dialog box to measure distance between two points on the toolpath. Till this point, we have simulated the tool path and checked for any error in the tool path. If the tool path is acceptable, then we are ready to generate the output file of the tool path so that the machine can work on it. The next topic discusses about generating the output files.

GENERATING OUTPUT FILES

There are two options in Creo Expert Machinist to generate the output files. You can generate output as cutter location data or you can create a post processed output file directly feed able to the machine. Both the methods are discussed next.

Generating Cutter Location Data

To generate cutter location data, select the tool path from the **Model Tree** and then click on the **Create CL File** tool from **Output** panel in the **Machining** tab of the **Ribbon**. On doing so, the **Save a Copy** dialog box will be displayed; refer to Figure-15. Specify the name of the file in the dialog box and then click on **OK** button from the dialog box to save the file. The file will be saved with an extension ***.ncl***. You can preview the file in any word processor. Figure-16 shows a cutter location data file in WordPad application of Microsoft Windows.

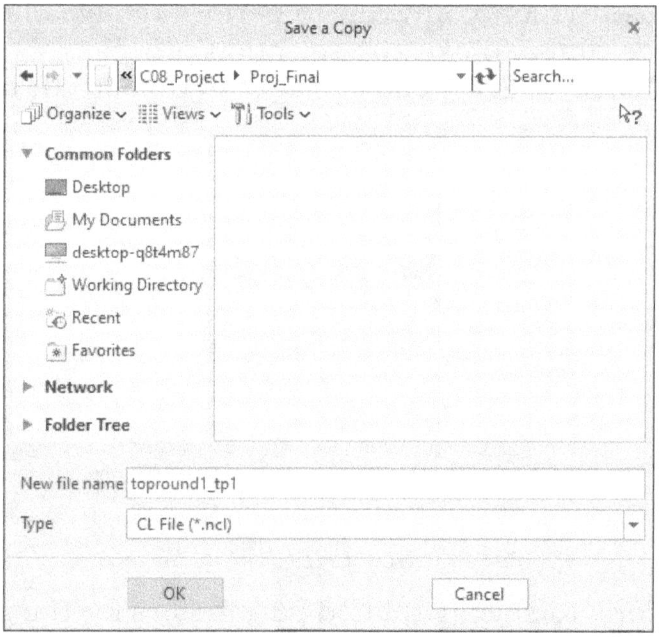

Figure-15. Save a Copy dialog box

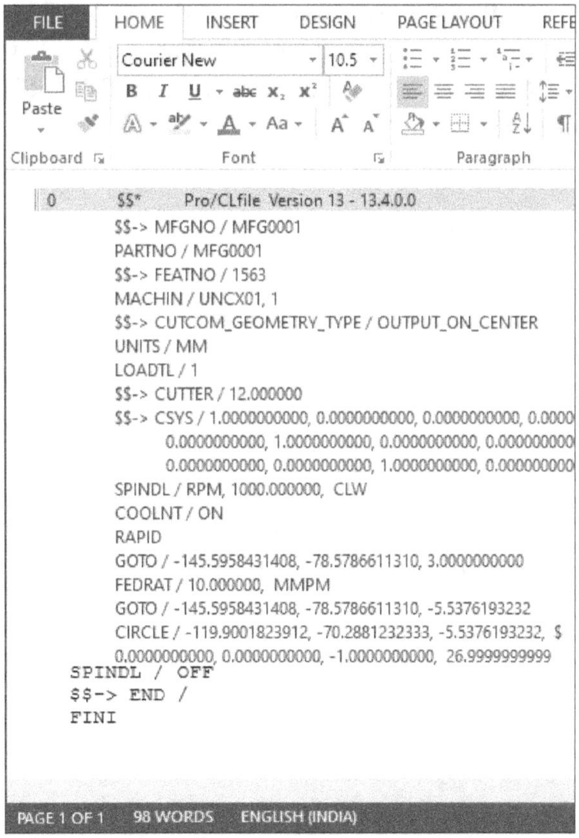

Figure-16. A cutter location data file opened in Microsoft WordPad

Here you can edit the file and then using any nc post processer application, you can generate the output file. The files that machines read are of ***.tap*** extension.

Generating post processed output file

Using this method, you can directly create the output file for the machine. The procedure to use this tool is discussed next.

- Click on the down arrow button adjacent in the **Output** panel of the **Machining** tab in the **Ribbon**.
- There are two tools available in this list i.e. **Automatic** and **Select Post**; refer to Figure-17.

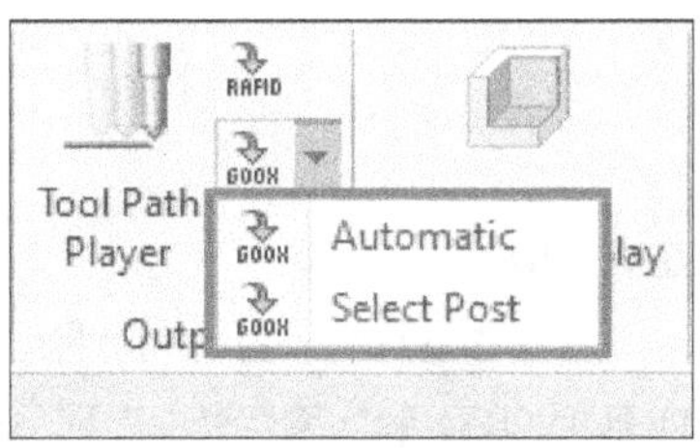

Figure-17. Tools for output

- On selecting the **Automatic** tool, the **Save a Copy** dialog box will be displayed and you are asked to save the cutter location file first. Click on the **OK** button from the dialog box and the output file with ***.tap*** extension will be saved in the same directory. Note that the post processor used for generating output will be the one specified while setting the machine in Machine Setup. This has been discussed earlier in chapter 4.

- On selecting the **Select Post** tool from the list, the **Save a Copy** dialog box is displayed and you are asked to save the CL file first. Save the file by clicking on the **OK** button. As soon as you save the file, the **POST PROCESSOR LIST (PP LIST) Menu Manager** is displayed; refer to Figure-18.

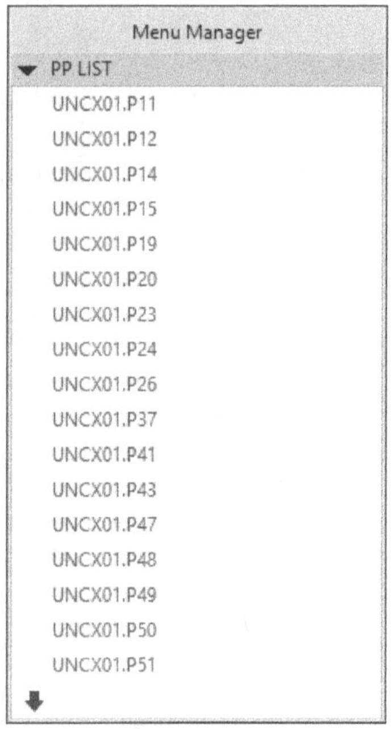

Figure-18. PP LIST Menu Manager

- Select a post processor of your choice from the list, an **INFORMATION WINDOW** with the information related to the output will be displayed; refer to Figure-19.

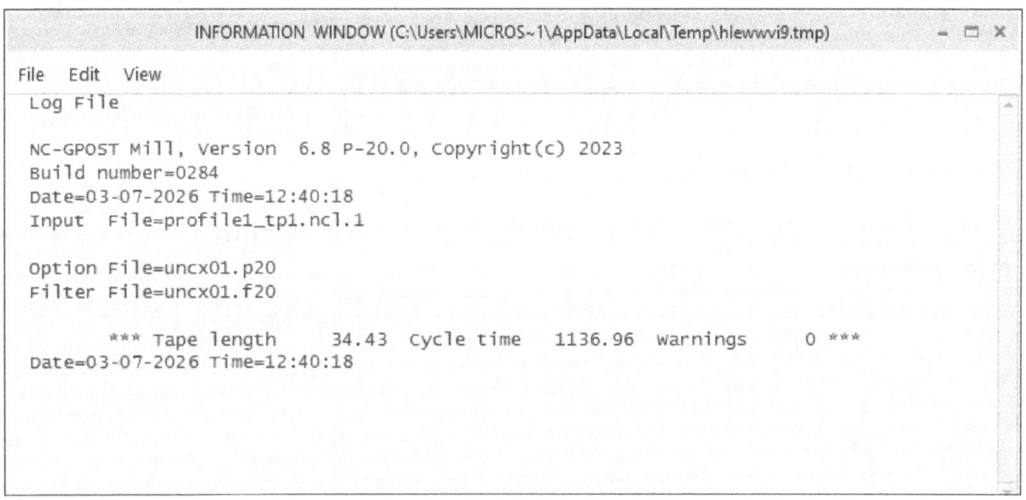

Figure-19. INFORMATION WINDOW

- Click on the **Close** button after reading the information and then open the file saved with ***.tap*** extension in a word processor to see the output of the tool path. Figure-20 shows the output of a tool path opened in WordPad application.

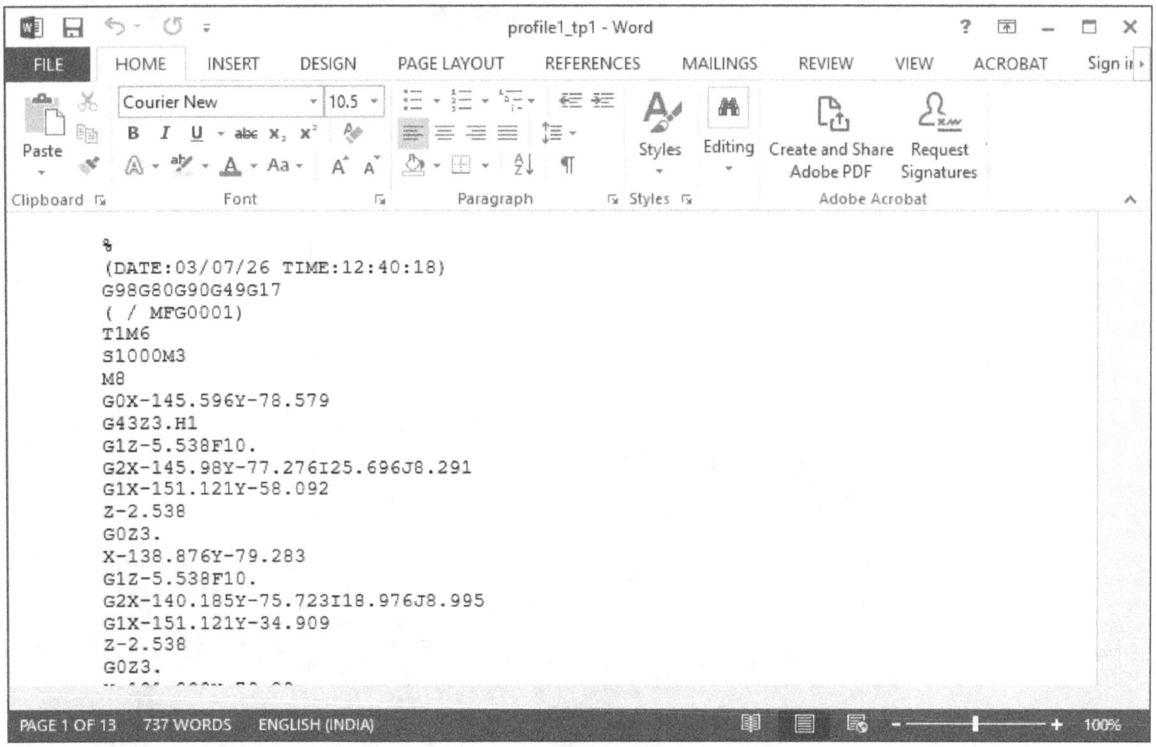

Figure-20. An output file with .tap extension opened in WordPad

Now, you can edit the file and then feed it to the machine to get the machining output.

> **Till this point, we have covered the generation of output after specifying all the parameters whether it is related to machine, workpiece, tool geometry, operation setting, or tool path. This is the point where I want the users of this book, to go back to previous chapters and then check the final output of same operation by using different settings applied in Machine Setup and Tool Setup. This will give an idea about, how the settings affect the output. For example, if we change the origin of operation; will the coordinates in output file be the same?**

You have used a post processor available by default in Expert Machinist. Now, is it sure that it will work for your machine? In many cases, the answer will be **No**. So, we need to create a post processor which is suitable for your machine.

Creating a post processor is a cumbersome job but we can modify a post processor in such a way that it understand the requirements of your machine. This is done by using the Option file. An Option file contains data related to the machine which will be used by Post Processor for generating output. To create an Option file for Expert Machinist, there is a separate App in Creo called **NC Post Processor**. To access this App, click on the **Applications** tab in the **Ribbon**; refer to Figure-21. All the manufacturing applications will be displayed in the **Ribbon**. Select the **NC Post Processor** button, a separate application will open named **Option File Generator**; refer to Figure-22.

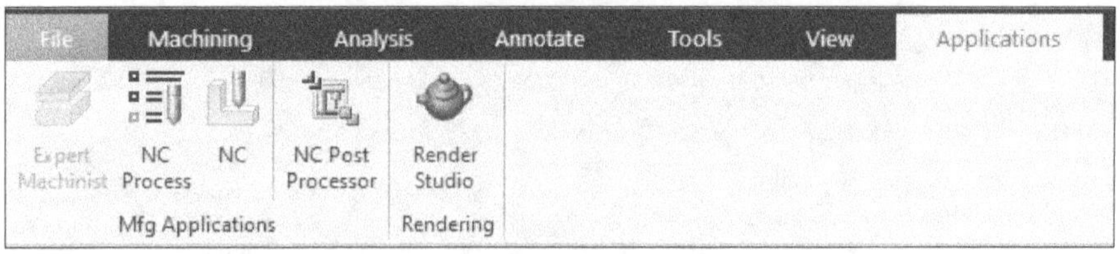

Figure-21. Applications tab with the Apps related to Manufacturing

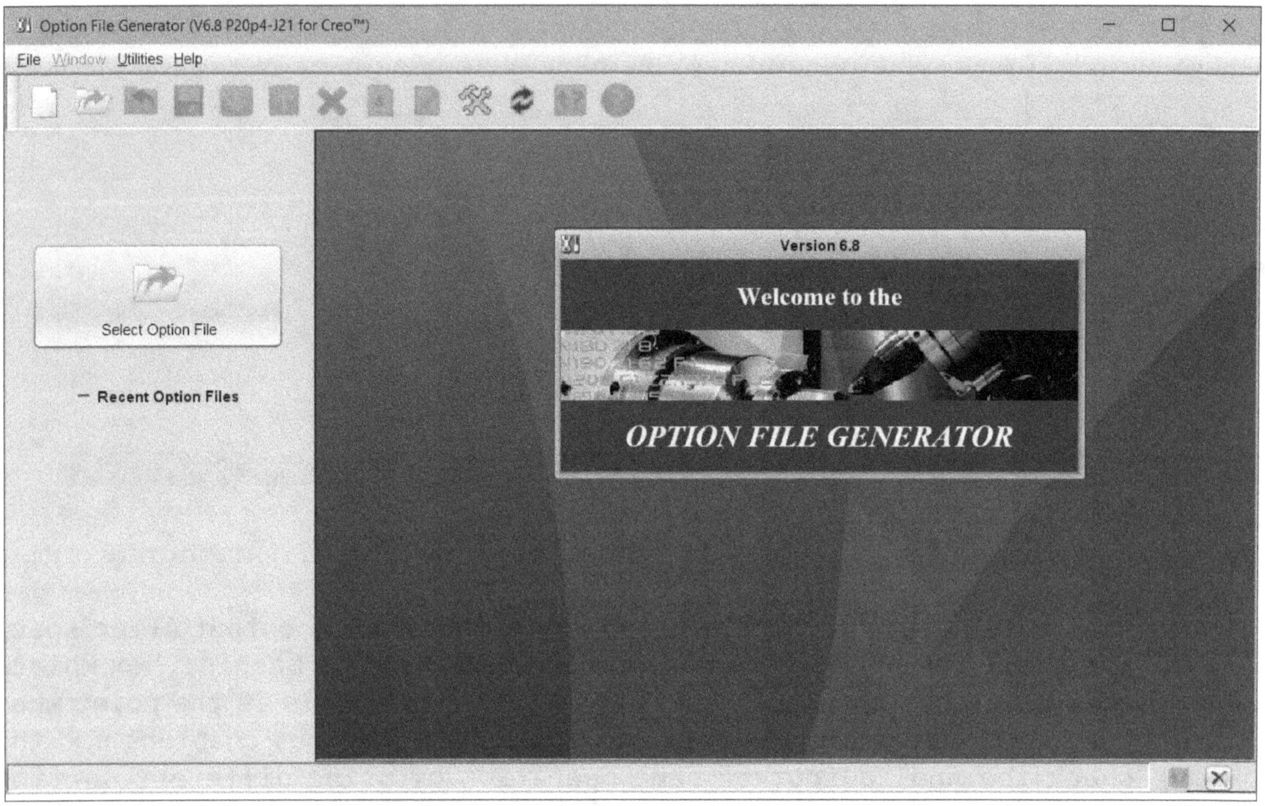

Figure-22. Option File Generator application

The options and their uses will be discussed later in this book.

TUTORIAL

In this tutorial, we will open the file created in Tutorial of Chapter 5. Now, we will create tool path and then the output file for this tutorial; refer to Figure-23 and Figure-24.

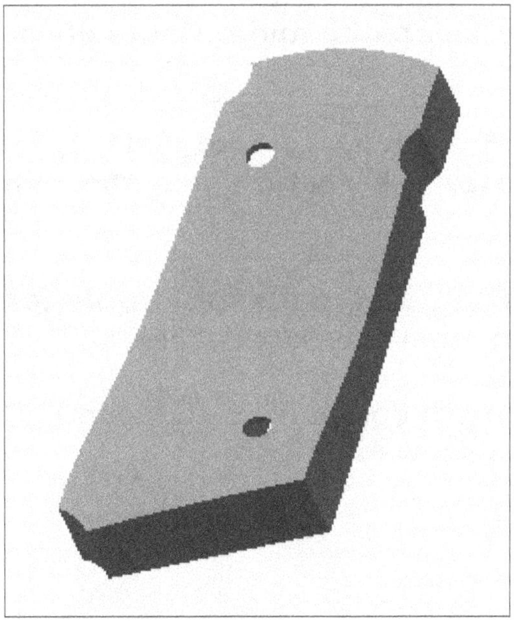

Figure-23. Model for Tutorial

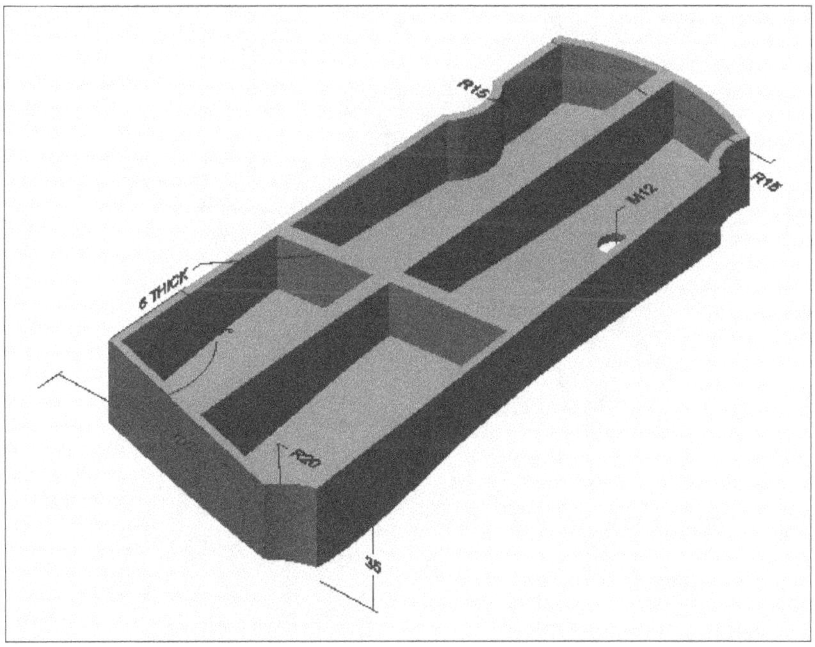

Figure-24. Backside of the model

Copying and Opening the tutorial file

- Copy the manufacturing assembly files created in Tutorial of Chapter 5.
- Create a new folder with the name **C06** and paste the files in this folder.
- Start Creo Parametric and open the **c05 tut1.asm** assembly file by using **Open** tool of the **Ribbon**.
- By default, Manufacturing app of Creo will open. Now, click on the **Applications** tab in the **Ribbon** and select the **Expert Machinist** button from the **Ribbon**; the file will open in Expert Machinist App.

In this file, we have created various NC features along with their respective operations. Now, we will generate the tool paths and outputs of each operation consisting of various nc features.

Note that in this tutorial, tool path creation and output will be explained for only one feature and the rest work is to be done by you.

Creating Tool path for Profile feature

- Select **PROFILE1[OP010]** from the **Model Tree** and right-click on it, a shortcut menu will be displayed.
- Select the **Create Toolpath** option from the menu. The **Profile Milling** dialog box will be displayed as shown in Figure-25.

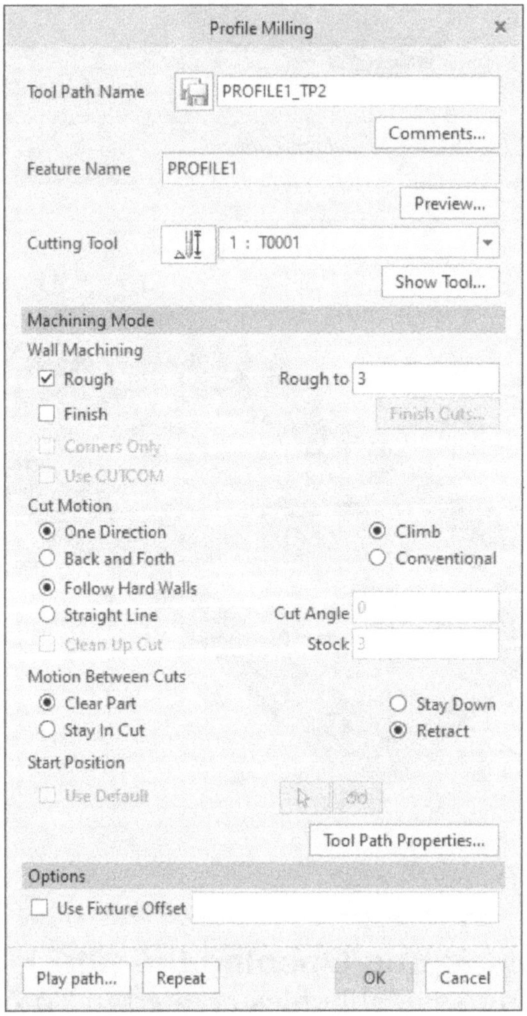

Figure-25. Profile Milling dialog box

- In this dialog box, click on the down arrow next to **Cutting Tool**; a list of tools created earlier will be displayed.
- Select the first tool from the list i.e. 1:END MILL ROUGH. You can preview the tool by selecting **Show Tool** button displayed adjacent to the down arrow.
- Now, we will specify depth of cut for this operation. Click in the **Rough to** edit box in the dialog box and specify the value as 1.
- Now, we will define the tool motion for cutting material. Select the **Back and Forth**

radio button from the dialog box so that the tool cuts material in both direction (forward and backward). Note that the tool type is an important factor for back and forth cutting.

- If the tool being used in machine is of very good quality then you can select the **Stay in Cut** radio button from the dialog box. On selecting this radio button, the tool will remain engaged with the material.
- If the parameters related to feed and spindle speed have not been defined for the machine then select the **Tool Path Properties** button from the dialog box; the **Tool Path Properties** dialog box will be displayed as shown in Figure-26.

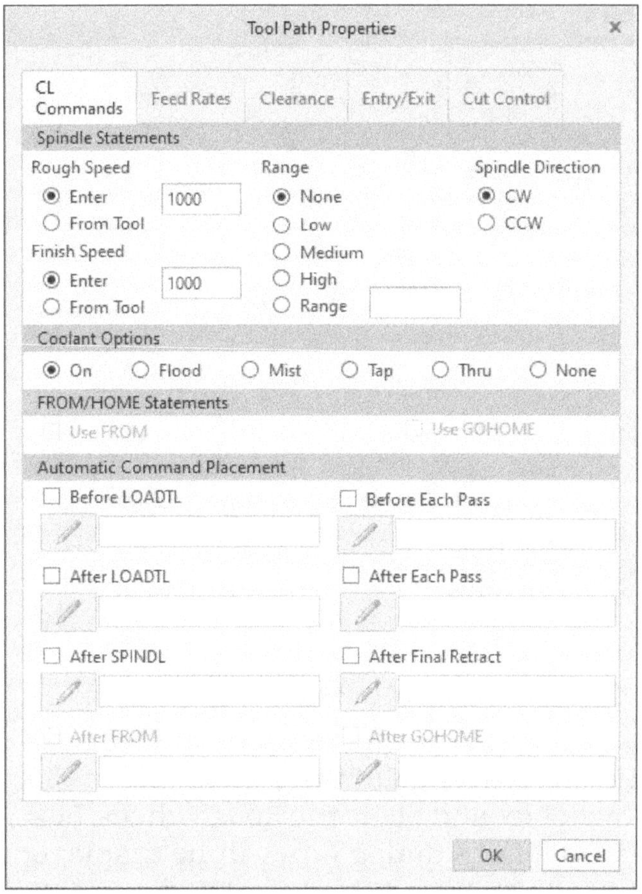

Figure-26. Tool Path Properties dialog box

- Specify the spindle speed for **Rough Speed** and **Finish Speed** as **2500** and **2800**, respectively.
- Click on the **Feed Rates** tab and specify desired feed rate values in the corresponding edit boxes.
- Click on the **Cut Control** tab and specify the value of **Depth of Cut** and **Stepover** as 2.
- Click on **OK** button from the dialog box and then **OK** button from the **Profile Milling** dialog box. The tool path will be created and added in the **Model Tree** with the name **PROFILE1 TP1[010]**.
- Click two times with a pause on its name and specify the name as Profile rough.

Now, we will create tool path to finish profile milling operation.
Right-click on **PROFILE1[OP010]** in the **Model Tree** and select the **Create Toolpath** option from the menu displayed. The **Profile Milling** dialog box will be displayed as shown in Figure-27.

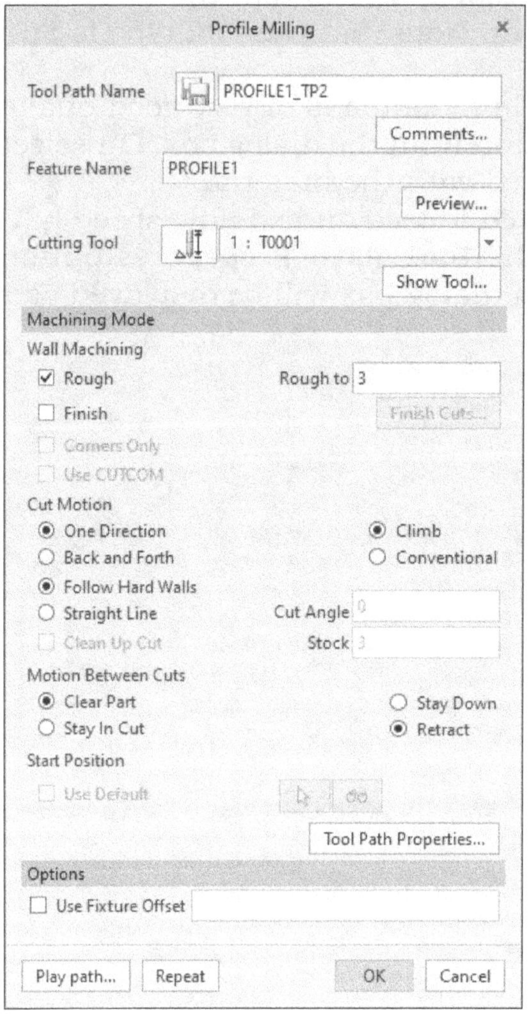

Figure-27. Profile Milling dialog box

- In **Tool Path Name** edit box, specify the name of tool path as **Profile Finish**.
- Select **END MILL FINISH** from the **Cutting Tool** list.
- Select the **Finish** check box and clear the **Rough** check box. Now, select the **Finish Cuts** button. The **Finish Cuts** dialog box will be displayed; refer to Figure-28.

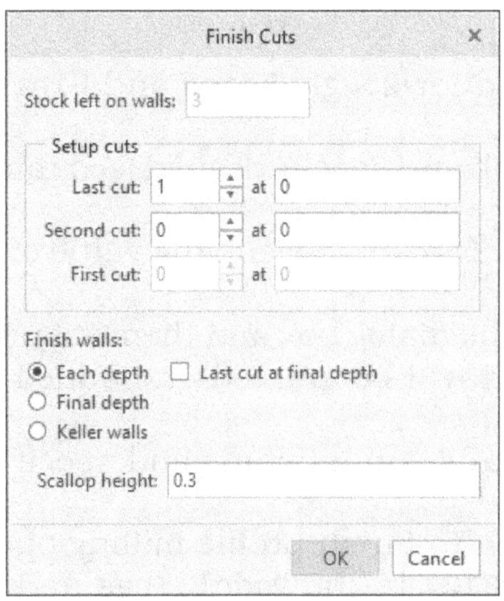

Figure-28. Finish Cuts dialog box

- Set the value as **2** in the **Last cut** spinner, select the **Last cut at final depth**, and then click on the **OK** button from the dialog box.
- Rest of the properties will remain unchanged. Now, select the **OK** button from the **Profile Milling** dialog box. The finishing tool path will be created.

Now, we will generate the output of the tool paths.

Generating tool path output

- Select the **PROFILE ROUGH** from the **Model Tree** and click on the **Select Post** tool from drop-down in the **Output** panel of the **Machining** tab in the **Ribbon**. The **Save a Copy** dialog box will be displayed.
- Save the file in desired directory. On saving the file, **PP List Menu Manager** is displayed with the list of Post Processor available in Creo.
- Select **UNCX01.P20** from the list and the output will be created in the directory in which you earlier saved the file using **Save a Copy** dialog box. Also, the INFORMATION WINDOW is displayed with the report of errors and warnings if any; refer to Figure-29.

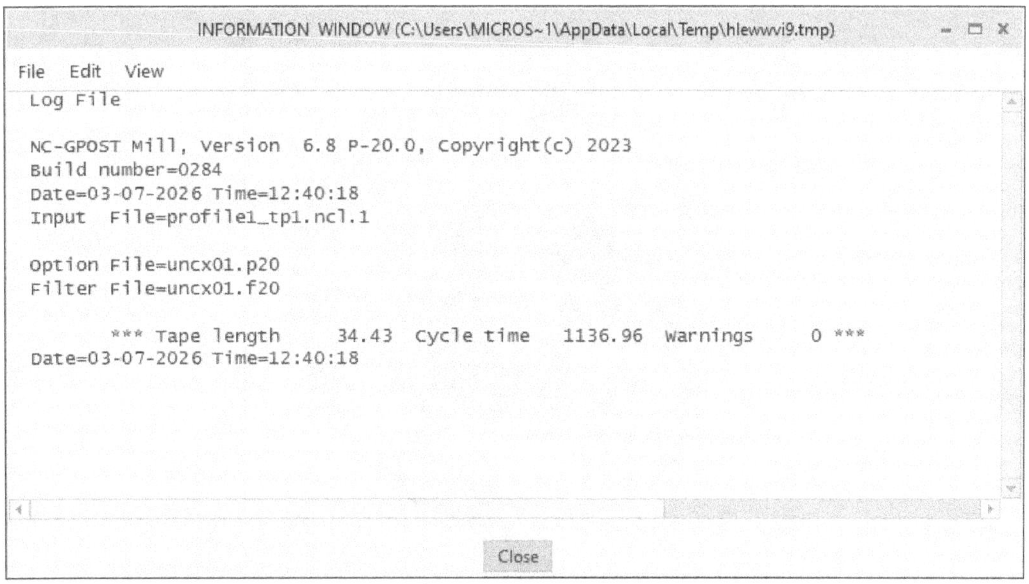

Figure-29. INFORMATION WINDOW

Similarly, you can create output for the PROFILE FINISH [OP010] toolpath.

In the same way, you can create tool path and output for the other operations. Note that manufacturing wise all the operations do not require roughing and finishing move. It mainly depends on the tolerance and surface finish in which the output is desired.

PROBLEM 1

In this problem, you will open the file created in Problem 1 of Chapter 5. In this file, you will generate all the tool paths and then you will create the outputs for **UNCX01.P43** Post Processor. Figure-30 and Figure-31 show the model.

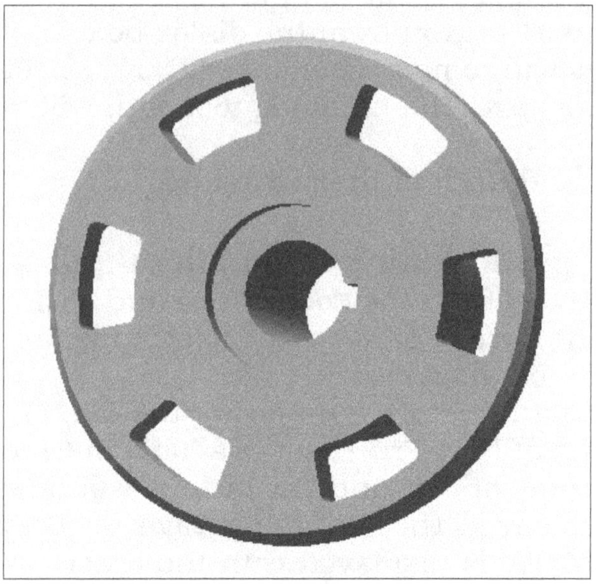

Figure-30. Isometric view of the model

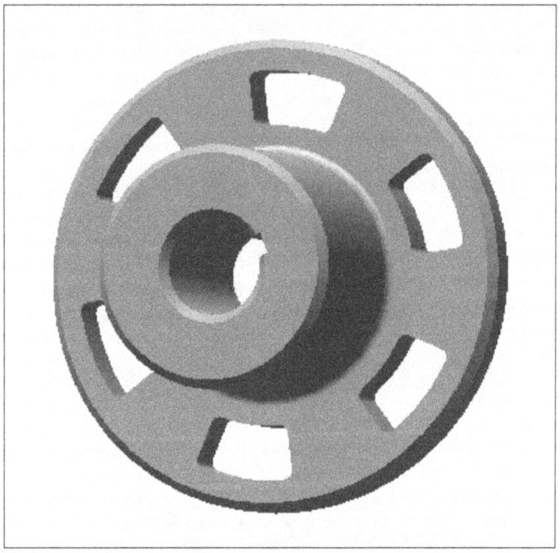

Figure-31. Reverse side view of the model

PROBLEM 2

In this problem, you will open the file created in Problem 2 of Chapter 5. Using this file, you will generate all the tool paths and then you will create the outputs for UNCX01.P43 Post Processor. Figure-32 and Figure-33 show the model.

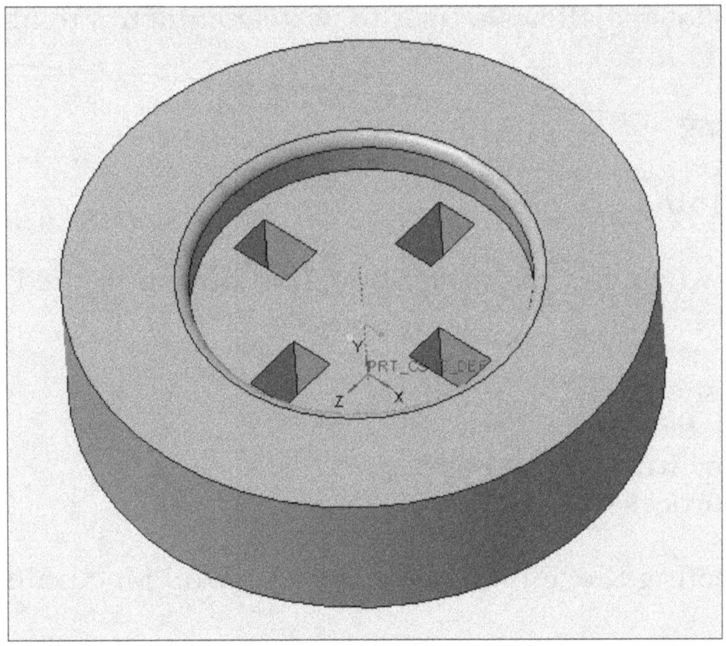

Figure-32. First view of Problem 2

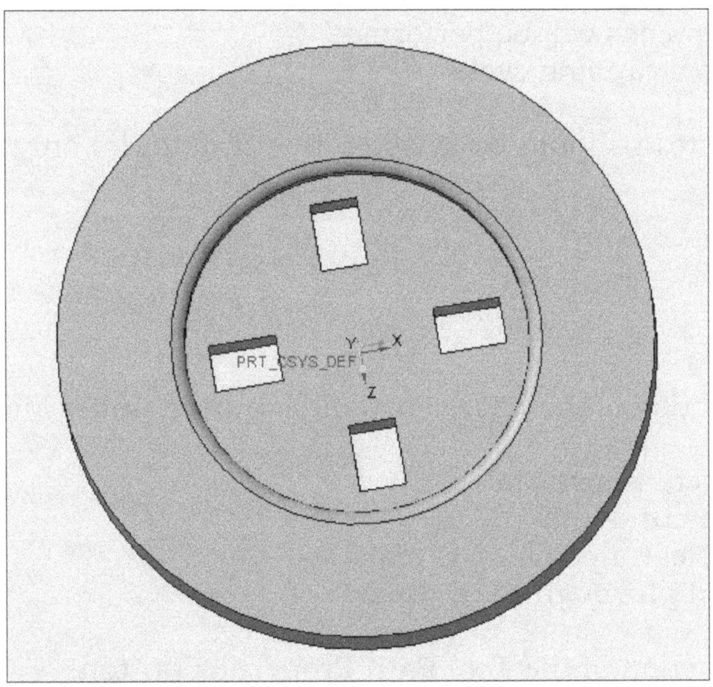

Figure-33. Second view of Problem 2

SELF-ASSESSMENT

Q1. What is the default format for naming a tool path in the Profile Milling dialog box?

A. OperationName Sequence ToolPath
B. FeatureName TPSequenceNumber [Operation Number]
C. TP FeatureName Operation
D. ToolPath Feature Sequence

Q2. Which of the following allows a user to write comments related to the tool path?

A. Tool Manager
B. Feature Name Box
C. Comments Button
D. CL Commands Tab

Q3. What happens when you click the Show Tool button in the Profile Milling dialog box?

A. A list of tools is shown
B. The tool gets deleted
C. A preview window with the tool appears
D. The machining process starts

Q4. What does selecting the 'Finish' check box in Wall Machining indicate?

A. Tool should only rough cut the part
B. Tool path will follow only the hard walls
C. Final finishing process will be performed
D. Tool will perform a tapping cycle

Q5. Which radio button should be selected to cut material only in one direction?

A. Back and Forth
B. Climb
C. One Direction
D. Straight Line

Q6. What is the function of the 'Clear Part' radio button under Motion Between Cuts?

A. Keeps tool engaged in material
B. Keeps tool at the cut depth
C. Retracts tool to clearance plane rapidly
D. Connects tool cuts through hard walls

Q7. What is the function of the Tool Path Properties button?

A. To save toolpath
B. To simulate cutting
C. To open a dialog box for toolpath configuration
D. To select another NC feature

Q8. What does the Use Fixture Offset check box do?

A. Adds a fixture to the model
B. Displays tool at a different location
C. Offsets toolpath due to fixture setup
D. Adds comments to toolpath

Q9. In the CL Commands tab, what does selecting the 'Enter' radio button under Rough Speed allow?

A. Automatically sets speed from tool
B. Ignores rough speed input
C. Allows user to manually enter RPM
D. Sets zero spindle speed

Q10. What does the 'Coolant ON' option indicate?

A. No coolant flow
B. Mist coolant enabled
C. Tool receives coolant from tool tip
D. Normal coolant flow through pipes

Q11. What is the purpose of the 'Use FROM' check box in FROM/HOME Statements?

A. Activates automatic CL output
B. Adds manual CL commands using FROM statement
C. Skips home position
D. Displays spindle direction

Q12. Which of the following is used to define feed rate manually for rough cutting?

A. From Tool
B. Enter
C. Edit
D. Measure

Q13. In Clearance settings, what does the 'Go Delta' option do?

A. Clears material around corners
B. Sets distance from last cut
C. Ignores clearance
D. Clears material vertically

Q14. What does selecting 'Soft Landing - Automatic' do in Entry/Exit settings?

A. Disables tool landing
B. Enables user to specify landing value
C. Applies landing automatically based on toolpath
D. Prevents lift and landing movement

Q15. What does the 'Side Clearance' edit box define?

A. Clearance along Z-axis
B. Distance from soft wall
C. Distance from hard walls
D. Cut depth

Q16. What does the Stepover value represent?

A. Vertical distance between cuts
B. Distance between passes in the toolpath
C. Horizontal distance between cuts
D. Distance from machine base

Q17. What does the Register edit box in CUTCOM Control define?

A. Tool number
B. Offset value for CUTCOM
C. Tool length
D. Spindle speed

Q18. What happens when the 'Allow Z Moves' check box is selected?

A. Allows vertical tool moves in CUTCOM
B. Prevents vertical tool movement
C. Ignores soft wall
D. Displays only horizontal motion

Q19. What is the use of the Tool Path Player tool?

A. Saves tool paths
B. Creates new NC feature
C. Simulates cutter motion along tool path
D. Generates .tap files

Q20. Which view mode displays the tool path in red lines?

A. Shaded Tool
B. Wireframe
C. Display Tool Tip
D. Display Tool

Q21. What does the NC Check option simulate?

A. Cutter with full collision detection
B. Toolpath on a virtual machine
C. Tool without material
D. Only spindle rotation

Q22. What does selecting the Display Tool Tip option do?

A. Displays length of tool
B. Highlights the toolpath trajectory
C. Enables tool setup
D. Adds new operation

Q23. Which menu is used to check tool clearance during simulation?

A. Gouge Check
B. Tool Path Properties
C. Tool Clearance
D. NC File

Q24. What file format is generated by the Create CL File tool?

A. .tap
B. .exe
C. .ncl
D. .cdl

Q25. Which tool is used to convert a CL file into an MCD file?

A. Output Panel
B. Save as MCD
C. Post Processor
D. CL Data

FOR STUDENT NOTES

Chapter 7

Introduction to CMM and Managing Post Processor

Topics Covered

The major topics covered in this chapter are:

- ***Introduction to CMM and its purpose.***
- ***CMM Machine Setting.***
- ***Use of default probe library and creation of probe model.***
- ***Creation of measuring operation.***
- ***Various options for measurement.***
- ***Creating output file.***
- ***Creating and Managing Post Processor***

INTRODUCTION TO CMM AND ITS PURPOSE

CMM is the short form of Coordinate Measuring Machine. As the name suggests, this machine is used to measure coordinates. Now, question is which coordinates and why? One of the good reason of using CMM is accuracy required to manufacture parts in today's world. The curvatures and shapes created by NC machines are very complicated and are required to be accurate. These NC machines are able to achieve that accuracy. But how to measure that accuracy? So, for measuring complicated shapes; CMM was introduced in production technology. A CMM works in the same way as does the NC machine. But, in CMM, in place of cutting tool there is a probe that runs over the workpiece and gives coordinates of each desired point on the workpiece. These coordinates together generate point cloud which can be converted to surface. This generated surface is then compared to the standard size required and then dimensional & geometric analysis is performed. In a simple way, a CMM finds out the difference between the coordinate sheet specified by the user and the real model. The CMM app of Creo Parametric is used to generate a sheet of coordinates that will be fed to the machine to perform dimensional and geometric analysis on the real model. Since working with CMM app is similar to the Expert Machinist so, the workflow for CMM will be the same. To start CMM app, click on the **New** button from the **Quick Access Toolbar** and select the **CMM** sub-type for **Manufacturing** type in the **New** dialog box. Set the other parameters as discussed earlier and click on the **OK** button from the dialog box. The process for generating Coordinates by this app is given in the steps discussed next.

Note that in this book, we will cover only the Introduction to CMM. So, we will be discussing about the steps that are mandatory for generating Coordinates for CMM.

Adding Reference Model

This is the first step to setup coordinate sheet. In this step, we define the model to be used for measurement.

- To add a reference model, click on the **Reference Model** drop-down in the **Components** panel of **Inspect** tab in the **Ribbon**. A list of tools will be displayed; refer to Figure-1.

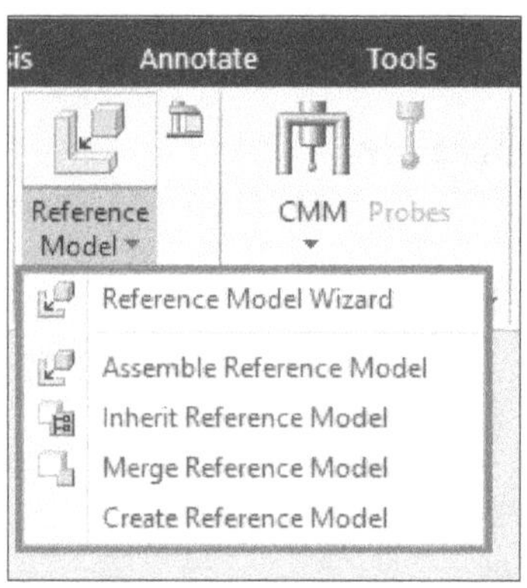

Figure-1. Reference Model drop down list

- Select the **Assemble Reference Model** option from the drop-down. The **Open** dialog box will be displayed; refer to Figure-2.

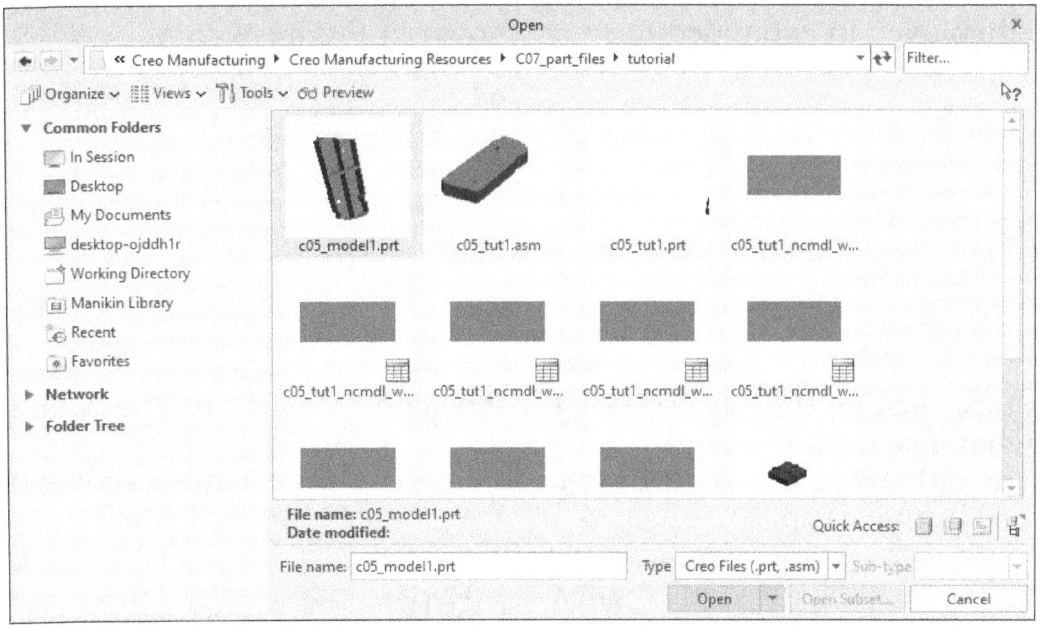

Figure-2. Open dialog box

- Select a model from the dialog box and then click on the **Open** button. The model will be displayed in Modeling area and you will be prompted to assemble the part with the assembly plane.
- Select the **Default** option from the **Constraint Type** drop-down in the **Placement** tab; refer to Figure-3. The reference model will be assembled at the default planes.

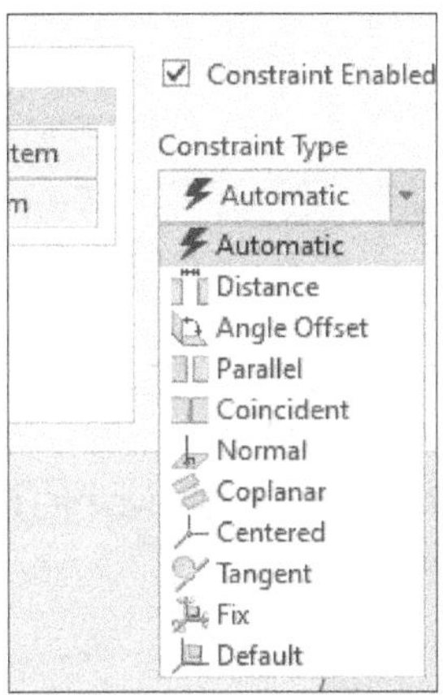

Figure-3. Constraint drop down with Default option highlighted

- Click on the **OK** button to accept the assembly. The reference model will be placed.

Setting Up a Fixture

After adding the reference model, you can add a fixture to hold the reference model. This step is optional and is performed when you want to check the interference of the probe with the fixture. The procedure to add a fixture is discussed next.

- Click on the **Fixture** button from **Components** panel in the **Ribbon**. The **Fixture Setup** contextual tab will become active.
- Here, you can set the models to be used as fixture for our current reference model.

To add model for the fixture, click on the **Components** tab in the **Ribbon**. The tab will be displayed in expanded form as shown in Figure-4.

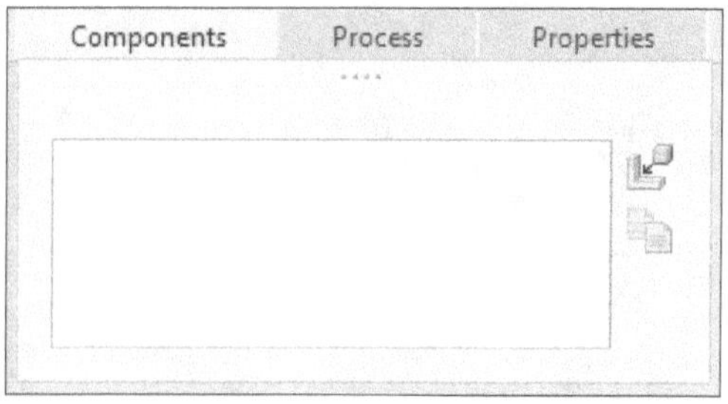

Figure-4. Expanded Components tab

- In this tab, click on the **Add a fixture component** button. The **Open** dialog box will be displayed again.
- Using the options in this dialog box, you can add an assembly model or part file as fixture in the setup.

CMM Setting

Till this point, we have a reference model and hopefully a fixture in the modeling area. Now, we need to setup a CMM so that the coordinate data to be generated is according to our CMM. The procedure to set up CMM is discussed next.

- Click on the **CMM** drop-down from **Inspection Machine** panel in the **Inspect** tab of the **Ribbon**. A list of tools will be displayed; refer to Figure-5.

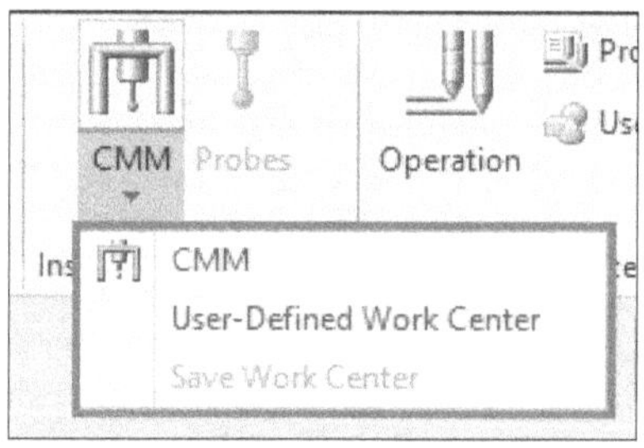

Figure-5. CMM drop-down list

- Click on the **CMM** tool from the list. The **CMM Work Center** dialog box will be displayed; refer to Figure-6.

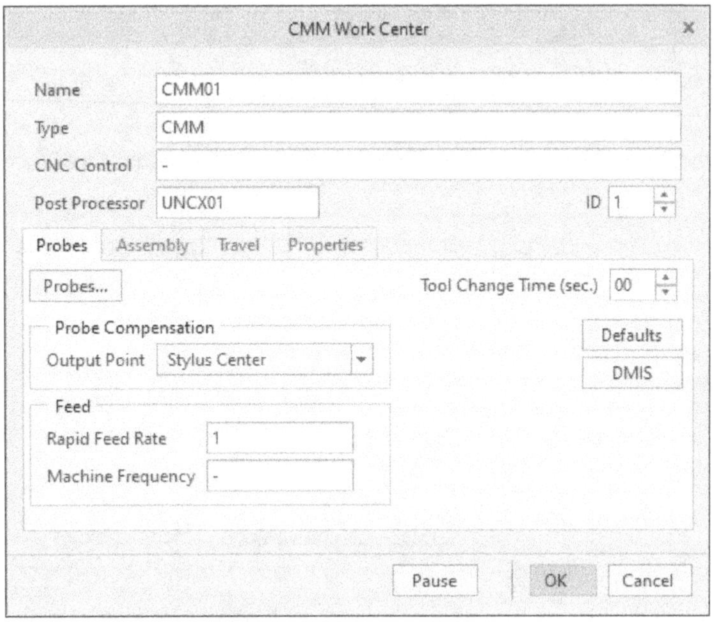

Figure-6. CMM Work Center dialog box

- The options in this dialog box are similar to the options discussed for **Milling Work Center** dialog box in Chapter 3.
- The main difference between the two dialog boxes is that; in **Milling Work Center** dialog box, a tool is required and in **CMM Work Center** dialog box, a probe is required in place of tool.

The options related to probe in this dialog box are discussed next.

Probe

A probe is a solid and sensitive tool which is used to map the surface of a component in the machine.

- To add a probe in the setup, click on the **Probes** button in the **Probes** tab of the **CMM Work Center** dialog box; refer to Figure-6. On selecting this button; the **Probe Setup** dialog box will be displayed; refer to Figure-7.

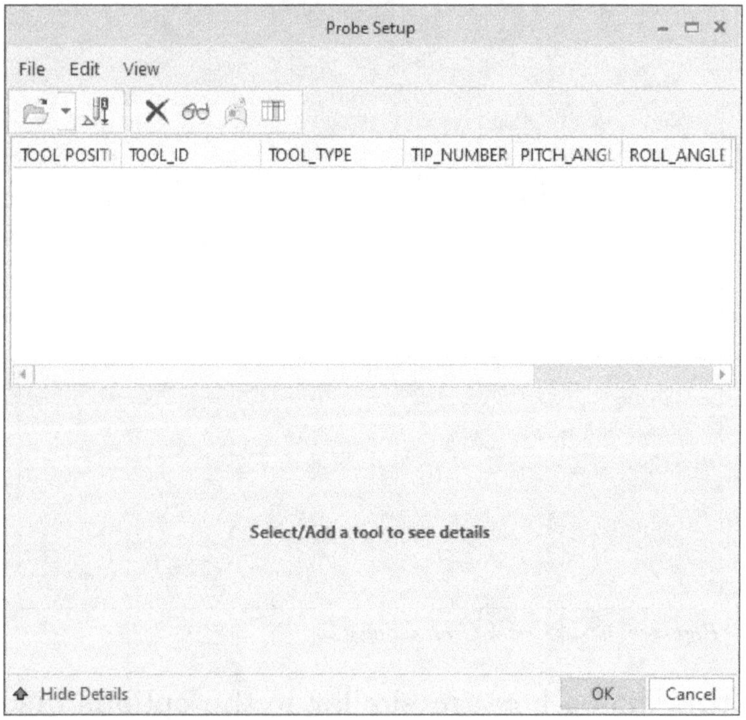

Figure-7. Probe Setup dialog box

- Now, you need to add an existing probe in the setup by using the **Open** button. On selecting the **Open** button, you will be asked to select model or assembly of the probe.
- You can also use default probes provided by Creo. To access the default probes, click on the **File** button in the menu bar of the **Probe Setup** dialog box. A menu will be displayed as shown in Figure-8.

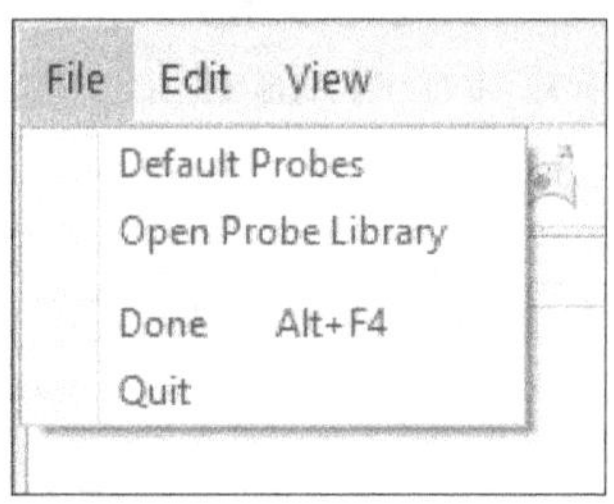

Figure-8. File menu

- Select the **Default Probes** option from the menu. The **Open** dialog box will be displayed with the folders of defaults probes; refer to Figure-9.

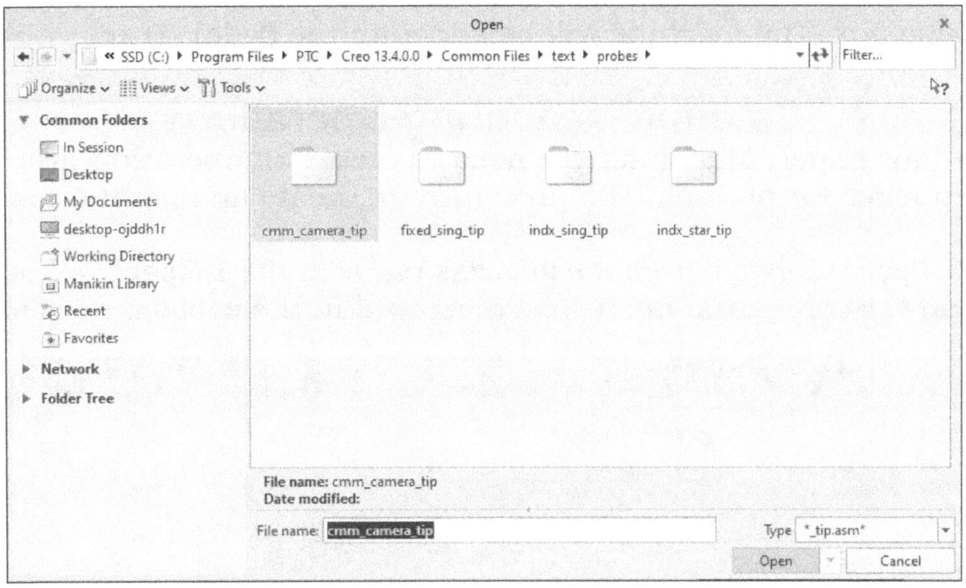

Figure-9. Open dialog box with the default probes in folders

- Open desired folder in the dialog box and select the assembly file from it. In our case, the **indx star tip** folder is opened and the assembly file in it has been selected.
- Now, click on the **Open** button from the dialog box. The **Probe Setup** dialog box will change as shown in Figure-10.

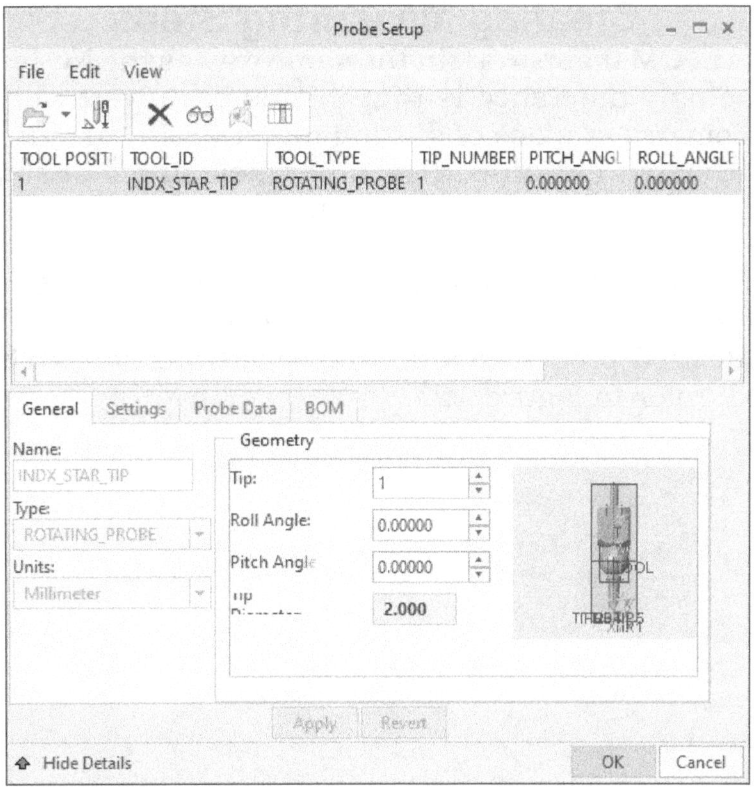

Figure-10. Probe Setup dialog box after selecting default Probe

- Specify desired settings in the dialog box and click on the **Apply** button.
- Now, click on the **OK** button from the dialog box. The probe will be added in the setup and the **CMM Work Center** dialog box will be displayed again.

Now, specify rest of the settings for the CMM Work Center and then click on **OK** button from the dialog box. The machine will be added in the **Model Tree**.

Creating Measuring Operations

As discussed for Expert Machinist, we need to create an operation first for creating tool path sequence for probing. The procedure to create an operation is given next.

- Select the **Operation** tool from the **Process** panel in the **Inspect** tab of the **Ribbon**. The **Operation** contextual tab will be displayed in the **Ribbon**; refer to Figure-11.

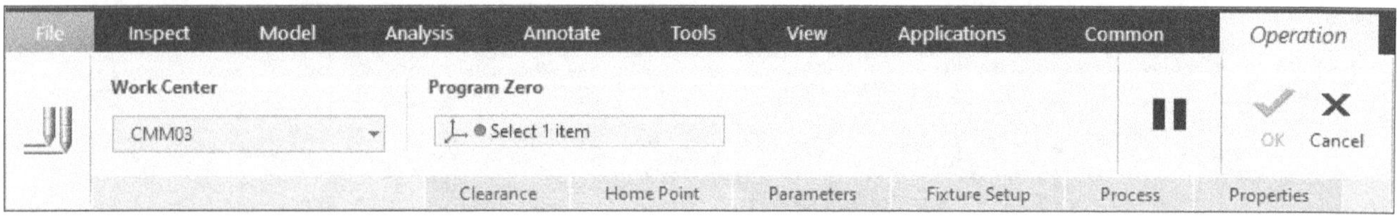

Figure-11. Operation contextual tab

- The CMM earlier created is already selected in **Work Center** drop-down in the **Ribbon**.
- Now, select a coordinate system from the modeling area. Note that the coordinate selected will be assumed as 0,0,0 position while measuring.
- Select the **OK** button from the **Ribbon** to create the operation. After creating the operation, most of the tools in the **Ribbon** will become active.

Creating Measuring Steps

Measurement steps in CMM app work in the same way as the NC features do in Expert Machinist app. The only difference is that in this case, you will be measuring the dimensions and geometry in place of cutting material. In this introductory chapter, only **Plane** measure step is explained. The other measurement steps will work in the same way. Creation of **Plane** measurement steps is explained next.

- After setting up probe, CMM, and operation; click on the **Plane** tool available in the **Measure** panel of the **Ribbon**. The **Probe Setup** dialog box is displayed.
- After selecting desired probe, click on the **OK** button. The **Edit Parameter** dialog box is displayed; refer to Figure-12.

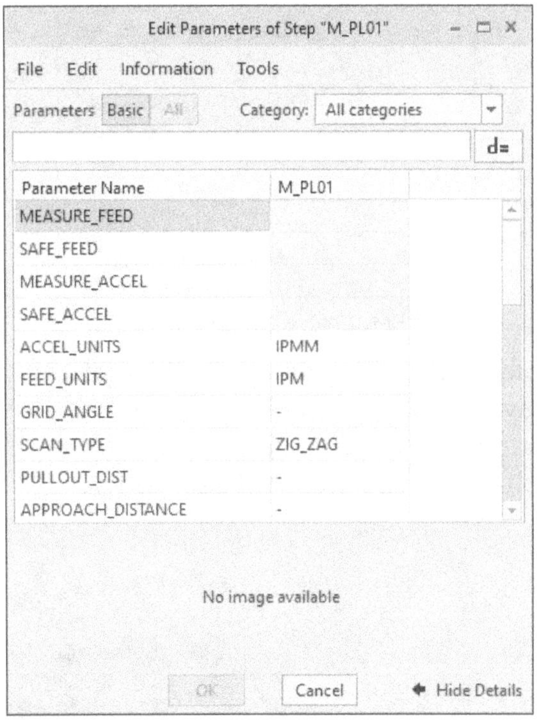

Figure-12. Edit Parameters of Step dialog box

- Now, specify the parameters for measurement in the fields of this dialog box like speed of measurement, acceleration, and so on. The fields that are highlighted in yellow color are compulsory to specify and the other fields are optional.
- After specifying desired parameters, click on the **OK** button from the dialog box. You will be asked to select a planar face for measurement.
- Select the face to be measured; refer to Figure-13.

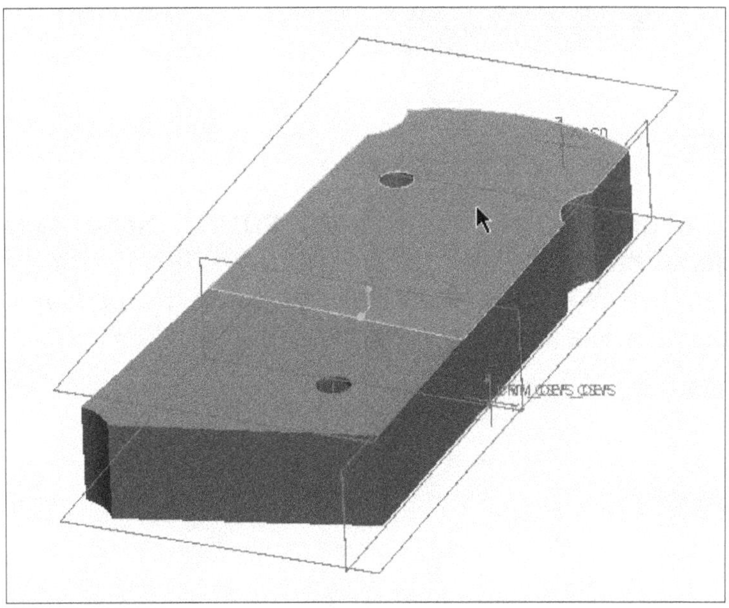

Figure-13. Face to be selected with cursor on it

- On selecting the face, **PTS AND PATH Menu Manager** will be displayed.
- Select **Automatic** option from the **ADD POINTS** section of **Menu Manager** displayed at the bottom in the **PTS AND PATH Menu Manager**. The **Probe Points** dialog box will be displayed; refer to Figure-14.

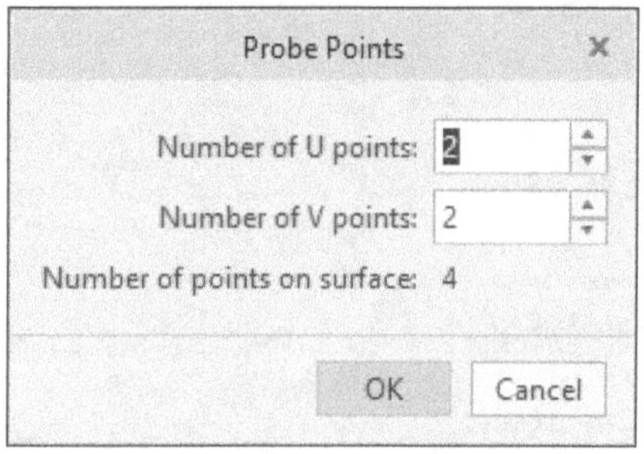

Figure-14. Probe Points dialog box

- Increase the number of points to be measured by probe in both U and V directions by using their respective spinners in this dialog box.
- Click on the **OK** button from the dialog box. Preview of the probe points will be displayed in the modeling area; refer to Figure-15.

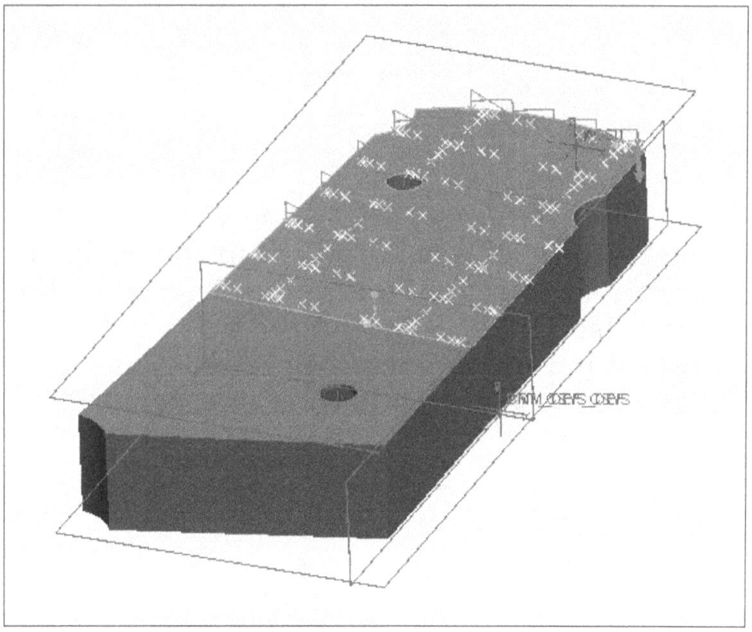

Figure-15. Preview of the probe points

- Select the **Done/Return** option from the **ADD POINTS Menu Manager** and then from **PTS and PATH Menu Manager**. The probe points will be added in the setup.
- Click on the **OK** button from the **MEASUREMENT STEP** dialog box displayed in the left of the application window; refer to Figure-16.

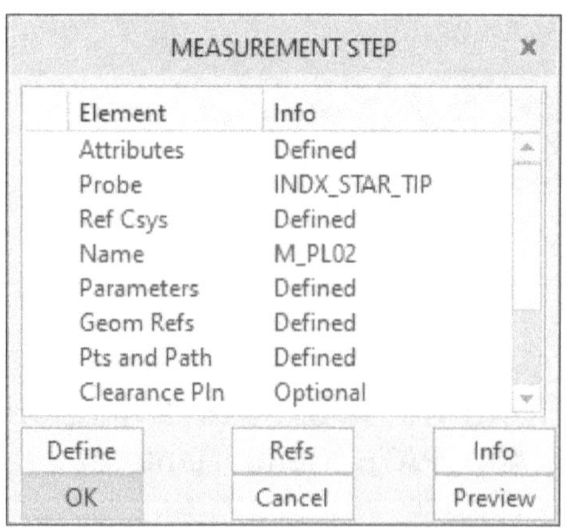

Figure-16. MEASUREMENT STEP dialog box

- On selecting the **OK** button, the step will be created and added in the **Model Tree** (and highlighted in blue color in the modeling area); refer to Figure-17.

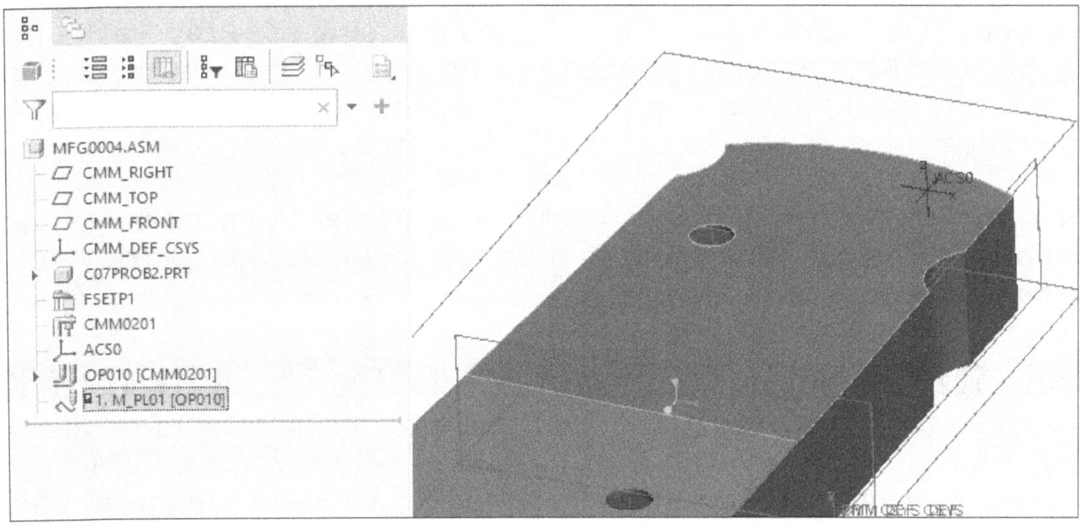

Figure-17. Measurement step created

You can create other measurement steps like surface, cylinder, cone, and so on in the same way.

Probe Path Output

After creating a measurement step, this is the time to generate output for the machine. The tool to generate output is available in the **Output** panel with the name **Probe Path**.

- Click on the **Probe Path** tool from the **Output** panel in the **Inspect** tab of the **Ribbon**. The **PROBE PATH Menu Manager** will be displayed.
- Now, you can create output for a complete operation having various measurement steps or you can create output for a specific step by using the options in this **Menu Manager**. The procedure for both the cases will be the same.
- To generate output for individual measurement step, select the **CMM Step** option from the **Menu Manager**. On doing so, list of available measurement steps will be displayed; refer to Figure-18.
- Select the step from the list displayed. The **Menu Manager** will get changed as shown in Figure-19.

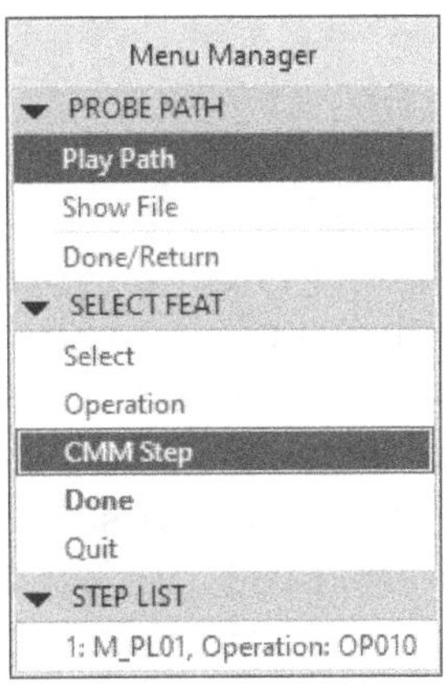

Figure-18. PROBE PATH Menu Manager

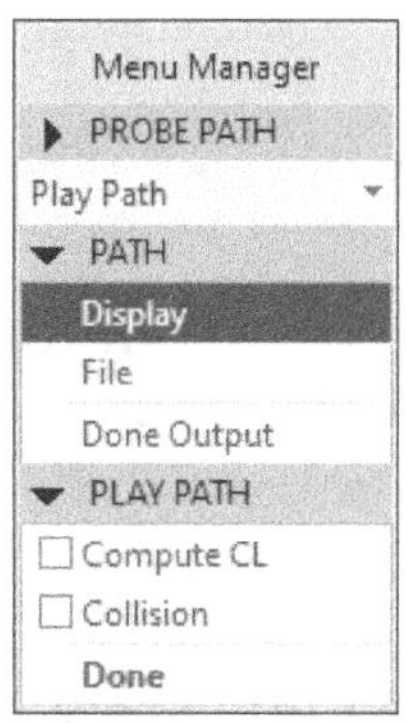

Figure-19. Modified PROBE PATH Menu Manager

- Select the **File** option from the **Menu Manager** to generate the output file. The **Save a Copy** dialog box will be displayed.

- Save the file at desired location. After saving the file, select the **Done** option from the **Menu Manager**. The **Menu Manager** will display two options: **Play Path** and **Show File**.
- You can check the simulation of probe path by using the **Play Path** option.
- Using the **Show File**, you can check the output file that you have saved.
- After selecting any of the two options (**Play Path** and **Show File**), select **CMM Step** and then desired step from the step list; the output will be displayed.

Tip: This is important to note that the CMM steps are used to perform geometric and dimensional analysis. So, make sure that you have applied geometric tolerances in the model as well.

CONSTRUCTING GEOMETRY FOR MEASUREMENT

The tools in the **Construct** panel are used to create geometries to be measured on the model; refer to Figure-20. There are instances when you can not locate points, lines, or other geometries on the surface of model for measurement. In such cases, it is easier to create a geometry on the surface of model for measurement.

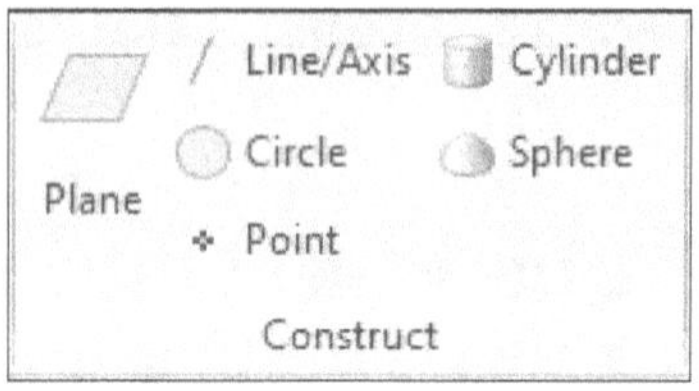

Figure-20. Construct panel

Various tools of this panel are discussed next.

Creating Plane for Measurement

The **Plane** tool is used to create a plane with respect to references selected from the model. The procedure to use this tool is given next.

- Click on the **Plane** tool from the **Construct** panel in the **Inspect** tab of **Ribbon**. The **CMM Plane Construct Step** contextual tab will be displayed; refer to Figure-21.

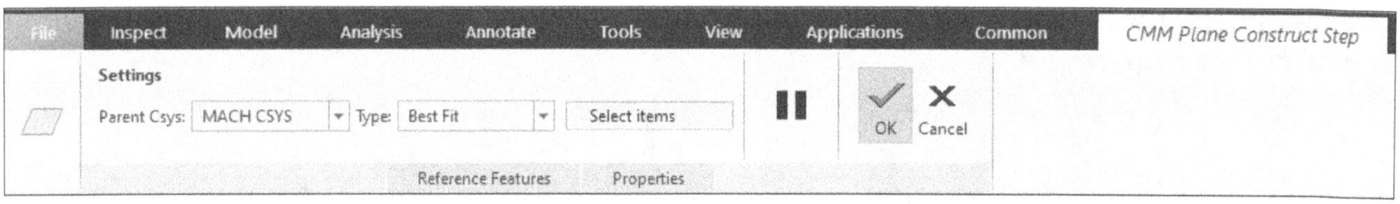

Figure-21. CMM Plane Construct Step contextual tab

- Select desired option from the **Type** drop-down to define type of plane to be created. Select the **Best Fit** option to automatically create the type of plane suitable based on selected geometries. Select the **Midplane** option from the drop-down to create a plane at the mid of two measurement/construction planes. Select the **Normal** option from the drop-down to create a plane perpendicular to selected plane/face and passing through selected point. Select the **Parallel** option from the drop-down to create plane parallel to selected plane/face and passing through a point. Select the **Theoretical** option from the drop-down to construct plane based on selected plane.

- After selecting desired option, select the geometry to be created based on information displayed in the status bar; refer to Figure-22.

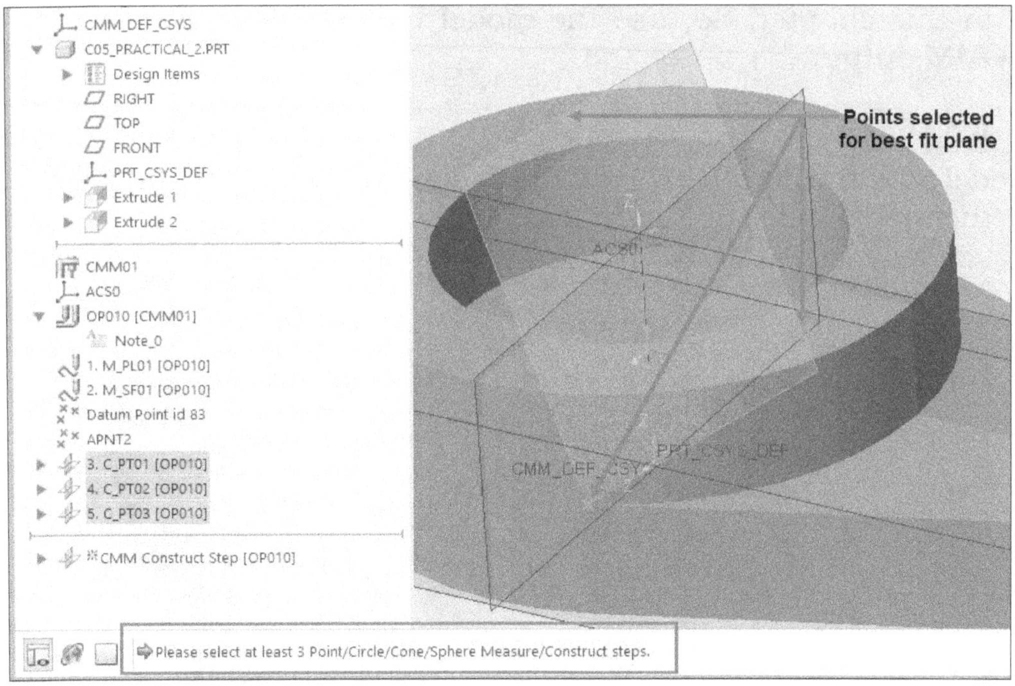

Figure-22. Points selected for best fit plane

- Click on the **Properties** in the contextual tab to provide comments for the operation.
- After setting desired parameters, click on the **OK** button from the **Ribbon**. The plane will be created.

Constructing Line/Axis

The **Line/Axis** tool in **Construct** panel is used to create a line/axis passing through two points. The procedure to use this tool is given next.

- Click on the **Line/Axis** tool from the **Construct** panel in the **Inspect** tab of the **Ribbon**. The **CMM Line Construct Step** contextual tab will be displayed in the **Ribbon**.
- Select desired option from the **Type** drop-down to define the type of line/axis to be created. Select the **Best Fit** option from the drop-down to create a line/axis passing through two selected points. Select the **Midline** option from the drop-down to use create an axis/line at the middle of two lines/cylinder/cone. Select the **Projection** option from the drop-down to use selected line/axis and project it on selected plane (construct or measurement). Select the **Intersect** option from the drop-down to create a line/axis at the intersect of two construct/measurement planes. Select the **Theoretical** option from the drop-down to create a line/axis based on selected line/axis.
- After selecting desired option from the drop-down, select the geometries based on information displayed in the Status bar.
- After setting desired parameters, click on the **OK** button from the **Ribbon** to create line/axis.

You can use the other tools in the **Construct** panel in the same way.

Problem 1

The models that we have earlier used can be check for CMM by using the tools discussed in this chapter. So, use the model files provided in the resource kit to check for CMM output.

Problem 2

Use the model with the name C07Prob2.prt as reference model and then create CMM output for the model; refer to Figure-23.

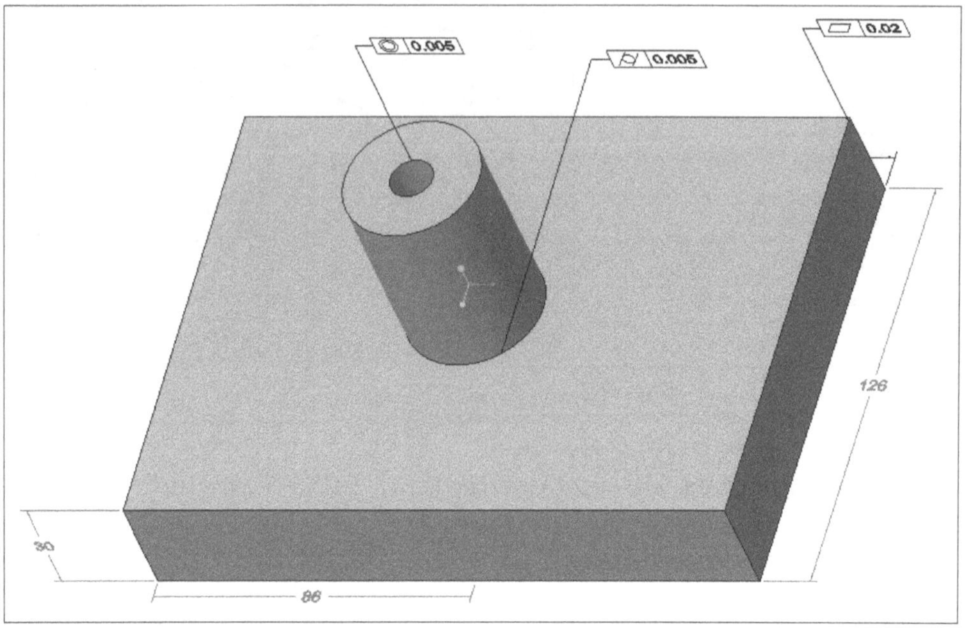

Figure-23. Model for Problem 2

CREATING AND MANAGING OPTION FILE FOR NC

The Option File Generator application is used to create post processor option file for generating cnc G-codes based on selected machine. To activate this application, click on the **NC Post Processor** tool from the **Manufacturing Applications** panel in the **Applications** tab of the **Ribbon** after starting Expert Machinist. The **Option File Generator** application window will be displayed; refer to Figure-24.

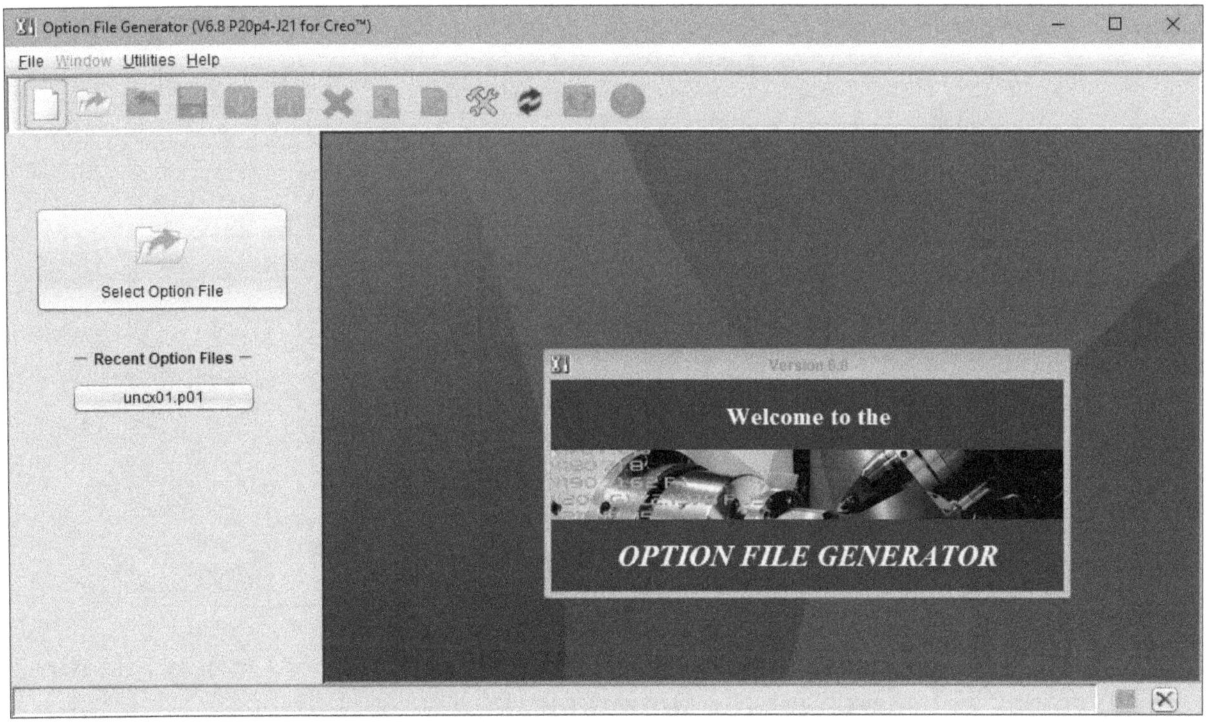

Figure-24. Option File Generator application

Creating a New Option File

The **New** tool in toolbar of **Option File Generator** application window is used to create NC post processor file. The procedure to create option file is given next.

- Click on the **New** tool from the toolbar. The **Define Machine Type** dialog box will be displayed; refer to Figure-25.

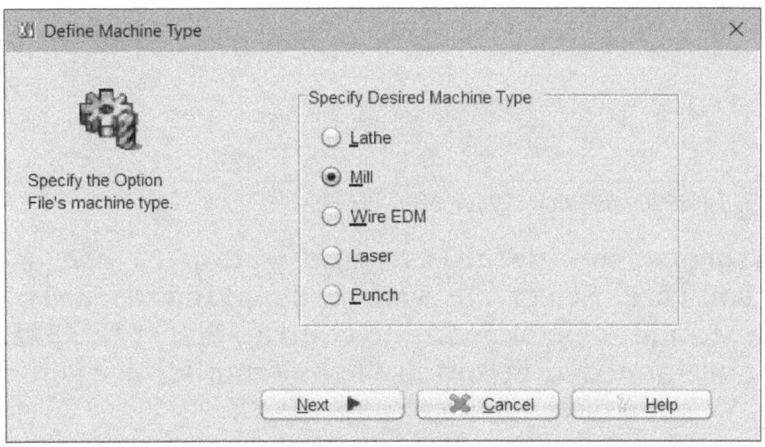

Figure-25. Define Machine Type dialog box

- Select desired radio button from the dialog box to define the type of machine for which you want to generate option file (Mill machine in our case) and click on the **Next** button. The **Define Option File Location** dialog box will be displayed; refer to Figure-26.

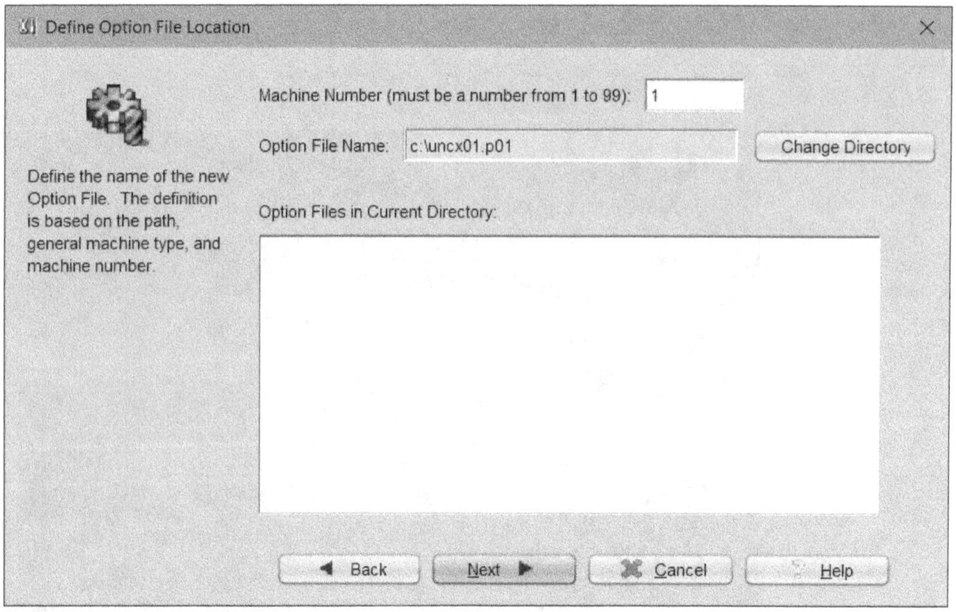

Figure-26. Define Option File Location dialog box

- Click on the **Change Directory** button to set the location of Option File directory where system will search for NC Option file.
- After setting parameters, click on the **Next** button. The **Option File Initialization** dialog box will be displayed; refer to Figure-27.

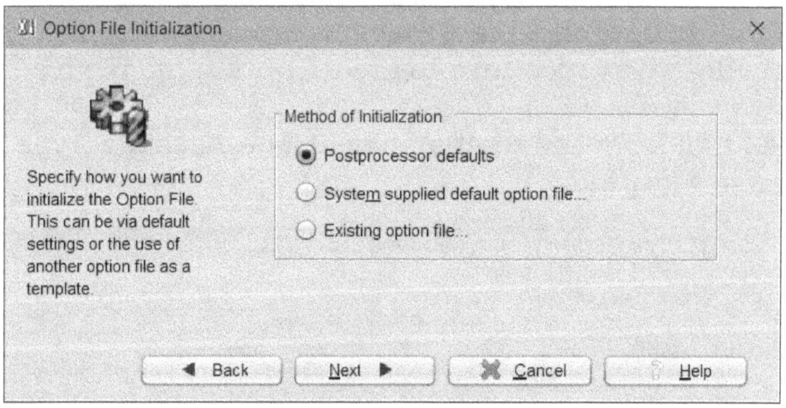

Figure-27. Option File Initialization dialog box

- Select the **Postprocessor defaults** radio button to use a default processor available with software. Select the **System supplied default option file** radio button to use a template file of machine control. Select the **Existing option file** radio button to use an existing option file as template for generating new Option file.
- If the **Postprocessor defaults** radio button is selected then on clicking **Next** button, the **Option File Title** dialog box will be displayed; refer to Figure-28. If the **System supplied default option file** radio button is selected then on clicking **Next** button, the **Select Option File Template** dialog box will be displayed; refer to Figure-29. Similarly, you can use the **Existing option file** radio button.

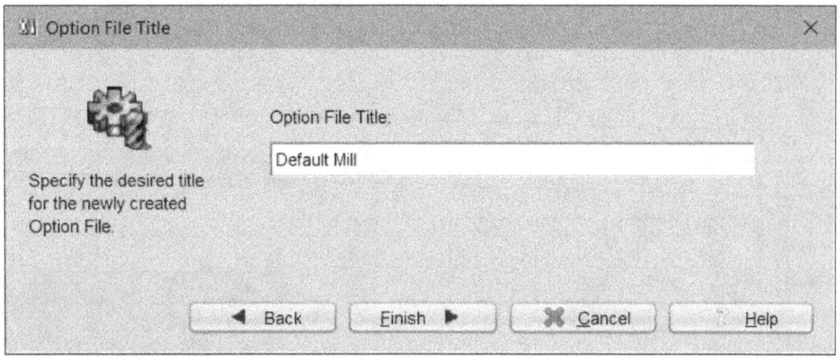

Figure-28. Option File Title dialog box

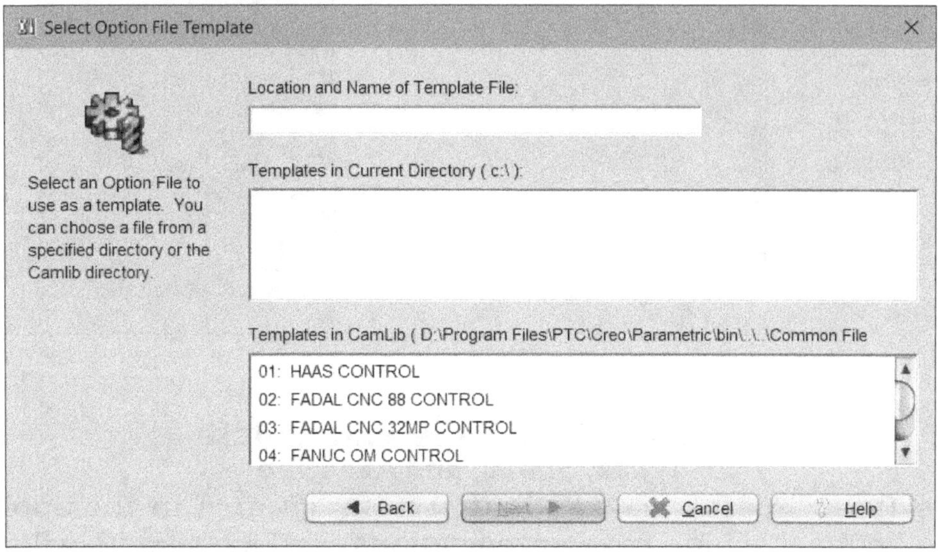

Figure-29. Select Option File Template dialog box

- Select desired template from the dialog box and click on the **Next** button. The **Option File Title** dialog box will be displayed.
- Specify desired title name of option file in the edit box and click on the **Finish** button. The options to define parameters for Option file will be displayed in the application window; refer to Figure-30.

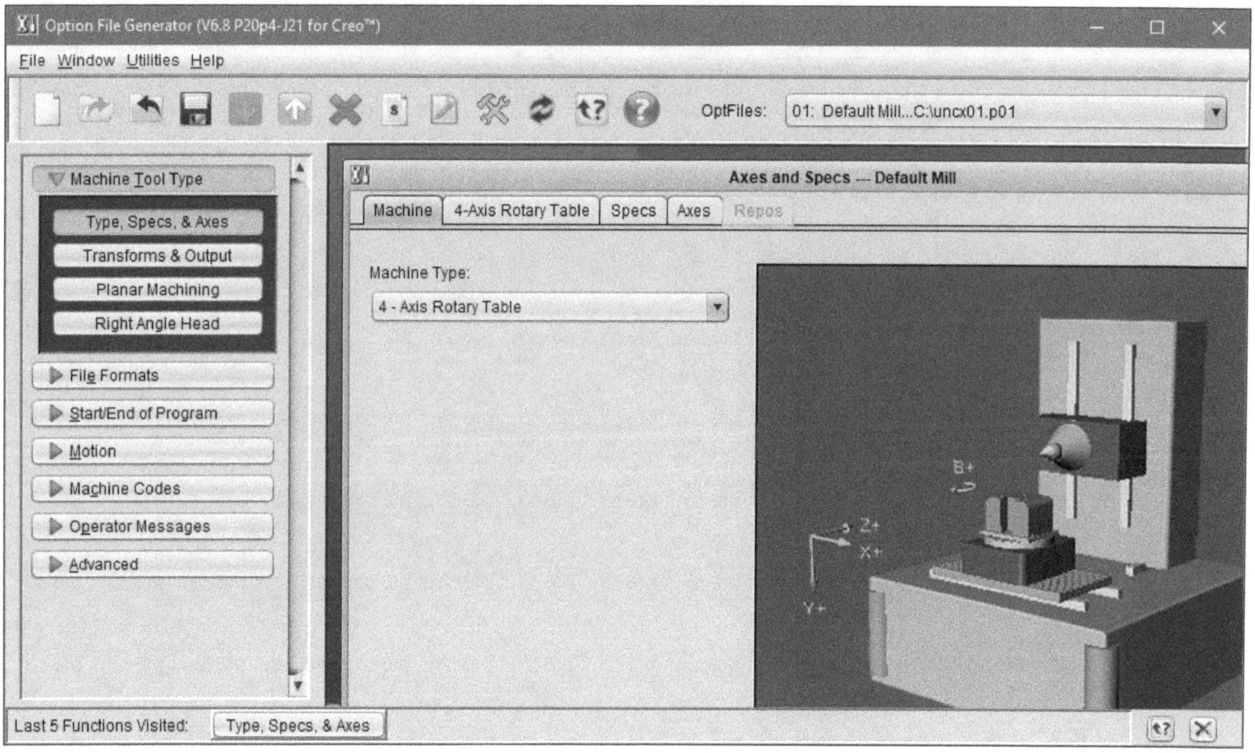

Figure-30. Parameters for Option file

Machine Tool Type Parameters

Types, Specs, and Axes Tab

- Select the **Type, Specs, & Axes** button from left area in the application. The options to define machine type, specifications, and axes limits will be displayed at the right in the application window.
- Make sure the **Machine** tab is selected at the right window and select the type of machine for which you want to create post processor. Preview of selected machine type will be displayed with their axes; refer to Figure-31.

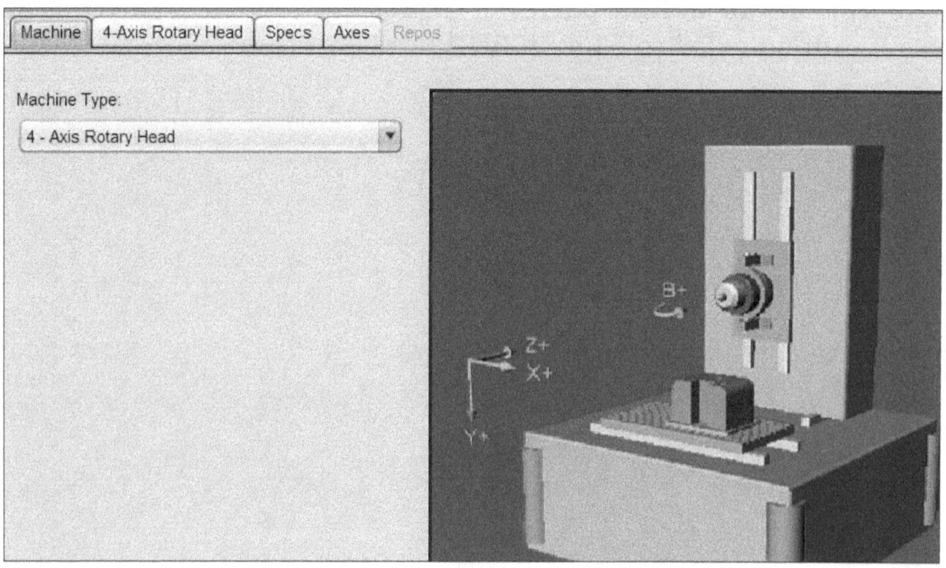

Figure-31. Preview of machine type

4-Axis Rotary Head Tab

- Click on the **4-Axis Rotary Head** tab (or other tab based on type of machine selected) from the right area in window. The options will be displayed as shown in Figure-32. Select desired option from the **Rotates About** drop-down in the **Axis & Rotation** area to define axis about which tool can rotate.

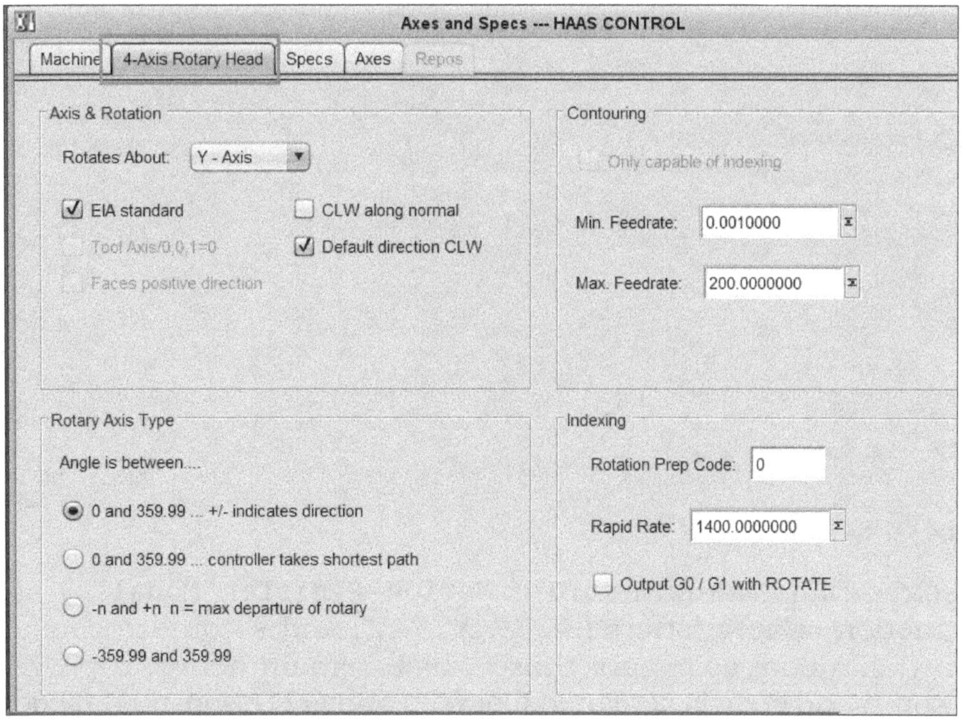

Figure-32. 4-Axis Rotary Head options

- Select the **EIA standard** check box to use Electronic Industries Alliance (EIA) standards for defining machine type and size. Select the **CLW along normal** check box to rotate the cutting tool clockwise. Select the **Default direction CLW** check box to make sure default direction of cutting tool rotation is clockwise.
- Specify desired values in the **Min. Feedrate** and **Max. Feedrate** edit boxes of **Contouring** area to define the range within which cutting tool will move for contour machining.
- Select desired radio button from the **Rotary Axis Type** area to define the angle range within which cutting tool can rotate.
- The options in the **Indexing** area of dialog box are used to define how machine activates the rotation of cutting tool. Specify desired value in the **Rotation Prep Code** edit box if your machine needs a special code for activating rotation of tool. Specify desired value in the **Rapid Rate** edit box to define speed at which indexer rotates when rapid feed rate is applicable. Select the **Output G0/G1 with ROTATE** check box to output G0/G1 codes for Rapid or the current Feed mode.

Specs Tab

- The options in the **Specs** tab are used to define accuracy parameters for various operations done by machine. Select the **Manually set resolution/maximum departure** check box to define the accuracy up to which your machine can make linear/rotary movements and maximum accurate distance travelled by cutting tool in respective edit boxes; refer to Figure-33.

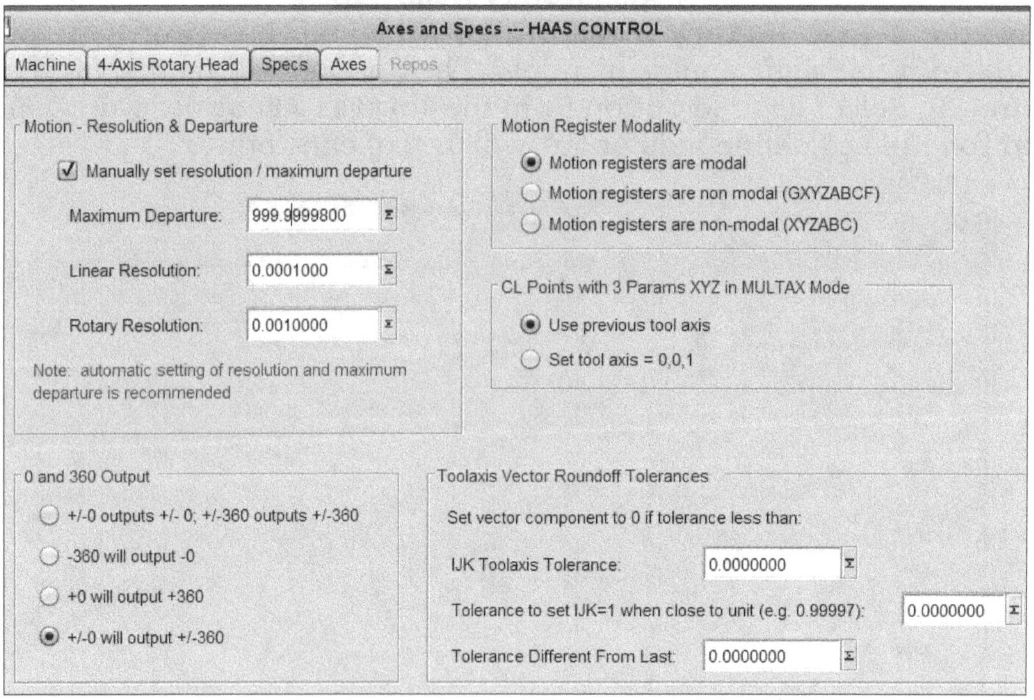

Figure-33. Specs tab

- Select desired radio button from the **Motion Register Modality** area to define whether motion related letters like G, X, Y, Z, and so on are considered modal or non-modal. Modal codes are those which remain active in program until an opposite command code is activated like G20 and G21. Non-modal codes are active only for its block like G04 F5 which applies a dwell of 5 seconds.
- The options in the **CL Points with 3 Params XYZ in MULTAX Mode** area are applicable for multi-axis machines only. Select the **Use previous tool axis** radio button if you want the system to use previously assigned tool axis angle when user has not specified axis angle while providing XYZ coordinates. Select the **Set tool axis = 0,0,1** radio button if you want to reset tool axis angle to Z axis.
- Select desired radio button from the **0 and 360 Output** area to define how outputs of angle values +/-0 and +/-360 will be considered.
- The options in the **Toolaxis Vector Roundoff Tolerance** area are used to define how tolerance will be round off when it is near to specified values in the edit boxes of this area.

Axes Tab

- The options in **Axes** tab are used to define whether axes limits will be checked when generating program or not. Select the **No limit checking** radio button if you do not want to check axes limits before generating NC program by postprocessor. Select the **Perform limit checking** radio button if you want to check for the axes limits and generate warning indicating which axis is violating limits. Note that in this case, the NC codes will still be generated so you need to manually modify the codes. Select the **Use automatic repositioning** radio button if you want the rotation axes to be automatically adjusted while linear axes are still output without corrective actions.

- Select the **ZW axis control** check box if you are working with ZW boring mills which have two collinear axes Z and W. This way your post processor can differentiate between Z axis and W axis. On selecting this check box, the **ZW Axis** tab will be added in the dialog box; refer to Figure-34. Set desired parameters in the W-Axis area to define limits, home position, address, and offset values for W axis. Select the **Axis retract** check box to allow retraction of cutting tool along W axis. Similarly, you can specify parameters for Z axis in the **Z-Axis** area of the tab.

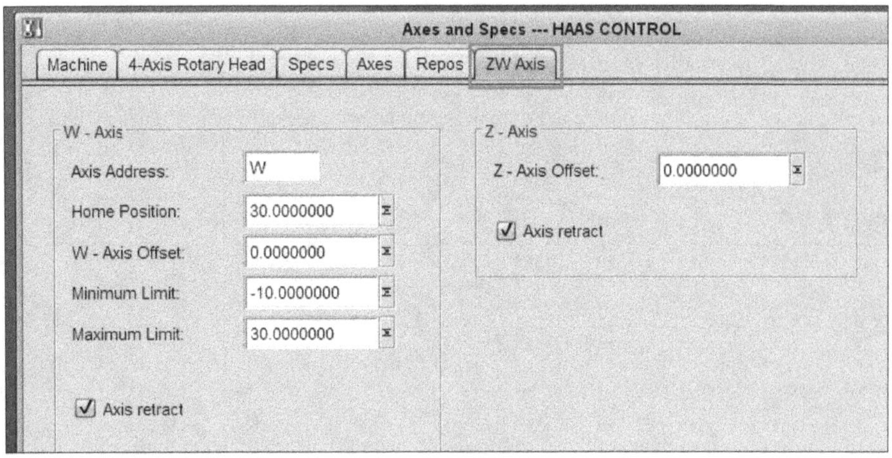

Figure-34. ZW Axis tab

- The edit boxes in **Axis Values and Limits** area of **Axes** tab are used to define limit values and home position for various axes of the machine.

Repos Tab

- The options in this tab are used for repositioning rotary axes controls when axis moves beyond the specified limits. Set desired parameters in various sub-tabs to define corrective actions for rotary axes.

Transformation and Output Parameters

Select the **Transforms & Output** option from the **Machine Tool Type** section at the left in the dialog box. The options in the dialog box will be displayed as shown in Figure-35.

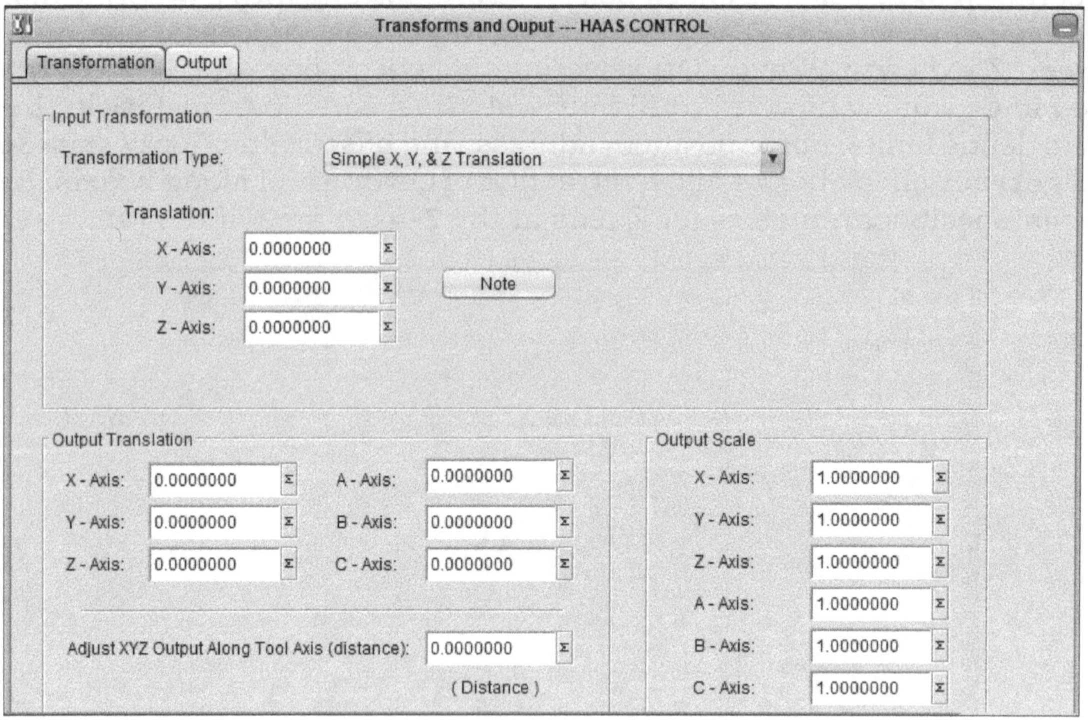

Figure-35. Transformation and Output options

Transformation Tab

The options in **Transformation** tab are used to define how post processor transforms CL points and tool axis data to generate coordinates for machine. Various options of this tab are discussed next.

- Select the **Simple X, Y and Z translation** option from the **Transformation Type** drop-down and specify desired values in **X - Axis**, **Y - Axis**, and **Z - Axis** edit boxes of the **Input Transformation** area. These values will be added in original CL points to get the final input CL point values.
- Select the **Point and Tool-Axis Transformation** option from the **Transformation Type** drop-down to apply transformation to points as well as tool axes. The options will be displayed as shown in Figure-36. Select the **General Trans** radio button if you want to apply desired transformation matrix to original CL data points. Select the **XY Rotation**, **YZ Rotation**, or **XZ Rotation** radio button to apply respective rotation to CL point along with transformation values.

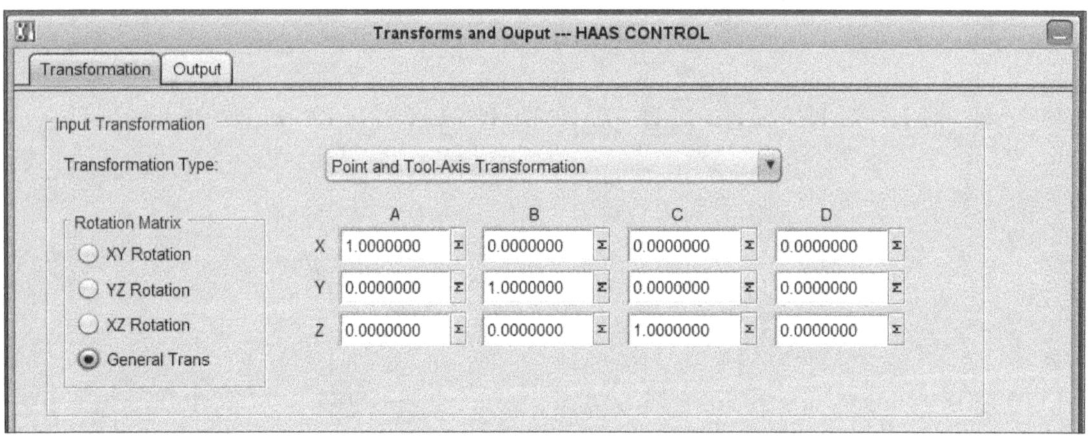

Figure-36. Point and Tool-Axis Transformation options

- Select the **Point only Transformation** option from the drop-down to apply transformation to input points only and not the tool axis.
- Select the **Tool-Axis only Transformation** option from the drop-down to apply transformation to input CL points of tool axis only.
- Similarly, you can apply transformation to output CL points and axes by using options in the **Output Translation** and **Output Scale** areas.

Output Tab

Select the **Output** tab to define how output CL points will be generated. The options will be displayed as shown in Figure-37.

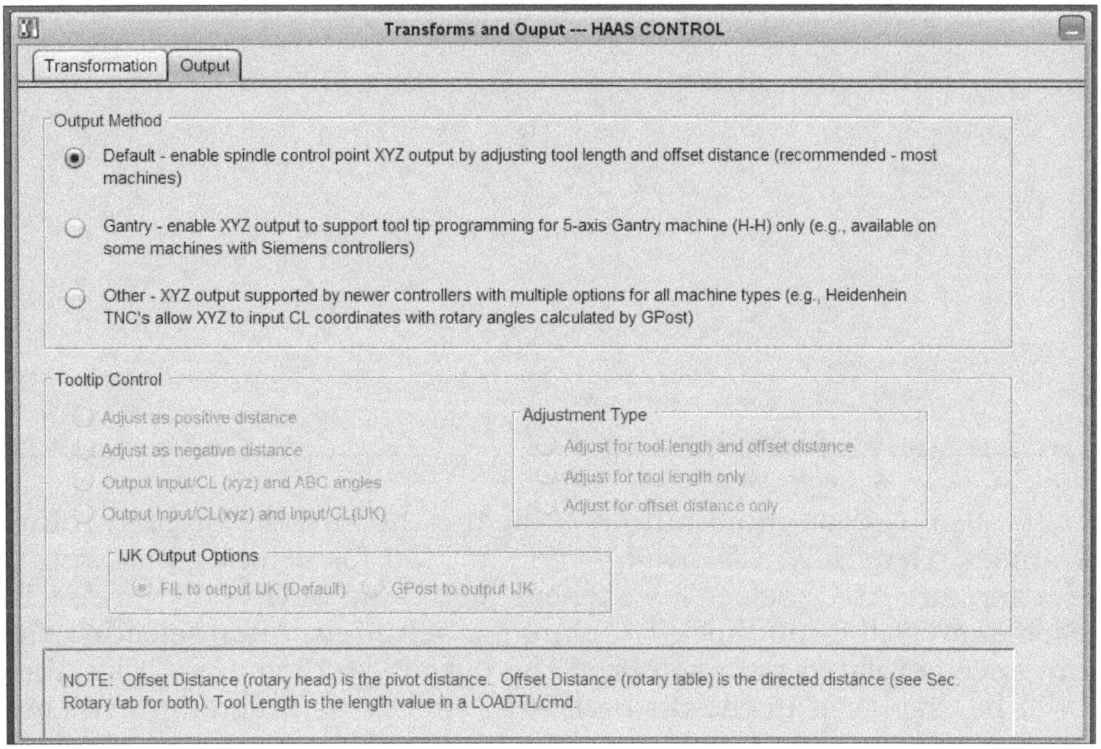

Figure-37. Output tab

- Select the **Default** radio button if you want the spindle to be used as reference for applying tool length adjustment and offset distance parameters in XYZ output. Select the **Gantry** radio button if you want the tool tip to be used as reference for applying tool length adjustment and offset distance parameters in XYZ output. Select the **Other** radio button to apply adjustments to tooltip and tool length for newer controllers. On selecting the **Other** radio button, options in **Tooltip Control**, **Adjustment Type**, and **IJK Output Options** areas will become active. Set the parameters based on your machine.

Planar Machining Parameters

Select the **Planar Machining** option from the left area to define parameters for rotating cutting tool perpendicular to spindle for performing planar machining if supported by your machine. Select the **Enable Planar Machining** check box to allow planar machining by post processor. The options will be displayed as shown in Figure-38.

- Select the **Off** or **On** option from the **Starting Mode** area to set PIVOT Z on or off for starting mode, respectively.

- Select desired option from the **Rotation Matrix Defined By** area to define the reference plane for rotation matrix.

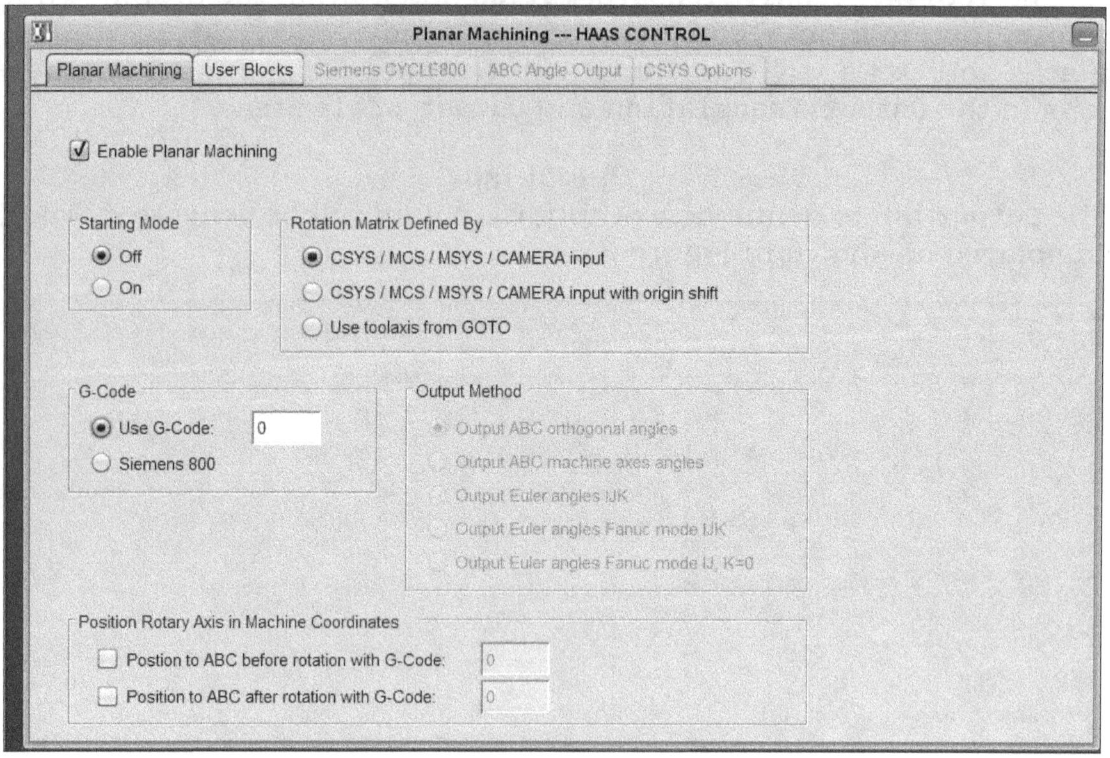

Figure-38. Planar Machining options

- Select the **Use G-Code** radio button to define the G code for plan rotation and letter angles. Generally, G7 or G68 code is used for defining plan rotation and angle letters are ABC. Select the **Siemens 800** radio button if your machine can use Siemens CYCLE800 block for planar machining. After selecting this radio button, specify related parameters in the **Output Method** area. Also, the related tabs will be displayed in the dialog box to specify parameters for Siemens 800 planar machining.

Right Angle Head Parameters

- Select the **Right Angle Head** option from the left area in dialog box if you have a 5 axis machine and the tool head is at 90 degree to spindle. Select the **Right angle head or holder support required** check box to activate the related options. The options will be displayed as shown in Figure-39.

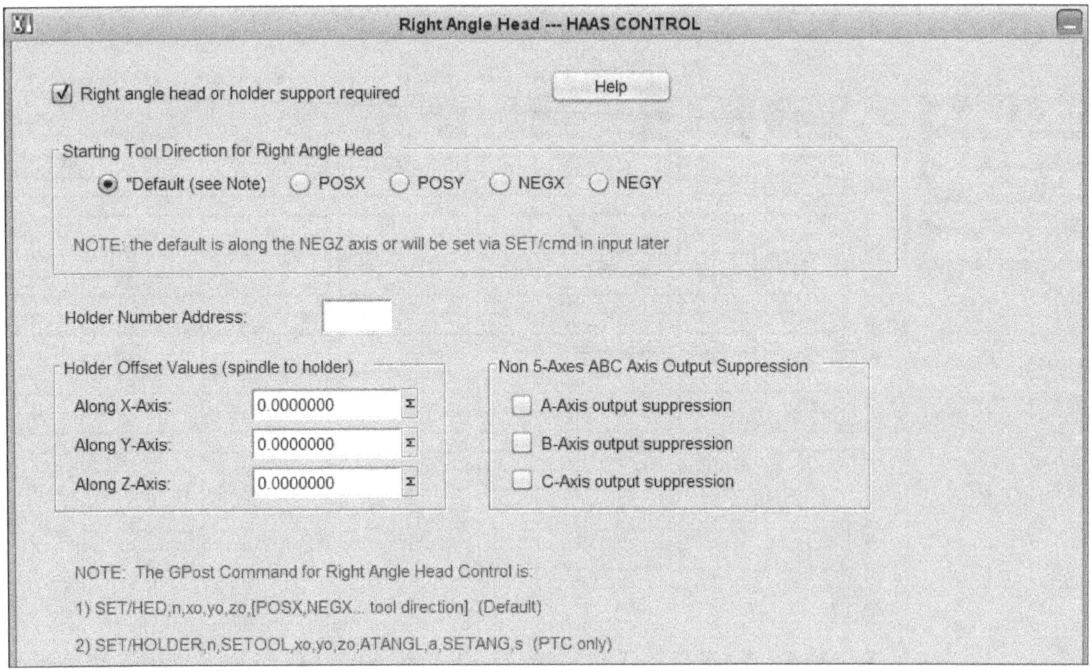

Figure-39. Right Angle Head options

- Select desired radio button from the **Starting Tool Direction for Right Angle Head** area to define the starting angle for Right Angle Head attached to machine. Select the **POSX** radio button if you want the head to be along positive X axis. Select the **NEGX** radio button if you want the head to be along negative X axis. Select the **Default** radio button if you want the head to be along default negative Z axis. Similarly, you can use other radio buttons for X axis.
- Specify desired value in the **Holder Number Address** edit box to define holder address value to be output by post processor with M or H code.
- Specify desired distance values in the **Along X-Axis**, **Along Y-Axis**, and **Along Z-Axis** edit boxes of the **Holder Offset Values (spindle to holder)** area to define distance by which holder will be away from spindle.
- Select desired check box(es) from the **Non 5-Axes ABC Axis Output Suppression** area to define the movement(s) which will not be output by post processor. For example, select the **A-Axis output suppression** check box if you do not want the machine to rotate along A-axis.

MCD File Format Parameters

Select the **File Formats** option from the left area to display options for modifying file format parameters. After selecting this option, select the **MCD File** option from the left area to define parameters related to MCD files. The options will be displayed as shown in Figure-40.

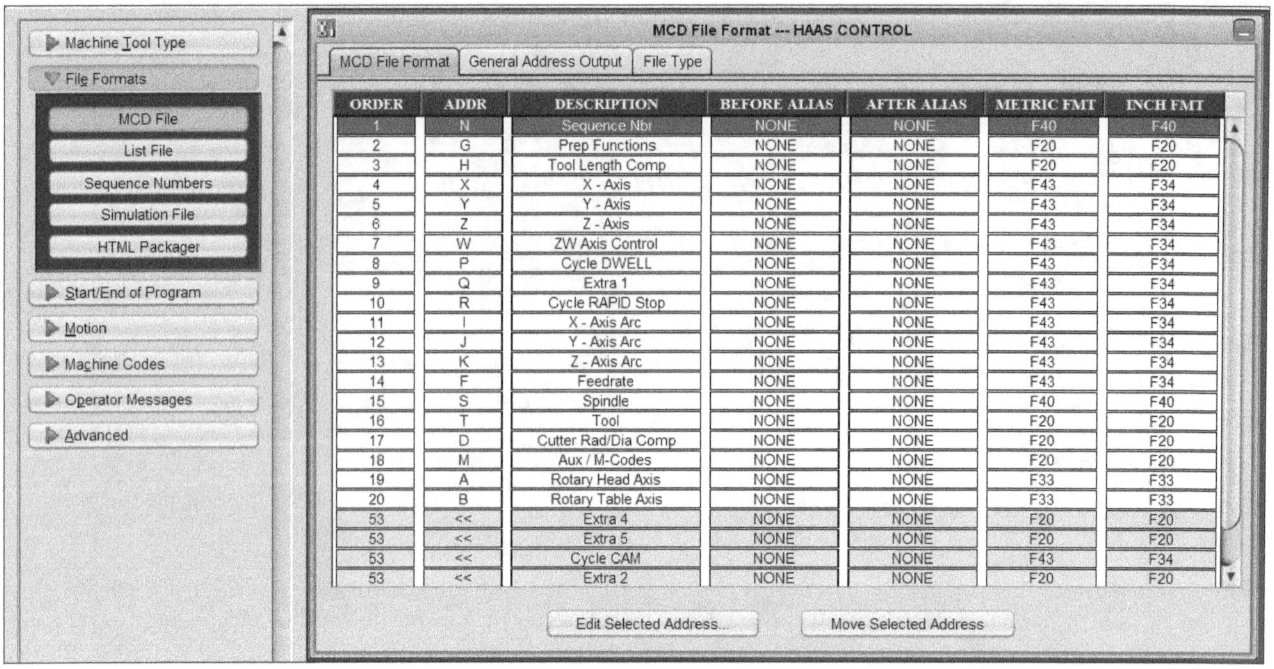

Figure-40. MCD File option

- Select desired value from the table and click on the **Edit Selected Address** button. The related **Register Settings** dialog box will be displayed; refer to Figure-41.

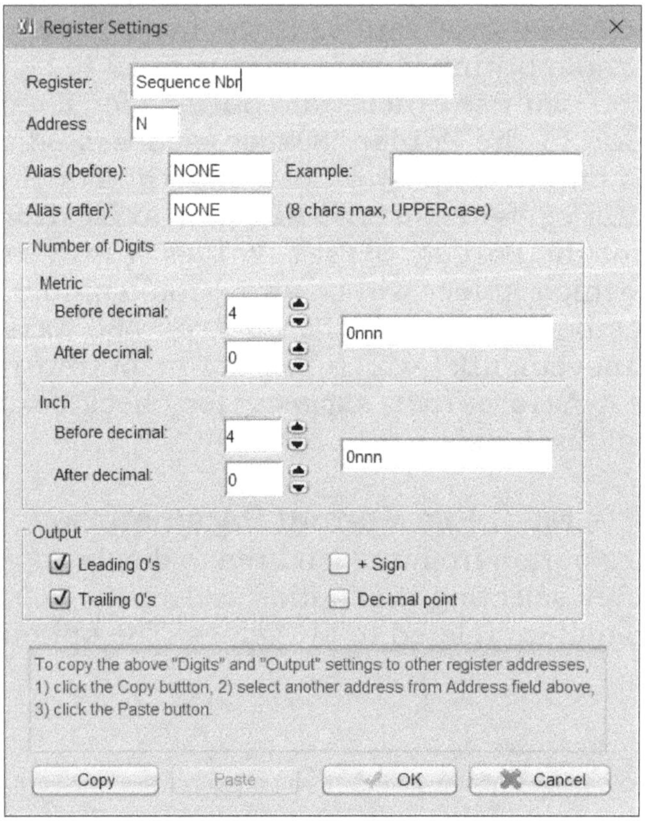

Figure-41. Register Settings dialog box

- Set desired parameters in the dialog box to define parameters for selected code to be output by Post Processor. For example, you can set the decimal points up to which the numbers will be output after the selected code. After setting desired parameters, click on the **OK** button to apply changes.

General Address Output Tab

- Select the **General Address Output** tab from the right area in the dialog box to define general address output parameters like how decimal points will be displayed in output; refer to Figure-42.

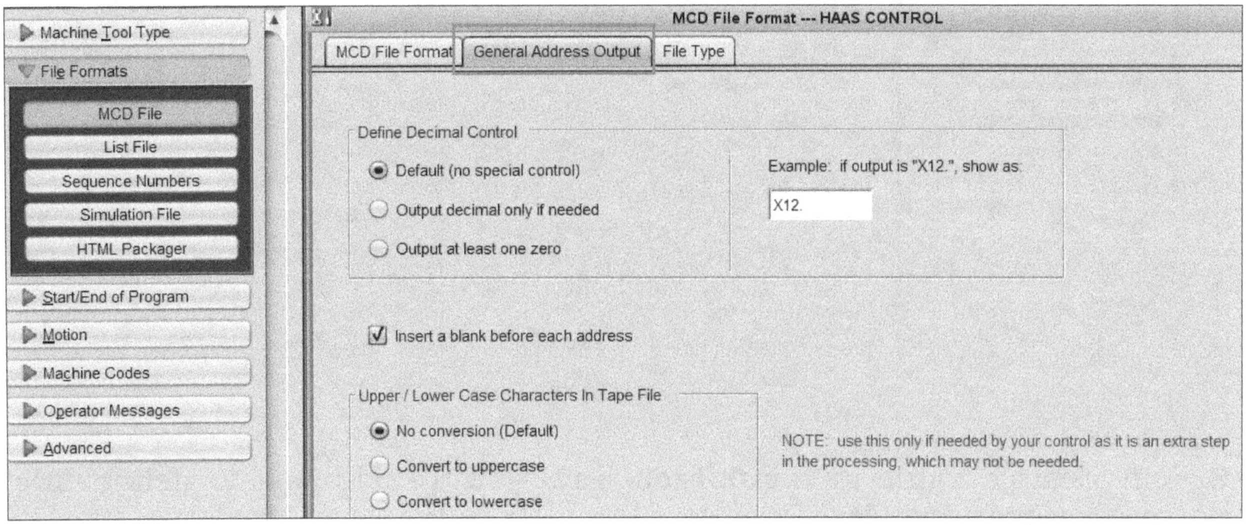

Figure-42. General Address Output tab

- Select the **Default** radio button from the **Define Decimal Control** area if you do not want to control the decimal in output by postprocessor. Select the **Output decimal only if needed** radio button if you want to output whole numbers without decimals. Select the **Output at least one zero** radio button if you want to display at least one zero after decimal in output generated by postprocessor.
- Select the **Insert a blank before each address** check box if you want to add a blank line in output before a new address code is generated in output file.
- Select desired radio button from the **Upper/Lower Case Characters In Tape File** area to define whether all the characters in output file will be in upper case, lower case, or uncontrolled by postprocessor.

File Type Tab

- Select the **Use system default** radio button to use default extension of file like *.tap, *.pu1, and so on for generating output of postprocessor.
- Select the **Specify extension** radio button to create a user defined extension for output file and specify the value in **Extension** edit box. Note that you can specify maximum 6 characters for extension.

List File Options

- Select the **List File** option from the left area to define parameters related to verification file listing. The options will be displayed as shown in Figure-43.

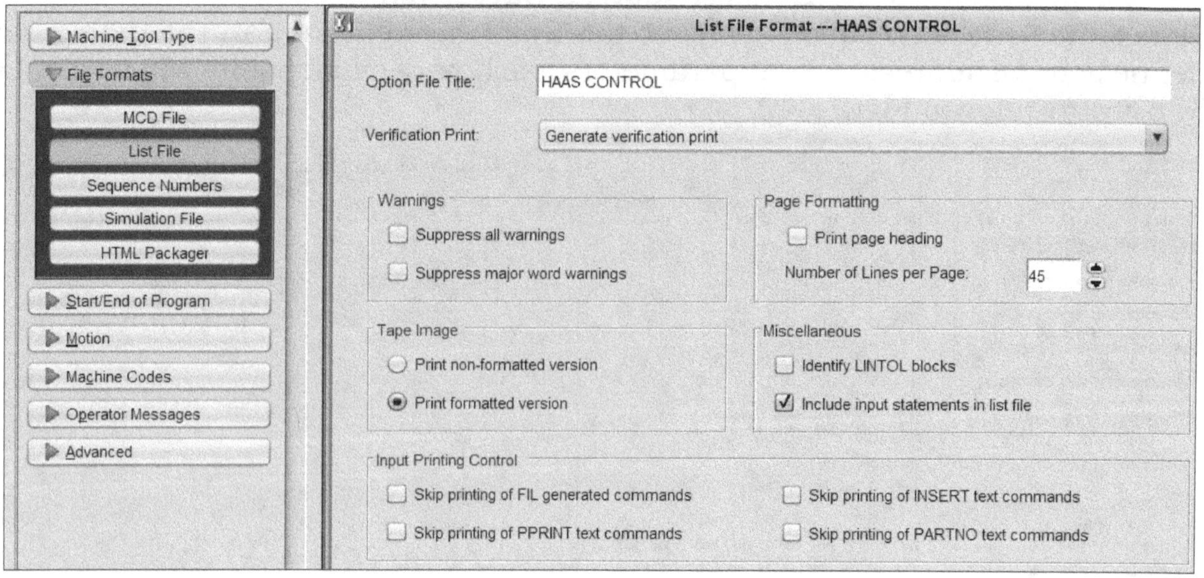

Figure-43. List File Format options

- Specify desired value in the **Option File Title** edit box to define title of postprocessor option file.
- Select desired option from the **Verification Print** drop-down to define which verification parameters will be generated in the output file.
- Select desired check boxes from the **Warnings** area to define which warning messages will be suppressed in the output file.
- Select desired radio button from the **Tape Image** area to define whether the output will be formatted or it will be generated as they are in CL file in the post processor output.
- Select the **Print page heading** check box from the **Page Formatting** area to display heading in each page of output file.
- Specify desired value in the **Number of Lines per Page** edit box to define total number of NC code lines in each page of output file.
- Select the **Identify LINTOL blocks** check box to identify multi-axes moves. Note that these moves will be identified in the list file and will not affect the machine control data file.
- Select the **Include input statements in list file** check box to also include the comments in the list file.
- Select the **Skip printing of FIL generated commands** check box if you do not want to generate FIL commands in the output file.
- Similarly, you can use other check boxes of the **Input Printing Control** area to skip respective commands in output of post processor.

Sequence Numbers Options

- Select the **Sequence Numbers** option from the left area in the dialog box. The options will be displayed as shown in Figure-44.

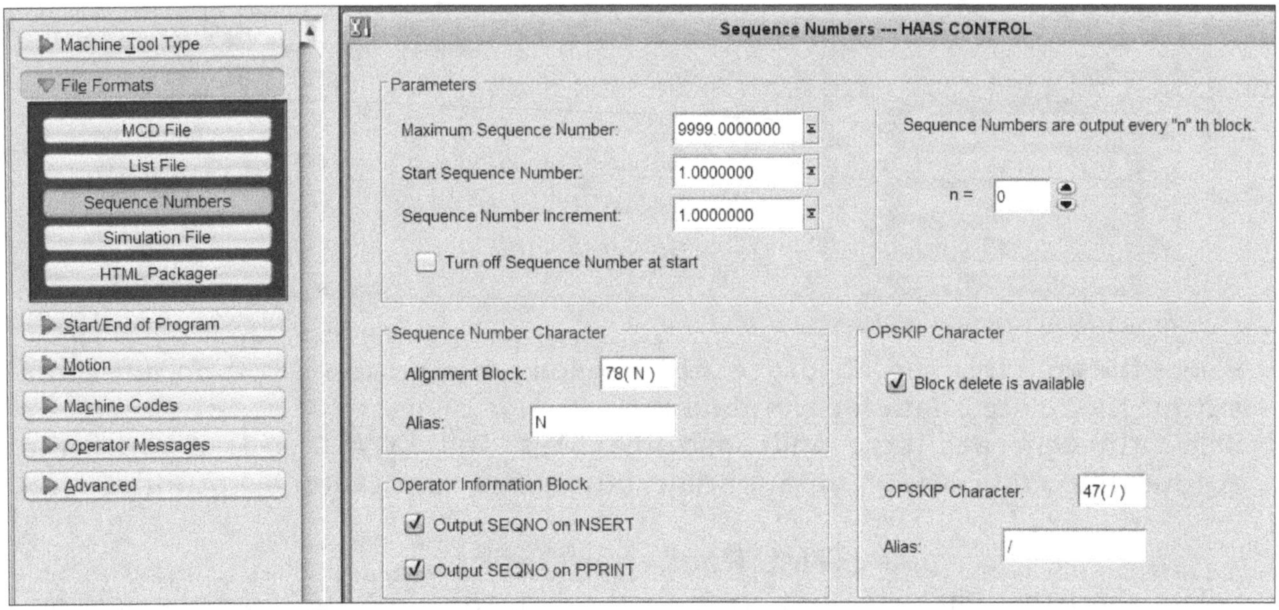

Figure-44. Sequence Numbers options

- Specify desired values in the **Maximum Sequence Numbers** and **Start Sequence Numbers** edit boxes to define the range of sequence numbers.
- Specify desired value in the **Sequence Number Increment** edit box to define the value by which sequence number will increase while going down in NC program.
- Select the **Turn off Sequence Number at start** check box if you do not want to output sequence number at the beginning of NC program.
- Specify desired value in the **Alignment Block** edit box to define sequence number to be displayed with address of next block in output. Specify desired value in **Alias** edit box to define alternate text/letter to be used in place of alignment blocks.
- Specify desired value in the **n=** edit box of **Sequence Numbers are output every "n" th block** area to define the interval at which sequence numbers will be generated in the output file.
- Select the **Block delete is available** check box if you want the postprocessor to generate block delete characters in the output when it encounters OPSKIP/ON and OPSKIP/OFF commands. You can specify delete characters in the edit boxes of **OPSKIP Character** area.
- Select the check boxes in **Operator Information Block** area to specify whether sequence numbers will be output with **INSERT** and **PPRINT** blocks.

Simulation File Options

- Select the **Simulation File** option from the left area to define whether you want to generate simulation as well along with regular NC program output file. On selecting this option, the options in the dialog box will be displayed as shown in Figure-45.

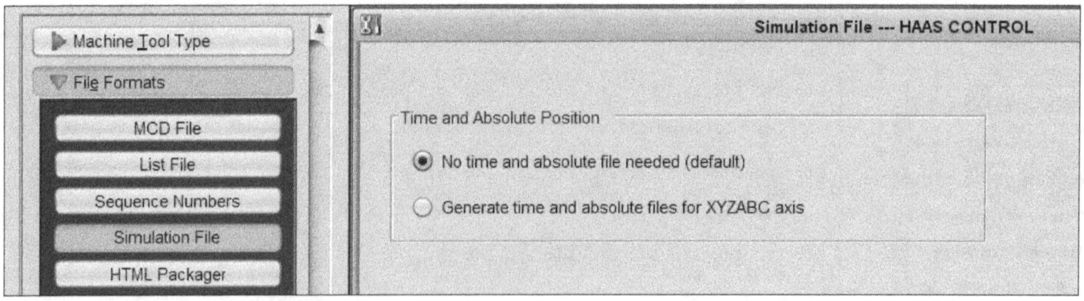

Figure-45. Simulation File options

- Select the **No time and absolute file needed** radio button if you do not want to output the related data for simulation.
- Select the **Generate time and absolute files for XYZABC axis** if you want to output time and position data for simulation in a simulation output file.

HTML Packager Options

- Select the **HTML Packager** option from the left area in **File Formats** section to create multiple HTML files at the output. The options will be displayed as shown in Figure-46.

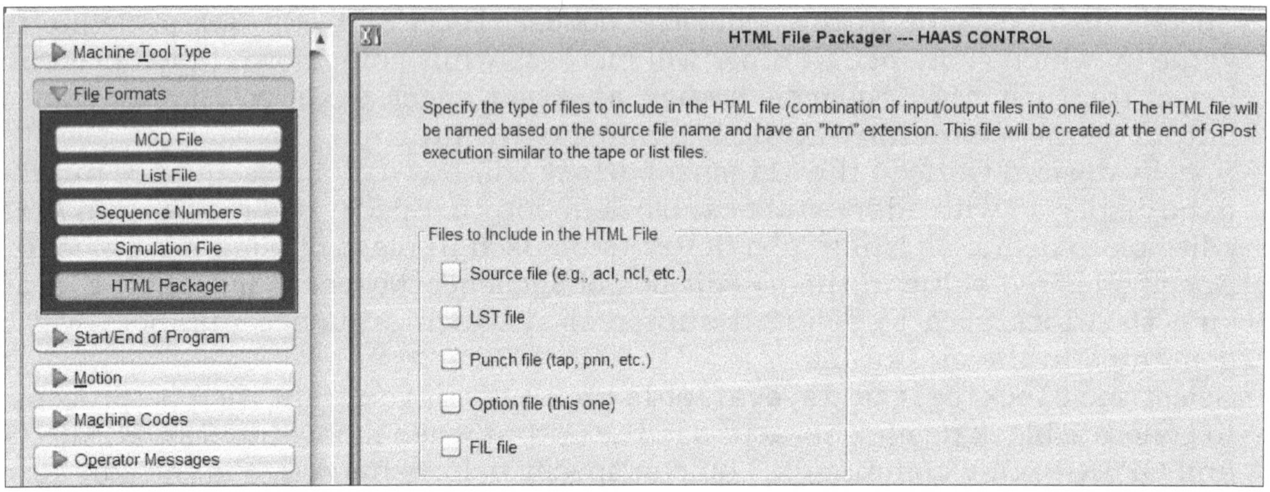

Figure-46. HTML Packager options

- Select check boxes for files to be included in the HTML package from the **Files to Include in the HTML File** area of the dialog box.

Start/End of Program Options

- Select the **Start/End of Program** option from the left area in the dialog box. The options will be displayed as shown in Figure-47.

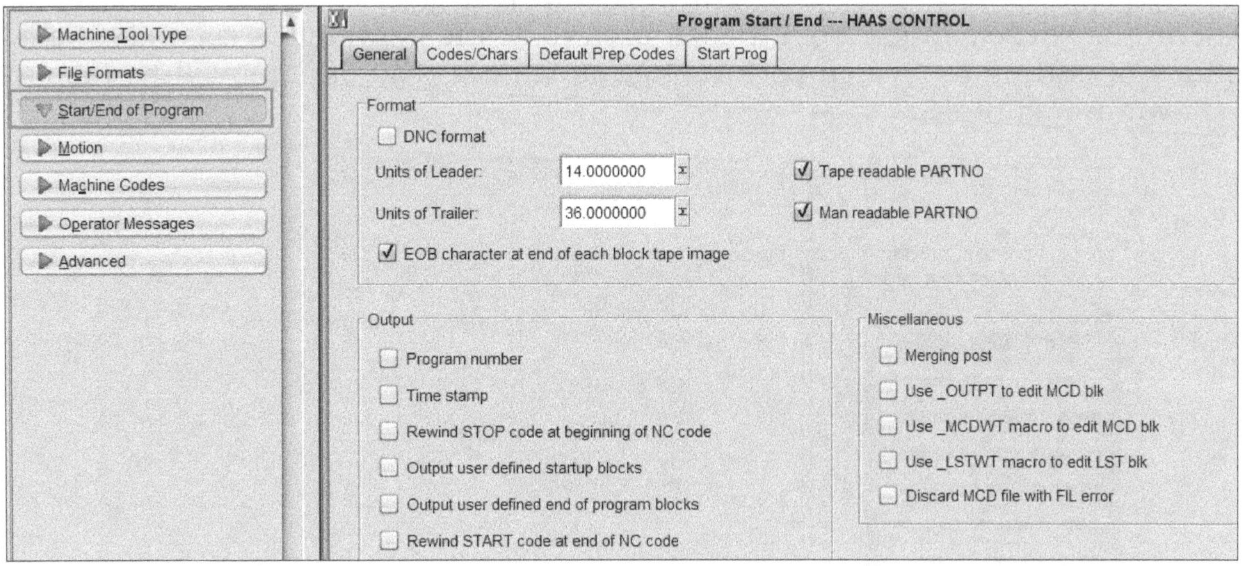

Figure-47. Start End of Program options

General Tab

- By default, the **General** tab from the dialog box to define general program parameters like unit of leaders, output parameters to be generated, and so on.
- Select the **DNC format** check box if you want to format the program output as per Distributed Numerical Control environment. Clear this check box if you want to manually define format for program and specify the parameters in **Format** area as desired.
- Select the **EOB character at end of each block tape image** check box to insert end of block character at the end of each block.
- Select check boxes from the **Output** area to define parameters to included in the output file.
- Select check boxes from the **Miscellaneous** area to perform respective operations on the output before generating output file.

Codes/Chars Tab

- Select the **Codes/Chars** tab from the dialog box to define code characters to be inserted in the program like End of Block (EOB) character, leader character, and so on.

Default Prep Codes Tab

- Select the **Default Prep Codes** tab from the dialog box to modify some basic preparation codes like code to change between inch and metric, code to change feedrate mode, and so on. Set the parameters in edit boxes of **Default Codes** area to define the G codes for respective functions.
- Select the **Output code to tape image** check boxes for desired codes if you want them to be recorded in tape image of output.
- In the **Post Units of Measure** area, specify the units to be used for input, output, and option files in respective drop-downs.

Similarly, you can define parameters in **Start Prog** and **Program Number** tabs of the dialog box.

Motion Parameters

Click on the **Motion** option from the left area to define parameters related to various motions of cutting tool when performing machining. The options will be displayed as shown in Figure-48.

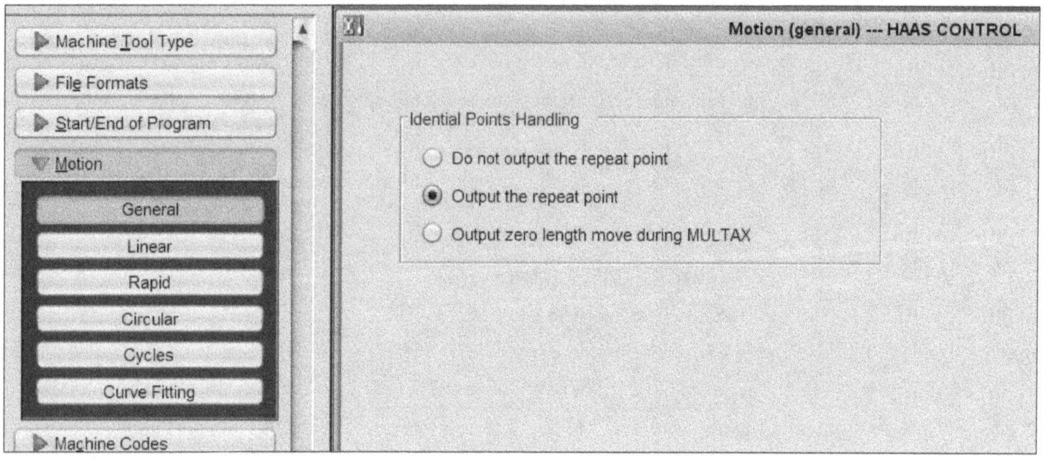

Figure-48. Motion parameters

By default, the **General** option is selected in the **Motion** section. Select the **Do not output the repeat point** radio button if you do not want to repeat the points having same coordinates for the same function lines. Select **Output the repeat point** radio button if you want to repeat same functions with same coordinates in the output file. Select the **Output zero length move during MULTAX** radio button if you want to output moves with zero length for multi-axis machine.

Linear Motion Options

Select the **Linear** option from the left area in **Motion** section to define parameters related to linear motion of cutting tool. The options will be displayed as shown in Figure-49.

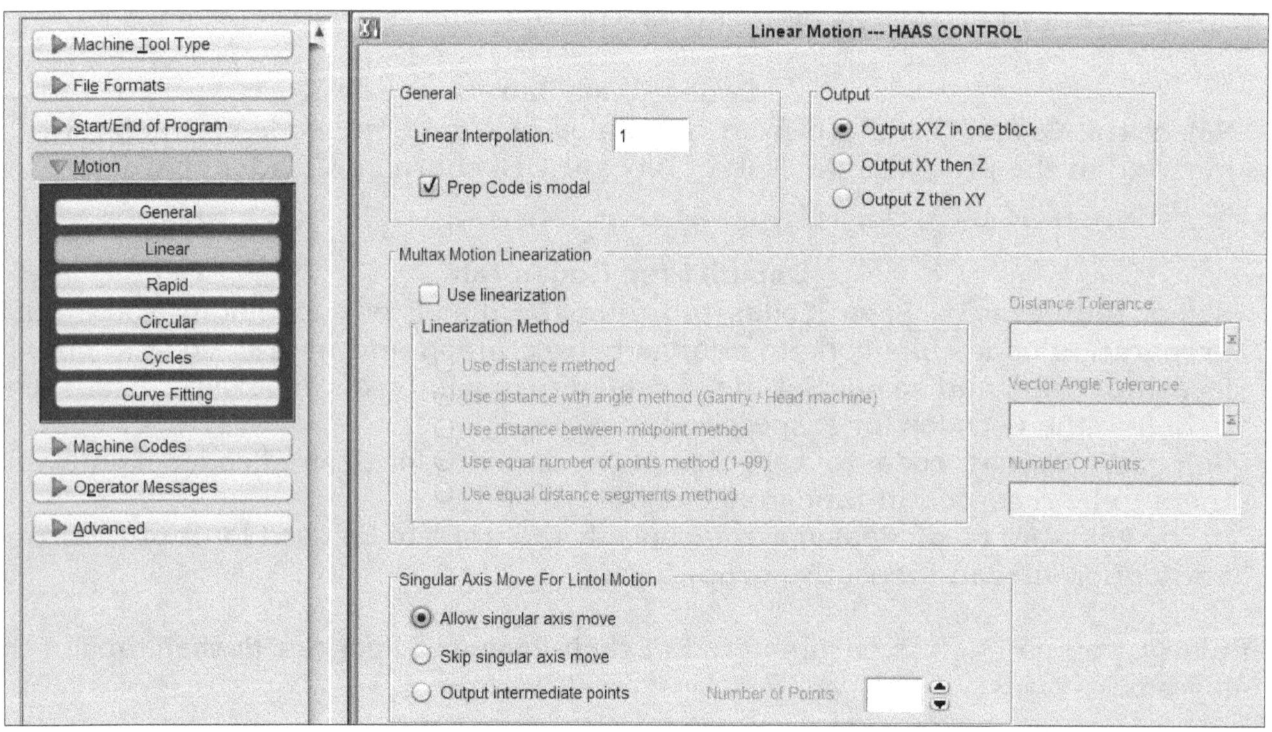

Figure-49. Linear options

- Specify desired value in the **Linear Interpolation** edit box. By default, **1** is specified in this edit box which means **G1** code is used for linear interpolation.
- Select the **Prep Code is modal** check box if you want to make the code active until an anti code is activated.
- Select desired radio button from the **Output** area to define how X, Y, and Z coordinates will be output in the file.
- Select the **Use linearization** check box to convert multi-axis motions into multiple linear motions. After selecting this check box, select desired radio button from the **Linearization Method** area. For example, if you want to convert a multi-axis movement into equal length linear motions then select the **Use equal distance segments method** radio button.
- Select desired radio button from the **Singular Axis Move For Lintol Motion** area to define how single axis movements are controlled in output.

Rapid Motion Options

- Select the **Rapid** option from the left area in the dialog box to define how rapid movements will be output by postprocessor; refer to Figure-50.

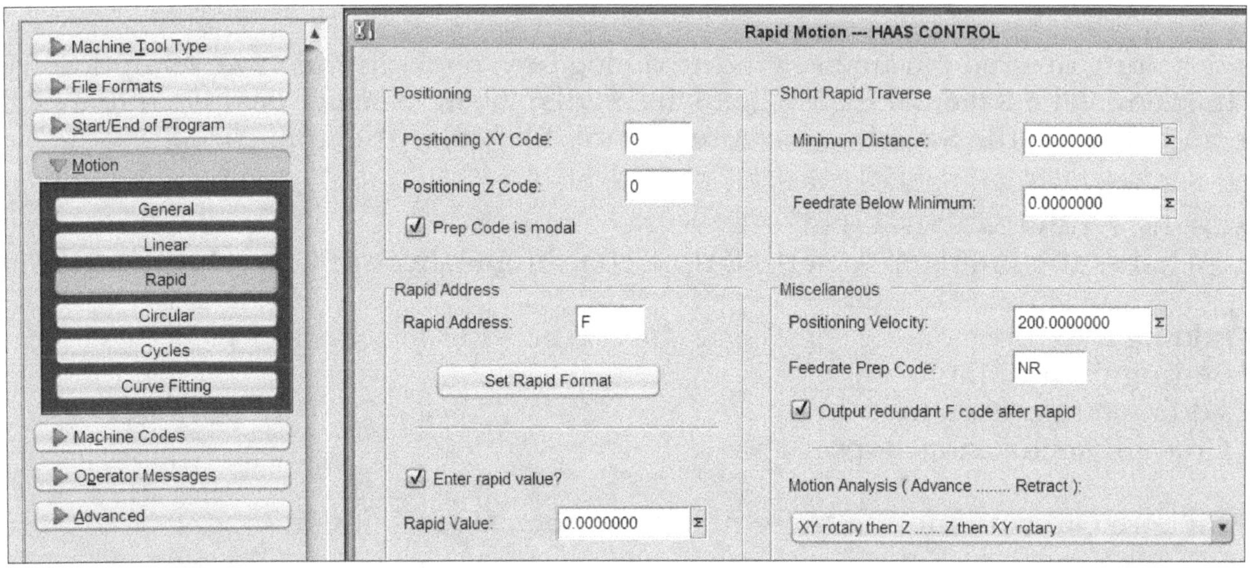

Figure-50. Rapid Motion options

- Set the code for rapid tool movement in the **Positioning XY Code** and **Positioning Z Code** edit boxes. By defaults, the value is 0 which makes the code G0.
- Similarly, specify desired parameters for other options related to motions.

Machine Codes Parameters

Select the **Machine Codes** option from the left area to define codes generated for various functions in the output; refer to Figure-51. These options can be used to define G-codes, M-codes, F-parameters, and so on.

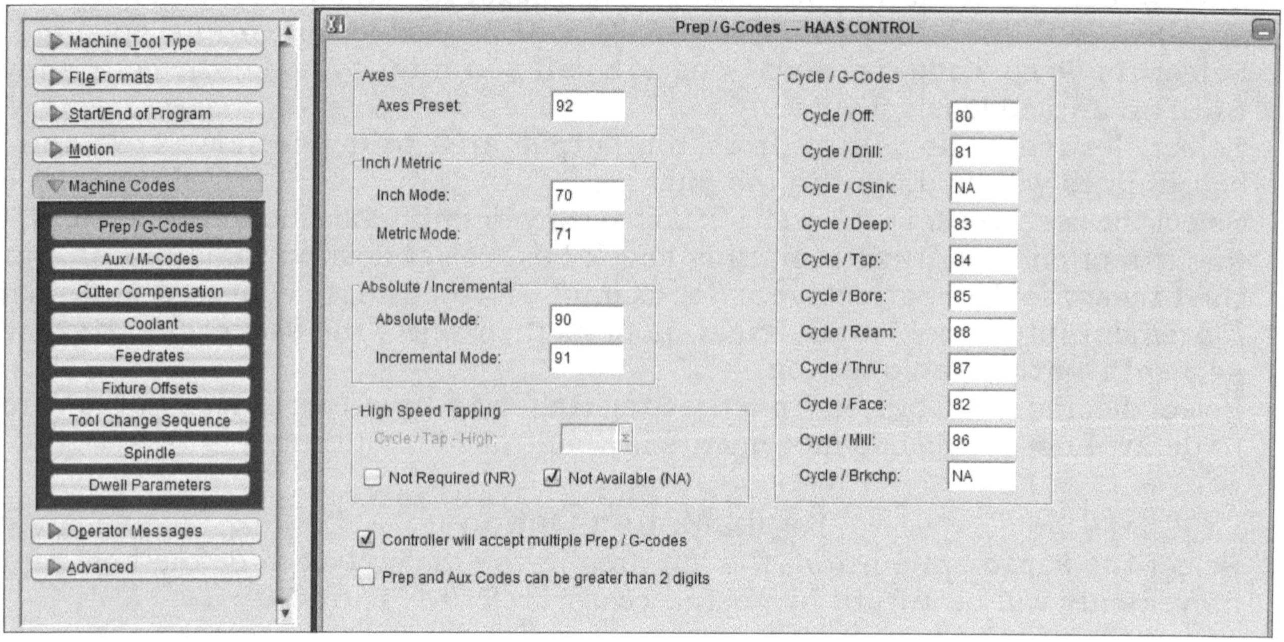

Figure-51. Machine Codes options

After setting desired parameters in the dialog box, click on the **Save As** option from **File** menu. The **Save As** dialog box will be displayed. Specify desired name of the file and click on the **Save** button. After saving file, close the application.

SELF-ASSESSMENT

Q1. What is the first step in setting up a coordinate sheet in Creo Manufacturing?

A. Adding a fixture
B. Setting up a CMM
C. Adding a reference model
D. Creating measuring steps

Q2. Where can you find the "Assemble Reference Model" option?

A. Output tab
B. Components panel in the Inspect tab
C. Measure panel in the Inspect tab
D. Tools menu

Q3. What does the "Default" option in Current Constraint Type do?

A. Aligns probe with fixture
B. Positions model arbitrarily
C. Assembles the model at default planes
D. Displays the model tree

Q4. What is the purpose of adding a fixture?

A. To add support geometry
B. To simulate probe interference
C. To generate NC code
D. To define coordinate origin

Q5. Where do you click to access CMM settings?

A. Construct tab
B. Probe Setup
C. CMM drop-down in Inspection Machine panel
D. Output panel

Q6. What is required in CMM Work Center instead of a tool?

A. G-code
B. Tool library
C. Fixture
D. Probe

Q7. How do you access default probes?

A. Through Fixture Setup
B. From the Components panel
C. Using the File button in Probe Setup dialog box
D. From the Measure panel

Q8. What does selecting the "Plane" tool in the Measure panel allow you to do?

A. Construct a geometry
B. Set fixture base
C. Create plane measurement step
D. Add CMM

Q9. Which fields in the Edit Parameter dialog box are compulsory?

A. All fields
B. Only fields with drop-downs
C. Fields highlighted in yellow
D. Fields with checkboxes

Q10. What is the function of the "Probe Path" tool?

A. Measure planes
B. Define probe geometry
C. Generate output file
D. Assemble model

Q11. What happens when you select "Play Path" from the Menu Manager?

A. Save file
B. Show code
C. Preview probe path
D. Return to Home tab

Q12. What is the "Construct Panel" used for?

A. Save probe path
B. Create measurement setup
C. Create geometry on model
D. Define coordinate system

Q13. What is the "Best Fit" option in Plane construction used for?

A. Project geometry
B. Align to coordinate system
C. Automatically choose plane based on selection
D. Center two faces

Q14. Which option in Line/Axis construction creates a line from two points?

A. Intersect
B. Best Fit
C. Midline
D. Projection

Q15. Which option constructs a plane at the midpoint of two planes?

A. Normal
B. Parallel
C. Theoretical
D. Midplane

Q16. What dialog box appears when you click on the "Probes" button in the CMM Work Center?

A. CMM Setup
B. Probe Selection
C. Probe Setup
D. Assembly Browser

Q17. What action must be taken after selecting the face for measurement?

A. Click Done/Return directly
B. Set probe parameters
C. Choose ADD POINTS → Automatic
D. Close the Probe Path

Q18. Which tool allows you to define an axis at the intersection of two planes?

A. Projection
B. Intersect
C. Midline
D. Best Fit

Q19. What must be selected from the status bar while constructing a plane?

A. Output file name
B. Coordinate system
C. Reference geometries
D. Measurement speed

Q20. What is the function of the "Add a fixture component" button?

A. Opens Probe Setup
B. Opens dialog to select model for fixture
C. Measures reference model
D. Assembles part to origin

Q21. What panel provides the "Line/Axis" and "Plane" tools?

A. Output panel
B. Process panel
C. Components panel
D. Construct panel

Q22. What type of geometry is typically selected for a Plane measurement step?

A. Cylindrical surface
B. Edges
C. Planar face
D. Datum axis

Q23. After completing a measurement step, what color highlights it in the modeling area?

A. Green
B. Blue
C. Red
D. Yellow

Q24. What tool must be used first before any measurement steps can be created?

A. Probe Path
B. Coordinate System
C. Operation tool
D. Output file

Q25. How can a user preview the created probe points on a surface?

A. By clicking Show File
B. By enabling Construction Geometry
C. By selecting Play Path
D. By clicking OK in the Probe Points dialog box

For Student Notes

Chapter 8

Project

Topics Covered

The major topics covered in this chapter are:

- ***Starting an Expert Machinist File.***
- ***Importing the reference model and creating the workpiece.***
- ***Creating Machine Setup.***
- ***Creating Operation Setup.***
- ***Creating Tool Setup.***
- ***Creating NC Features.***
- ***Creating Toolpaths.***

PROJECT

Starting an Expert Machinist File

- Start Creo Parametric by using the icon on desktop or by using the **Start** menu.
- Select the **New** button from the **Data** panel in the **Home** tab of **Ribbon**. The **New** dialog box will be displayed.
- Select the **Manufacturing** radio button from the **Type** area and **Expert Machinist** radio button from the **Sub-type** area.
- Specify the name as **Project** in the **Name** edit box of this dialog box and clear the **Use default template** check box. After specifying all the settings, the updated **New** dialog box will be displayed; refer to Figure-1.

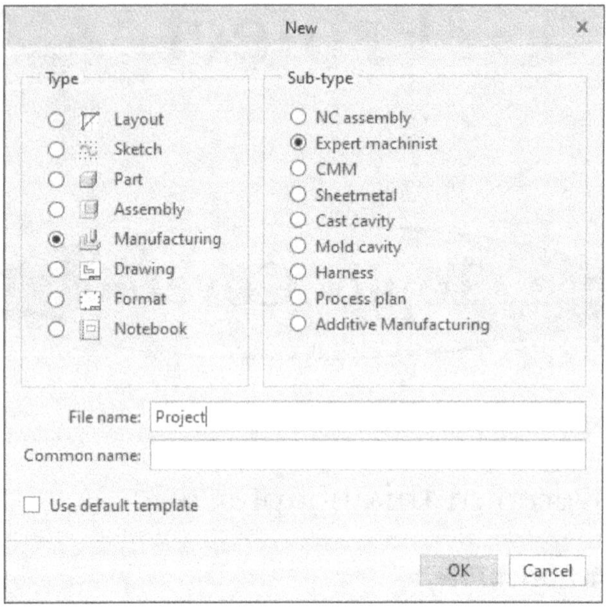

Figure-1. New File Options dialog box

- Click on the **OK** button from the dialog box. The **New File Options** dialog box will be displayed; refer to Figure-2.

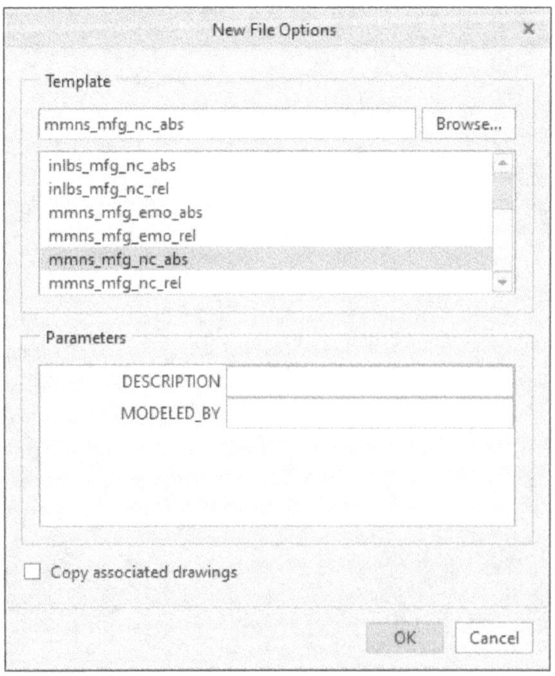

Figure-2. New File Options dialog box

- Select **mmns mfg nc abs** template from the list, enter your name in the **MODELED BY** edit box in the **Parameters** area of this dialog box and then click on the **OK** button. On doing so, the interface of Expert Machinist is displayed.
- Click on the **Quit NC-Wizard** button to exit the **NC-WIZARD** dialog box displayed in the right. This will increase the view area. You can skip this step if you want to see the tips related to current operation.

Importing the reference model and creating the workpiece

- Click on the **Create Model** tool from the **NC Model** panel in the **Machining** tab of the **Ribbon**; refer to Figure-3. The prompt will be displayed to specify the name of the nc model that will be used for machining; refer to Figure-4.

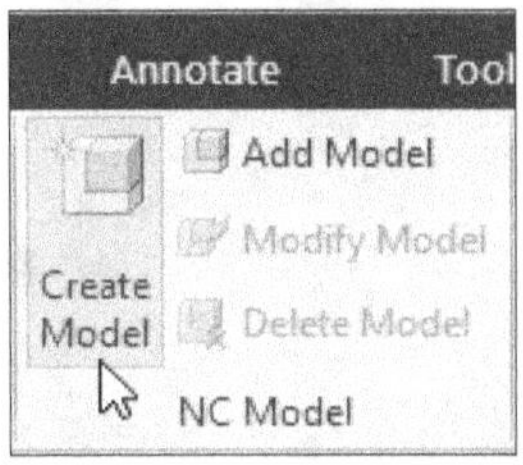

Figure-3. Create Model tool

Figure-4. Prompt for specifying name of the nc model

- Click on the **Accept value** button to accept default name displayed as **[PROJECT NCMDL]** or you can specify desired name and then click on the **Accept value** button. On selecting the button, the **Open** dialog box will be displayed along with the **Menu Manager**; refer to Figure-5.

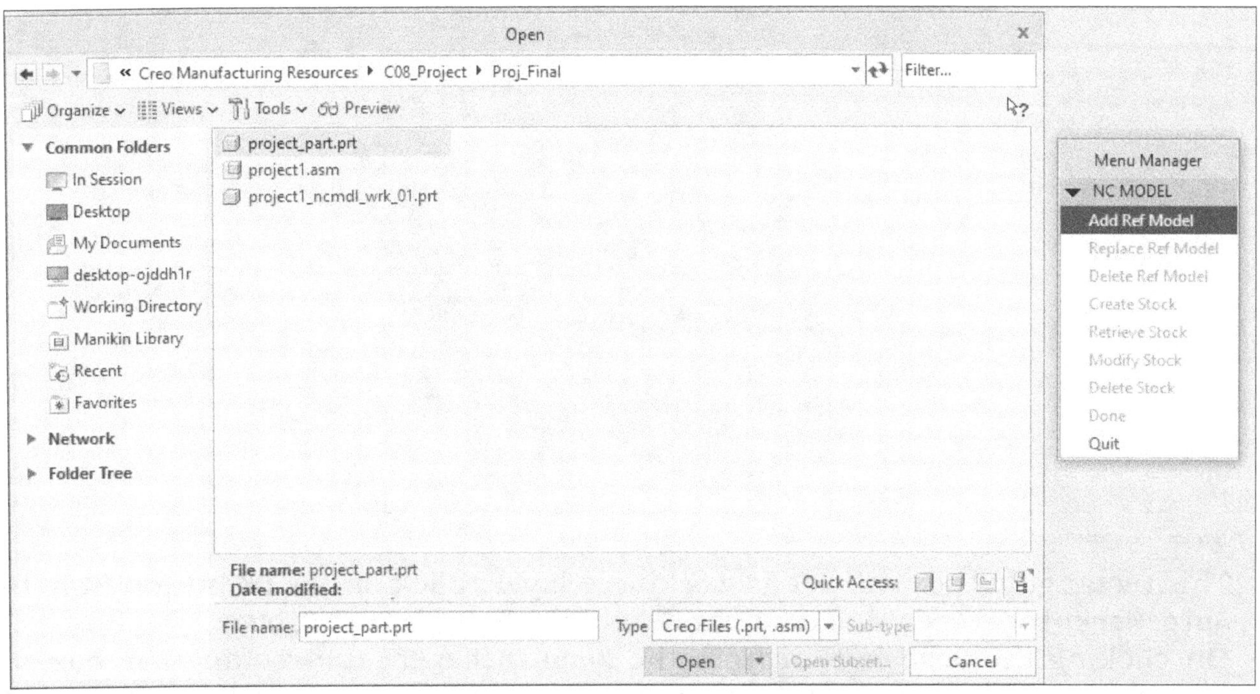

Figure-5. Open dialog box with NC MODEL Menu Manager

- Select the **project part.prt** file from the downloaded resource kit and then click on **Open** button from the **Open** dialog box. The model will be displayed in the Expert Machinist interface; refer to Figure-6.

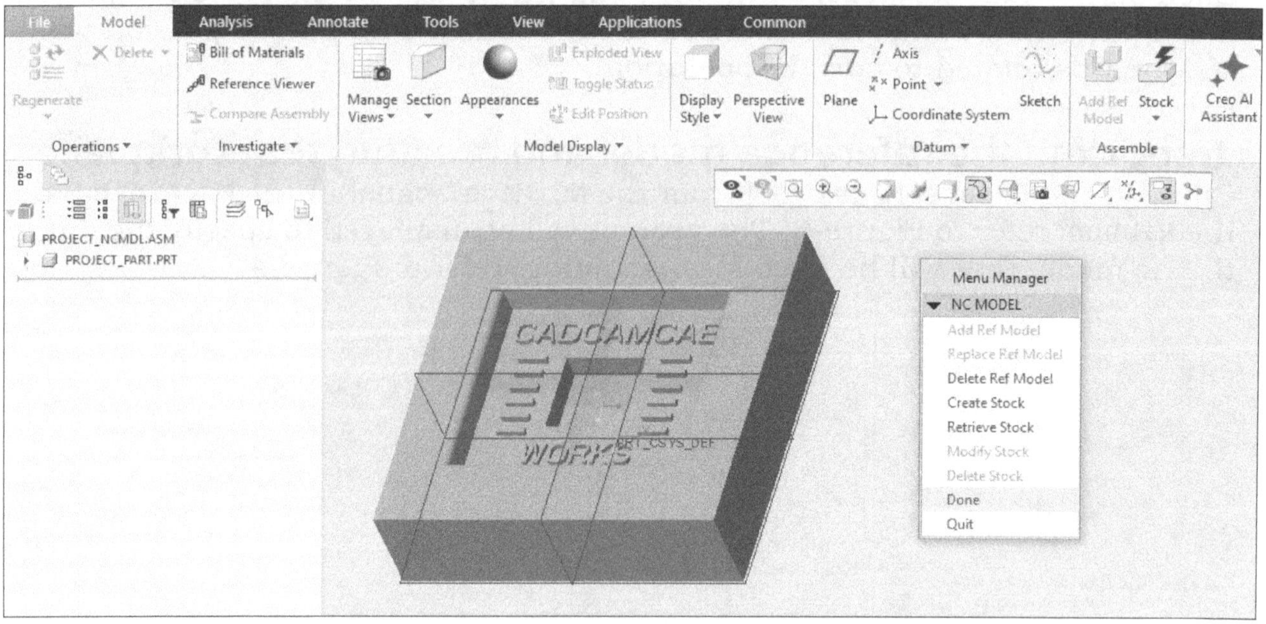

Figure-6. Expert machinist interface with the imported model and the active NC MODEL Menu Manager

- Click on the **Create Stock** option from the **Menu Manager**. The imported model (also called reference model) will be packaged by a rectangular box; refer to Figure-7.

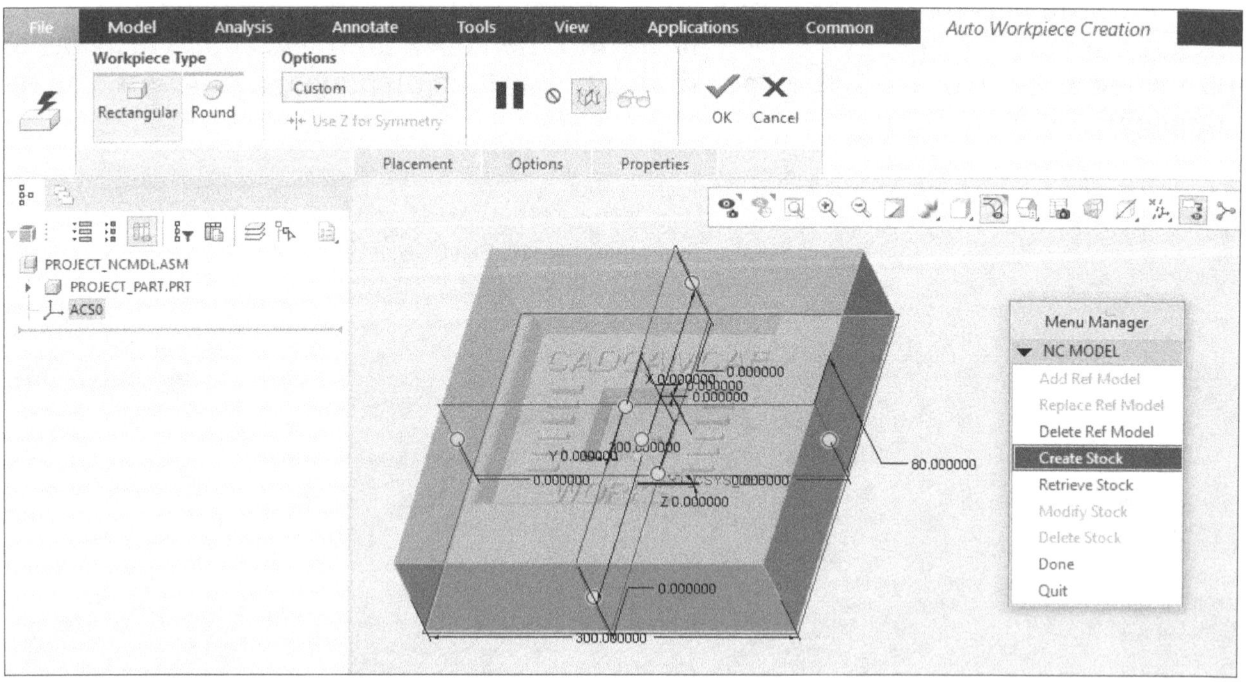

Figure-7. Creating stock for the reference model

- This rectangular box will act as workpiece layer. Click on the **OK** button from the **Auto Workpiece Creation** contextual tab displayed in the **Ribbon**.
- On clicking the **Done** button from the **Menu Manager**, the rectangular box will be locked as the workpiece. Click on the **Done** button from the **Menu Manager** to accept the workpiece. On doing so, the **Component Placement** contextual tab will be displayed in the **Ribbon**.

- Select the **Default** option from the **Constraint Type** drop-down in this contextual tab; refer to Figure-8. The workpiece along with the reference model is placed at the origin of Expert Machinist coordinate system.

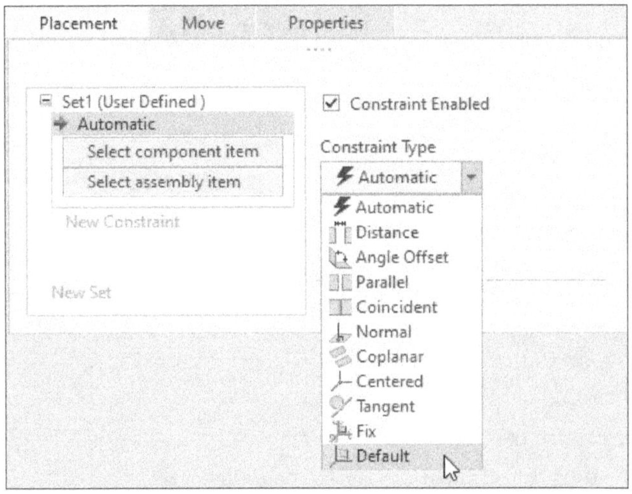

Figure-8. Option to be selected from Constraint Type drop down

- Click on the **OK** button from the **Ribbon** to accept the placement.
- Click on the **Material Removal Display** button from the **Display** panel of **Machining** tab in the **Ribbon** for a better visualization of workpiece. On selecting this button, the workpiece will be displayed as shown in Figure-9.

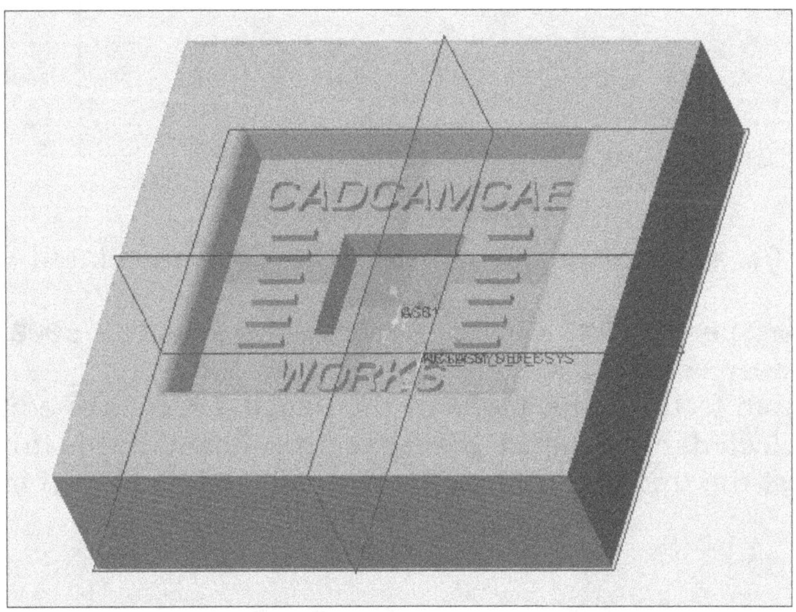

Figure-9. Workpiece displayed after selecting Material Removal Display button

Creating Machine Setup

- Click on the **Machine Tool Manager** tool from the **Work Center** drop-down in the **Setup** panel of **Machining** tab in the **Ribbon**. The **Milling Work Center** dialog box will be displayed as shown in Figure-10.
- Specify the name of machine as **VMC015** in the **Name** edit box. (Now, the machine setup being created will be saved with the name VMC015).
- In the **CNC Control** edit box, specify the name of controller as **HAAS**.

- Select the **5 Axis** option from the **Number of Axes** drop-down.
- In the **Output** tab of this dialog box, retain all the default settings as shown in Figure-10.

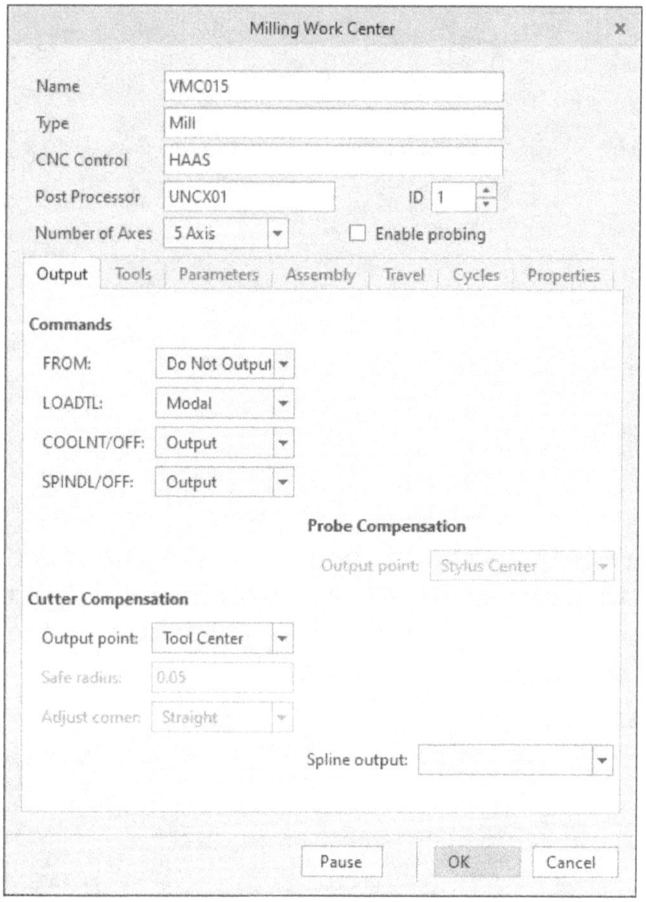

Figure-10. Milling Work Center dialog box

- Click on the **Parameters** tab to activate the options related to parameters of machine.
- In the **Maximum Speed (RPM)** edit box, specify the speed as **8000**.
- In the **Horsepower** edit box, specify the value as **30**.
- Specify the rapid feed rate as **14000** in the **Rapid Feed Rate** edit box. Make sure that **MMPM** is selected in the **Rapid Traverse** drop-down in this tab. After specifying all parameters, the updated dialog box is displayed as shown in Figure-11.

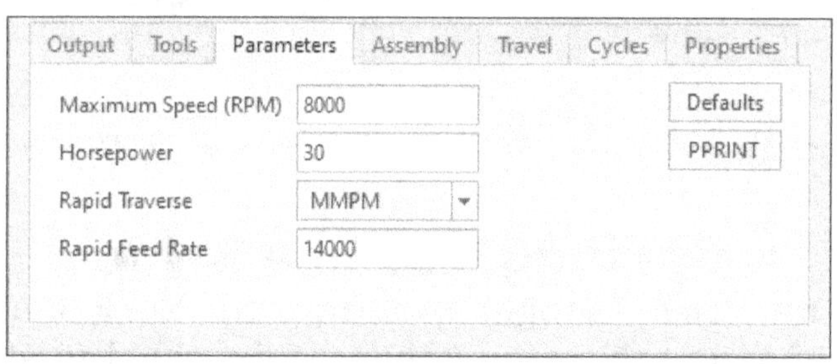

Figure-11. Parameters tab of Milling Work Center dialog box

- Click on the **Travel** tab to specify the limits of machine.
- Specify the value of X travel as **700**, Y travel as **400**, and Z travel as **500**. Refer to Figure-12 for specifying the values.

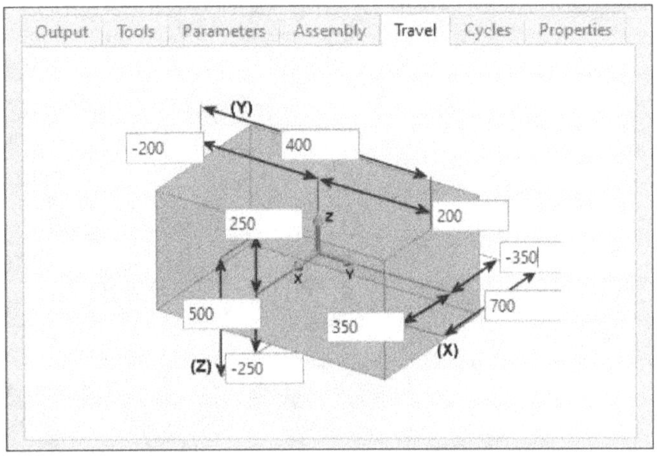

Figure-12. Travel tab of Milling Work Center dialog box

- Click on the **OK** button to accept all the specified settings and create the machine. On doing so, the machine will be added in the **Model Tree** with the name **VMC015**.

Creating Operation Setup

- Click on the **Operation** tool from the **Setup** panel in the **Ribbon**. The options of **Operation** tab will be displayed in the **Ribbon**; refer to Figure-13.

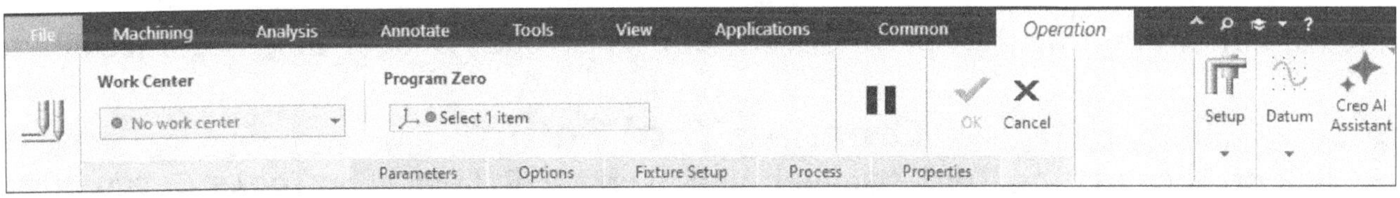

Figure-13. Operation tab and its options

- Click on the **Work Center** drop-down and select the **VMC015** option. (the machine we created earlier)
- Click on the **Datum** drop-down (displayed in the right of the **Ribbon**) and click on the **Coordinate System** button, the **Coordinate System** dialog box will be displayed; refer to Figure-14.

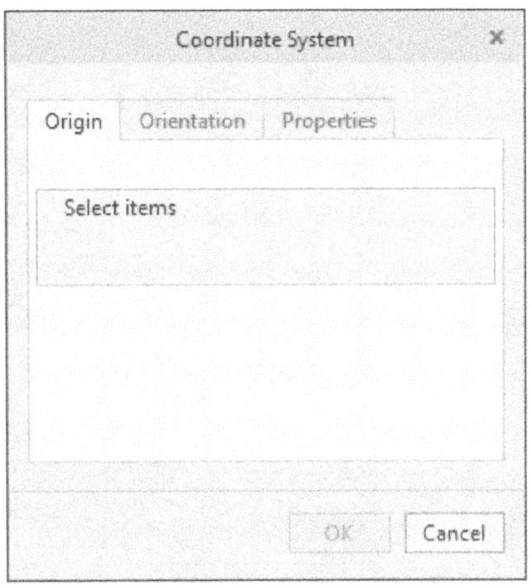

Figure-14. Coordinate System dialog box

- Select the top face of the workpiece to place the coordinate system.
- Select the two boundary edges and specify the distance value as **0** for both; refer to Figure-15.

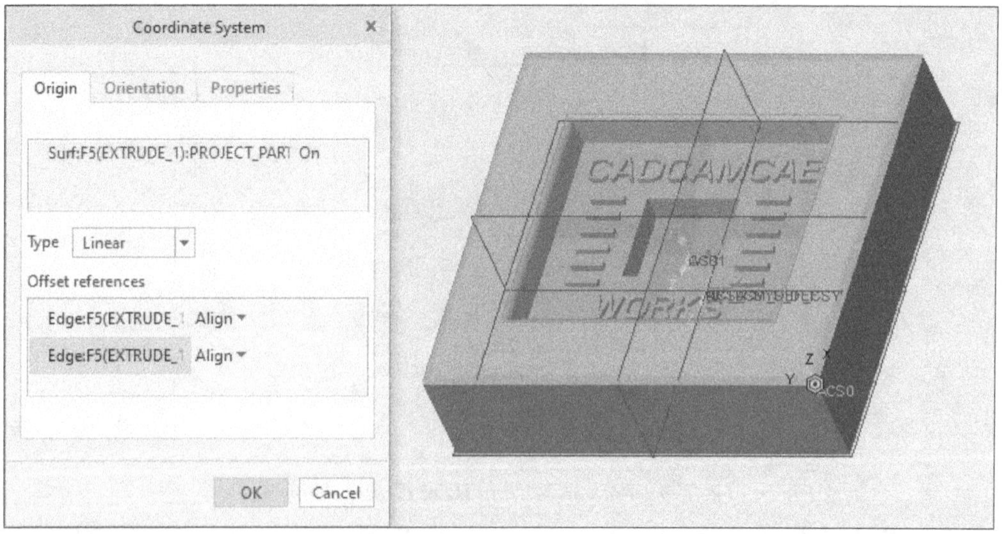

Figure-15. Creating the Coordinate System

- Click on the **OK** button from the **Coordinate System** dialog box, the coordinate system will be placed at the specified location.
- Click on the **Resume** button from the **Ribbon** to activate the **Operation** tab again.
- Select the coordinate system recently created and then click on the **OK** button from the **Ribbon** to create the operation.

Note that after creating the operation, the **Cutting Tool Manager** also becomes active.

Creating Tool Setup

- Click on the **Cutting Tool Manager** tool from the **Ribbon**. The **Tools Setup** dialog box will be displayed as shown in Figure-16.

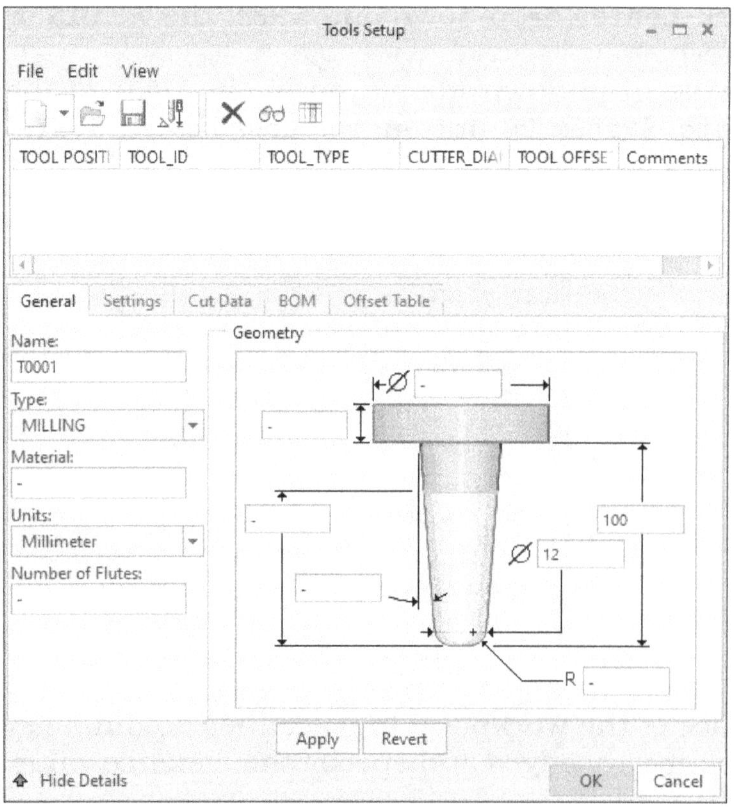

Figure-16. Tools Setup dialog box

- Click in the **Name** edit box of this dialog box and specify **END MILL ROUGH**.
- Click on the down arrow of **Type** drop-down and select the **END MILL** option.
- In the **Geometry** area of the dialog box, specify the values as shown in Figure-17.

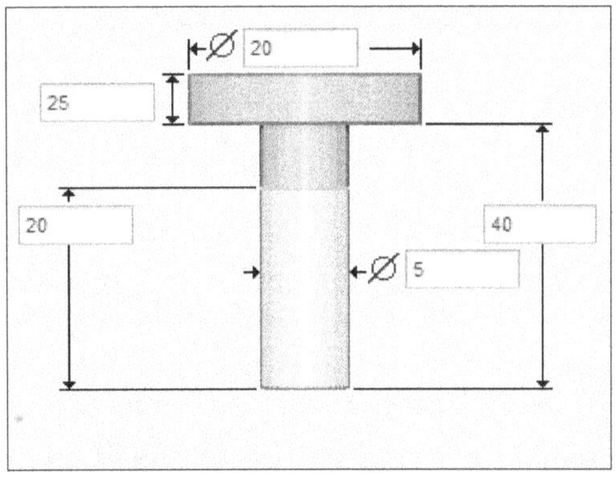

Figure-17. Value to be specified

- Click on the **Cut Data** tab; the options in the tab will be displayed as shown in Figure-18.

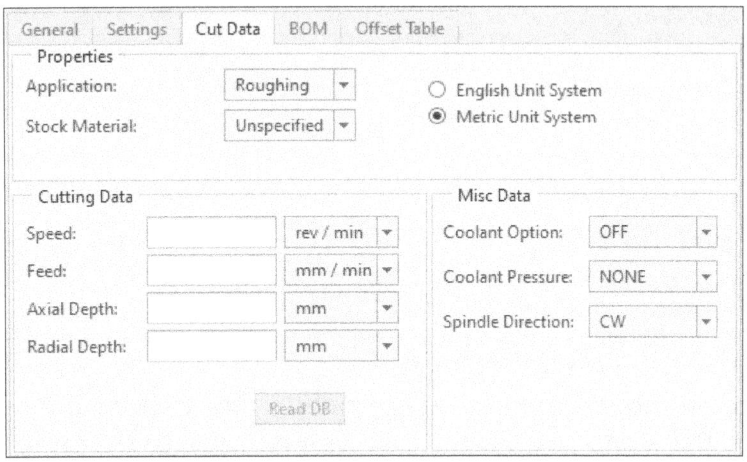

Figure-18. Options of the Cut Data tab

- Click in the **Speed** edit box and specify the value as **4500**.
- Click in the **Feed** edit box and specify the value as **250**.
- Click in the **Axial Depth** edit box and specify the value as **2**.
- Click in the **Radial Depth** edit box and specify the value as **2**.
- Click on the down arrow of **Coolant Option** drop-down and select the **FLOOD** option from the list.
- Click on the down arrow of **Coolant Pressure** drop-down and select the **MEDIUM** option from the list.
- Click on the down arrow of the **Spindle Direction** drop-down and select the **CCW** option from the list.
- Now, click on the **Apply** button to create the tool, the tool will be added in the tool list of **Tools Setup** dialog box.

For Finishing and embossing the text, we need to add a finishing tool also. Following steps can be used for creating the finishing tool.

- Click on the **General** tab if any other tab is selected.
- Click in the **Name** edit box and specify the name as **END MILL FINISH**.
- Select **END MILL** option from the **Type** drop-down if not selected.

- Specify the parameters of the tool as shown in Figure-19.

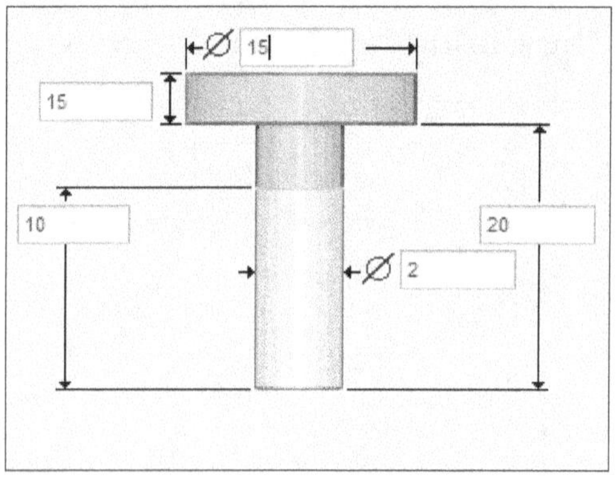

Figure-19. Parameters to be specified for tool

- Click on the **Settings** tab, the options in the **Settings** tab will be displayed as shown in Figure-20.

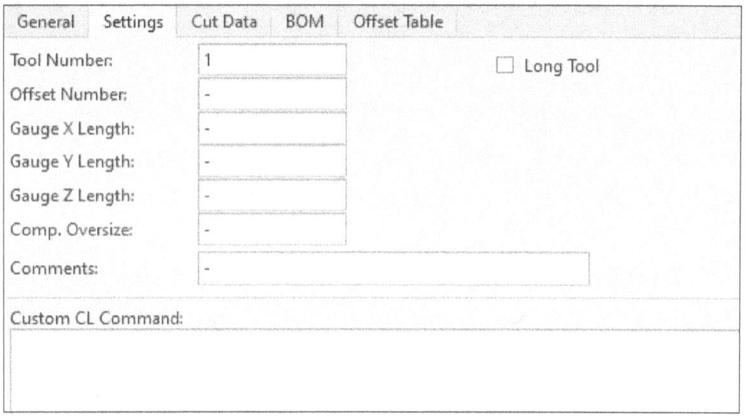

Figure-20. Options in the Settings tab

- Click in the **Tool Number** edit box and specify the value as **2**.
- Click on the **Cut Data** tab to display options related to cutting; refer to Figure-21.

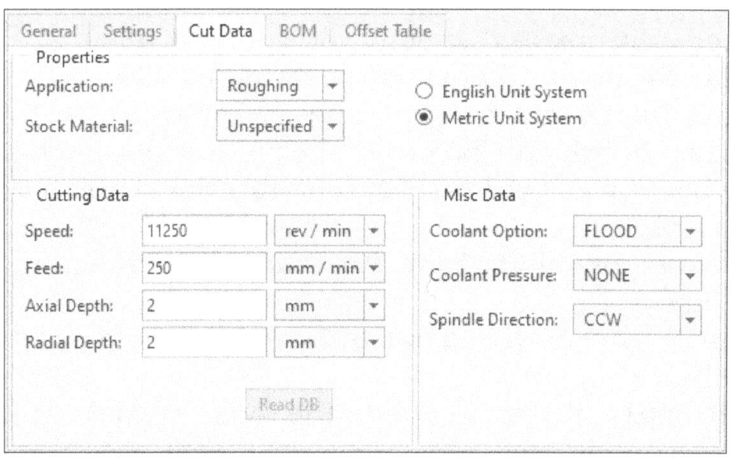

Figure-21. Options in the Cut Data tab

- Click on the down arrow of **Application** drop-down and select the **Finishing** option from the list.
- Specify the rotational speed of tool as **5000** in the **Speed** edit box.
- Click on the down arrow of **Coolant Pressure** drop-down and select the **MEDIUM** option from the list.
- Specify the rest of the options as in Figure-21.

Now, click on the **Apply** button to add the tool in the list. The reference part also has fillet at the corners. To create fillet in the workpiece, we need a special type of tool. The procedure to add this tool is given next.

- Click on the **General** tab if not selected.
- Click in the **Name** edit box and specify **FILLET TOOL**.
- Click on the down arrow of **Type** drop-down and select the **CORNER ROUNDING** option from the list; the tool and its parameters will be displayed accordingly.
- Specify the parameters of the tool as shown in Figure-22.

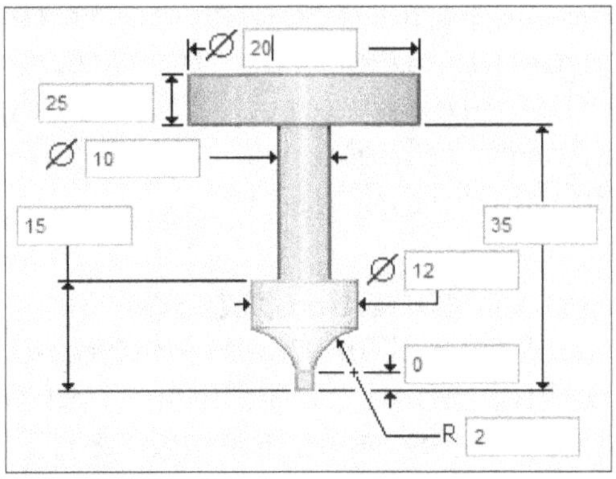

Figure-22. Parameters to be specified for tool

- Click on the **Settings** tab and specify the tool number as **3** in the **Tool Number** edit box.
- Click on the **Cut Data** tab, the options to specify cutting parameters will be displayed.
- Specify the cutting parameters as shown in Figure-23.

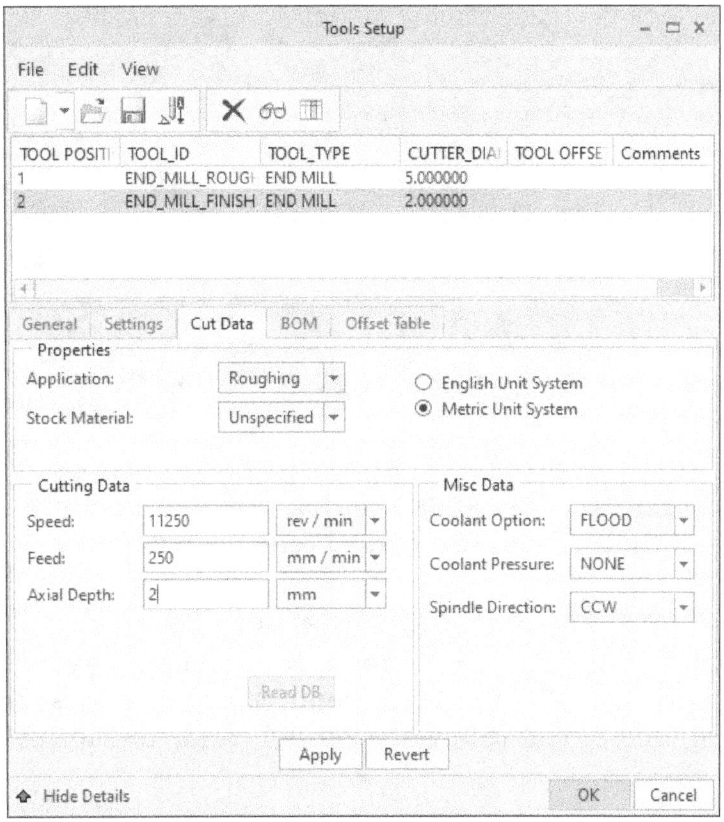

Figure-23. Specifying parameters for Fillet tool

- Click on the **Apply** button to add the tool in the list.
- Now, click on the **OK** button from the **Tools Setup** dialog box to create the tool setup. On doing so, the options in the **NC Features & Machining** panel will become active.

Now, we are ready to create material cutting features (NC Features) to remove the material.

Creating NC Features

In this section, we will create the nc features to remove material from the workpiece. Selection of the nc features mainly based on the interpretation of user. There can be various ways to remove the same material. The selection of features will also be dependent on type of machinery being used and the tool setup. The NC Features used in the project are for ideal conditions.

Round Feature

- Click on the **Top Round** tool from **Top Chamfer** drop-down in the **NC Features & Machining** panel of **Machining** tab in the **Ribbon**. The **TOP ROUND** dialog box will be displayed along with **SELECT SRFS Menu Manager** and **Select** dialog box.
- Select the round faces of the workpiece to create the NC feature; refer to Figure-24 and then press the **MMB** (Middle Mouse Button) twice.

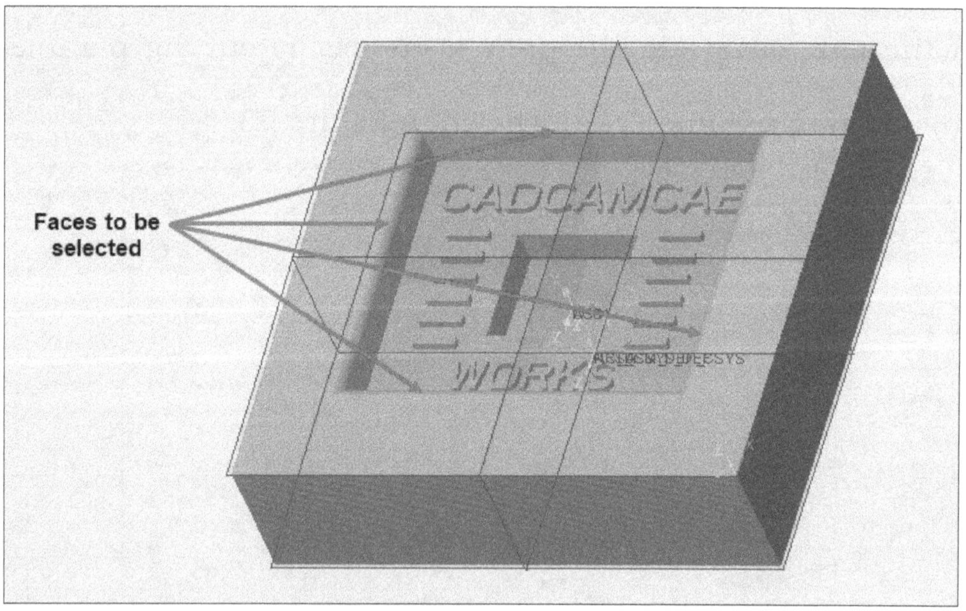

Figure-24. Faces to be selected for Top Round feature

- Now, the **OK** button of the **TOP ROUND** dialog box will become active. Click on the **OK** button from the dialog box, the round feature will be created.

Pocket Feature

- Click on the **Pocket** tool from the **Ribbon**, the **Pocket Feature** dialog box will be displayed along with the **SELECT SRFS Menu Manager** and **Select** dialog box.
- Select the bottom face of the reference model; refer to Figure-25.

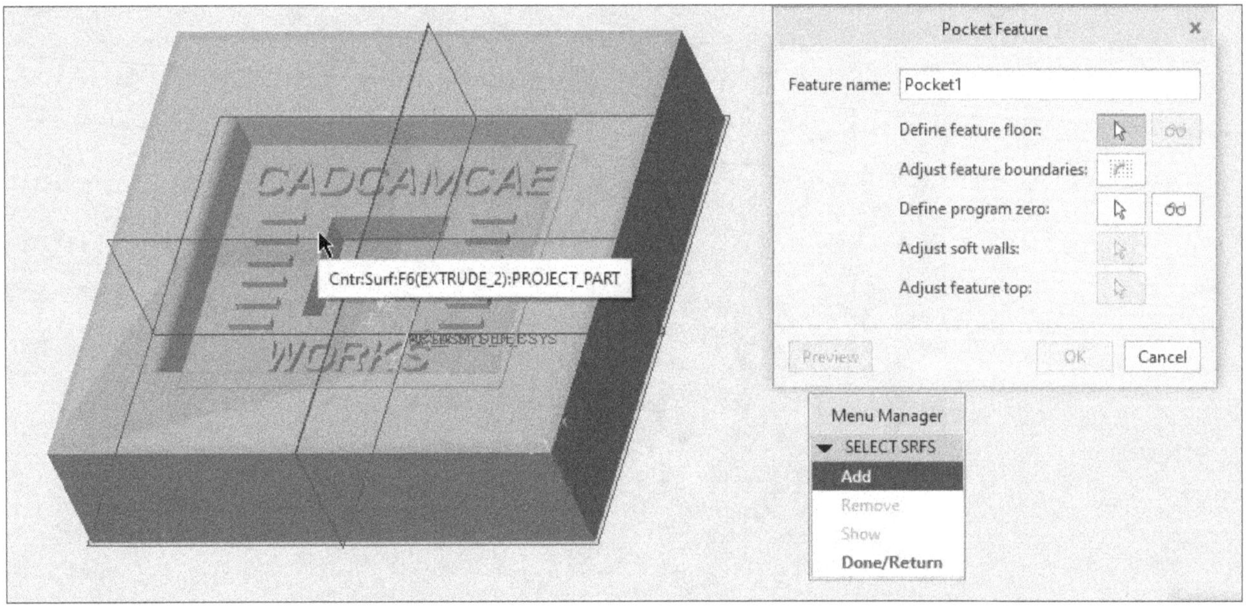

Figure-25. Face to be selected for Pocket feature

- Press the **MMB** twice, preview of the pocket feature will be displayed as shown in Figure-26.

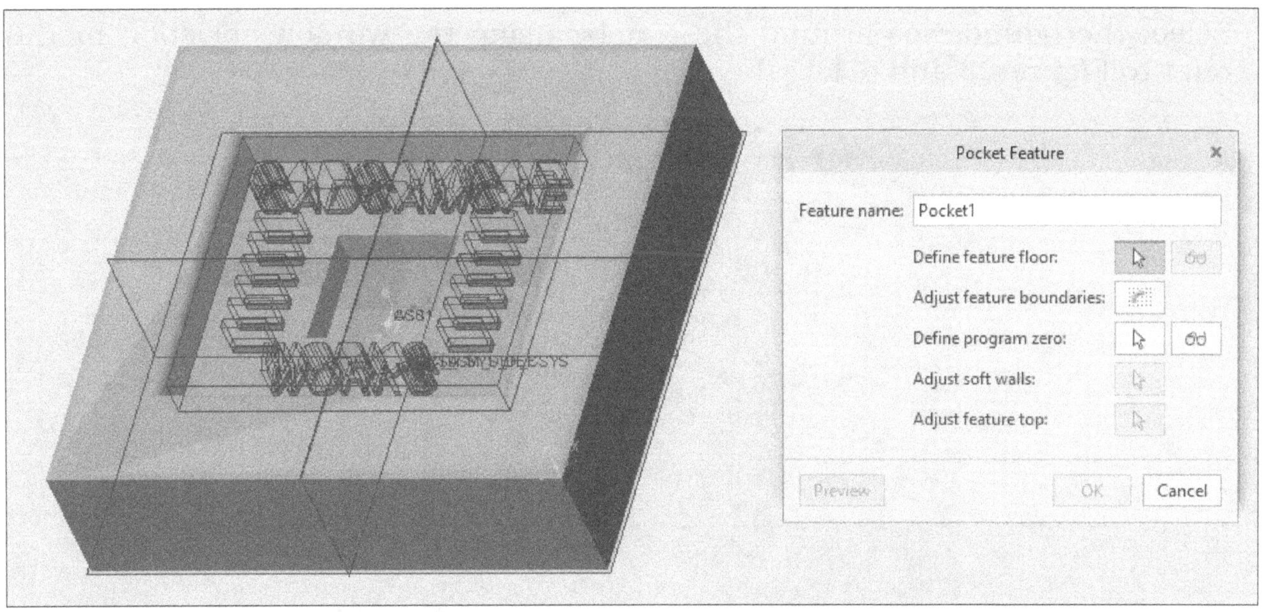

Figure-26. Preview of pocket feature

At some places, the feature will not be according to our requirement, so we need to modify the boundaries of the feature.

- Click on the **Adjust feature boundaries** button from the dialog box, the sketcher environment of Creo will open; refer to Figure-27.

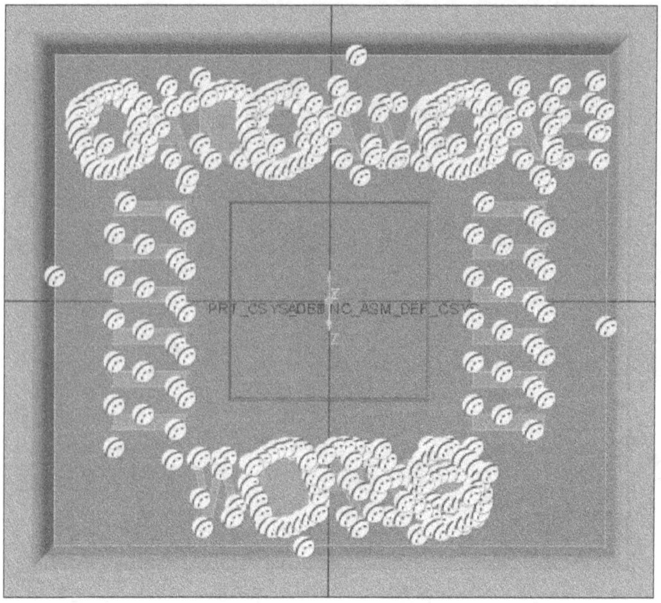

Figure-27. Pocket feature boundaries in sketcher

Machining of the text is difficult job and cannot be achieved by our roughing tool. So, we need to exclude it from the current pocket feature.

- Select the boundaries around the text by using the window selection method; refer to Figure-28 and delete them.

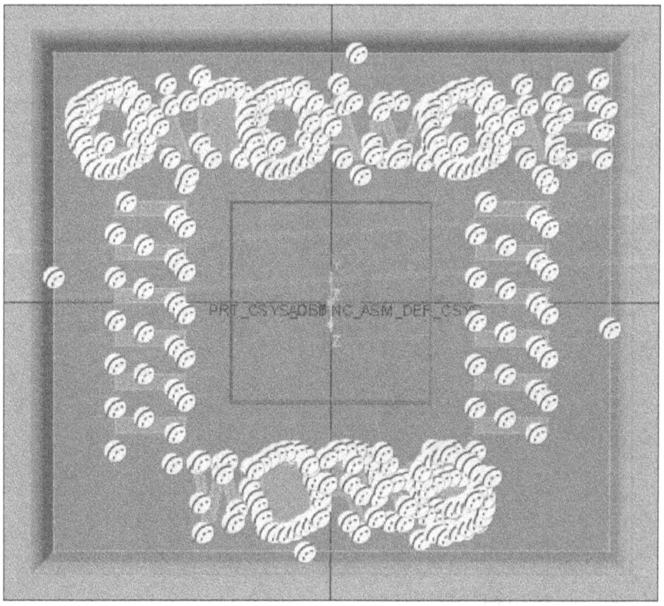

Figure-28. Boundaries to be selected

- Change the display style to **Hidden Line** by using the **In-Graphics Toolbar**; refer to Figure-29. On doing so, the model will be displayed as shown in Figure-30.

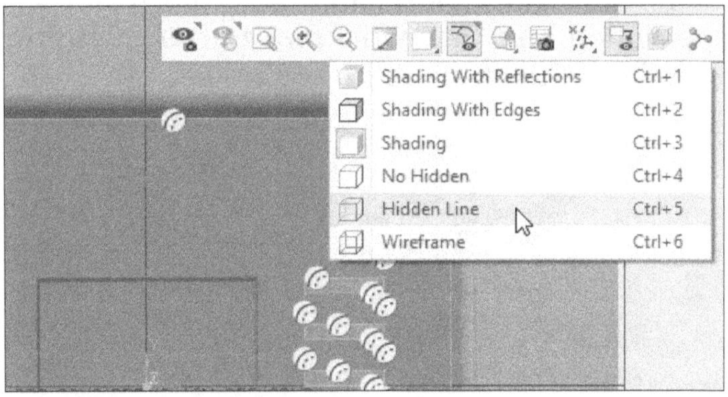

Figure-29. In-Graphics Toolbar with the option to be selected

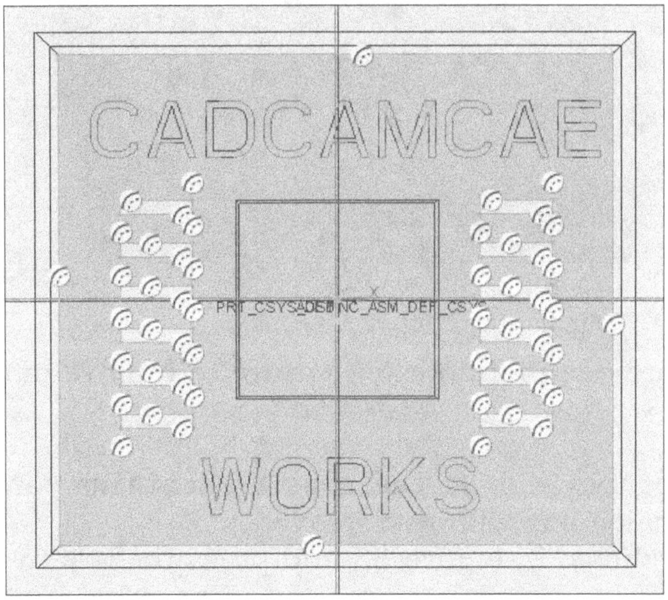

Figure-30. Model after deleting boundaies and selecting the Hidden Line style

- Delete the outer boundary of the pocket feature and project the lower edges of fillet as boundary lines; refer to Figure-31.

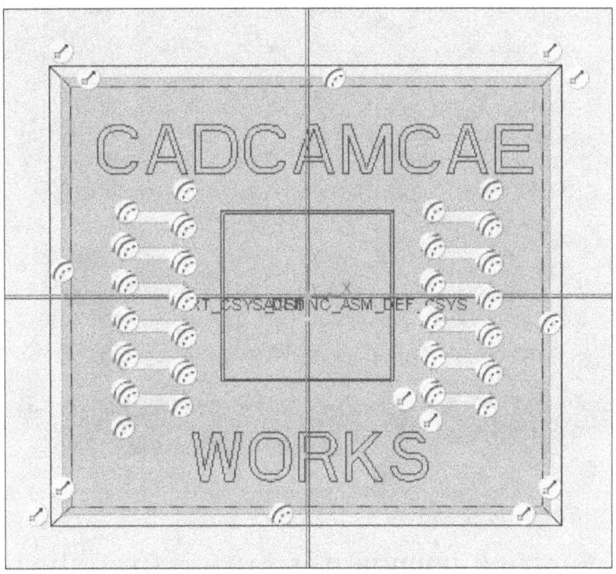

Figure-31. Lower edges of fillet projected

- Click on the **OK** button from the **Sketch** contextual tab and then **OK** button from the **Pocket Feature** dialog box. The workpiece after switching to **Shading** display style will be displayed as shown in Figure-32.

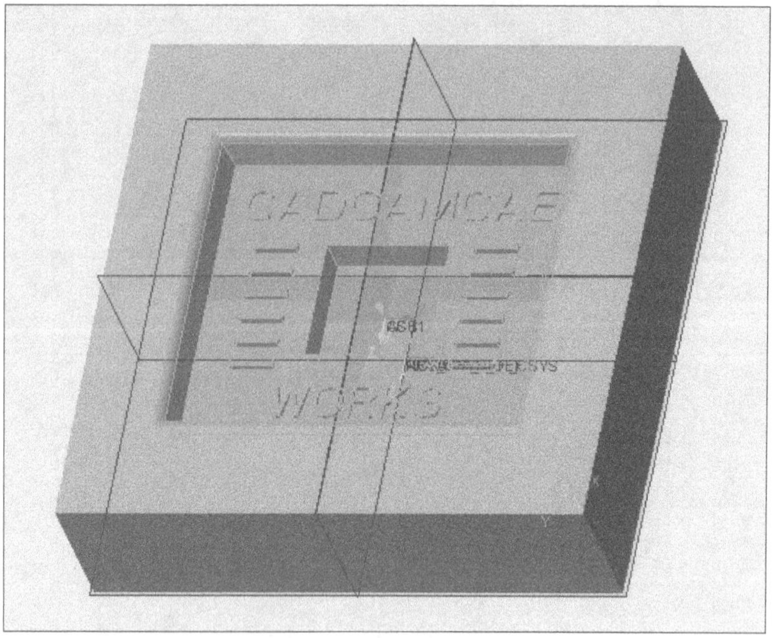

Figure-32. Workpiece after creating pocket feature

Now, we need to create one more pocket feature to remove material from the inner pocket.

- Click on the **Pocket** tool from **NC Features & Machining** panel in the **Ribbon**. The **Pocket Feature** dialog box will be displayed.
- Select the face as shown in Figure-33 and press the **MMB** twice.

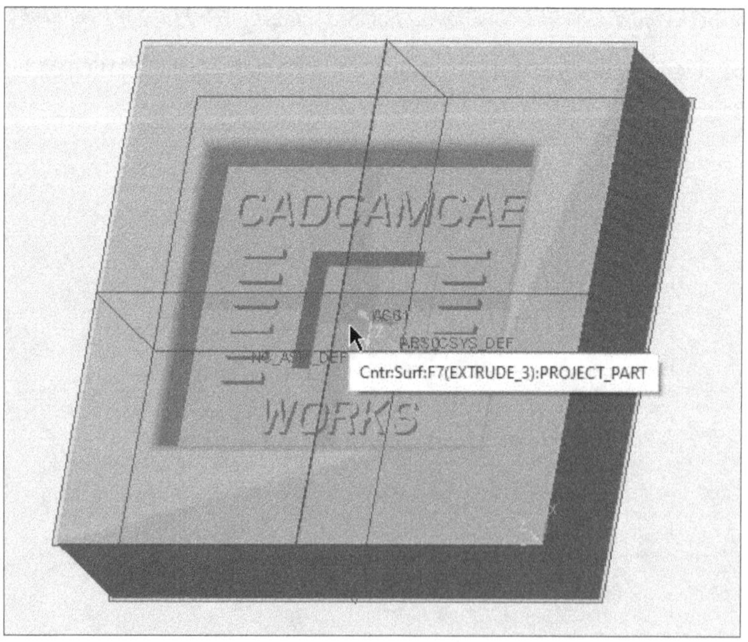

Figure-33. Face to be selected

- Click on the **Adjust feature boundaries** button from the dialog box, the sketcher environment will be displayed.

- Delete the older boundary and project the top boundary of the cavity; refer to Figure-34.

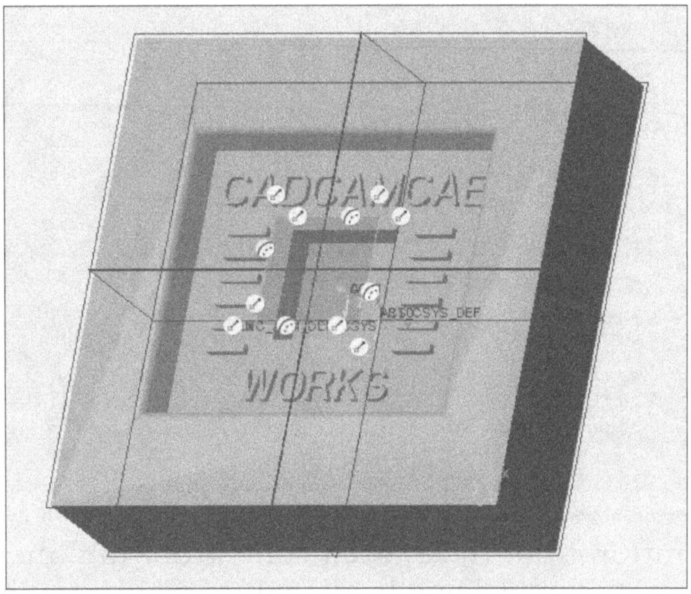

Figure-34. Projected top boundary of the cavity

- Click on the **OK** button from the **Sketch** contextual tab and then click on the **OK** button from the **Pocket Feature** dialog box.

Slab Feature

- Click on the **Slab** tool from the list displayed on clicking the down arrow next to **Flange** tool in the **Ribbon**. The **Slab Feature** dialog box will be displayed along with the **SELECT SRFS Menu Manager** and **Select** dialog box.
- Select top face of the rib feature; refer to Figure-35.

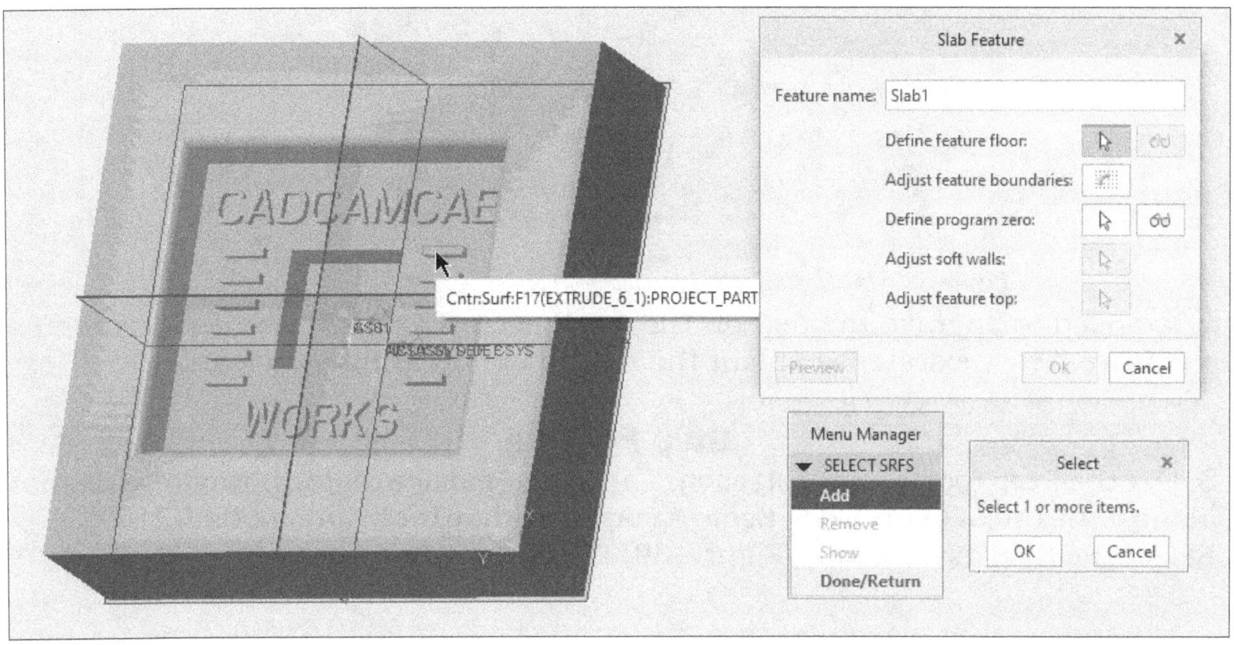

Figure-35. Face to be selected for slab feature

- Press the **MMB** twice and then click on the **Adjust feature boundaries** button from the **Slab Feature** dialog box, the sketcher environment will be displayed; refer to Figure-36.

- Click on the **Project** tool from the **Ribbon** and project all the material boundaries by selecting them. Also, create rectangle around the text; refer to Figure-37.

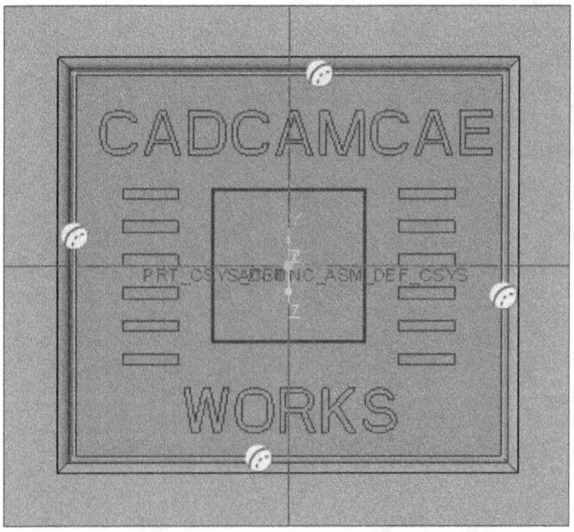

Figure-36. Sketcher environment for slab feature

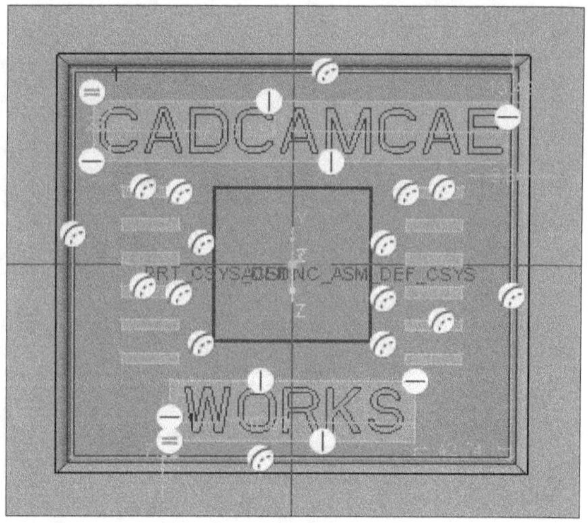

Figure-37. After projecting boundaries

- Click on the **OK** button from the **Sketch** contextual tab and then from the **Slab Feature** dialog box, the model will be displayed as shown in Figure-38.

Figure-38. Model after creating the Slab feature

Now, we need to engrave the text on the workpiece. To do so, we need to create the step feature. The next steps explain the method of creating step feature.

Step Feature

- Select the **Step** tool from the **Ribbon**. The **Step Feature** dialog box will be displayed along with the **SELECT SRFS Menu Manager** and **Select** dialog box.
- Select the face as shown in Figure-39. Press the **MMB** twice.

Figure-39. Face to be selected for Creating step feature

- Click on the **Adjust feature boundaries** button from the **Step Feature** dialog box, the sketcher environment will be displayed.
- Zoom in and project the inner boundaries of character 'A', '0', 'R' and 'D'; refer to Figure-40.

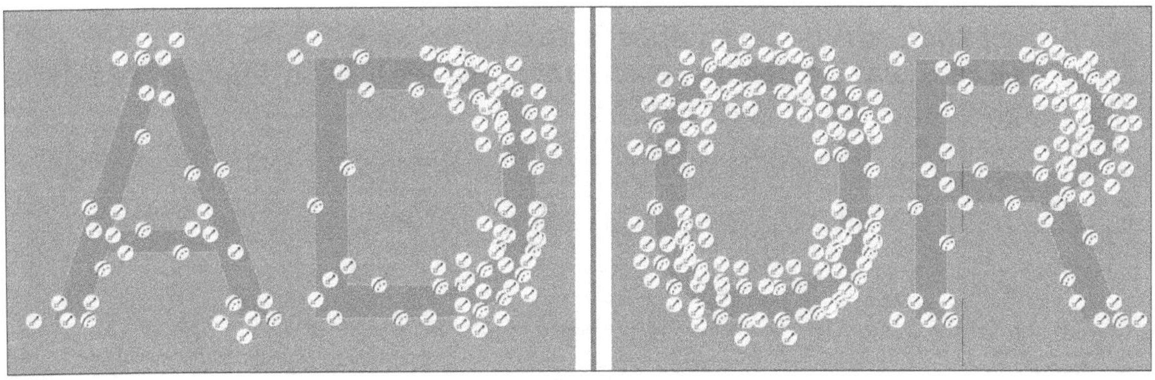

Figure-40. Characters after projecting

- Click on the **OK** button from the **Sketch** contextual tab and then **OK** button from the **Step Feature** dialog box.

The NC feature creation is complete till this point. Now, we need to generate tool path for the NC features.

Creating Toolpaths

In this section, we will create the toolpath to remove material from the workpiece by using respective NC features.

Toolpath for Round Feature

- Select **TOPROUND1 [OP010]** from the **Model Tree** and right-click on it, a shortcut menu will be displayed.
- Click on the **Create Toolpath** option from the list. The **Top Round and Chamfer Milling** dialog box will be displayed as shown in Figure-41.

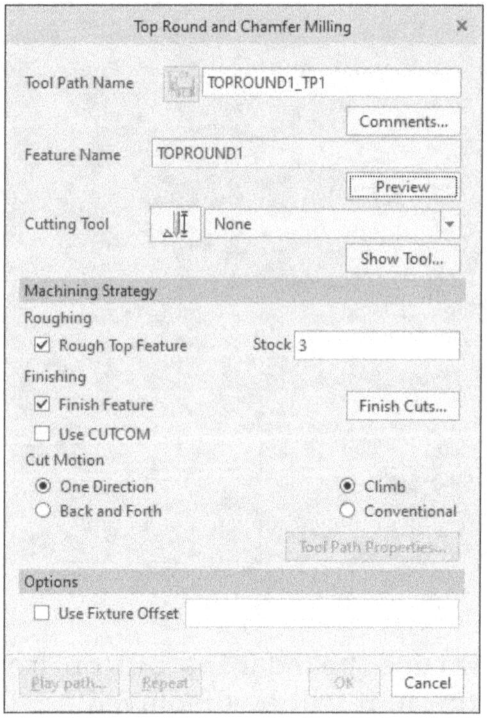

Figure-41. Top Round and Chamfer Milling dialog box

- Click on the down arrow of **Cutting Tool** list and select the **3:FILLET TOOL** from the list.
- Click in the **Stock** edit box and specify the value as **0**.
- Click on the **Tool Path Properties** button, the **Tool Path Properties** dialog box will be displayed; refer to Figure-42.

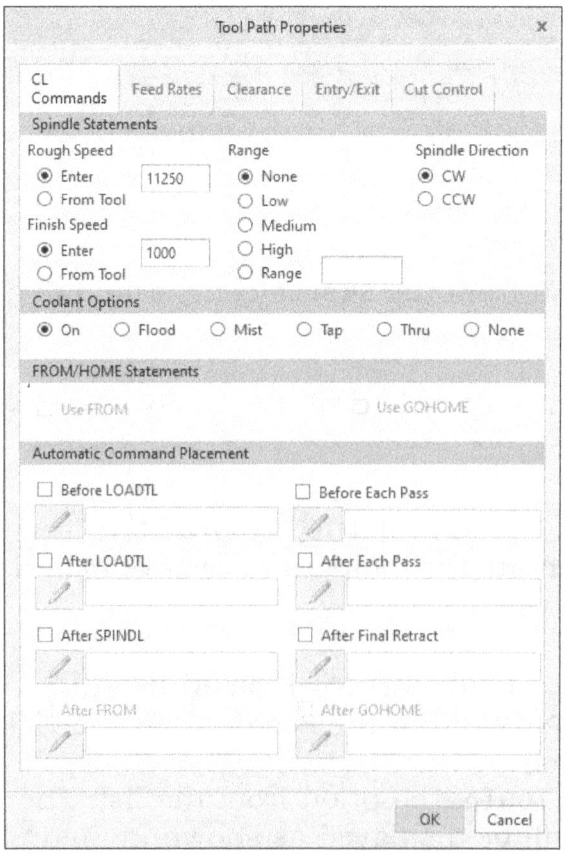

Figure-42. Tool Path Properties dialog box

- Select the **From Tool** radio button for both **Rough Speed** and **Finish Speed** in the **Spindle Statements** area of the dialog box.
- Select the **Flood** radio button from the **Coolant** options.
- Click on the **Feed Rates** tab, the dialog box will be displayed as shown in Figure-43.

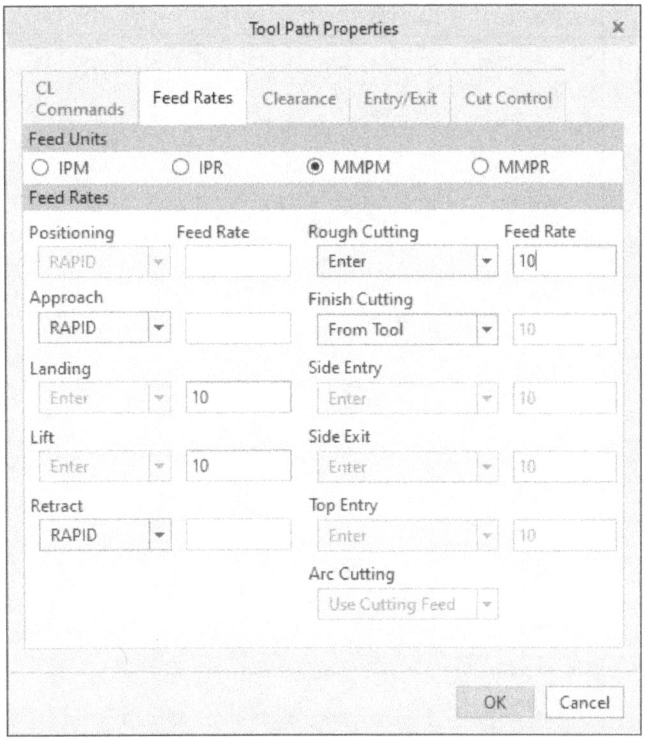

Figure-43. Tool Path Properties dialog box with the Feed Rates tab selected

- Click on the down arrow displayed below **Rough Cutting** and select the **From Tool** option from the list displayed.
- Click on the **OK** button from the **Tool Path Properties** dialog box and then from the **Top Round and Chamfer Milling** dialog box, the tool path will be created and will be added below **TOPROUND1 [OP010]** NC feature in the **Model Tree**.
- You can play the tool path simulation by selecting the **Tool Path Player** option from the shortcut menu. This shortcut menu is displayed on right-clicking on the tool path in the **Model Tree**.

Toolpath for Pocket Feature

- Select **POCKET1 [OP010]** from the **Model Tree** and right-click on it, a shortcut menu will be displayed.
- Select the **Create Toolpath** option from the list, the **Pocket Milling** dialog box will be displayed as shown in Figure-44.

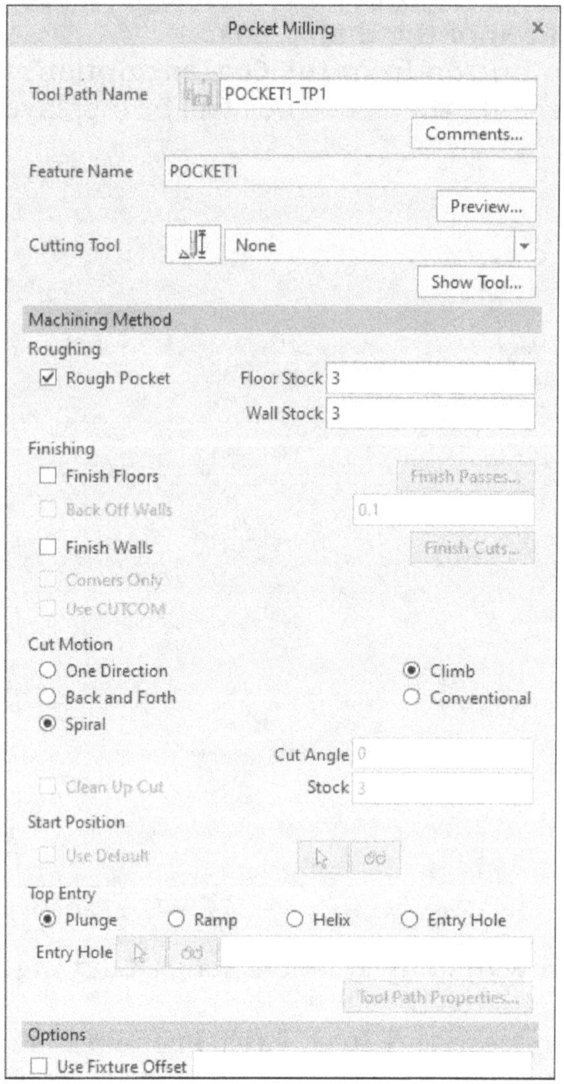

Figure-44. Pocket Milling dialog box

- Click on the down arrow of **Cutting Tool** list and select the **1:END MILL ROUGH** from the list.
- Specify the value as **0** in both the **Floor Stock** and the **Wall Stock** edit boxes.
- Set the tool path properties similar to those specified for round feature.
- Click on the **OK** button from the dialog box to create the tool path for the pocket milling feature.

Similarly, you can create tool paths of other features. Make sure that for the **Step1 [OP010]** nc feature, you select **2:END MILL FINISH** tool from the **Cutting Tool** list.

Creating Output Files

Till this point, we have simulated the tool path and we have checked it for errors. Now, we need to generate the output files by using the tool paths. In this section, we will generate the output files by using respective tool paths. To create an output file specific to a machine, we need to have a post processor specific to that machine. In this project, we will be using UNCX01.P12 as the post processor for our machine.

- Select the **TOPROUND1 TP1 [OP010]** from the **Model Tree** and then click on the **Select Post** button from drop-down button of **Output** panel in the **Ribbon**. The **Save a Copy** dialog box will be displayed; refer to Figure-45.

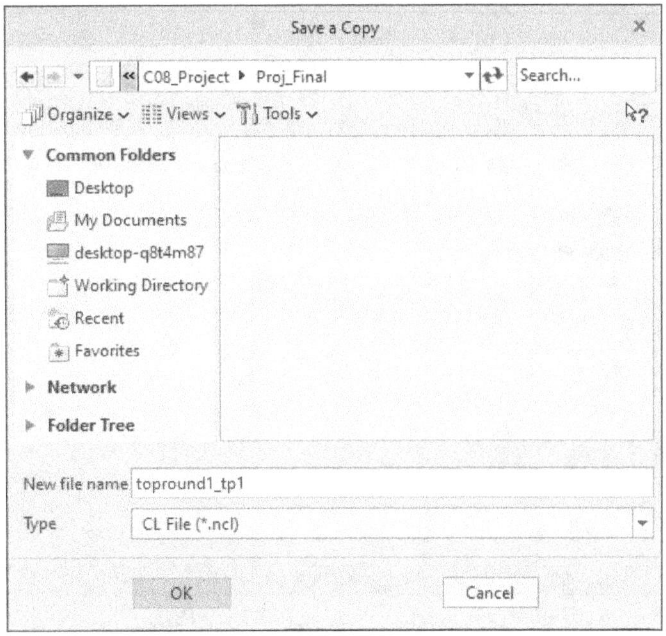

Figure-45. Save a Copy dialog box

- Save the CL file at desired location by using the options in this dialog box.
- On clicking the **OK** button from the **Save a Copy** dialog box, the **PP LIST Menu Manager** (Post Processor List Menu Manager) will be displayed; refer to Figure-46.

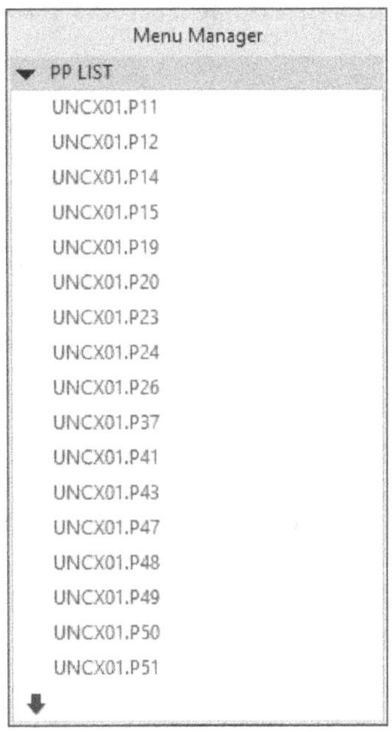

Figure-46. PP LIST Menu Manager

- Select the **UNCX01.P12** option from the **Menu Manager**, the **INFORMATION WINDOW** will be displayed and the output file will be saved at the location earlier specified in **Save a Copy** dialog box.
- Click on the **Close** button from the **INFORMATION WINDOW**.
- To check the output, open the location specified earlier and then open the output file with .tap extension by using any word processor; refer to Figure-47.

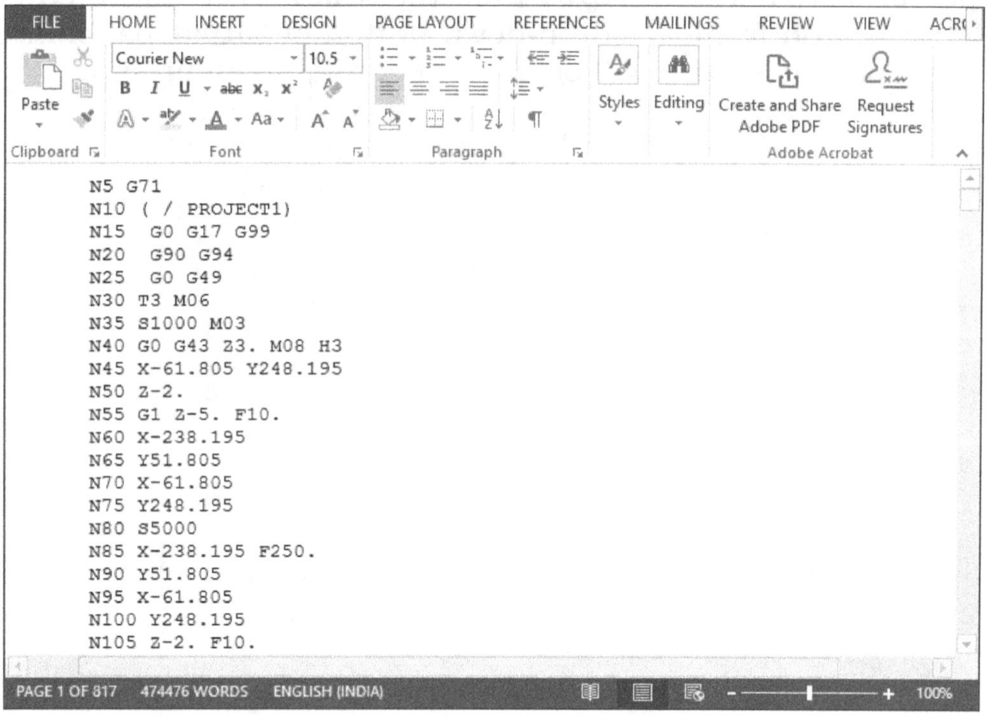

Figure-47. An output file with .tap extension opened in WordPad

- In the same way, you can generate and check the output files for the other tool paths.

SELF-ASSESSMENT

Q1. What is the purpose of creating NC features in Creo Manufacturing?
A. For design validation
B. To reduce file size
C. To remove material from the workpiece
D. To check tolerance values

Q2. Which tool is used to create the round feature on a workpiece?
A. Slab Tool
B. Pocket Tool
C. Top Round Tool
D. Step Tool

Q3. What dialog box appears when creating a round feature?
A. POCKET
B. TOP ROUND
C. SLAB FEATURE
D. STEP FEATURE

Q4. What is required after selecting faces for a round feature?
A. Left-click once
B. Press the Middle Mouse Button (MMB) twice
C. Select Done from Menu
D. Click Cancel

Q5. What must be done before confirming a Pocket Feature?
A. Assign the spindle speed
B. Exclude all top boundaries
C. Adjust feature boundaries
D. Change display style to wireframe

Q6. What tool in Creo opens when adjusting feature boundaries?
A. Feature Editor
B. NC Manager
C. Sketcher
D. Measurement Module

Q7. Which method is used to remove text from a pocket feature?
A. Hidden Line conversion
B. Window selection and delete
C. Right-click hide
D. Create offset curve

Q8. To remove material from the inner pocket, which face is selected?
A. Top fillet edge
B. Inner bottom face
C. Side rib face
D. Chamfer edge

Q9. How is the outer boundary deleted during pocket feature creation?
A. Trim tool
B. Cut tool
C. Delete and project new edges
D. Sketch with rectangle

Q10. What is the purpose of the Slab Feature tool?
A. To cut vertical slots
B. To engrave characters
C. To create a flat slab around geometry
D. To add chamfers

Q11. What tool is used to project the material boundaries in a slab feature?
A. Line
B. Offset
C. Project
D. Trim

Q12. Why is a step feature created?
A. To adjust depth
B. To remove ribs
C. To engrave text
D. To simulate cooling

Q13. Which toolpath dialog appears when creating path for a round feature?
A. Step Milling
B. Pocket Drilling
C. Top Round and Chamfer Milling
D. Slab Simulation

Q14. What coolant option is selected for round feature toolpath?
A. Dry
B. Flood
C. Mist
D. Water Jet

Q15. What tab allows feed rate configuration?
A. Speed & Feed
B. Operation
C. Feed Rates
D. Toolpath

Q16. What cutting tool is used for Pocket1 feature toolpath?
A. Fillet Tool
B. End Mill Finish
C. Engraving Cutter
D. End Mill Rough

Q17. Which tool is used to post-process the output file?
A. TOOLOUT.XP01
B. CLPOSTGEN
C. UNCX01.P12
D. FINALCUT.EXE

Q18. What is the extension of the output file created for the machine?
A. .dat
B. .step
C. .tap
D. .nc

Q19. What is required before generating output files?
A. Simulate toolpath and check for errors
B. Generate STL
C. Export .DWG file
D. Apply fixture constraints

Q20. What file format is opened using a word processor to view output?
A. .dwg
B. .tap
C. .prt
D. .asm

Chapter 9

Starting with NC Assembly

Topics Covered

The major topics covered in this chapter are:

- ***Setting Reference Model.***
- ***Inherit Reference Model.***
- ***Automatic Workpiece.***
- ***Assemble Workpiece.***
- ***Workpiece Wizard.***

INTRODUCTION TO NC ASSEMBLY

Creo Parametric **NC Assembly** application creates the data necessary to drive an NC machine tool to machine a part for desired purpose. This application provide the tools to let the manufacturing engineers follow a logical sequence of steps to progress from a design model to ASCII CL data files that can be post-processed into NC machine data.

STARTING NC ASSEMBLY

There are two ways to start **NC Assembly** application which are discussed next.

Using New button

- Start the **Creo Parametric** if not started yet.
- Click on the **New** button from **File** menu of Creo Parametric window. The **New** dialog box will be displayed; refer to Figure-1.

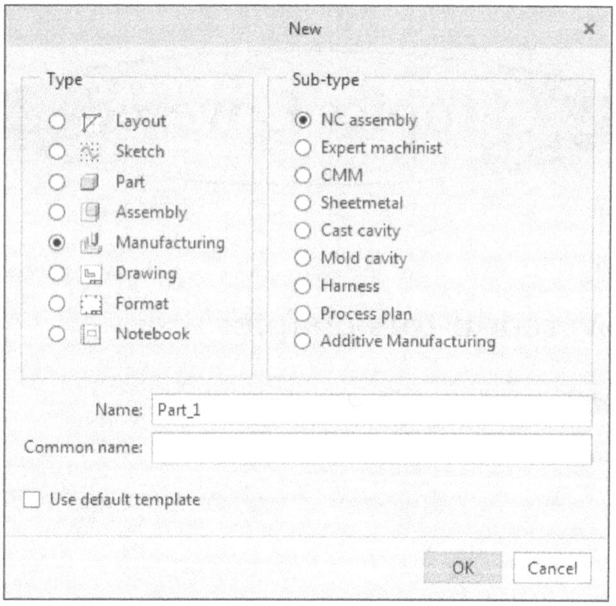

Figure-1. New dialog box

- Select the **Manufacturing** radio button from **Type** area and select **NC assembly** radio button from **Sub-type** area.
- Click in the **Name** edit box and specify desired name of file or part.
- Click in the **Common name** edit box and specify the description about the part. This option is optional.
- Clear the **Use default template** check box if you want to set the template according to your need.
- Now, click on the **OK** button from **New** dialog box. The **New File Options** dialog box will be displayed; refer to Figure-2, where you need to select template for your part.

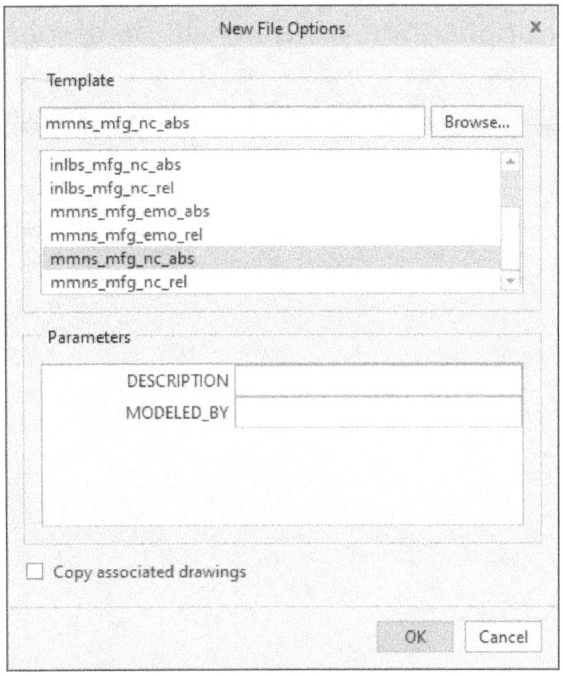

Figure-2. New File Options dialog box

- Select desired template from **Template** section.
- If you want to add more template to **Template** section then click on the **Browse** button. The **Choose Template** dialog box will be displayed; refer to Figure-3.

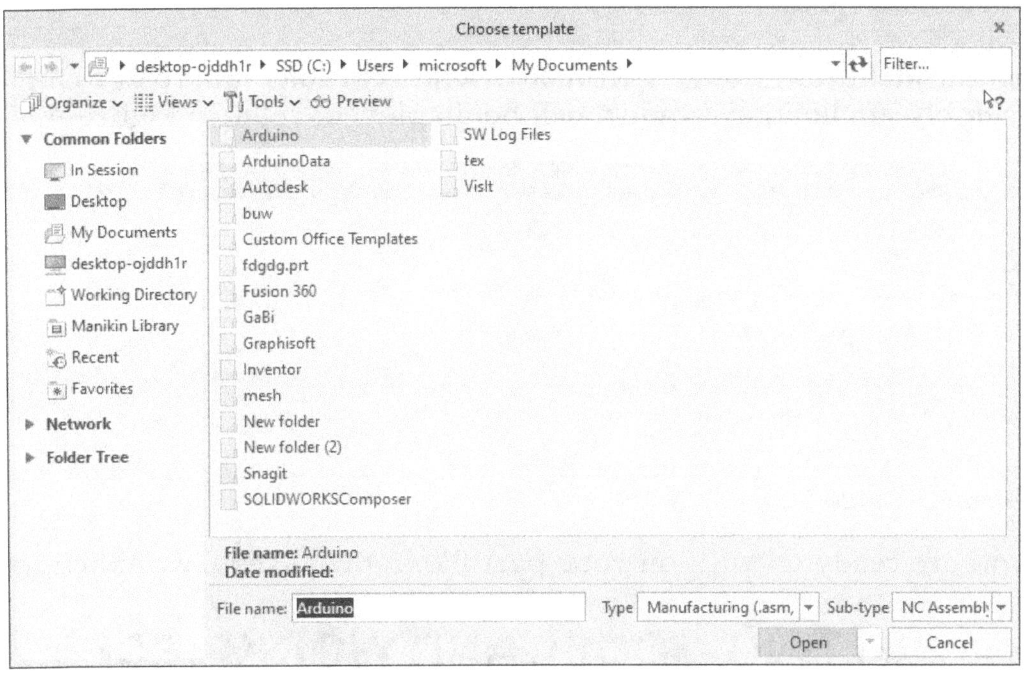

Figure-3. Choose Template dialog box

- Select desired template and click on **Open** button. The new template will be added in **Template** section of **New File Options** dialog box.
- Click on the **MODELED BY** edit box of **Parameters** section and enter the detail of creator of this part. You can also add description in the **DESCRIPTION** edit box. These two options are optional.
- Select the **Copy associated drawings** check box if you want to copy all the associated drawing files for the selected template. Otherwise, clear the check box.

- After specifying the parameters, click on **OK** button from **New File Options** dialog box. The **NC Assembly** application window will be displayed; refer to Figure-4.

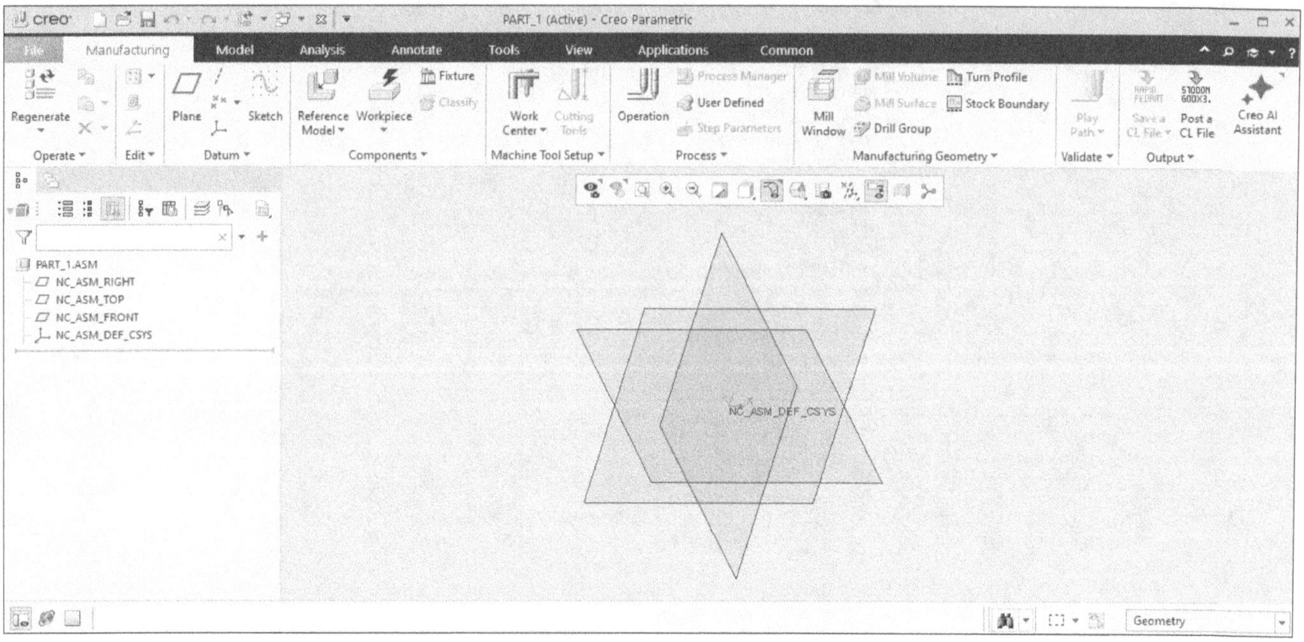

Figure-4. NC Assembly application window

Using NC button

While working on part file, there is also an option to open the **NC Assembly** application which is discussed next.

- Click on the **NC** button from the **Ribbon** of **Applications** tab; refer to Figure-5. The NC Assembly application window will be displayed; refer to Figure-4.

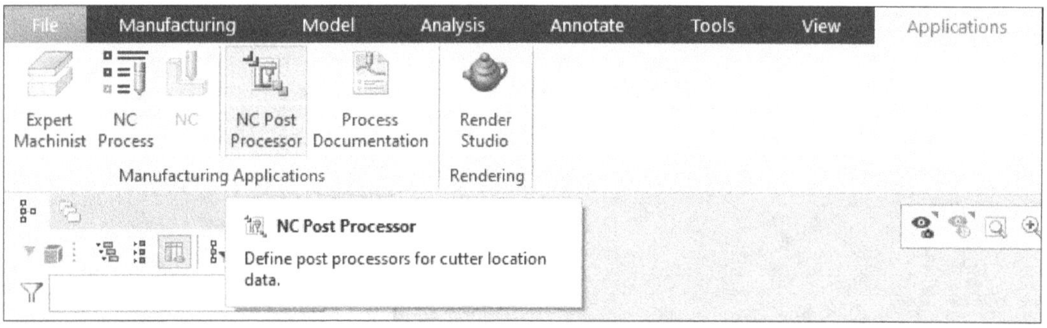

Figure-5. NC button

- Now, you are ready to work on your part file in **NC Assembly** application.

SETTING MODEL AND WORKPIECE

In this section, we will discuss the procedure of setting up a reference model and workpiece.

Setting up a reference model

- Click on the **Assemble Reference Model** button from **Reference Model** drop-down of **Components** panel; refer to Figure-6. The **Open** dialog box will be displayed; refer to Figure-7.

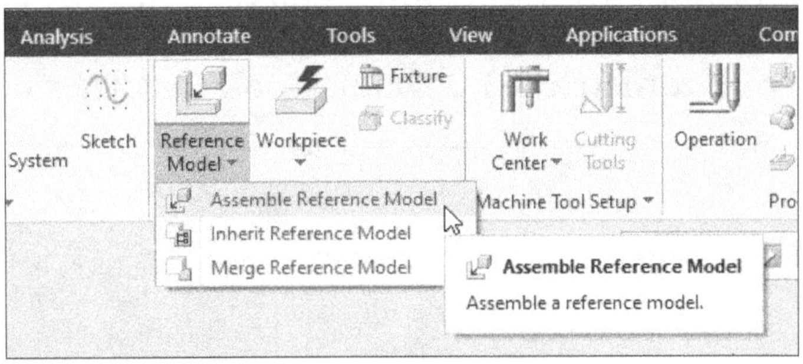

Figure-6. Assemble Reference Model button

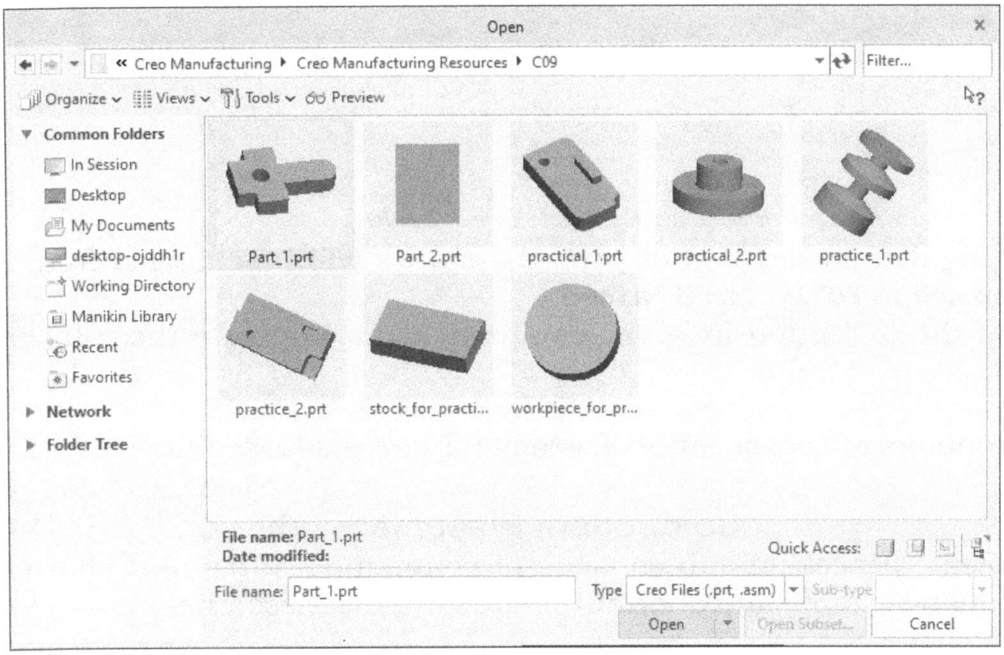

Figure-7. Open dialog box for reference model

- Select desired part file and click on the **Open** button. The **Component Placement** contextual tab will be displayed; refer to Figure-8. Using the options in this tab, you need to constrain the model.

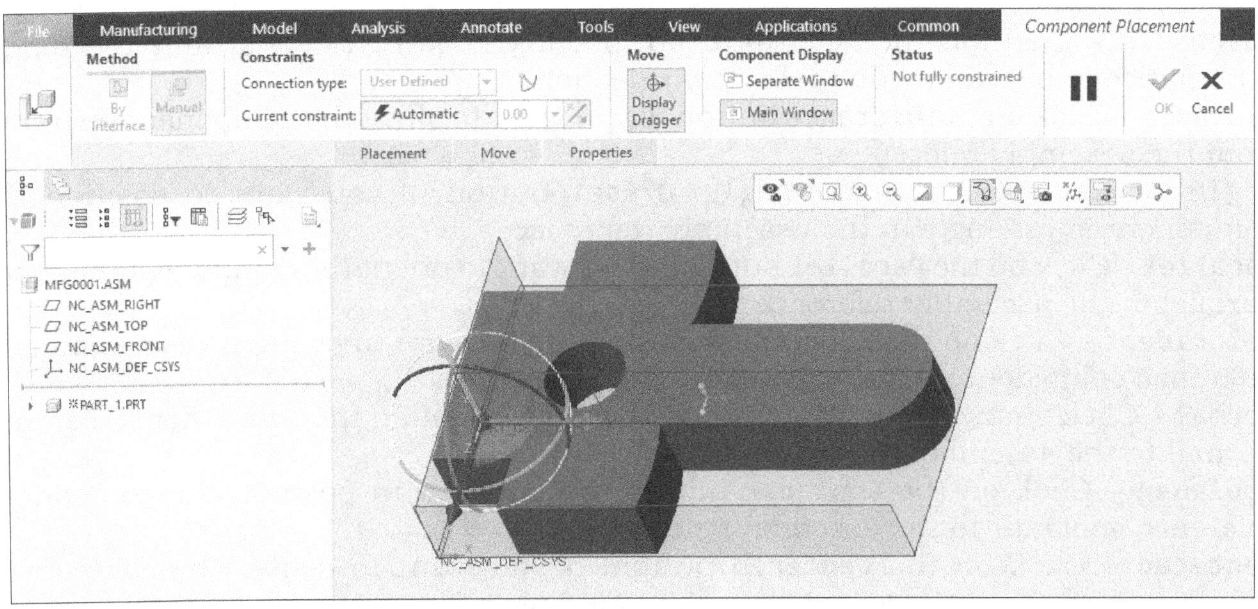

Figure-8. Component Placement tab

- Click on **Default** option from **Current constraint** drop-down of **Component Placement** tab to set the location of model to default position; refer to Figure-9. Please refer to Creo Parametric 13.0 Black Book for other constraining options.

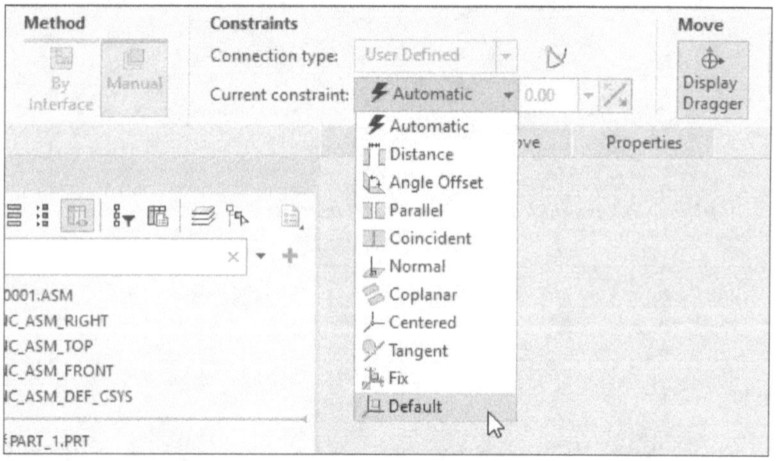

Figure-9. Assembling component to Default location

- On setting default location of part, the status will be changed from **Not fully constrained** to **Fully constrained**.
- Click on the **OK** button from the component tab to create the fully constrained model.

The other options of **Component Placement** tab are discussed next.

Component Placement tab

The **Component Placement** tab consists of commands, tabs, and shortcut menus. These commands, tabs, and shortcut menus are discussed next.

Constraint drop-down

This drop-down contains the constraints applicable for the selected model or set. By default, **User Defined** option is selected in the **Constraint Set** drop-down and **Automatic** is selected in the **Constraint** drop-down. The various constraint of **Constraint** drop-down are discussed next.

Automatic - Click on the **Automatic** button, if you want to constraint the model automatically based on your geometry selection.
Distance - Click on the **Distance** button, if you want to offset the component reference from the assembly reference.
Angle Offset - Click on the **Angle Offset** button, if you want to position the component at an angle to the assembly reference.
Parallel - Click on the **Parallel** button, if you want to orient the component reference parallel to the assembly reference.
Coincident - Click on the **Coincident** button, if you want to position the component reference coincident with the assembly reference.
Normal - Click on the **Normal** button, if you want to position the component reference normal to the assembly reference.
Coplanar - Click on the **Coplanar** button, if you want to position the component reference coplanar to the assembly reference.
Centered - Click on the **Centered** button, if you want to center the component reference between the selected assembly references.

Tangent - Click on the **Tangent** button, if you want to position two references tangent to each other.

Fix - Click on the **Fix** button, if you want to fix the current location of a component that was moved or packaged.

Default - Click on the **Default** button if you want to align the component coordinate system with the default assembly coordinate system.

If you want to flip the direction of offset then click on **Change Orientation of Constraint** button.

The **Display Dragger** button is used to hide/show the 3D Dragger from screen.

The **Status** option is used to check the status of part or model. There are four types of status i.e. No constraints, Not fully constrained, Fully constrained and Constraints Invalid.

- No constraints is displayed in **Status** section, when no constraints are applied to the model.
- Not fully constrained is displayed in **Status** section, when the model is partially constrained. This happens when some motions of part are constrained.
- Fully constrained is displayed in **Status** section, when the model is fully constrained. This happens when all motions of part are constrained.
- Constraints Invalid is displayed in **Status** section, when the constraints of the model are invalid.

The **Separate Window** button in the **Component Display** area is used to display the component in its own window as you define constraints.

The **Main Window** button in the **Component Display** area is used to display the component in the graphics window and updates component placement as you define constraints.

Placement tab

The **Placement** tab is used to enable and display component placement and connection definition. There are various options in this tab which are discussed next.

Navigation and Collection area — This section displays **sets** and **constraints**; refer to Figure-10. Translation references and motion axes are displayed for predefined constraint sets. The first constraint in a set activates automatically. A new constraint activates automatically after a valid pair of references is selected, until the component is fully constrained.

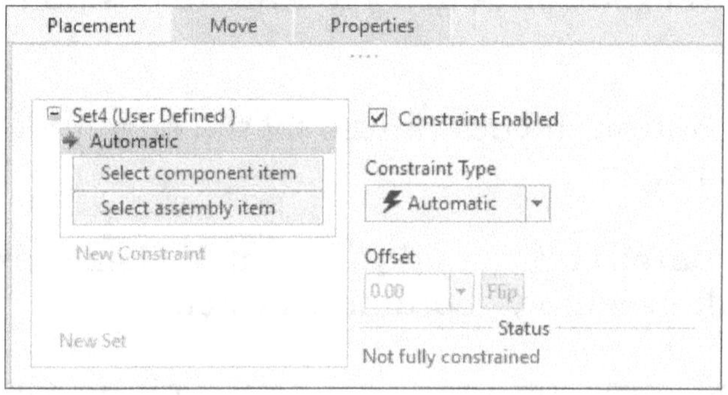

Figure-10. Placement tab

- Select the **Constraint Enabled** check box to enable the **Automatic** option of **Set1** section. This **Automatic** option allow to set the reference.
- Select desired constraint from **Constraint Type** drop-down.
- To set the reference, you need to click on **Select component item** selection box and select the reference for component side.
- Click on **Select assembly item** selection box and select the assembly side reference for the model. Assembly side reference is the geometry of model already existing before inserting the new component.
- On selecting the **Default** option of **Constraint** drop-down from **Component Placement** tab, the updated **Placement** tab will be displayed; refer to Figure-11.

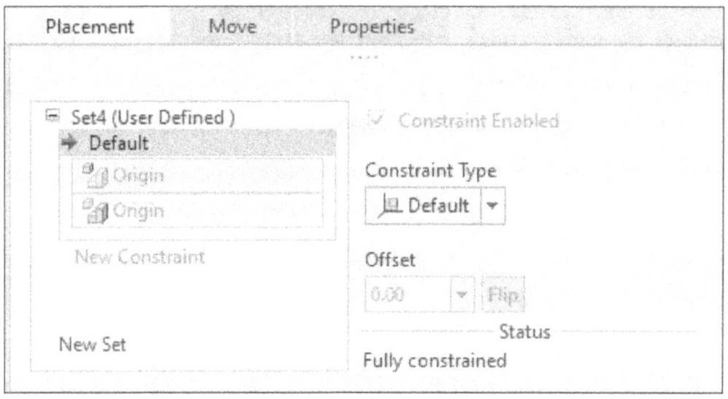

Figure-11. Updated Placement tab

Move tab

The **Move** tab is used to move the component being assembled for easier access; refer to Figure-12. When the **Move** tab is active, all other component placement operations are paused.

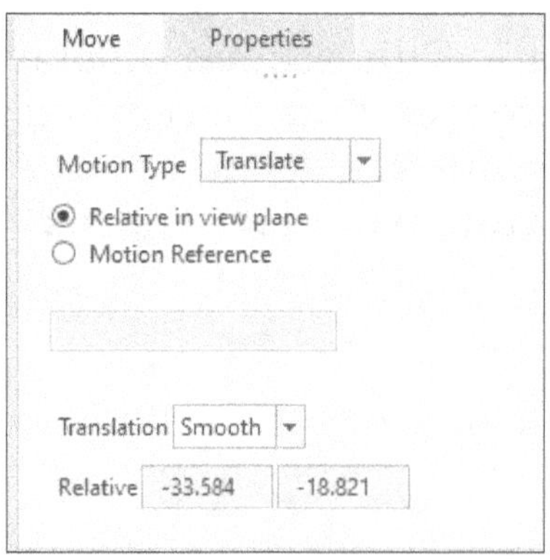

Figure-12. Move tab

- Select the **Orient Mode** option from **Motion Type** drop down to reorient the view.
- Select the **Translate** option from **Motion Type** drop-down to move the component.
- Select the **Rotate** option from **Motion Type** drop-down to rotate the component.
- Select the **Adjust** option from **Motion Type** drop-down to adjust the component position.
- Select the **Relative in view plane** radio button to move the component relative to the viewing plane.
- Select the **Motion Reference** radio button to move the component relative to a component or reference. On selecting this radio button, reference selection is enabled where you need to select the reference from the screen.
- Select the **Smooth** button from the **Translation** drop-down to move/rotate the model smoothly.
- Click on the model and place the model at desired location. While moving the model, the coordinate will be shown in **Relative** option.

After specifying the parameters for constrained model, click on the **OK** button from the **Component Placement** tab. The NC Assembly application window will be displayed with more enabled tools; refer to Figure-13.

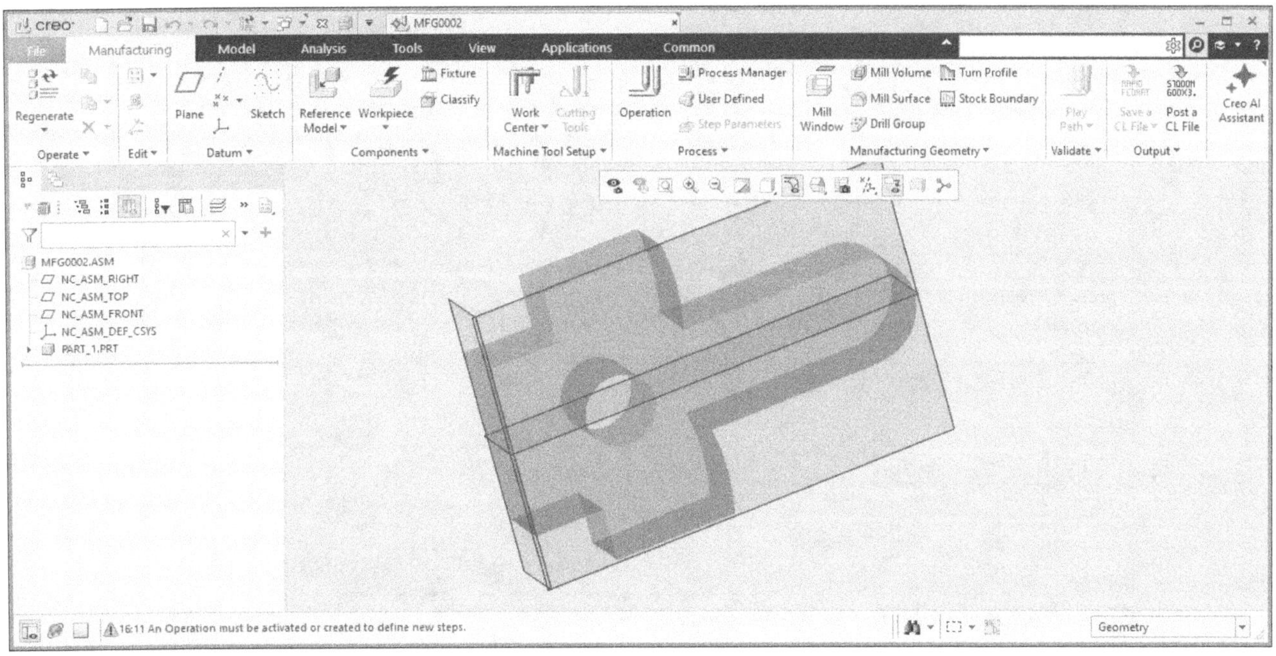

Figure-13. Updated NC Assembly application window

Properties tab

The **Properties** tab displays the information regarding the working model; refer to Figure-14.

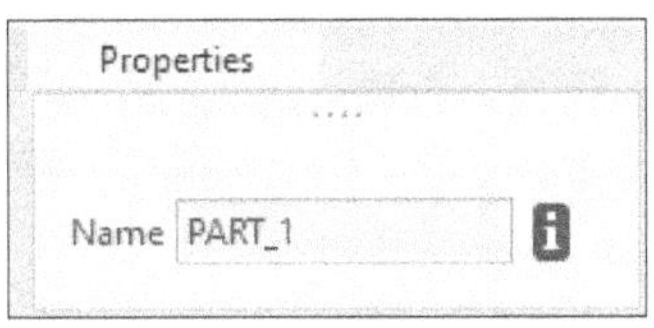

Figure-14. Properties tab

- The **Name** box displays the name of model.
- Click on the **Displays information for this feature** button to know more information about the current model.

Inherit Reference Model

This button is used to add some inherit feature. The procedure to use this button is discussed next.

- Click on the **Inherit Reference Model** button from **Reference Model** drop-down of **Components** panel; refer to Figure-15. The **Open** dialog box will be displayed; refer to Figure-16.

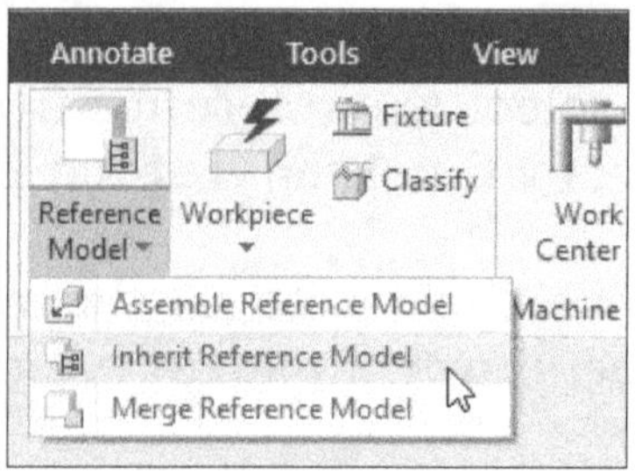

Figure-15. Inherit Reference Model button

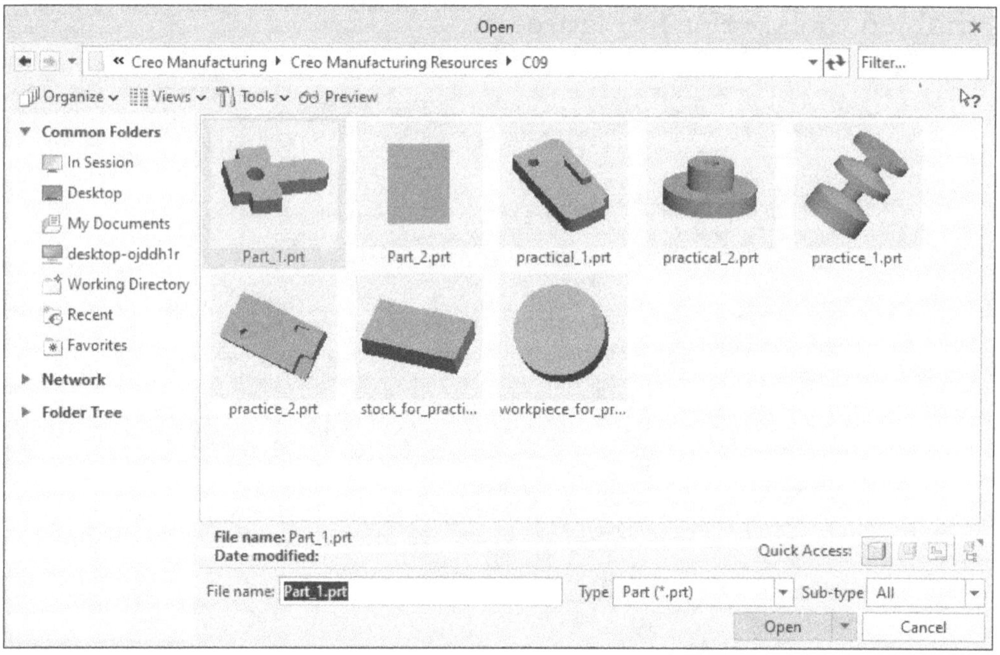

Figure-16. Open dialog box for reference model

- Select the file and click on the **Open** button. The **Component Placement** tab will be displayed which was discussed earlier.
- Select the **Default** option from **Constraint** drop-down and click on the **OK** button. The **Create Reference Model** dialog box will be displayed; refer to Figure-17.

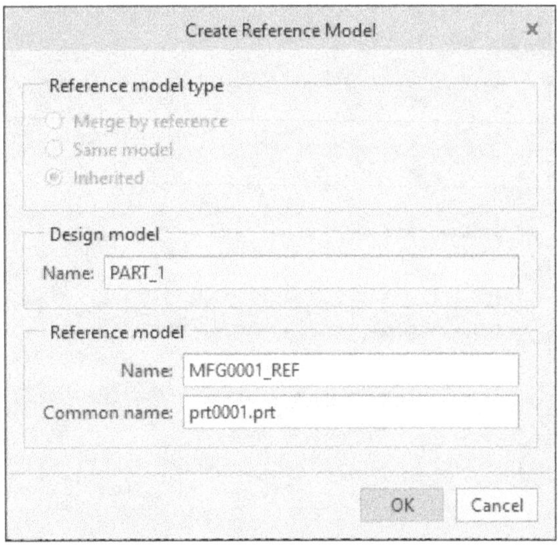

Figure-17. Create Reference Model dialog box

- Click in the **Name** edit box of **Reference model** section and change the name as desired.
- Click in the **Common name** edit of **Reference model** section and change the name as desired.

After specifying the parameters, click on the **OK** button to complete the process. The model will be added as manufacturing reference model.

Merge Reference Model

The **Merge Reference Model** tool is used to create a reference model with geometry merged from the selected model. The procedure to use this tool is discussed next.

- Click on the **Merge Reference Model** button from **Reference Model** drop-down of **Components** panel in the **Manufacturing** tab; refer to Figure-18. The **Open** dialog box will be displayed.

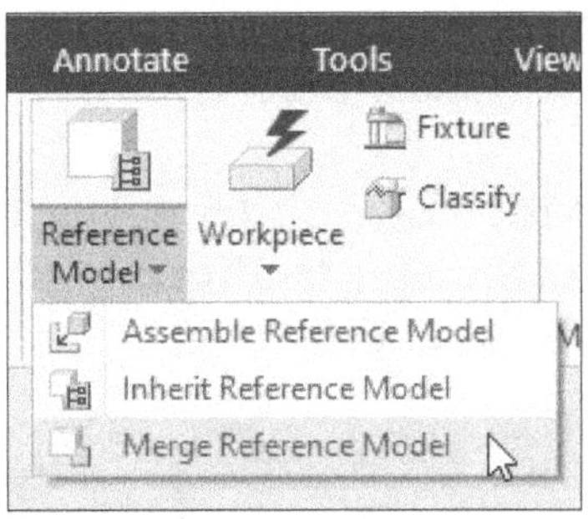

Figure-18. Merge Reference Model button

- Select the part file from **Open** dialog box and click on the **Open** button. The **Component Placement** tab will be displayed which was discussed earlier.
- Select **Default** option from **Constraint** drop-down to fully constrained the model.
- Click on the **OK** button from the **Component Placement** tab. The **Create Reference Model** dialog box will be displayed; refer to Figure-19.

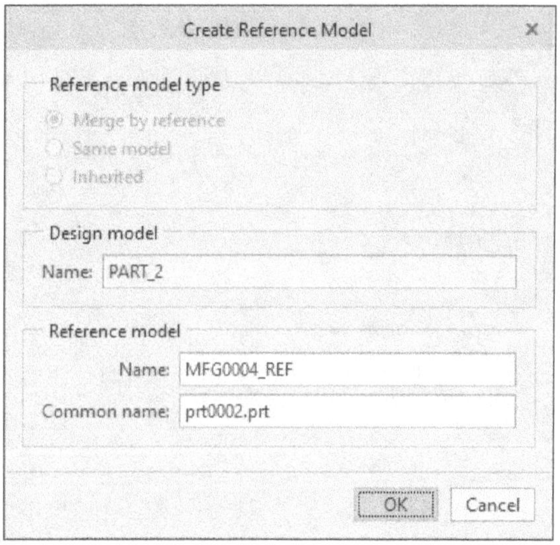

Figure-19. Create Reference Model dialog box to merge by reference

The options of this dialog box have been discussed earlier. After specifying the parameters, click on the **OK** button to complete the process.

CREATING WORKPIECE

The workpiece represents the raw material or stock that is going to be machined by the manufacturing operations. The use of workpiece is optional in **Creo NC Assembly** application. **NC Assembly** application allows you to create or assemble the workpiece. You can manually create the workpiece (manual workpiece) or allow **NC Assemby** to automatically create it using standard shapes and your choice of dimensions (automatic workpiece). Alternatively, you can assemble the workpiece using an existing design model. In this case, the workpiece can have features inherited or merged from the design model.

Automatic Workpiece

The **Automatic Workpiece** button is used to create workpiece automatically. The procedure to use this tool is discussed next.

- Click on the **Automatic Workpiece** button from **Workpiece** drop-down of **Components panel** in the **Manufacturing** tab; refer to Figure-20. The **Auto Workpiece Creation** tab will be displayed; refer to Figure-21.

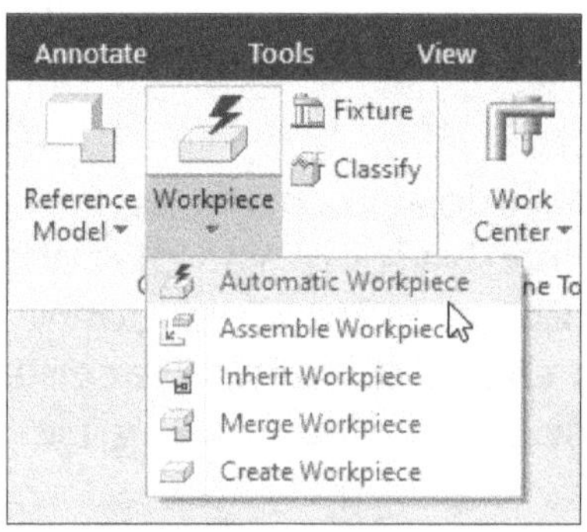

Figure-20. Automatic Workpiece button

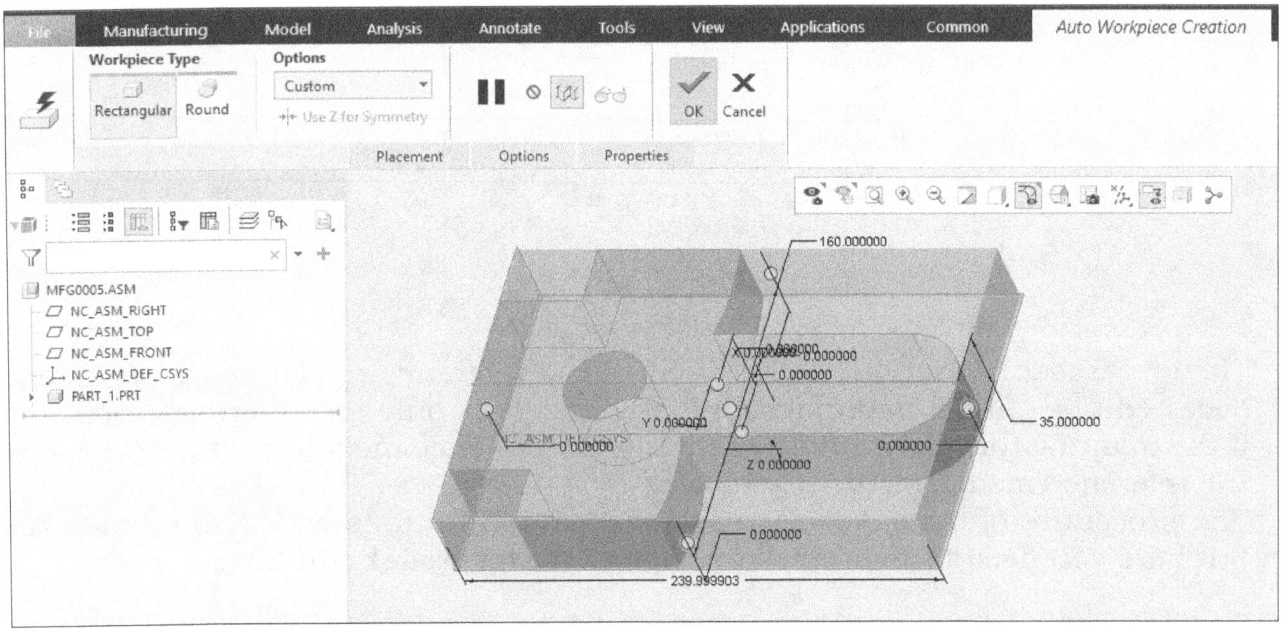

Figure-21. Auto Workpiece Creation tab

Workpiece Type area

- Select the **Rectangular** button if you want to create a rectangular or billet shape workpiece.
- Select the **Round** button if you want to create a bar or round shape workpiece.

Options area

- Select the **Custom** button from the **Sub-shape** drop-down to define overall dimensions and offsets of the workpiece; refer to Figure-22.

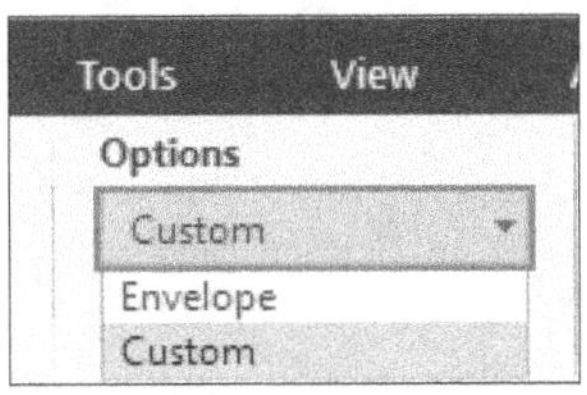

Figure-22. Sub-shape drop-down

- Select the **Envelope** button from the **Sub-shape** drop-down to define the minimum offsets and angular offsets. You can use **Envelope** button to reset the current offsets to the minimum values.

Placement tab

The **Placement** tab is used to specify the coordinate system and the reference model using their respective collectors.

- The **NC Assembly** application automatically specifies the coordinate system of the reference model in the **Coordinate System** edit box.
- If there is no reference model, or multiple reference models, or if you have removed the coordinate system, you need to specify it from the model.
- If you want to remove the coordinate system from selection then, right-click on the **Coordinate System** selection box and click on **Remove** button; refer to Figure-23.

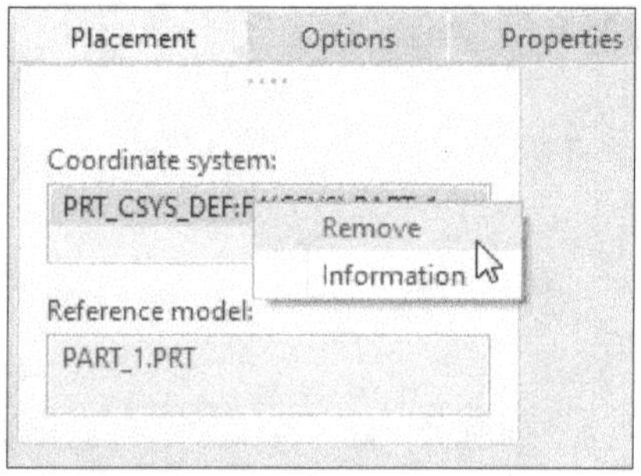

Figure-23. Placement tab

- The **NC Assembly** automatically specifies the reference model in the **Reference Model** edit box, if the manufacturing assembly has only one reference model.
- If the manufacturing assembly has multiple reference model, you need to specify the reference model for the workpiece.
- The procedure of using **Remove** and **Information** buttons was discussed earlier but here you need to right-click on the **Reference Model** edit box.

Options tab

The **Options** tab is used to specify values for the units, overall dimensions, and stock offsets. The options in **Options** tab are different for rectangular and round workpiece. On selecting the **Rectangular** button from **Workpiece Type** area, the **Options** tab is displayed as shown in Figure-24. The options for rectangular workpiece are discussed next.

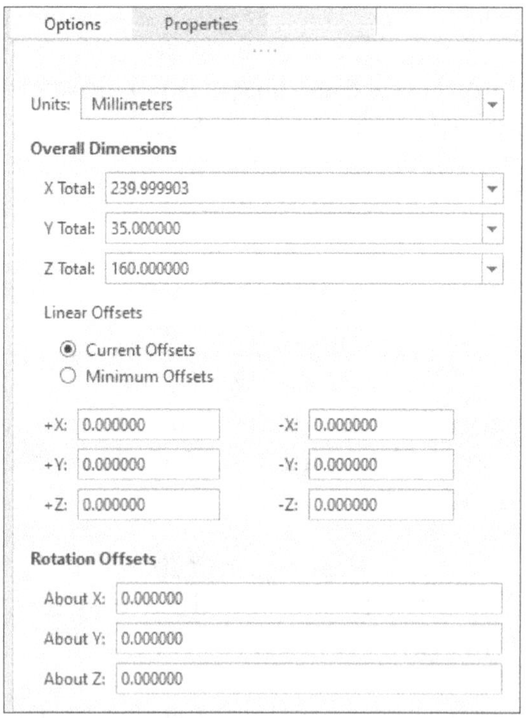

Figure-24. Options tab of rectangular workpiece

- Select the **Millimeters** button from **Units** drop-down if you want to set the unit in millimeters.
- Select the **Inches** button from **Units** drop-down if you want to set the unit in inches.
- Click on the **X Total** edit box of **Overall Dimensions** section and specify the overall dimensions for the workpiece in the x-direction. This value applies only for a billet workpiece.

- Click on the **Y Total** edit box of **Overall Dimensions** section and specify the overall dimensions for the workpiece in the y-direction. This value applies only for a billet workpiece.
- Click on the **Z Total** edit box of **Overall Dimensions** section and specify the overall dimensions for the workpiece in the z-direction. This value applies only for a billet workpiece.
- Select the **Current Offsets** radio button of **Linear Offsets** section if you want to specify the stock offsets of the workpiece around the reference model and along the positive and negative x-axis, y-axis, and z-axis.
- Select the **Minimum Offsets** button of **Linear Offsets** section if you want to specify the minimum values of stock offsets of the workpiece around the reference model along the positive and negative x-axis, y-axis, and z-axis.
- Click on **About X** button of **Rotation Offsets** section if you want to specify the angular stock offset of the workpiece around the x-axis of the reference model.
- Click on **About Y** button of **Rotation Offsets** section if you want to specify the angular stock offset of the workpiece around the y-axis of the reference model.
- Click on **About Z** button of **Rotation Offsets** section if you want to specify the angular stock offset of the workpiece around the y-axis of the reference model.
- Click in the **Diameter total** edit box and specify the diameter of the workpiece.
- Click in the **Length total** edit box and specify the length of the workpiece.

Other options of the **Options** tab have been discussed earlier.

Properties tab

The **Properties** tab is used to specify general information regarding the part file.

- Click in the **Workpiece name** edit box and specify desired name.
- Click in the **Workpiece common name** edit box and specify desired name by which it will be displayed in **Model Tree**.

After specifying the parameters, click on the **OK** button from **Auto Workpiece Creation** contextual tab. The workpiece will be displayed as shown in Figure-25.

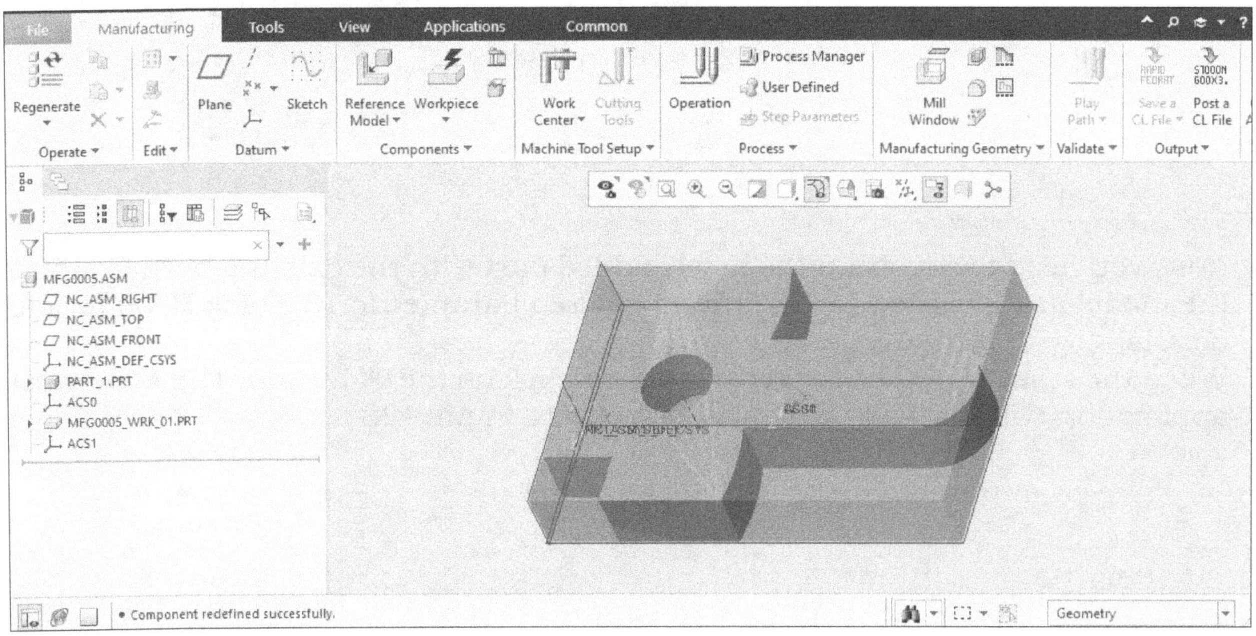

Figure-25. NC Assembly application window after creating workpiece

Assemble Workpiece

The **Assemble Workpiece** button is used to assemble or add a workpiece with the existing workpiece. The procedure to use this button is discussed next.

- Click on the **Assemble Workpiece** tool from **Workpiece** drop-down of **Components** panel; refer to Figure-26. The **Open** dialog box will displayed.

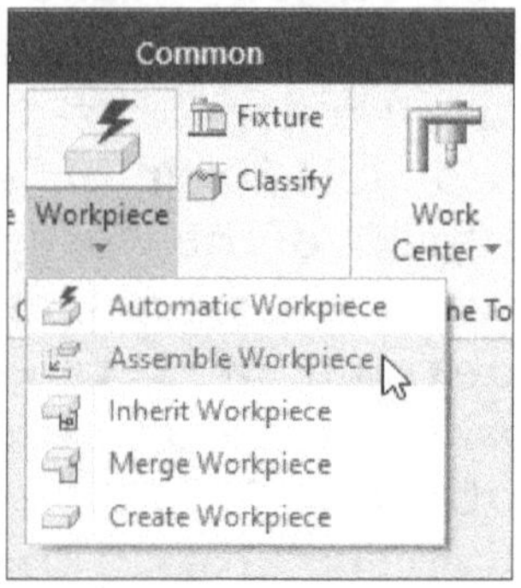

Figure-26. Assemble Workpiece tool

- Select the part file which you want to add or assemble and then click on the **Open** button. The **Component Placement** tab will be displayed; refer to Figure-27.

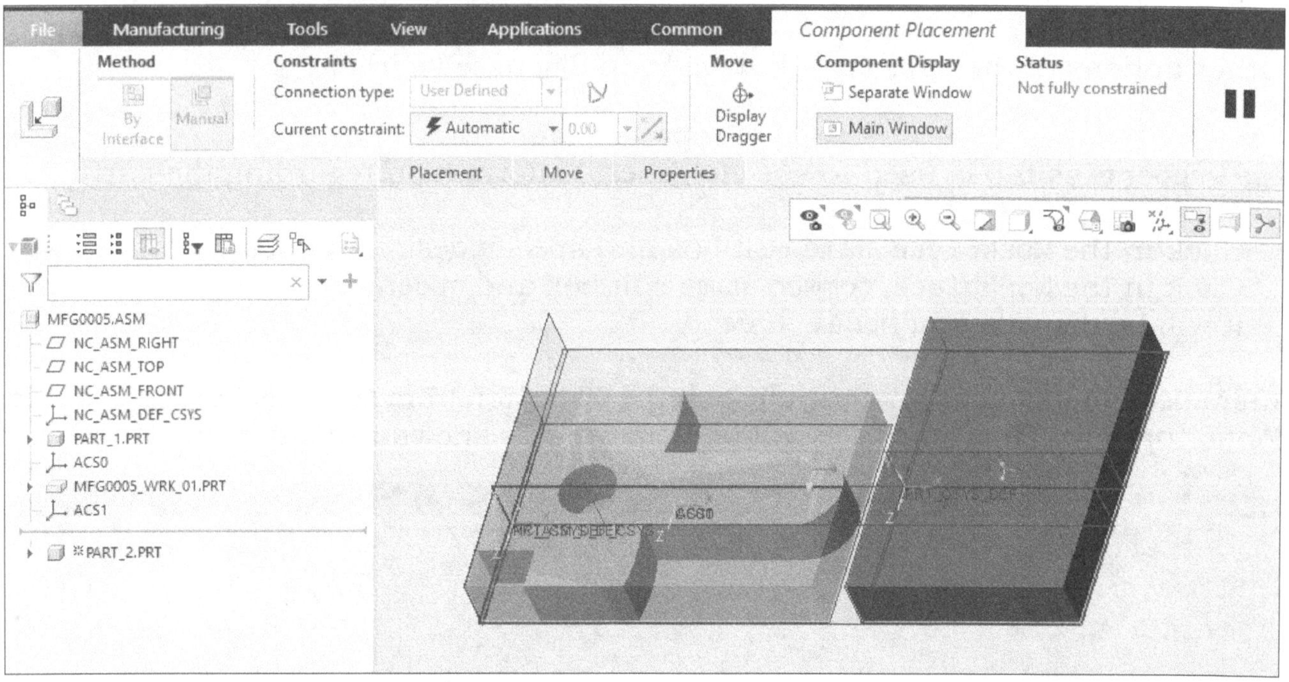

Figure-27. Assembling the part file

- Now, you need to constrain the newly added part with the existing part. Constrain the model as discussed earlier. (Refer to Creo Parametric 13 Black Book for more details).
- When the status is **Fully Constrained** then click on the **OK** button. The **NC Assembly** application window will be displayed; refer to Figure-28.

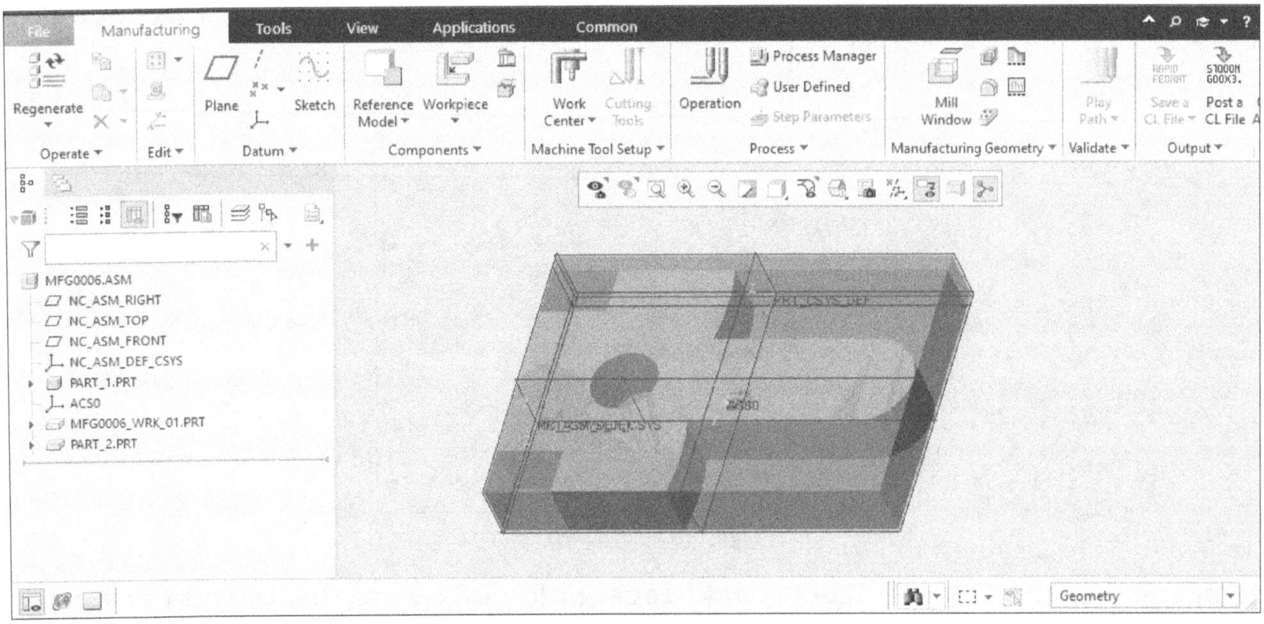

Figure-28. NC Assembly application window after adding part

Inherit Workpiece

The Inherit Workpiece is used for inherit features. The procedure to use this tool is discussed next.

- Click on the **Inherit Workpiece** tool from **Workpiece** drop-down of **Components** panel; refer to Figure-29. The **Open** dialog box will be displayed.

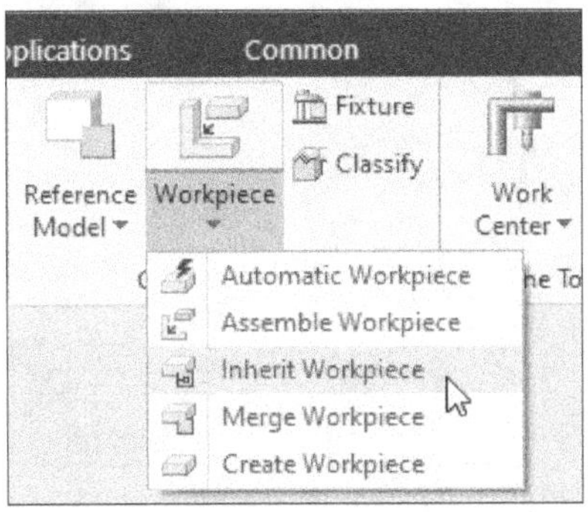

Figure-29. Inherit Workpiece button

- After selecting the part file for inherit feature, you need to click on the **Open** button. The **Component Placement** tab will be displayed which was discussed earlier.
- Click on the **OK** button from **Component Placement** tab. The **Create Stock-workpiece** dialog box will be displayed; refer to Figure-30.

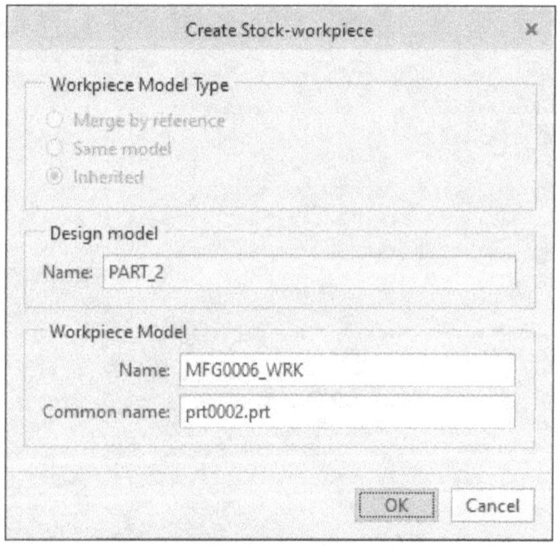

Figure-30. Create Stock-workpiece dialog box

The options of the **Create Stock-workpiece** dialog box were discussed earlier.

Merge Workpiece

The **Merge Workpiece** tool is used to merge features. The procedure to use this tool is discussed next.

- Click on the **Merge Workpiece** tool from **Workpiece** drop-down of **Components** panel; refer to Figure-31. The **Open** dialog box will be displayed.

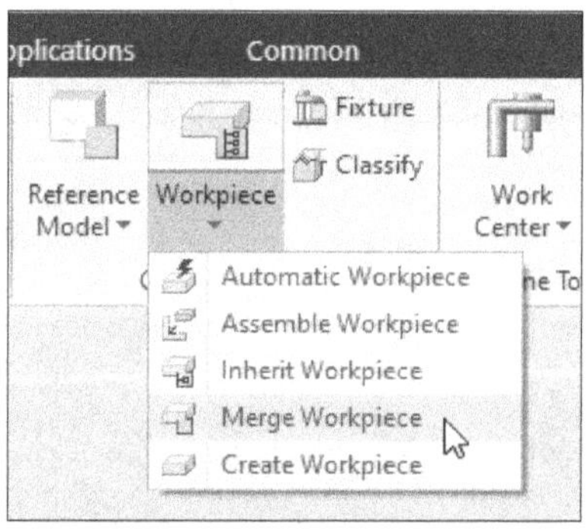

Figure-31. Merge Workpiece tool

- After selecting the part file for merge feature, you need to click on the **Open** button. The **Component Placement** tab will be displayed which was discussed earlier.
- In this window, you need to fully constrain the part file with newly added part; refer to Figure-32.

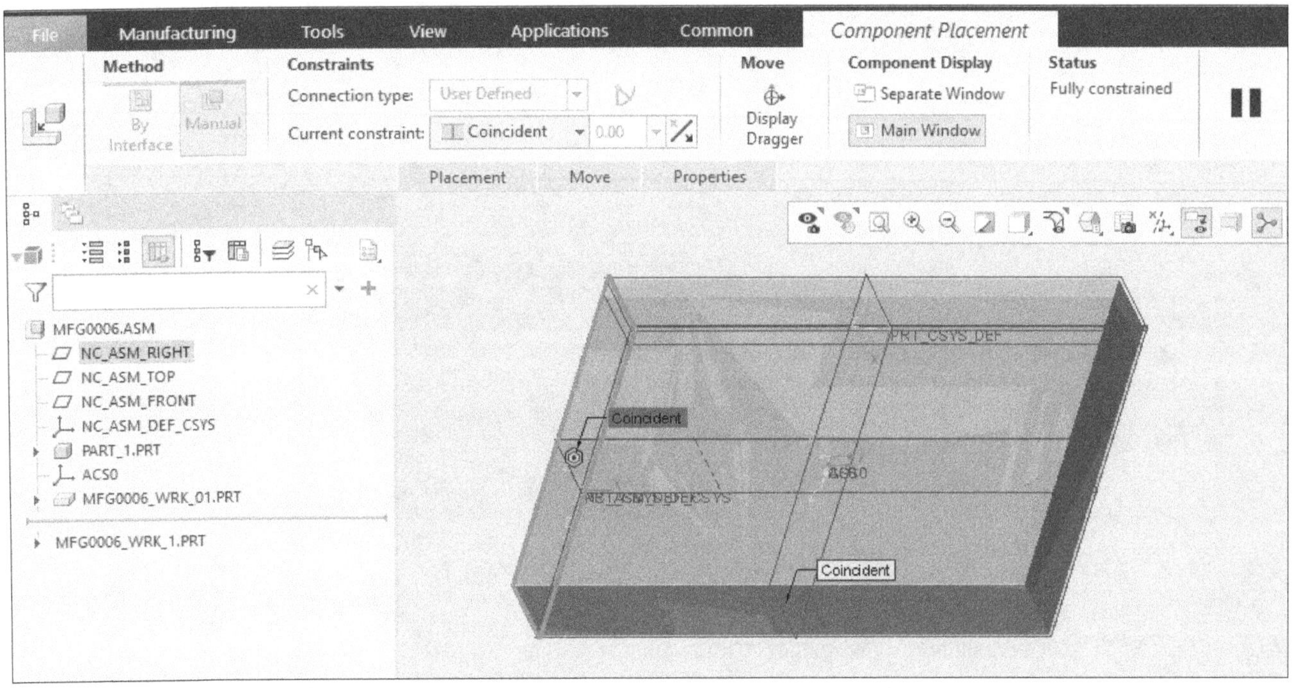

Figure-32. Fully constrained part

- After specifying the parameters, click on the **OK** button. The **Create Stock-workpiece** dialog box will be displayed; refer to Figure-33.

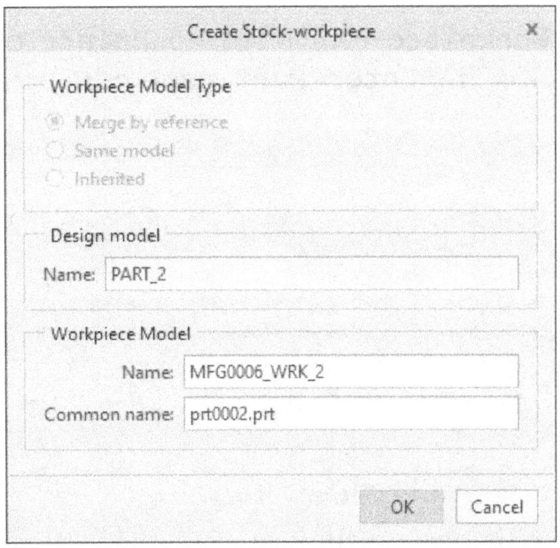

Figure-33. Create Stock-workpiece dialog box for merge feature

- The options of the **Create Stock-workpiece** dialog box were discussed earlier.
- After specifying the parameters, click on **OK** button. The **NC Assembly** application window will be displayed; refer to Figure-34.

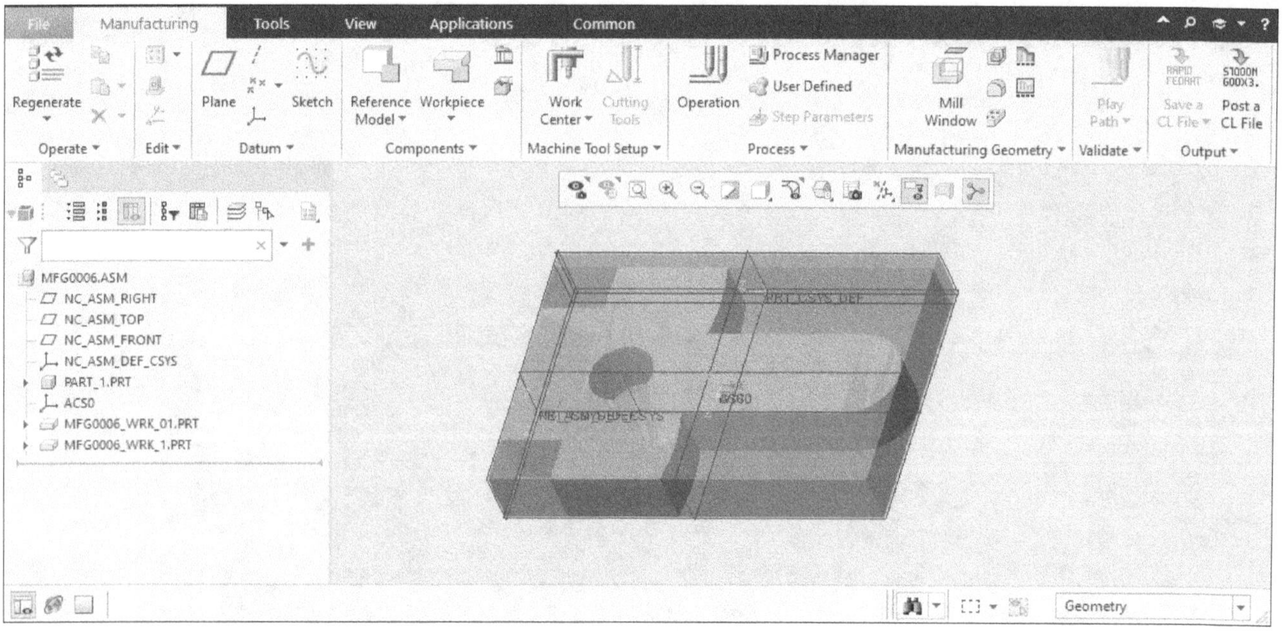

Figure-34. The NC Assembly window after merge feature

Create Workpiece

The **Create Workpiece** tool is used to create a workpiece manually. The procedure to use this tool is discussed next.

- Click on the **Create Workpiece** tool from **Workpiece** drop-down of **Components** panel; refer to Figure-35. The **Enter Part name** edit box will be displayed on the application window.

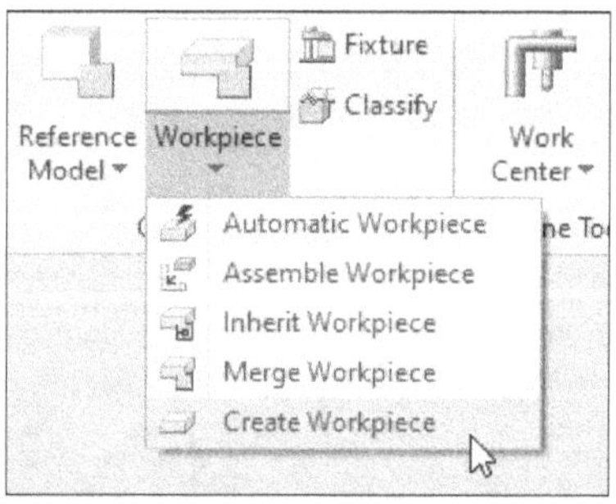

Figure-35. Create Workpiece tool

- Enter the name in the edit box or click on the ✓ button to use the default name of part. The **FEAT CLASS Menu Manager** will be displayed; refer to Figure-36.

Figure-36. FEAT CLASS Menu Manager

- Select the face of part to be used as base plane; refer to Figure-37.

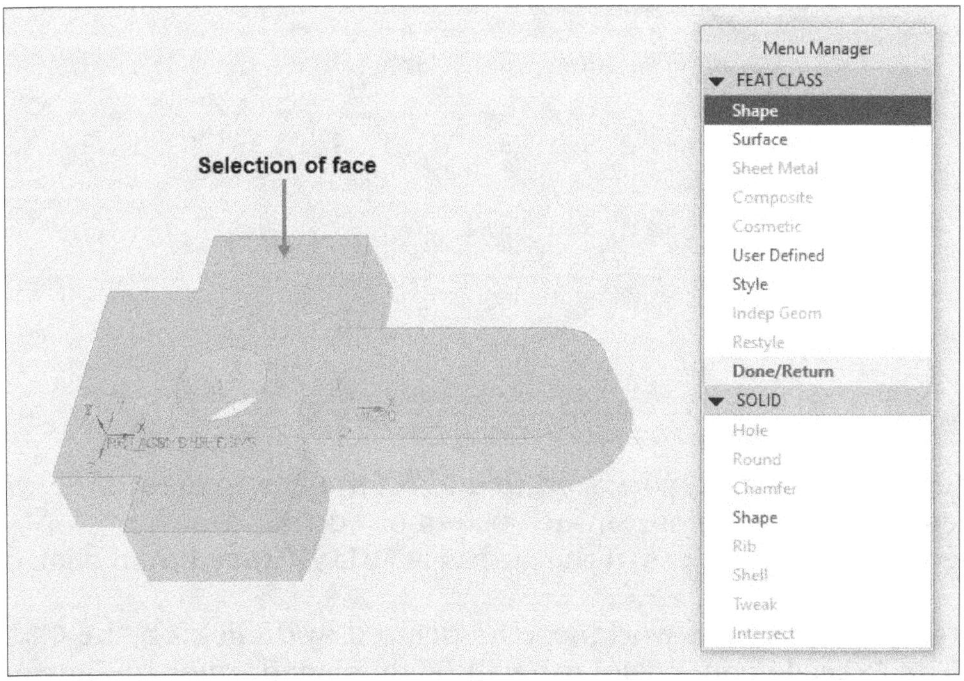

Figure-37. Selection of face for creating workpiece

- After selection of plane, you need to click on **Shape** button from **SOLID** section of **Menu Manager**. The **SOLID OPTS Menu Manager** will be displayed; refer to Figure-38.

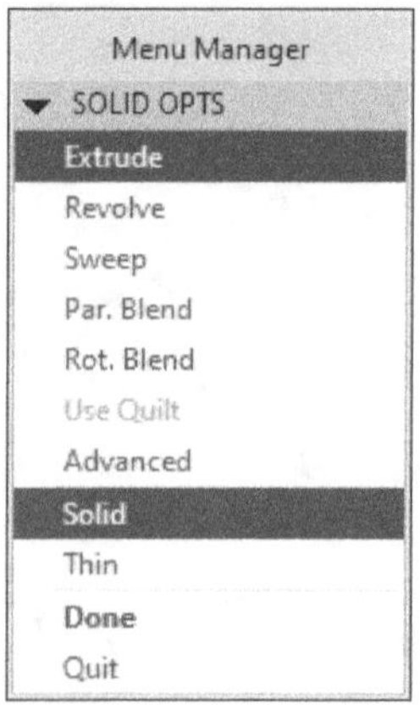

Figure-38. Updated Menu Manager

- Here, you need to select the type of workpiece you are going to make. Select **Extrude** and **Solid** button.
- After specifying the parameters, click on **Done** button from the **Menu Manager**. If there are no clear references specified then the **References** dialog box will be displayed; refer to Figure-39.

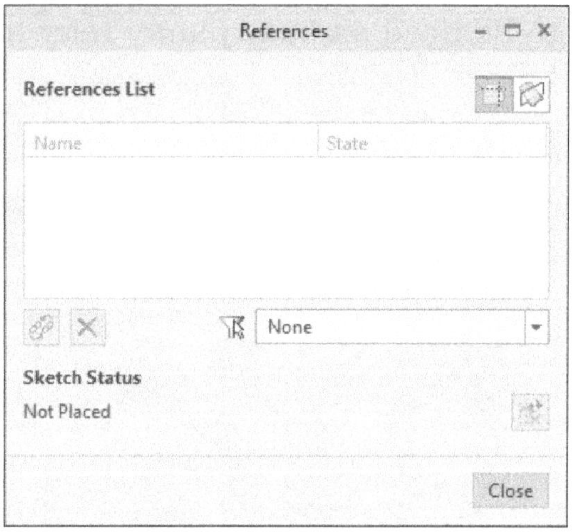

Figure-39. References dialog box

- In **References** dialog box, you need to add references to create the workpiece. In references, you can add coordinate system or edges.
- After selecting the references, if the status is **Fully Placed** then click on the **Close** button.
- Now, create the sketch of workpiece as desired and click on the **OK** button from **Ribbon**. The **Extrude** contextual tab will be displayed; refer to Figure-40.

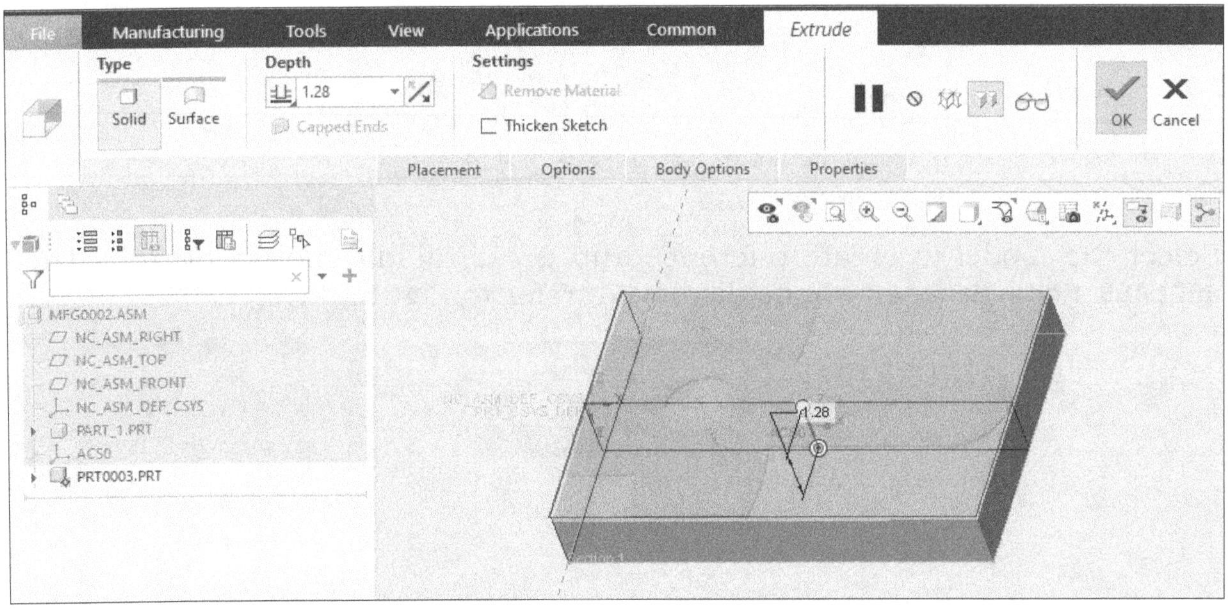

Figure-40. Creating workpiece with extrude button

- Adjust the dimension of extrude for workpiece as desired and click on the **OK** button. The **NC Assembly** application window will be displayed along with part and recently created workpiece; refer to Figure-41.

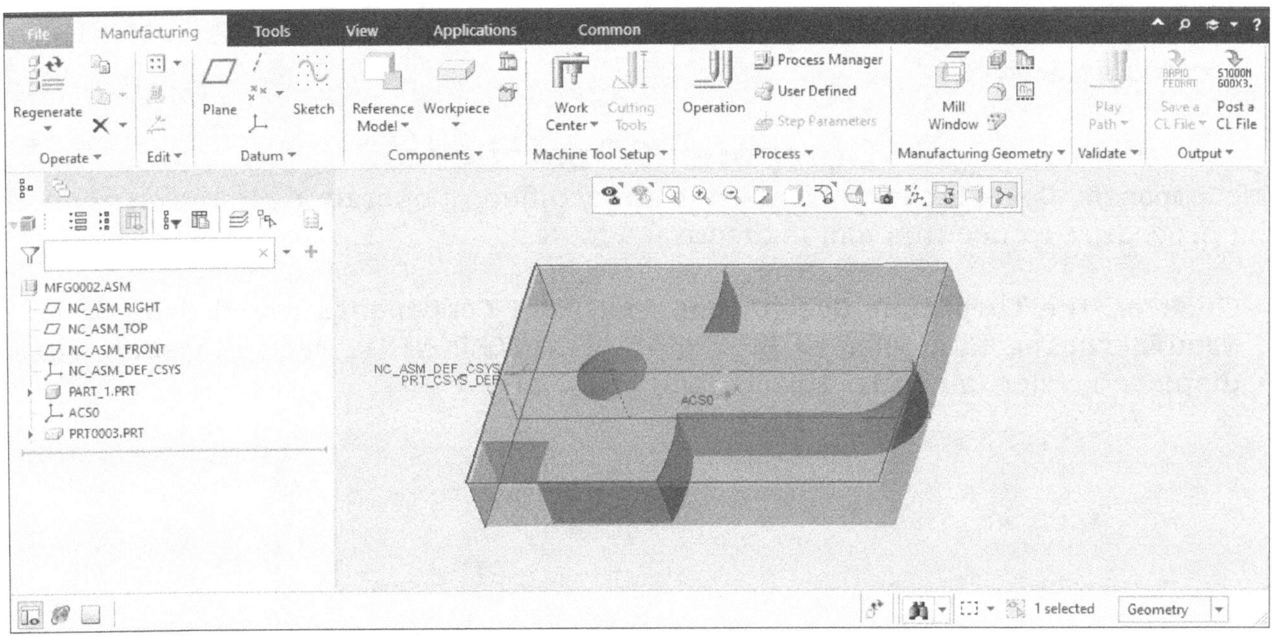

Figure-41. NC Assembly application window after creating workpiece

Classify

The **Classify** tool is used to classify the model as reference, fixture, or workpiece. The procedure to use this tool is discussed next.

- Click on the **Classify** tool of **Components** panel from **Manufacturing** tab; refer to Figure-42. The **Select** dialog box will be displayed; refer to Figure-43.

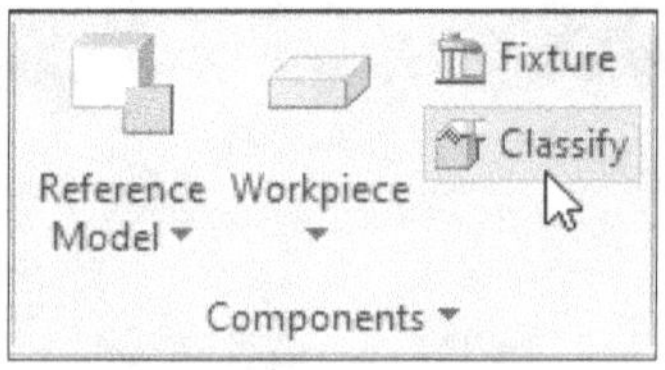

Figure-42. Classify tool

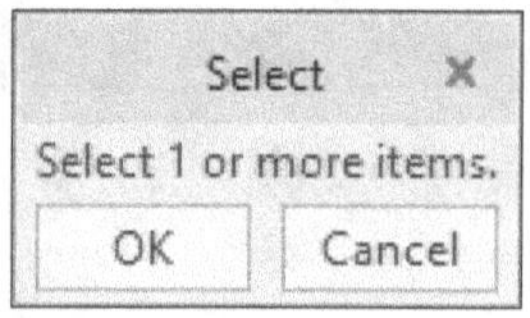

Figure-43. Select dialog box

- Select the model to create reference and press middle mouse button. The **MFG RECLASS Menu Manager** will be displayed; refer to Figure-44.

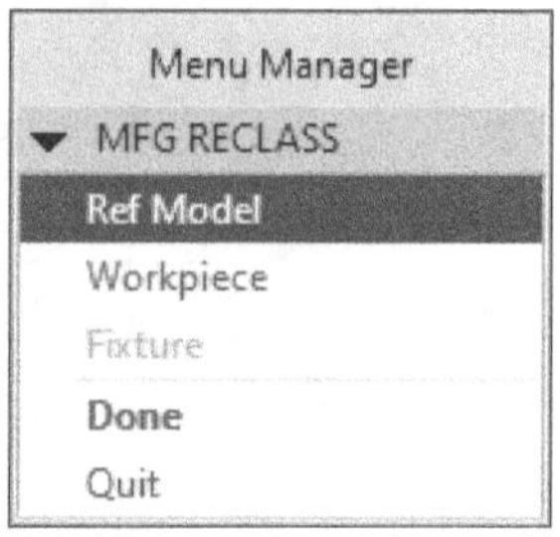

Figure-44. MFG RECLASS Menu Manager

- Select **Ref Model** button from **Menu Manager** if you want to create the selected model as reference model.
- Select **Workpiece** button from **Menu Manager**, if you want to create the selected model as workpiece.
- After selection of specific button, click on the **Done** button. The model will be created as desired.

Component Operations

The **Component Operations** tool is used to apply different operations to the component. The procedure to use this tool is discussed next.

- Click on the **Component Operations** tool from **Components** panel drop-down of **Manufacturing** tab; refer to Figure-45. The **COMPONENT Menu Manager** will be displayed; refer to Figure-46.

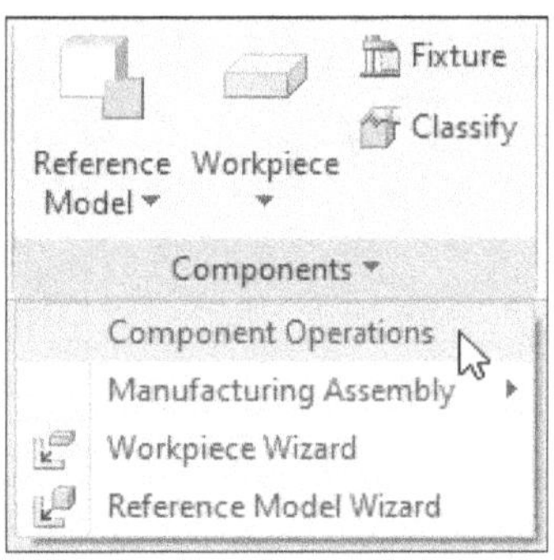

Figure-45. Component Operations tool

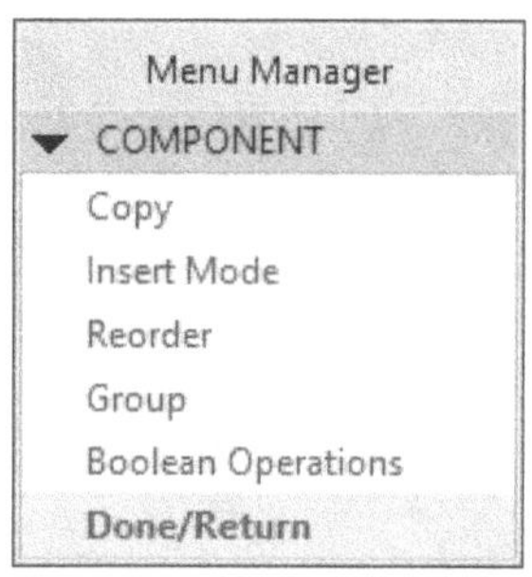

Figure-46. COMPONENT Menu Manager

Copy button

The **Copy** button is used to copy component with respect to coordinate system. The procedure to use this tool is discussed next.

- Click on the **Copy** button from **COMPONENT Menu Manager**. The updated **COMPONENT Menu Manager** will be displayed; refer to Figure-47.

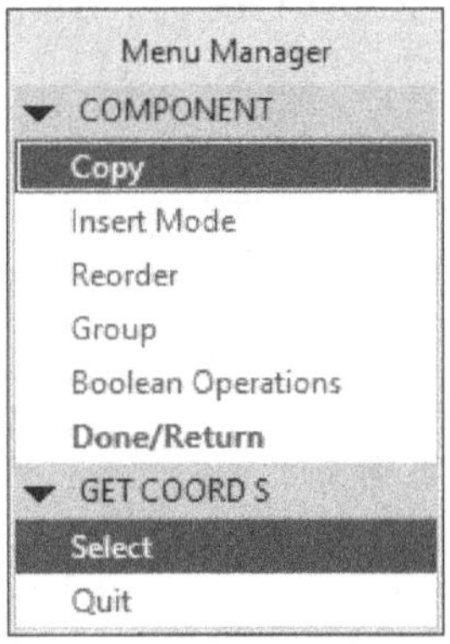

Figure-47. Updated COMPONENT Menu Manager

- Select the **Coordinate system** from the application window. The **Select** dialog box will be displayed; refer to Figure-48.

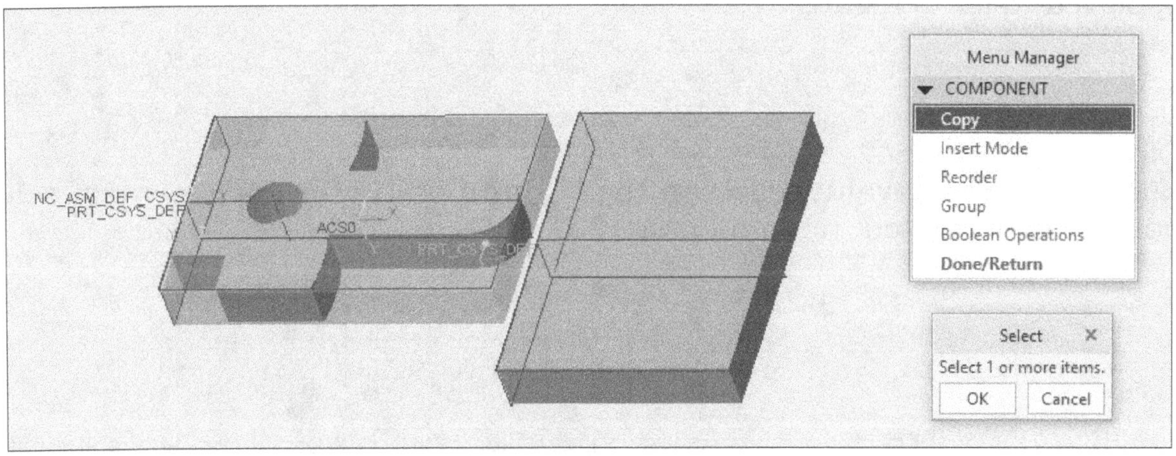

Figure-48. Selection of coordinate system for copy command

- Select the part to copy and press middle mouse button. The updated **COMPONENT Menu Manager** will be displayed; refer to Figure-49.

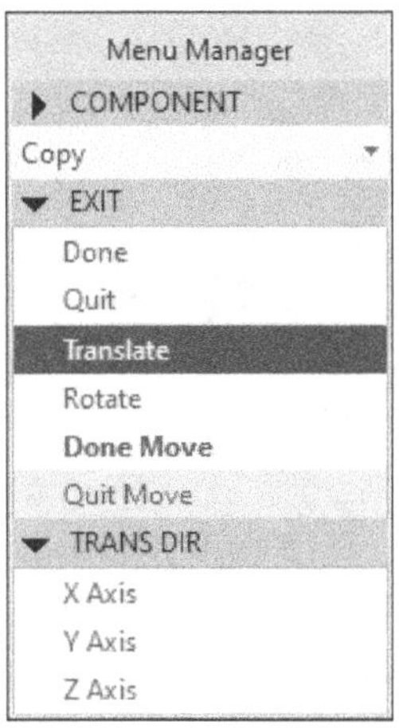

Figure-49. Updated COMPONENT Menu Manager

- Select the transfer axis from **TRANS DIR** section. The **Input distance** box will be displayed on the canvas screen; refer to Figure-50.

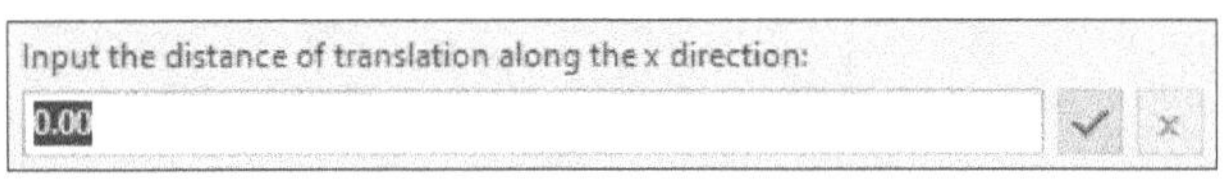

Figure-50. Input distance box

- After inserting the distance, click on the button. The updated **COMPONENT Menu Manager** will be displayed; refer to Figure-51.

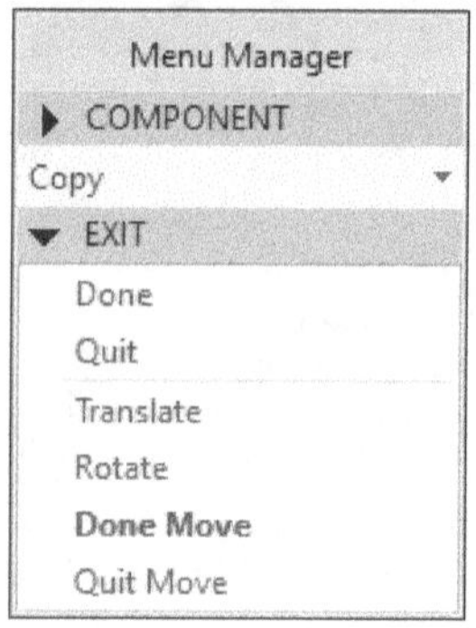

Figure-51. Updated COMPONENT Menu Manager

- Click on the **Done Move** button. The **Enter number of Instances** box will be displayed; refer to Figure-52.

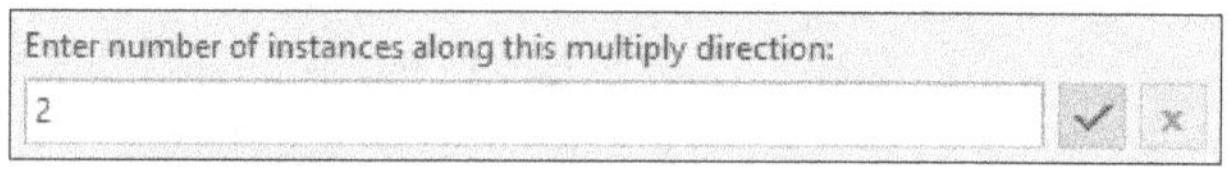

Figure-52. Enter number of instances

- After inserting the value, click on the button. The multiple copy of selected model will be created; refer to Figure-53.

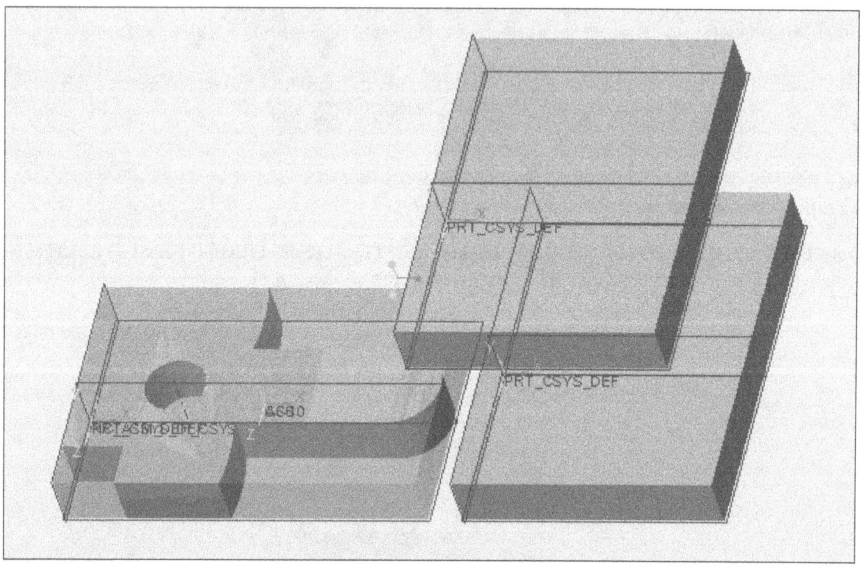

Figure-53. Creating multiple copy

Insert Mode

The **Insert Mode** tool is used to roll back assembly to insert one component before the current component. The procedure to use this tool is discussed next.

- Click on the **Insert Mode** button from **COMPONENT Menu Manager**. The **INSERT MODE Menu Manager** will be displayed; refer to Figure-54.

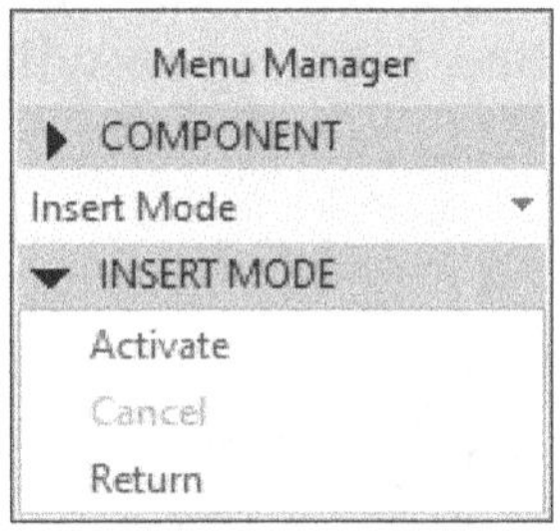

Figure-54. INSERT MODE Menu Manager

- Click on **Activate** button. The **SELECT FEAT** section will be displayed.
- Now, select the component from the **Model Tree** to activate the insert mode; refer to Figure-55.

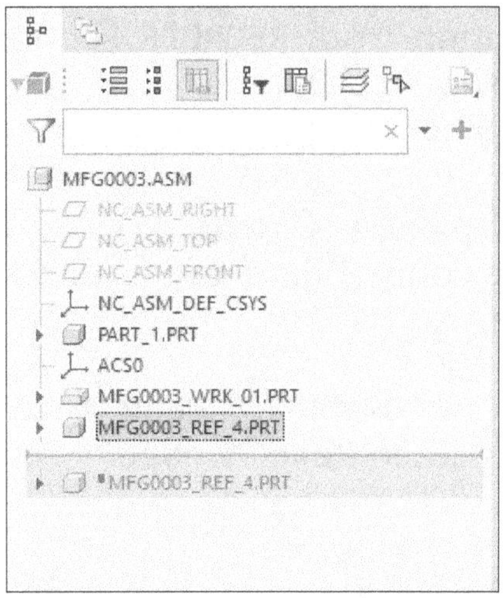

Figure-55. Selection of Component for Insert Mode

- The commands or action below the selected component will be hidden until **Insert Here** button is selected by right clicking on the component.
- You can also do this process by drag and drop commands with the help of left key of mouse.

Reorder

The **Reorder** tool is used to reorder the sequence of component generation. The procedure to use this tool is discussed next.

- Click on the **Reorder** button from **COMPONENT Menu Manager**. The updated **Component Menu Manager** will be displayed along with **Select** dialog box; refer to Figure-56.

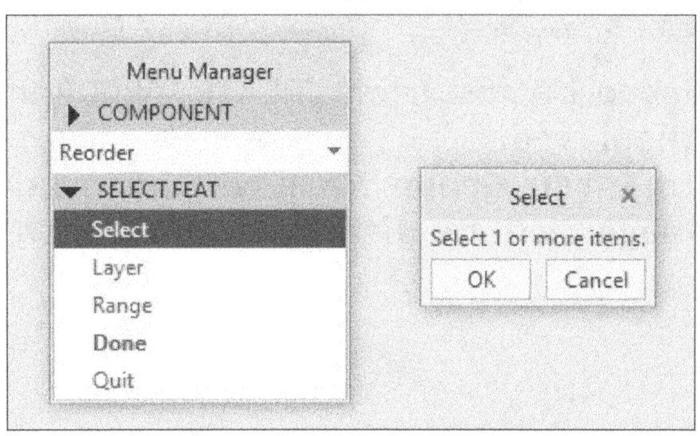

Figure-56. COMPONENT Menu Manager for Reorder

- Select the part or action which you want to reorder. After selection, click on **Done** button. The updated **REORDER Menu Manager** will be displayed; refer to Figure-57.

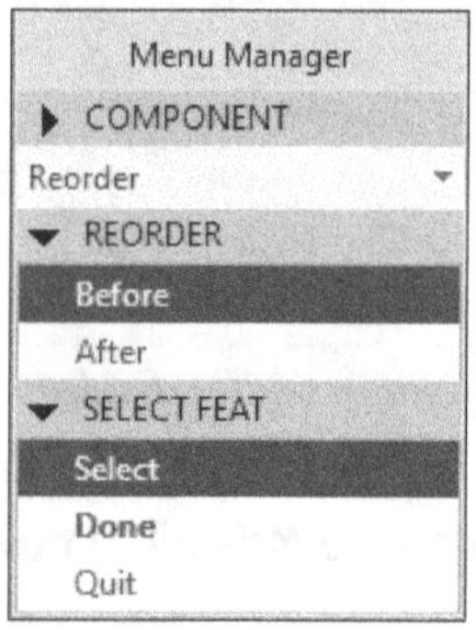

Figure-57. Updated REORDER Menu Manager

- Select **Before** or **After** option from **REORDER** section and click on the action or command for reordering from **Model Tree**.
- Click on the **Done** button. The action will be reordered.

Group

The **Group** tool is used to group components and assemble the features. The procedure to use this tool is discussed next.

- Click on the **Group** button of **COMPONENT Menu Manager**. The **Open** dialog box will be displayed along with updated **Menu Manager**; refer to Figure-58.

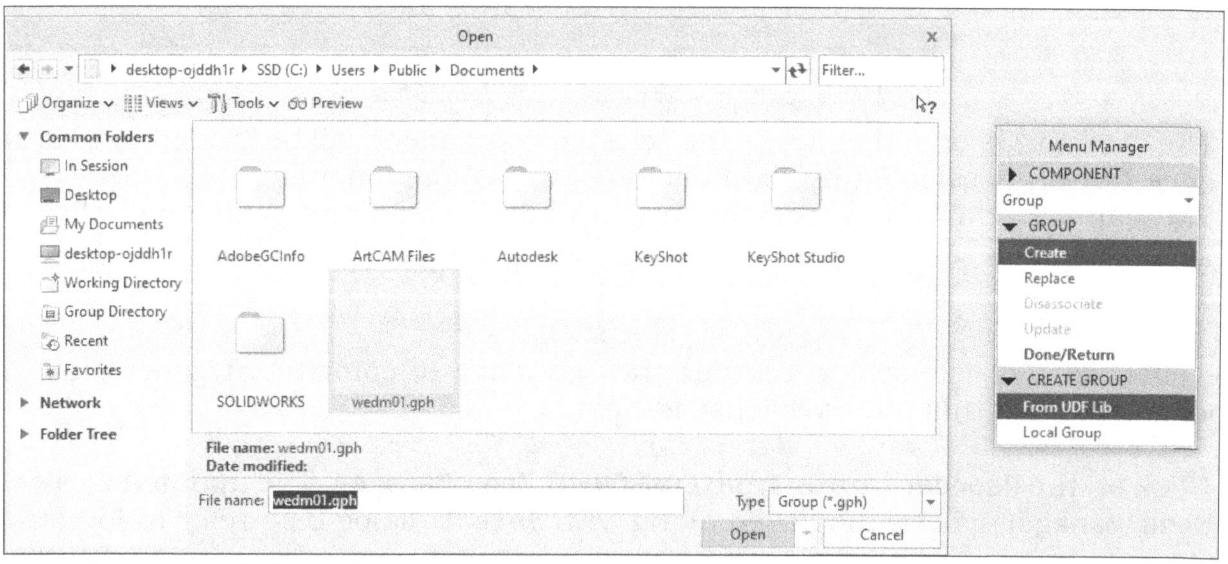

Figure-58. Updated COMPONENT Menu Manager for Group option with Open dialog box

- Click on the **Local Group** button from **CREATE GROUP** section. The **Enter Group Name** edit box will be displayed.
- Enter desired name in **Enter Group Name** edit box and click on the  button. The updated **Menu Manager** will be displayed along with **Select** dialog box; refer to Figure-59.

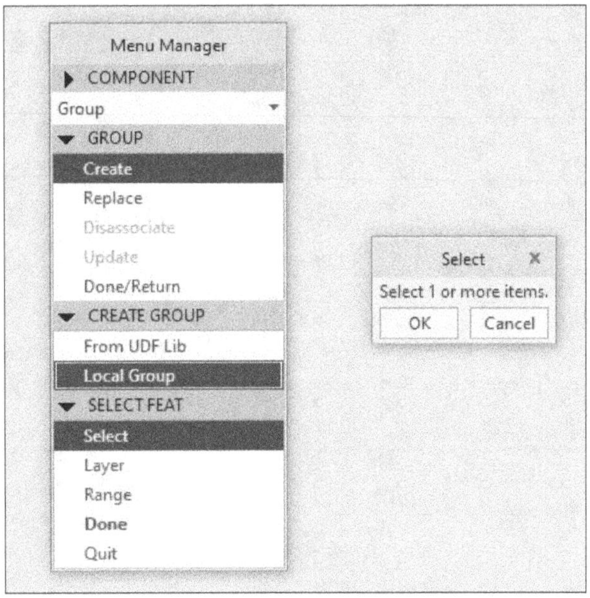

Figure-59. Updated GROUP Menu Manager

- Select the command or action while holding **CTRL** key from **Model Tree** and click on **Done** button from **Select Feat** section.
- The **Group** will be created in the **Model Tree**.

Boolean Operator

The **Boolean Operator** button is used for boolean operation. The procedure to use this tool is discussed next.

- Click on the **Boolean Operations** button of **COMPONENT Menu Manager**. The **Boolean Operations** dialog box will be displayed along with updated **COMPONENT Menu Manager**; refer to Figure-60.

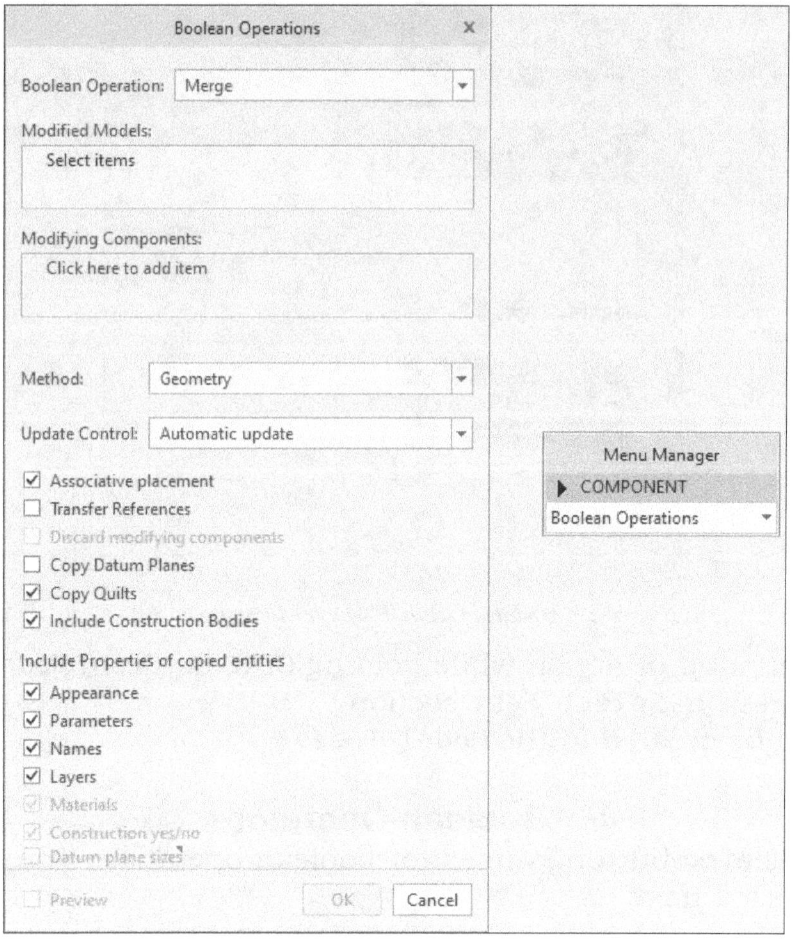

Figure-60. Boolean Operations dialog box

Boolean Operations drop-down

- Select **Merge** option from **Boolean Operations** drop-down of **Boolean Operations** dialog box, if you want to merge the selected component from selected model.
- Select **Add Bodies** option from **Boolean Operations** drop-down of **Boolean Operations** dialog box, if you want to add the bodies in the selected model.
- Select **Cut** option from **Boolean Operations** drop-down of **Boolean Operations** dialog box, if you want to cut the selected component from selected model.
- Select the **Intersect** option from **Boolean Operations** drop-down of **Boolean Operations** dialog box, if you want to intersect the selected component from selected model.

Update Control drop-down

- Select **Automatic update** option from **Update Control** drop-down, if you want to update the feature automatically.
- Select the **Manual update** option from **Update Control** drop-down, if you want to update the feature upon request.
- Select **No dependency** option from **Update Control** drop-down, if you do not want to create any dependency between a feature and the modifying component.
- Check the **Associative placement** check box, if you want to update the resulting cut according to the placement of modifying component.
- Check the **Copy Datum Planes** check box, if you want to copy Datums to the modified model as a part of cut.

- Check the **Copy Quilts** check box, if you want to copy quilts to the modified model as a part of Cut.
- Select the **Appearance** check box to apply the appearance in the source geometry to the copied geometry.
- Select the **Parameters** check box to copy the parameters of the copied entities to the target entities and lock them in the target.
- Select the **Names** check box to copy the names of the copied entities to the target model.
- Select the **Layers** check box to copy layers, layers states, include entities in corresponding layers.
- Select the **Datum plane sizes** check box to copy the datum planes with their original defined sizes.
- After specifying the parameters, click on the **Preview** button. If preview of your model is as per your need then click on the **OK** button from the **Boolean Operations** drop-down. The boolean operation will be created.

Manufacturing Assembly

The **Manufacturing Assembly** tool is used to assemble and classify the model. There are two tools in **Manufacturing Assembly** cascading menu which are discussed next; refer to Figure-61.

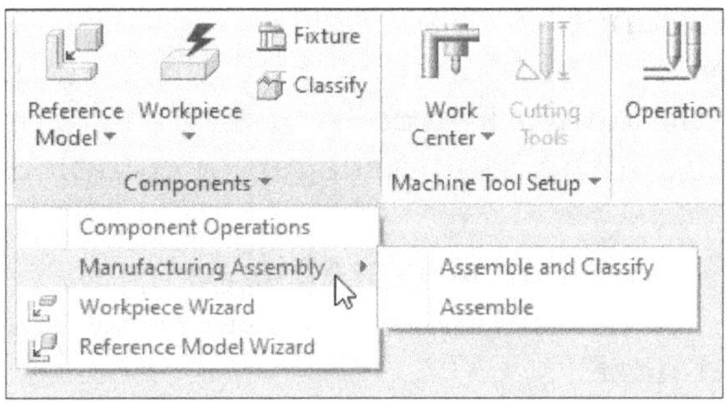

Figure-61. Manufacturing Assembly cascading menu

Assembly and Classify

- Click on the **Assemble and Classify** tool of **Manufacturing Assembly** cascading menu from **Components** drop-down. The **Open** dialog box will be displayed.
- Select the assembly part file from **Open** dialog box and click on **Open** button. The **Component Placement** contextual tab will be displayed.
- Set the constrain of recently added assembly to **Default** from **Constraint** drop-down. You can also constraint the model with assembly by yourself.
- Click on the **OK** button from **Component Placement** contextual tab. The **NC Assembly** application window will be displayed along with **MFG CLASS Menu Manager**; refer to Figure-62.

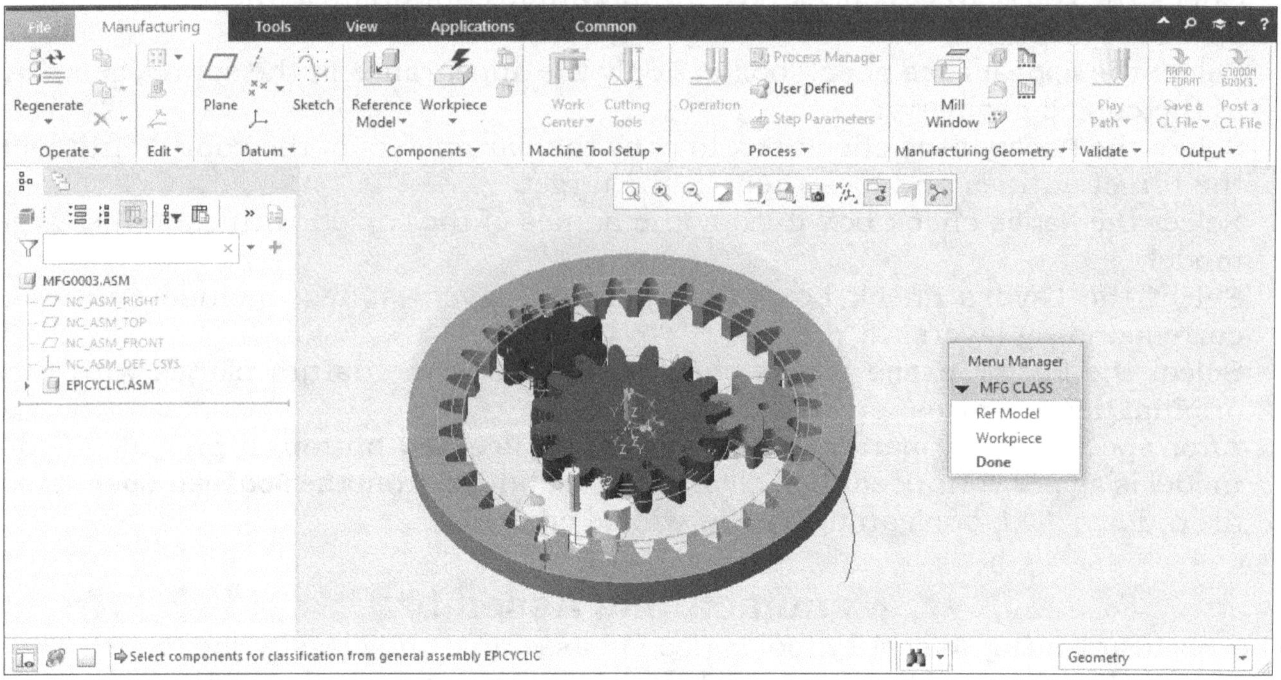

Figure-62. NC Assembly application window with MFG CLASS Menu Manager

- Select the **Ref Model** or **Workpiece** from **MFG CLASS Menu Manager** and select the model or part from reference as required.
- Note that you can even set some components of assembly as reference and other components of assembly as workpiece by using these options.
- Click on **Done** button from the **Menu Manager** to complete the process.

Assemble

The **Assemble** tool is used to assemble a manufacturing assembly. The procedure to use this tool is discussed next.

- Click on the **Assemble** tool of **Manufacturing Assembly** cascading menu from **Components** drop-down. The **Open** dialog box will be displayed.
- Select the assembly part file from **Open** dialog box and click on **Open** button. The **Component Placement** tab will be displayed.
- Set the constrain of recently added assembly to **Default** from **Constraint** drop-down.
- Click on **Done** button from **Component Placement** tab. The **NC Assembly** application window will be displayed along with the added assembly.

Workpiece Wizard

The **Workpiece Wizard** tool is used to assemble workpiece using the Same model, or with features inherited or merged from another model. The procedure to use this tool is discussed next.

- Click on the **Workpiece Wizard** tool from the expanded **Components** panel of **Manufacturing** tab in the **Ribbon**; refer to Figure-63. The **Open** dialog box will be displayed.

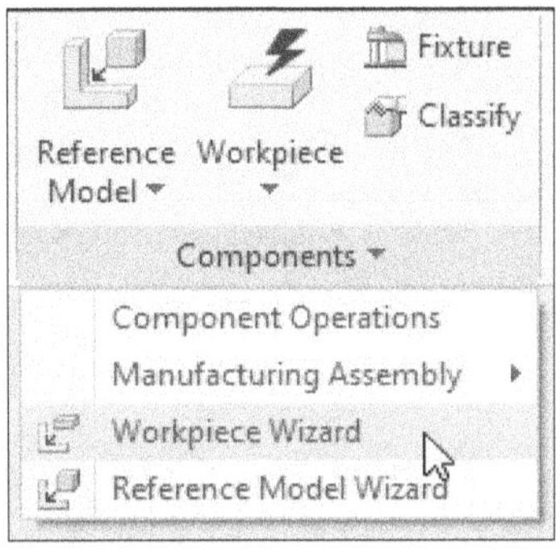

Figure-63. Workpiece Wizard tool

- Select the specific workpiece for model from **Open** dialog box and click on **Open** button. The **Component Placement** tab will be displayed.
- Click on **Default** from **Constrain** drop-down or you can constrain the workpiece manually and click on the **OK** button. The **Create Stock-workpiece** dialog box will be displayed; refer to Figure-64.

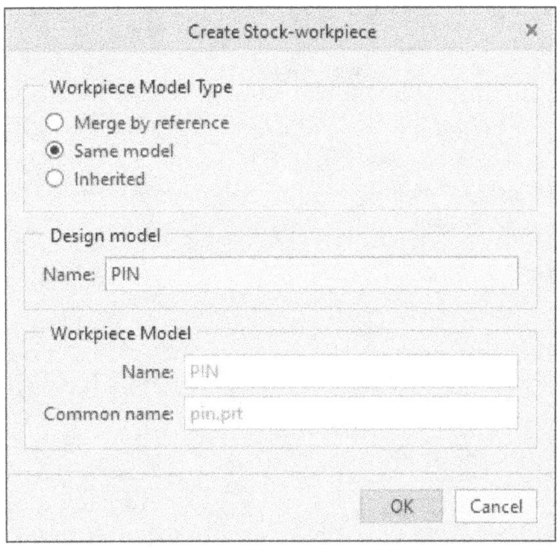

Figure-64. Create Stock-workpiece dialog box for Workpiece Wizard

- Select the **Merge by reference** radio button of **Workpiece Model Type** section, if you want to assemble a workpiece using merge features.
- Select the **Same model** radio button of **Workpiece Model Type** section, if you want to assemble a workpiece using same model.
- Select the **Inherited** radio button of **Workpiece Model Type** section, if you want to assemble a workpiece using inherited features.
- Click in the **Name** edit box of **Workpiece Model** section and specify the name.
- Click in the **Common name** edit box of **Workpiece Model** section and specify the common name for workpiece.
- After specifying the various parameters, click on the **OK** button from **Create Stock-workpiece** dialog box. The workpiece will be created with desired features.

Reference Model Wizard

The **Reference Model Wizard** tool is used to assemble a reference model. The procedure to use this tool is discussed next.

- Click on the **Reference Model Wizard** tool of expanded **Components** panel from **Manufacturing** tab; refer to Figure-65. The **Open** dialog box will be displayed.

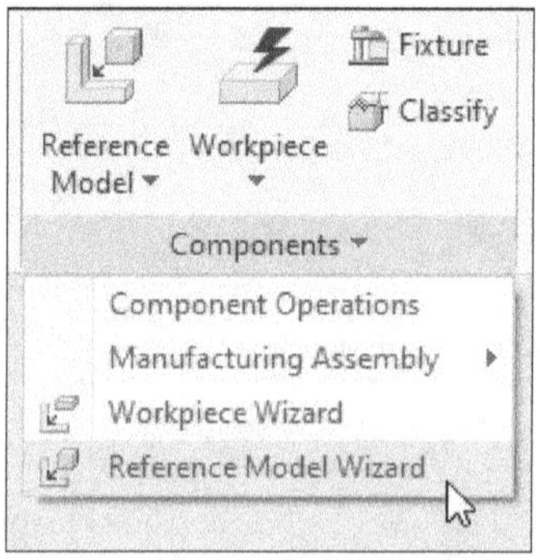

Figure-65. Reference Model Wizard tool

- Select the file to add as reference model and click on **Open** button from **Open** dialog box. The **Component Placement** tab will be displayed.
- Click on **Default** button from **Constrain** drop-down or constrain the reference model manually.
- Click on the **OK** button. The **Create Reference model** dialog box will be displayed; refer to Figure-66.

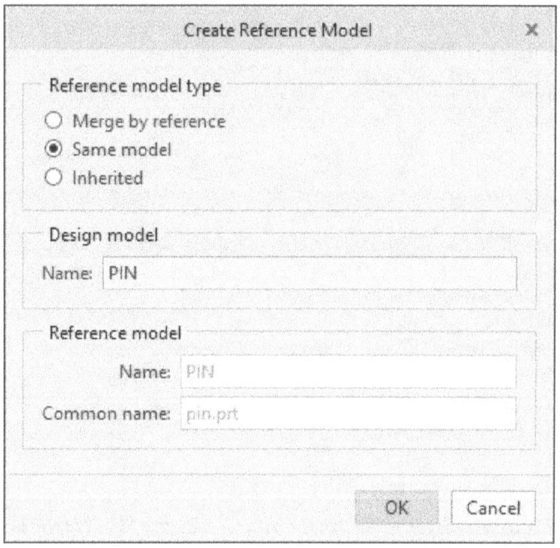

Figure-66. Create Reference Model dialog box

- The options of this dialog box have been discussed earlier.
- After specifying various parameters, click on the **OK** button to complete this process. The reference model will be added on **NC Assembly** application window.

PRACTICAL 1

Create a reference model as given in Figure-67 and also create the workpiece for the model.

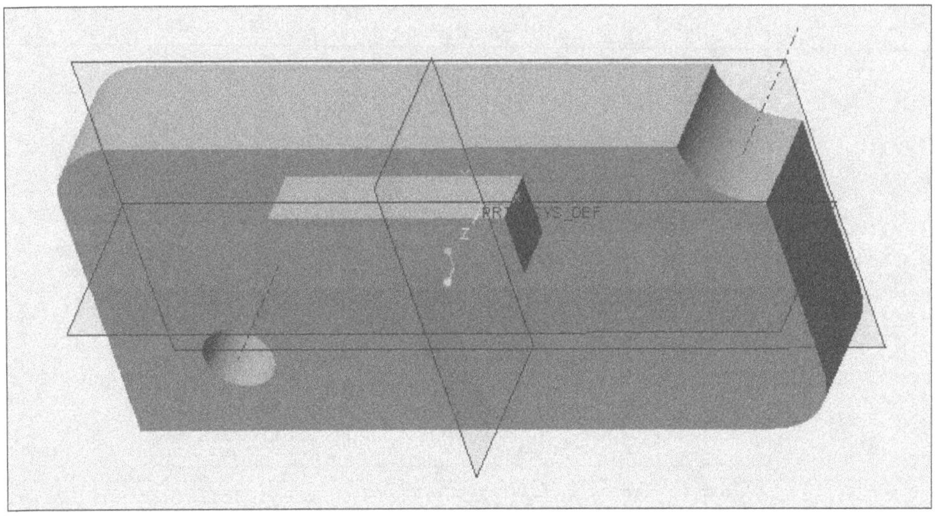

Figure-67. Practical 1

Starting the NC Assembly

- Double-click on **Creo Parametric** icon from your computer's desktop or **Start** menu. The creo parametric application window will be displayed; refer to Figure-68.

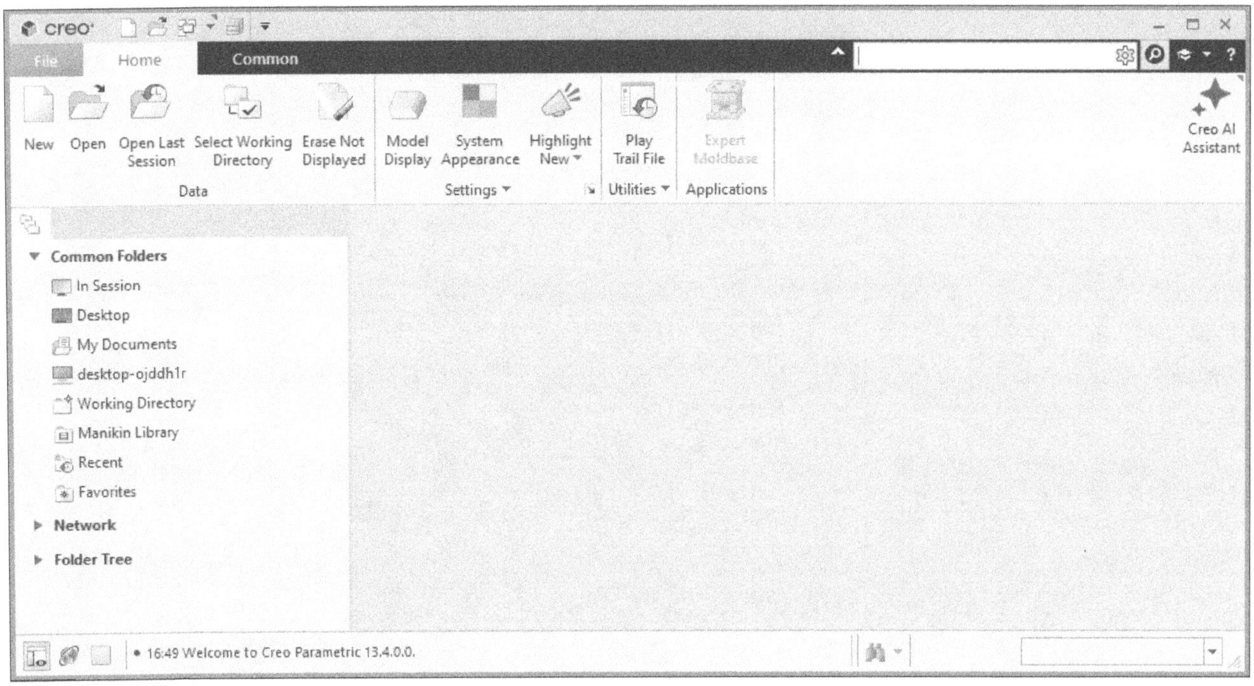

Figure-68. Creo Parametric starting window

- Click on the **New** button from **Ribbon**. The **New** dialog box will be displayed; refer to Figure-69.

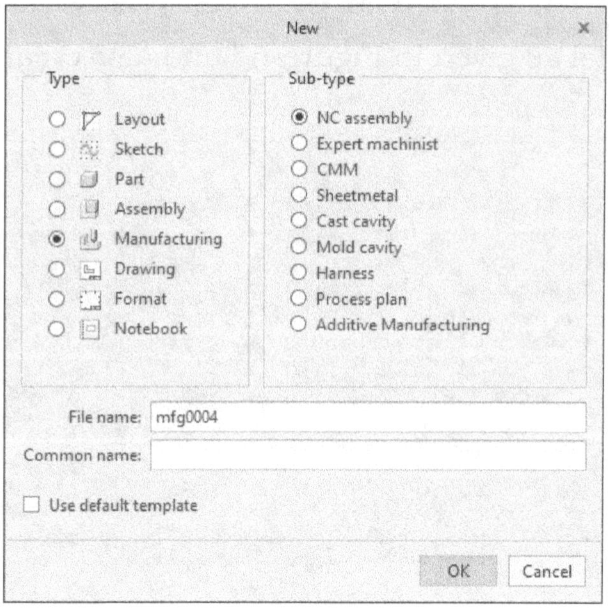

Figure-69. New File Options dialog box

- Click on the **Manufacturing** radio button from **Type** area and **NC assembly** radio button from **Sub-type** area.
- Click on the **File name** edit box and type **Practical 1** as the name of file.
- Clear the **Use default template** check box from **New** dialog box.
- Click on **OK** button from **New** dialog box. The **New File Options** dialog box will be displayed; refer to Figure-70.

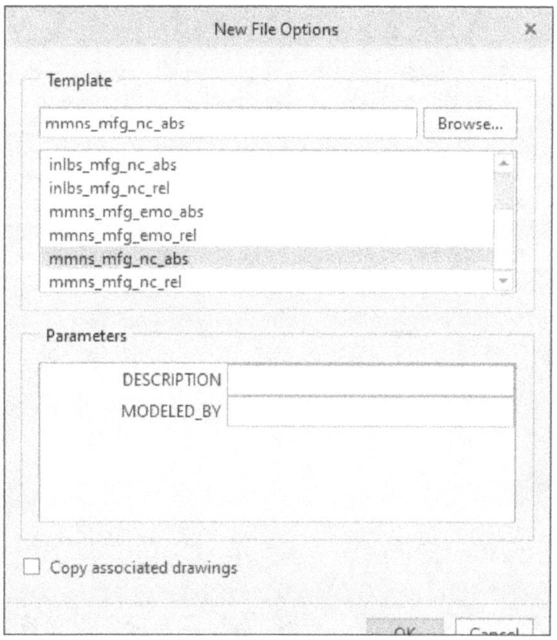

Figure-70. New File Options dialog box

- Click on **mmns mfg nc abs** option from **Template** section and specify the required details of **Parameters** section.
- Click on **OK** button from **New File Options** dialog box. The **NC Assembly** application window will be displayed; refer to Figure-71.

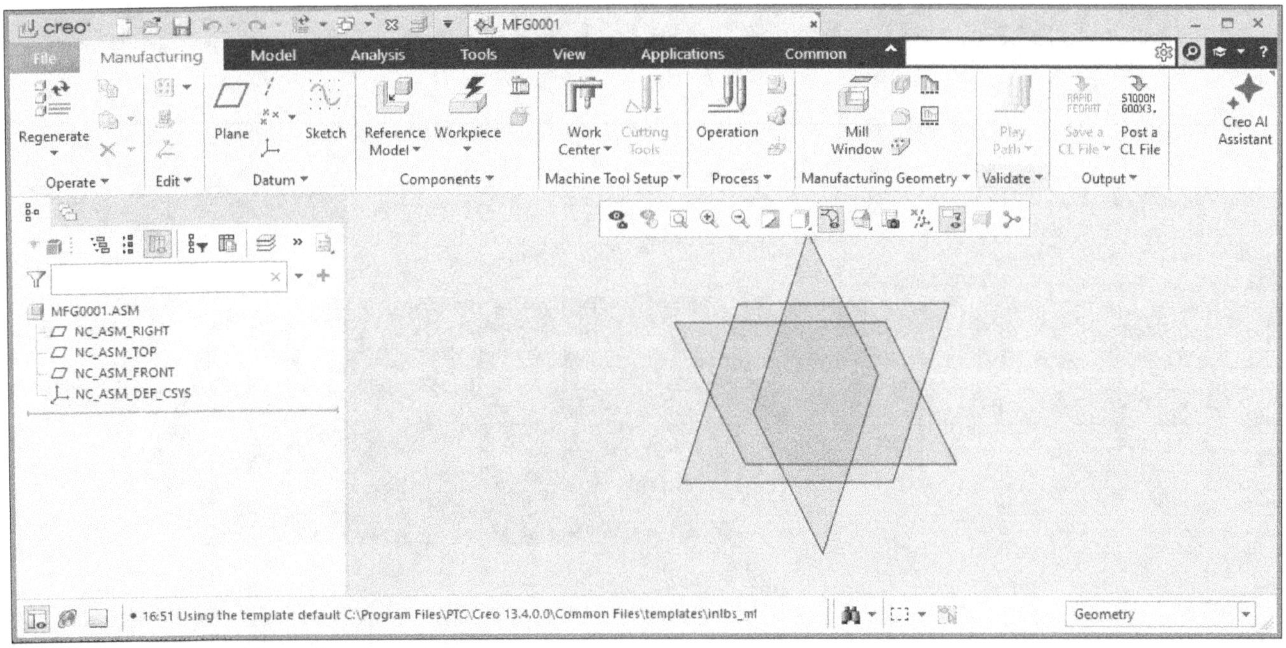

Figure-71. NC Assembly application window

Adding Reference Model

- Click on **Assemble Reference Model** button of **Reference Model** drop-down from **Manufacturing** tab. The **Open** dialog box will be displayed; refer to Figure-72.

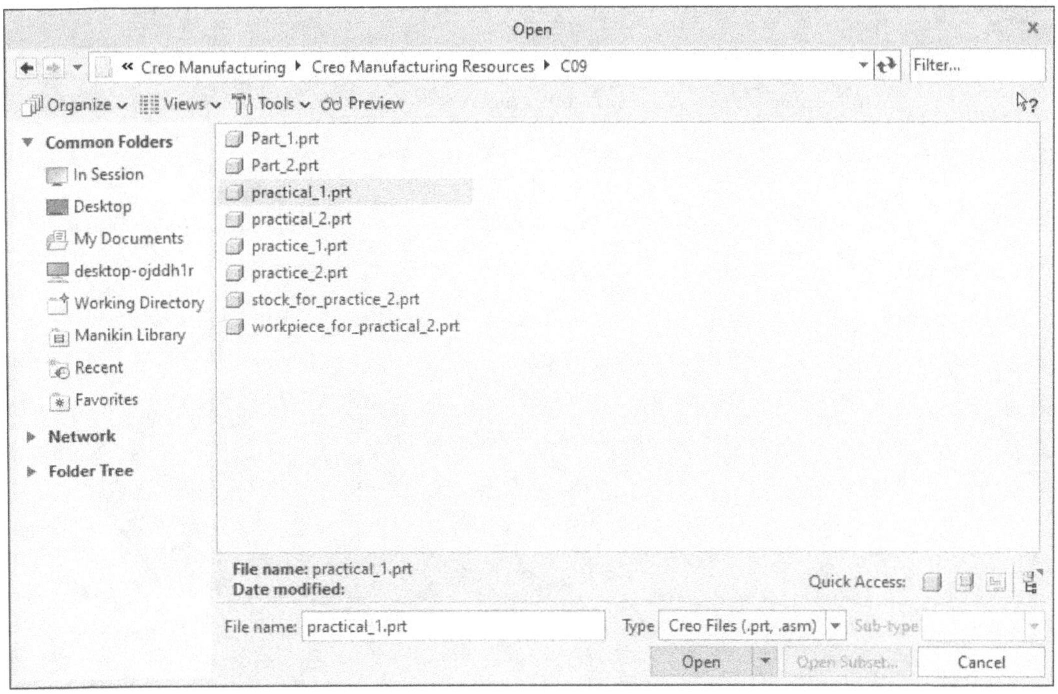

Figure-72. Open dialog box

- Select the **Practical 1** file from resource kit folder and click on **Open** button from **Open** dialog box.
- The **Component Placement** contextual tab will be displayed along with the model; refer to Figure-73.

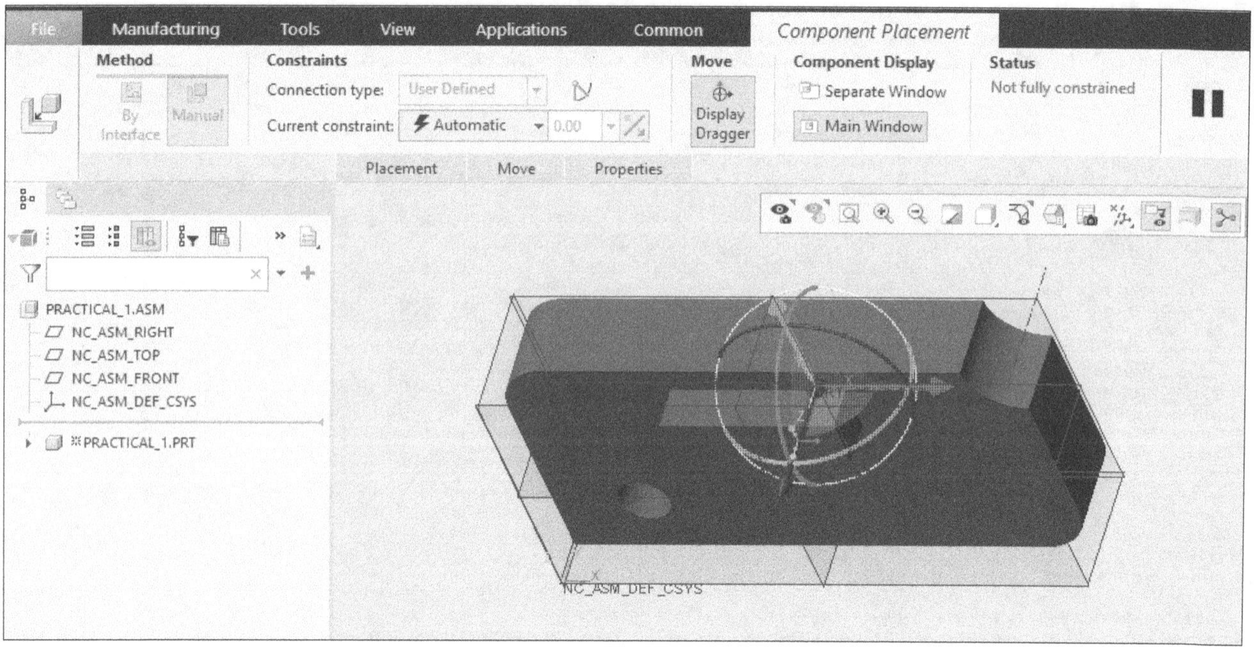

Figure-73. Component Placement contextual tab

- Click on the **Constraint** drop-down from the **Component Placement** contextual tab and select **Default** button. The **STATUS** will be changed to **Fully constrained**.
- Click on the **OK** button from **Component Placement** contextual tab. The **NC Assembly** application window will be displayed along with the reference model; refer to Figure-74.

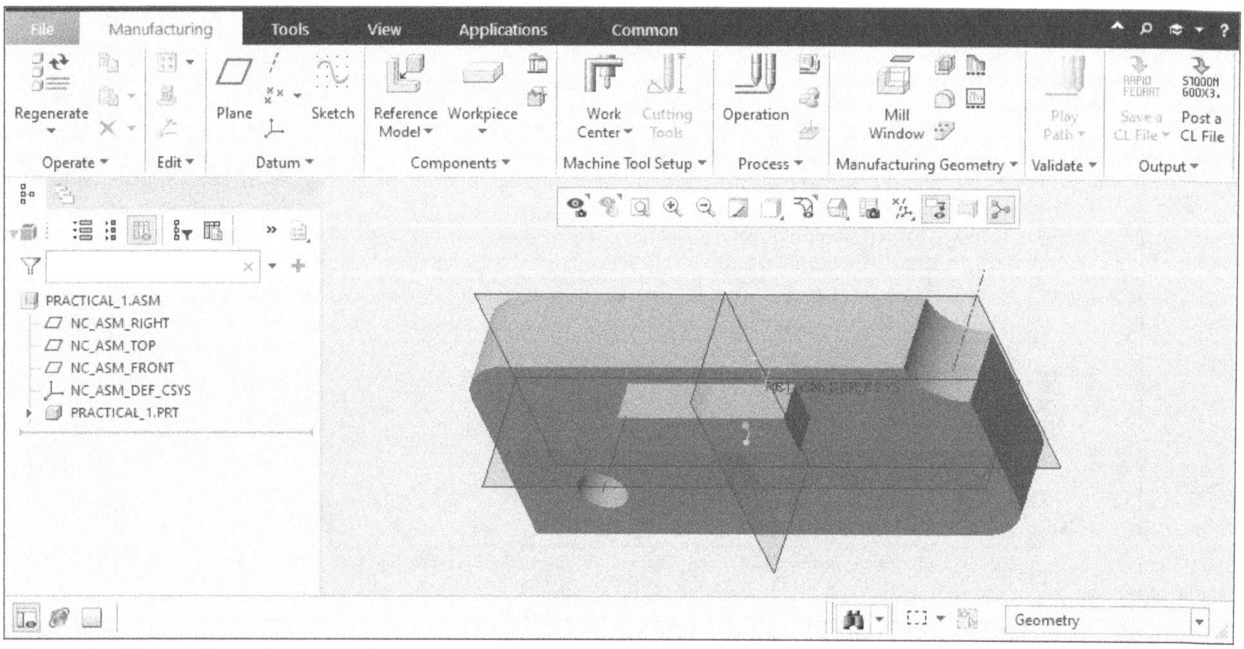

Figure-74. Practical 1 reference model

Creating Workpiece

- Click on the **Automatic Workpiece** button of **Workpiece** drop-down from **Manufacturing** tab. The **Auto Workpiece Creation** contextual tab will be displayed; refer to Figure-75.

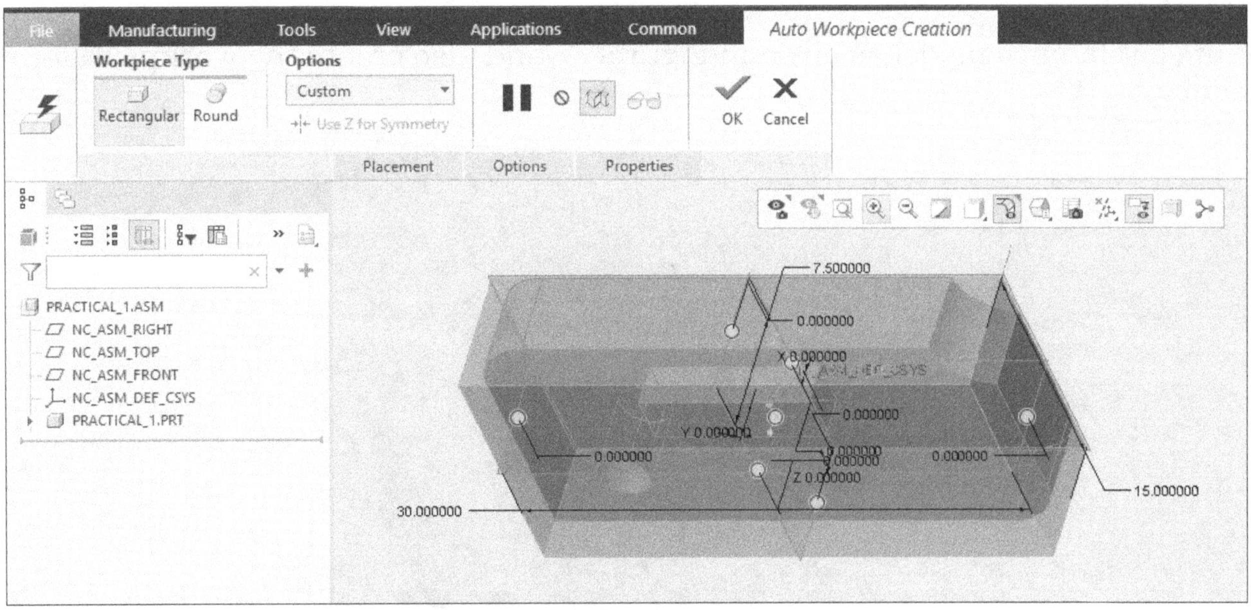

Figure-75. Auto Workpiece Creation contextual tab for Practical 1

- Click on the **OK** button from **Auto Workpiece Creation** contextual tab. The **NC Assembly** workpiece will be added to reference model; refer to Figure-76.

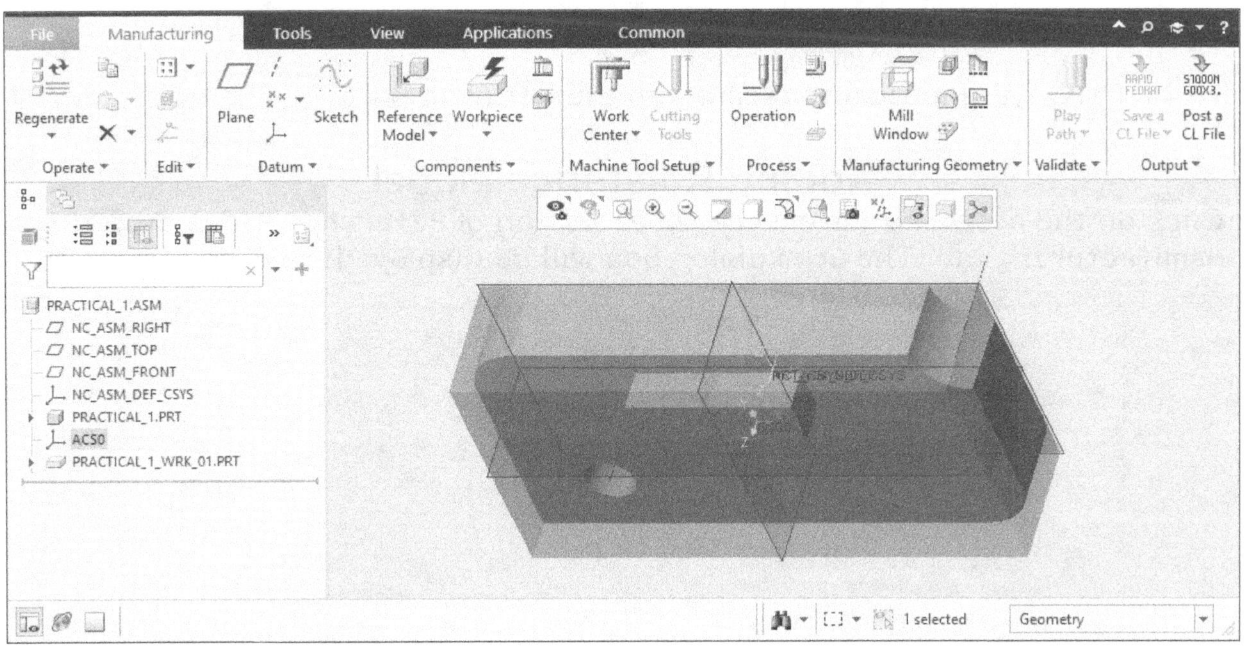

Figure-76. Model along with workpiece

PRACTICAL 2

Create a reference model as given in Figure-77 and also create the workpiece for the model.

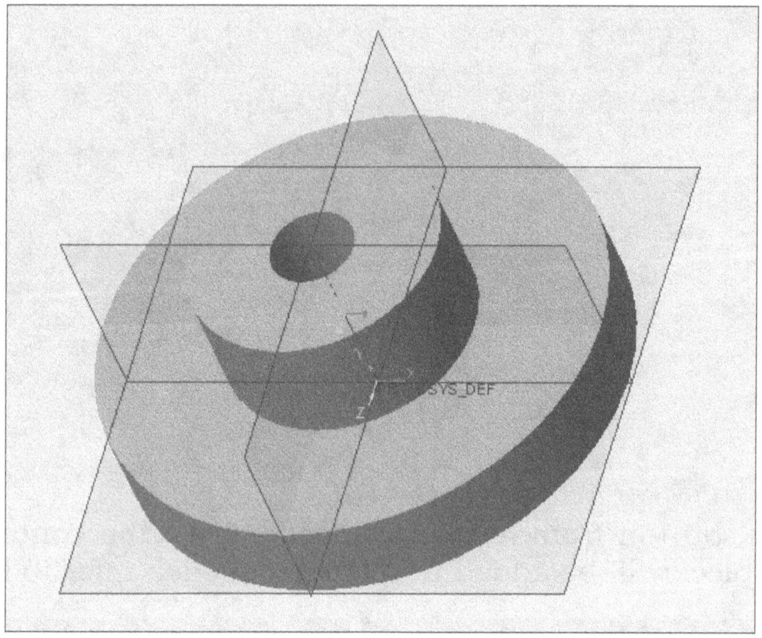

Figure-77. Practical 2

Start the Creo Parametric and create a manufacturing part.

Adding Reference Model

- Click on the **Assemble Reference Model** button of **Reference Model** drop-down of **Manufacturing** tab. The **Open** dialog box will be displayed; refer to Figure-78.

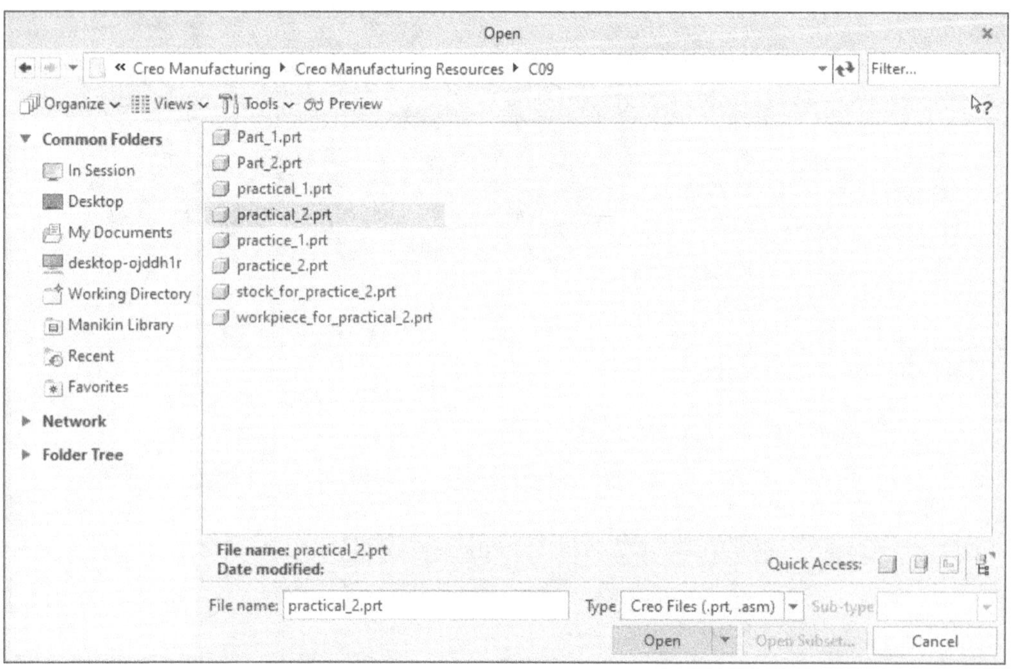

Figure-78. Open dialog box for Practical 2

- Select the **Practical 2** file and click on **Open** button from **Open** dialog box. The **Component Placement** contextual tab will be displayed along with the reference model; refer to Figure-79.

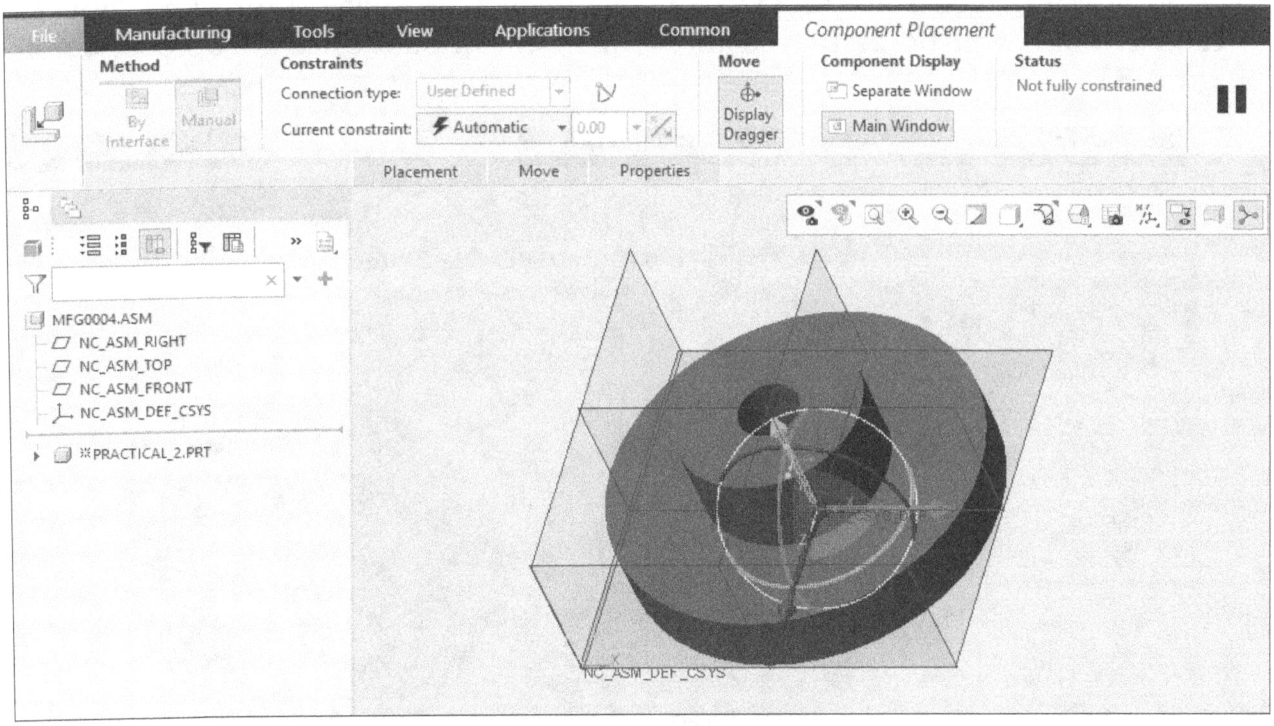

Figure-79. Component Placement contextual tab along with Practical 2 model

- Click on the **Constraint** drop-down of **Component Placement** contextual tab and select **Default** option. The **STATUS** will be changed to **Fully constrained**.
- Click on the **OK** button from **Component Placement** contextual tab. The **NC Assembly** application window will be displayed along with the reference model; refer to Figure-80.

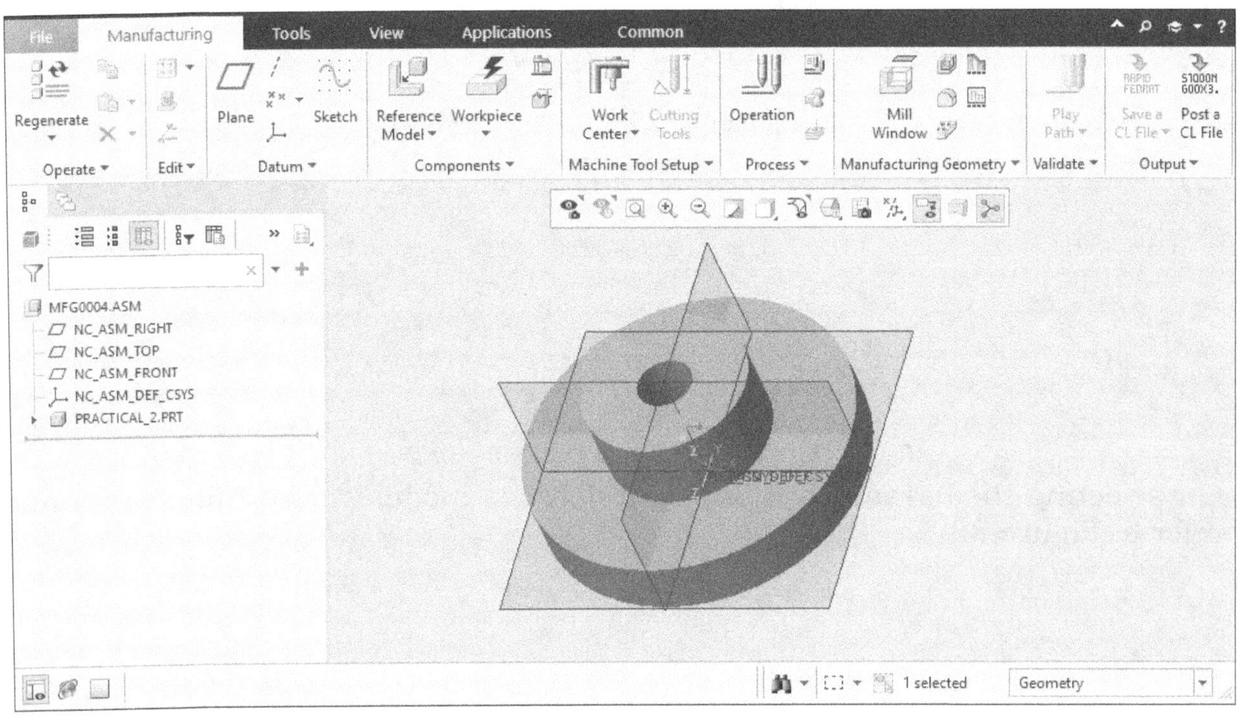

Figure-80. NC Assembly application window after adding model

Adding Workpiece

- Click on **Assemble Workpiece** button from **Workpiece** drop-down of **Manufacturing** tab. The **Open** dialog box will be displayed.
- Select the **Workpiece for Practical 2** file and click on **Open** button. The **Component Placement** tab will be displayed along with the model and workpiece; refer to Figure-81.

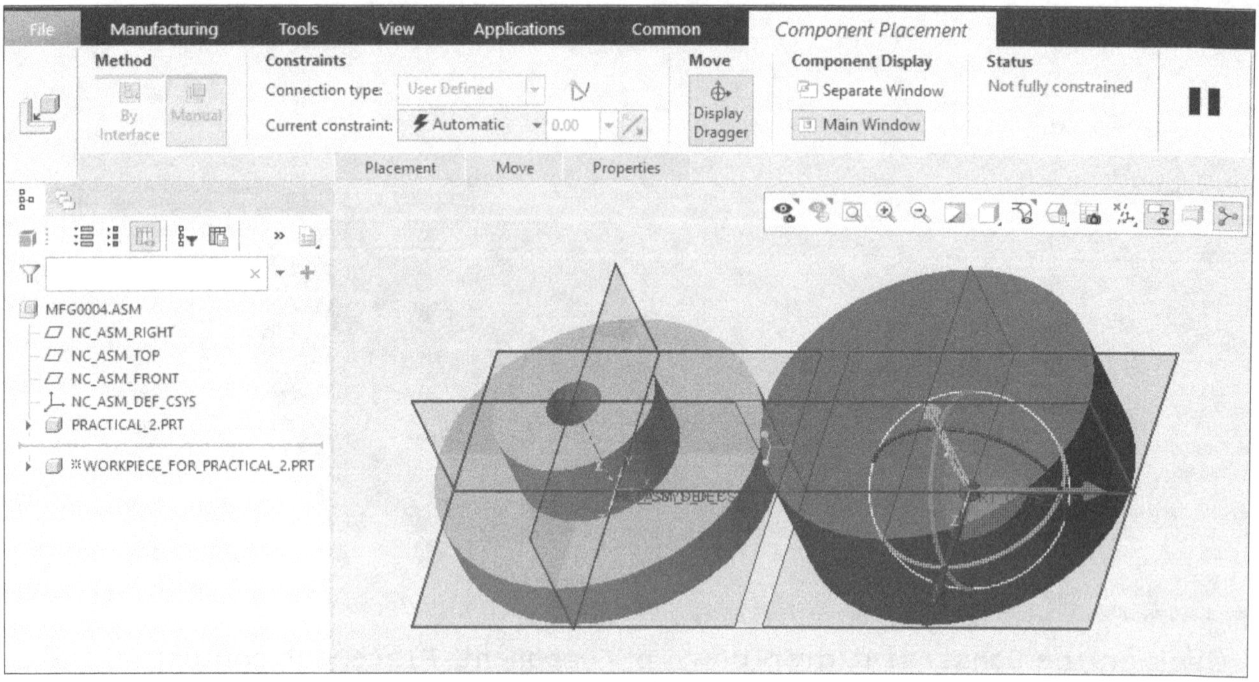

Figure-81. Component Placement contextual tab along with model and workpiece

- Select **Default** option from **Constraint** drop-down of **Component Placement** contextual tab; refer to Figure-82.

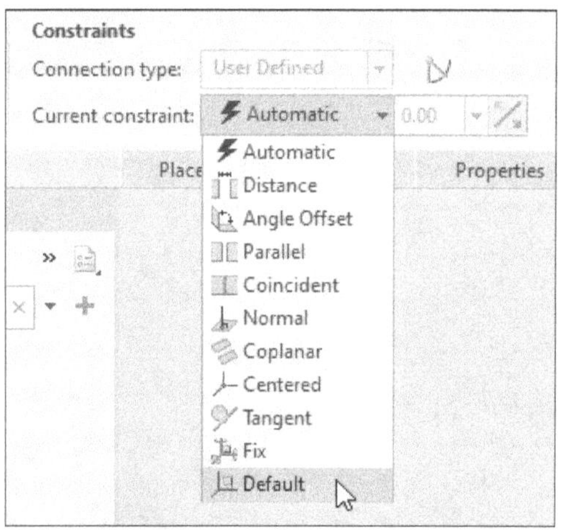

Figure-82. Default option from Constraint drop down

- On selecting the **Default** button, the reference model will be fully constrained; refer to Figure-83.

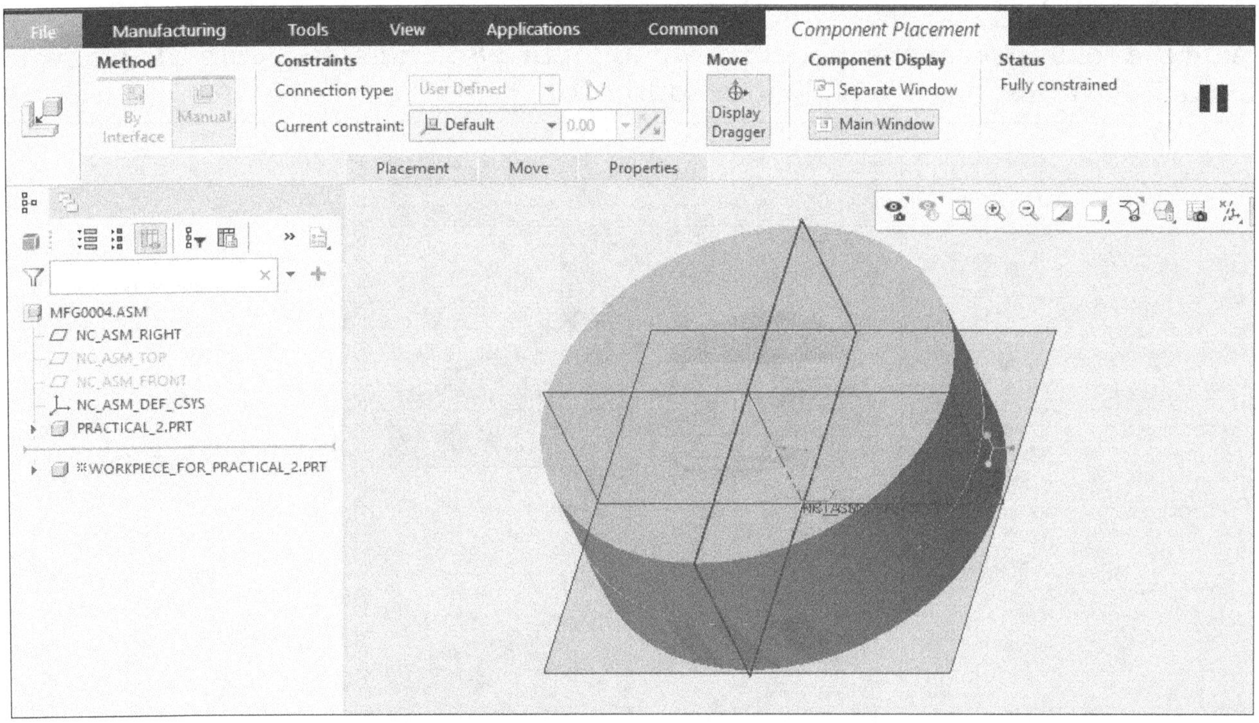

Figure-83. Fully constrained model

- Click on the **OK** button from **Component Placement** contextual tab. The **NC Assembly** application window will be displayed along with the model; refer to Figure-84.

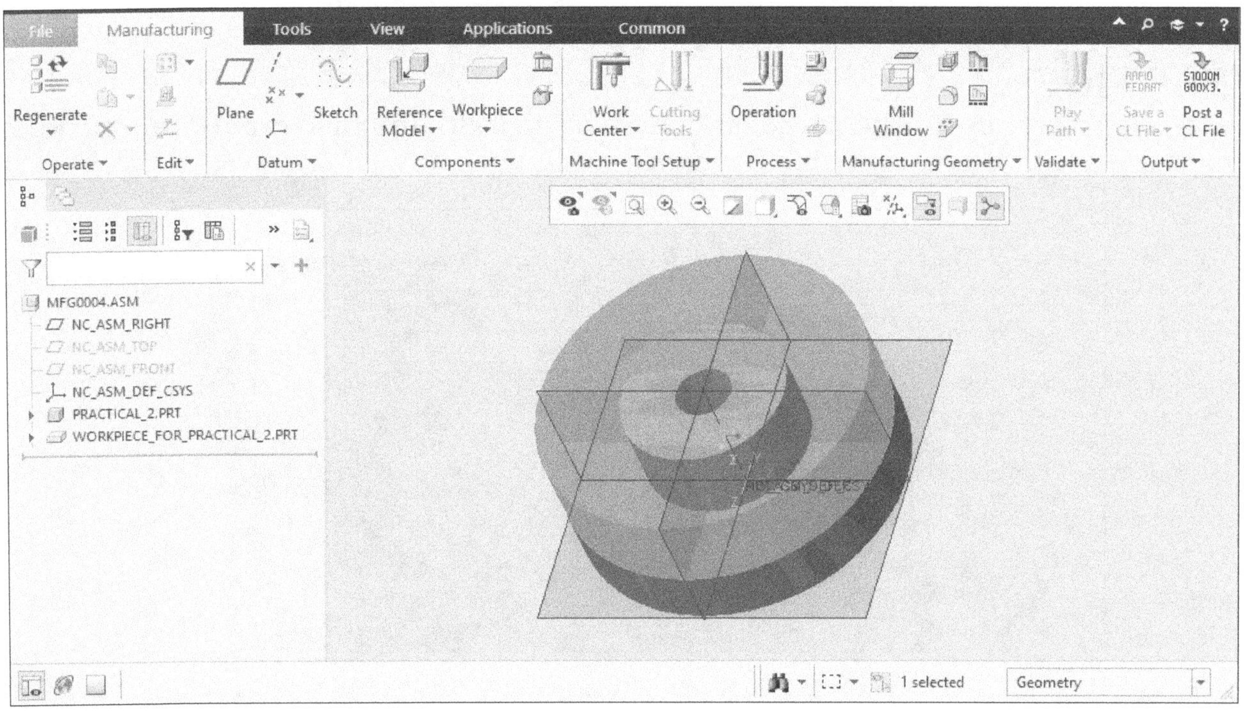

Figure-84. NC Assembly application window for Practical 2

Practice 1

Create the reference for the model shown in Figure-85 and also create the workpiece of model. Part files are available in resource kit.

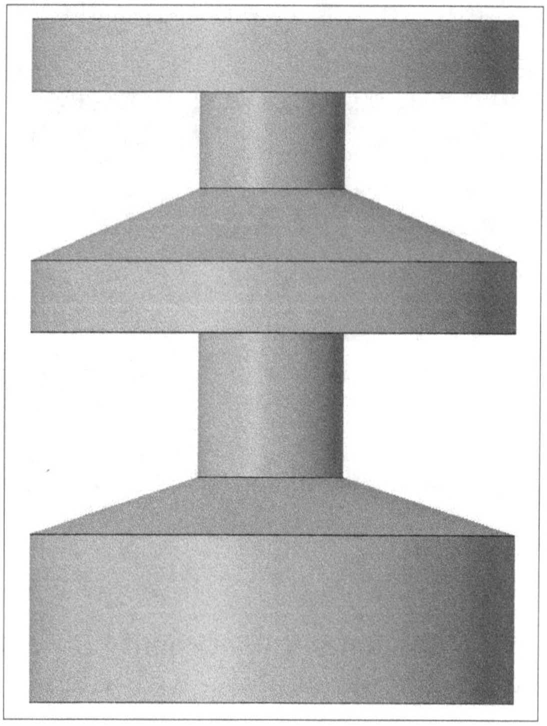

Figure-85. Practice 1

Practice 2

Create the reference for the model shown in Figure-86 and also create the workpiece of model. Part files are available in resource kit.

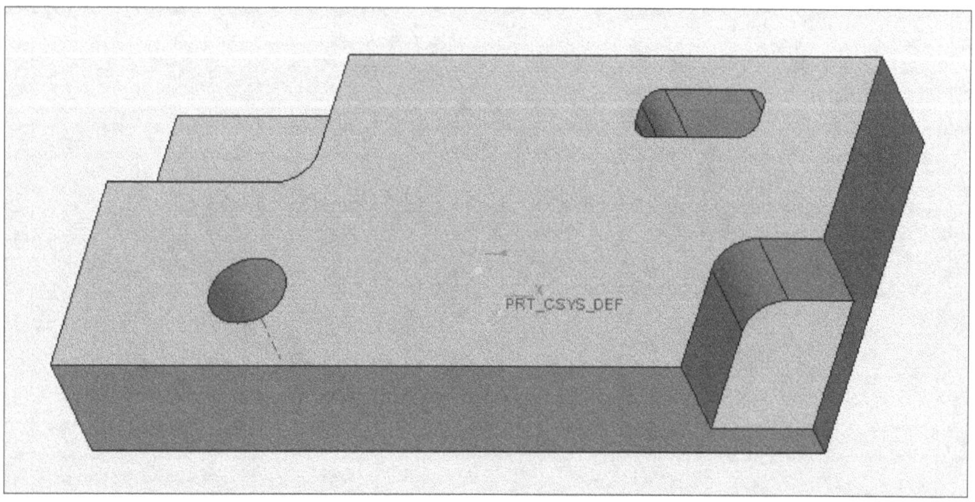

Figure-86. Practice 2

SELF-ASSESSMENT

Q1. What happens when you click on the NC button from the Applications tab?

A. It opens the Component Placement tab
B. It launches the Creo Drawing environment
C. It opens the NC Assembly application window
D. It opens the Part Modeling environment

Q2. Which button is used to insert a reference model in the NC Assembly?

A. Place Component
B. Assemble Reference Model
C. Create Workpiece
D. Insert Model

Q3. What is the status of a part when all its motions are constrained?

A. Not fully constrained
B. No constraints
C. Constraints Invalid
D. Fully constrained

Q4. What is the function of the 'Fix' option in the Constraint drop-down?

A. Rotate the model
B. Automatically position the model
C. Fix the component's current location
D. Constrain the component tangent to reference

Q5. Which tab in Component Placement allows enabling and displaying component placement?

A. Move tab
B. Placement tab
C. Constraint tab
D. Properties tab

Q6. What is the purpose of the Move tab in the NC Assembly?

A. Display file properties
B. Define reference models
C. Pause component placement operations to reposition parts
D. Finalize constraints

Q7. Which motion type option is used to rotate the component during move operations?

A. Orient Mode
B. Rotate
C. Adjust
D. Translate

Q8. What does the 'Relative in view plane' option in Move tab allow?

A. Move the component in the z-direction
B. Move relative to a selected model
C. Move component relative to the viewing plane
D. Move along x-axis only

Q9. What is the use of the 'Properties' tab?

A. Define constraints
B. Display and edit model information
C. Change assembly color
D. Add custom macros

Q10. What does the Inherit Reference Model tool do?

A. Combines models with no constraints
B. Adds inherit features from a selected part
C. Shows the component tree
D. Displays model in main window

Q11. What type of shape can be selected using Automatic Workpiece tool?

A. Polygonal and round
B. Cubic and square
C. Rectangular and round
D. Spherical and circular

Q12. What does the Envelope button do in the Options area of Automatic Workpiece?

A. Sets stock offset to user-defined value
B. Sets the coordinate system
C. Resets offsets to minimum values
D. Converts to billet shape

Q13. Which units can be set in the Options tab of Automatic Workpiece?

A. Feet and meters
B. Millimeters and inches
C. Centimeters and feet
D. Inches and yards

Q14. What does the Assemble Workpiece button do?

A. Combines all components
B. Deletes all workpieces
C. Assembles an existing design model as a workpiece
D. Generates machining code

Q15. What is required after selecting a part file for merging in Merge Workpiece tool?

A. Running the default assembly
B. Creating a drawing
C. Constraining the part
D. Exporting a STEP file

Q16. Which tool is used for manual creation of a workpiece?

A. Merge Workpiece
B. Inherit Workpiece
C. Create Workpiece
D. Automatic Workpiece

Q17. What allows specifying the model's name and common name for display in Model Tree?

A. Display Tab
B. Reference Model Tab
C. Properties Tab
D. Assembly Tab

Q18. What happens when the Default option is selected from the Constraint drop-down?

A. Sets constraints based on selected geometry
B. Fixes the part's position
C. Aligns component with default coordinate system
D. Offsets the part at a specific distance

Q19. What is the first step to manually create a workpiece in Creo NC Assembly?

A. Select the face to be extruded
B. Open Component Placement tab
C. Click on the Create Workpiece tool
D. Set the coordinate system

Q20. Which Menu Manager appears after selecting the workpiece shape in the Create Workpiece process?

A. COMPONENT Menu Manager
B. SOLID OPTS Menu Manager
C. REORDER Menu Manager
D. BOOLEAN Operations Menu

Q21. Which feature is used to classify a model as a workpiece or reference in Creo?

A. Group tool
B. Classify tool
C. Assembly tool
D. Move tab

Q22. In the Component Operations tool, which function allows duplication of a component along a defined axis?

A. Insert Mode
B. Boolean Operation
C. Copy
D. Reorder

Q23. What does the Insert Mode tool allow the user to do?

A. Copy and paste multiple parts
B. Insert a component before the current component
C. Merge two models
D. Delete unused models

Q24. How is a group of features created in NC Assembly?

A. By using the Classify tool
B. By using the Merge option in Boolean
C. By selecting Local Group in Group tool
D. By enabling the Move tab

Q25. What is the purpose of the Boolean Operator tool?

A. Constraint setting
B. Applying material
C. Combining geometries like merge, cut, add
D. Animating model motion

Q26. Which option in Boolean Operator is used to remove material from a model?

A. Add Bodies
B. Merge
C. Cut
D. Intersect

Q27. What does the "Associative placement" checkbox do in Boolean operations?

A. Removes all dependencies
B. Locks the model in place
C. Updates resulting cuts based on component position
D. Adds multiple references

Q28. What is the function of the Manufacturing Assembly tool?

A. To sketch a model
B. To animate model movement
C. To assemble and classify models
D. To cut and merge components

Q29. Which tool lets you assemble and simultaneously classify model components?

A. Assemble
B. Classify
C. Assemble and Classify
D. Reference Model Wizard

Q30. What must be selected from Constraint drop-down while using Assemble and Classify tool?

A. Fully Constrained
B. Merge
C. Default
D. Coplanar

Q31. Which tool is used when you want to assemble a workpiece using inherited features?

A. Workpiece Wizard
B. Component Operations
C. Reference Model Wizard
D. Insert Mode

Q32. What must be selected in Workpiece Wizard to assemble workpiece with merge features?

A. Inherited radio button
B. Same model radio button
C. Merge by reference radio button
D. Workpiece copy option

Q33. What must be done after selecting a file in Reference Model Wizard?

A. Define group name
B. Use Group tool
C. Set constraints
D. Open the FEAT CLASS Menu

Q34. What dialog box appears after clicking OK in the Reference Model Wizard?

A. Create Stock-workpiece
B. FEAT CLASS
C. Boolean Operations
D. Create Reference model

Chapter 10

Machine Setup

Topics Covered

The major topics covered in this chapter are:

- ***Mill.***
- ***Mill -Turn.***
- ***Lathe.***
- ***Wire EDM.***
- ***Process Manager.***
- ***Mill Window.***
- ***Turn Profile.***
- ***Stock Boundary.***
- ***Practice and Practical.***

CREATING MACHINE TOOL

By creating machine tool in software, we define the real machine to be used for manufacturing part. In this chapter, we will learn about the basics of creating machine tool and procedure to create cutting tools of Mill, Lathe, Mill-Turn, and Wire EDM machine.

WORK CENTER

The **Work Center** tool is used to create different type of machines like Milling machine, Lathe machine, Mill-Turn machine, and Wire EDM machine. The procedure to create these machines is discussed next.

Mill

The milling machine is used to remove material from workpiece by using rotary motion of the tool. The procedure to create a milling machine setup is discussed next.

- Click on the **Mill** tool from **Work Center** drop-down in the **Ribbon**; refer to Figure-1. The **Milling Work Center** dialog box will be displayed; refer to Figure-2.

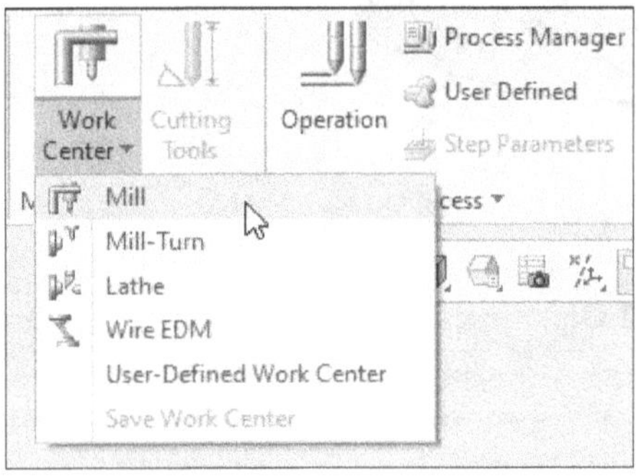

Figure-1. Mill tool

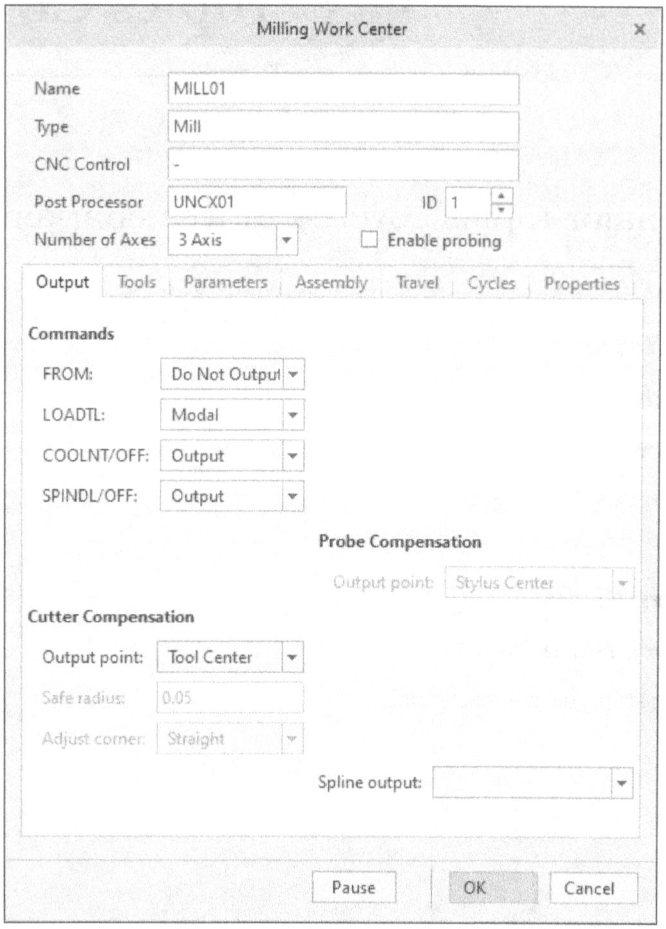

Figure-2. Milling Work Center dialog box

- Click in the **Name** edit box and specify the name for milling machine.
- Click in the **CNC Control** edit box and enter the controller name.
- Click in the **Post Processor** edit box and specify the default name of post processor.
- Click in the **ID** edit box and set a post-processor ID from the list. The **ID** may be from 1 to 99.

- Click on the **Number of Axes** drop-down and select **3-Axis**, **4-Axis** or **5-Axis** for machine.
- Select the **Enable probing** check box, if you want to allow CMM step definition within an NC session. To use this option, you must have the CMM license.

The other options of **Milling Work Center** dialog box have been discussed earlier in **Tool Setting** chapter.

Mill-Turn

The procedure to create a **Mill-Turn** machine is discussed next.

- Click on the **Mill-Turn** tool from **Work Center** drop-down in the **Ribbon**; refer to Figure-3. The **Mill-Turn Work Center** dialog box will be displayed; refer to Figure-4.

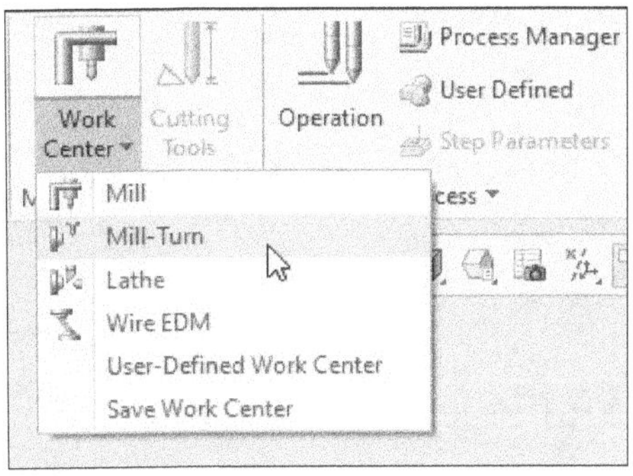

Figure-3. Mill-Turn tool

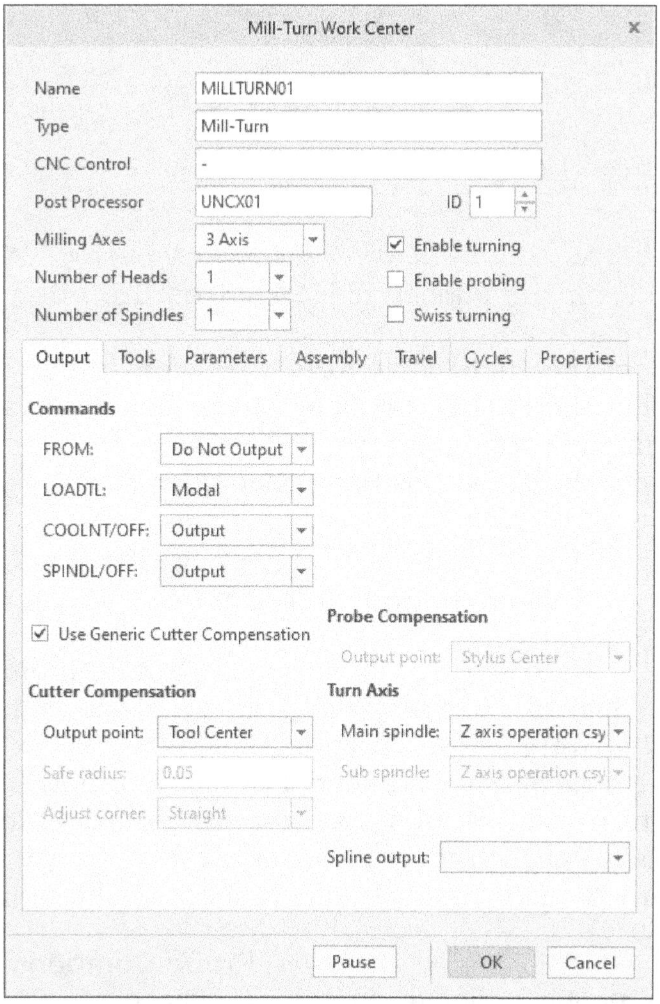

Figure-4. Mill-Turn Work Center dialog box

- Click on the **Number of Heads** drop-down and specify the number of head that enables you to set up the cutting tools associated with a machine tool head like if we select **2** from **Number of Heads** drop-down then in **Tools** tab, there will be two **Head** sections; refer to Figure-5.

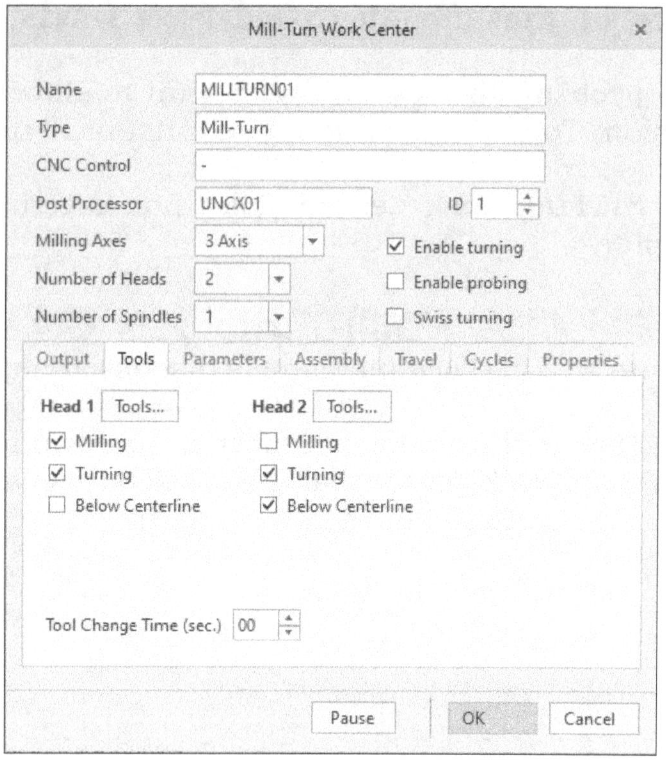

Figure-5. Head section of Tools tab

- Click on the **Number of Spindles** drop-down and select the number of spindle for machine.
- Select the **Enable turning** check box if you want to enable turning for machine.
- Select the **Enable probing** check box if you want to add a probe or default probe from the probe library.
- Select the **Swiss turning** check box if you want to enable the swiss style turning.

Output tab

There are various options in **Output** tab which are discussed next.

Sub-spindle

- The **Sub-spindle** area is displayed in the dialog box on selecting 2 from the **Number of Spindles** drop-down.
- Select **Main Spindle Program Zero** option from **Program zero** drop-down, if you want to output all steps using the main spindle program zero.
- Select **Per Spindle Program Zero** option from **Program zero** drop-down, if you want to output steps with respect to the spindle used to create the steps.

Probe Compensation

- The **Probe Compensation** area is active in the dialog box only if you have selected the **Enable probing** check box.
- Select **Stylus Center** option from **Output point** drop-down, if you want to select stylus center as the output point.
- Select **Contact Point** option from **Output point** drop-down, if you want to select contact point of machine as the output point.
- Select **Use Generic Cutter Compensation** check box to use common values for mill and turn.

Tools tab

There are various tool in this tab which are discussed next.

Head 1

- Select the **Milling** check box if you want to make available milling on a particular head. This is the default selection for **Head 1**.
- Select the **Turning** check box if you want to make available turning on a particular head. This check box is selected by default for all head.
- Select the **Below Centerline** check box, if you want to enable turning below the spindle centerline.
- Click in the **Tool Change Time (sec.)** edit box and specify the value of time needed for changing a tool, in seconds. This option is optional.
- Click on the **Tools** button of **Tools** tab from **Mill-Turn Work Center** dialog box; refer to Figure-6. The **Tools Setup (Head 1)** dialog box will be displayed; refer to Figure-7.

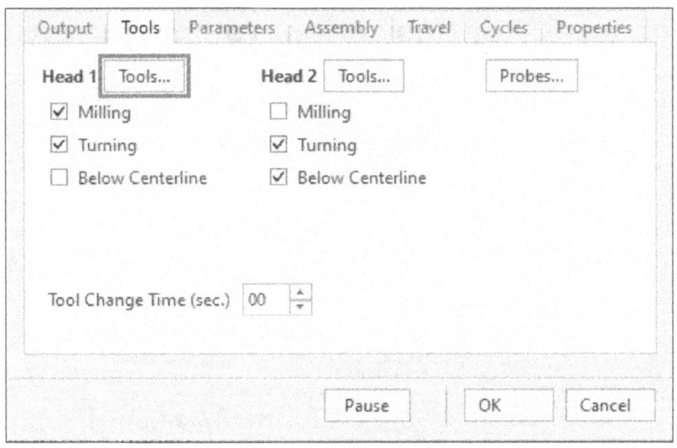

Figure-6. Tools tab

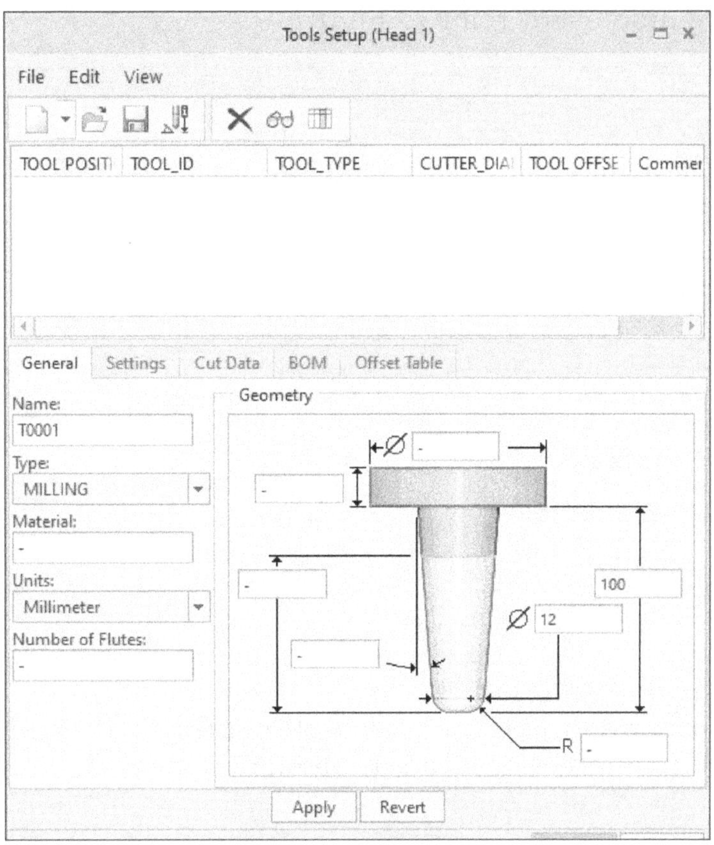

Figure-7. Tools Setup (Head 1) dialog box

The procedure to create a tool was discussed earlier in this book.

- After creating the tool for Head 1, click on **Apply** button. The tool will be created and displayed in the tool list. Note that the tools added in the list will be assumed as installed on the machine as per their tool position in this list.
- Click on **OK** button from **Tool Setup(Head 1)** dialog box.
- The procedure to add or create **Probe** has been discussed earlier in this book.

Parameters tab

- Click in the **Maximum Speed (RPM)** edit box of **Sub Spindle** section and enter the value of maximum rotating speed of spindle.
- Click in the **Horsepower** edit box of **Sub Spindle** section and enter the value of horsepower for spindle.
- Click in the **Machine Frequency** edit box of **Sub Spindle** section and enter the value of frequency for machine.
- Click on the **DMIS** button of **Parameters** tab. The **DMIS TEXT Menu Manager** will be displayed; refer to Figure-8. For this option, you must have CMM Probing enabled.

Figure-8. DMIS TEXT Menu Manager

- Click on the **Create** button of **DMIS TEXT Menu Manager**. The **Activate DMIS Text** dialog box will be displayed; refer to Figure-9.

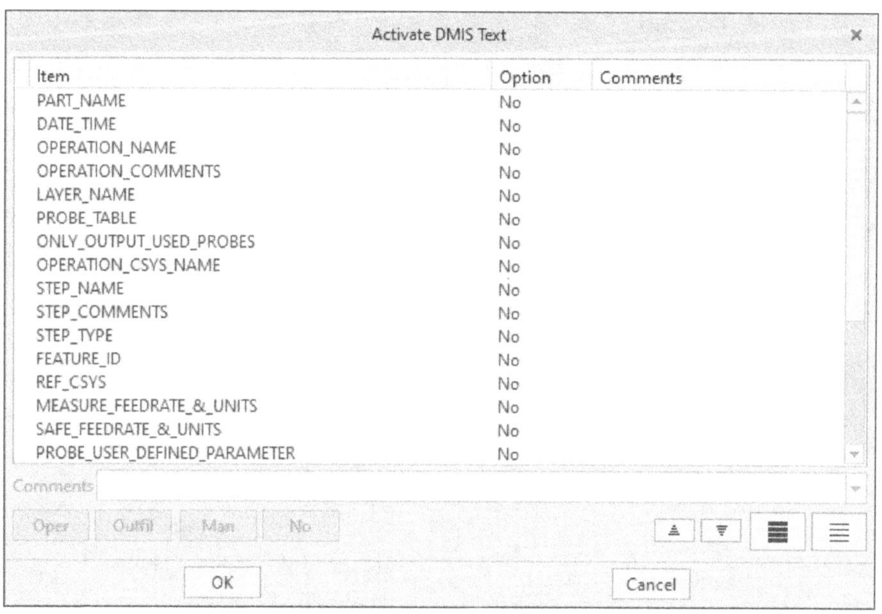

Figure-9. Activate DMIS Text dialog box

- Select the specific command from **Item** section and enter the text in **Comments** edit box. The comment will be displayed in **Comments** section.

- Click on the **Oper** button from **Activate DMIS text** dialog box, if you want to display DMIS Text to CMM screen.
- Click on **Outfil** button from **Activate DMIS text** dialog box, if you want to include DMIS TEXT statement in CMM Output.
- Click on the **Man** button from **Activate DMIS text** dialog box, if you want to display DMIS TEXT statement to CMM operator.
- Click on the **No** button from **Activate DMIS text** dialog box, if you do not want to output or display DMIS TEXT statement.
- After specifying the parameters, click on **OK** button. The **DMIS TEXT Menu Manager** will be displayed again. Click on the **Done/Return** button from **Menu Manager**. The **Mill-Turn Work Center** dialog box will be displayed.

The other options of this dialog box have been discussed earlier in this book. Click on **OK** button. The milling machine will be added in **Model Tree**.

Lathe

- Click on the **Lathe** tool of **Work Center** drop-down from **Ribbon**; refer to Figure-10. The **Lathe Work Center** dialog box will be displayed; refer to Figure-11.

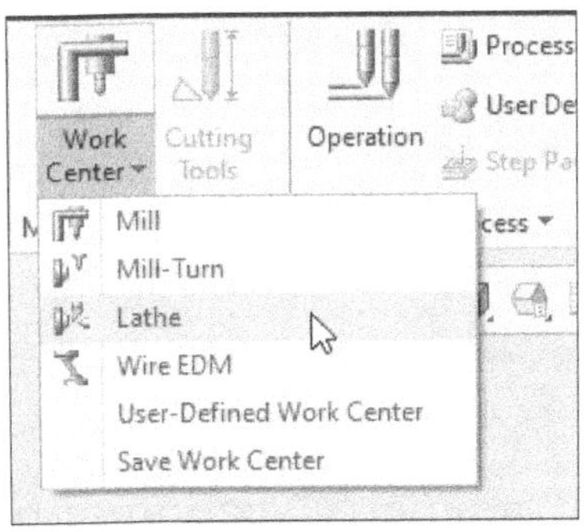

Figure-10. Lathe tool

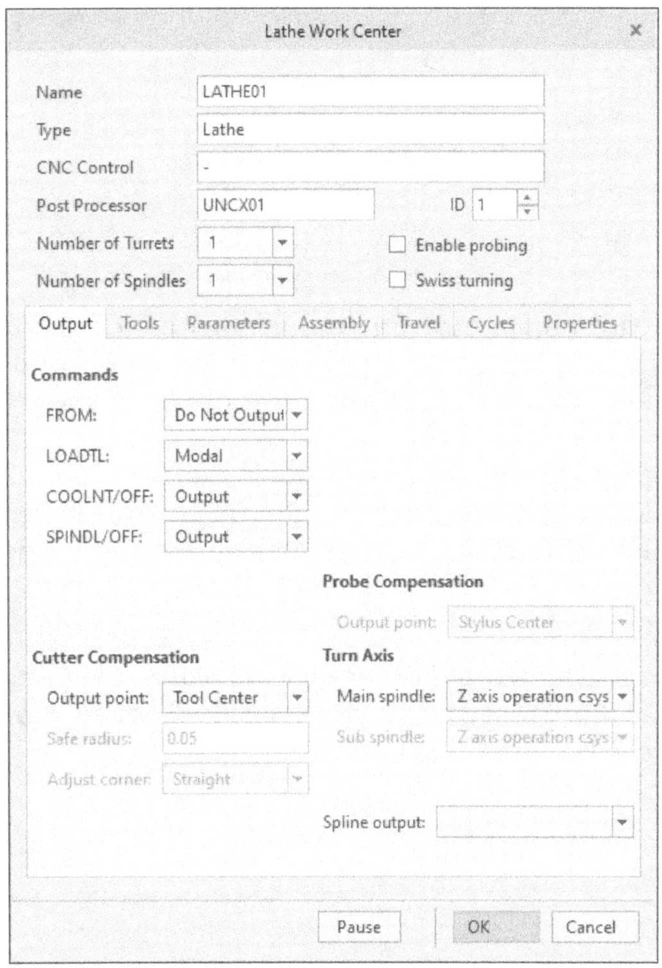

Figure-11. Lathe Work Center dialog box

- Select the number of turret applicable for your machine from the **Number of Turrets** drop-down in the **Lathe Work Center** dialog box.
- Select the number of spindle applicable for your machine from the **Number of Spindles** drop-down in **Lathe Work Center** drop-down.

Tools tab

- Click on the **Turret 1** button of **Tools** tab from **Lathe Work Center** dialog box. The **Tools Setup** dialog box will be displayed; refer to Figure-12.

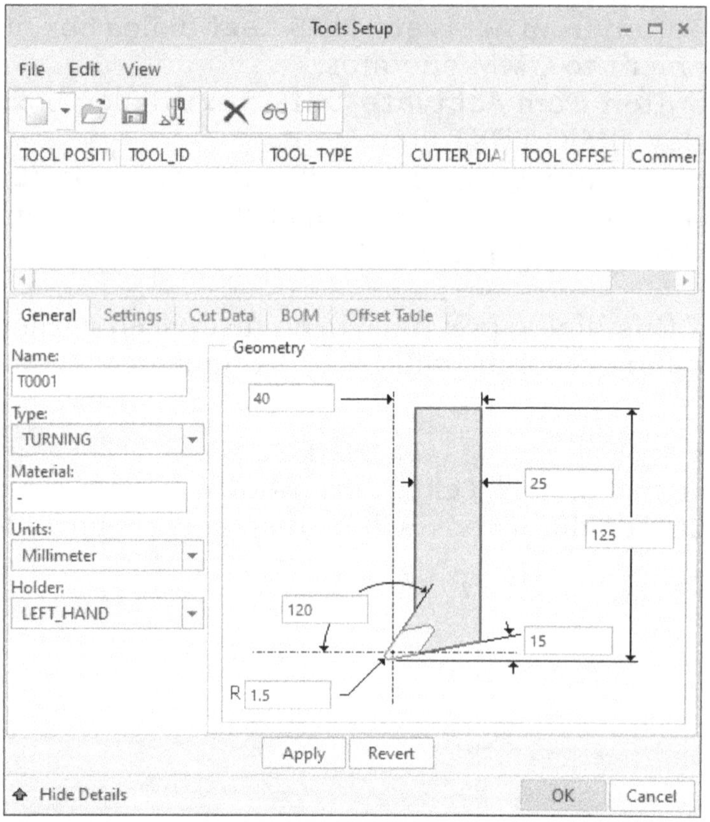

Figure-12. Tools Setup dialog box for turret

- Enter the parameter for tool in specific edit box of geometry section and click on **Apply** button. The tool will be added in **Record** section.
- After specifying the parameters, click on the **OK** button from **Tools Setup** dialog box.
- The other options of **Lathe Work Center** dialog box are same as discussed earlier in this book. Now, click on the **OK** button from **Lathe Work Center** dialog box to complete this process. The machine will be added in **Model Tree**.

Wire EDM

- Click on the **Wire EDM** tool from **Work Center** drop-down of **Manufacturing** tab; refer to Figure-13. The **WEDM Work Center** dialog box will be displayed; refer to Figure-14.

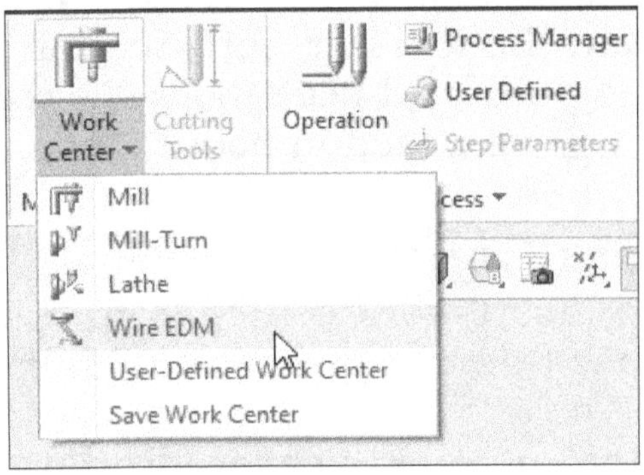

Figure-13. Wire EDM tool

Figure-14. WEDM Work Center dialog box

Tools tab

- Click on the **Tools** button of **Tools** tab from **WEDM Work Center** dialog box. The **Tools Setup** dialog box will be displayed; refer to Figure-15.

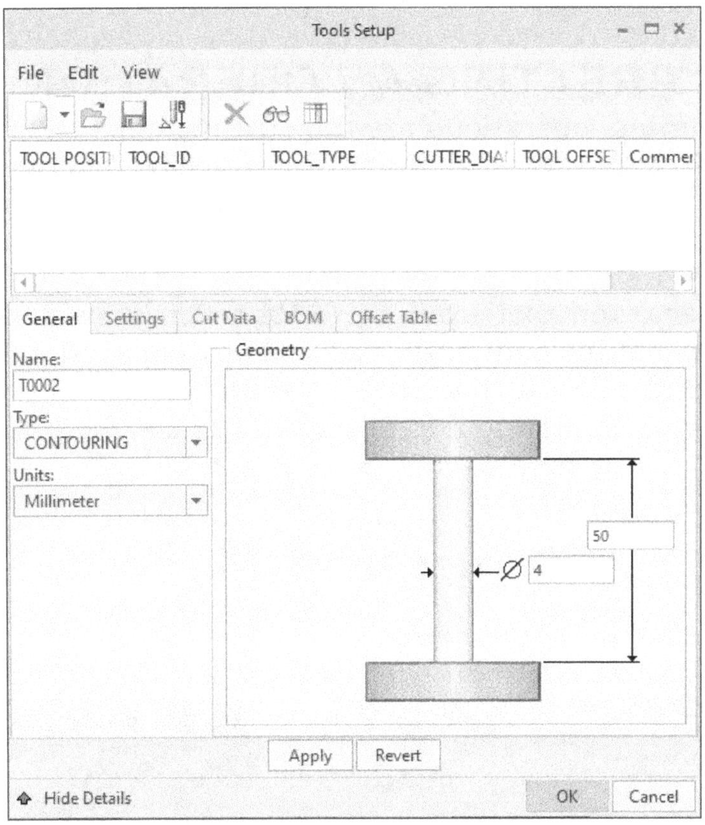

Figure-15. Tools Setup for Wire EDM

- Enter the parameter as required in the specific edit box of **Geometry** section of **General** tab and click on **Apply** button to add the tool in record section.
- Click on the **OK** button of **Tools Setup** dialog box and **WEDM Work Center** dialog box to complete the process. The machine will be added in **Model Tree**.

User-Defined Work Center

The **User-Defined Work Center** tool is used to insert work center from a library of user defined work centers. The procedure to use this tool is discussed next.

- Click on the **User-Defined Work Center** tool of **Work Center** drop-down from **Manufacturing** tab; refer to Figure-16. The **Open** dialog box will be displayed.

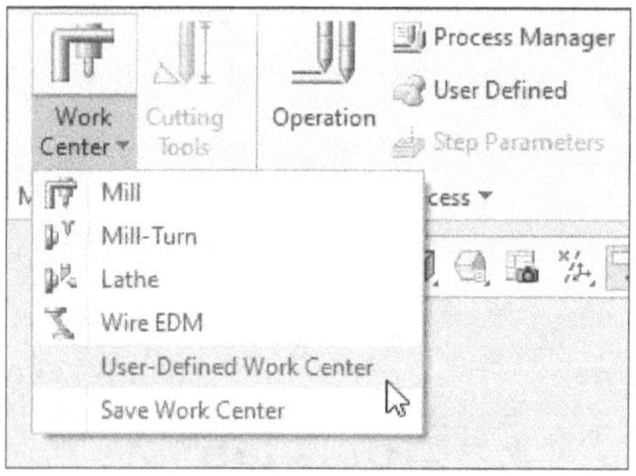

Figure-16. User-Defined Work Center tool

- Select the part file from **Open** dialog box and click on **Open** button. The work center will be added in application window.

CREATING AN OPERATION

In any kind of machining, operations are the cutting steps to get desired shape and size from the workpiece. It is possible that a single operation cuts only a small portion of the workpiece and it may also possible that a single operation can cut almost all the workpiece to get desired parameters in one go.

- Click on the **Operation** tool from the **Ribbon** of **Manufacturing** tab; refer to Figure-17. The **Operation** contextual tab will be displayed; refer to Figure-18 and you will be asked to select a coordinate system.

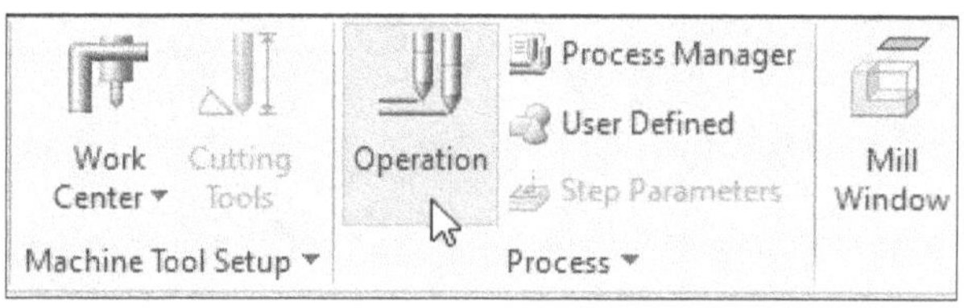

Figure-17. Operation tool

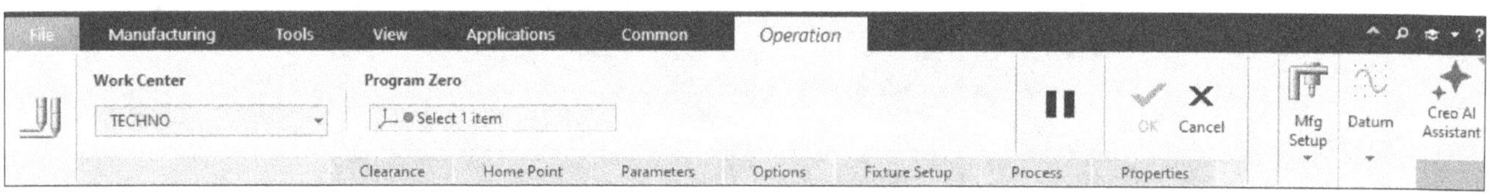

Figure-18. Operation contextual tab

- Select the coordinate system to specify orientation of machine and workpiece.

Operation tab

There are various options in **Operation** tab which are discussed next.

Clearance tab

- The options in the **Clearance** tab are used to specify the reference to which the tool will move during retract motion.
- Click on the **Clearance** tab from **Operation** tab; refer to Figure-19.

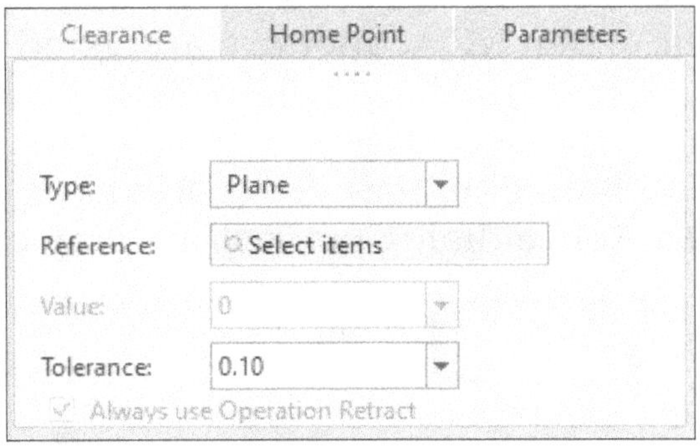

Figure-19. Clearance tab

- Select **Plane** from **Type** drop-down in **Clearance** tab if you want to define a plane for tool retract.
- Select **Cylinder** from **Type** drop-down in **Clearance** tab if you want to define a cylindrical surface for tool retract.
- Select **Sphere** from **Type** drop-down in **Clearance** tab if you want to define a spherical surface for tool retract.
- Select **Surface** from **Type** drop-down in **Clearance** tab if you want to use selected surface for tool retract.
- After selecting desired option from the **Type** drop-down, click in the **Reference** selection box and select desired geometry.
- Click in the **Value** edit box and specify the offset value or radius.
- Click in the **Tolerance** edit box and enter the value of tolerance.
- Clear the **Always use Operation Retract** check box, if you want to use the operation retract only when tool axis orientation changes.

Home Point tab

- Click on the **Home Point** tab from **Operation** contextual tab; refer to Figure-20.

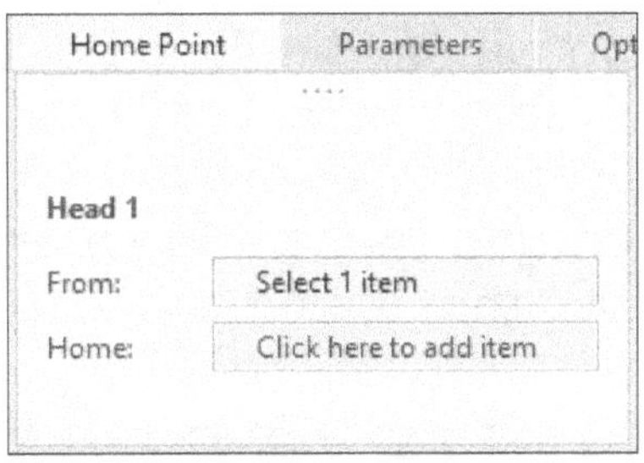

Figure-20. Home Point tab

- Click in the **From** selection box from **Home Point** tab and select the operation starting location.
- Click in **Home** button from **Home Point** tab and select operation end location.

The other options of **Operation** tab have been discussed earlier.

After specifying the parameters, click on the **OK** button from **Operation** contextual tab. The operation will be added in **Modal Tree**. Note that a new tab will be added in the **Ribbon** based on your machine. Like if you have set Milling machine for operations then **Mill** tab will be added.

Process Manager

The **Process Manager** functionality is based on the process table, which lists all the manufacturing process objects, such as workcells, operations, fixture setups, tooling, and NC sequences. When NC sequences are listed in the process table, they are called steps.

- Click on the **Process Manager** tool from **Ribbon**; refer to Figure-21. The **Manufacturing Process Table** dialog box will be displayed; refer to Figure-22.

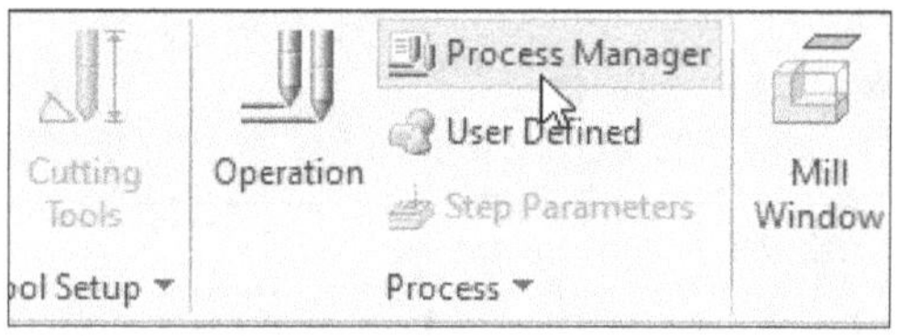

Figure-21. Process Manager tool

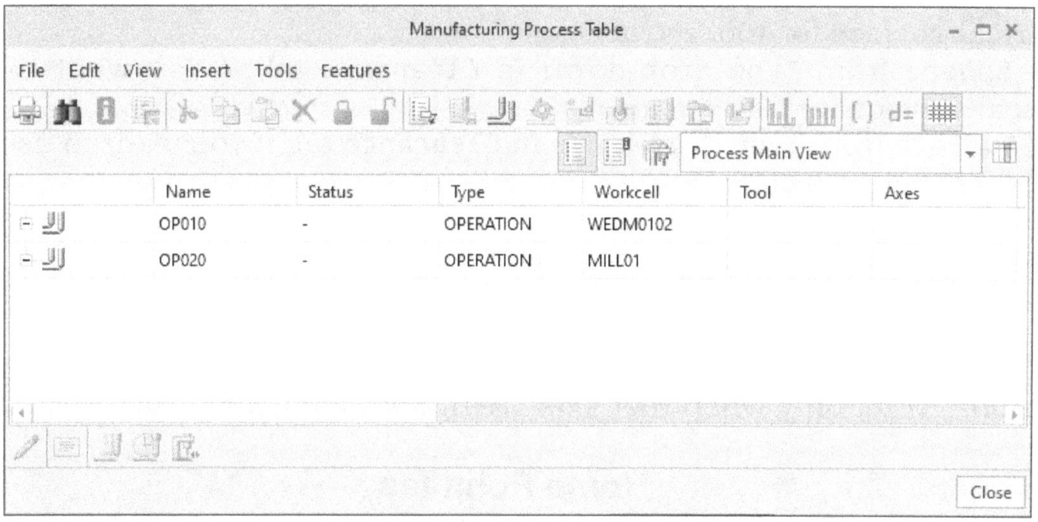

Figure-22. Manufacturing Process Table dialog box

- The list of machine operation will be displayed in the table.
- In **Manufacturing Process Table** dialog box, you can also rename the machine operations.
- To rename, click on the operation name and enter desired name.
- Click on **Close** button to close this dialog box.

PREPARING GEOMETRY FOR MANUFACTURING

There are various tools which help us to prepare geometry for manufacturing of part.

Mill Window

The **Mill Window** tool is used to specify the region in which the tool will move while cutting. The procedure to use this tool is discussed next.

- Click on the **Mill Window** tool from the **Ribbon** of **Manufacturing** tab; refer to Figure-23. The **Mill Window** contextual tab will be displayed; refer to Figure-24.

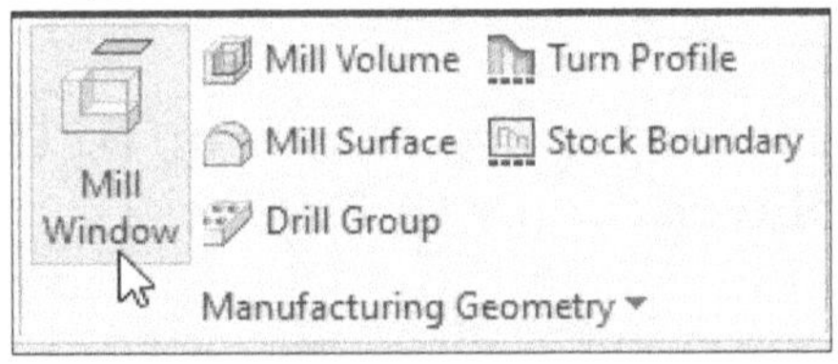

Figure-23. Mill Window tool

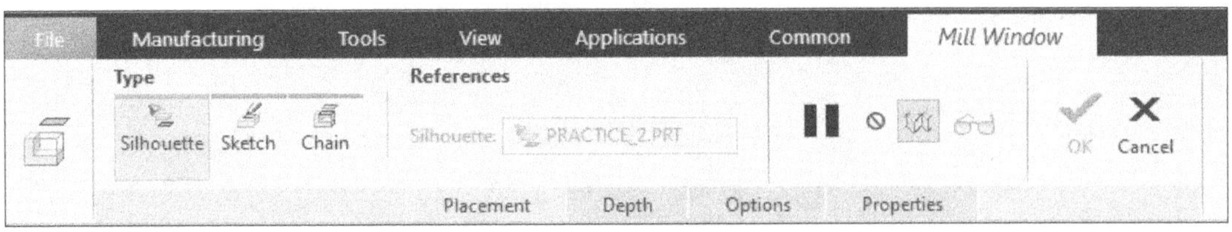

Figure-24. Mill Window contextual tab

- The **Silhouette** button allows you to create the window by projecting the silhouette of the reference part on the **Mill Window** start plane, in the direction parallel to the z-axis of the **Mill Window** coordinate system.
- The **Sketch** button allows you to define the **Mill Window** by sketching a closed contour.
- The **Chain** button allows you to define the **Mill Window** by selecting edges or curves that form a closed contour.
- The other options of this contextual tab are same as discussed earlier in this book.
- Click on the **OK** button from **Mill Window** contextual tab. The mill window will be added in **Model Tree**.

Mill Volume

The **Mill Volume** tool is used to define the volume of a part to be machined. The procedure to use this tool is discussed next.

- Click on the **Mill Volume** button from **Ribbon** of **Manufacturing** tab; refer to Figure-25. The **Mill Volume** contextual tab will be displayed; refer to Figure-26.

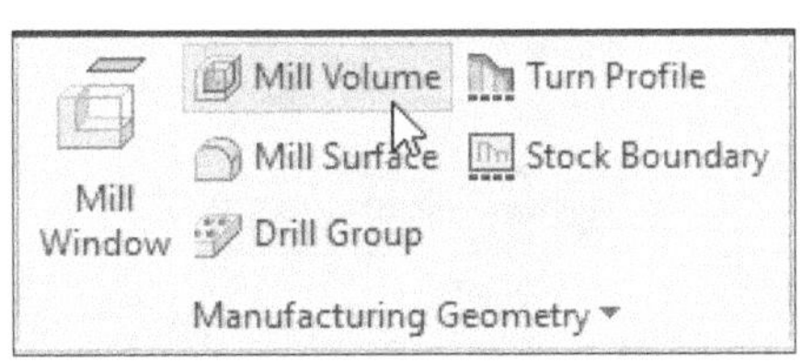

Figure-25. Mill Volume tool

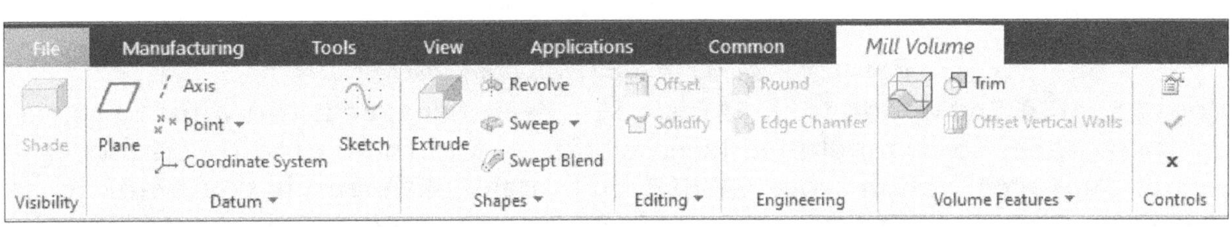

Figure-26. Mill Volume contextual tab

Gather Volume Tool

The **Gather Volume Tool** is used to create the volume for milling operations. The procedure to use this tool is discussed next.

- Click on the **Gather Volume Tool** button from **Mill Volume** tab. The **VOL GATHER Menu Manager** will be displayed; refer to Figure-27.

Figure-27. VOL GATHER Menu Manager

- Select the **Select** check box of **GATHER STEPS** section, if you want to select surfaces to be machined.
- Select the **Exclude** check box of **GATHER STEPS** section, if you want to ignore the outer loops or exclude some of the selected surfaces from the volume.
- Select the **Fill** check box of **GATHER STEPS** section, if you want to ignore the inner loops on the selected surfaces.
- Select the **Close** check box of **GATHER STEPS** section, if you want to specify ways of closing the volume, other than the default way described above.

Select desired check box and click on **Done** button from **Menu Manager**. The updated **Menu Manager** will be displayed; refer to Figure-28.

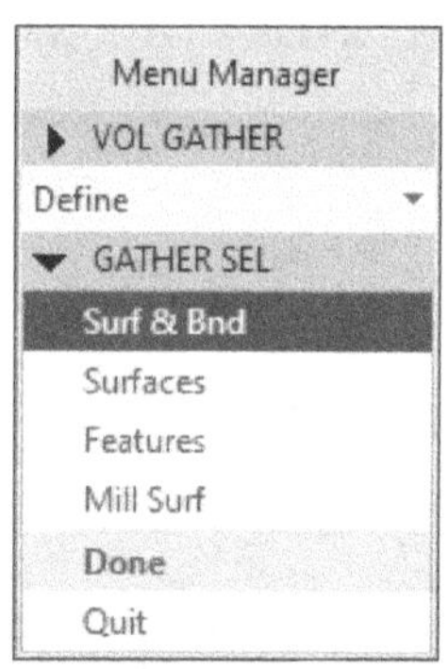

Figure-28. Updated VOL GATHER Menu Manager

- Select **Surf & Bnd** option from **GATHER SEL Menu Manager** if you want to select one of the surfaces to be machined (seed surface), and the bounding surfaces.
- Select **Surfaces** option from **GATHER SEL Menu Manager** if you want to select continuous surfaces to be machined. All the selected surfaces are included in the volume definition.
- Select **Features** option from **GATHER SEL Menu Manager** if you want to select features to be machined. All the surfaces of selected features are included in the volume definition.

- Select **Mill Surf** option from **GATHER SEL Menu Manager** if you want to select a pre-defined mill surface from a list.

In our case, we are selecting **Features** option. After selecting the option, click on **Done** button from **GATHER SEL Menu Manager**. The updated **Menu Manager** will be displayed along with **Select** dialog box; refer to Figure-29.

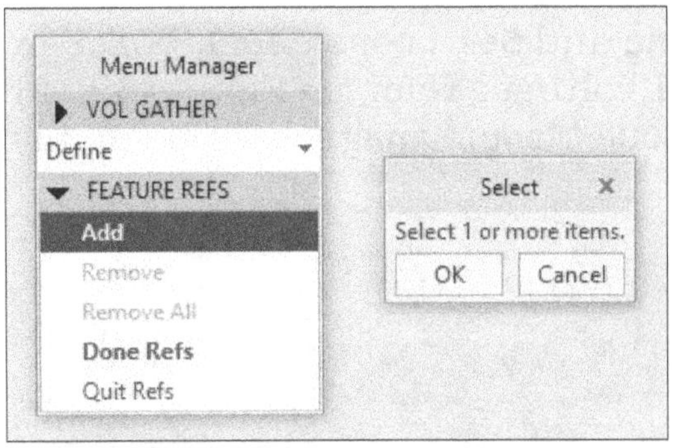

Figure-29. VOL GATHER Menu Manager with Select dialog box

- Select the inner volume of part; refer to Figure-30.

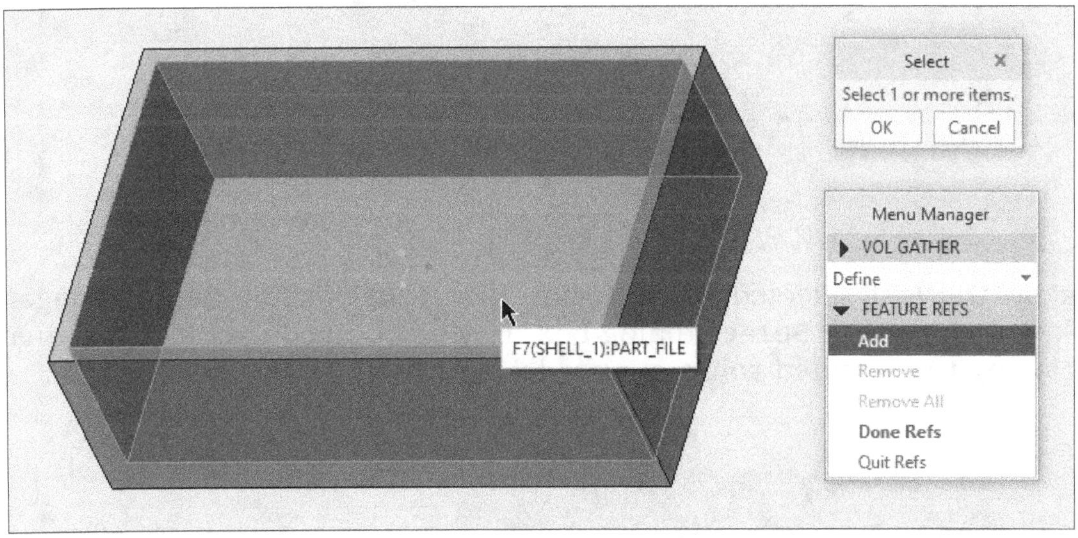

Figure-30. Selection of volume

- After selecting volume, click on the **Done Refs** button from **FEATURE REFS Menu Manager**. The **CLOSURE Menu Manager** will be displayed; refer to Figure-31.

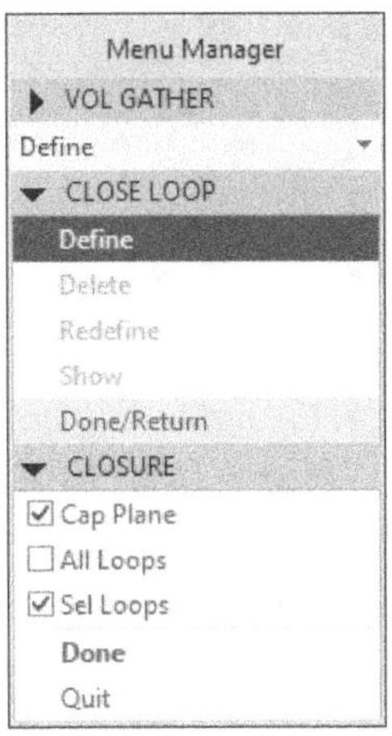

Figure-31. CLOSURE Menu Manager

- Select **Cap Plane** check box of **CLOSURE Menu Manager** if you want to define cap plane of closure.
- Select **All Loops** check box of **CLOSURE Menu Manager** if you want to select all holes in selected surface to close.
- Select the **Sel Loops** check box of **CLOSURE Menu Manager** if you want to use bounding loops to close the selected volume.

We have selected **Cap Plane** and **Sel Loops** check boxes in our case. Select the plane which closes the selected volume; refer to Figure-32. After selection, click on the **Done** button. The **CLOSE LOOP Menu Manager** will be displayed.

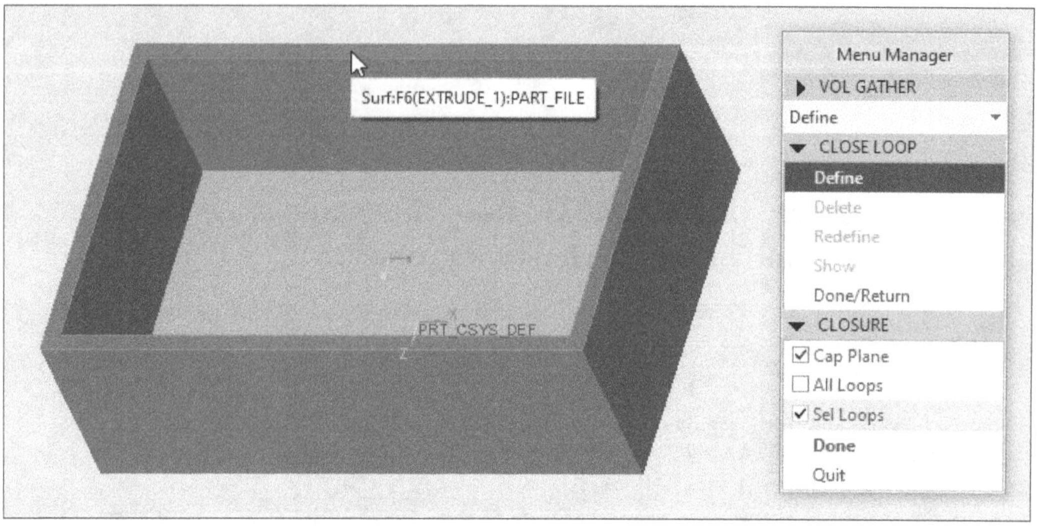

Figure-32. Selection of surface

- Click on the last selected plane again. The **CLOSE LOOP Menu Manager** will be displayed along with **Select** dialog box. Here, you need to select the edges which are closing the selected volume; refer to Figure-33.

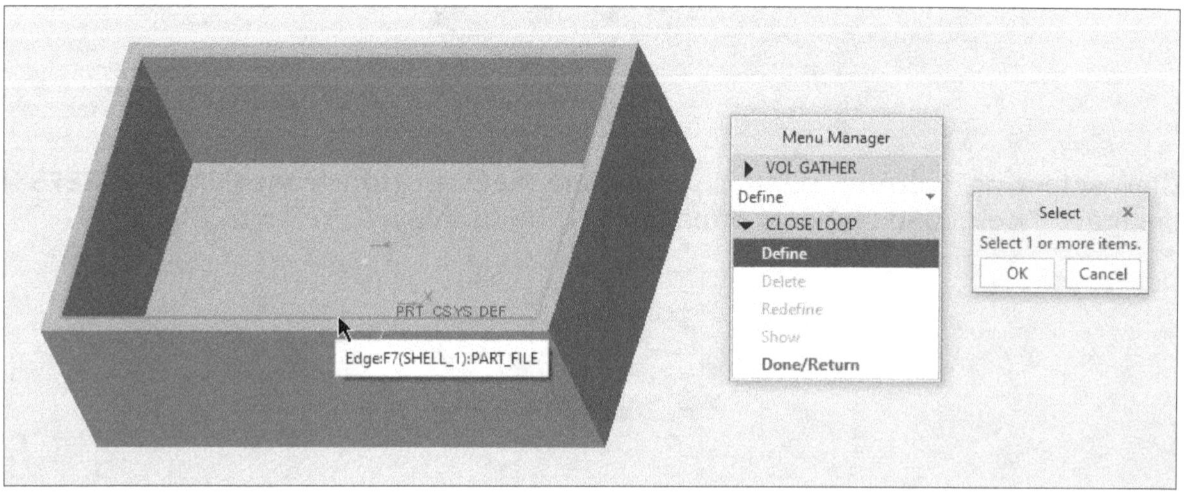

Figure-33. Selection of edges

- After selection of edges, click on **Done/Return** button from the **CLOSE LOOP Menu Manager** and **Done** button from the **VOL GATHER Menu Manager**. The gathered volume will be displayed; refer to Figure-34.

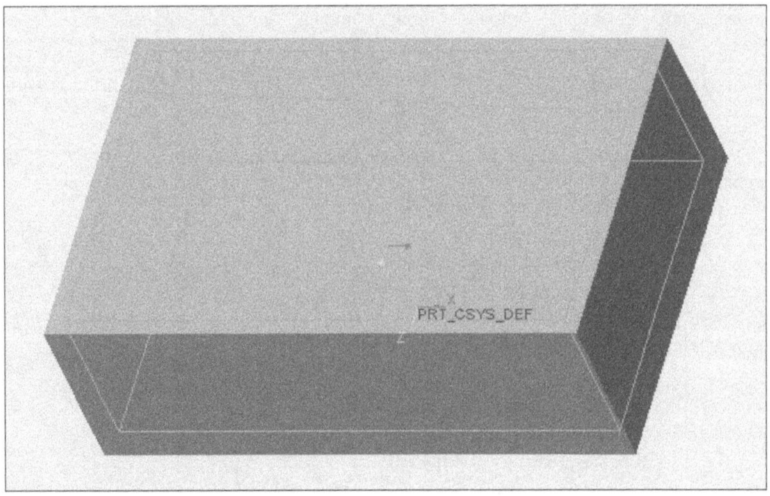

Figure-34. Gathered volume

- Click on the **OK** button from **Mill Volume** tab to apply or save the changes. The gathered volume will be added in **Model Tree**.

Mill Surface

The **Mill Surface** tool is used to select/create surfaces on which mill machining is to be performed. The procedure to use this tool is discussed next.

- Click on the **Mill Surface** tool of **Manufacturing** tab from **Ribbon**; refer to Figure-35. The **Mill Surface** tab will be displayed; refer to Figure-36.

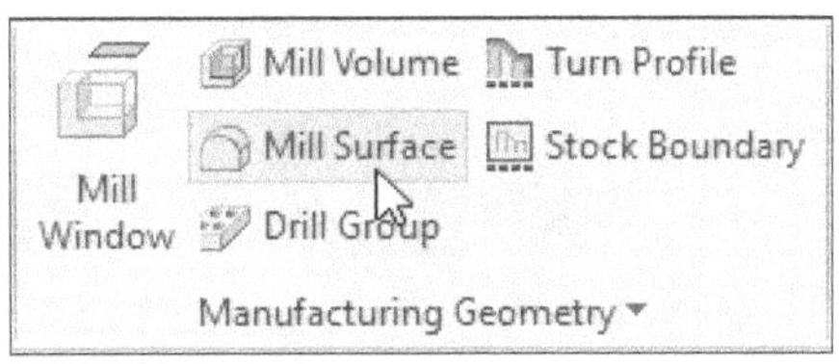

Figure-35. Mill Surface tool

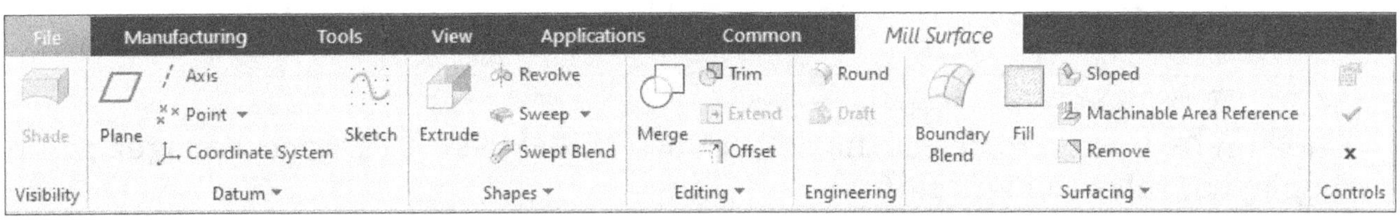

Figure-36. Mill Surface tab

Most of the tools in this tab are the modeling tools. To know more about these tools, please refer to our other book Creo Parametric 13.0 Black Book.

Sloped

The **Sloped** tool is used to easily adjust machining strategy for finish milling based on the orientation of the surface. The procedure to use this tool is discussed next.

- Click on the **Sloped** tool from the **Mill Surface** contextual tab; refer to Figure-37. The **SURFACE** dialog box will be displayed along with **Select** dialog box; refer to Figure-38.

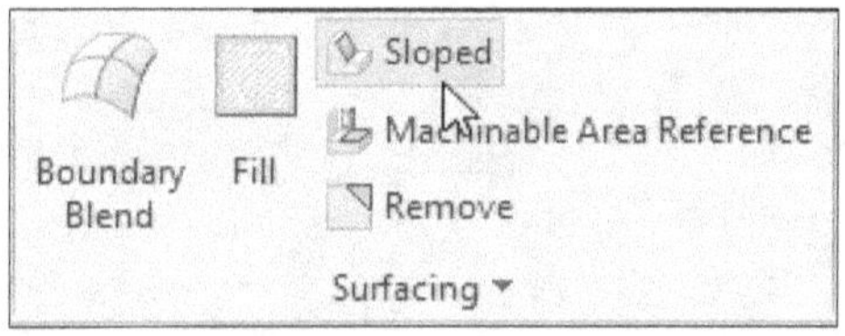

Figure-37. Sloped tool

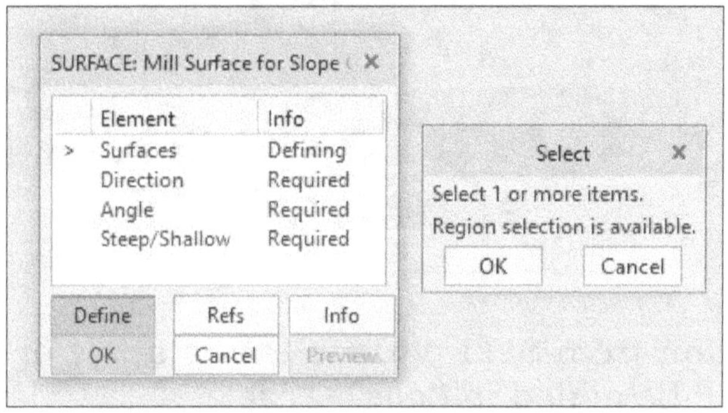

Figure-38. SURFACE dialog box along with Select dialog box

- Here, you need to select the surface for sloped feature. Select the surface as displayed; refer to Figure-39.

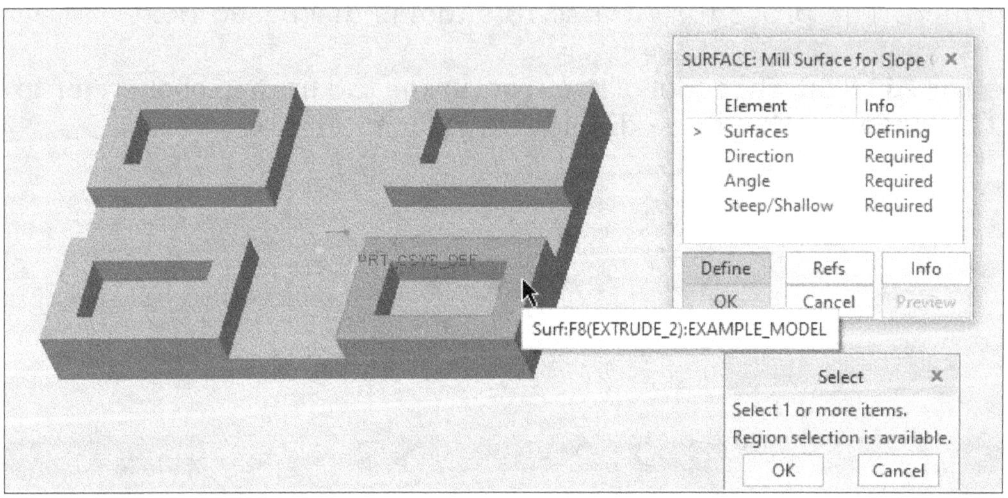

Figure-39. Selection of surface for Sloped tool

- Click on **OK** button to select the selection. The **GEN SEL DIR Menu Manager** will be displayed; refer to Figure-40.

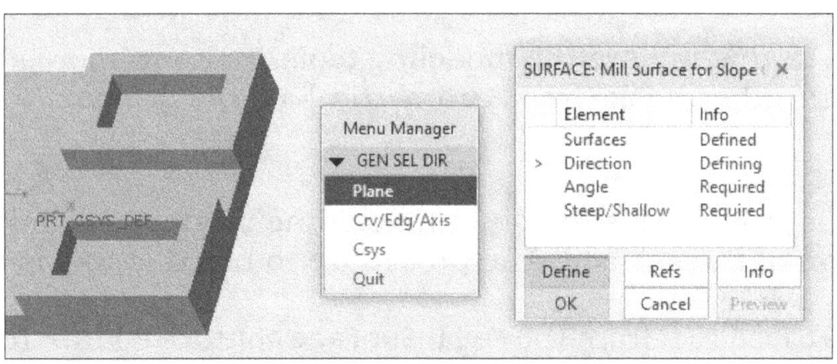

Figure-40. GEN SEL DIR Menu Manager

- Select **Plane** option from **GEN SEL DIR Menu Manager** if you want to select plane as a reference for direction of sloped feature.

- Select **Crv/Edg/Axis** option from **GEN SEL DIR Menu Manager** if you want to select curve, edge, or axis as a reference for direction of sloped feature.
- Select **Csys** option from **GEN SEL DIR Menu Manager** if you want to select coordinate system as a reference for direction of sloped feature.

In our case, we are selecting **Crv/Edg/Axis** option. Click on the edge of part as shown in Figure-41. The **DIRECTION Menu Manager** will be displayed; refer to Figure-42.

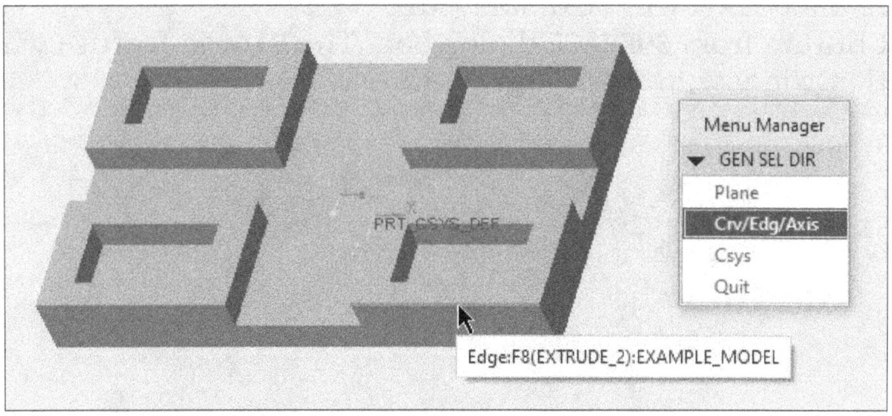

Figure-41. Selection of edge for sloped feature

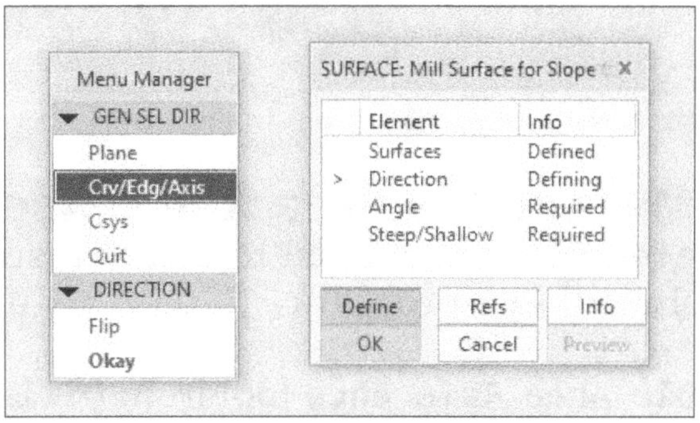

Figure-42. DIRECTION Menu Manager

- Click on **Flip** option of **DIRECTION Menu Manager**, if you want to flip or reverse the selected direction. Otherwise, click on **Okay** button. The **Enter draft angle** edit box will be displayed; refer to Figure-43.

Figure-43. Enter draft angle edit box

- Enter the value of draft angle in **Enter draft angle** edit box and click on the button. The **SHALLOW OR STEEP SIDE Menu Manager** will be displayed; refer to Figure-44.

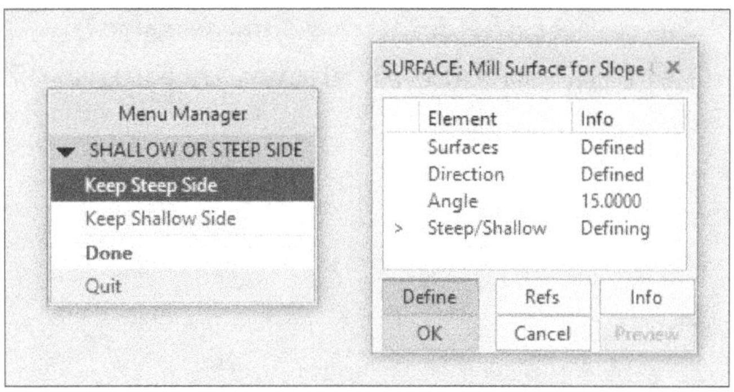

Figure-44. SHALLOW OR STEEP SIDE Menu Manager

- Select **Keep Steep Side** option from **SHALLOW OR STEEP SIDE Menu Manager** if you want to keep only those portions of the selected surface where the angle between the surface normal and the direction vector is greater than specified angle value.
- Select **Keep Shallow Side** option from **SHALLOW OR STEEP SIDE Menu Manager** if you want to keep only those portions of the selected surfaces where the angle between the surface normal and the direction vector is less than the specified Angle value.
- In our case, we are selecting **Keep Steep Side** option and click on **Done** button. The **SURFACE** dialog box will be displayed.
- Click on **OK** button from **SURFACE** dialog box. The **Sloped** feature will be displayed on application window; refer to Figure-45.

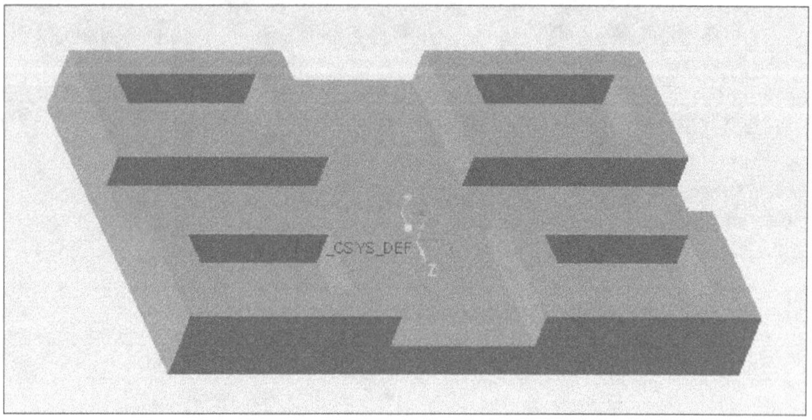

Figure-45. Sloped feature

Machinable Area Reference

The **Machinable Area Reference** tool is used to create a surface that only includes areas that are to be machined. The procedure to use this tool is discussed next.

- Click on the **Machinable Area Reference** tool from **Mill Surface** contextual tab. The **SURFACE: Machinable Area** dialog box will be displayed along with **Select** dialog box; refer to Figure-46.

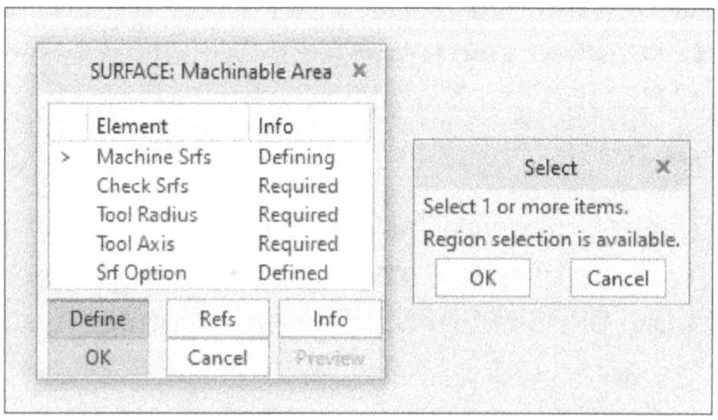

Figure-46. SURFACE Machinable Area dialog box

- Here, you need to select the surface as shown in Figure-47.

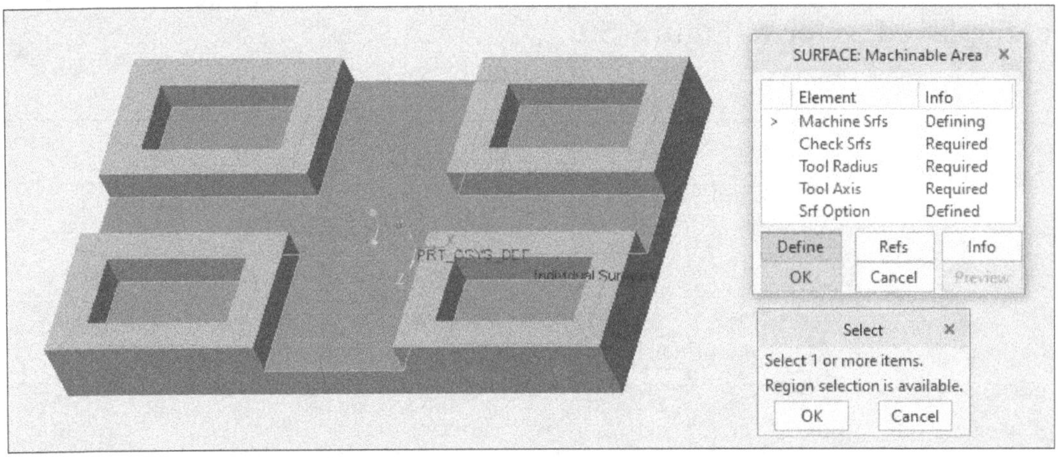

Figure-47. Selection of surface for machine

- Click on **OK** button from **Select** dialog box. The **SELECT SRFS Menu Manager** will be displayed along with **Select** dialog box; refer to Figure-48.

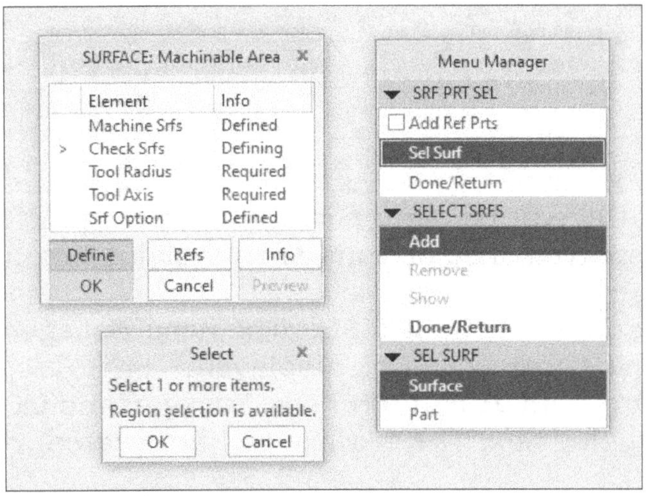

Figure-48. SELECT SRFS Menu Manager along with Select dialog box

- Select the surface as reference to check gouging agent from the part as shown in Figure-49.

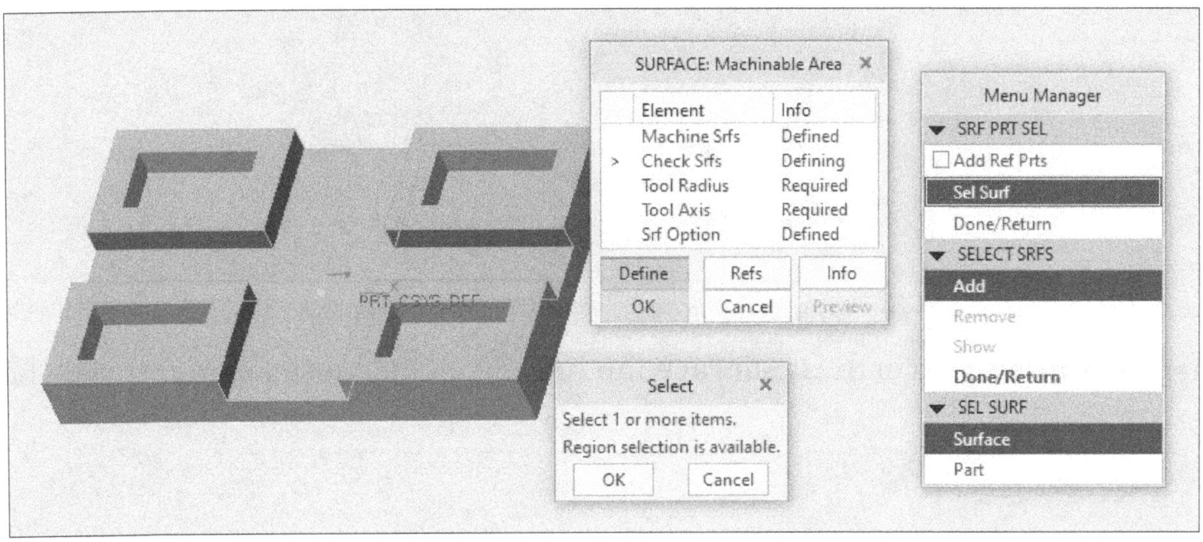

Figure-49. Selection of surfaces

- Click on **OK** button from **Select** dialog box. The updated **SELECT SRFS Menu Manager** will be displayed; refer to Figure-50.

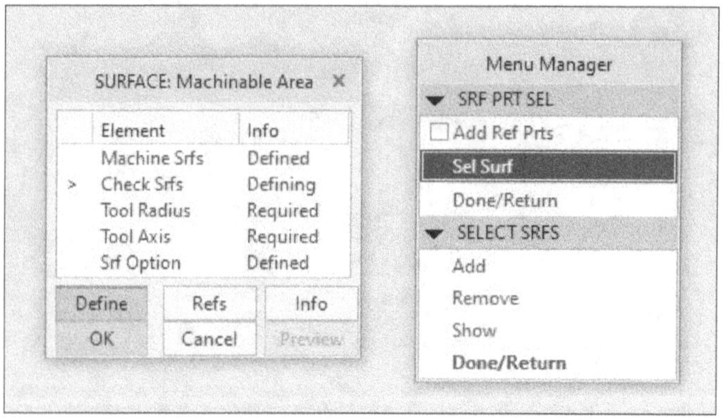

Figure-50. Updated SELECT SRFS Menu Manager

- Click on **Done/Return** button from the **Menu Managers**. The **Enter radius of ball end mill for calculating Machinable Area** edit box will be displayed; refer to Figure-51.

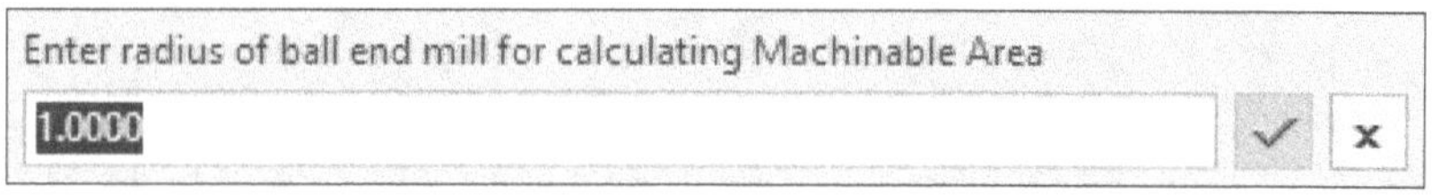

Figure-51. Enter radius of ball end mill for calculating machinable area

- Enter the value in the edit box and click on **Done** button. The **GEN SEL DIR Menu Manager** will be displayed. The options of this dialog box are same as discussed earlier.
- Click on the **Plane** option from **GEN SEL DIR Menu Manager** and select the plane. The **DIRECTION Menu Manager** will be displayed.
- Click on **Okay** button from **DIRECTION Menu Manager** and **OK** button from **SURFACE: Machinable Area** dialog box. The surface will be created; refer to Figure-52.

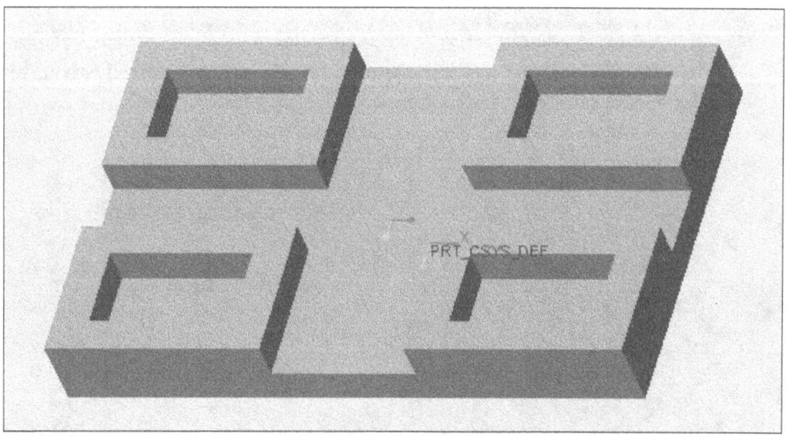

Figure-52. Surface created after using machinable area reference tool

Other tools or options of **Mill Surface** tab have been discussed earlier in this book.

- After specifying the parameters, click on the **OK** button of **Mill Surface** contextual tab. The commands will be added in **Model Tree**.

Drill Group

The **Drill Group** tool is used to define group of holes to be created by drilling machine. The procedure to use this tool is discussed next.

- Click on the **Drill Group** tool from **Ribbon** of **Manufacturing** tab; refer to Figure-53. The **Drilling Group** dialog box will be displayed; refer to Figure-54.

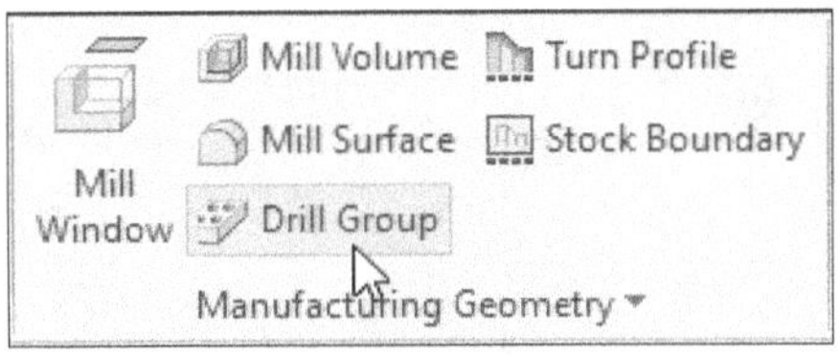

Figure-53. Drill Group tool

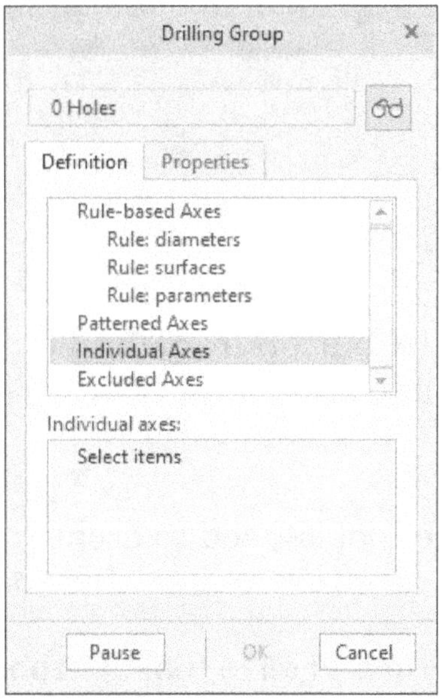

Figure-54. Drilling Group dialog box

- Select **Rule diameters** option from **Definition** section if you want to select holes of specified diameter.
- Select **Rule surfaces** option from **Definition** section if you want to select holes of specified surfaces.
- Select **Rule parameters** option from **Definition** section if you want to select holes of specified feature parameters.
- Select **Patterned Axes** option from **Definition** section if you want to select hole in a specific pattern.
- Select **Individual Axes** option from **Definition** section if you want to select individual holes from drill group.
- Select **Excluded Axes** option from **Definition** section if you want to exclude holes from drill group.
- In our case, we are selecting the **Individual Axes** option. Select the axis of holes while holding **CTRL** key. The selected axes will be listed in **Individual axes** section; refer to Figure-55.

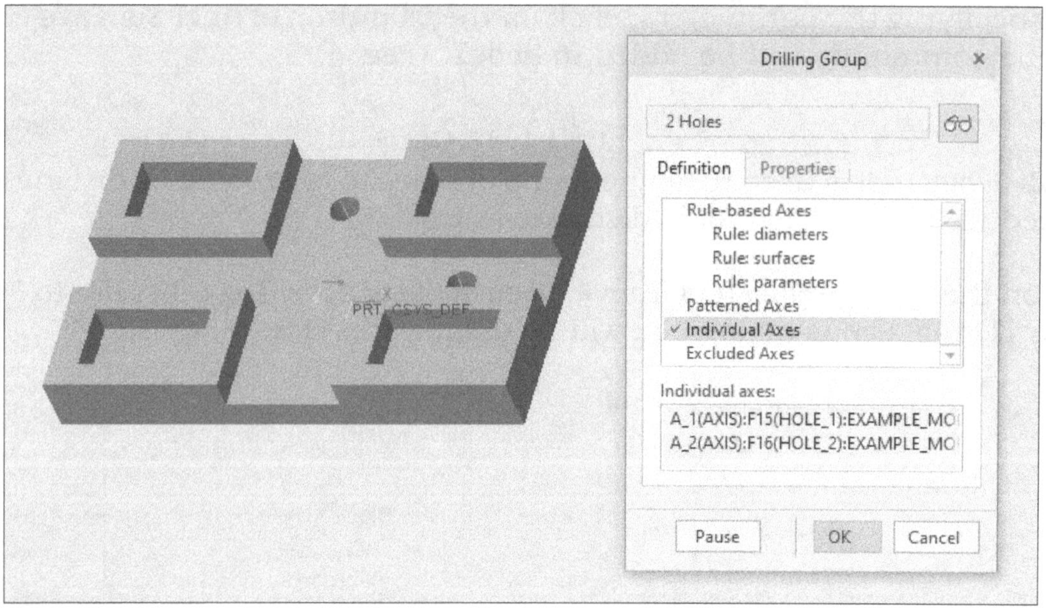

Figure-55. Selection of axes

- Click on the **OK** button from **Drilling Group** dialog box to apply the changes. The command will be added in **Model Tree**.

Turn Profile

The **Turn Profile** tool is used to create a cut on part using turning operation on lathe machine. The procedure to use this tool is discussed next.

- Click on the **Turn Profile** tool of **Ribbon** from **Manufacturing** tab; refer to Figure-56. The **Turn Profile** contextual tab will be displayed; refer to Figure-57.

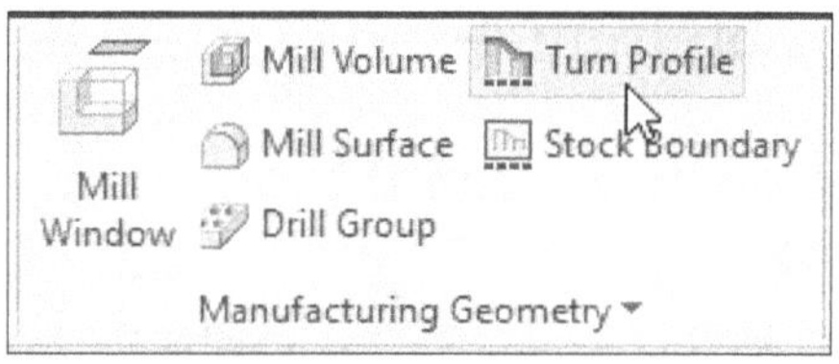

Figure-56. Turn Profile tool

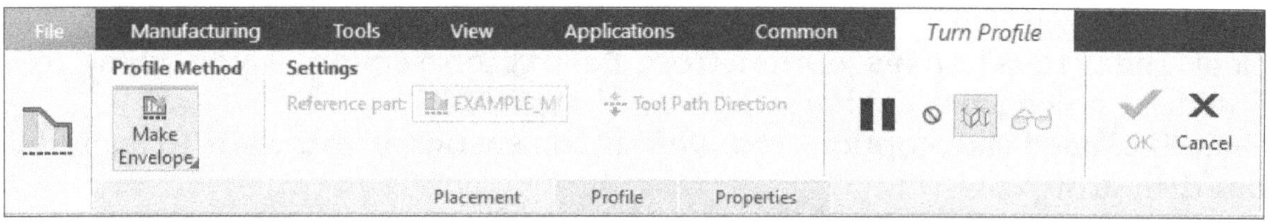

Figure-57. Turn Profile contextual tab

- Select **Make Envelope** option from drop-down in the **Profile Method** area if you want to define a turn profile by creating an envelope on the fly.
- Select **Envelope Feature** option from drop-down in the **Profile Method** area if you want to select an existing envelope to create a turn profile.
- Select **Surface** option from drop-down in the **Profile Method** area if you want to define turn profile by specifying **From** and **To** surfaces on a reference model.
- Select the **Chain** option from drop-down in the **Profile Method** area if you want to define turn profile along the segments of a datum curve or another turn profile.

- Select the **Sketch** option from drop-down in the **Profile Method** area if you want to sketch a turn profile.
- Select the **Cross Section** option from drop-down in the **Profile Method** area if you want to define a turn profile by section.

Here, we are going to sketch the turn profile, so select the **Sketch** option from drop-down. Select the coordinate system to be used for machining; refer to Figure-58.

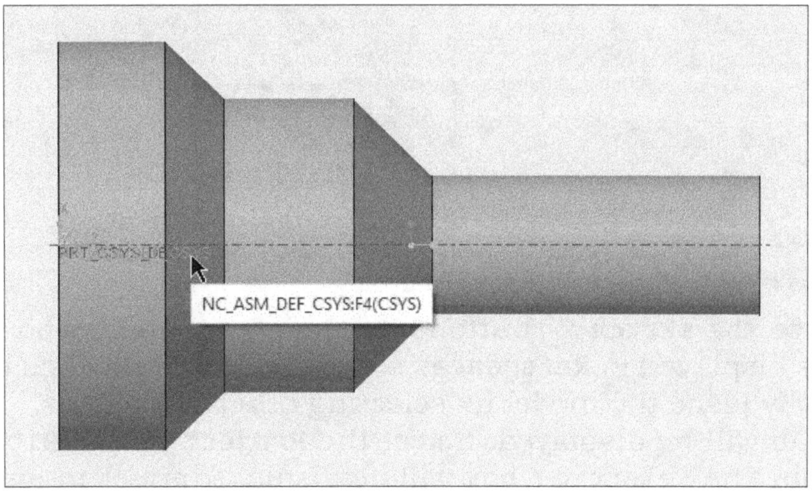

Figure-58. Selecting coordinate system

- Now, click on the **Sketch** button from **Settings** area of contextual tab. The **Sketch** dialog box will be displayed.
- Click on the **Sketch** button from **Sketch** dialog box. The **References** dialog box will be displayed; refer to Figure-59.

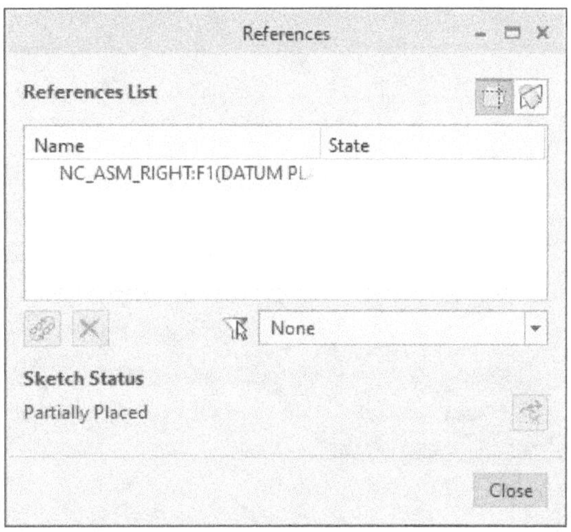

Figure-59. References dialog box

- Here, you need to select the reference to fully place the model. Select the coordinate system as reference as shown in Figure-60.

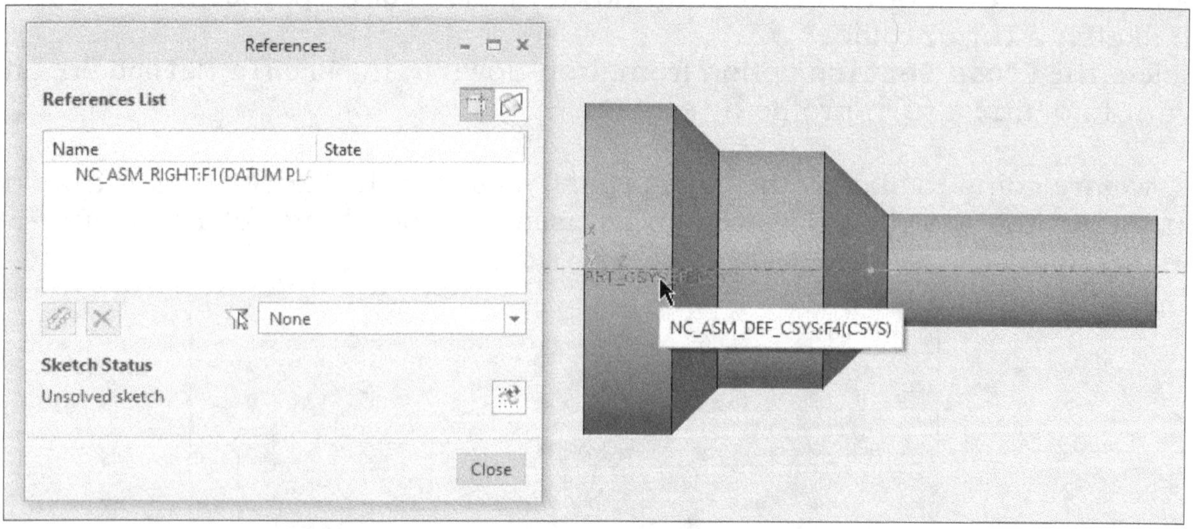

Figure-60. Selection of coordinate system as reference

- Click on **Update the sketch** button from **References** dialog box. If **Fully Placed** notification is displayed in **References** status section then click on **Close** button. Otherwise, fully place the model by selecting other references.
- The **Sketch** tab will be displayed. Select the **Project** tool of **Ribbon** from **Sketch** contextual tab. The **Selection box** will be displayed; refer to Figure-61.

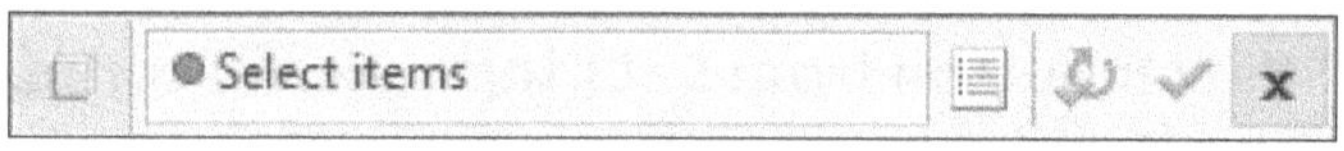

Figure-61. Selection box

- Select the edges of part as shown in Figure-62 and click on **OK** button from **Sketch** tab. The **Turn Profile** tab will be displayed again.

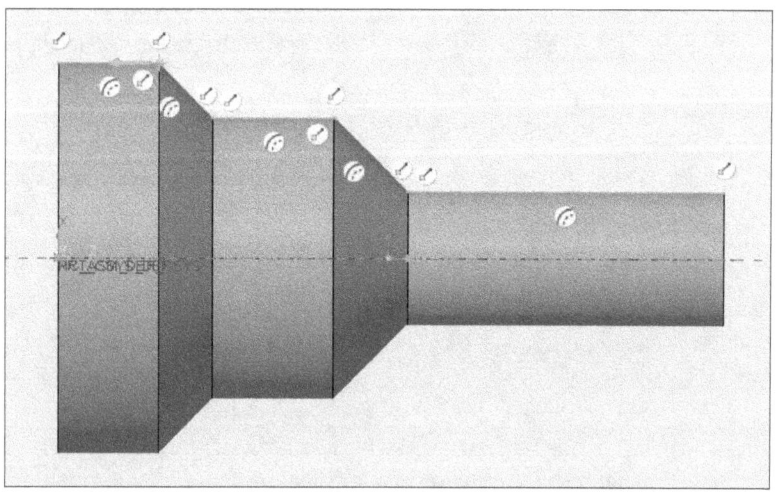

Figure-62. Selection of sketch

- Click on **OK** button from **Turn Profile** tab. The profile command will be added to **Model Tree**.

Stock Boundary

The **Stock Boundary** tool is used to create the boundary of stock or workpiece. The procedure to use this tool is discussed next.

- Click on the **Stock Boundary** tool of **Ribbon** from **Manufacturing** tab; refer to Figure-63. The **Stock Boundary** contextual tab will be displayed; refer to Figure-64.

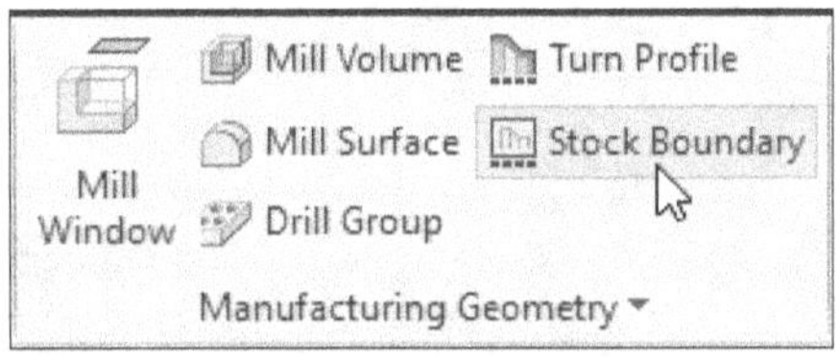

Figure-63. Stock Boundary tool

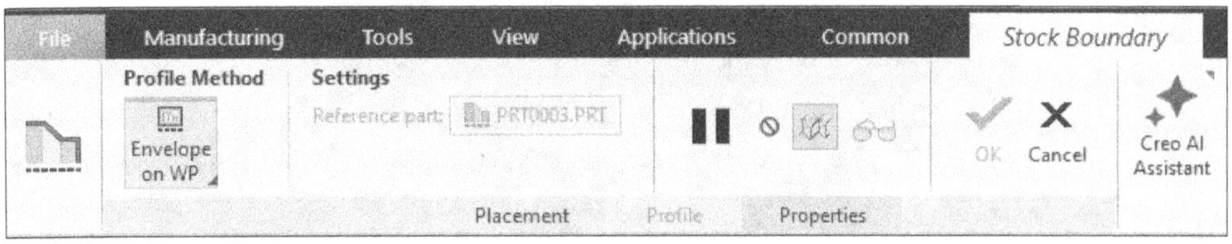

Figure-64. Stock Boundary tab

- Select the coordinate system from part as a reference. The **Stock Boundary** will be created automatically; refer to Figure-65.

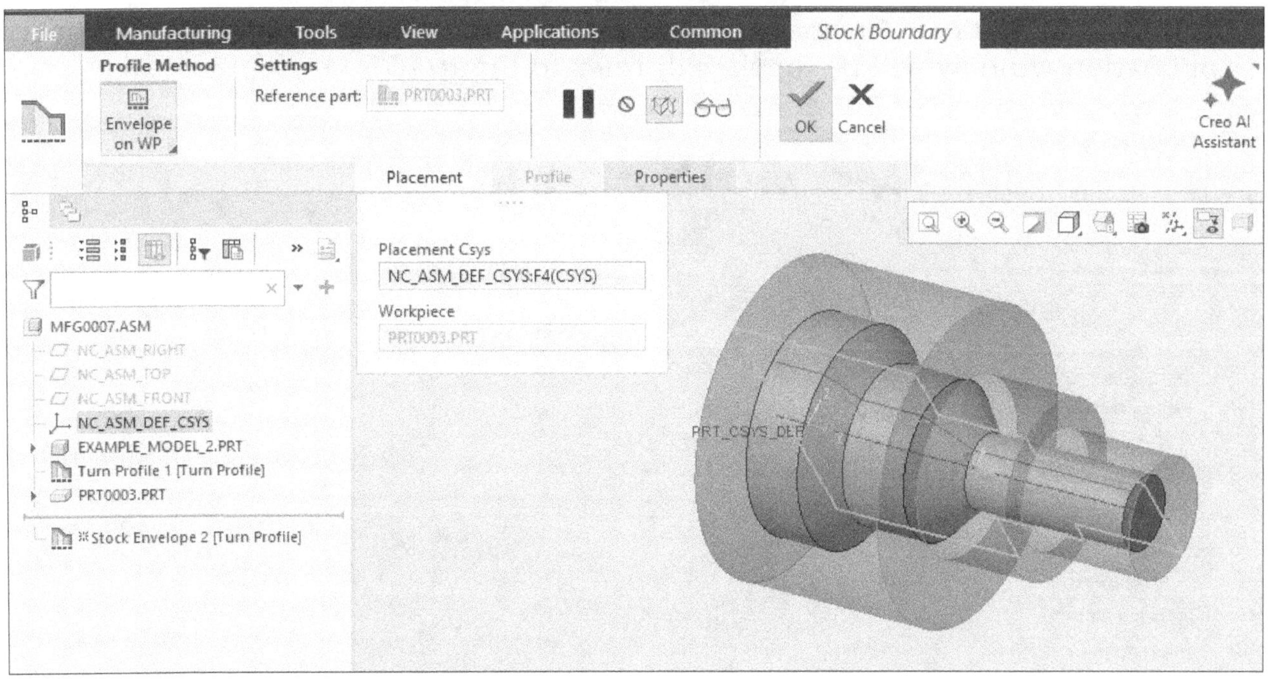

Figure-65. Stock Boundary

- Select the **Envelope on WP** button from **Profile Method** section if you want to create the boundary for workpiece automatically.
- Select the **Sketched envelope** button from **Profile Method** section if you want to create a boundary for workpiece with the help of sketch.
- After specifying the parameters for **Stock Boundary**, click on **Done** button from **Stock Boundary** tab. The boundary will be added in **Model Tree** with the name of **Stock Envelope**.

PRACTICAL 1

Create the milling operation for the model as shown in Figure-66.

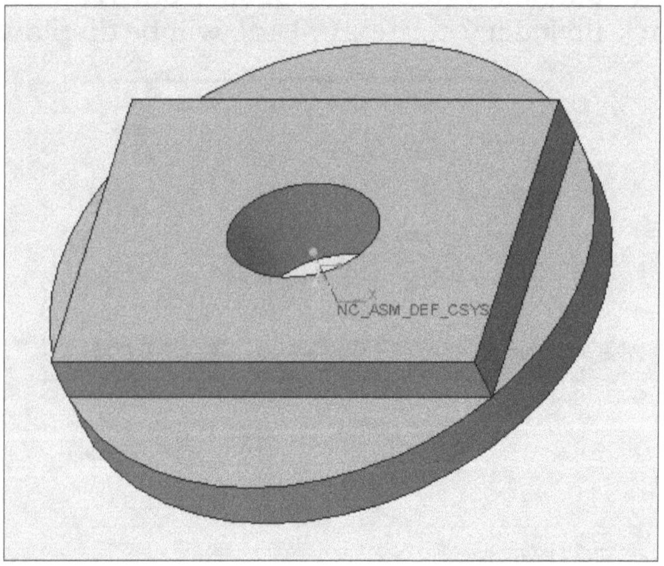

Figure-66. Practical 1

Starting the NC Assembly

- Double-click on **Creo Parametric** icon from your desktop. The **Creo Parametric** application window will be displayed; refer to Figure-67.

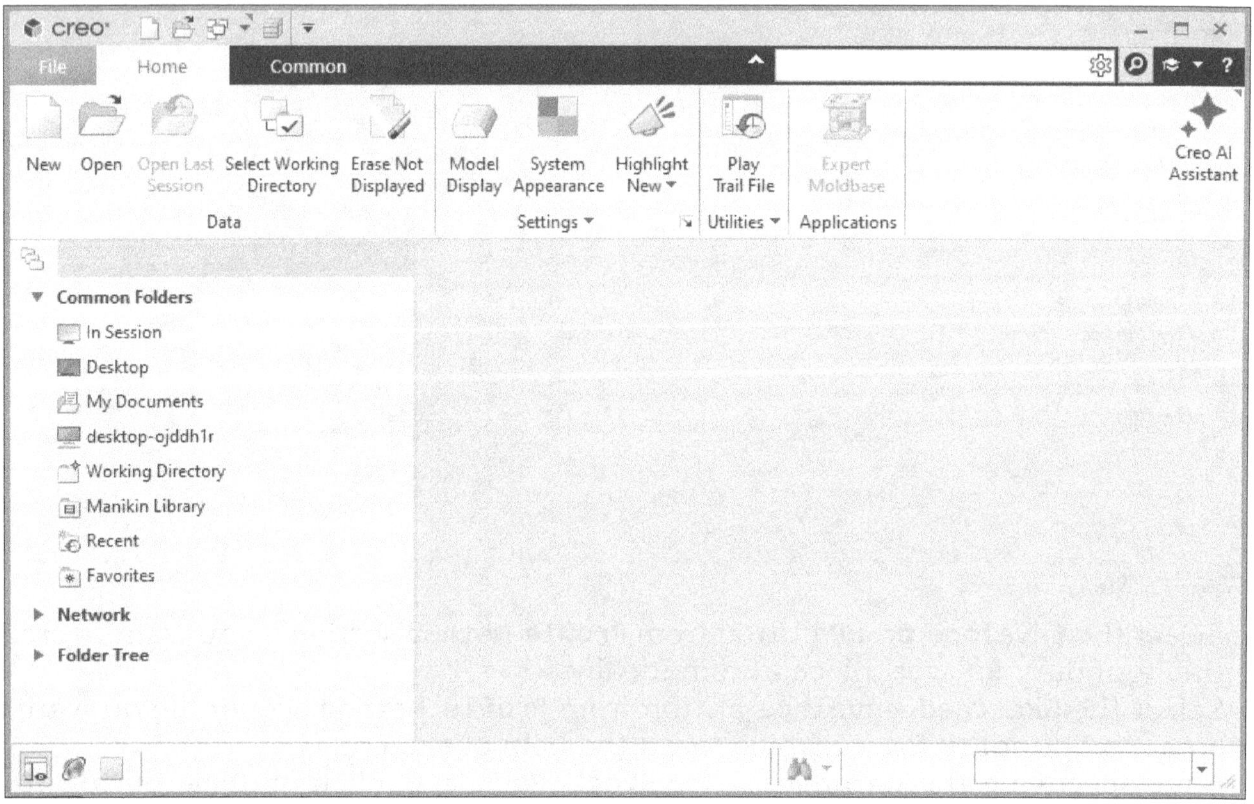

Figure-67. Creo Parametric starting window

- Click on the **New** button from **Ribbon**. The **New** dialog box will be displayed; refer to Figure-68.

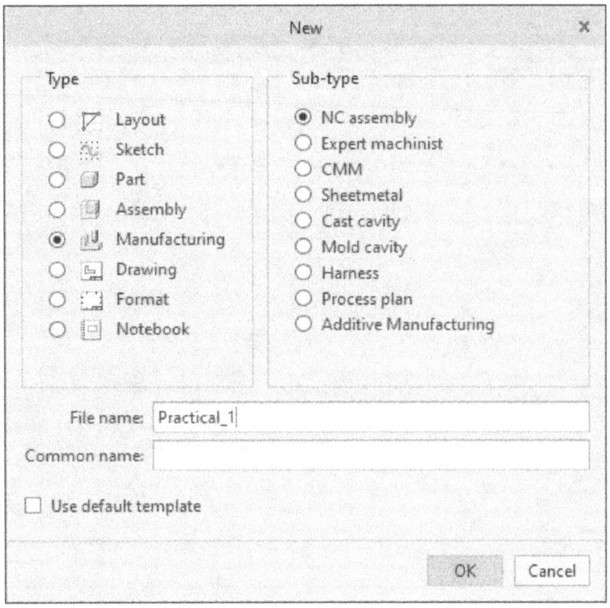

Figure-68. New dialog box

- Select the **Manufacturing** radio button from **Type** area and **NC assembly** radio button from **Sub-Type** area.
- Click on the **Name** edit box and enter **Practical 1** as the name of file.
- Clear the **Use default template** check box from **New** dialog box.
- Click on **OK** button from **New** dialog box. The **New File Options** dialog box will be displayed; refer to Figure-69.

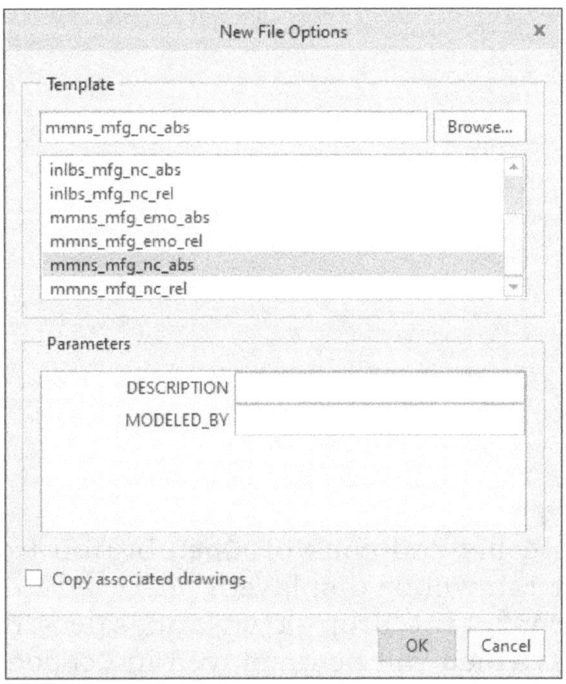

Figure-69. New File Options dialog box

- Click on **mmns mfg nc abs** option from **Template** section and specify the required details of **Parameters** section.
- Click on the **OK** button from **New File Options** dialog box. The **NC Assembly** application window will be displayed; refer to Figure-70.

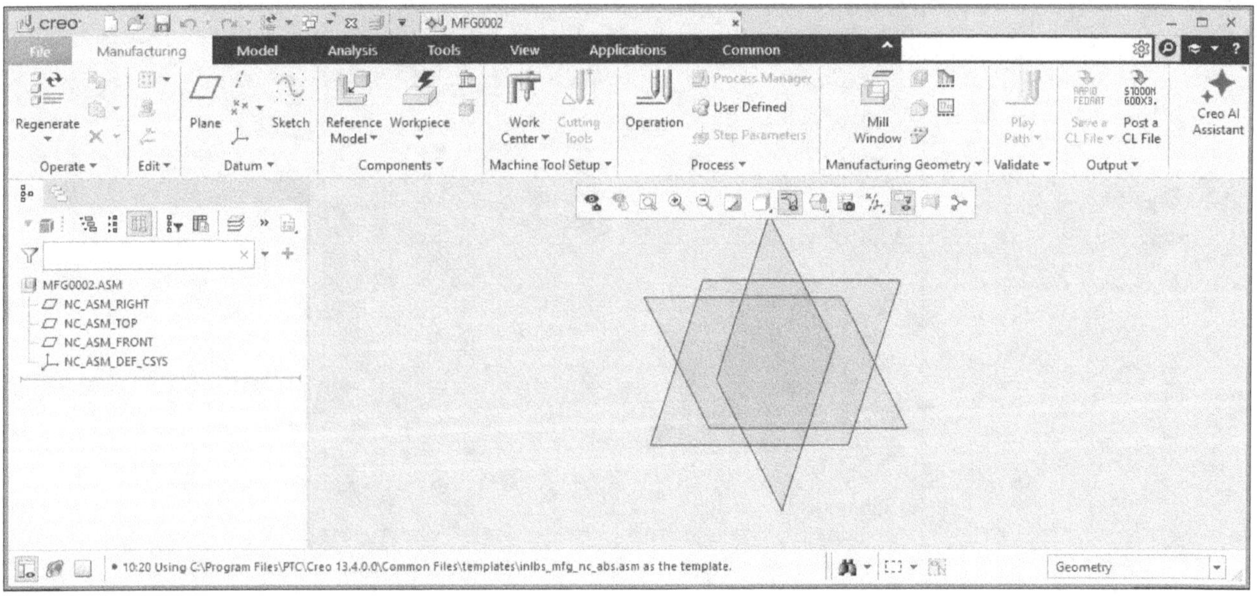

Figure-70. NC Assembly application window

Adding Reference Model

- Click on **Assemble Reference Model** button of **Reference Model** drop-down from **Manufacturing** tab. The **Open** dialog box will be displayed; refer to Figure-71.

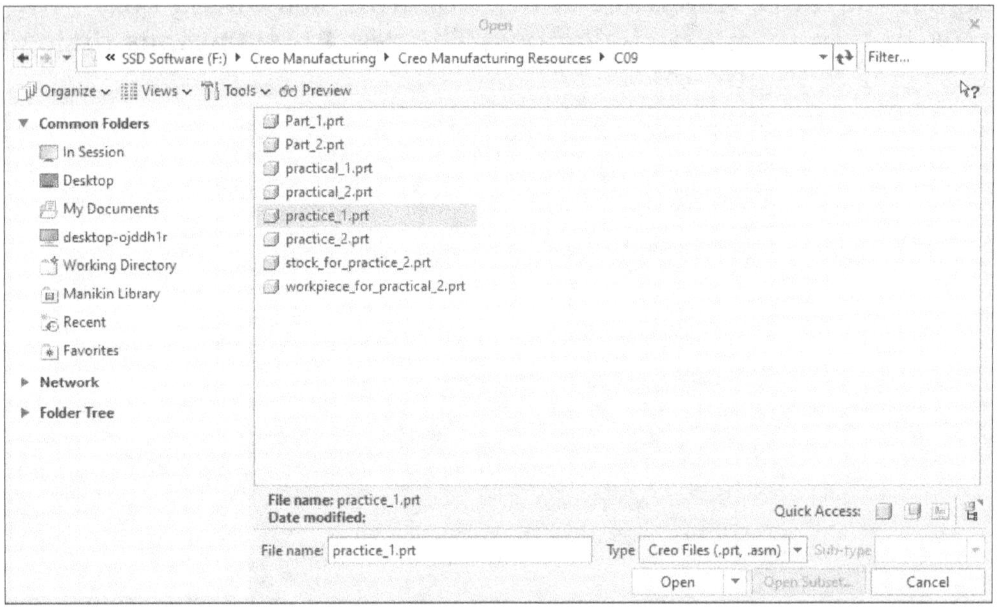

Figure-71. Open dialog box

- Select the **Practical 1** file and click on **Open** button from **Open** dialog box. The **Component Placement** tab will be displayed.
- Click on **Current constraint** drop-down and select the **Default** button. The **STATUS: Fully constrained** will be displayed in **Component Placement** tab; refer to Figure-72.

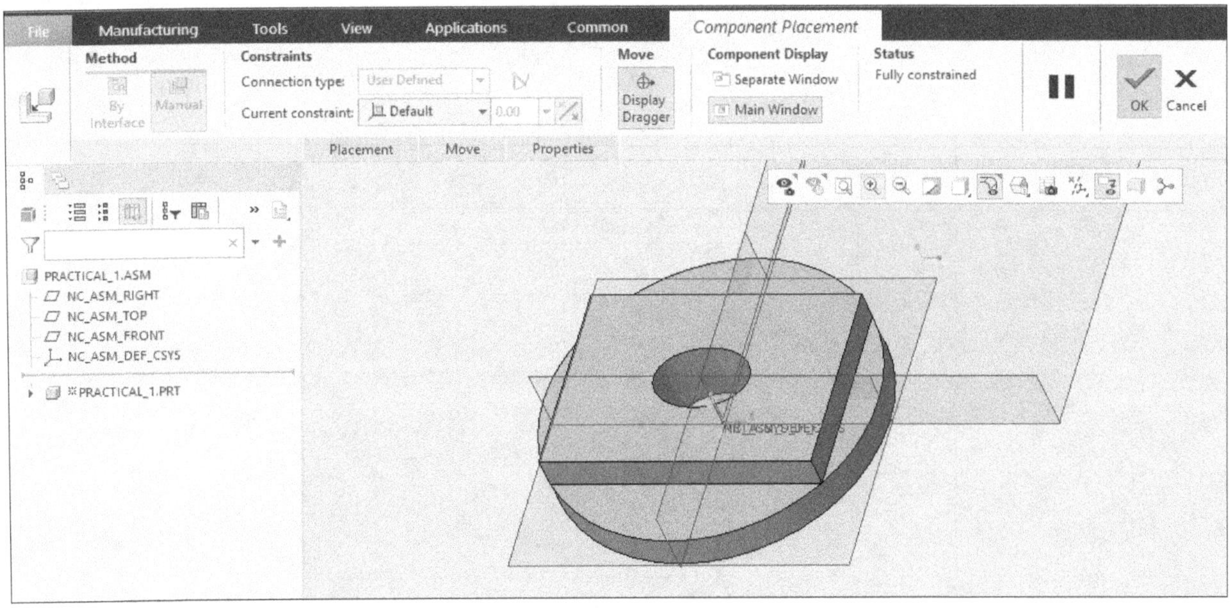

Figure-72. Fully constrained model

- Click on **OK** button from **Component Placement** contextual tab. The **NC Assembly** application window will be displayed along with the constrained model.

Creating Workpiece

- Click on the **Automatic Workpiece** button of **Workpiece** drop-down from **Manufacturing** tab. The **Auto Workpiece Creation** tab will be displayed; refer to Figure-73.

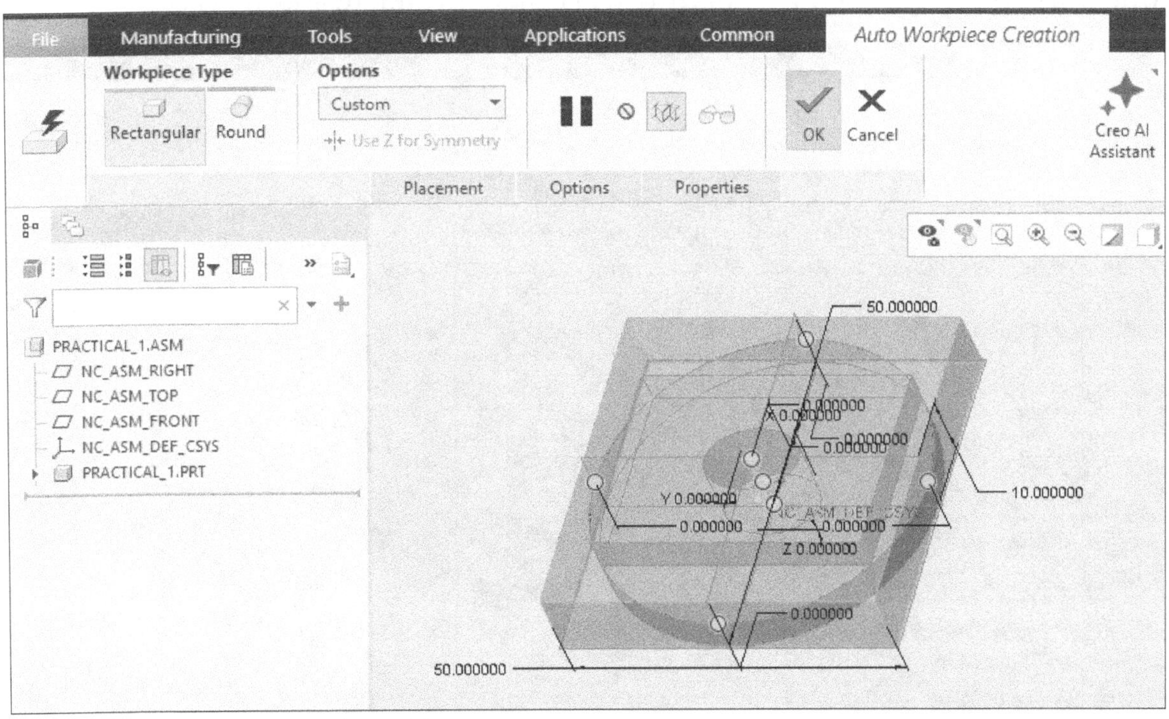

Figure-73. Creating workpiece for model

- Select **Round** option from **Workpiece Type** area of the **Auto Workpiece Creation** contextual tab.
- Click on **Options** tab of **Auto Workpiece Creation** contextual tab.
- Click on **About X:** edit box of **Rotation Offsets** section and enter the value as **90**; refer to Figure-74.

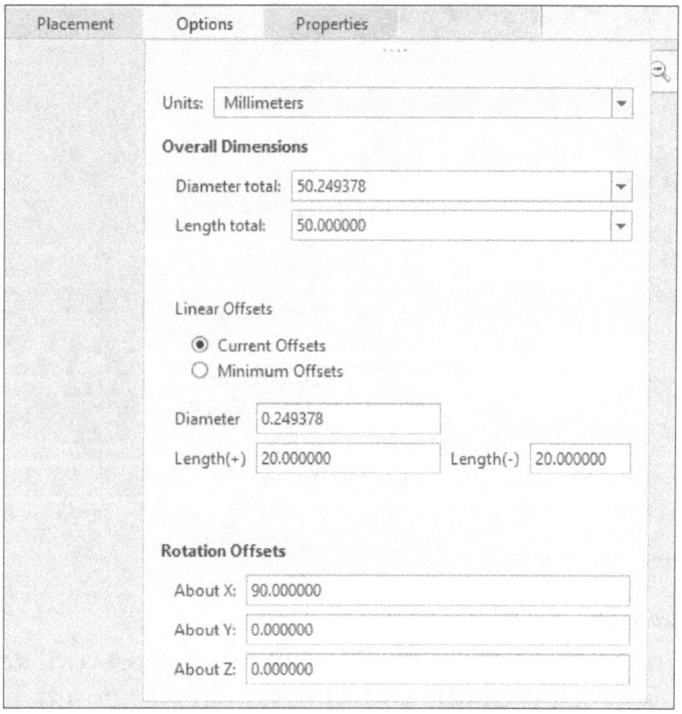

Figure-74. Options tab

- Click on **Length(+)** button of **Options** tab and enter the value as **0**.
- Click on **Length(-)** button of **Options** tab and enter the value as **0**.
- After specifying the parameters, click on the **OK** button from **Auto Workpiece Creation** contextual tab. The **NC Assembly** application window will be displayed along with the reference model and workpiece; refer to Figure-75.

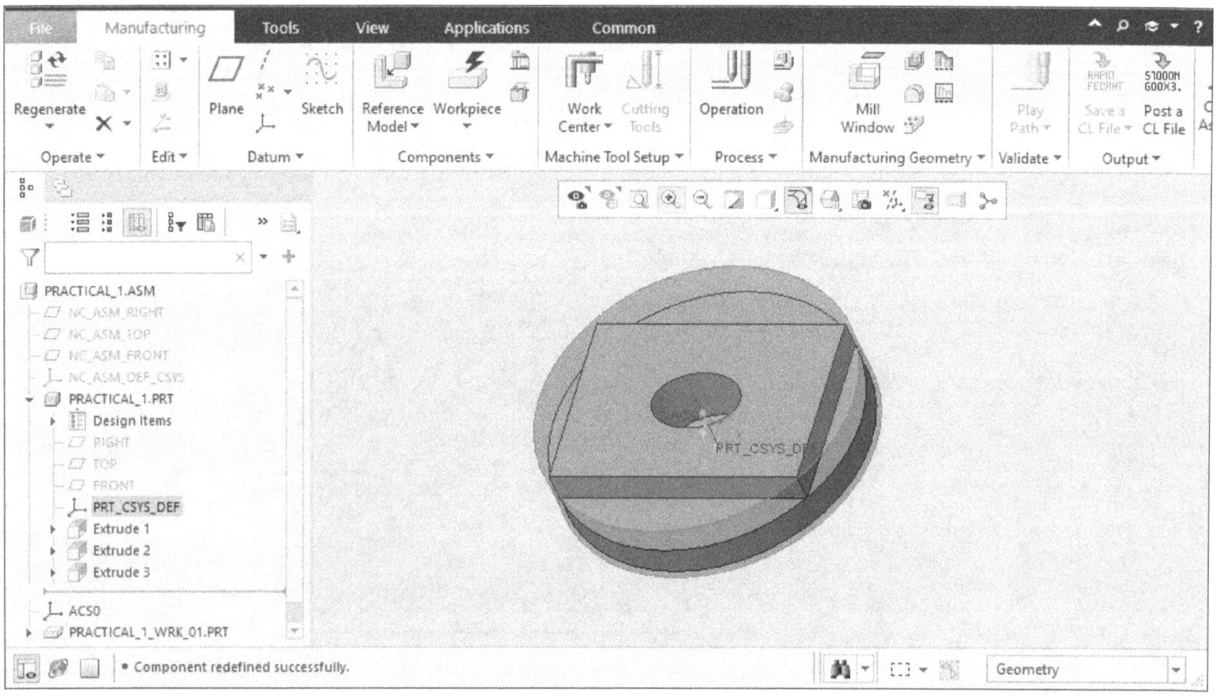

Figure-75. NC Assembly application window along with model and workpiece

Machine Tool Setup

- Click on the **Mill** tool from **Work Center** drop-down of **Manufacturing** tab. The **Milling Work Center** dialog box will be displayed; refer to Figure-76.

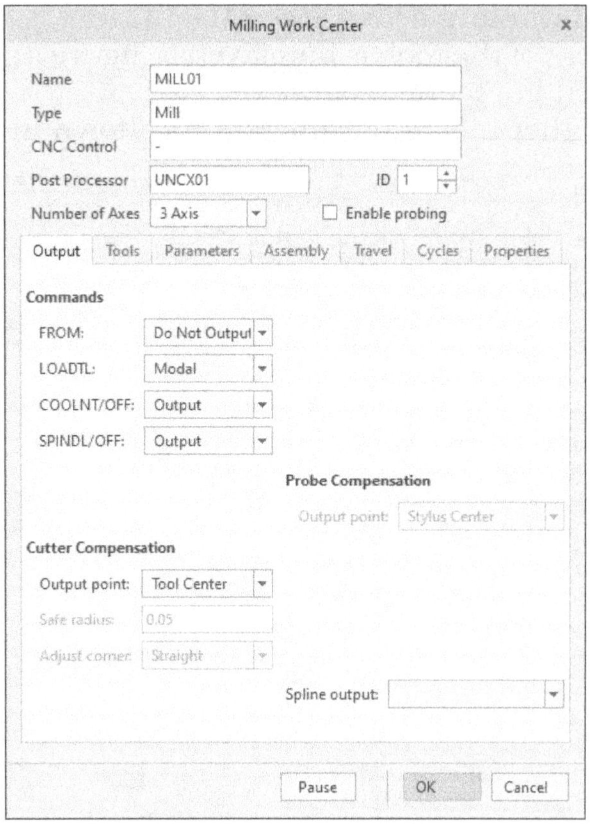

Figure-76. Milling Work Center dialog box

- Click on **Name** edit box and type **TECHNO** as the name of machine.
- Click on **Tools** button of **Tools** tab from **Milling Work Center** dialog box. The **Tools Setup** dialog box will be displayed; refer to Figure-77.

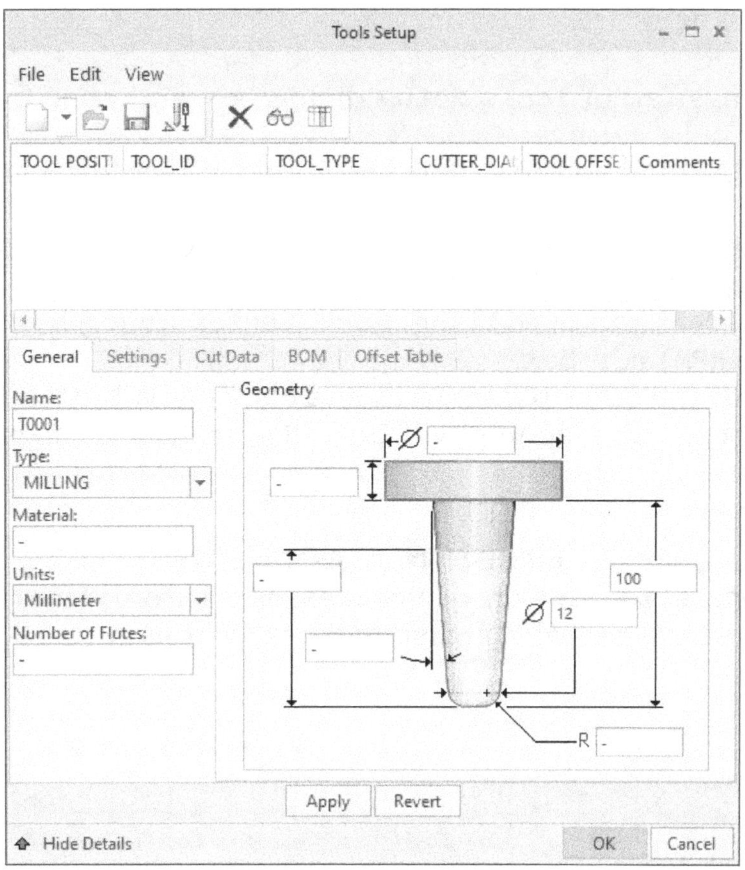

Figure-77. Tools Setup dialog box for Practical 1

- Click on **Type** drop-down and select **END MILL** button.
- Specify the parameters of the tool as displayed in figure and click on **Apply** button. The tool will be added in record section.
- Similarly, create another tool of parameters as shown in Figure-78.

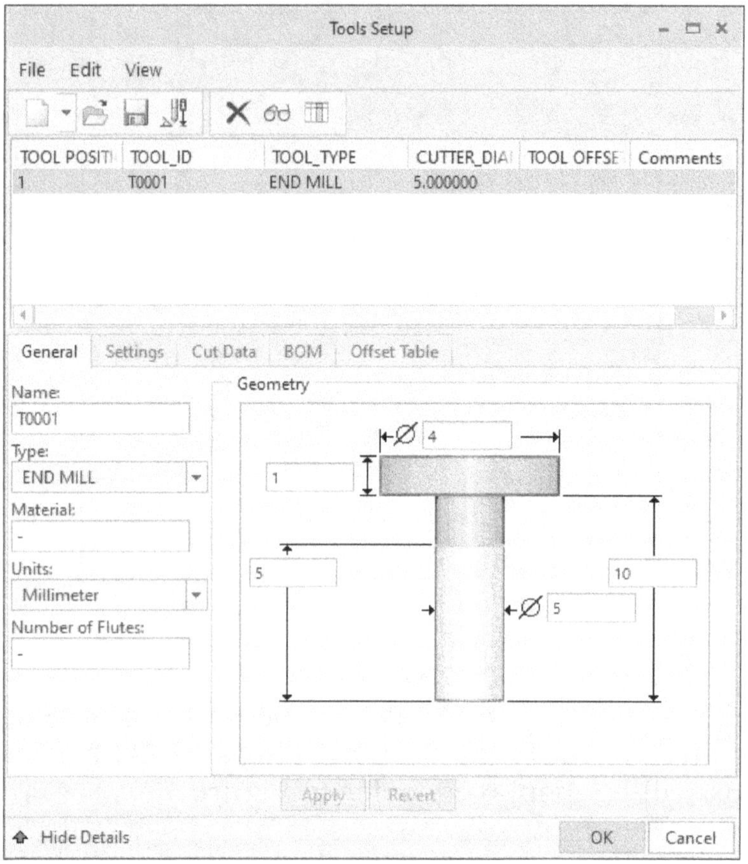

Figure-78. Creating another tool

- Click on **Settings** tab of **Tools Setup** dialog box and specify **2** in **Tool Number** edit box.
- Click on **Apply** button and the tool will be added in records section of **Tools Setup** dialog box.
- After specifying the parameters, click on **OK** button from **Tools Setup** dialog box. The **Milling Work Center** dialog box will be displayed.
- Click on **Parameters** tab of **Milling Work Center** dialog box and enter **6000** in **Maximum Speed(RPM)** edit box.
- Similarly, specify the other parameters and click on **OK** button from **Milling Work Center** dialog box. The machine will be added in **Model Tree** with the name as **TECHNO**.

Creating Operation

- Click on the **Operation** button of **Process** panel from **Manufacturing** tab. The **Operation** contextual tab will be displayed; refer to Figure-79.

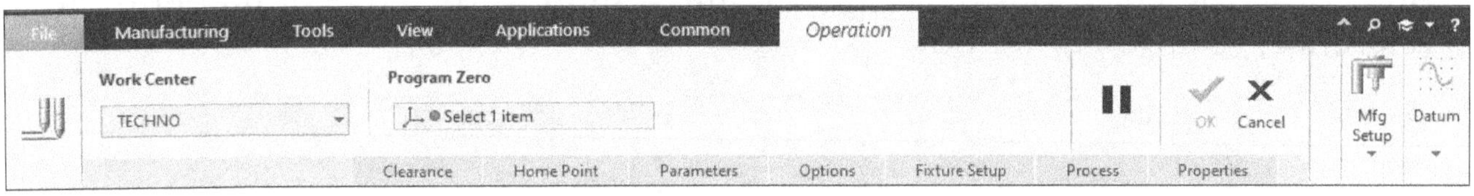

Figure-79. Operation contextual tab

- Click on **Datum** button from **Ribbon** and select **Coordinate System** button; refer to Figure-80. The **Coordinate System** dialog box will be displayed; refer to Figure-81.

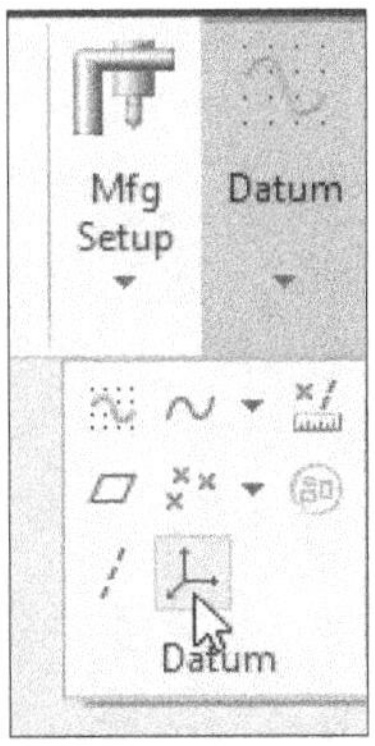

Figure-80. Coordinate System tool

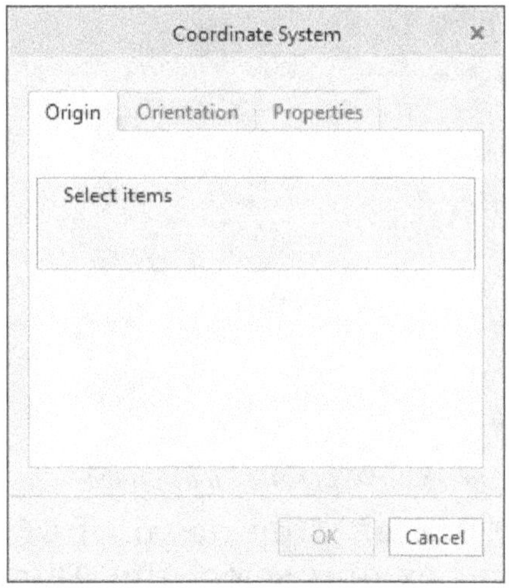

Figure-81. Coordinate System dialog box

- Select the surface of model as shown in Figure-82. The coordinate system will be displayed on selected surface.

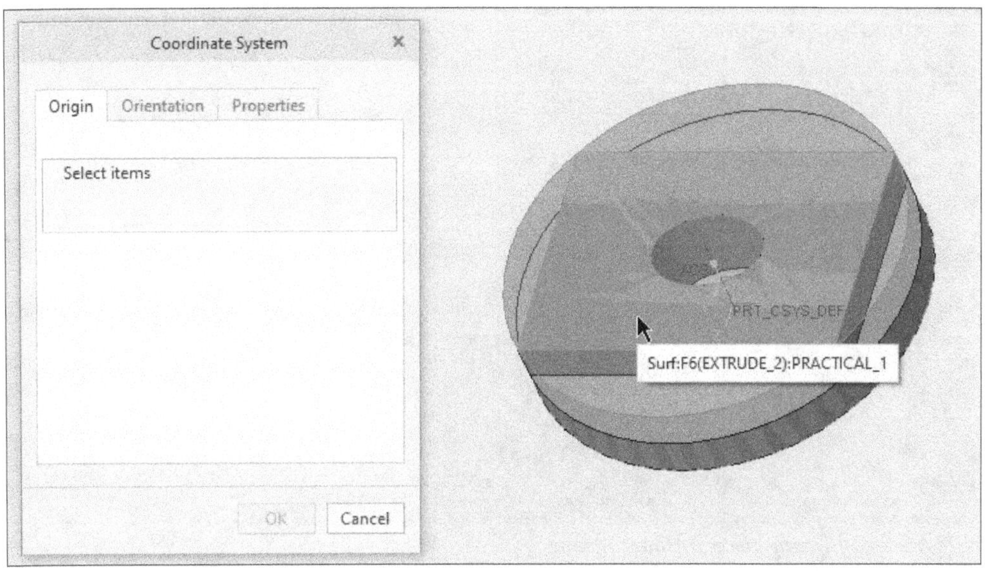

Figure-82. Selection of surface for Coordinate System

- Now, drag the green button of coordinate system to the edge of model to define reference; refer to Figure-83.

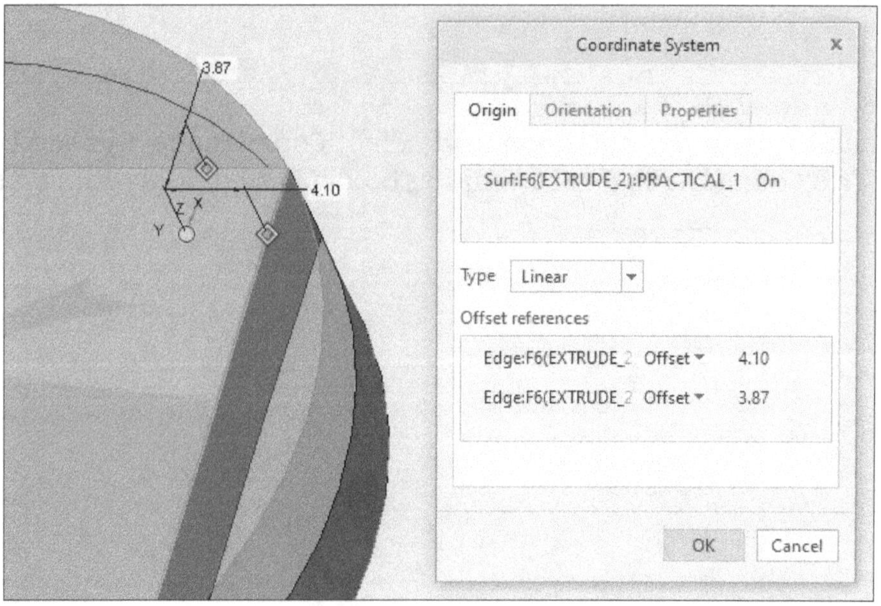

Figure-83. Placing coordinate system

- Click on the **Offset** drop-down of **Offset** references section from **Coordinate System** dialog box and select the **Align** option in both the drop-down; refer to Figure-84.

Figure-84. Aligning the coordinate system

- Click on **Orientation** tab of **Coordinate system** dialog box and select **Y** from **to project** drop-down.
- Click on **Flip** button of **to project** section. The direction of coordinate system will be changed in such a way that **Z** axis is perpendicular to the milling face of model; refer to Figure-85.

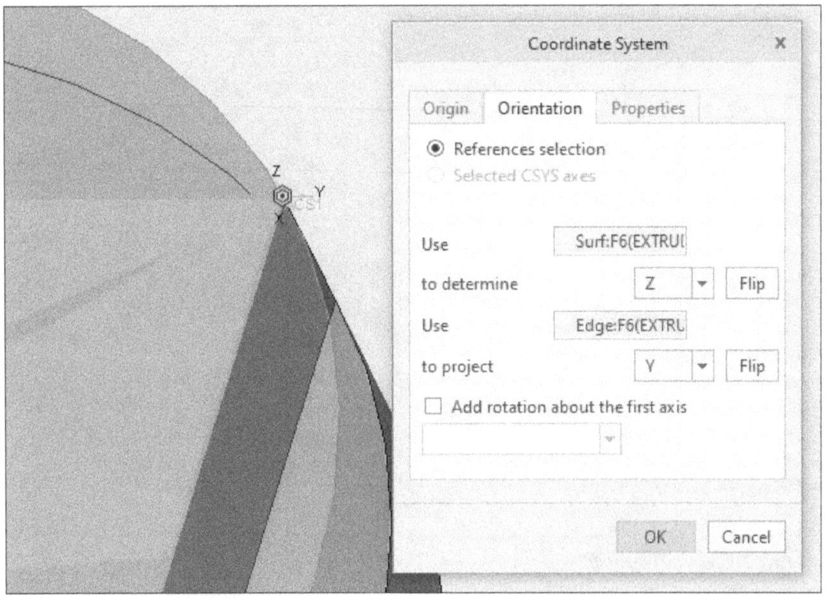

Figure-85. Change of direction of coordinate system

- Click on **OK** button from **Coordinate System** dialog box. The **Operation** tab will be displayed.
- Click on **Resume** button from **Operation** tab and the newly created coordinate system will be selected automatically.
- Click on **OK** button from the **Operation** contextual tab. The operation command will be added in **Model Tree** with the name as **OP010[TECHNO]**.

Creating Mill Window

- Click on **Mill Window** button of **Manufacturing Geometry** panel from **Manufacturing** tab. The **Mill Window** contextual tab will be displayed; refer to Figure-86.

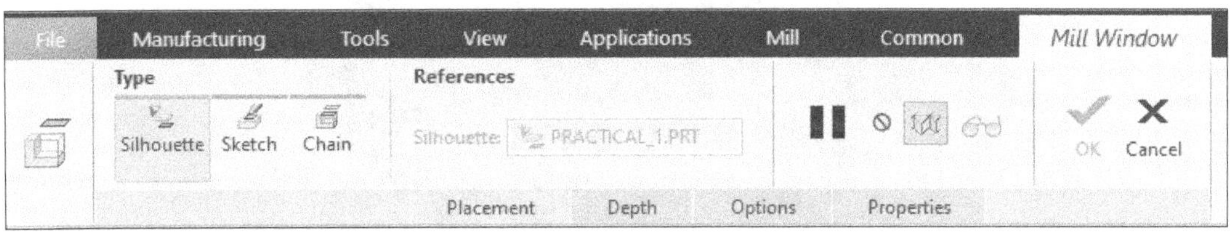

Figure-86. Mill Window contextual tab

- Click on **Window Plane** selection box of **Placement** tab and click on upper face of workpiece; refer to Figure-87.

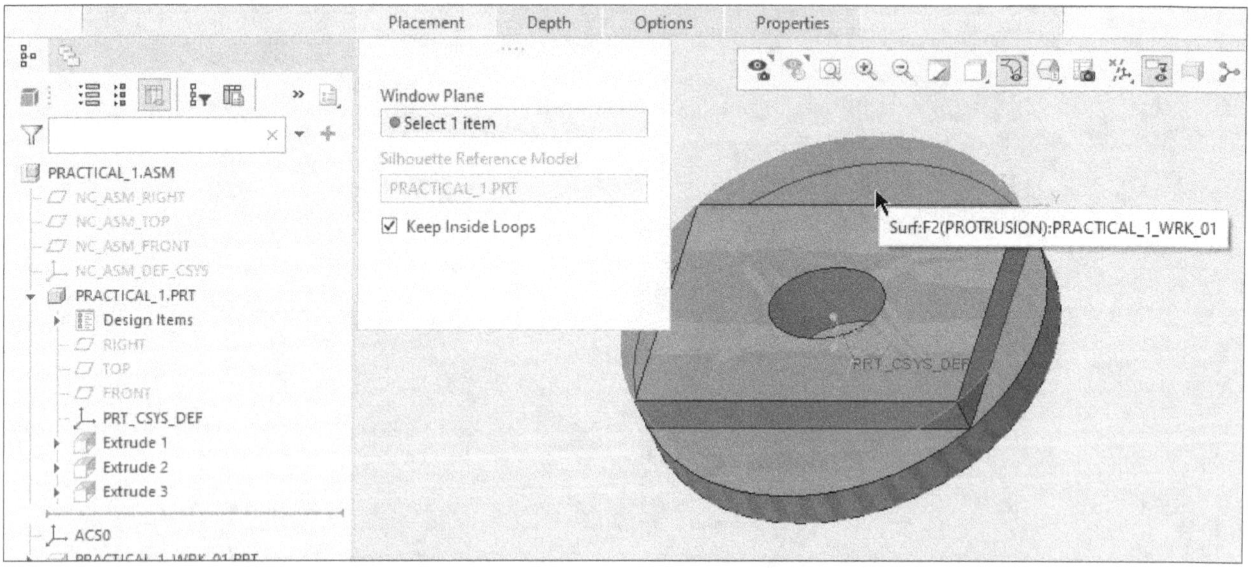

Figure-87. Selection of face in Mill Window

- Click on **OK** button from **Mill Window** contextual tab. The **NC Assembly** application window will be displayed.

PRACTICAL 2

Apply the Lathe operation in Figure-88.

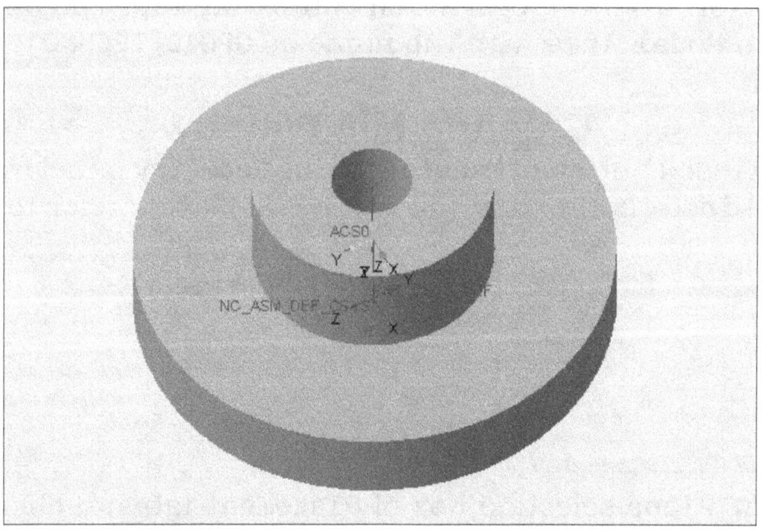

Figure-88. Practical 21

Start the NC Assembly application as discussed earlier.

Adding Reference Model

- Click on **Assemble Reference Model** button of **Reference Model** drop-down from **Manufacturing** tab. The **Open** dialog box will be displayed; refer to Figure-89.

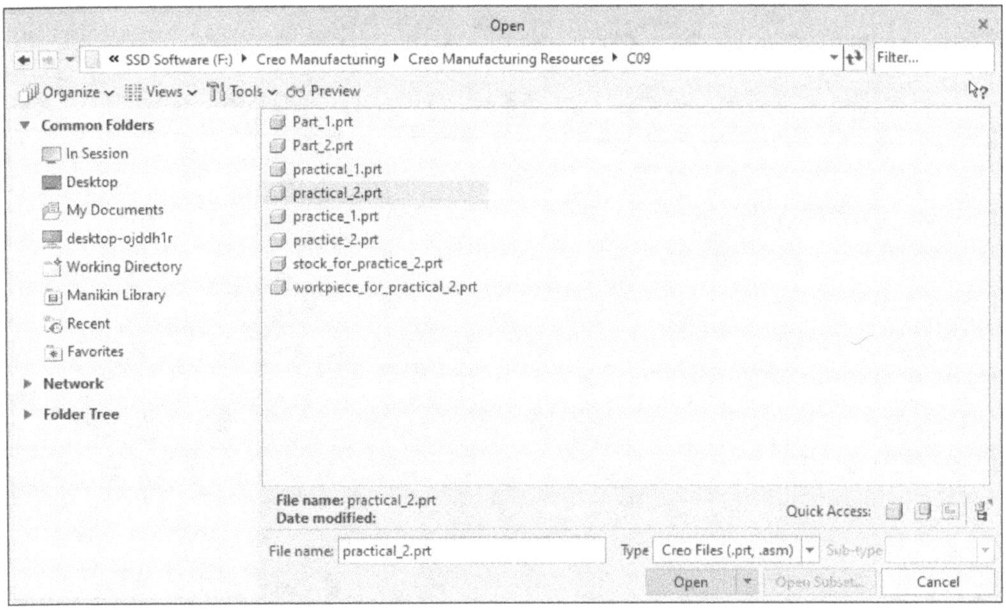

Figure-89. Open dialog box

- Select the **Practical 2** file and click on **Open** button from **Open** dialog box. The **Component Placement** contextual tab will be displayed.
- Click on **Current constraint** drop-down and select the **Default** option. The **Status: Fully constrained** will be displayed in **Component Placement** contextual tab; refer to Figure-90.

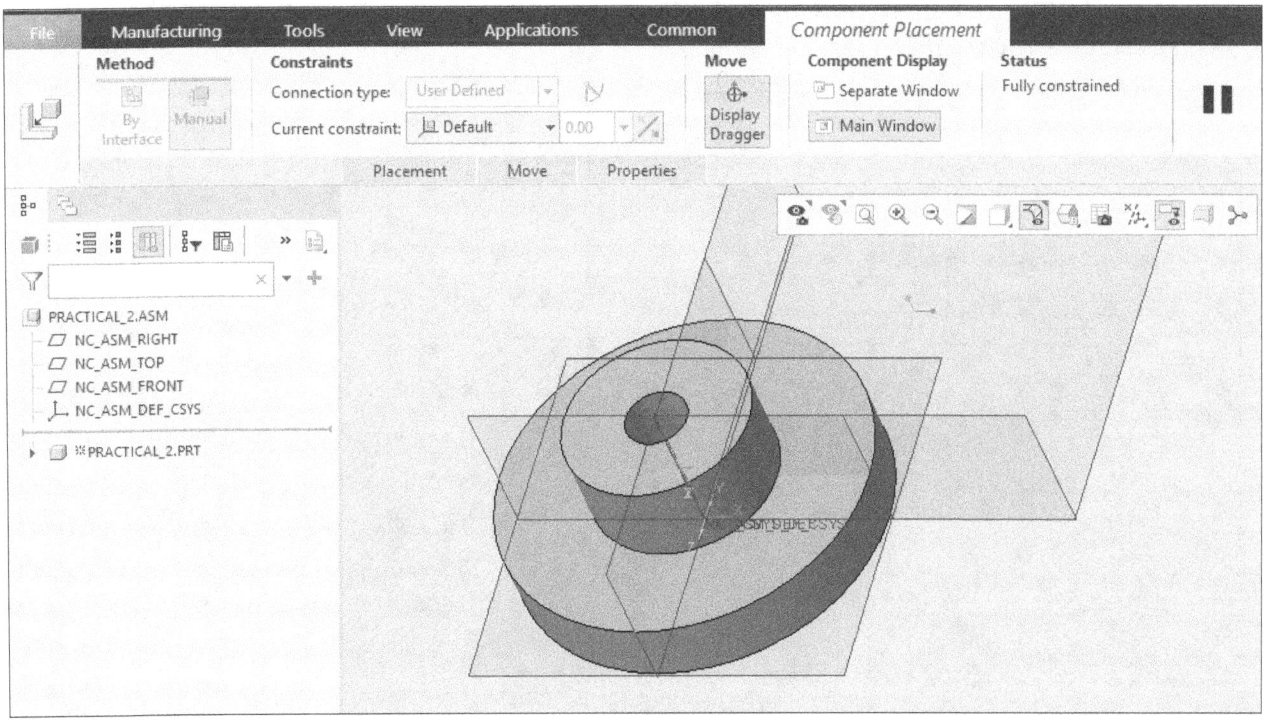

Figure-90. Constraining Practical 2

- Click on **OK** button from **Component Placement** contextual tab. The **NC Assembly** application window will be displayed along with the constrained model.

Creating Workpiece

- Click on the **Automatic Workpiece** button from **Workpiece** drop-down of **Manufacturing** tab. The **Auto Workpiece Creation** contextual tab will be displayed; refer to Figure-91.

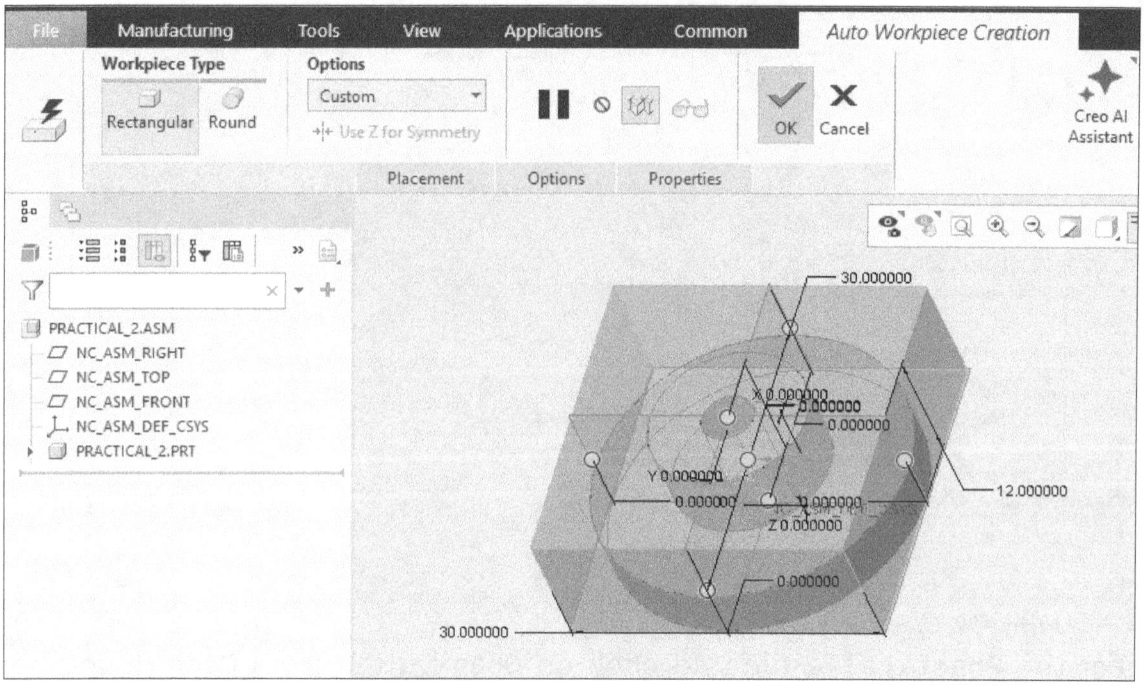

Figure-91. Creating workpiece for Practical 2 model

- Select **Round** option from **Workpiece Type** area of the **Auto Workpiece Creation** contextual tab.
- Click on the **Options** tab of **Auto Workpiece Creation** contextual tab.
- Click on **About X:** edit box of **Rotation Offsets** section and enter the value as **90**; refer to Figure-92.

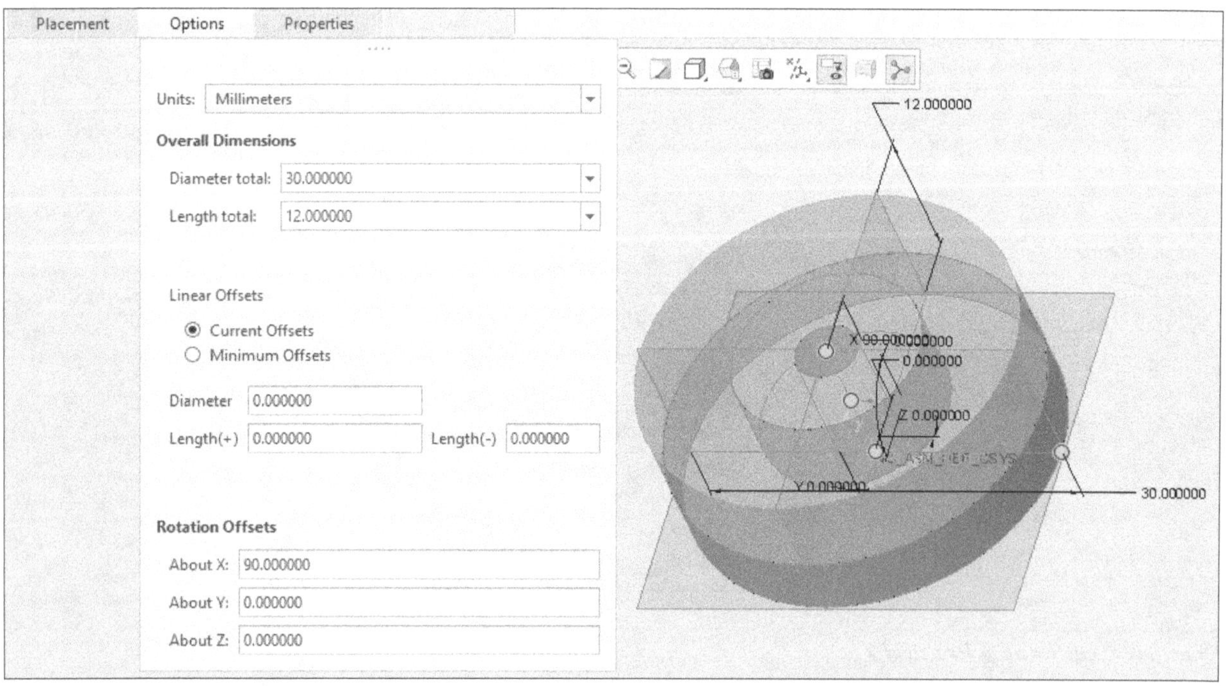

Figure-92. Creating round workpiece for model

- Click on **Length(+)** button of **Options** tab and enter the value as **0**.
- Click on **Length(-)** button of **Options** tab and enter the value as **0**.
- Click on the **OK** button from **Auto Workpiece Creation** contextual tab. The **NC Assembly** application window will be displayed along with model and workpiece.

Creating Lathe Operation

- Click on the **Lathe** tool from **Work Center** drop-down of **Manufacturing** tab. The **Lathe Work Center** dialog box will be displayed; refer to Figure-93.

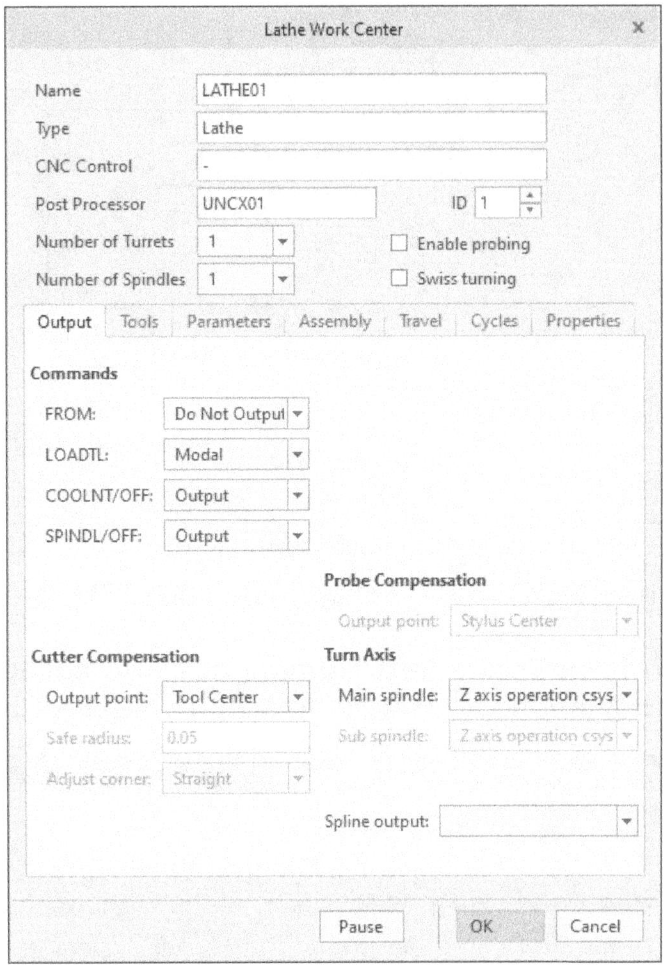

Figure-93. Lathe Work Center dialog box

- Click in the **Name** edit box and enter **TMT LATHE** as the name of machine.
- Click on **Tools** tab of **Lathe Work Center** dialog box and click on **Turret 1** button of **Tools** tab. The **Tools Setup** dialog box will be displayed.
- Enter the parameters of tool as shown in Figure-94.

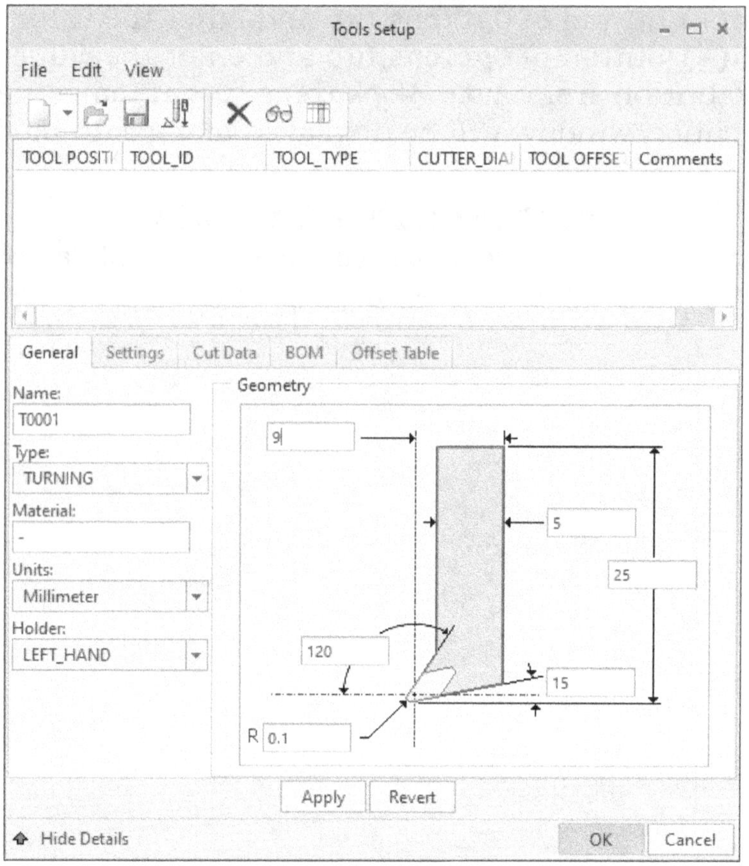

Figure-94. Tools Setup dialog box for Lathe

- Click on **Apply** button from **Tools Setup** dialog box. The tool will be added in the list.
- Click on **OK** button from **Tools Setup** dialog box and **Lathe Work Center** dialog box. The **NC Assembly** application window will be displayed; refer to Figure-95.

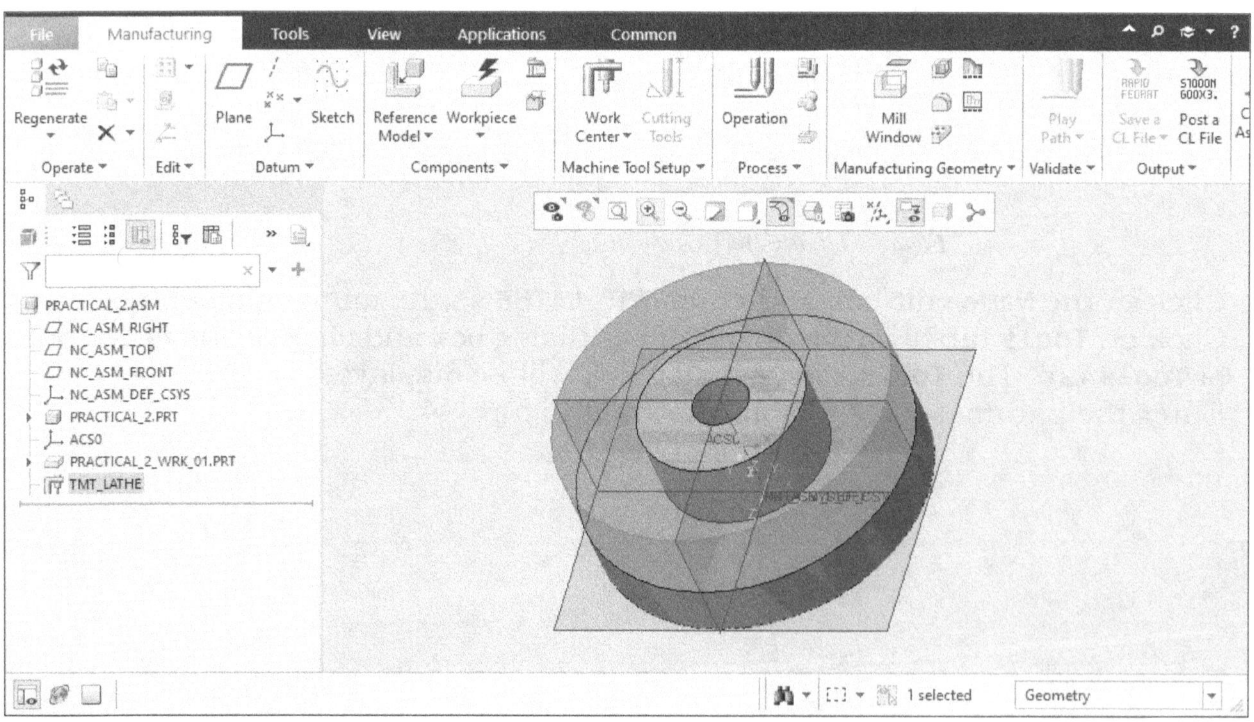

Figure-95. Model after adding machine

Creating Operation

- Click on the **Operation** button of **Process** panel from **Manufacturing** tab. The **Operation** contextual tab will be displayed; refer to Figure-96.

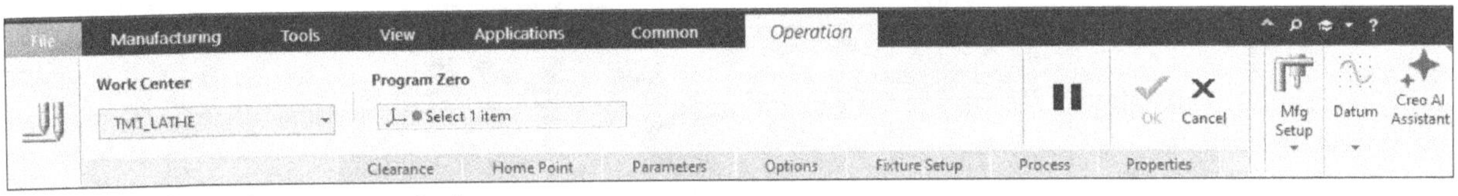

Figure-96. Operation contextual tab

- Click on coordinate system from model to set the program zero point and click on **OK** button from **Operation** contextual tab.

Creating Turn Profile

- Click on **Turn Profile** tool from **Manufacturing Geometry** panel of **Manufacturing** tab. The **Turn Profile** contextual tab will be displayed; refer to Figure-97.

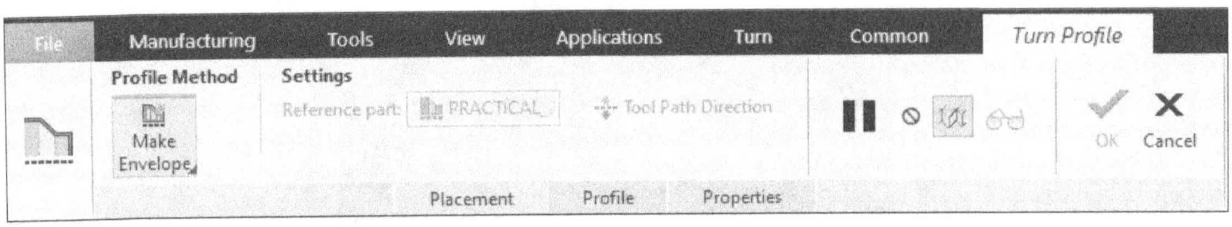

Figure-97. Turn Profile contextual tab

- Click on the **Placement** tab of **Turn Profile** contextual tab and select the coordinate system.
- Make sure the **Z** direction of your coordinate system is perpendicular to the flat face of model; refer to Figure-98.

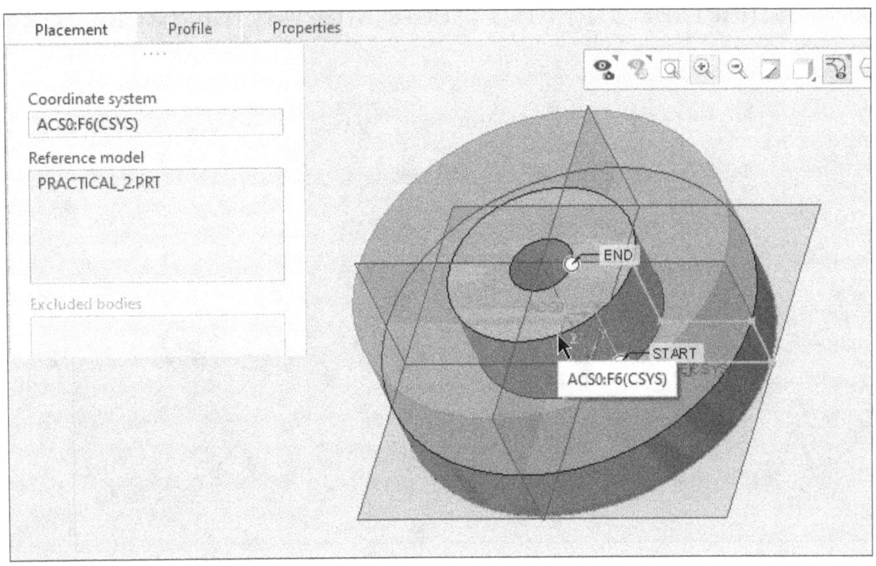

Figure-98. Selection of coordinate system

- Click on the **OK** button from **Turn Profile** contextual tab. The **Turn Profile** operation will be added in **Model Tree**.

PRACTICE 1

Create a tool in Lathe machine and also create its turn profile; refer to Figure-99.

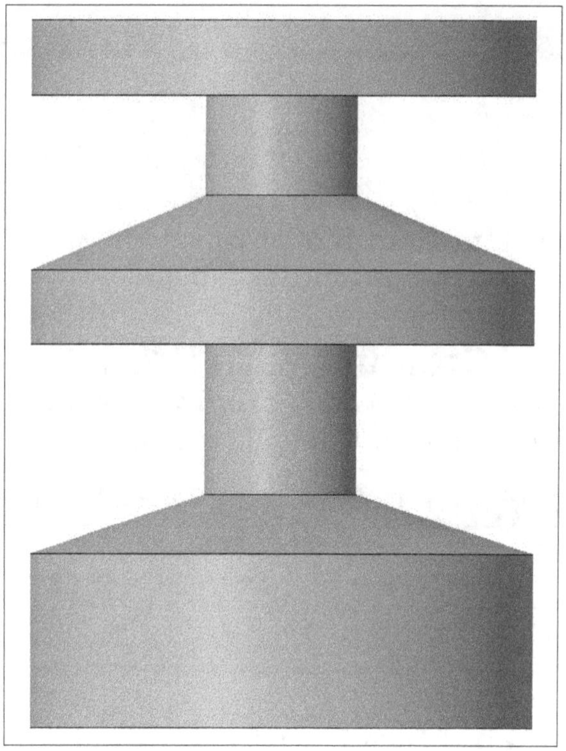

Figure-99. Practice 1

PRACTICE 2

Create a tool in Mill machine and also create Mill Window; refer to Figure-100.

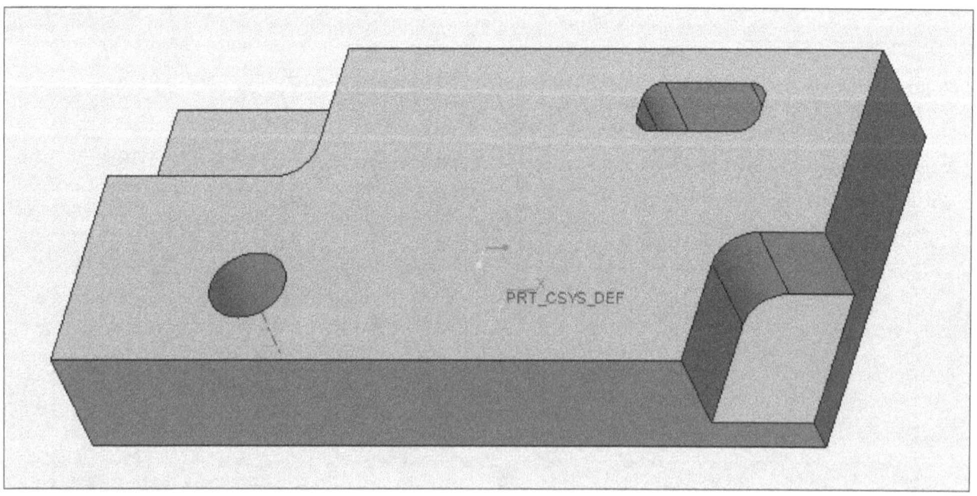

Figure-100. Practice 2

SELF-ASSESSMENT

Q1. What is the primary use of the Work Center tool in Creo?

A. To edit existing manufacturing operations
B. To generate tool paths automatically
C. To create various types of machine setups
D. To import machine models

Q2. Which of the following is NOT a machine type created using the Work Center tool?

A. Milling Machine
B. CNC Router
C. Lathe Machine
D. Wire EDM Machine

Q3. In the Milling Work Center, which field is used to specify the name of the CNC controller?

A. ID edit box
B. Post Processor edit box
C. Name edit box
D. CNC Control edit box

Q4. What does selecting the 'Enable probing' checkbox in Milling Work Center allow?
A. Multi-axis machining
B. Toolpath optimization
C. Defining CMM steps within an NC session
D. Faster tool changes

Q5. In the Mill-Turn setup, selecting 2 heads from the 'Number of Heads' drop-down results in:

A. Two milling tools being created automatically
B. Two sections appearing in the Tools tab for tool setup
C. The machine running in dual mode
D. Dual spindles being activated

Q6. What happens when you select 2 spindles from the 'Number of Spindles' drop-down in Mill-Turn setup?

A. Both spindles rotate simultaneously
B. Output tab enables Sub-spindle options
C. Head 2 is activated
D. Tool change time is reduced

Q7. What does the 'Per Spindle Program Zero' option in Output tab do?

A. Assigns zero to the first spindle only
B. Outputs steps with respect to the spindle that created them
C. Combines program zero for all spindles
D. Disables sub-spindle support

Q8. Which output point option selects the stylus center in probe compensation?

A. Stylus Center
B. Contact Point
C. Surface Point
D. Mid Point

Q9. What happens if you clear the 'Use Generic Cutter Compensation' checkbox?

A. Generic compensation values are applied
B. Separate cutter compensation values must be specified
C. Cutter compensation is disabled
D. Tool radius is auto-calculated

Q10. What is the default head setting for enabling milling in Mill-Turn Work Center?

A. Head 2 – Turning
B. Head 1 – Milling
C. Head 1 – Swiss Turning
D. Head 2 – Below Centerline

Q11. Which parameter defines the speed of the Sub-Spindle in Mill-Turn Parameters tab?

A. Horsepower
B. Machine Frequency
C. Maximum Speed (RPM)
D. Tool Change Time

Q12. What is the function of the 'DMIS' button in the Parameters tab?

A. Launches tool setup window
B. Displays toolpath animation
C. Opens DMIS TEXT Menu Manager
D. Enables custom post-processing

Q13. What does the 'Man' button do in Activate DMIS Text dialog box?

A. Outputs DMIS text to file
B. Displays text to CMM operator
C. Disables DMIS text
D. Displays machine frequency

Q14. In the Lathe Work Center, what does selecting the number of turrets define?

A. Number of tools in spindle
B. Number of tool holding heads
C. Number of turret stations on lathe
D. Number of work offsets

Q15. What does the Mill Window tool help define in a machining setup?

A. Tool radius
B. Region where tool can cut
C. Feed rate
D. Tolerance value

Q16. Which Mill Window method projects the part's shape along the Z-axis?

A. Chain
B. Sketch
C. Silhouette
D. Loop

Q17. In the Clearance tab of Operation, which option is used to define a cylindrical retract region?

A. Plane
B. Surface
C. Cylinder
D. Sphere

Q18. What does the Home Point tab allow you to set?

A. Maximum feed rate
B. Location for tool offset
C. Starting and ending position of the tool
D. Depth of cut

Q19. What is listed in the Manufacturing Process Table?

A. Machine specifications
B. All NC sequences and process steps
C. Only milling operations
D. Only toolpath simulations

Q20. What is the function of the User-Defined Work Center tool?

A. Customize the spindle parameters
B. Import work centers from a pre-saved library
C. Automatically set tool change values
D. Create custom machine parts

Q21. What is the main function of the Mill Volume tool in Creo?

A. To sketch toolpaths manually
B. To define a volume of the part to be machined
C. To simulate the CNC program
D. To assign materials to the part

Q22. Which button launches the volume creation process within the Mill Volume tab?

A. Create Feature Tool
B. Generate Milling Surface
C. Gather Volume Tool
D. Boundary Tool

Q23. What is the purpose of selecting the Exclude checkbox in the GATHER STEPS section?

A. To close all loops in the surface
B. To exclude outer loops or selected surfaces from the volume
C. To define a cap plane
D. To select edges for boundary

Q24. Which option in the GATHER SEL Menu Manager is used to include all surfaces of a selected feature in volume definition?

A. Mill Surf
B. Surfaces
C. Features
D. Surf & Bnd

Q25. What is the function of the Cap Plane checkbox in the CLOSURE Menu Manager?

A. To exclude top faces from milling
B. To define a reference for depth
C. To define the cap plane for volume closure
D. To filter the surface loops

Q26. What is the final step to confirm the gathered volume in the Mill Volume tool?

A. Click Done from CLOSURE Menu Manager
B. Click Close from Menu
C. Click OK from Mill Volume tab
D. Click Cancel from Feature Refs

Q27. What is the use of the Sloped tool under the Mill Surface contextual tab?

A. To sketch inclined features
B. To create tool axis manually
C. To adjust machining strategy based on surface orientation
D. To close sloped surface gaps

Q28. Which option in the GEN SEL DIR Menu Manager allows the selection of a curve, edge, or axis for direction reference?

A. Csys
B. Plane
C. Crv/Edg/Axis
D. Direction Point

Q29. In the Sloped tool, what does selecting Keep Steep Side mean?

A. Keep regions with angle less than specified
B. Ignore all flat regions
C. Keep only surface areas with angle greater than specified
D. Invert the direction vector

Q30. What is the purpose of the Machinable Area Reference tool?

A. Create a reference for drilling
B. Select an area that defines the fixture
C. Create a surface that includes only areas to be machined
D. Assign machine parameters

Q31. Which value needs to be entered in the Machinable Area dialog for gouging checks?

A. Tool clearance
B. Radius of ball end mill
C. Machining depth
D. Angle of entry

Q32. In Machinable Area Reference, which option is selected from GEN SEL DIR Menu Manager for plane direction?

A. Crv/Edg/Axis
B. Axis System
C. Plane
D. Coordinate Datum

Q33. What is the main purpose of the Drill Group tool in Creo?

A. Define surface machining parameters
B. Create a group of holes for drilling operations
C. Generate tool paths for lathe tools
D. Assign cutting speed to drills

Q34. Which option in the Definition section allows selection of holes by diameter?

A. Rule surfaces
B. Rule parameters
C. Patterned Axes
D. Rule diameters

Q35. Which Drill Group option is used when selecting specific holes manually?

A. Rule parameters
B. Individual Axes
C. Patterned Axes
D. Excluded Axes

For Students Notes

Chapter 11

Milling Operations

Topics Covered

The major topics covered in this chapter are:

- ***Milling Operations.***
- ***Profile Milling.***
- ***Surface Milling.***
- ***2-Axis Trajectory.***
- ***Standard Drilling Tool.***
- ***Deep Drilling Tool.***
- ***Practice and Practical.***

INTRODUCTION

In previous chapters, we have learned the procedure of setting up a machine for particular operation. In this chapter, we will learn about various operations and tools of mill machine.

SETUP A MILLING OPERATIONS

The procedure to setup a milling operation is discussed next.

- Click on the **Operation** tool from **Process** panel of **Manufacturing** tab; refer to Figure-1. The **Operation** contextual tab will be displayed; refer to Figure-2.

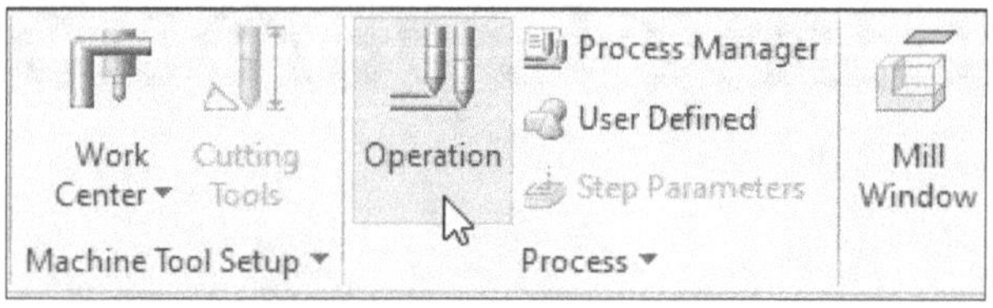

Figure-1. Operation tool

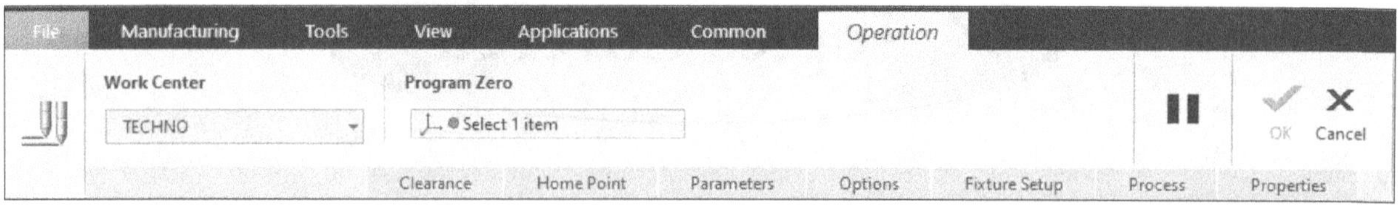

Figure-2. Operation contextual tab

- Select the coordinate system as a program zero point and click on **OK** button from **Operation** contextual tab. The **Mill** tab will be displayed after **Applications** tab; refer to Figure-3.

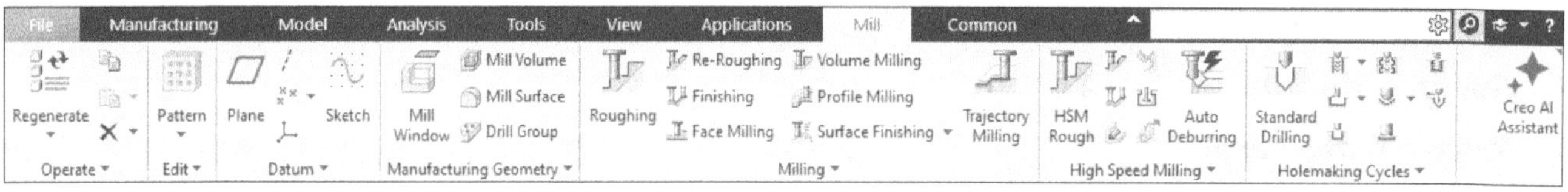

Figure-3. Mill tab

Note- The **Mill** tab is displayed when you have selected a milling machine to perform operations.

MILLING OPERATION

There are various milling operation in Creo Parametric like Face Milling, Surface Milling, Profile Milling, and so on. These operations are discussed next.

Roughing Toolpath

The **Roughing** tool is used to remove unwanted material from workpiece. The procedure to use this tool is discussed next.

- Click on the **Roughing** tool from **Milling** panel of **Mill** tab; refer to Figure-4. The **Roughing** contextual tab will be displayed; refer to Figure-5.

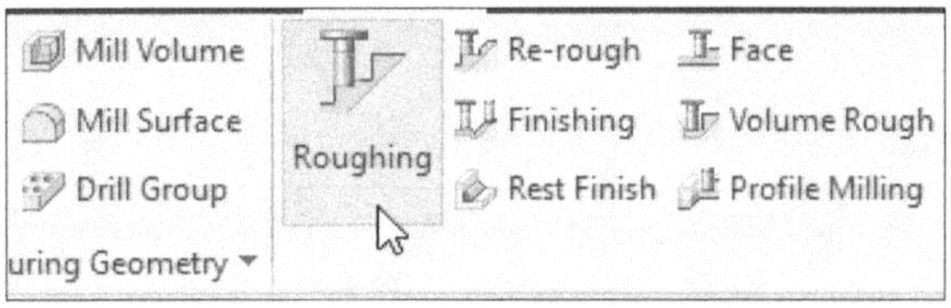

Figure-4. Roughing tool

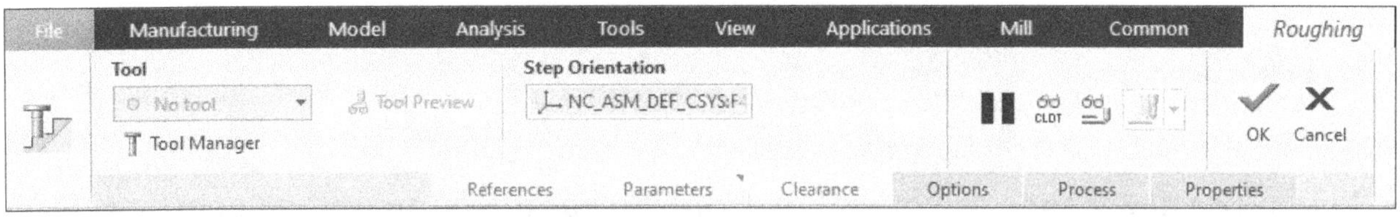

Figure-5. Roughing contextual tab

- Select the specific tool for roughing from **Tool** drop-down which you have created earlier.
- Click on the **References** tab of **Roughing** contextual tab. The earlier created **Mill Window** for workpiece will be automatically selected; refer to Figure-6. If not selected automatically, then select it.

Figure-6. References tab

- Now, click on the **Parameters** tab of **Roughing** contextual tab and specify the parameters for the roughing operations; refer to Figure-7.

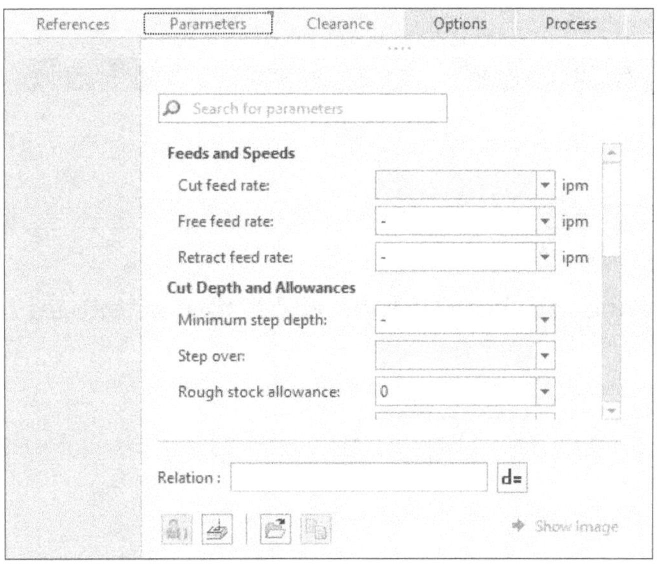

Figure-7. Parameters tab of Roughing contextual tab

- Click on the **Clearance** tab of **Roughing** contextual tab; refer to Figure-8.

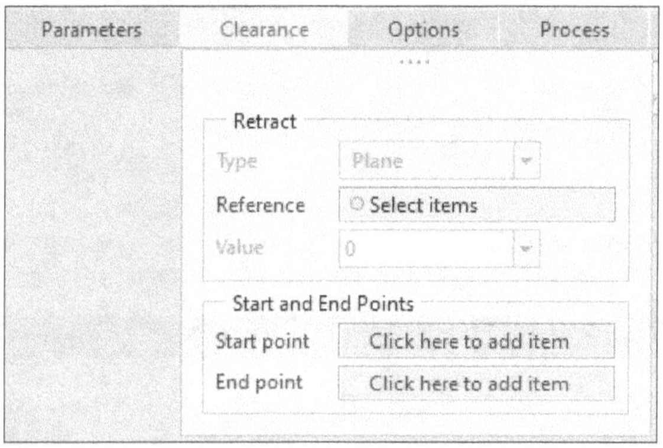

Figure-8. Clearance tab

- Click in the **Reference** selection box from **Retract** section and select the reference for cutting tool.
- After specifying the parameters, click on the **OK** button from **Roughing** contextual tab. The **Roughing** toolpath will be added in **Model Tree**.

Volume Milling

The **Volume Milling** tool is used to rough large amount of stock material. The procedure to use this tool is discussed next.

- Click on the **Volume Milling** tool from **Milling** panel in the **Mill** tab; refer to Figure-9. The **Volume Milling** contextual tab will be displayed; refer to Figure-10.

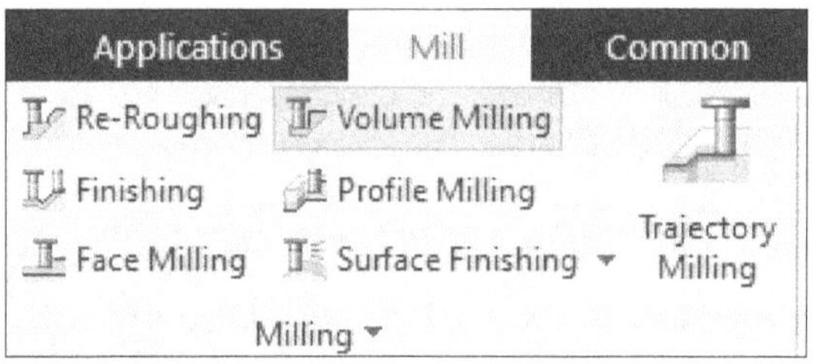

Figure-9. Volume Milling tool

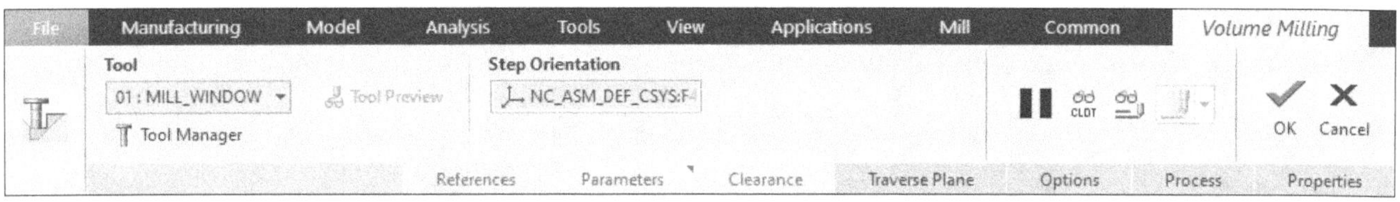

Figure-10. Volume Milling contextual tab

- Click on the **Reference** tab from **Volume Milling** contextual tab; refer to Figure-11.

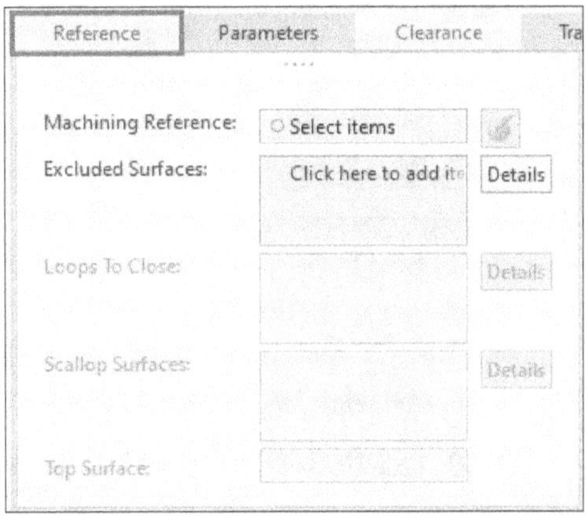

Figure-11. Reference tab for Volume Milling

- Click in the **Machining Reference** selection box of **Volume Milling** tab and select the top surface of workpiece.
- Click on the **Parameters** tab of **Volume Milling** contextual tab and specify the necessary parameters.
- Click on the button from **Volume Milling** contextual tab, if you want to see the toolpath for part.
- After specifying the parameters, click on the **OK** button. The **Volume Milling** toolpath will be added in **Model Tree**.

Face Milling

The **Face Milling** tool is used to apply a face milling operation on the workpiece. The procedure to use this tool is discussed next.

- Click on the **Face Milling** tool from **Mill** tab; refer to Figure-12. The **Face Milling** contextual tab will be displayed; refer to Figure-13.

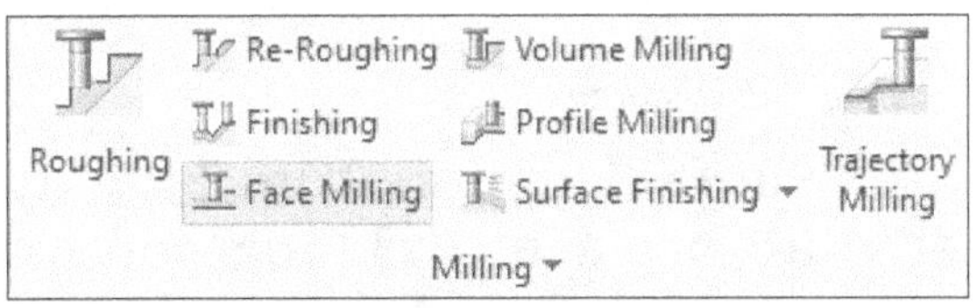

Figure-12. Face Milling tool

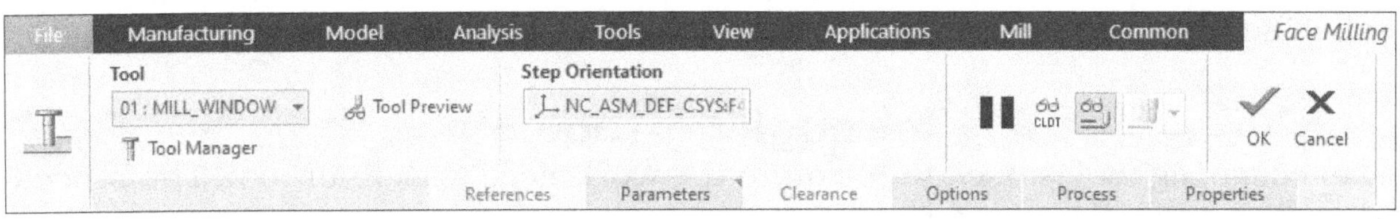

Figure-13. Face Milling contextual tab

- Click on the **Reference** tab of **Face Milling** contextual tab; refer to Figure-14.

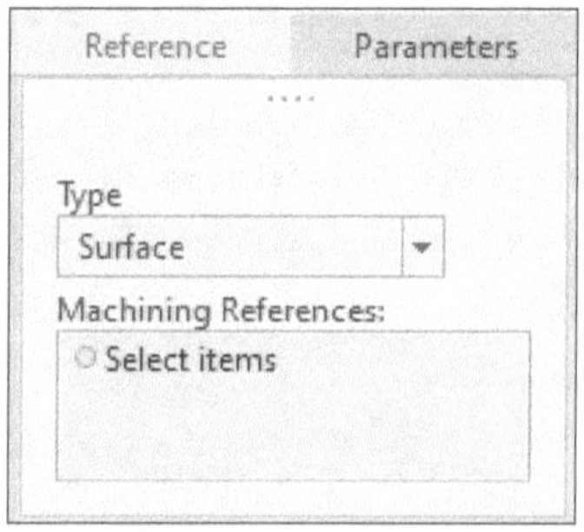

Figure-14. Reference tab for Face Milling

- Select the **Surface** option from **Type** drop-down if you want to select the surface as a reference.
- Select the **Mill Window** option from **Type** drop-down if you want to select the mill window as a machining reference.
- In our case, we are selecting **Mill Window**. Click on the **Machining References** selection box and select the earlier created mill window from **Model Tree**; refer to Figure-15.

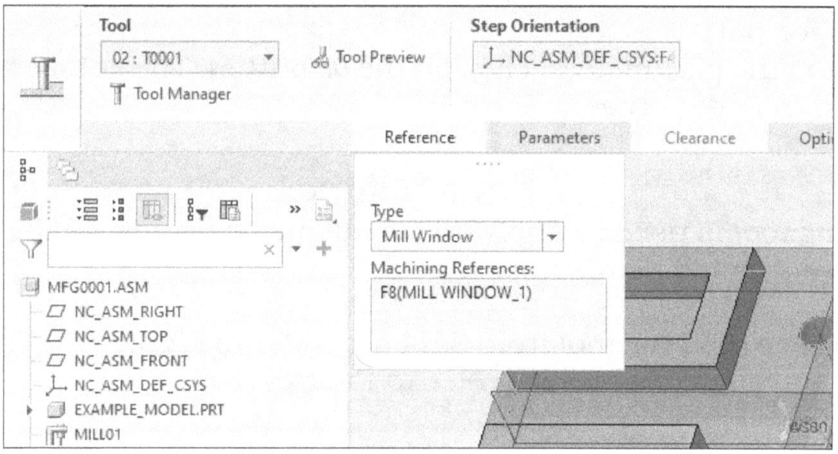

Figure-15. Selection of mill window

- Similarly, you can use the **Surface** option from **Type** drop-down.
- Click on the **Parameters** tab of **Face Milling** contextual tab and specify the necessary parameters.
- After specifying the parameters, click on **OK** button from **Face Milling** contextual tab. The **Face Milling** operation will be added in **Model Tree**.

Re-roughing Toolpath

The **Re-roughing** tool is used to re-rough the workpiece with finer tool. The procedure to use this tool is discussed next.

- Click on the **Re-roughing** tool from **Mill** tab; refer to Figure-16. The **Re-Roughing** contextual tab will be displayed; refer to Figure-17.

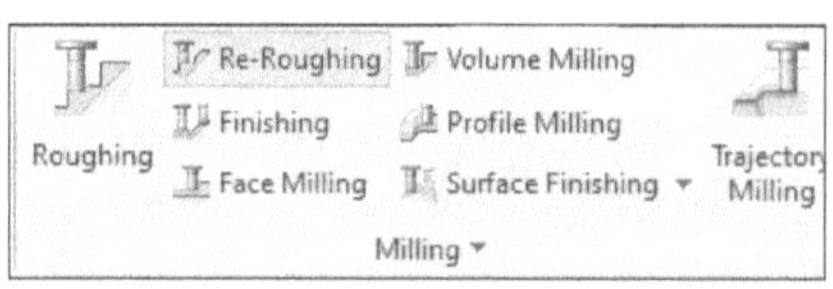

Figure-16. Re-Roughing tool

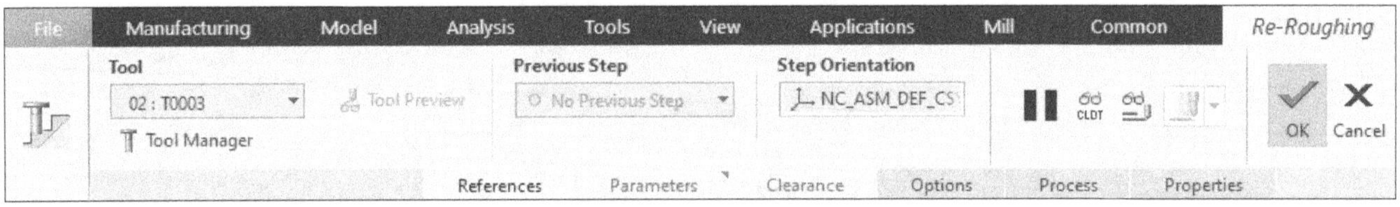

Figure-17. Re-Roughing contextual tab

- Select the machining tool from **Tool** drop-down.
- Select the roughing operation earlier performed from the **Previous Step** drop-down in the **Re-Roughing** contextual tab of **Ribbon**.
- Click on the **Parameters** tab from **Re-Roughing** contextual tab and specify the necessary parameters for machining process.
- After specifying the parameters, click on the **OK** button. The re-roughing operation will be added in **Model tree**.

Profile Milling

The **Profile Milling** tool is used to remove material from outer walls of the workpiece. The procedure to use **Profile Milling** tool is discussed next.

- Click on the **Profile Milling** tool from **Mill** tab; refer to Figure-18. The **Profile Milling** contextual tab will be displayed; refer to Figure-19.

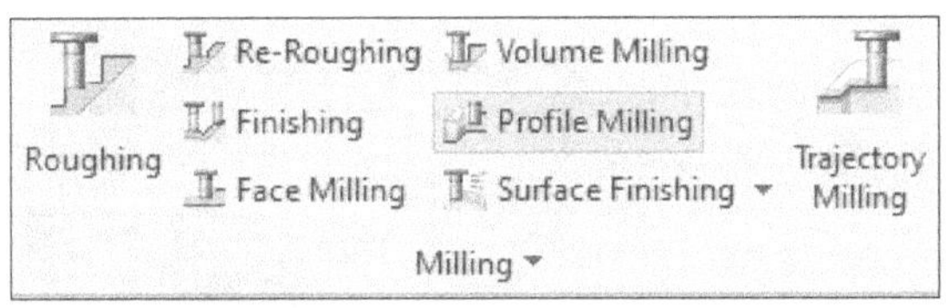

Figure-18. Profile Milling tool

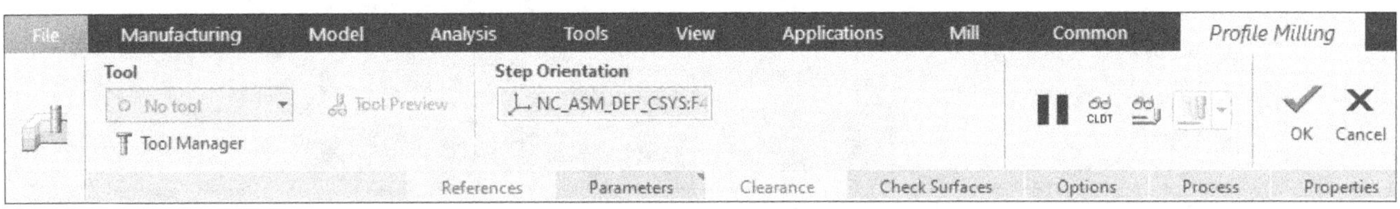

Figure-19. Profile Milling contextual tab

- Select the tool from **Tool** drop-down.
- Click on the **Reference** tab from **Profile Milling** contextual tab; refer to Figure-20.

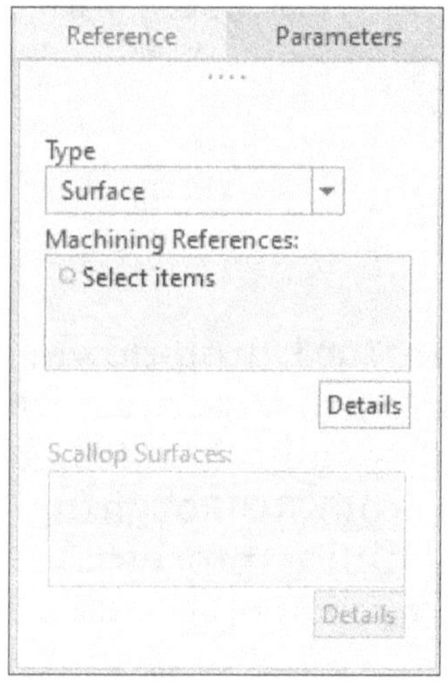

Figure-20. Reference tab of Profile Milling

- Select the **Surface** option from **Type** drop-down.
- Click in the **Machining References** section and select the surface of workpiece; refer to Figure-21.

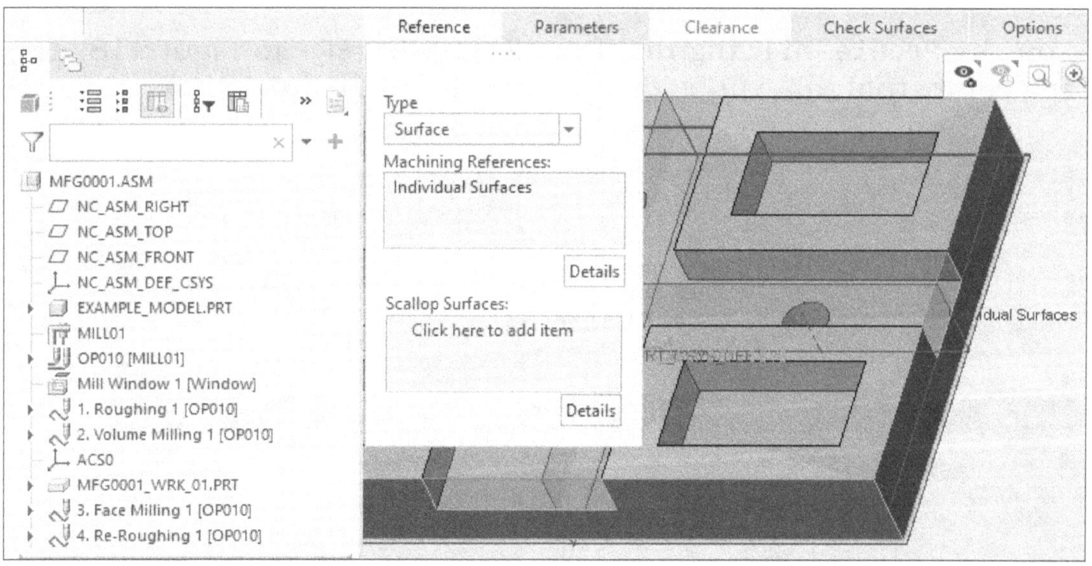

Figure-21. Selection of surface for profile milling

- Click on the **Parameters** tab and specify necessary parameters for profile milling.
- After specifying the parameters, click on the **OK** button from **Profile Milling** contextual tab. The profile milling operation will be added in **Model Tree**.

Surface Finishing Toolpath

The **Conventional Milling** tool is usually used to semi-finish or finish the surfaces. The procedure to use this tool is discussed next.

- Click on the **Conventional Milling** tool from the **Surface Finishing** drop-down in the **Milling** panel of **Mill** tab in **Ribbon**; refer to Figure-22. The **Conventional Milling** contextual tab will be displayed; refer to Figure-23

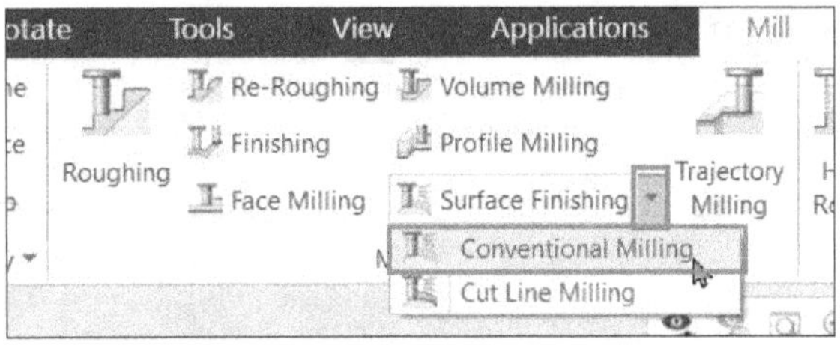

Figure-22. Surface Milling tool

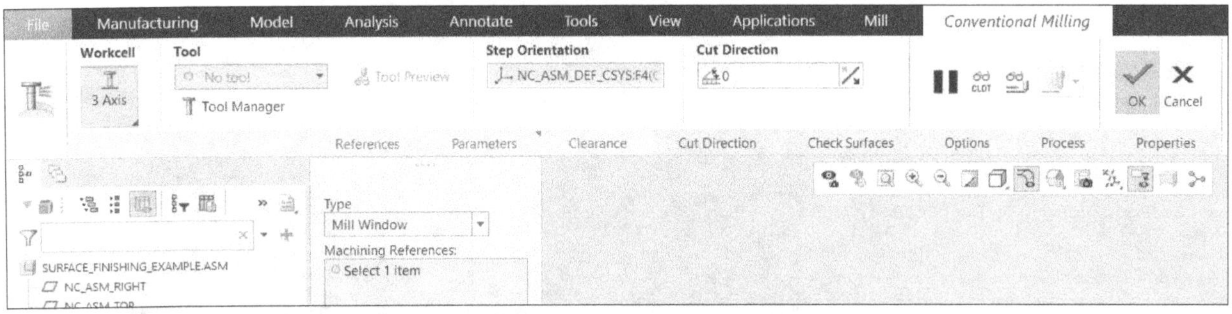

Figure-23. Conventional Milling contextual tab

- Select desired machine type to be used for generating surface toolpaths from the **Workcell** drop-down. Based on selected machine, there will be additional variables for A and B angles in G-code output.
- Select a ball end mill or other round tip cutting tool from the **Tool** drop-down in the **Ribbon**.
- Select the **Mill Window** option from the **Type** drop-down in the **References** tab to use earlier created mill window as reference region to be machined. Select the **Surface** option from the drop-down to select surface to be machined. Select the reference geometry from model in graphics area after selecting desired option from the drop-down.
- Click in the **Scallop Surfaces** selection field of the **References** tab and select surfaces that you want to exclude from scallop height calculation. Scallop height is the distance between peak of surface ridge and depth of valley on the irregular surface.
- Set desired parameters like cutting feed rate, cutting depth, allowances, cutting motion and so on in the fields of **Parameters** tab as discussed earlier.
- Define clearance plane where tool will move after each cutting pass to ensure safety of workpiece using the options in **Clearance** tab as discussed earlier.
- After setting desired parameter, click on the **Preview mode** button from **Ribbon**. The preview of toolpath will be displayed; refer to Figure-24.
- Click on the **OK** button from the **Ribbon** to generate the toolpath.

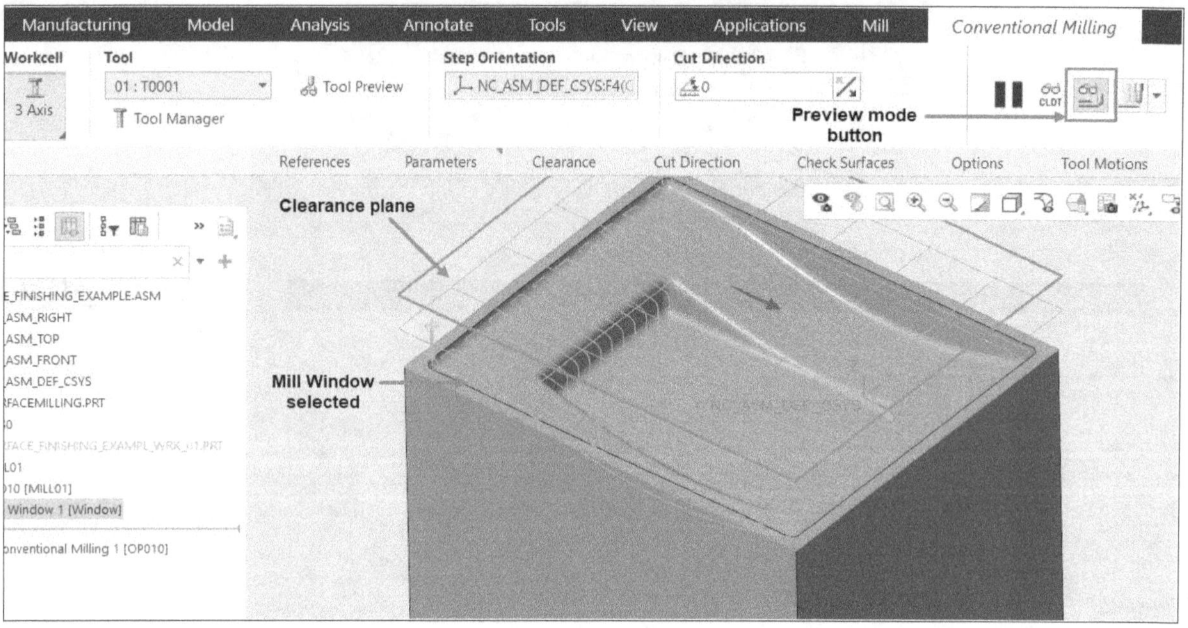

Figure-24. Preview of conventional milling toolpath

Finishing

The **Finishing** tool is used to give the final touch to the workpiece. The procedure to use this tool is discussed next.

- Click on the **Finishing** tool from **Milling** panel in the **Mill** tab; refer to Figure-25. The **Finishing** contextual tab will be displayed; refer to Figure-26.

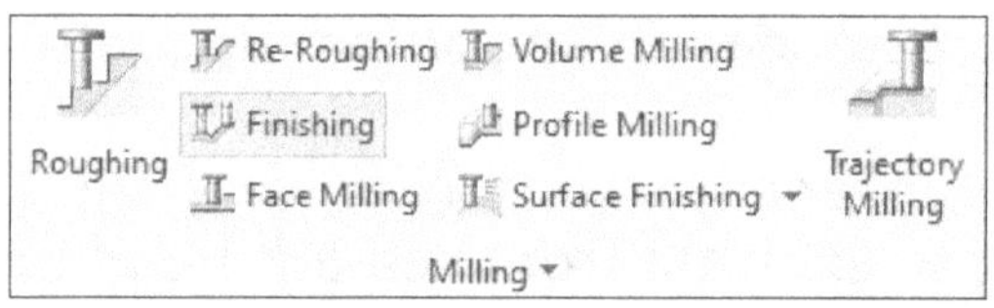

Figure-25. Finishing tool

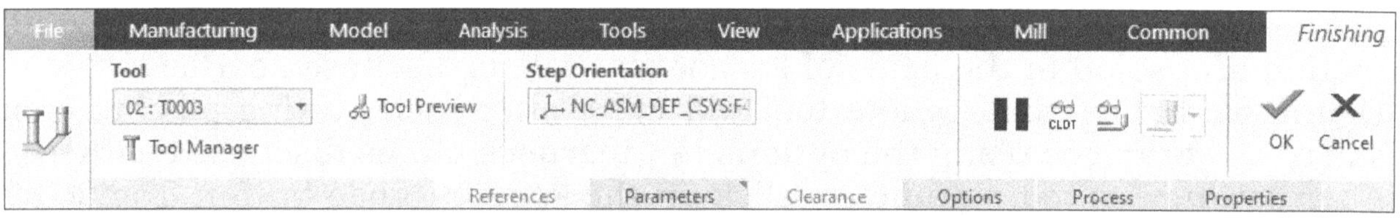

Figure-26. Finishing contextual tab

- Click on **Tool** selection box and select desired tool.
- Click on **References** tab and select the **Mill Window**.
- Click on **Parameters** tab and specify desired parameters for machining.
- If clearance plane has not been defined earlier then set desired clearance plane.
- Click on **OK** button from **Finishing** contextual tab. The **Finishing** operation will be added in **Model Tree**; refer to Figure-27.

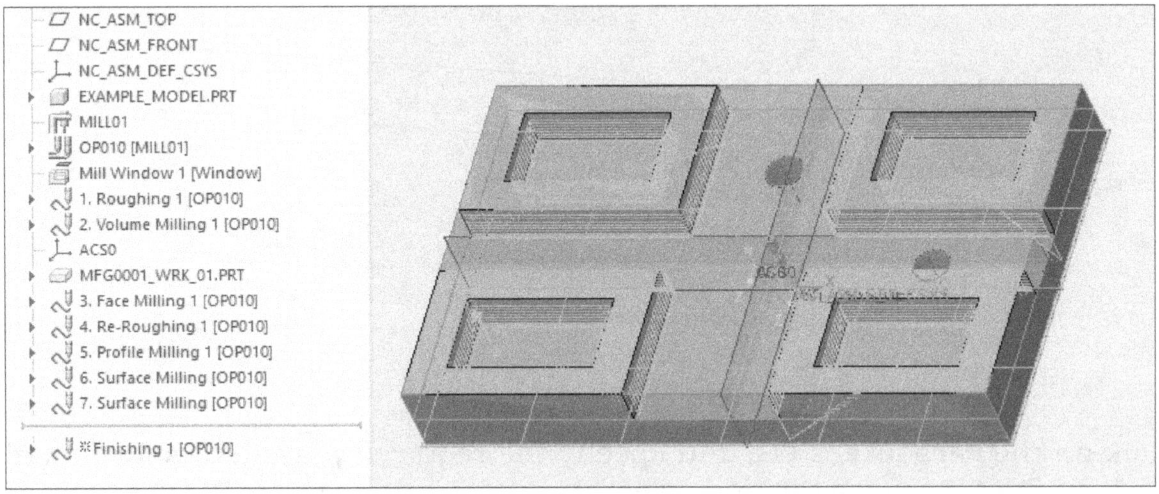

Figure-27. Preview of toolpath

Corner Finishing

The **Corner Finishing** tool is used on corners of workpiece. The procedure to use this tool is discussed next.

- Click on the **Corner Finishing** tool from **Milling** expanded panel of **Mill** tab; refer to Figure-28. The **Corner Finishing** contextual tab will be displayed; refer to Figure-29.

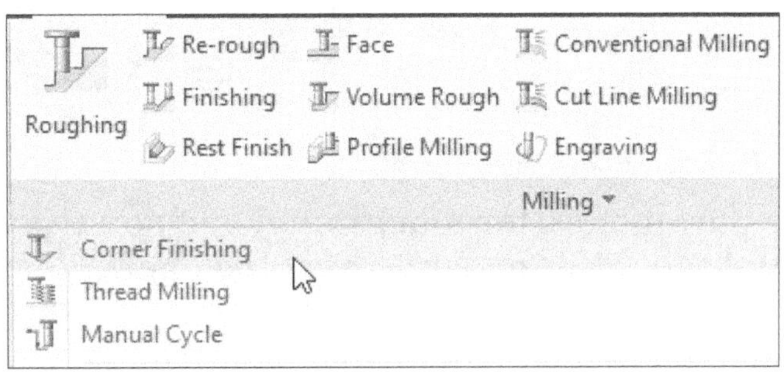

Figure-28. Corner Finishing tool

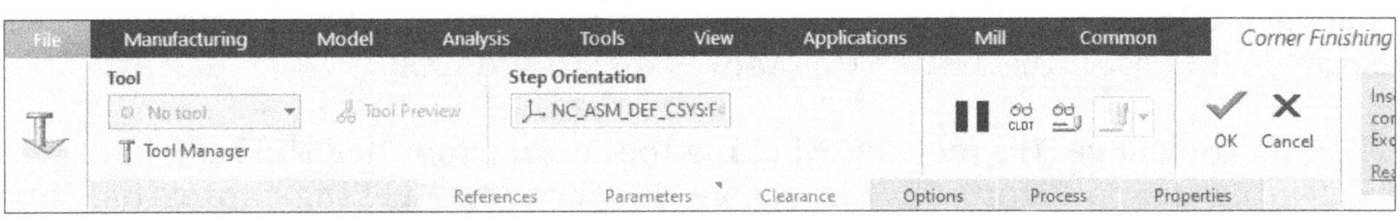

Figure-29. Corner Finishing contextual tab

- Click on the **Tool** drop-down and select desired tool for machining.
- Click on the **References** tab of **Corner Finishing** contextual tab and select desired tool in **Reference Cutting Tool** drop-down; refer to Figure-30.

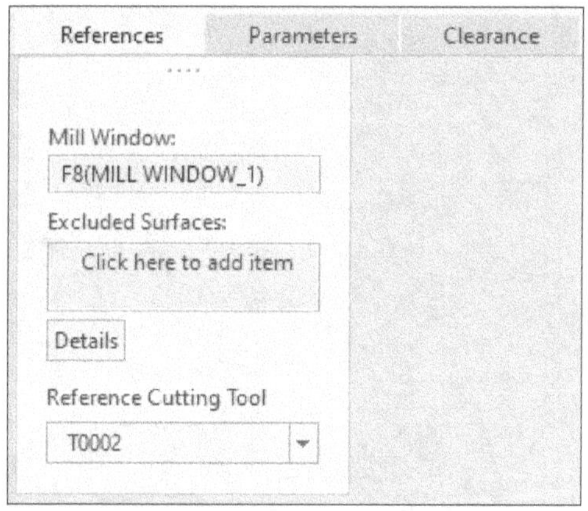

Figure-30. References tab of corner finishing

- Click on the **Parameters** tab and specify the required parameters for machining.
- Click on the **Clearance** tab and select the retract plane using **Reference** selection box of **Retract** section; refer to Figure-31.

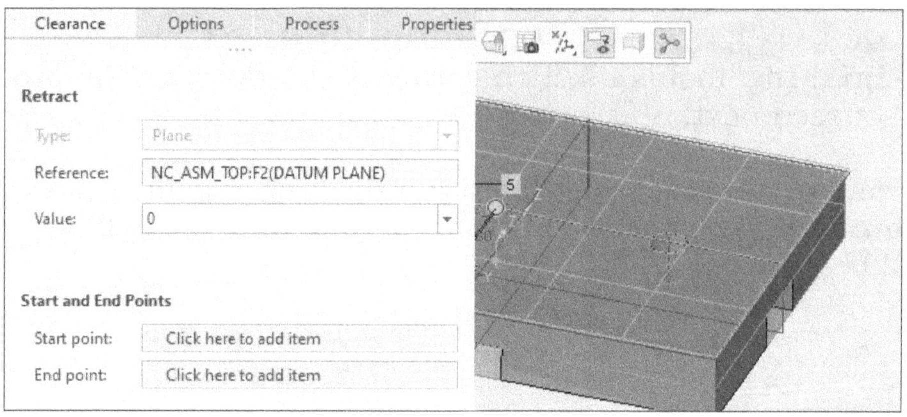

Figure-31. Selection of retract plane

- After specifying the parameters for machining, click on the **OK** button from **Corner Finishing** contextual tab. The **Corner Finishing** operation will be added in **Model Tree**.

2-Axis Trajectory Toolpath

The **Curve Trajectory Milling** tool is used to remove material by following a selected trajectory. The procedure to use this tool is discussed next.

- Click on the **Curve Trajectory Milling** tool from expanded **Milling** panel in the **Mill** tab; refer to Figure-32. The **Curve Trajectory Milling** contextual tab will be displayed; refer to Figure-33.

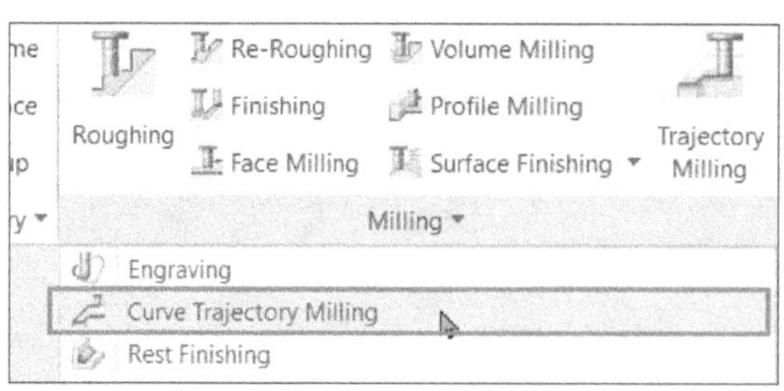

Figure-32. Curve Trajectory Milling tool

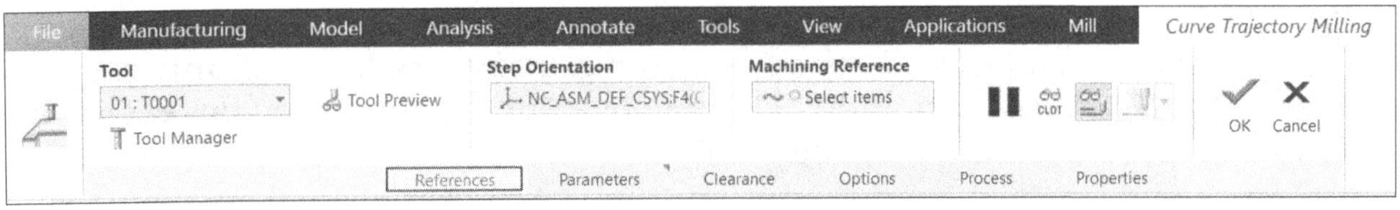

Figure-33. Curve Trajectory Milling contextual tab

- Click on the **Tool** drop-down and select the required tool for machining.
- Click on the **References** tab of **Curve Trajectory Milling** contextual tab. Click on the **Machining Reference** selection box and select the reference for trajectory; refer to Figure-34. To select multiple references, click on the **Details** button and select the references while holding the **CTRL** key.

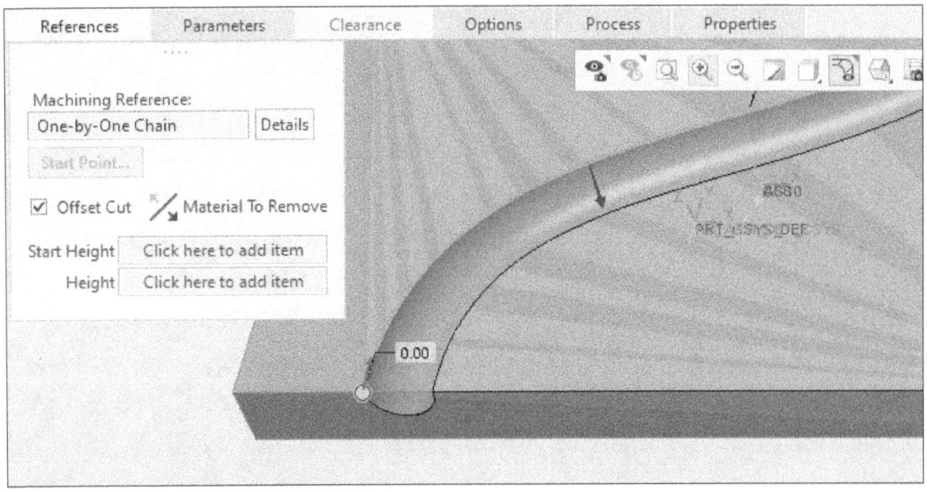

Figure-34. Selection of reference for trajectory

- Click on **Parameters** tab and specify desired parameters for machining.
- After specifying the parameters, click on **OK** button from **Curve Trajectory Milling** contextual tab. The curve trajectory operation will be added in **Model Tree**.

Trajectory Milling

The procedure to use **Trajectory Milling** tool is discussed next.

- Click on the **Trajectory Milling** tool from **Milling** panel in the **Mill** tab; refer to Figure-35. The **Trajectory Milling** contextual tab will be displayed; refer to Figure-36.

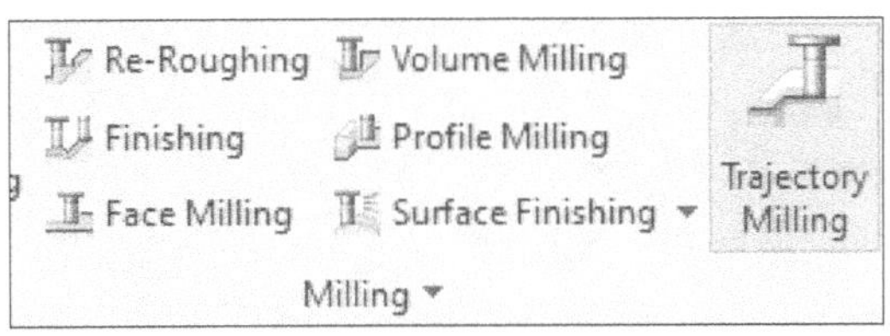

Figure-35. Trajectory Milling tool

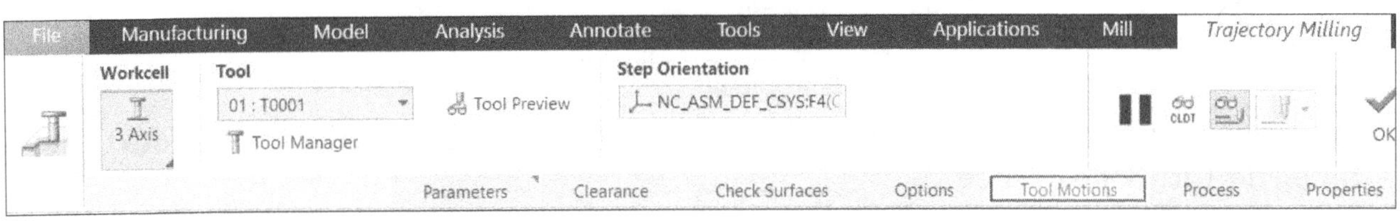

Figure-36. Trajectory Milling contextual tab

- Select desired tool for machining from tools selection box.
- Click on **Parameters** tab and specify desired parameters for machining.
- Click on **Tool Motions** tab and click on **Curve Cut** button. The **Curve Cut** dialog box will be displayed; refer to Figure-37.

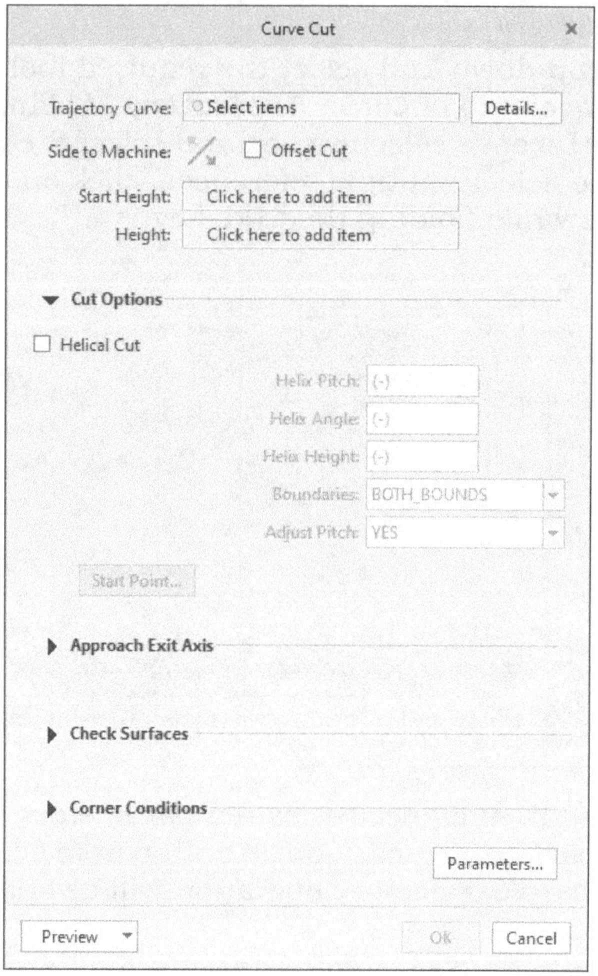

Figure-37. Curve Cut dialog box

- Click in the **Trajectory Curve** selection box and select the trajectory for machining.
- Set the other parameters as desired and click on **OK** button from the **Curve Cut** dialog box and **Tool Motions** tab will be displayed; refer to Figure-38.

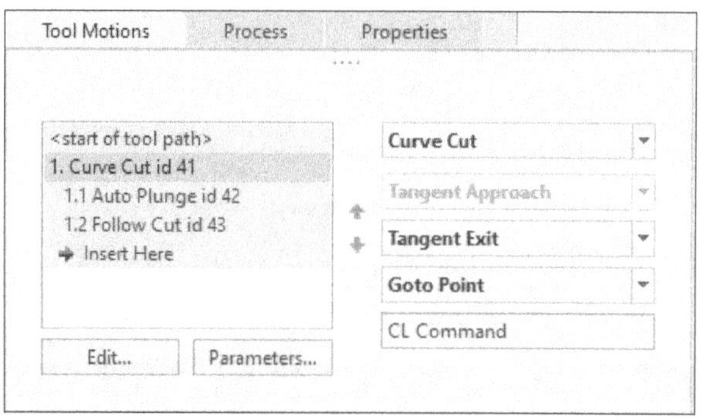

Figure-38. Tool Motions tab

- Click on **OK** button from **Trajectory** contextual tab. The trajectory operation will be added in **Model Tree**.

Engraving

The **Engraving** tool is used to machine grooves or curves on the metal surface. This can also be used to machine letters on the surface of metal. The procedure to use this tool is discussed next.

- Click on the **Engraving** tool from expanded **Milling** panel of **Mill** tab; refer to Figure-39. The **Engraving** contextual tab will be displayed; refer to Figure-40.

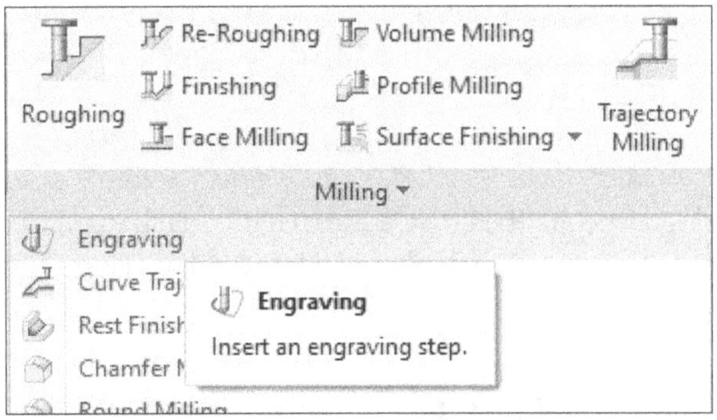

Figure-39. Engraving tool

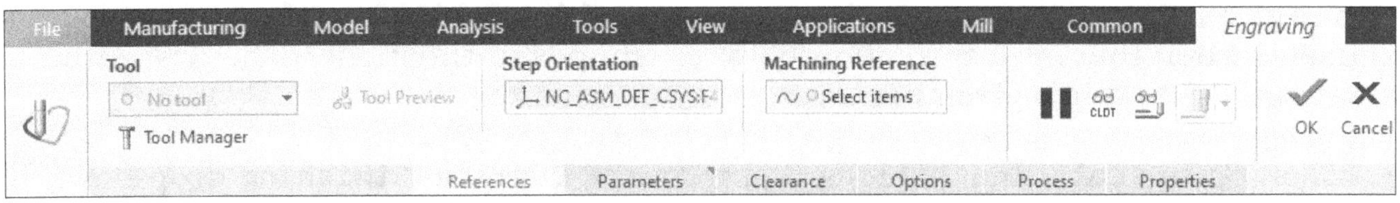

Figure-40. Engraving contextual tab

- Click on the **Tool** drop-down and select desired tool for machining.
- Click on the **References** tab and select the groove to be machined; refer to Figure-41.

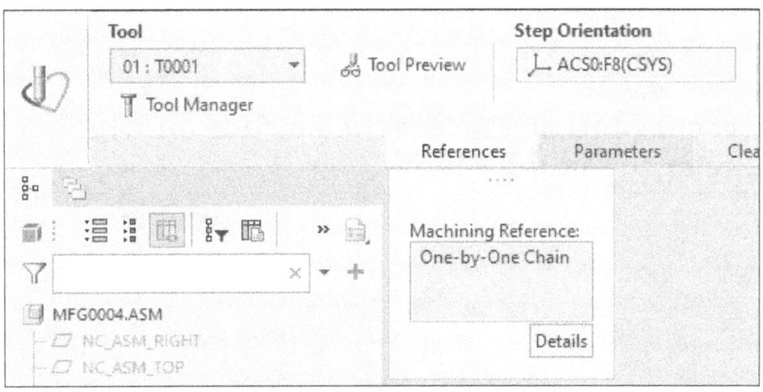

Figure-41. References tab for engraving tool

- Click on the **Parameters** tab and specify desired parameters as discussed earlier.
- Click on the **Clearance** tab and select the retract plane in **References** section; refer to Figure-42.

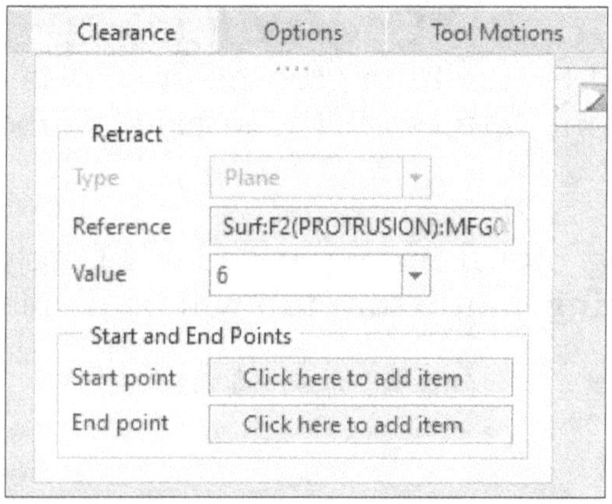

Figure-42. Selection of retract plane for engraving

- Click in the **Value** edit box of **Retract** section and specify the value for retract.
- After specifying the parameters, click on the **OK** button. The **Engraving operation** will be added in **Model Tree**.

Cut Line Milling

The **Cut Line Milling** tool is used to create toolpath which follows selected edges/ curves as reference for cutting tool contact point with machining surface. This toolpath is useful when there is a transition between shapes in the model. The procedure to create this toolpath is given next.

- Click on the **Cut Line Milling** tool from the **Surface Finishing** drop-down in the **Milling** panel of the **Ribbon**. The **Cut Line Milling** contextual tab will be displayed in the **Ribbon**; refer to Figure-43.

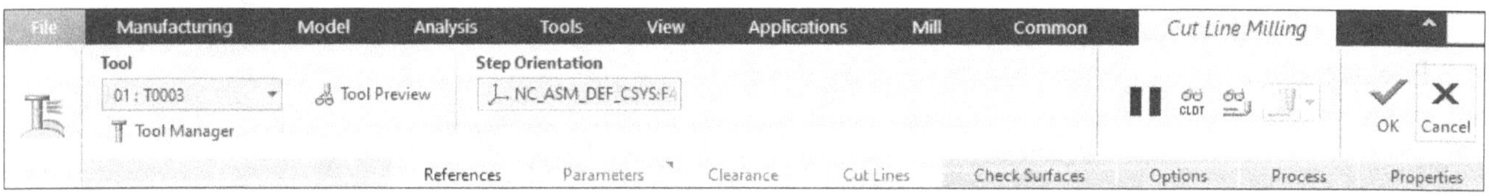

Figure-43. Cut Line Milling contextual tab

- Click on the **Reference** tab and select the surface on which you want to perform cut line milling; refer to Figure-44.

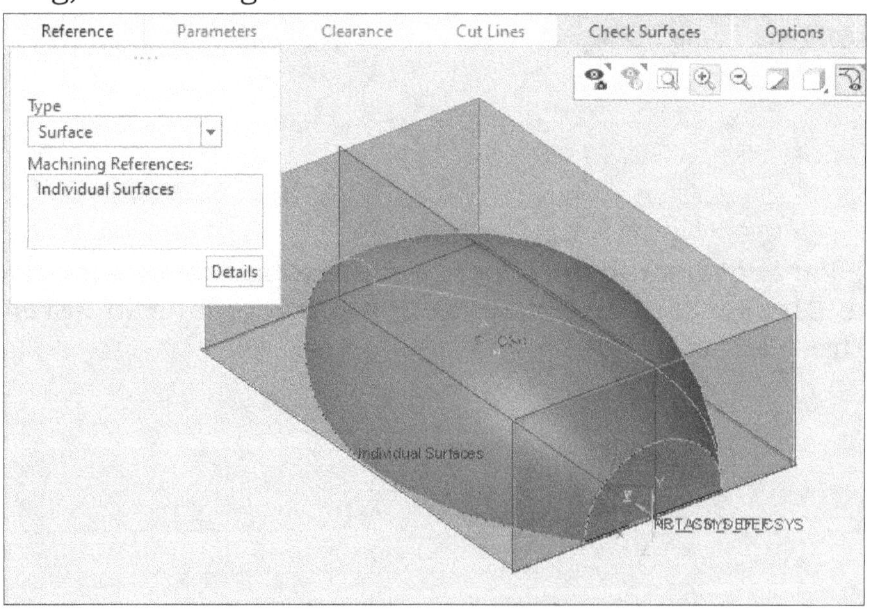

Figure-44. Surface selected

- Click on the **Clearance** tab and set desired location for retraction plane as discussed earlier.
- Click on the **Cut Lines** tab and select the curves to be used as reference for cutting tool contact points; refer to Figure-45. Click on the ***New Cutline** option from the tab to add more cut lines.
- Select the **Auto Cut Line** check box to automatically select/create cut lines for the model.
- Select the **Tool Center Curve** check box to generate the profile of model which can be machined by current cutting tool and milling machine. You can then select the cut lines from generated profile.
- Specify other parameters as discussed earlier and click on the **OK** button. The toolpath will be generated.

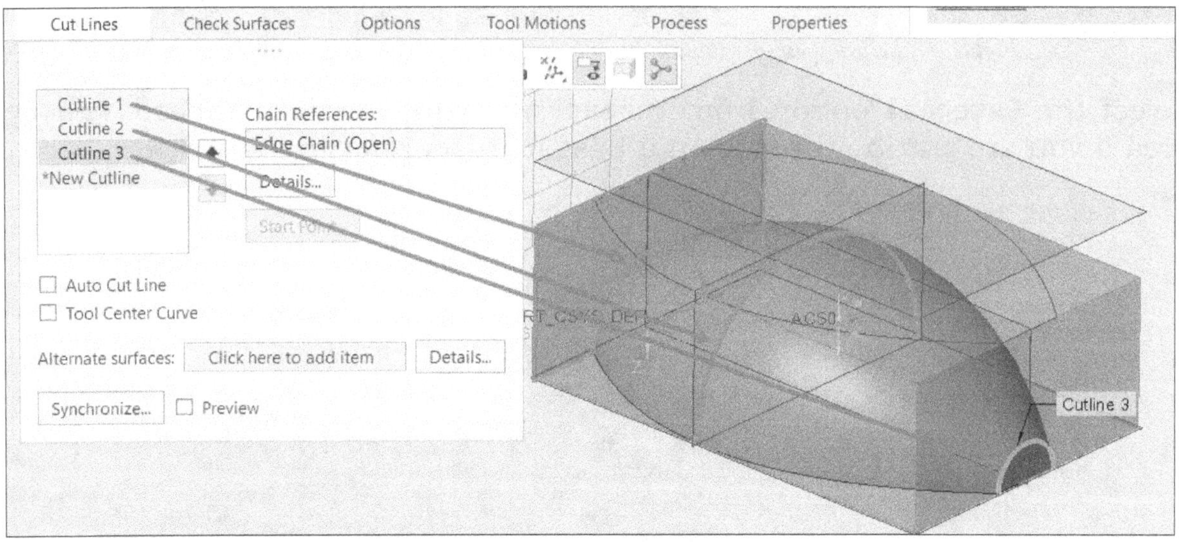

Figure-45. Cut lines selected

Thread Milling

The **Thread Milling** tool is used to create threads in holes or boss features in the model. The procedure to use this tool is given next.

- Click on the **Thread Milling** tool from the expanded **Milling** panel of **Mill** tab in the **Ribbon**. The **Thread Milling** contextual tab will be displayed; refer to Figure-46.

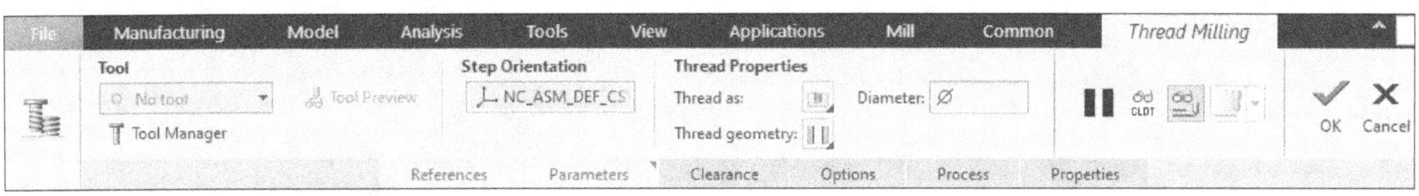

Figure-46. Thread Milling contextual tab

- Click in the **Tool** drop-down and select desired thread cutting tool from the list. If there is no tool available for threading then select the **Edit Tools** option from drop-down and create desired cutting tool.
- Click on the **References** tab and select axis of the boss/hole feature on which you want to cut threads; refer to Figure-47.

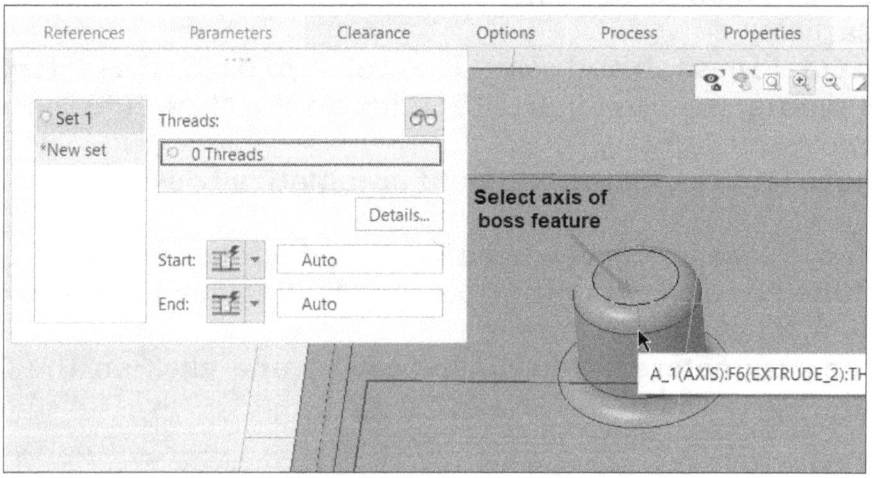

Figure-47. Selecting axis for thread

- Select the **External** option from **Thread as** flyout menu of **Thread Properties** area if you are cutting threads on a boss feature; refer to Figure-48.

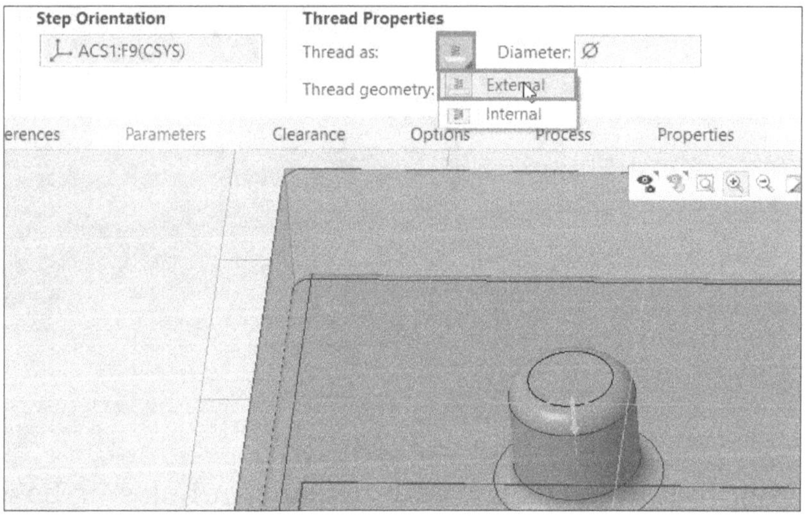

Figure-48. External thread option

- Select the **Internal** option from **Thread as** flyout menu if you are cutting threads on walls of a hole; refer to Figure-49.

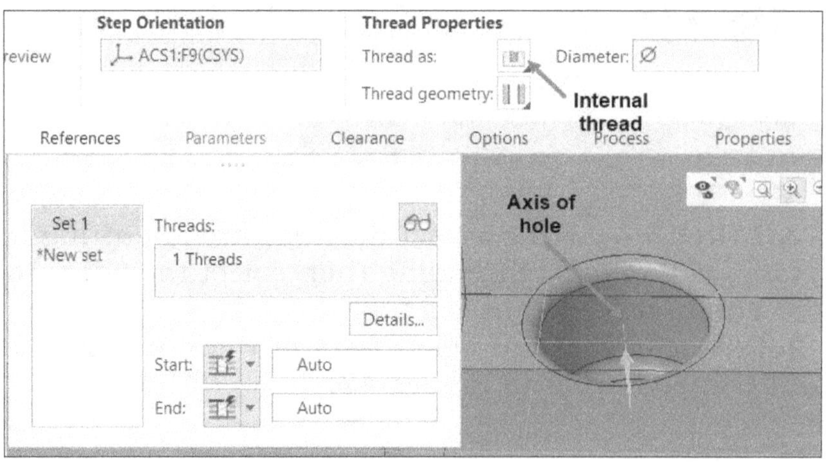

Figure-49. Internal thread option

- Click in the **Diameter** edit box of contextual tab and specify diameter of thread. Preview of internal thread will be displayed; refer to Figure-50.

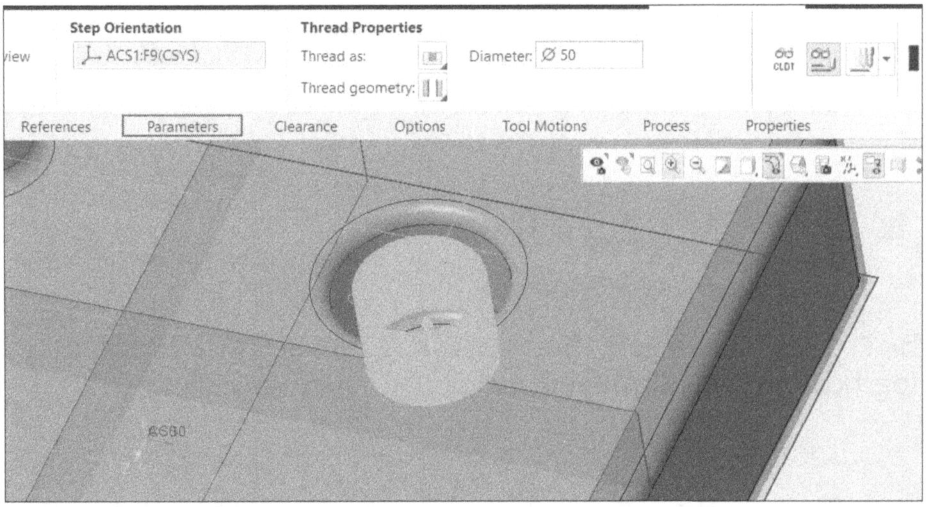

Figure-50. Preview of internal thread

- Select desired option from the **Thread Geometry** flyout to define shape of thread; refer to Figure-51.

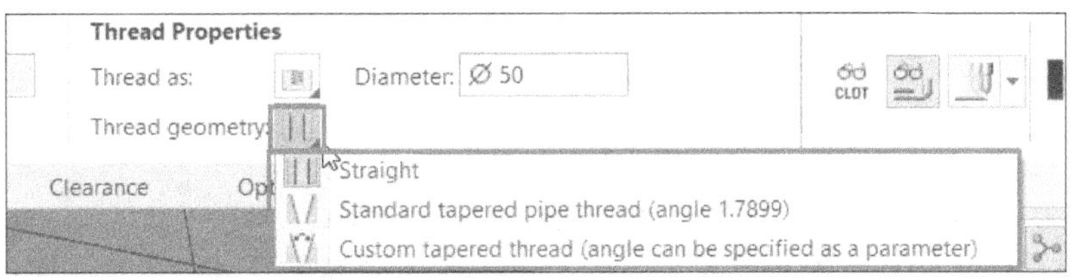

Figure-51. Thread geometry flyout

- Set the other parameters as discussed earlier and click on the **OK** button to create the thread toolpath.

Manual Cycle Toolpath

The **Manual Cycle** tool is used to manually define steps of tool motion. The procedure to use this tool is given next.

- Click on the **Manual Cycle** tool from the expanded **Milling** panel of **Mill** tab in the **Ribbon**. The **Manual Cycle** contextual tab will be displayed in the **Ribbon**; refer to Figure-52.

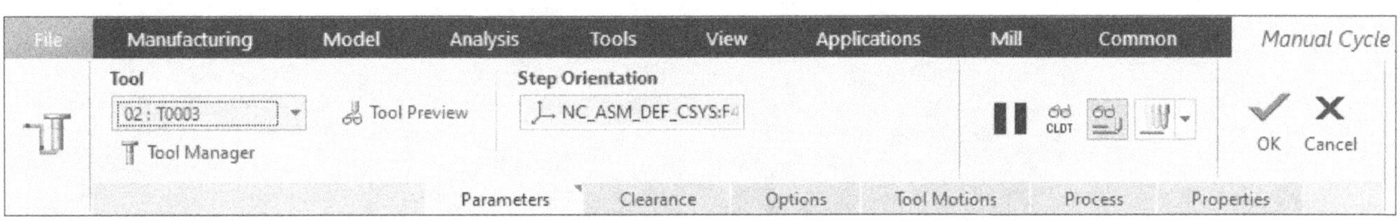

Figure-52. Manual Cycle contextual tab

- Select desired cutting tool and specifying cutting parameters as discussed earlier.
- Click on the **Tool Motions** tab to define steps of motion. The options will be displayed as shown in Figure-53.

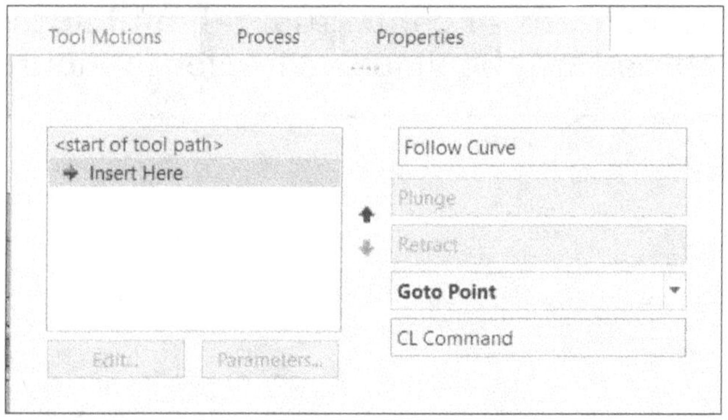

Figure-53. Tool Motions tab

- Click on the **Follow Curve** selection button from the **Tool Motions** tab. The **Follow Curve** dialog box will be displayed; refer to Figure-54.

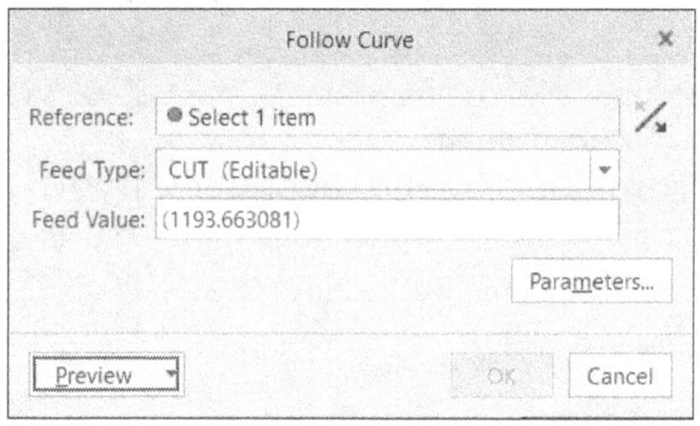

Figure-54. Follow Curve dialog box

- Select desired curve feature from the model so that cutting tool follows the selected curve during operation. Set the other related parameters in dialog box and click on the **OK** button to create motion step.
- Click on the **Retract** button from the **Tool Motions** tab if you want the tool to retract after performing motion.
- Similarly, select other motion step type from the **Motion Type** drop-down; refer to Figure-55 and specify related parameters.

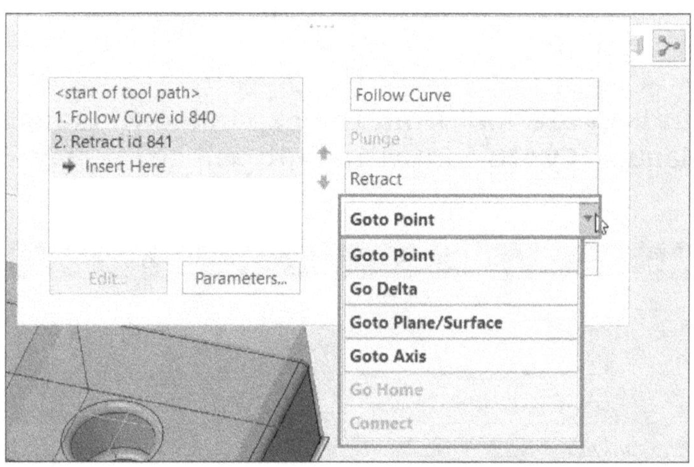

Figure-55. Motion type drop-down

- After creating desired motion steps, click on the **OK** button from **Ribbon** to create the toolpath.

Similarly, you can use other tools in **Milling** panel of **Mill** tab to create related toolpaths.

Standard Drilling

The **Standard Drilling** tool is used to drill holes in the workpiece. The procedure to use this tool is discussed next.

- Click on the **Standard Drilling** tool from **Holemaking Cycles** panel in the **Mill** tab; refer to Figure-56. The **Drilling** contextual tab will be displayed; refer to Figure-57.

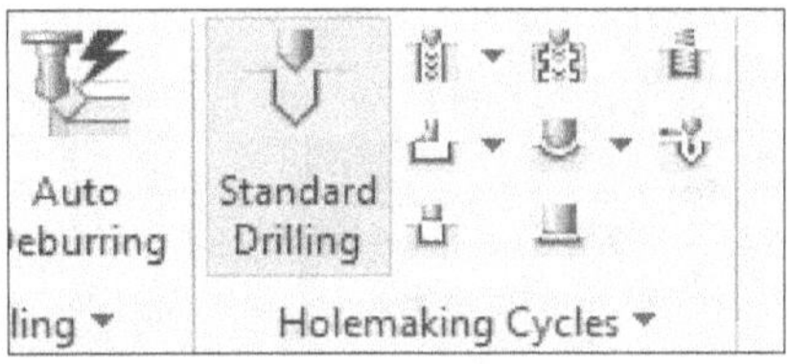

Figure-56. Standard tool

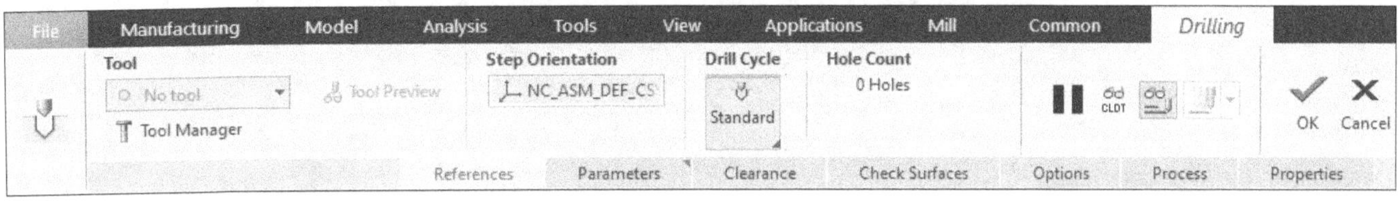

Figure-57. Drilling contextual tab

- Click on the **Tool** drop-down from **Drilling** contextual tab and select the required tool for drilling.
- Click on **References** tab of **Drilling** contextual tab; refer to Figure-58.

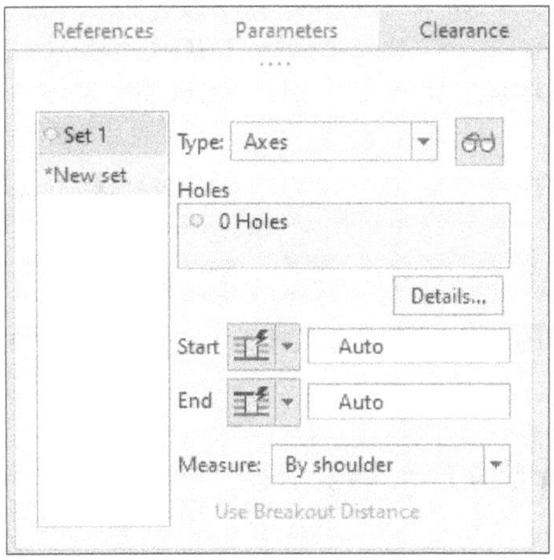

Figure-58. References tab of Drilling contextual tab

- Select **Axes** option from **Type** drop-down, if you want to select axes as references for drilling.
- Select **Points** option from **Type** drop-down, if you want to select points as references for drilling.
- Select **Geometry** option from **Type** drop-down, if you want to select geometry as reference for drilling.
- In our case, we are selecting **Axes** option from **Type** drop-down.
- Click in the **Holes** selection box and select the axes of hole for drilling.
- Click on the **Parameters** tab and specify the required parameters for drilling.
- After specifying the parameters for drilling, click on **OK** button from **Drilling** contextual tab. The drilling operation will be added in **Model Tree**.

Deep Drilling

The **Deep Drilling** tool is used to drill through the workpiece. The procedure to use this tool is discussed next.

- Click on the **Deep Drilling** tool from **Pecking** drop-down in the **Holemaking Cycles** panel of **Mill** tab; refer to Figure-59. The **Drilling** contextual tab will be displayed; refer to Figure-60.

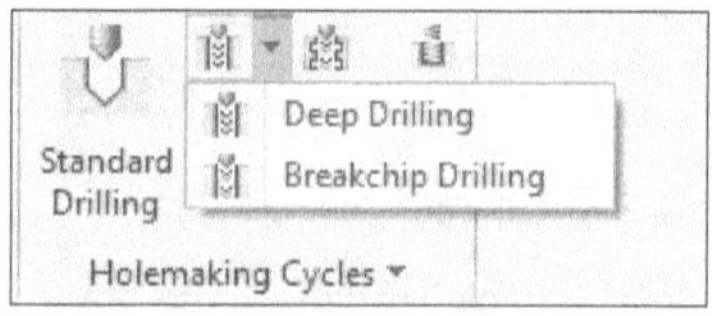

Figure-59. Deep Drilling tool

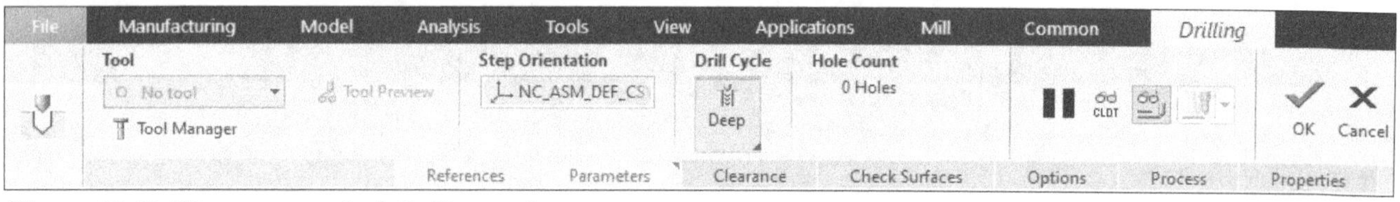

Figure-60. Drilling contextual tab for Deep tool

- Click on the **Tool** drop-down and select the required tool for deep drilling.
- Click on the **References** tab of **Drilling** contextual tab and select the required option from **Type** drop-down.
- Click in the **Holes** selection box and select the axes of hole. You can also select multiple holes with the use of **CTRL** key.
- Click on the **Parameters** tab and specify the required parameters for drilling.
- Click on the **Clearance** tab and select the retract plane for workpiece as discussed earlier.
- After specifying the parameters, click on **OK** button from **Drilling** contextual tab.

Breakchip Drilling

The **Breakchip Drilling** tool is used to create a breakchip drilling cycle. The procedure to use this tool is discussed next.

- Click on the **Breakchip Drilling** tool from **Pecking** drop-down in the **Holemaking Cycles** panel of **Mill** tab; refer to Figure-61. The **Drilling** contextual tab will be displayed.

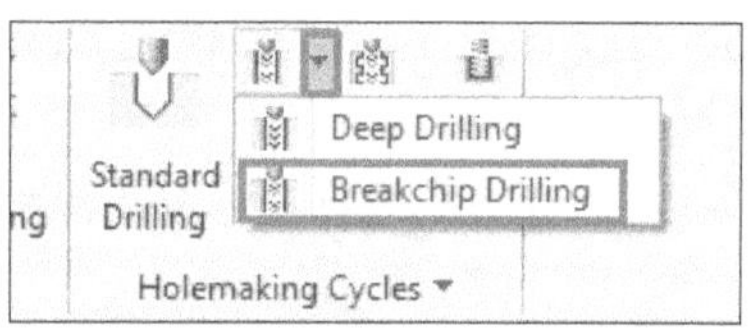

Figure-61. Breakchip tool

- Click on the **Tool** drop-down and select the required tool for drilling.
- Click on the **References** tab and select the axes for holes.
- Click on the **Parameters** tab and specify the required parameters for drilling.
- After specifying the parameters, click on the **OK** button from **Drilling** contextual tab. The **Drilling** operation will be added in **Model Tree**.

Similarly, you can use other tools of **Holemaking Cycles** panel in the **Mill** tab of **Ribbon**.

PRACTICAL 1

In this practical, we will create toolpath for the given model; refer to Figure-62.

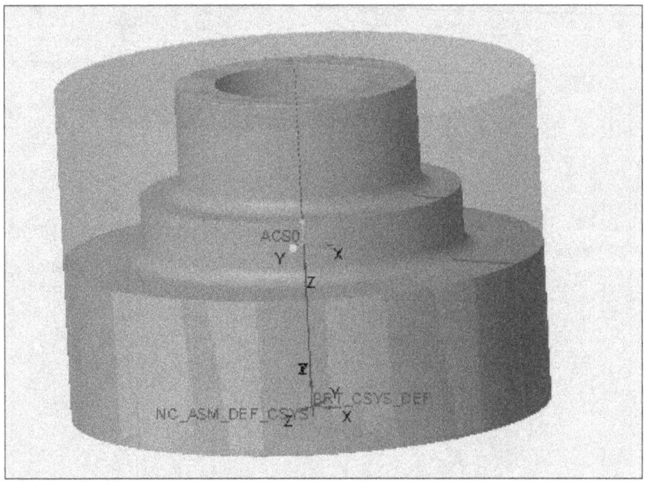

Figure-62. Practical 1

The first step before we start machining is to identify the operation that are required to machine the part. We can identify from the part that there is turning and drilling operations required. Note that these basic machining operations can be sub-divided into multiple operations based on the capabilities of the CAM software.

Starting the NC Assembly

- Double-click on **Creo Parametric** icon from your computer's desktop. The **Creo Parametric** application window will be displayed; refer to Figure-63.

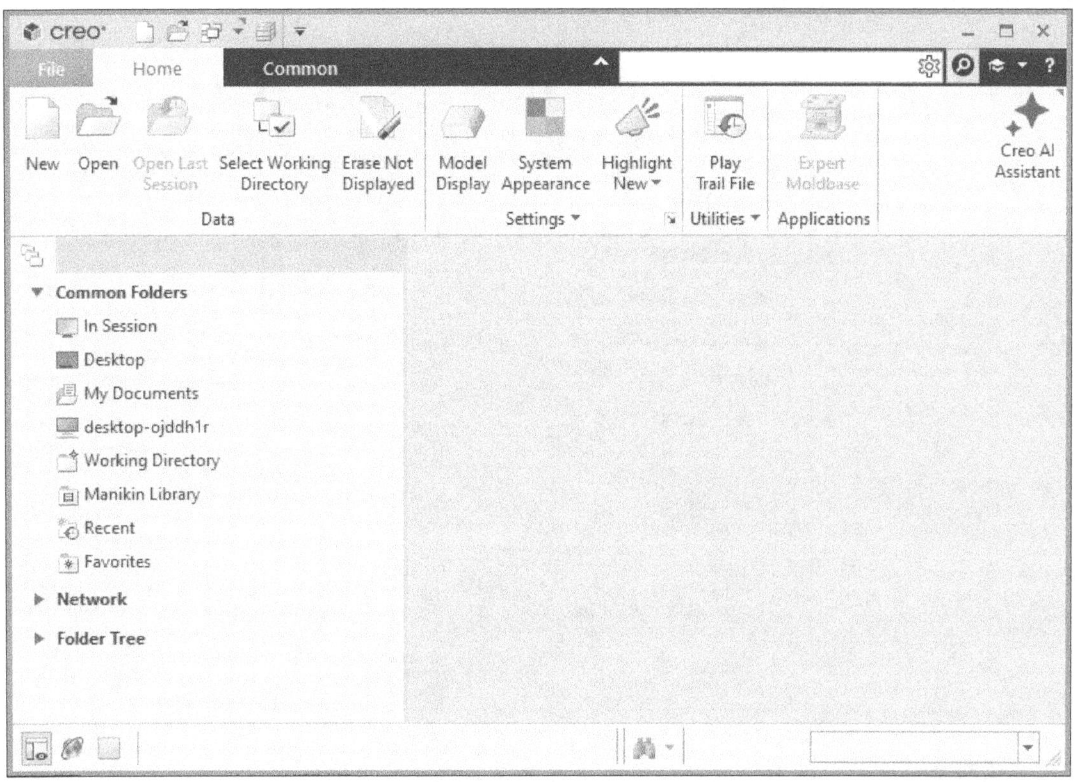

Figure-63. Creo Parametric starting window

- Click on the **New** button from **Ribbon**. The **New** dialog box will be displayed; refer to Figure-64.

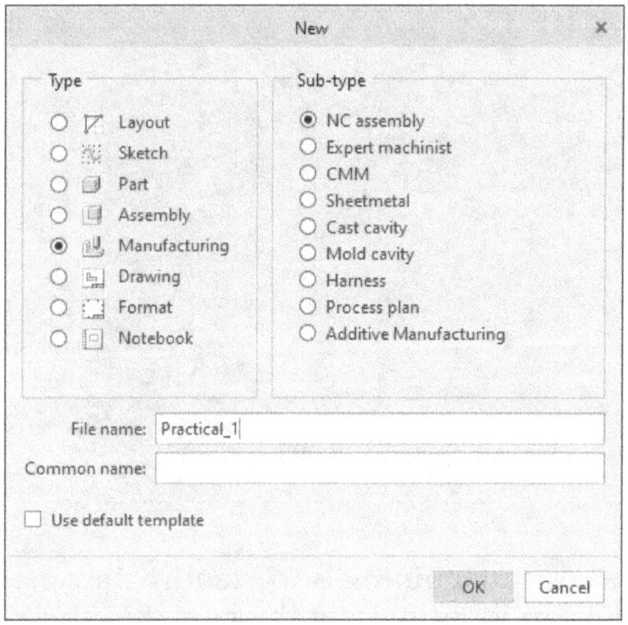

Figure-64. New dialog box

- Click on **Manufacturing** radio button from **Type** area and **NC Assembly** radio button from **Sub-Type** area.
- Click on the **File name** edit box and enter **Practical 1** as the name of file.
- Clear the **Use default template** check box from **New** dialog box.
- Click on **OK** button from **New** dialog box. The **New File Options** dialog box will be displayed; refer to Figure-65.

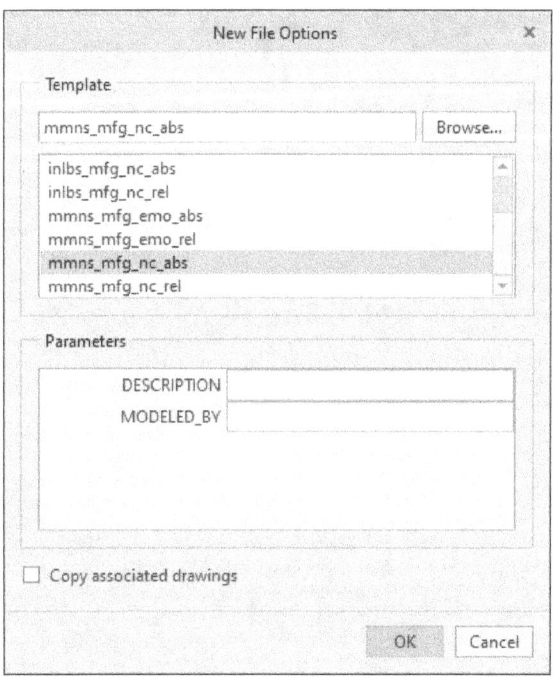

Figure-65. New File Options dialog box

- Click on **mmns mfg nc abs** option from **Template** section and specify the required details of **Parameters** section.

- Click on **OK** button from **New File Options** dialog box. The **NC Assembly** application window will be displayed; refer to Figure-66.

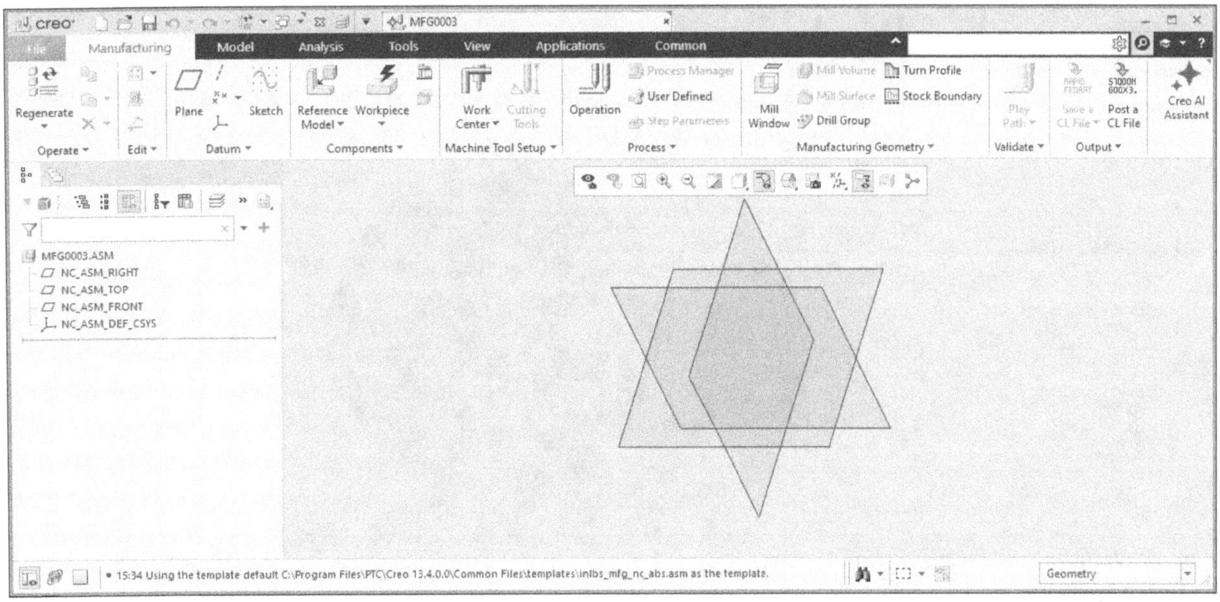

Figure-66. NC Assembly application window

Adding Reference Model

- Click on **Assemble Reference Model** button of **Reference Model** drop-down from **Manufacturing** tab. The **Open** dialog box will be displayed; refer to Figure-67.

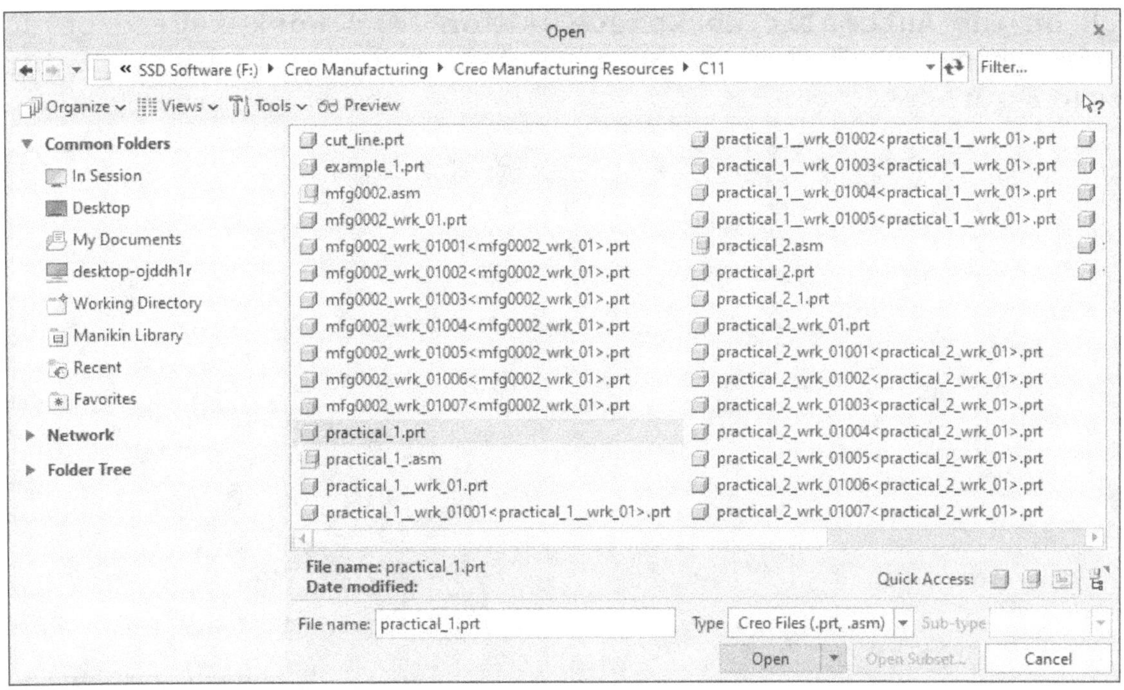

Figure-67. Open dialog box

- Select **Practical 1** file from resource folder and click on **Open** button. The **Component Placement** contextual tab will be displayed along with the reference model; refer to Figure-68.

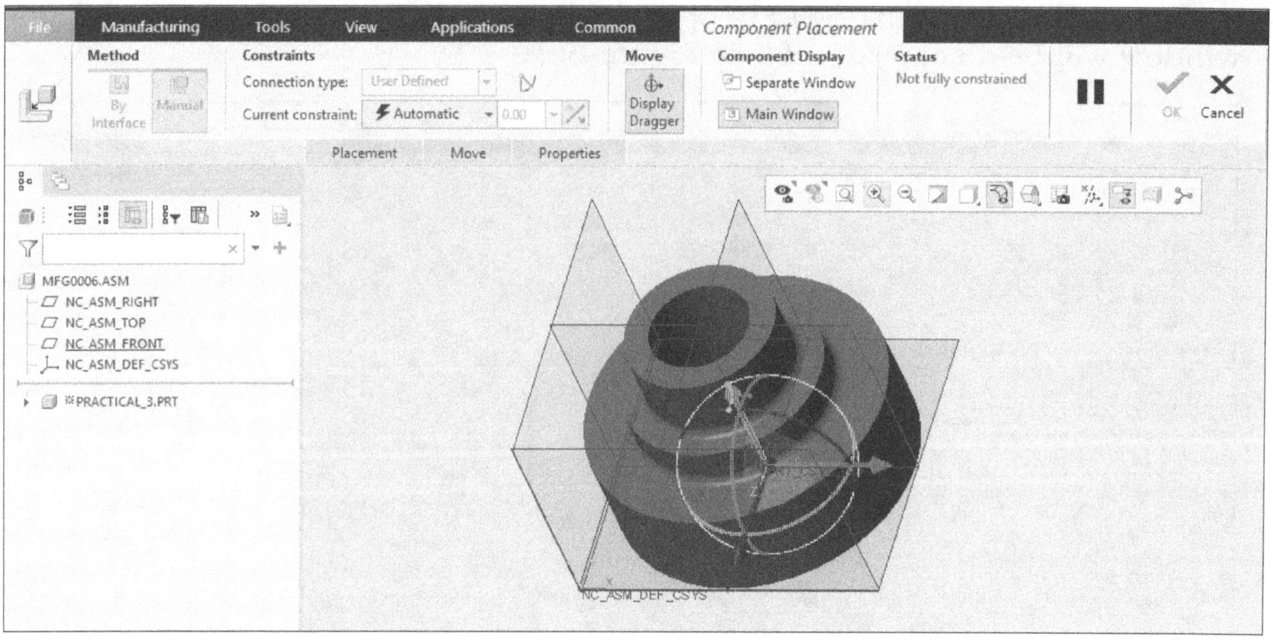

Figure-68. Reference model of Practical 1

- Select **Default** option from **Current constraint** drop-down and the **STATUS** will be changed from **Not Fully Constrained** to **Fully Constrained**.
- Click on **OK** button from the contextual tab, the **NC Assembly** application window will be displayed.

Creating Workpiece

- Click on the **Automatic Workpiece** button from **Workpiece** drop-down of **Manufacturing** tab. The **Auto Workpiece Creation** contextual tab will be displayed; refer to Figure-69.

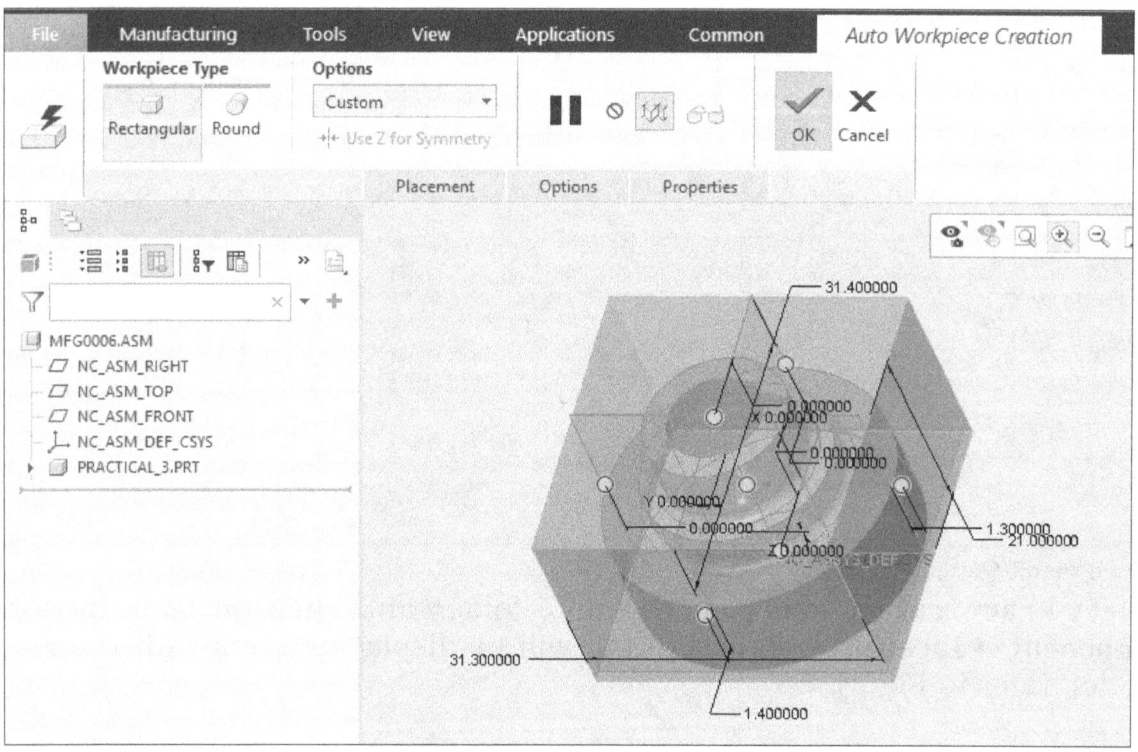

Figure-69. Creating workpiece of Practical 1

- Select **Round** option from **Workpiece Type** area of **Auto Workpiece Creation** contextual tab.
- Click on **Options** tab of **Auto Workpiece Creation** contextual tab.
- Click on **About X** edit box of **Rotation Offsets** section and enter the value as **90**; Figure-70.

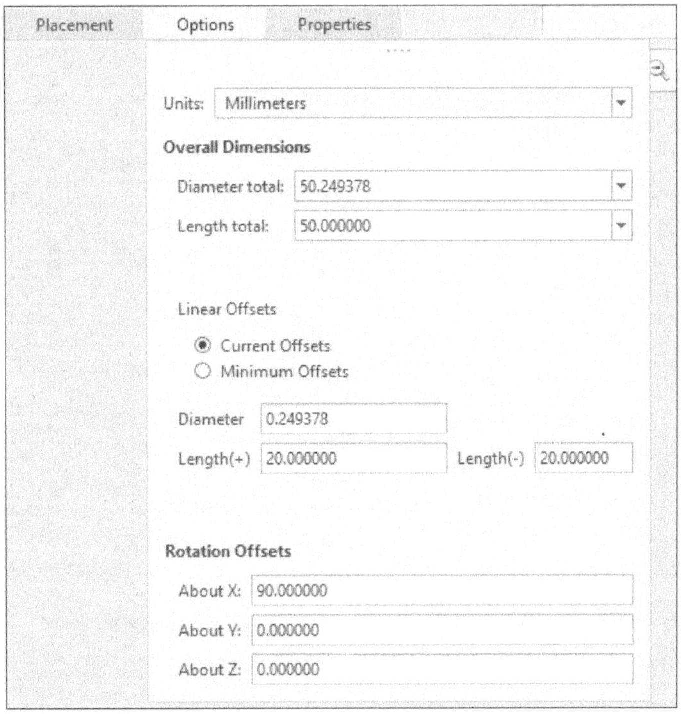

Figure-70. Options tab

- Click on **Length(+)** button of **Options** tab and enter the value as **0**.
- Click on **Length(-)** button of **Options** tab and enter the value as **0**.
- After specifying the parameters, click on **OK** button from **Auto Workpiece Creation** contextual tab.
- The **NC Assembly** application window will be displayed along with the reference model and workpiece; refer to Figure-71.

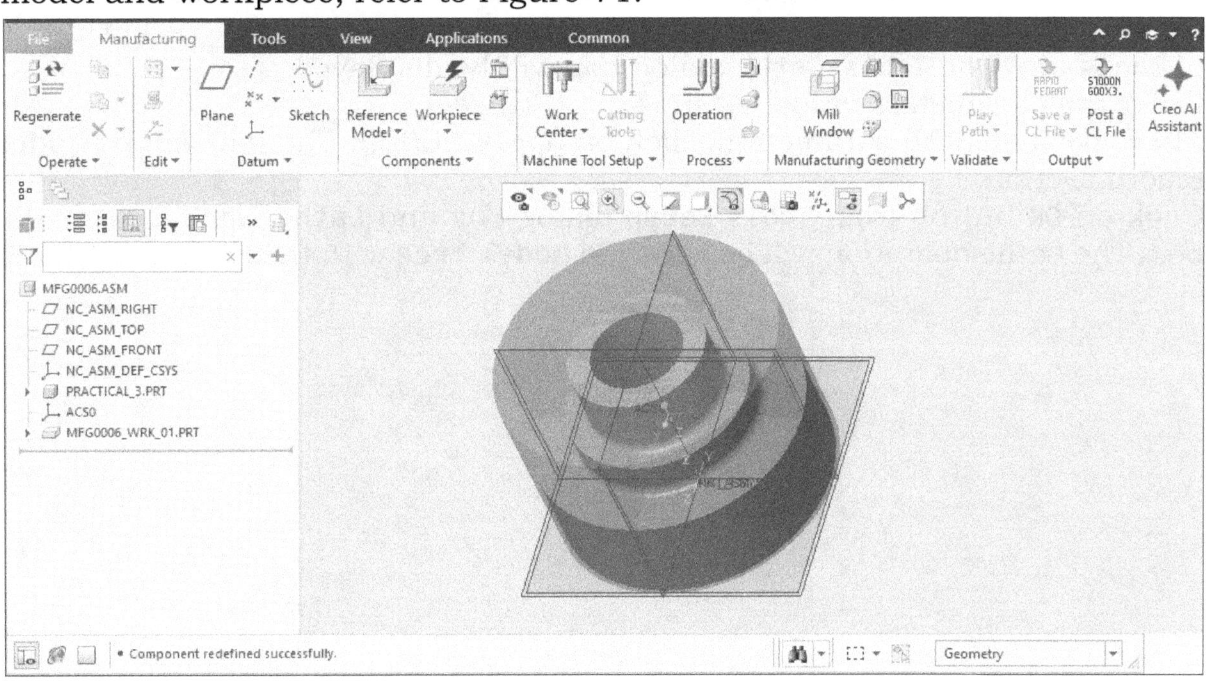

Figure-71. NC Assembly application window after adding model and workpiece

Machine Tool Setup

- Click on **Lathe** tool from **Work Center** drop-down. The **Lathe Work Center** dialog box will be displayed; refer to Figure-72.

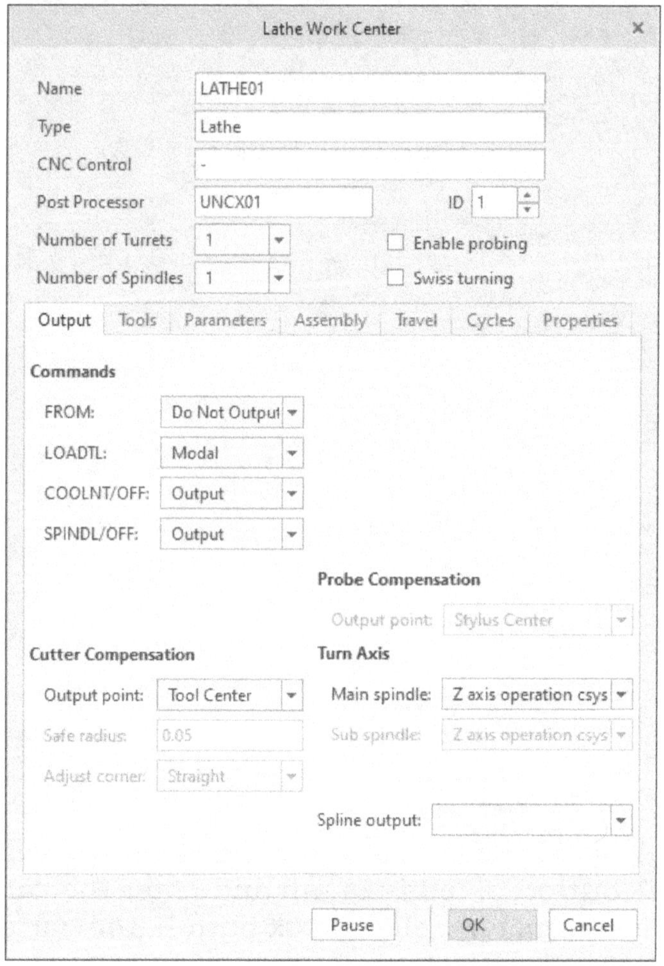

Figure-72. Lathe Work Center dialog box

- Click in the **Name** edit box and enter **TMT LATHE** as the name of machine.
- Click on **Tools** tab of **Lathe Work Center** dialog box and click on **Turret 1** button of **Tools** tab. The **Tools Setup** dialog box will be displayed.
- Enter the parameters of tool as shown in Figure-73.
- After specifying the parameters, click on **Apply** button. The tool will be added in record section.
- Click on **OK** button from **Tools Setup** dialog box and **Lathe Work Center** dialog box. The Lathe operation will be added in **Model Tree** with the name as **TMT LATHE**.

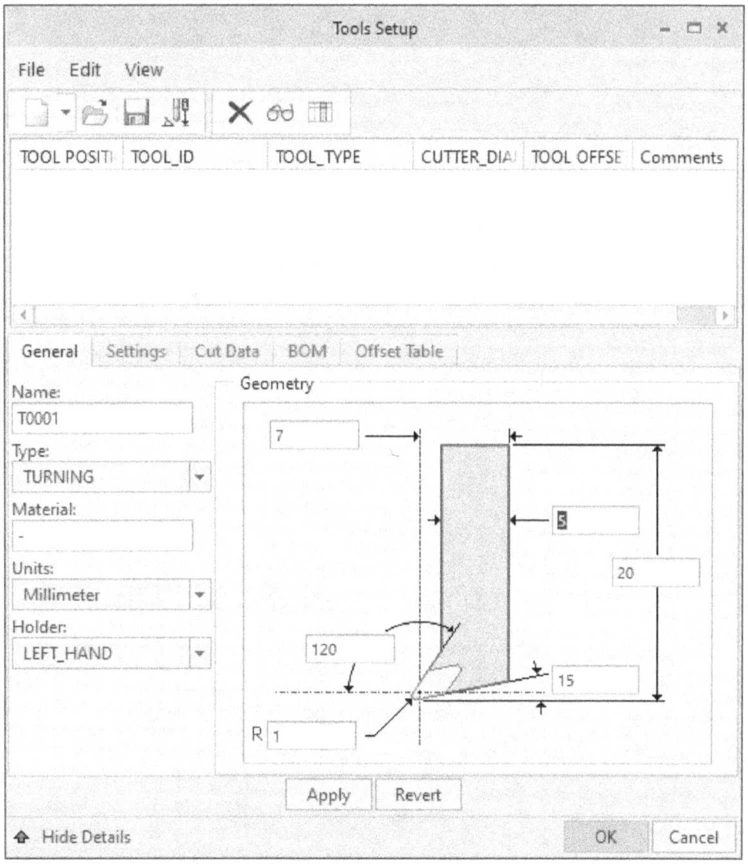

Figure-73. Tools Setup dialog box for Lathe

Creating Operation

- Click on the **Operation** button of **Process** panel from **Manufacturing** tab. The **Operation** contextual tab will be displayed; refer to Figure-74.

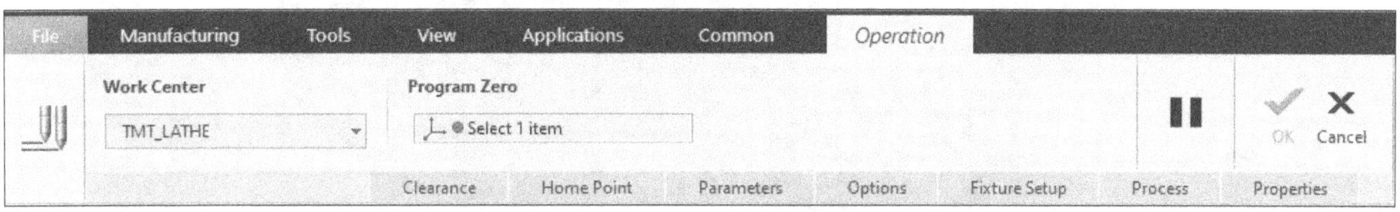

Figure-74. Operation contextual tab

- Click on coordinate system from model to set the program zero point and click on **OK** button from **Operation** contextual tab. The **Turn** tab will be added after **Applications** tab; refer to Figure-75.

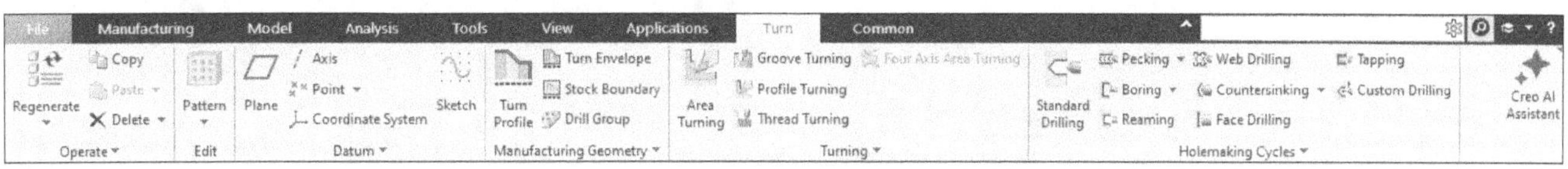

Figure-75. Turn tab

Creating Turn Profile

For lathe machine, you need to create a turn profile. The procedure to create profile is discussed next.

- Click on the **Turn Profile** button from **Manufacturing Geometry** panel of **Manufacturing** tab. The **Turn Profile** contextual tab will be displayed; refer to Figure-76.

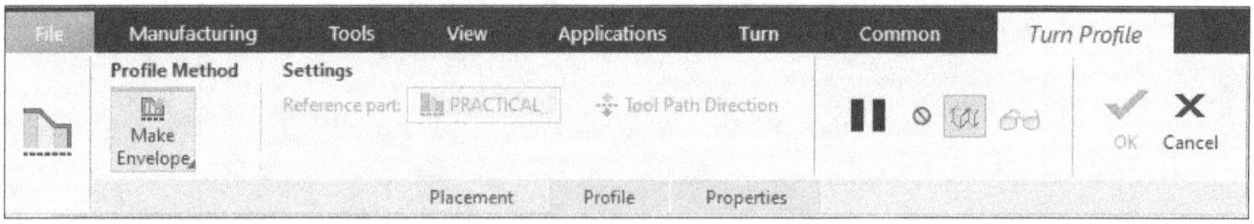

Figure-76. Turn Profile contextual tab

- Select the **Sketch** option from **Profile Method** drop-down in **Ribbon** and click on **Sketch** button which is highlighted in Figure-77. The **Sketch** tab will be displayed.

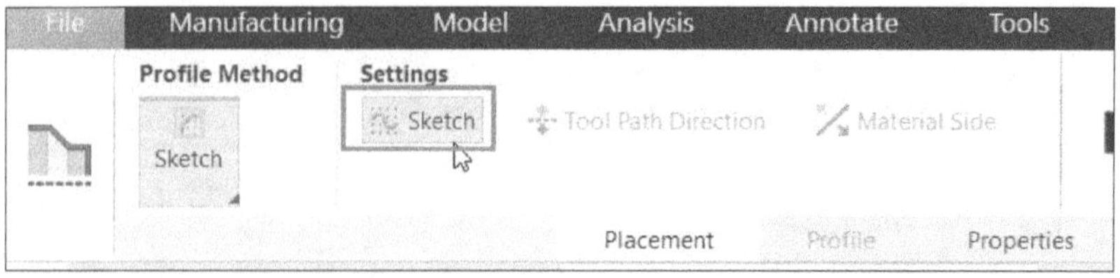

Figure-77. Sketch button

- Project the model on sketching plane as shown in Figure-78.

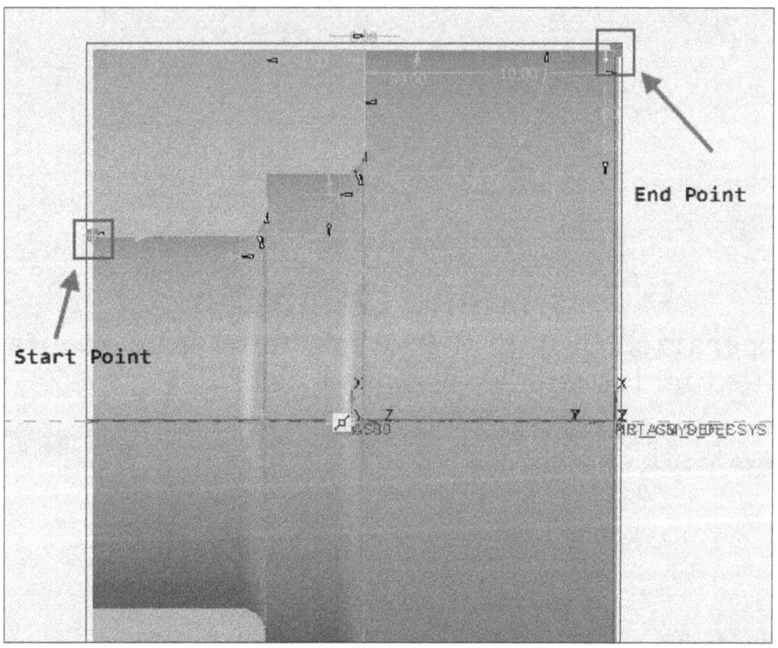

Figure-78. Projecting the sketch

- After projecting, click on **OK** button from **Sketch** tab. The **Turn Profile** contextual tab will be displayed; refer to Figure-79.

Figure-79. Turn Profile contextual tab along with projected model

- Click on **OK** button from **Turn Profile** contextual tab. The Turn Profile operation will be added in **Model Tree**.

Creating Turning Operation

- Click on **Area Turning** tool from **Turning** panel of **Turn** tab. The **Area Turning** contextual tab will be displayed; refer to Figure-80.

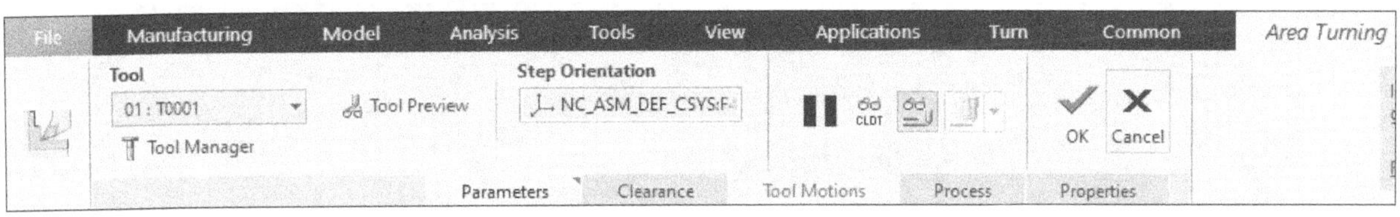

Figure-80. Area Turning contextual tab

- Click on **Tool** drop-down and select the **T0001** tool for turning.
- Click on **Parameters** tab and specify the parameters as shown in Figure-81.

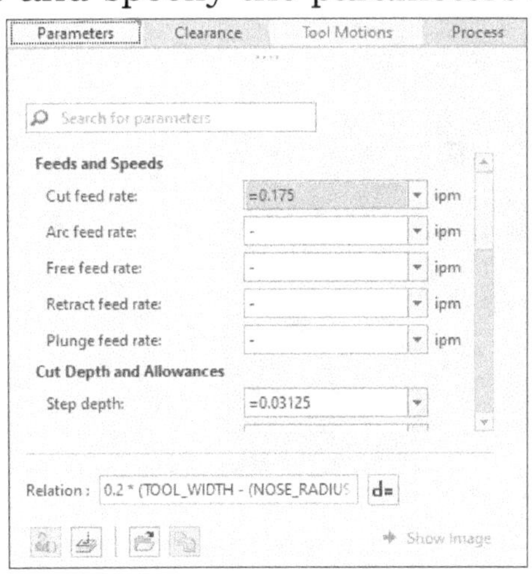

Figure-81. Parameters tab of area turning

- Click on **Area Turning Cut** button from **Tool Motions** tab. The **Area Turning Cut** dialog box will be displayed; refer to Figure-82.

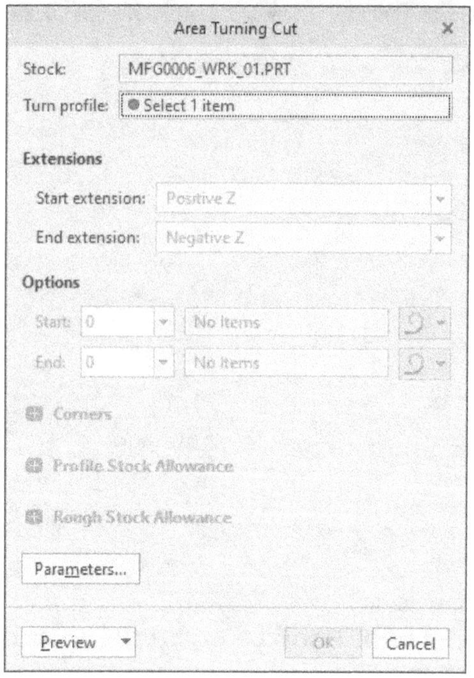

Figure-82. Area Turning Cut dialog box

- Click on **Turn profile** selection box of **Area Turning Cut** dialog box and select the recently created turn profile; refer to Figure-83. Preview of toolpath will be displayed; refer to Figure-84.

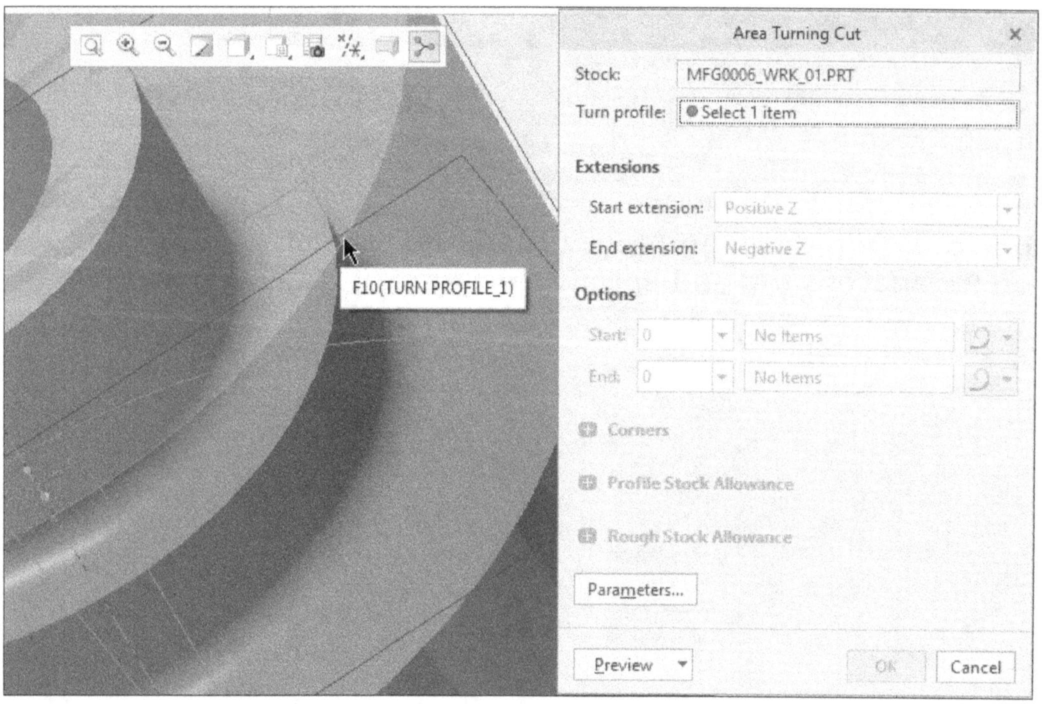

Figure-83. Selection of turn profile

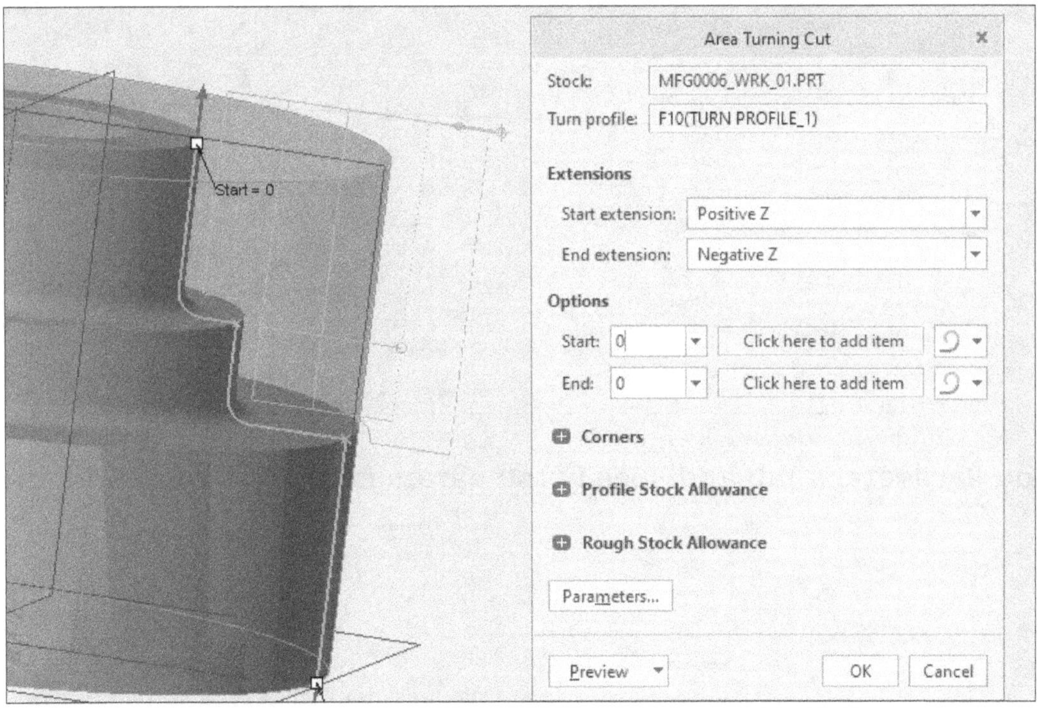

Figure-84. Selection for turn profile

- Click on **OK** button from **Area Turning Cut** dialog box and **OK** button from **Area Turning** contextual tab. The Area Turning operation will be added in **Model Tree** as **Area Turning 1**.

Creating Drilling Operation

- Click on **Standard Drilling** tool of **Holemaking Cycles** panel from **Turn** tab. The **Drilling** contextual tab will be displayed.
- Click on **Tool** drop-down from **Drilling** contextual tab and select the **Edit Tools** option. The **Tools Setup** dialog box will be displayed.
- Create the Drill and Boring tool with parameters as shown in Figure-85.

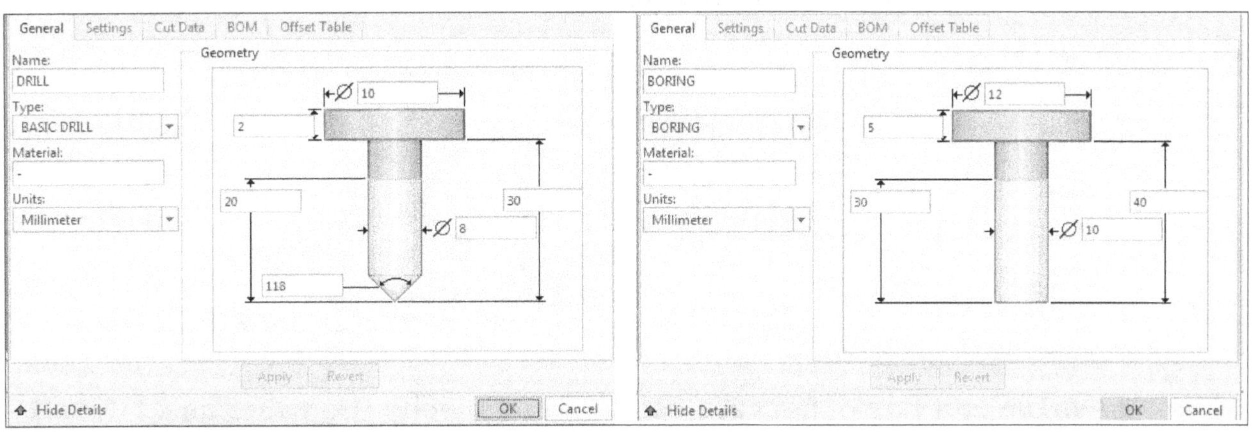

Figure-85. Drill and Boring tool

- After creating the tools, click on **OK** button from **Tools Setup** dialog box. Both the tools will be created and added in tools selection list.
- Click on **References** tab from **Drilling** contextual tab and select **Axes** from **Type** drop-down.
- Click on **Holes** selection box and select the axes of hole from model; refer to Figure-86.

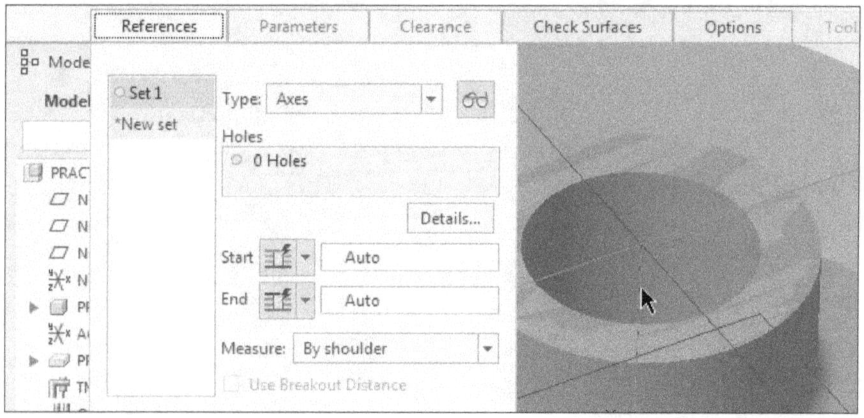

Figure-86. Selection of axes

- Click on **Parameters** tab and specify the parameters as shown in Figure-87.

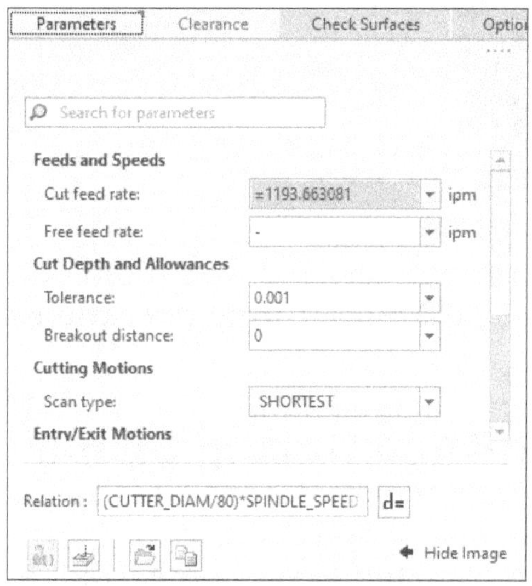

Figure-87. Parameters tab of Drilling

- Click on **Reference** selection box of **Clearance** tab from **Drilling** tab and select the face of workpiece as shown in Figure-88.

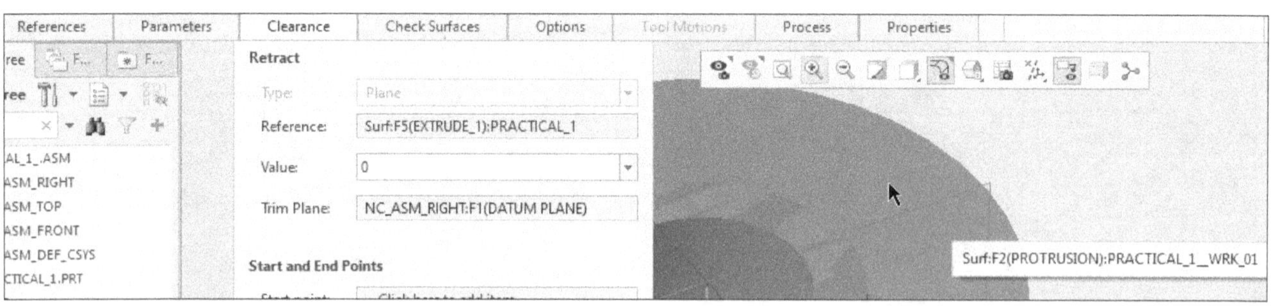

Figure-88. Selection of retract plane for drilling

- Click on **Value** edit box of **Retract** section and specify the value as **4**.
- After specifying the various parameters, click on **OK** button from **Drilling** contextual tab. The drilling operation will be added in **Model Tree** with the name as **Drilling 1**.

Creating Boring Operation

- Click on the **Boring** tool from **Holemaking Cycles** panel of **Turn** tab. The **Boring** contextual tab will be displayed; refer to Figure-89.

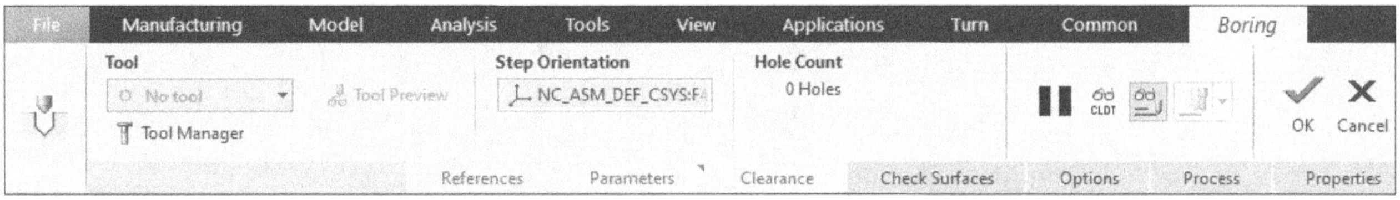

Figure-89. Boring contextual tab

- Click on the **Tool** drop-down and select the **Boring** tool.
- Click on **References** tab from **Boring** contextual tab and select **Axes** from **Type** drop-down.
- Click on **Holes** selection box and select the axes of hole from model which were used earlier for drilling hole.
- Click on **Parameters** tab and specify the parameters as shown in Figure-90.

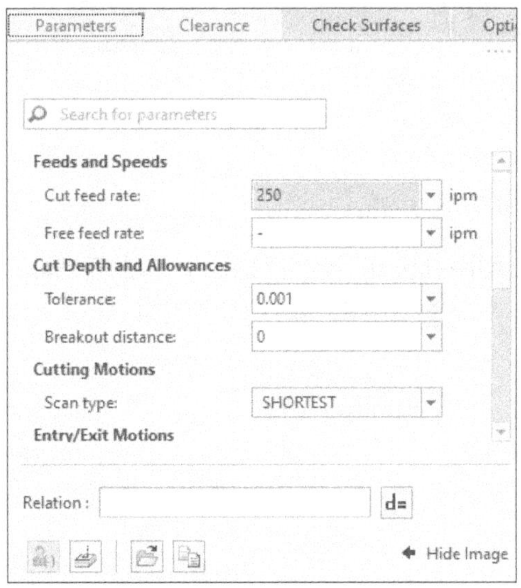

Figure-90. Parameters tab of Drilling

- After specifying the parameters, click on **OK** button from **Boring** contextual tab. The **Boring** operation will be added in **Model Tree** with the name as **Boring 1**.

Simulating Material Removal

The process of creating part from workpiece is competed. Now, you can simulate the cutting material from workpiece by using the **Material Removal Simulation** tool and the procedure is discussed next.

- Right-click on OPO10[TECHNO] or operation name. A shortcut menu will be displayed; refer to Figure-91.

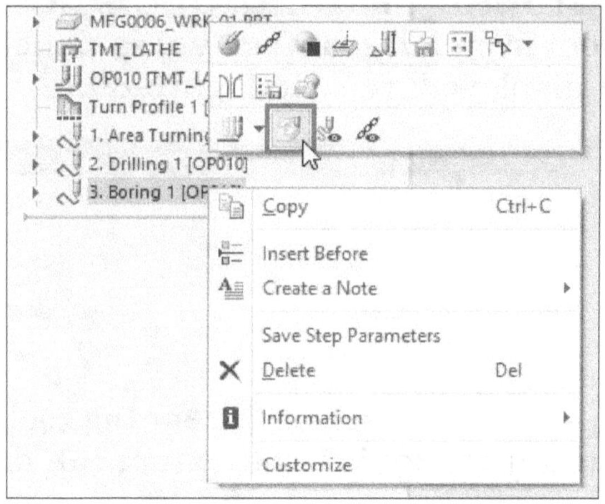

Figure-91. Material Removal Simulation button

- Click on **Material Removal Simulation** button from menu. The **Material Removal** contextual tab will be displayed; refer to Figure-92.

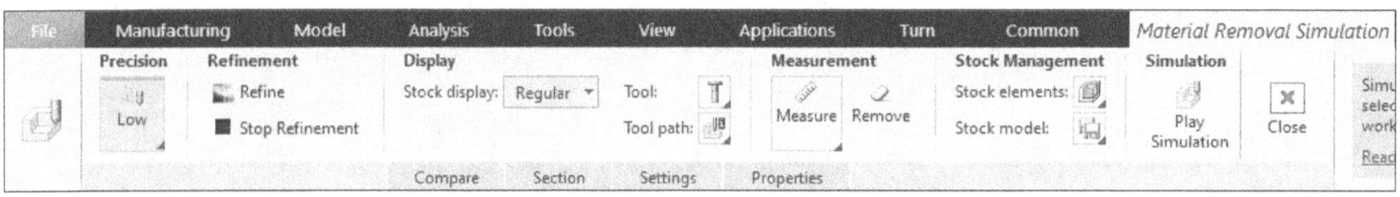

Figure-92. Material Removal contextual tab

- Click on **Play Simulation** button from **Material Removal** contextual tab. The **Play Simulation** dialog box will be displayed; refer to Figure-93.

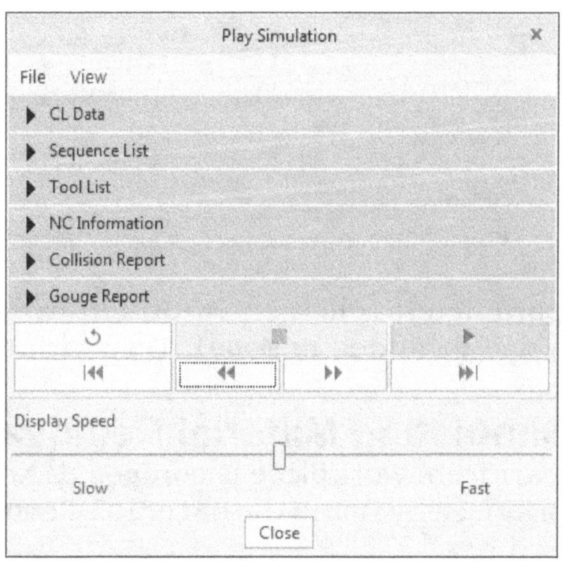

Figure-93. Play Simulation dialog box

- Now, adjust the speed as required from **Display Speed** section and click on **Play** button. The animation will start; refer to Figure-94.

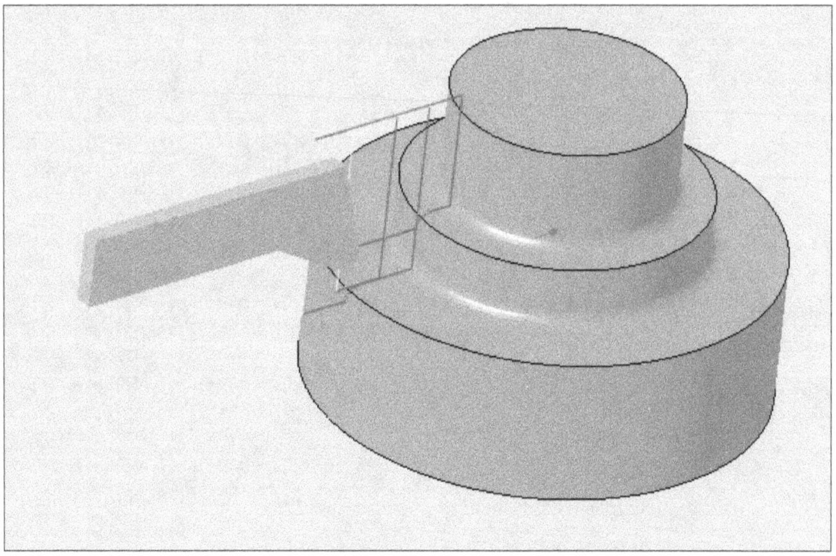

Figure-94. Animation of tool cutting

PRACTICAL 2

In this practical, we will create toolpath for the given model; refer to Figure-95.

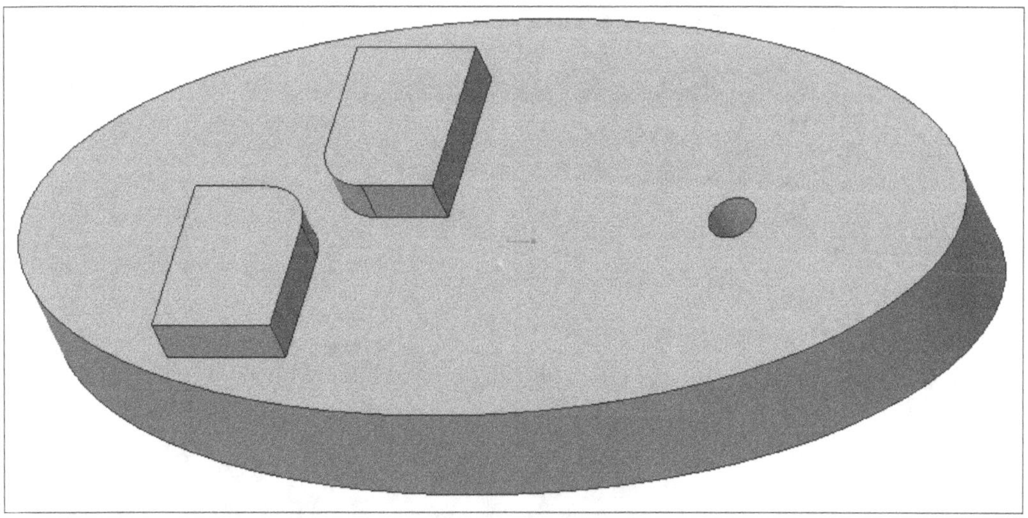

Figure-95. Practical 2

The first step before we start machining is to identify the operation that are required to machine the part. We can identify from the part that there is milling and drilling operations required. Note that these basic machining operations can be sub-divided into multiple operations based on the capabilities of the CAM software. We will start with various operations one by one.

Start the **NC Assembly** application window as discussed earlier.

Adding Reference Model

- Click on **Assemble Reference Model** button of **Reference Model** drop-down from **Manufacturing** tab. The **Open** dialog box will be displayed; refer to Figure-96.

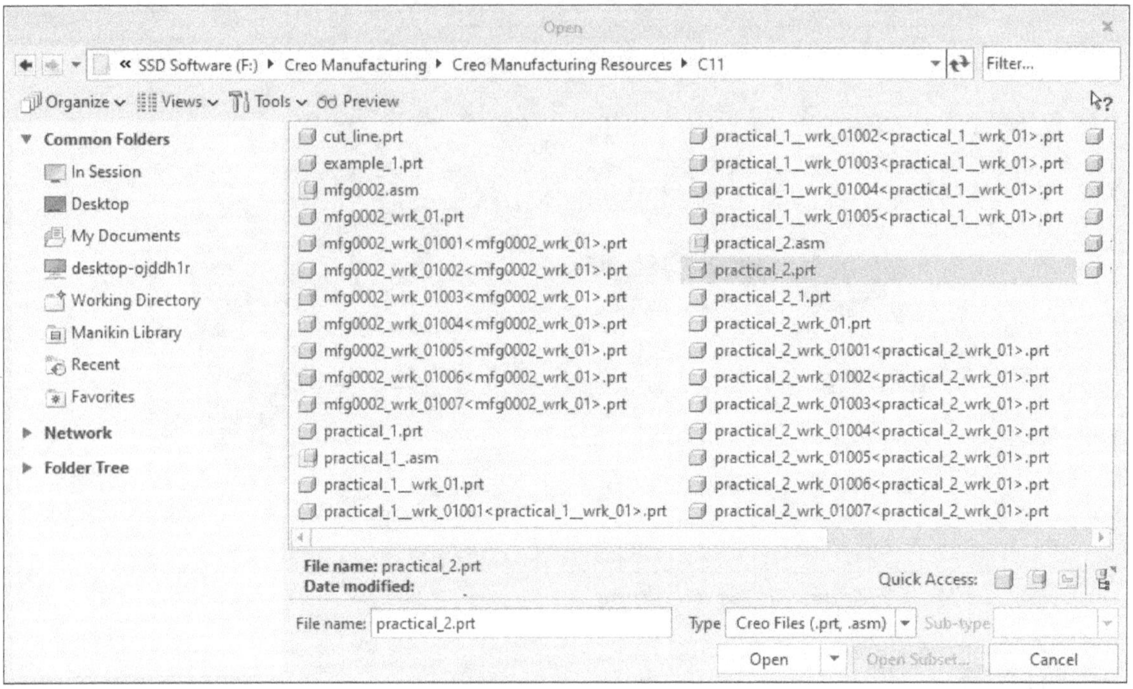

Figure-96. Open dialog box

- Select the **Practical 2** part file and click on **Open** button. The **Component Placement** contextual tab will be displayed along with the model; refer to Figure-97.

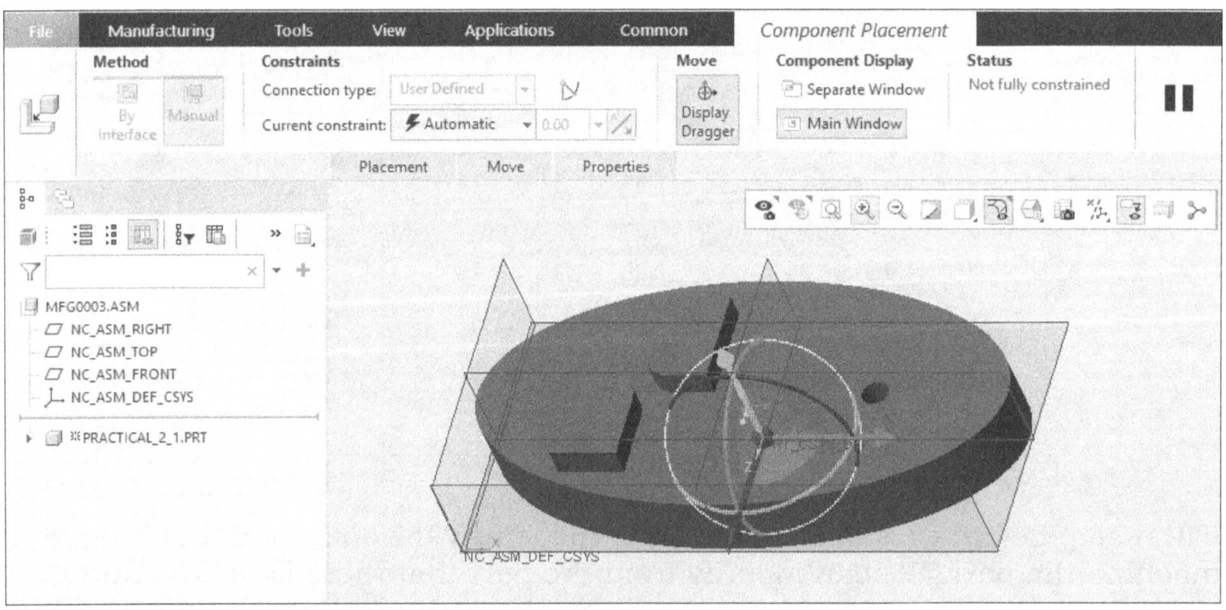

Figure-97. Component Placement contextual tab along with Practical 2

- Select **Default** option from **Current constraint** drop-down of **Component Placement** contextual tab and click on **OK** button. The **Manufacturing** tab will be displayed along with reference model; refer to Figure-98.

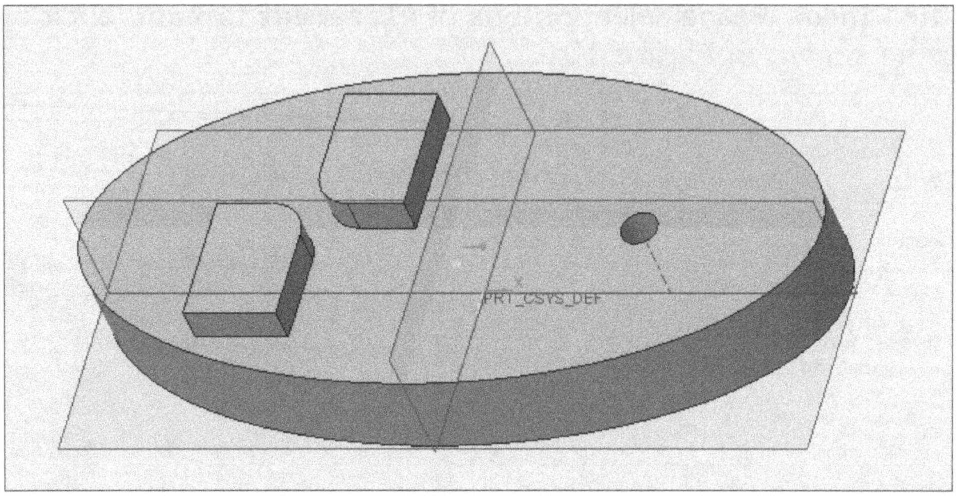

Figure-98. Manufacturing tab with model

Creating Workpiece

- Click on the **Automatic Workpiece** tool from **Workpiece** drop-down. The **Auto Workpiece Creation** contextual tab will be displayed; refer to Figure-99.

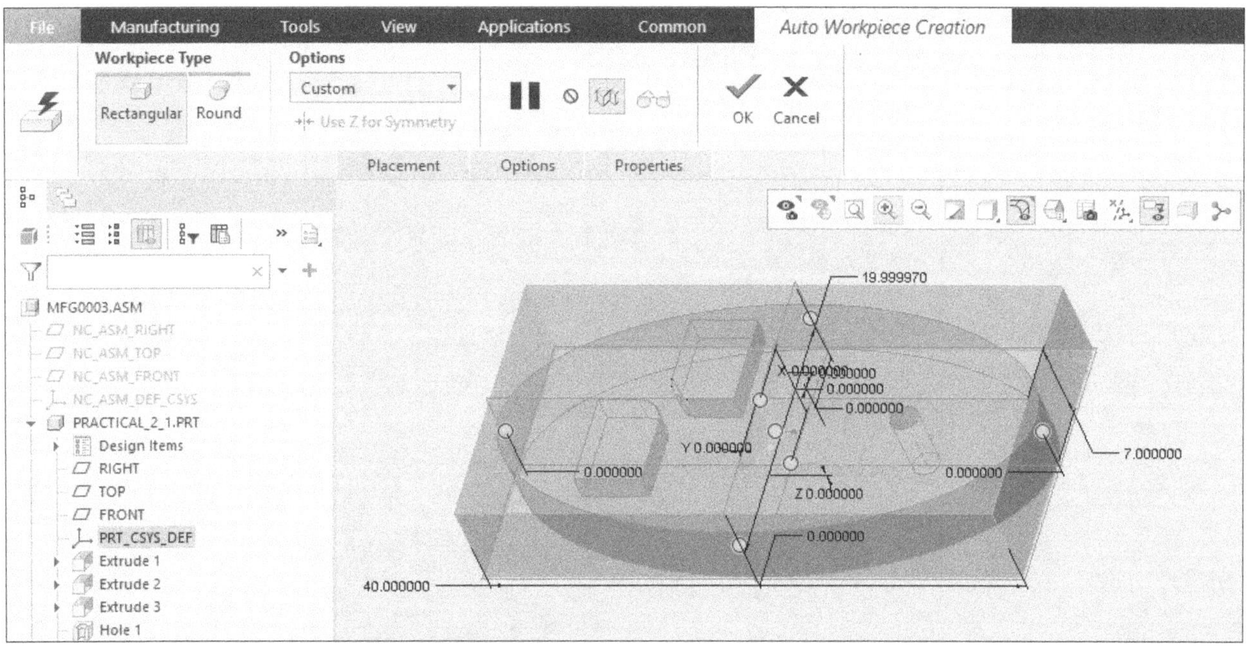

Figure-99. Creating workpiece for Practical 2

- Click on **OK** button from **Auto Workpiece Creation** contextual tab. The model will be displayed along with workpiece.

Creating Mill Window

- Click on **Mill Window** tool of **Manufacturing Geometry** panel of **Manufacturing** tab. The **Mill Window** contextual tab will be displayed; refer to Figure-100.

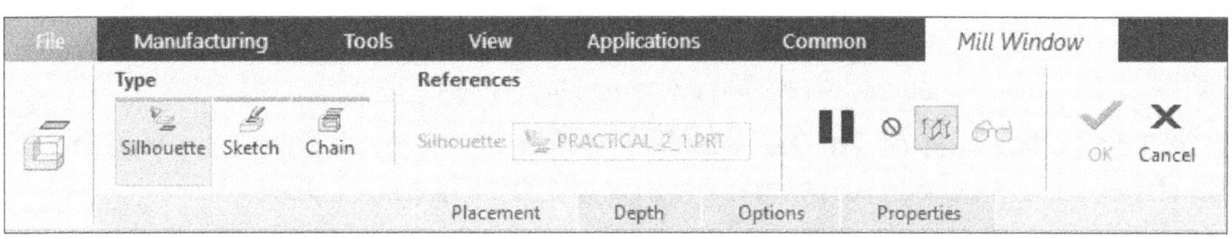

Figure-100. Mill Window contextual tab

- Click in the **Window Plane** selection box of **Placement** tab and click on top face of workpiece as shown in Figure-101.

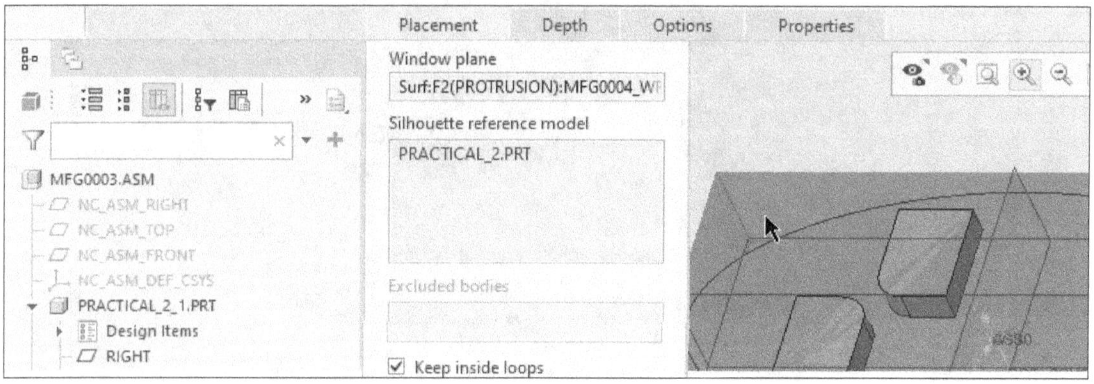

Figure-101. Selection for window plane

- Click on **OK** button from **Mill Window** contextual tab. The **NC Assembly** application window will be displayed.

Creating Mill Machine

- Click on **Mill** tool from **Work Center** drop-down. The **Milling Work Center** dialog box will be displayed; refer to Figure-102.

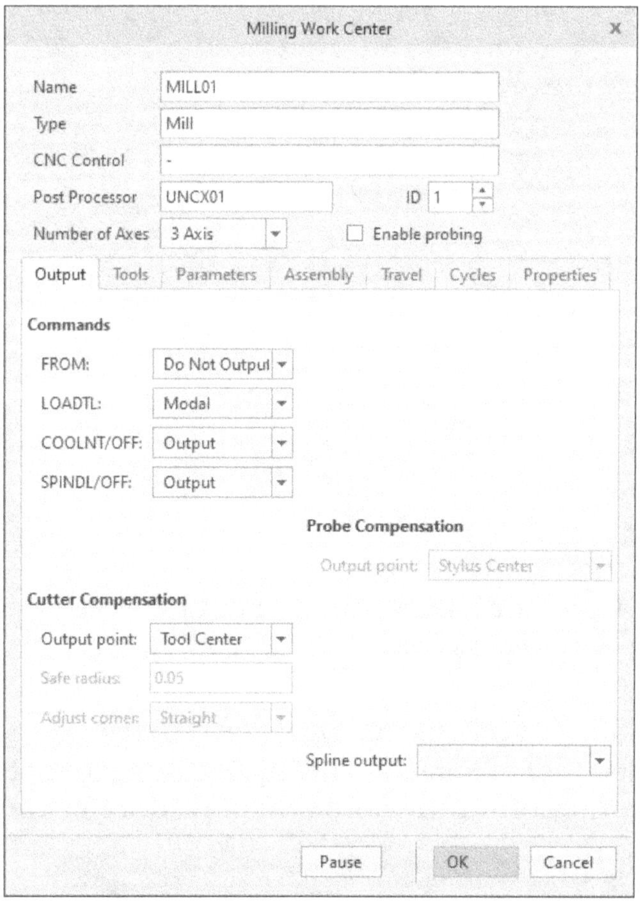

Figure-102. Milling Work Center dialog box

- Click on **Tools** button of **Tools** tab. The **Tools Setup** dialog box will be displayed.
- Create three tools of parameters as shown in Figure-103.

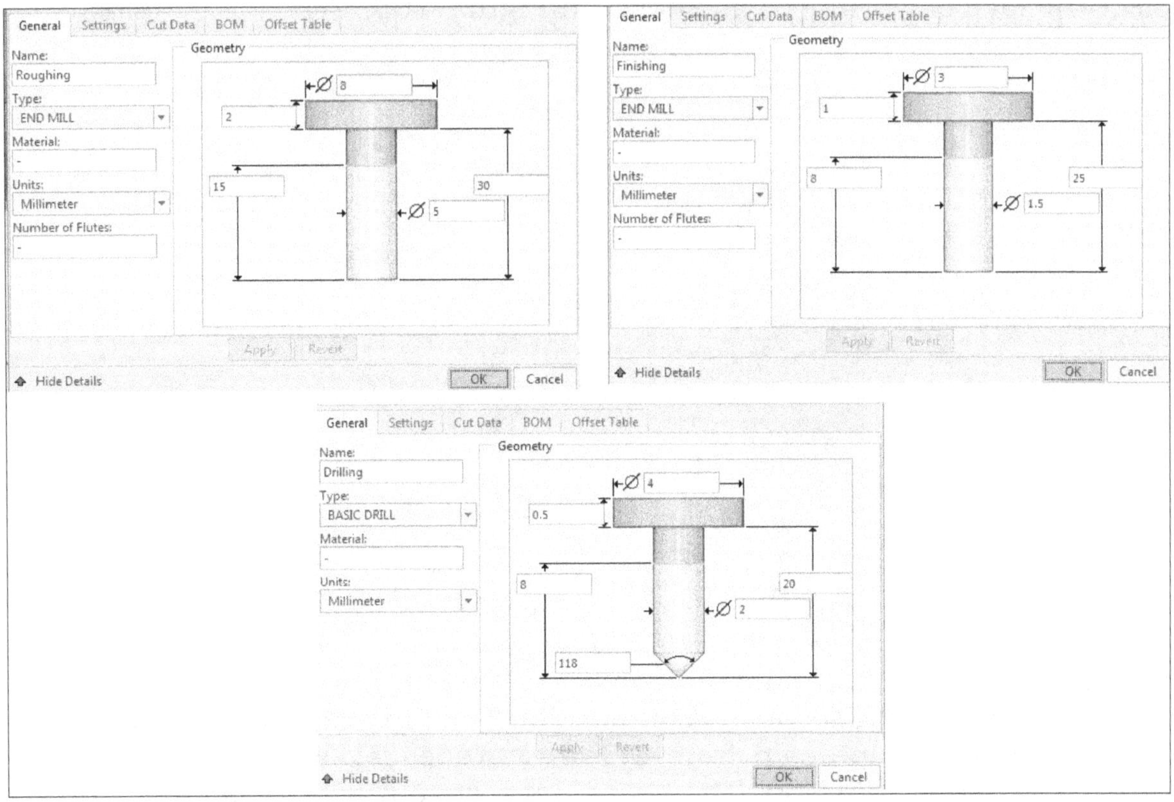

Figure-103. Parameters of tools

- After specifying the parameters, click on **Apply** button. These tools will be added in records section of **Tools Setup** dialog box; refer to Figure-104.

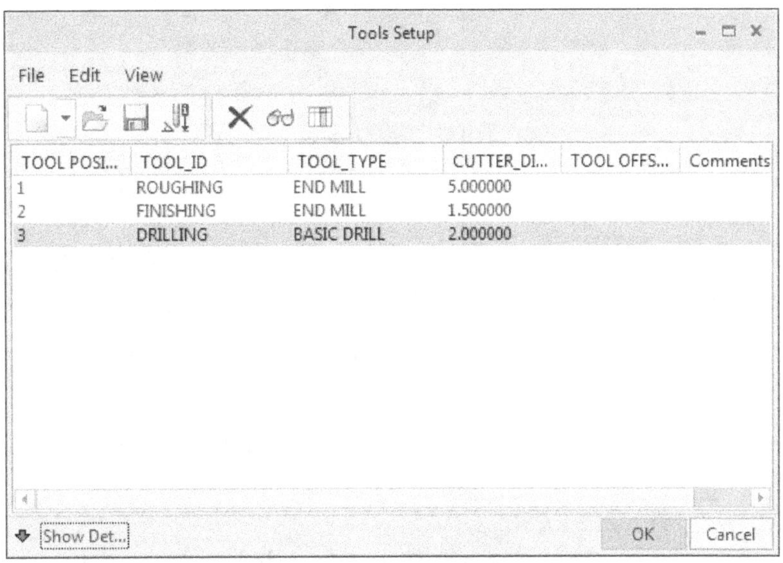

Figure-104. Records section of Tools Setup dialog box

- Click on **OK** button from **Tools Setup** dialog box and **Milling Work Center** dialog box. The **Mill** machine will be added in **Model Tree**.

Creating Operation

- Click on **Operation** tool from **Process** panel of **Manufacturing** tab. The **Operation** contextual tab will be displayed.
- Click on **Coordinate System** button from **Datum** drop-down. The **Coordinate System** dialog box will be displayed.

- Select the face of workpiece as shown in Figure-105.

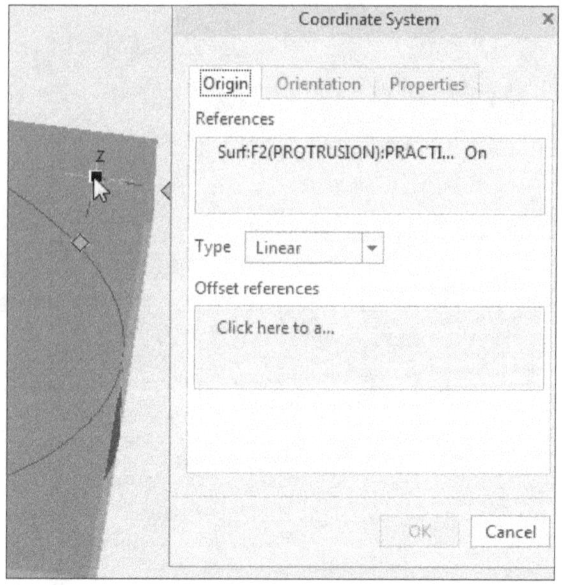

Figure-105. Placing coordinate system

- Pick one of the green handle of coordinate system and place it to nearby edge. Similarly, repeat with second green handle. The **Origin** tab will be updated.
- Click on **Offset** drop-down from **Offset references** section and select **Align** button; refer to Figure-106. The coordinate system will be aligned to the edge; refer to Figure-107.

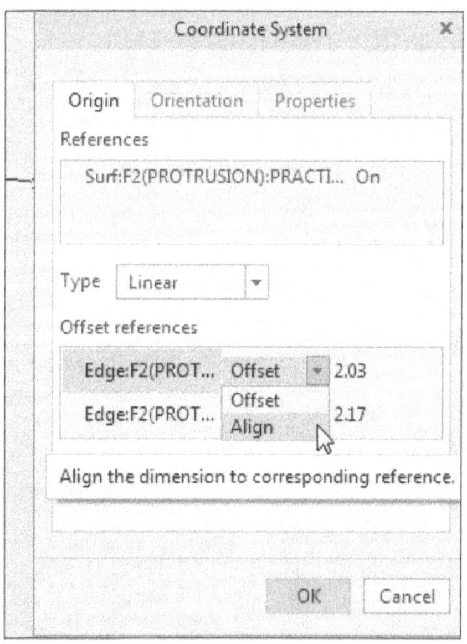

Figure-106. Setting up coordinate system

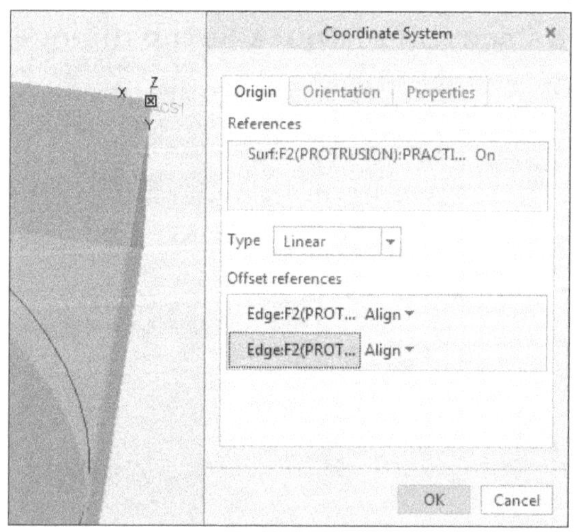

Figure-107. Correctly aligns coordinate System

- Click on **OK** button from **Coordinate System** dialog box and **Resume** button from **Operation** contextual tab.
- The coordinate system will be selected automatically. Click on **OK** button from **Operation** contextual tab.

Creating Mill Machine Operations

Roughing

- Click on **Roughing** tool from **Milling** panel of **Mill** tab. The **Roughing** contextual tab will be displayed; refer to Figure-108.

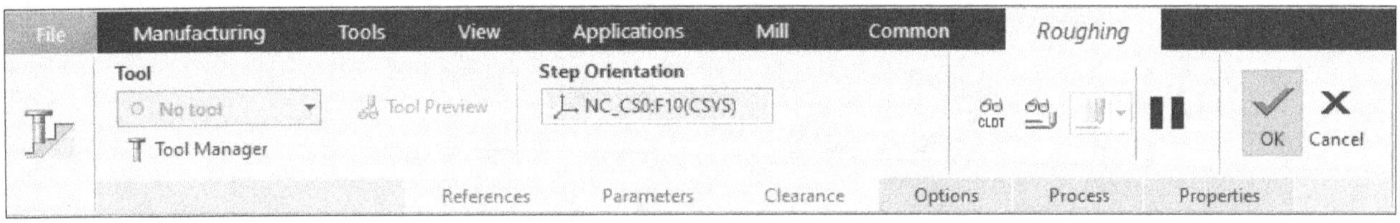

Figure-108. Roughing contextual tab

- Click on **Tool** drop-down and select **Roughing** tool.
- Click on **Mill Window** selection box from **References** tab and select the recently mill window created earlier.
- Click on **Parameters** tab and specify the required parameters as shown in Figure-109.

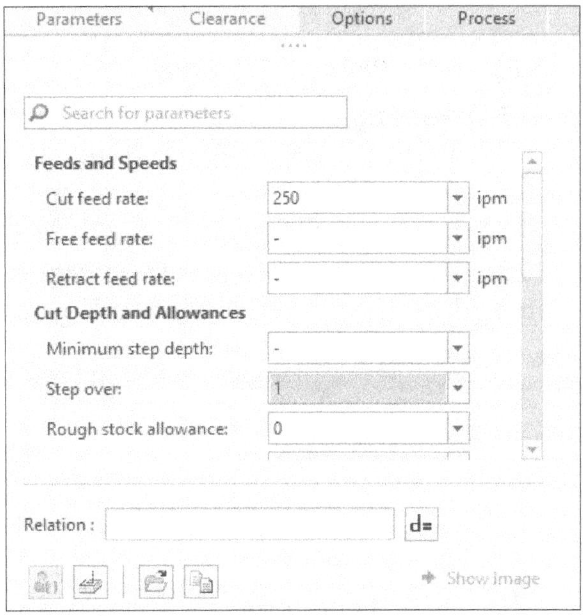

Figure-109. Parameters for roughing

- Click on reference selection box of **Clearance** tab from **Roughing** contextual tab and select the upper face of workpiece.
- Click on the **Value** edit box of **Retract** section and enter the value as **4**.
- After specifying the parameters, click on **OK** button from **Roughing** contextual tab. The roughing operation will be added in **Model Tree** with the name as **Roughing 1**.

Finishing

- Click on **Finishing** tool from **Milling** panel of **Manufacturing** tab. The **Finishing** contextual tab will be displayed; refer to Figure-110.

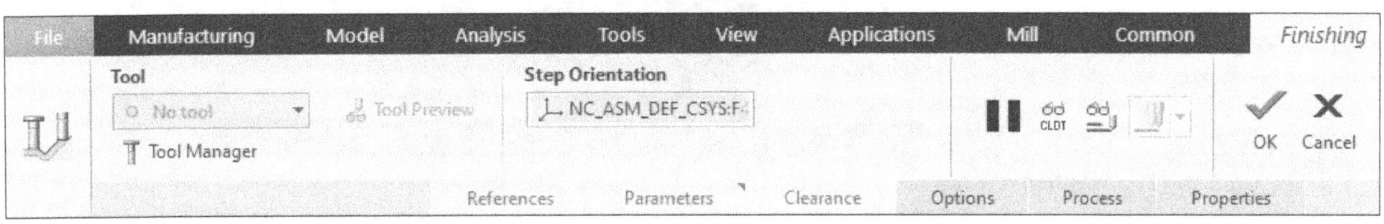

Figure-110. Finishing contextual tab

- Select **Mill Window** in references tab as discussed earlier.
- Click on **Parameters** tab and specify the required parameters; refer to Figure-111.

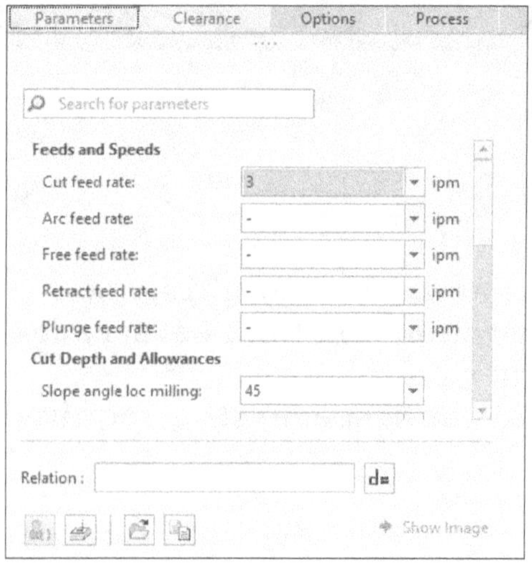

Figure-111. Parameters for finishing

- Click on **OK** button from **Finishing** contextual tab. The **Finishing** operation will be added in **Model Tree** with the name as **Finishing 1**.

Drilling

- Click on **Standard Drilling** tool from **Holemaking Cycles** panel of **Mill** tab. The **Drilling** contextual tab will be displayed; refer to Figure-112.

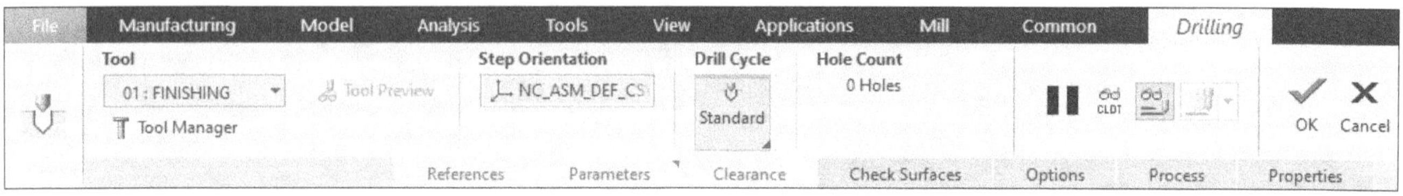

Figure-112. Drilling contextual tab

- Click in **Holes** selection box of **References** tab from **Drilling** contextual tab and select the axes of hole from model; refer to Figure-113.

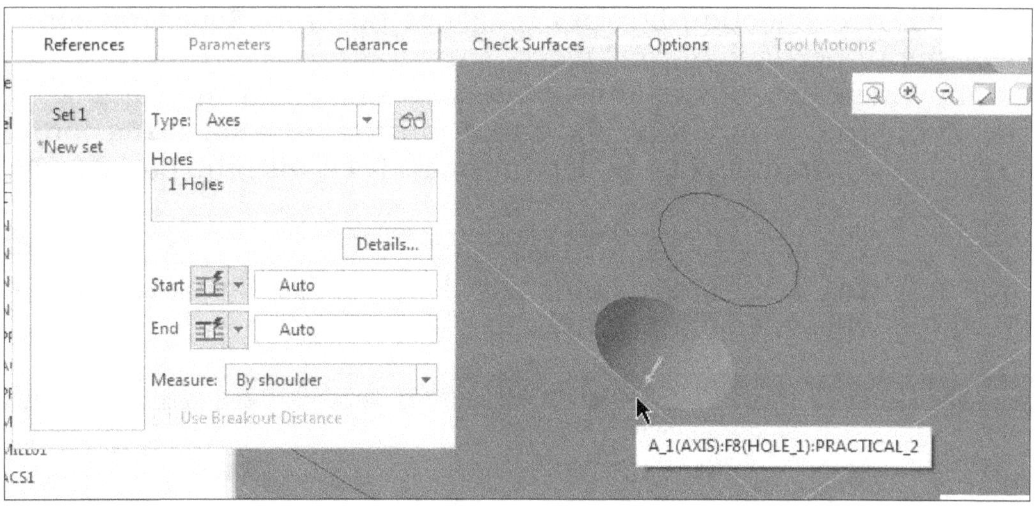

Figure-113. Selection of hole

- Click on **Parameters** tab of **Drilling** contextual tab and specify the parameters as shown in Figure-114.

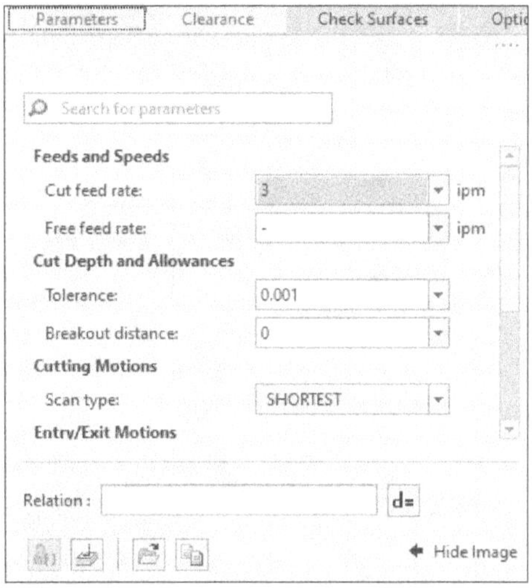

Figure-114. Parameters for drilling

- After specifying the parameters, click on **OK** button from **Drilling** contextual tab. The **Drilling** operation will be added in **Model Tree** with the name as **Drilling 1**.

If you want to simulate the material removal based on created operations then repeat the simulation steps as discussed in previous practical.

PRACTICE 1

Create the Mill machining process and toolpath of the given Figure-115.

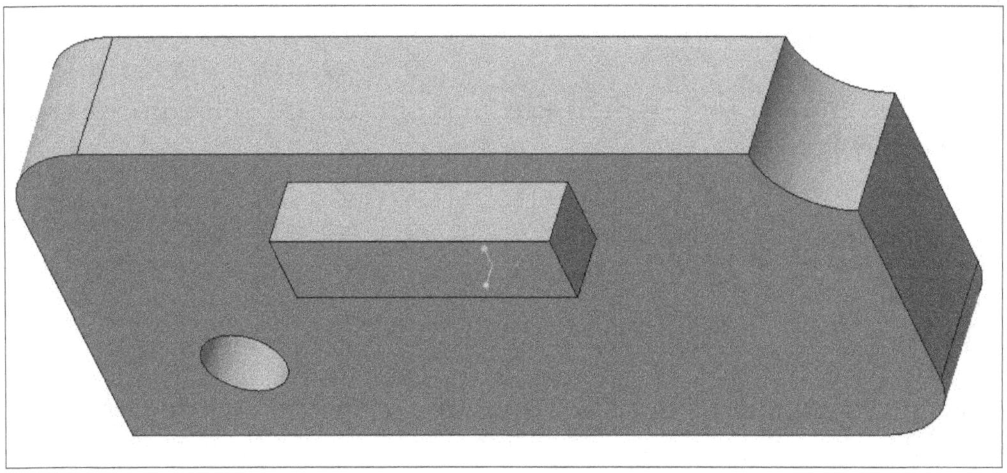

Figure-115. Practice 1

PRACTICE 2

Create the Lathe machining process and toolpath of the given Figure-116.

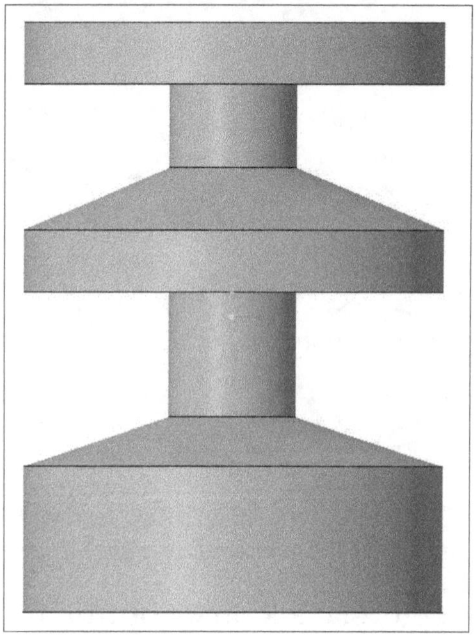

Figure-116. Practice 2

SELF-ASSESSMENT

Q1. What is the main function of the Roughing tool in Creo Parametric?

A. To finish outer walls
B. To rough large volume of material
C. To remove unwanted material
D. To apply draft angle

Q2. In the Volume Rough tool, which surface should be selected in the Machining Reference selection box?

A. Side wall
B. Top surface of workpiece
C. Bottom plane
D. Inside face

Q3. Which option is selected from the Type drop-down in the Face Milling operation in the example?

A. Surface
B. Feature
C. Plane
D. Mill Window

Q4. What is the Re-rough tool primarily used for?

A. Finishing small corners
B. Re-roughing with finer tool
C. Roughing large volume
D. Applying surface isolines

Q5. In Profile Milling, what type is selected to remove material from outer walls?

A. Mill Window
B. Axis
C. Surface
D. Curve

Q6. Which tool is commonly used for semi-finishing or finishing flat surfaces?

A. Face tool
B. Surface Milling tool
C. Roughing tool
D. Profile Milling tool

Q7. In the Surface Milling operation, what is selected to machine along lines defining the surface?

A. Surface Pattern
B. Projected Cuts
C. From Surface Isolines
D. Rough Reference

Q8. What does the Finishing tool primarily do?

A. Re-rough surface
B. Create trajectory
C. Apply final machining touches
D. Define the mill window

Q9. In Corner Finishing, which tab allows the selection of retract plane?

A. Tool tab
B. Parameters tab
C. References tab
D. Clearance tab

Q10. Which tool is used to remove material by following a specific path?

A. Profile Milling
B. 2-Axis Trajectory
C. Volume Rough
D. Face Milling

Q11. What is the purpose of the Trajectory tool in Creo Parametric?

A. Create a straight drilling path
B. Follow a defined curve for machining
C. Drill deep holes
D. Mill large flat surfaces

Q12. Which operation is specifically used to engrave letters or grooves on a metal surface?

A. Trajectory
B. Thread Milling
C. Engraving
D. Standard

Q13. What happens when the Auto Cut Line checkbox is selected in Cut Line Milling?

A. It restricts cut lines to curves only
B. It avoids generating toolpath
C. It automatically selects or creates cut lines
D. It mirrors the surface

Q14. In Thread Milling, what option is selected to cut threads on a boss feature?

A. Internal
B. Circular
C. External
D. Radial

Q15. Which tab in the Manual Cycle tool allows you to define motion steps like "Follow Curve"?

A. References
B. Clearance
C. Parameters
D. Tool Motions

Q16. In Standard drilling, what reference type is selected to drill using hole axes?

A. Geometry
B. Points
C. Surface
D. Axes

Q17. Which drilling tool is designed to drill completely through a workpiece?

A. Deep
B. Standard
C. Breakchip
D. Manual Cycle

Q18. What is the primary function of the Breakchip drilling tool?
A. Smooth edge drilling
B. Create a series of broken chip cycles
C. Deep cut into solid block
D. 3D curved drilling

Q19. During NC Assembly creation, which template option is selected in the New File Options dialog box?

A. mmns mfg nc abs
B. simple asm mm
C. std prt mm
D. iso metric solid

Q20. What option is used to rotate the workpiece by 90 degrees during creation?

A. X Scale edit box
B. About X edit box
C. Orientation drop-down
D. Y Offset input

Q21. Which tab in the Engraving tool allows you to define the retract plane?

A. Parameters
B. References
C. Clearance
D. Tool Motions

Q22. What is the use of the Conventional Milling tool?

A. To engrave on curved surfaces
B. To ignore holes and machine only flat surfaces
C. To drill internal threads
D. To machine external bosses

Q23. In Cut Line Milling, which tab lets you select curves for cutting tool contact?

A. Tool Motions
B. Cut Lines
C. Clearance
D. Geometry

Q24. What does the Tool Center Curve checkbox do in Cut Line Milling?

A. Creates a tool centerline drawing
B. Mirrors the cut lines
C. Generates a machinable profile using the tool
D. Selects holes automatically

Q25. In Thread Milling, which option is chosen from the Thread as flyout menu to define threads in a hole?
A. Surface
B. External
C. Internal
D. Middle

Q26. What must be specified in the Diameter edit box during thread milling?

A. Thread pitch
B. Cutting depth
C. Thread diameter
D. Tool speed

Q27. Which tab in Manual Cycle provides different types of motion steps like Retract?

A. Parameters
B. Tool Motions
C. References
D. Setup

Q28. In Manual Cycle, which option is used to ensure the tool follows a selected curve?

A. Follow Surface
B. Edge Contact
C. Follow Curve
D. Curve Path

Q29. What is the first step after launching Creo Parametric to start NC Assembly?

A. Open Reference Model
B. Click on Mill Tab
C. Click on New and choose Manufacturing type
D. Import Workpiece

Q30. Which constraint status must be achieved while placing the reference model in NC Assembly?

A. Under-constrained
B. Free
C. Fully Constrained
D. Locked

Chapter 12

Multi-Axis Milling Operations

Topics Covered

The major topics covered in this chapter are:

- ***Introduction to Multi-axis milling.***
- ***High Speed Milling Toolpaths.***
- ***5-Axis Milling Toolpaths.***
- ***Practice and Practical.***

INTRODUCTION

In previous chapters, you have learned to perform various milling operations using conventional milling toolpaths. In this chapter, you will learn to create high speed milling toolpaths and multi-axis toolpaths. These toolpaths are discussed next.

HSM TOOLPATHS

The HSM toolpaths are used to machine surface of part at high speed. The tools to generate these toolpaths are available in the **High Speed Milling** panel of **Mill** tab in the **Ribbon**; refer to Figure-1. There are four HSM toolpaths provided by ModuleWorks for high speed milling: HSM Rough, HSM Rest Rough, HSM Finish, and HSM Rest Finishing. These toolpaths are discussed next.

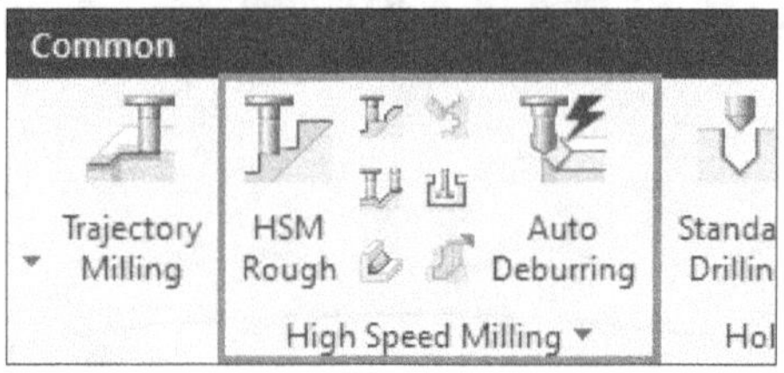

Figure-1. High Speed Milling panel

Creating HSM Rough Toolpaths

The **HSM Rough** tool is used to remove large portion of material without tight tolerance at high speed machines. The procedure to use this tool is given next.

- Click on the **HSM Rough** tool from the **High Speed Milling** panel in the **Mill** tab of the **Ribbon**. The **HSM Rough** contextual tab will be displayed; refer to Figure-2.

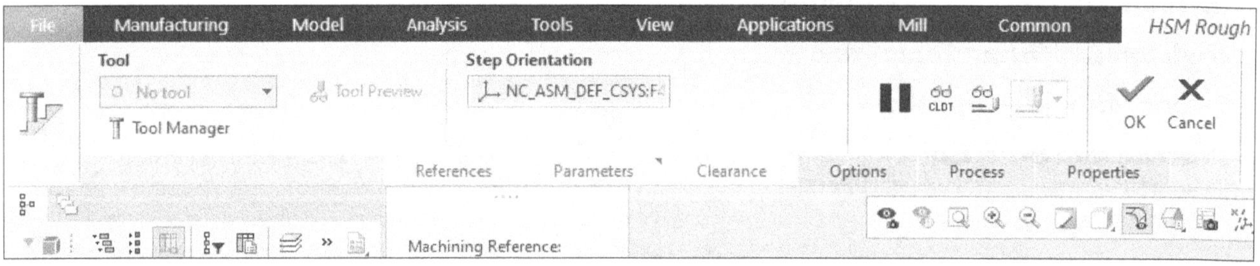

Figure-2. HSM Rough contextual tab

- Select desired cutting tool from the **Tool** drop-down in the contextual tab of **Ribbon**.
- Select the Mill Window, Mill Surface, or Mill Volume from the graphics area which is to be machined; refer to Figure-3.
- Click on the **Parameters** tab from the contextual tab to specify cutting parameters; refer to Figure-4.

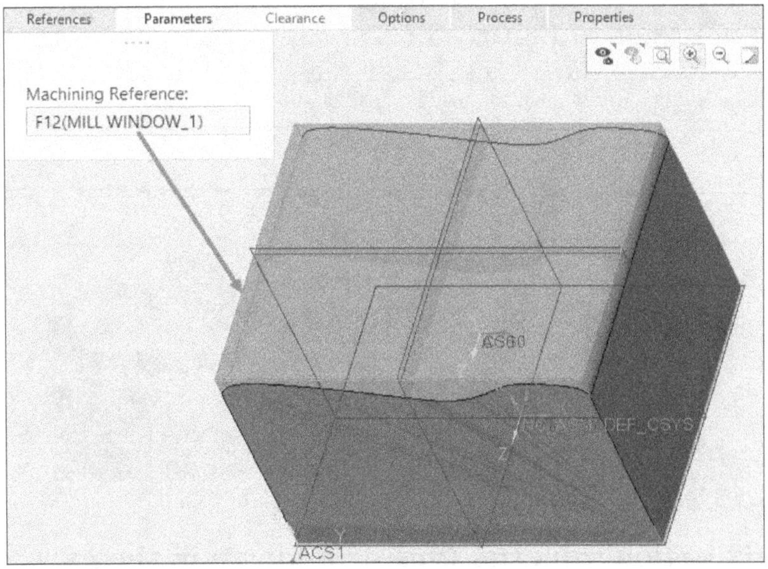

Figure-3. Mill window selected

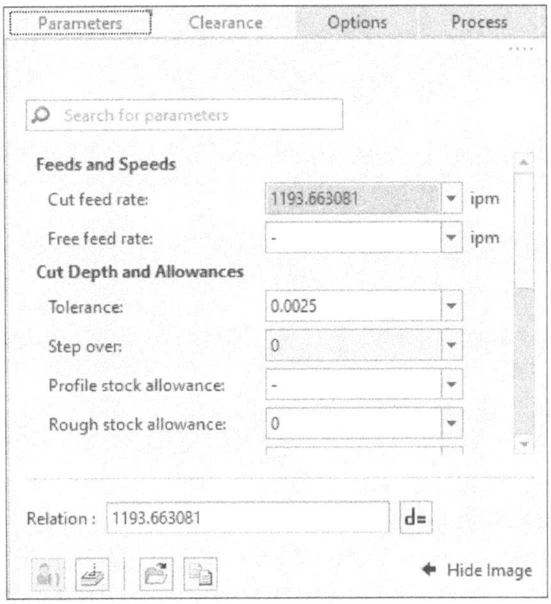

Figure-4. Parameters tab for HSM Rough

- Specify desired value in the **CUT feed rate** edit box to define feed rate at which tool will move while cutting.
- Similarly, specify free movement speed of cutting tool when it is not cutting in the **FREE feed rate** edit box.
- Select the **CONSTANT LOAD** option from the **Scan type** drop-down in the **Parameters** tab to keep the load on cutting tool constant while maintaining balance of cutting depth, feed rate, and so on. This option ensures more material removal with lesser machining time. Select the **TYPE SPIRAL** option from the drop-down to generate spiral cutting path. Select the **TYPE 1** option from the drop-down to create parallel cuts at multiple depths.
- Select the **ROUGH AND PROF** option from the **Roughing option** drop-down in **Parameters** tab to generate roughing as well as profiling toolpath. Select the **ROUGH ONLY** option from the drop-down to generate only roughing toolpath.
- Set the other parameters in **Parameters** tab as discussed earlier.

- Select the **Clearance** tab from the contextual tab in **Ribbon** and set desired location of clearance plane; refer to Figure-5.

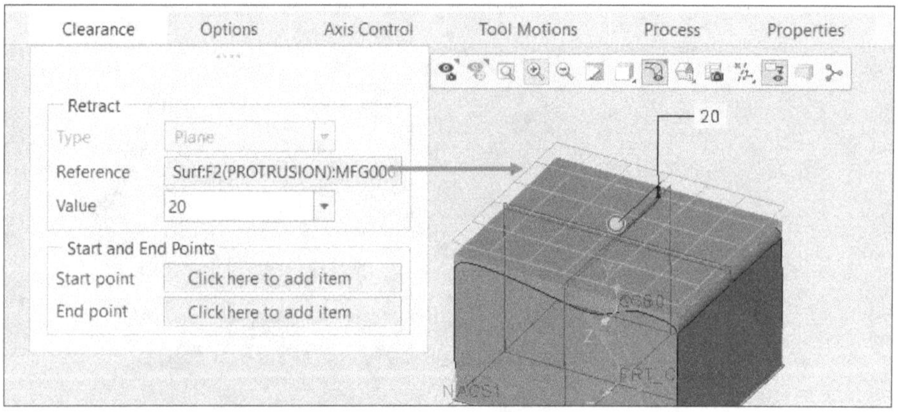

Figure-5. Setting clearance plane

- Select the **3 Axis** option from the **Type** drop-down in the **Axis Control** tab of the **Ribbon** to generate 3-axis high speed toolpath; refer to Figure-6.

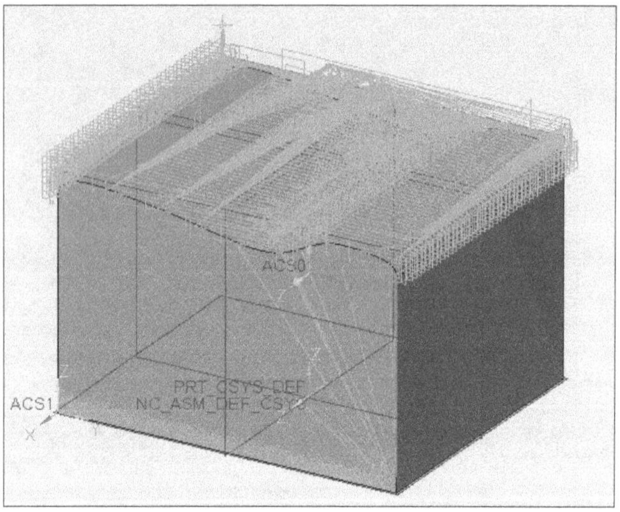

Figure-6. 3-axis toolpath

- Select the **3+2 Axis** option from the **Type** drop-down in the **Axis Control** tab to generate 5-axis milling toolpath. The options in **Axis Control** tab will be displayed as shown in Figure-7.

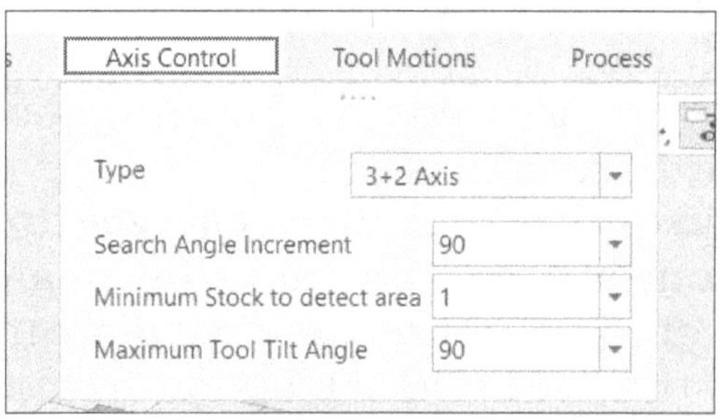

Figure-7. Axis Control tab for 5-axis

- Set desired angle value in the **Search Angle Increment** edit box to define the amount by which cutting tool tilt angle will increase/decrease to find optimum orientation while cutting. Specify desired value in the **Maximum Tool Tilt Angle** edit boxes to define the maximum angle upto which cutting tool can tilt to perform 5 axis milling operation.

- Specify desired value in the **Minimum Stock to detect area** edit box to define the minimum amount of stock to be available before 5 axis milling can be performed on the workpiece. The toolpath for 5 axis milling will be generated similar to shown in Figure-8.

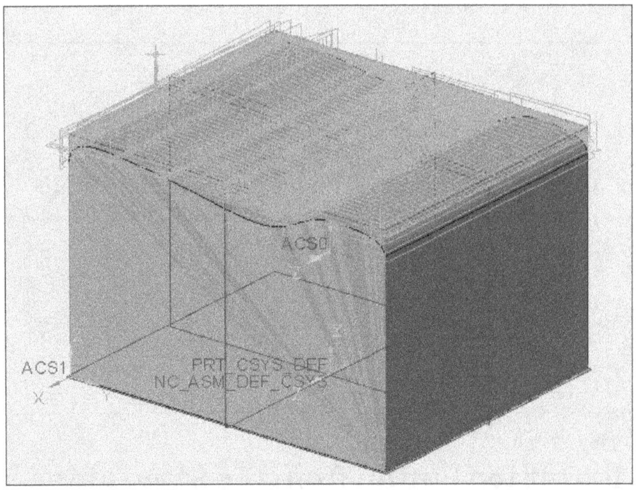

Figure-8. 5-axis HSM Rough toolpath

- Other options of the contextual tab have been discussed in earlier chapters. Click on the **OK** button from the **Ribbon** to generate the toolpath.

Material Removal Simulation and In-Process Stock Management

The In-process stocks are generally used for simulation and presentation purpose. In Creo Manufacturing, you can create and use In-process stocks in Material Removal Simulation environment. Consider a scenario when after generating toolpaths, you want to check material removal simulation of finish toolpath but want to use stock left after rough toolpath as starting stock. The process to create and manage material removal simulation is discussed next.

- After generating toolpaths, right-click on the rough milling toolpath from **Navigation Trees**. A shortcut menu will be displayed as shown in Figure-9.

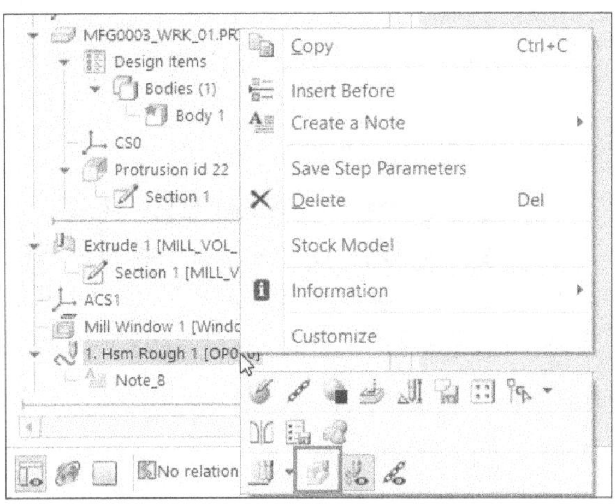

Figure-9. Shortcut menu for HSM rough toolpath

- Select the **Material Removal Simulation** button from the shortcut menu. The simulation environment will be displayed; refer to Figure-10.

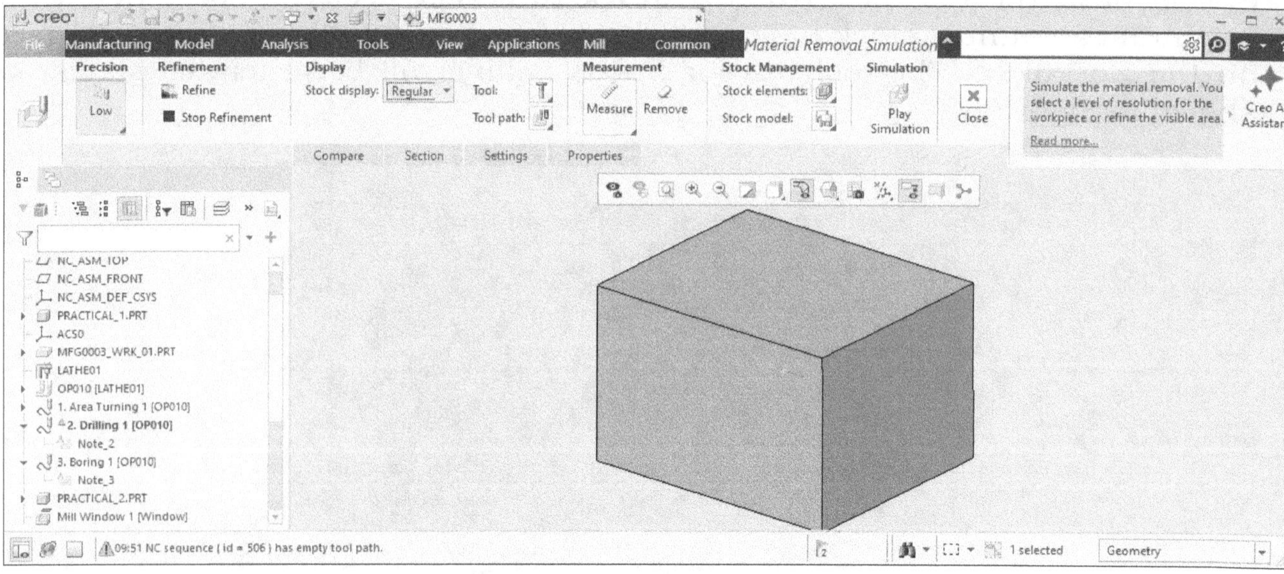

Figure-10. Material Removal simulation

- Click on the **Play Simulation** button from the **Simulation** section in the **Material Removal** contextual tab of **Ribbon**. The **Play Simulation** dialog box will be displayed.
- Click on the **Play Simulation** button from the dialog box. The toolpath simulation will be displayed; refer to Figure-11.

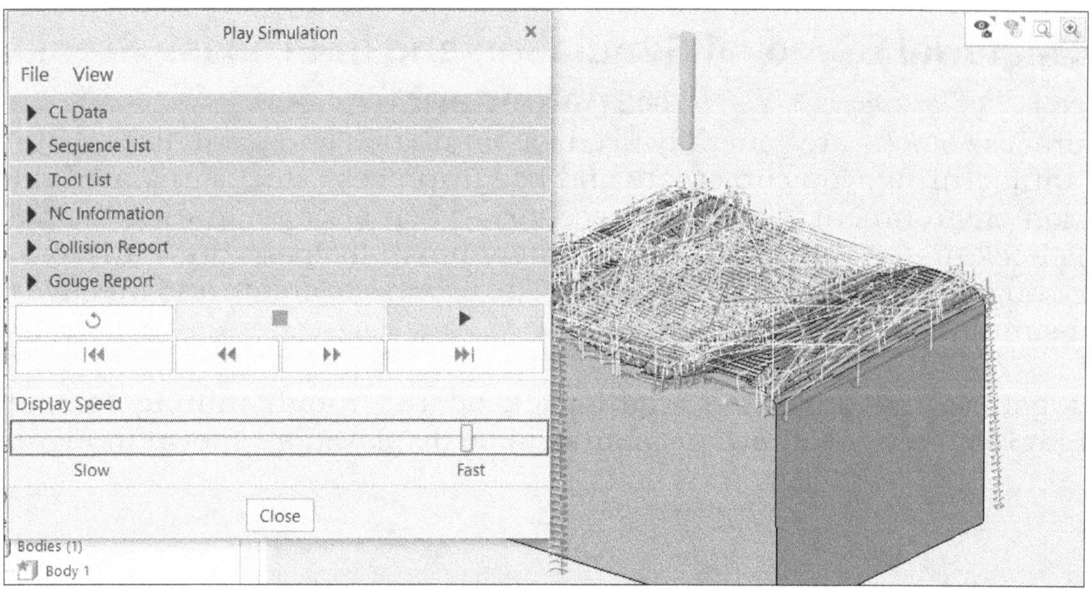

Figure-11. After performing material removal simulation

Saving In-Process Stock

- Click on the **Save In-Process Stock** option from the **Stock model** drop-down in the **Material Removal Simulation** contextual tab of **Ribbon**; refer to Figure-12. The **Save current stock** dialog box will be displayed; refer to Figure-13.

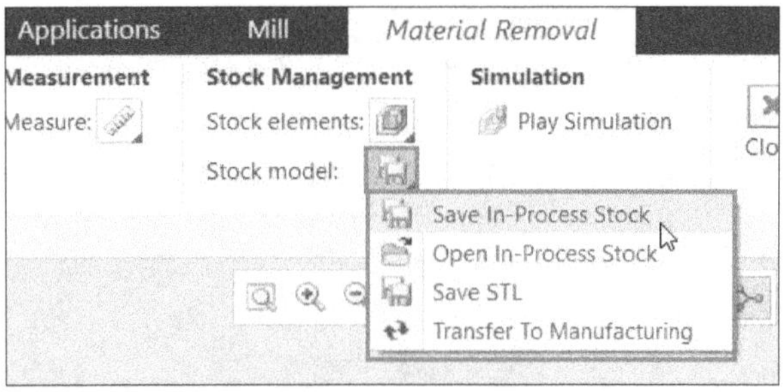

Figure-12. Stock model drop-down

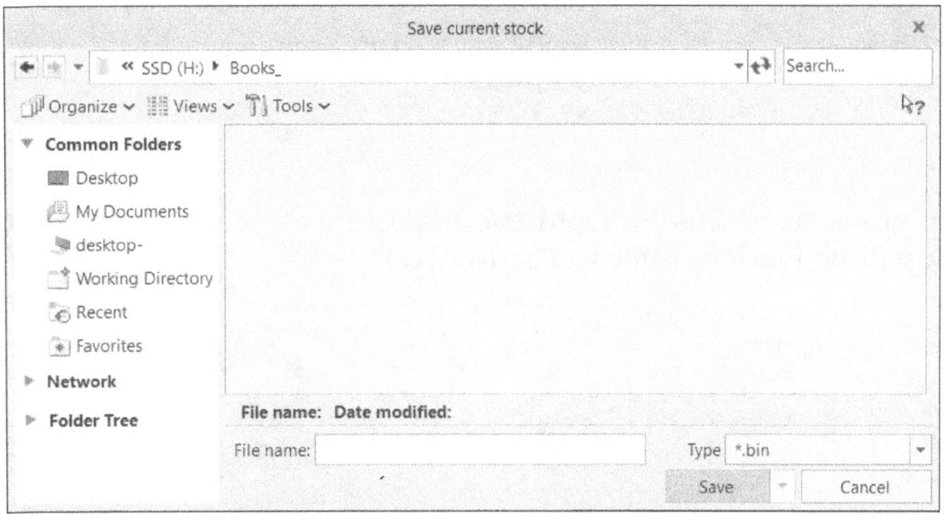

Figure-13. Save current stock dialog box

- Specify desired name of in-process stock in the **File name** edit box and click on the **Save** button. The stock after roughing will be saved at specified location.
- Click on the **Close** button from the **Material Removal Simulation** contextual tab to exit the simulation environment.

Loading In-Process Stock

- After generating roughing & finishing toolpaths and saving the In-process stock of roughing toolpath, right-click on finish toolpath to display shortcut menu as discussed earlier.
- Select the **Material Removal Simulation** button from the shortcut menu. The **Material Removal** contextual tab will be displayed in the **Ribbon**.
- Click on the **Open In-Process Stock** option from the **Stock model** drop-down in the **Ribbon**. The **Load stock** dialog box will be displayed; refer to Figure-14.

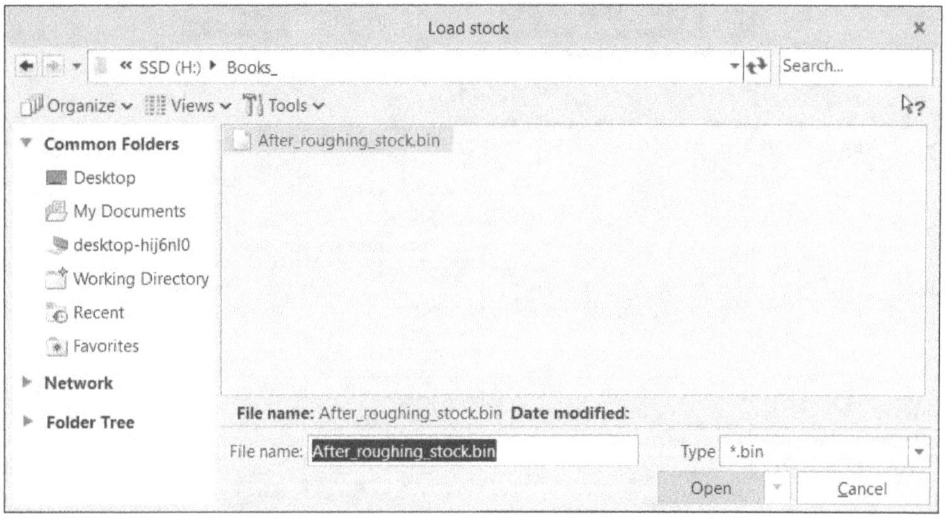

Figure-14. Load stock dialog box

- Select the stock to be loaded from the dialog box and click on the **Open** button. The stock will be loaded; refer to Figure-15.

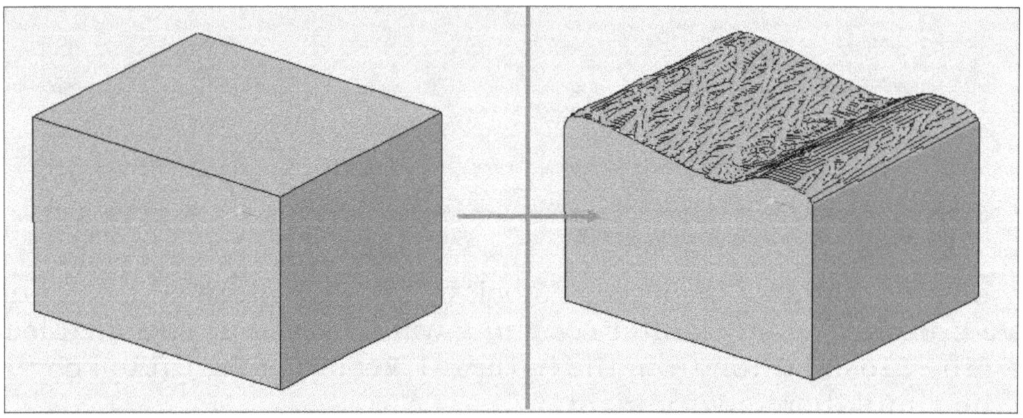

Figure-15. Stock after loading in-process stock

- Click on the **Play Simulation** button to check the simulation of toolpath.

Generating Stock for Rest Roughing

The stock required for rest roughing is generally the stock left after previous operations. You can generate stock after any operation in Creo Manufacturing. The procedure to generate the stock is given next.

- Right-click on the toolpath from **Navigation Trees** after which you want to generate the stock and select the **Stock Model** option from the shortcut menu; refer to Figure-16. The **Stock Model** contextual tab will be displayed; refer to Figure-17 and you will be asked to select previous stock/boundary.

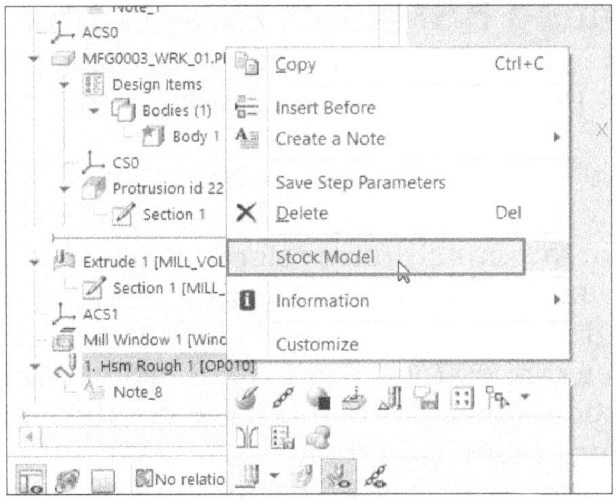

Figure-16. Stock Model option

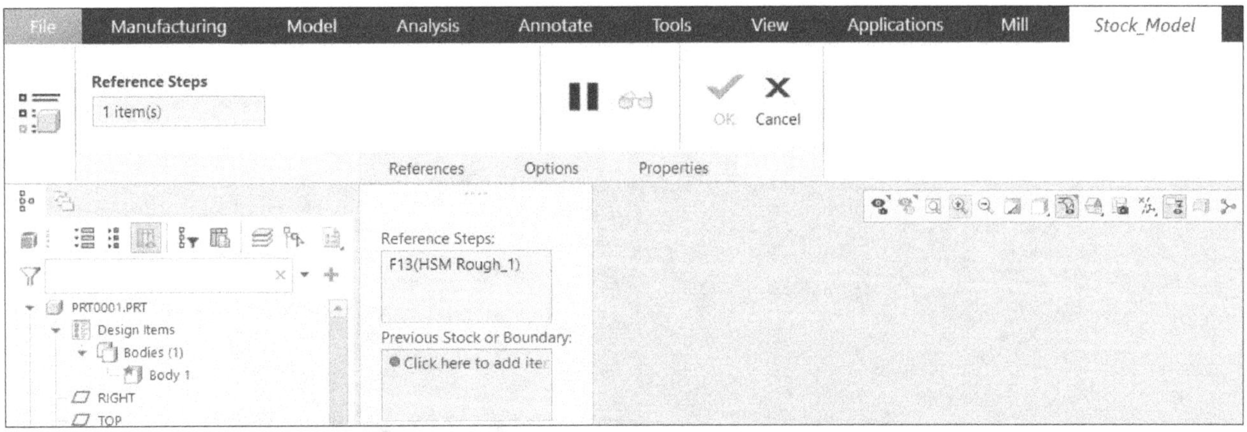

Figure-17. Stock Model contextual tab

- Select workpiece (stock) earlier created from the graphics area to use as reference.
- Click on the **Export Stock Model** option from the **Options** tab in the **Ribbon**. The **Export** dialog box will be displayed; refer to Figure-18.

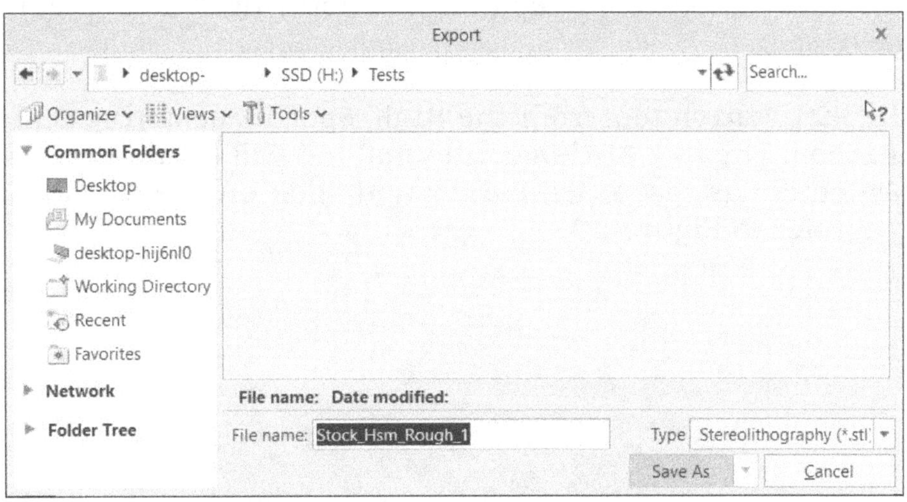

Figure-18. Export dialog box

- Specify desired name of the stock file in the **File name** edit box and click on the **Save As** button to save the stock file at desired location.
- Click on the **OK** button from the **Ribbon** to create the stock feature in **Navigation Trees** as well.

Creating HSM Rest Rough Toolpath

The **HSM Rest Rough** tool is used to remove material left by previous toolpaths at high speed. The procedure to use this tool is given next.

- Click on the **HSM Rest Rough** tool from the **High Speed Milling** panel in the **Mill** tab of the **Ribbon**. The **HSM Rest Rough** contextual tab will be displayed.
- Select the cutting tool and machining reference geometry as discussed earlier.
- Click on the **Select Rough Stock File** button from the **References** tab to use earlier saved stocked file as initial stock for current operation. Alternatively, you can select the reference stock from the **Stock Model Ref** drop-down in the **Reference** tab of **Ribbon**. Make sure you have created stock model as discussed in previous topic before using this tool.
- Set the other parameters as discussed earlier and click on the **OK** button from the **Ribbon** to create the toolpath; refer to Figure-19.

Figure-19. HSM Rest Rough toolpath

Creating HSM Finish Toolpath

The HSM Finish toolpath is used to perform finishing operation on rough machined workpiece to achieve tighter tolerance in manufacturing. The procedure to use this tool is given next.

- Click on the **HSM Finish** tool from the **High Speed Machining** panel in the **Mill** tab of the **Ribbon**. The **HSM Finish** contextual tab will be displayed in the **Ribbon**.
- Set the parameters as discussed earlier and click on the **OK** button to generate the toolpath; refer to Figure-20.

Figure-20. HSM Finish toolpath

Creating HSM Rest Finish Toolpath

The HSM Rest Finish toolpath is similar to HSM Rest Rough toolpath with only difference being tighter tolerances. Note that to use generate HSM Rest Finish toolpath, there must be an HSM Rest Rough toolpath already created.

Creating HSM 5 Axis Swarf Finish

The HSM 5 Axis Swarf Finish is used to generate toolpath for finishing tapered or irregular surface walls using the side of cutting tool instead of using only tip of the cutting tool. The procedure to use this tool is discussed next.

- Click on the **HSM 5 Axis Swarf Finish** tool from the **High Speed Milling** panel in the **Mill** tab of the **Ribbon**. The **HSM Swarf Finish** contextual tab will be displayed; refer to Figure-21.

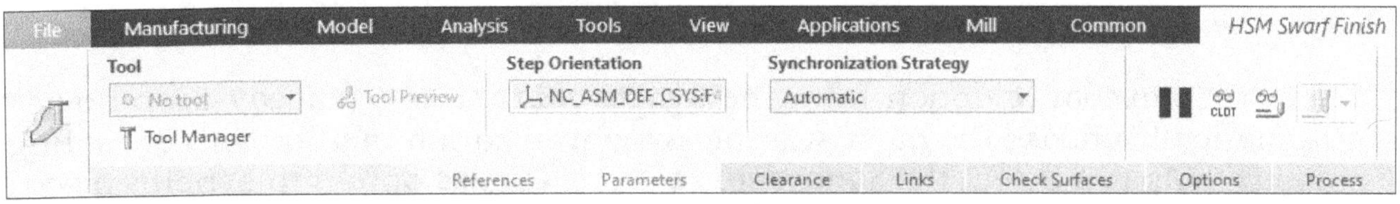

Figure-21. HSM Swarf Finish contextual tab

- Select the cutting tool, coordinate system, and other settings as discussed earlier.
- Click on the **Reference** tab in **Ribbon** and select Surface option from the Selection type drop-down of Swarf References section to define surface reference to be machined using swarf milling. The options will be displayed as shown in Figure-22.

Figure-22. Reference tab

- Select desired surface(s) to be machined; refer to Figure-23. Similarly, select desired reference from **Floor References** section to define floor of toolpath.

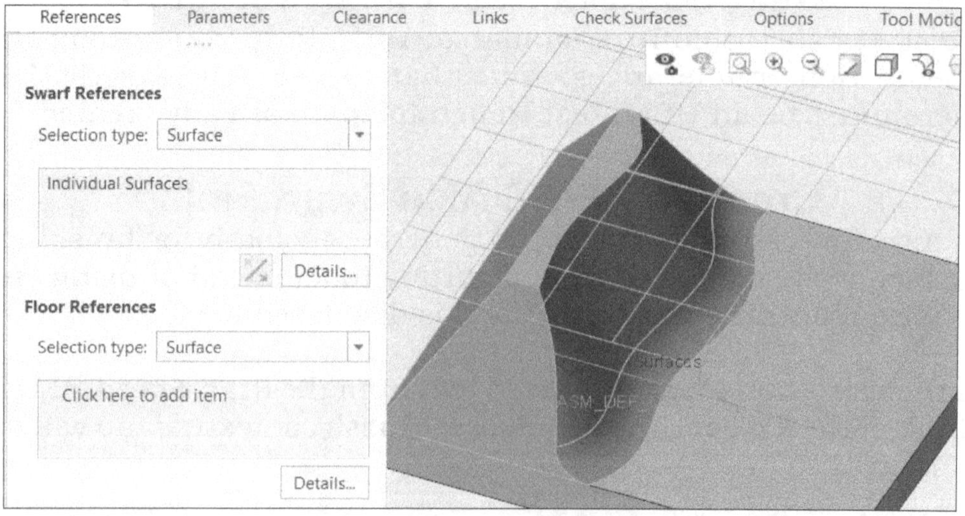

Figure-23. Surfaces selected for swarf milling

- Select the **Automatic** option from the **Synchronization Strategy** drop-down to automatically choose the most suitable synchronization method for generating a smooth toolpath. Select the **Synchronize Tilt Curves** option to synchronize the tool movement based on the selected tilt curves and maintain a consistent tool tilt. Select the **Synchronize Guide Curves** option to synchronize the toolpath with the selected guide curves for accurate machining. Select the **Shortest Distance** option to synchronize the tool orientation by following the shortest distance between the drive and guide surfaces. Select the **Iso Curves** option to synchronize the toolpath along the isoparametric (U or V) curves of the selected surface. Select the **Normal to Guide Curves** option to keep the cutting tool normal to the selected guide curves throughout the machining operation.
- Specify other parameters as discussed earlier and check the preview of toolpath; refer to Figure-24. Click on the **OK** button from the **Ribbon** to create toolpath and exit the tool. Note that you can use swarf toolpaths to machine turbine blades and similar geometries.

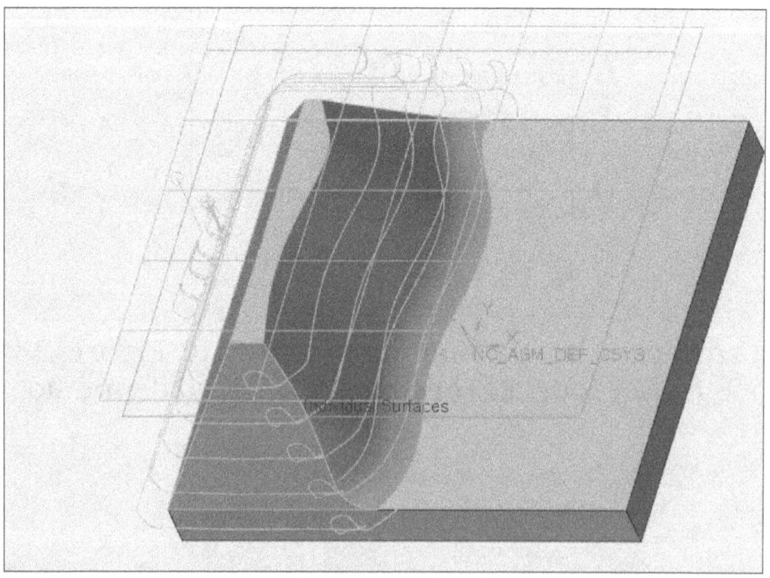

Figure-24. Preview of swarf toolpath

Creating Auto Deburring Toolpath

The Auto Deburring toolpath is used to remove burr from sharp edges of the workpiece after performing other cutting operations. The procedure to create this toolpath is given next.

- Click on the **Auto Deburring** tool from the **High Speed Milling** panel in the **Mill** tab of the **Ribbon**. The **Auto Deburring** contextual tab will be displayed; refer to Figure-25.

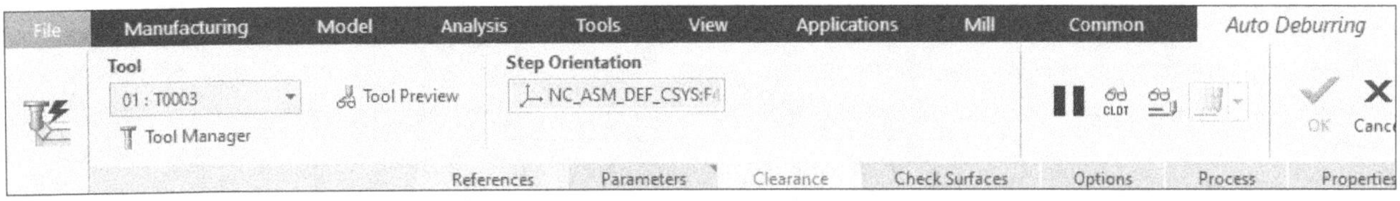

Figure-25. Auto Deburring contextual tab

- Select desired option from the **Axes** drop-down in **Workcell** section of the **Ribbon** to define the number of axes to be used for generating deburring toolpath; refer to Figure-26. Note that this option is available for 5-axis machines.

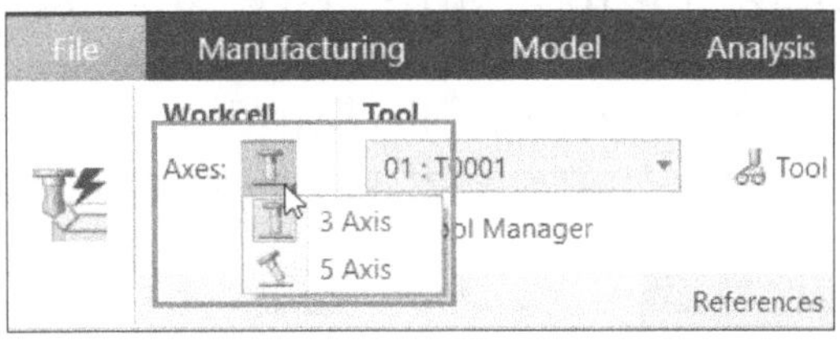

Figure-26. Axes drop-down

- Click on the **References** tab in **Ribbon** and select the **Include all edges** button to deburr all the edges of the model. Deselect this button if you want to select the edges to be deburred manually. After deselecting this button, click in the **Include edges** selection box of **References** tab and select the edges to be deburred from the model (Press and Hold **CTRL** key for selecting multiple edges).
- Set the other parameters as discussed earlier and click on the **OK** button. The toolpath will be created.

Creating HSM 5 Axis Rough Toolpath

The HSM 5 Axis Rough toolpath is created to remove large portion of stock using multi-axis tool movement. The procedure to create this toolpath is given next.

- Click on the **HSM 5 Axis Rough** tool from the **High Speed Milling** panel of the **Mill** tab in the **Ribbon**. The **HSM Multi Axis Rough** contextual tab will be displayed in the **Ribbon**.
- Select the cutting tool and coordinate system as discussed earlier.
- Click on the **Reference** tab in the **Ribbon** to define the geometry to be machined. The options will be displayed as shown in Figure-27.

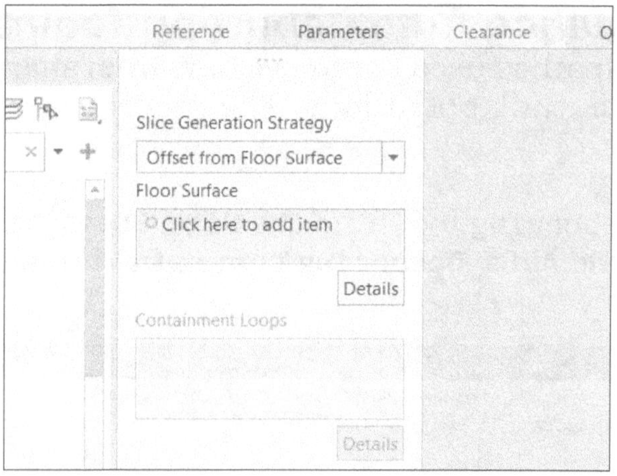

Figure-27. Reference tab for multi axis rough

- Select the **Offset from Floor Surface** option from the **Slice Generation Strategy** drop-down in the tab to use curvature of selected floor surface of model as template for generating toolpath. Select the **Offset from Ceiling Surface** option to use curvature of top surface of model as template for generating toolpaths. Select the **Morph** option from the drop-down to blend selected ceiling face and floor face of the model when generating toolpaths. (We have selected **Offset from Floor Surface** option in our case.)
- Click in the **Floor Surface** selection box and select the surfaces to be used as reference template for generating offset toolpaths; refer to Figure-28.

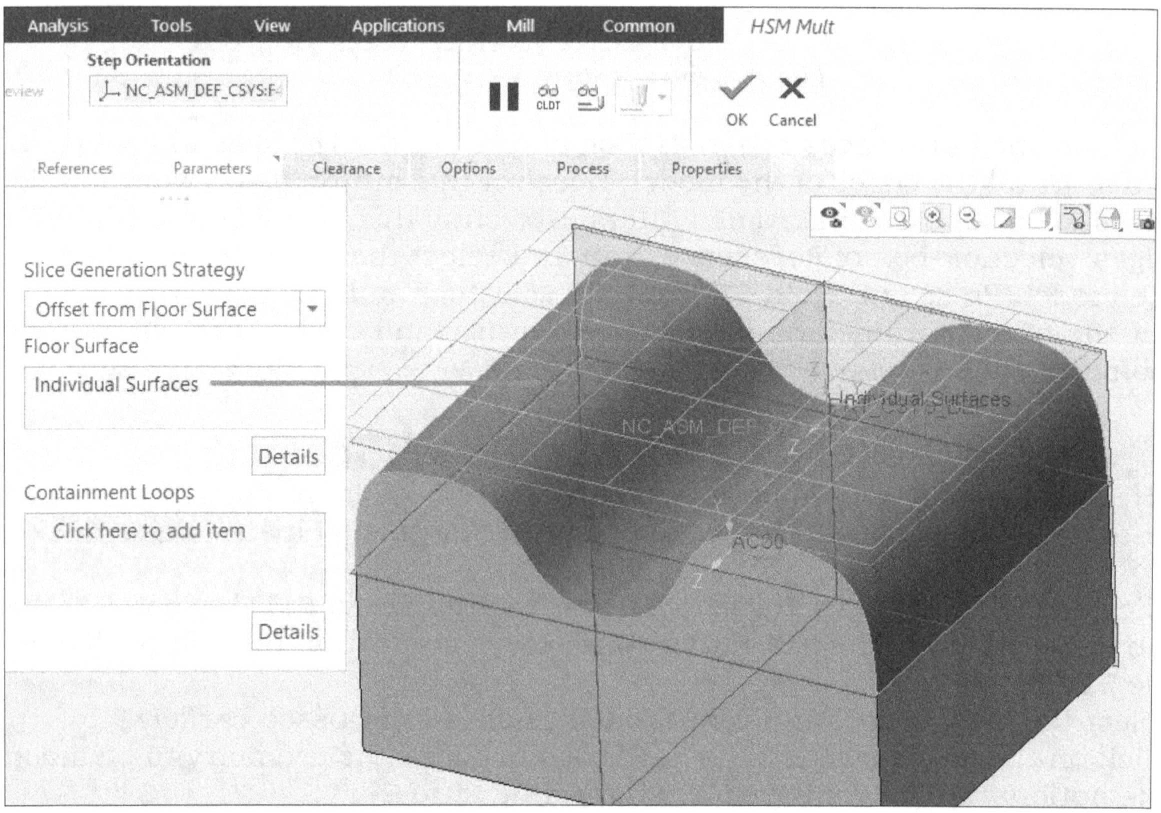

Figure-28. Surfaces selected for multi-axis rough machining

- Set the other parameters as discussed earlier and click on the **OK** button to generate the toolpath; refer to Figure-29.

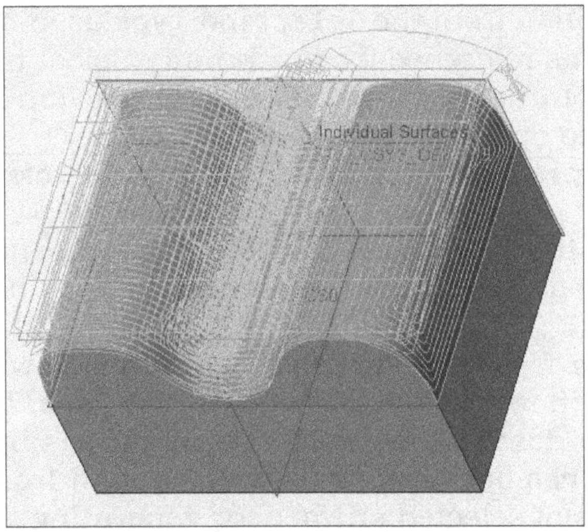

Figure-29. Preview of multi-axis rough toolpath

Similarly, you can create HSM multiaxis Rest Rough toolpaths using the **HSM 5 Axis Rest Rough** tool from **High Speed Milling** panel in the **Mill** tab of **Ribbon**.

Geodesic 5 Axis Finish Toolpath

The **Geodesic 5 Axis Finish** tool is used to perform finishing operation on complex 3D parts using multi-axis tool motion. The procedure to use this tool is given next.

- After performing desired roughing operations on the model, click on the **Geodesic 5 Axis Finish** tool from the **High Speed Milling** panel of **Mill** tab in the **Ribbon**. The **Geodesic Finish** contextual tab will be displayed.

Reference tab

- Click on the **Reference** tab to select the geometry to be machined; refer to Figure-30.

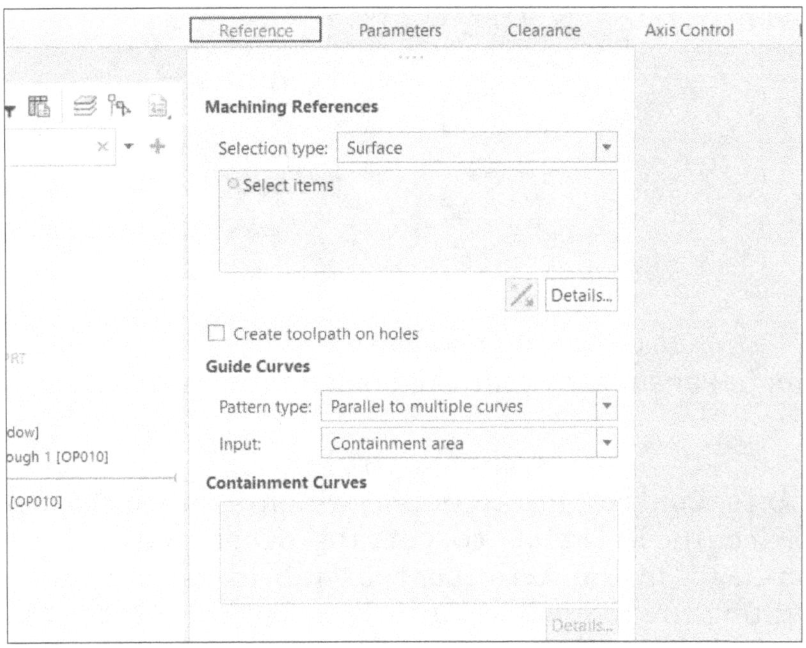

Figure-30. Reference tab for geodesic finish

- Select the **Surface** option from the **Selection type** drop-down in **Reference** tab to use selected surface as reference for machining. Select the **Previous Step** option from the drop-down to use surface selected in previous geodesic toolpath. (We have selected **Surface** option in our case).
- Select the surfaces/previous step based on option selected in **Selection type** drop-down.
- Select the **Create toolpath on holes** check box to create finishing toolpath on filled holes as well. Note that you cannot select the holes to be machined individually in this case.
- Select desired option from the **Pattern type** drop-down to define how cutting passes will be oriented in the toolpath. Select the **Parallel to multiple curves** option from the drop-down to generate cutting passes by offsetting all the guide curves. Select the **Morph between two curves** option from the drop-down to use two boundary curves of selected surface for generating toolpath.
- By default, **Containment area** option is selected in the **Input** drop-down of **Reference** tab so boundaries of containment area are used to define pattern of toolpath. To select the containment area, click in the **Containment Curves** selection box of **Reference** tab and select the curves to be used for defining pattern from the drawing area while holding the **CTRL** key.
- Select the **User defined** option from the **Input** drop-down to select the curves to be used for defining pattern of toolpath. On selecting this option, the **Input** selection box is displayed in the **Reference** tab. Click in the **Input** selection box and select desired curves from the drawing area; refer to Figure-31.

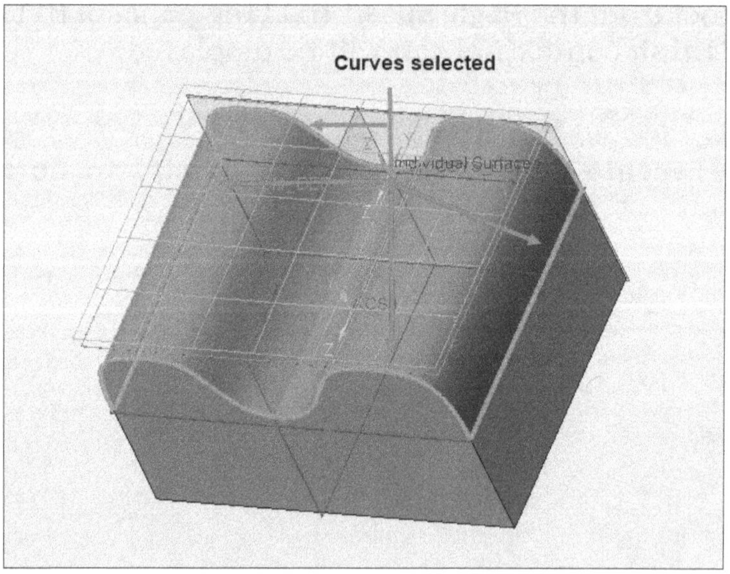

Figure-31. Curves selected as guide curves

- Set the options in **Parameters** and **Clearance** tabs as discussed earlier.

Axis Control tab

- Click on the **Axis Control** tab to define which axis will be used for tilting the cutting tool. Select the **Relative to cutting direction** option from the **Tilting strategy** drop-down in the **Axis Control** tab to use current tool direction as reference for tilting the tool while cutting. Select the **Tilt with fixed angle to axis** option from the **Tilting strategy** drop-down to define the axis to be used as reference for tilt direction. Set the other parameters in this tab as discussed earlier.

Links tab

- Select the **Links** tab from the **Ribbon** to define how cutting passes will be linked at the end points where cutting tool changes direction. The options will be displayed as shown in Figure-32.
- Select the **Automatic arc** option from the **Lead-in** drop-down to automatically select the arc type at the start of cutting pass. Select the **Vertical tangential arc** option from the drop-down to create an arc vertically tangent to the plunge direction at the start of toolpath. Select the **Horizontal tangential arc** option from the drop-down to create horizontally tangent arc at the start of cutting pass.
- Select the **Tangent arc** option from the drop-down to create a tangent arc at entry when direction of entry is neither horizontal nor vertical.
- Similarly, you can set parameters in the **Lead-out** drop-down to define exit motion of cutting passes.
- Specify desired value in the **Lead Radius** edit box to define arc radius at entry and exit points of cutting passes. Select the **In percentage of tool diameter** option from the drop-down next to **Lead Radius** edit box to specify radius of arc in percentage of cutting tool diameter. Select the **Value (in model units)** option to specify the radius of lead in/out arcs in default unit.

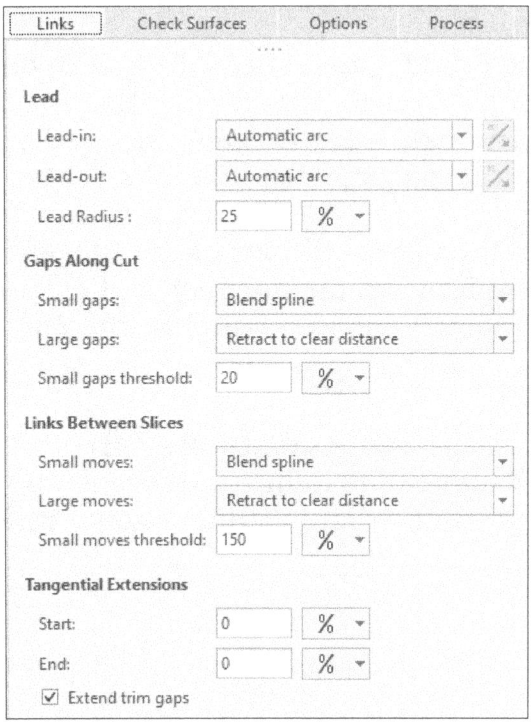

Figure-32. Options in Links tab

- Select desired option from the **Small gaps** drop-down to define how cutting tool will process small gaps in the model when generating cutting passes. Select the **Blend Spline** option from the drop-down to create tangential arcs connecting the open ends of toolpath. Select the **Direct** option from the drop-down to connect the cutting passes with straight line. Select the **Follow Surface** option from the drop-down if you want the tool to follow current surface curvature then machining gap. Select the **Retract to clear distance** option from the drop-down to retract the tool over the gap by clearance distance and then continue the toolpath. Select the **Retract to rapid distance** option from the drop-down to retract the tool upto rapid movement height over the gap and then continue the cutting toolpath. Select the **Retract to clearance** option from the drop-down to make the cutting tool retract to clearance plane when encountered with gap. Refer to Figure-33.

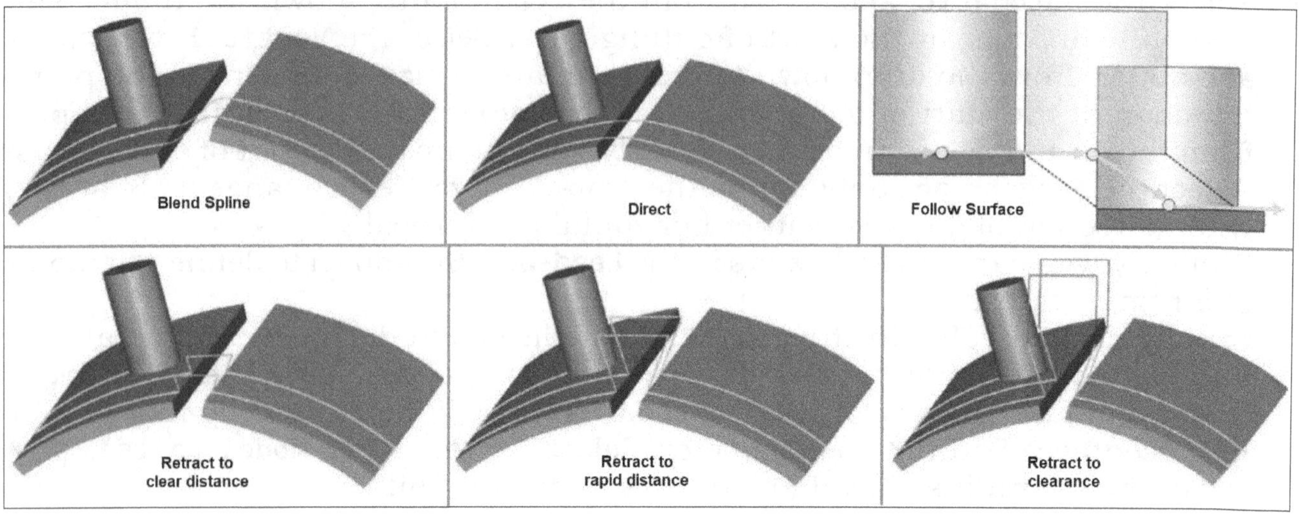

Figure-33. Small gap link options

- Set desired value in the **Small gaps size** edit box to define the size of gap below which gaps will be considered as small gap. Set the parameters as discussed earlier in the drop-down next to **Small gaps size** edit box.
- Similarly, you can set the parameters in **Links Between Slices** section of the **Link** tab of the **Ribbon**.
- Specify desired value in the **Start** edit box of the **Tangential Extensions** section of the tab to define the length by which start point of cutting passes will be extended or trimmed. Similarly, specify desired value in the **End** edit box for end points of cutting passes.

Check Surfaces tab

- Click on the **Check Surfaces** tab to define the faces to be avoided when performing machining. The options will be displayed as shown in Figure-34.

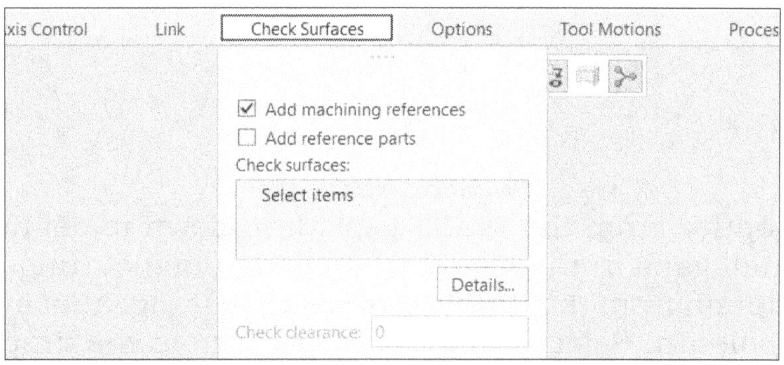

Figure-34. Check Surfaces tab

- Select the **Add machining references** check box to avoid all the machining references like fixtures, machine table, and so on.
- Select the **Add reference parts** check box to add model and related parts in the list of geometry to be avoided when created toolpath. On selecting this check box, all the model entities in graphics area will be selected.

- Set the other parameters as discussed earlier and click on the **OK** button to generate the toolpath; refer to Figure-35.

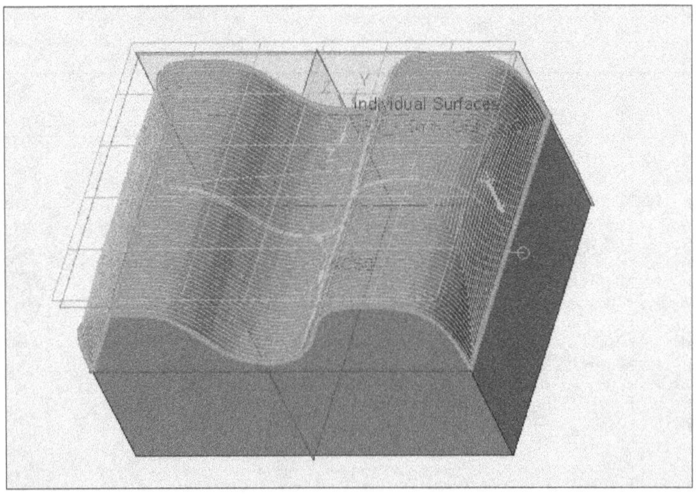

Figure-35. Preview of geodesic finish toolpath

Creating 5 Axis Wall Finishing Toolpath

The **Wall 5 Axis Finish** tool is used to generate toolpath for finishing walls of the model in tight tolerance. The procedure to use this tool is given next.

- Click on the **Wall 5 Axis Finish** tool from the **High Speed Milling** panel in the **Mill** tab of the **Ribbon**. The **Wall Finish** contextual tab will be displayed in the **Ribbon**.
- Make sure the **Surface** option is selected in the **Selection type** drop-down of **Wall References** section in the **Reference** tab of **Ribbon** and select the side walls of the model to be finished; refer to Figure-36.

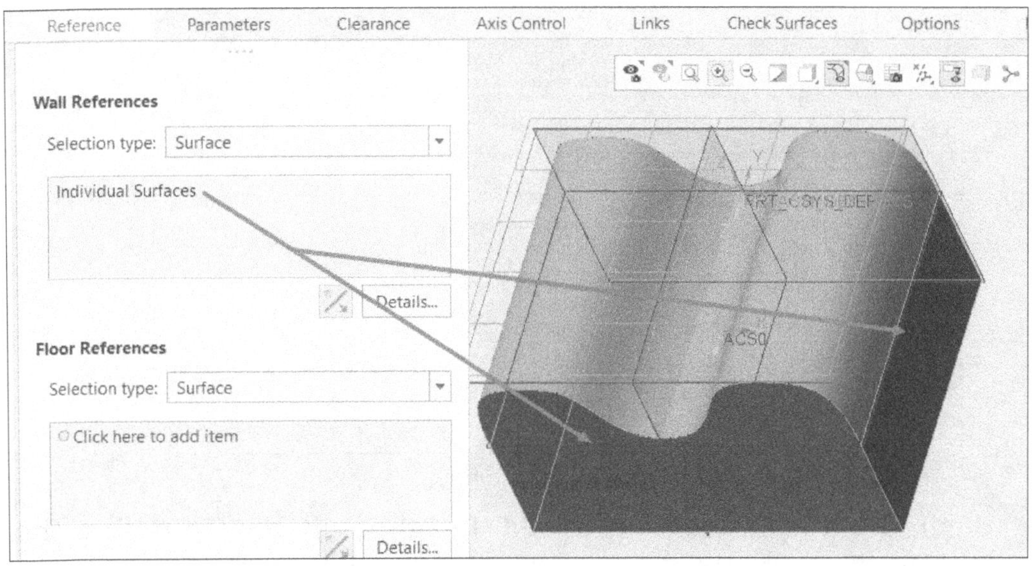

Figure-36. Wall surfaces selected

- Select the **Surface** option from drop-down in the **Floor References** section and click in the selection box of the section to select floor surface of model. Alternatively, select the **Previous Step** option from the **Selection type** drop-down and select previous operation from the **Navigation Trees** to use floor of previous operation; refer to Figure-37.

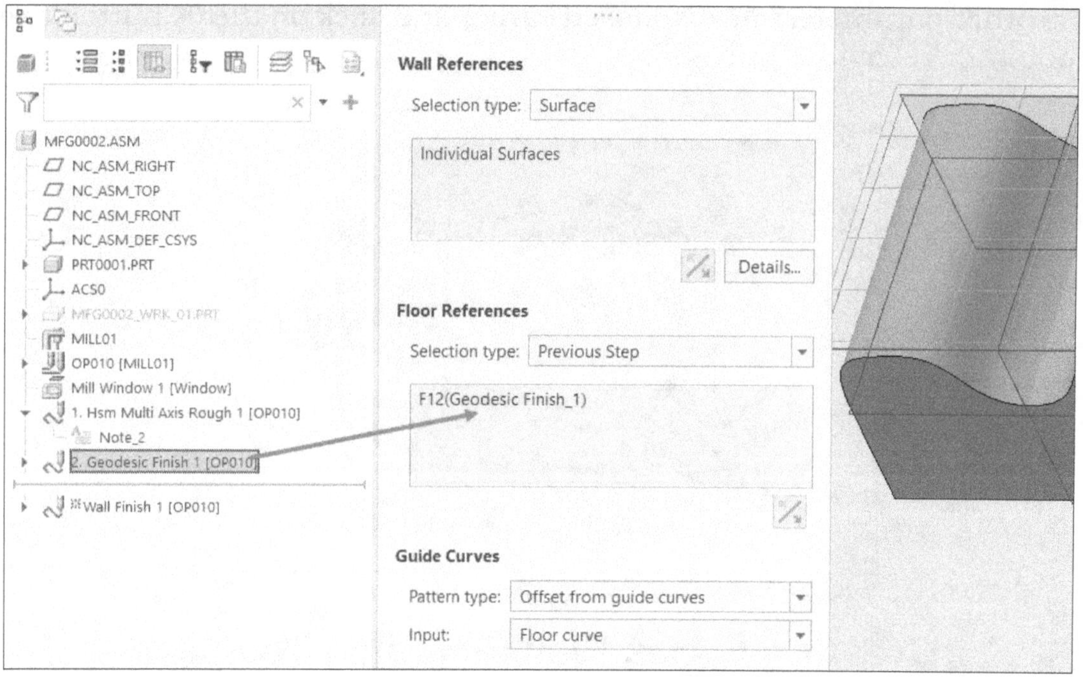

Figure-37. Selecting previous operation

- Click on the **Axis Control** tab in the **Ribbon** to define the maximum tilt angles allowed in toolpath. The options will be displayed as shown in Figure-38.

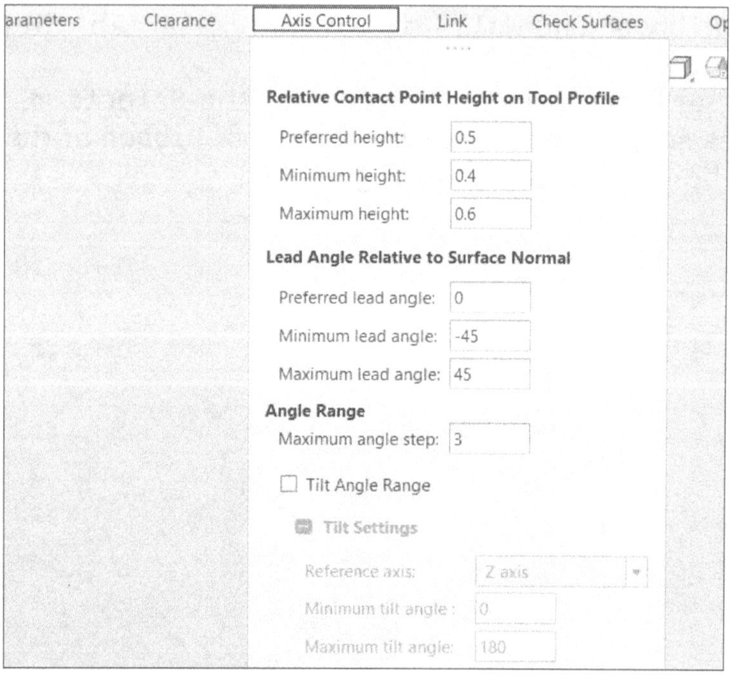

Figure-38. Axis Control tab for wall finish

- Specify desired value in the **Preferred height** edit box to define the point on cutting tool profile to be used as reference point for creating cutting passes.
- Specify desired value in the **Minimum height** edit box to define minimum height of reference point on cutting tool profile. Similarly, specify maximum height of reference point in the **Maximum height** edit box.
- Specify the preferred angle at which cutting passes will start in the **Preferred lead angle** edit box. Similarly, specify the maximum and minimum angle limit values for lead angle in the **Maximum lead angle** and **Minimum lead angle** edit boxes, respectively.

- Specify desired value in the **Maximum angle step** edit box to define the minimum amount by which angle will change.
- Select the **Tilt Angle Range** check box to define the range within which cutting tool can tilt.
- Specify other parameters as discussed earlier and click on the **OK** button from the **Ribbon** to generate the toolpath; refer to Figure-39.

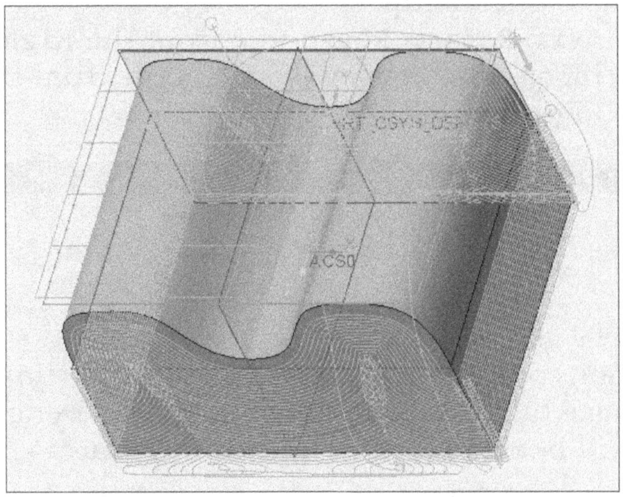

Figure-39. Wall finish 5-axis toolpath

Creating Floor 5 Axis Finish Toolpath

The **Floor 5 Axis Finish** tool is used to create toolpath for finishing base of the model within tight tolerances. The procedure to use this tool is given next.

- Click on the **Floor 5 Axis Finish** tool from the **High Speed Milling** panel in the **Mill** tab of the **Ribbon**. The **Floor Finish** contextual tab will be displayed in the **Ribbon**.
- Set the parameters as discussed earlier and click on the **OK** button. The toolpath will be created; refer to Figure-40.

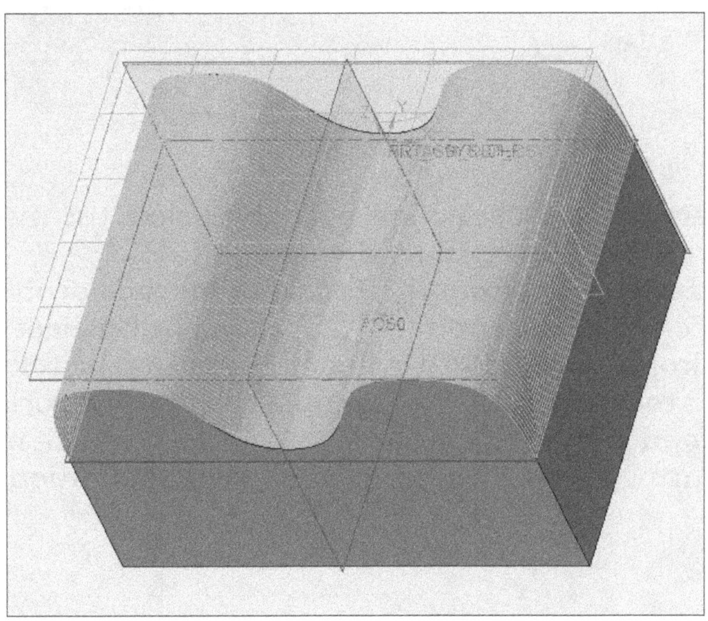

Figure-40. Floor finish toolpath

Creating HSM 4 Axis Rotary Rough

The **HSM 4 Axis Rotary Rough** tool is used to create toolpath for machining faces of irregular cylindrical objects like turbine blades, cam shafts, crank shafts, and so on. The procedure to use this tool is given next.

- Open the part on which you want to perform 4-axis milling operation and create a 4 axis, 5-axis or mill-turn setup.
- Click on the **HSM 4 Axis Rotary Rough** tool from the **High Speed Milling** panel of **Mill** tab in the **Ribbon**. The **Rotary Rough** contextual tab will be displayed in the **Ribbon**; refer to Figure-41.

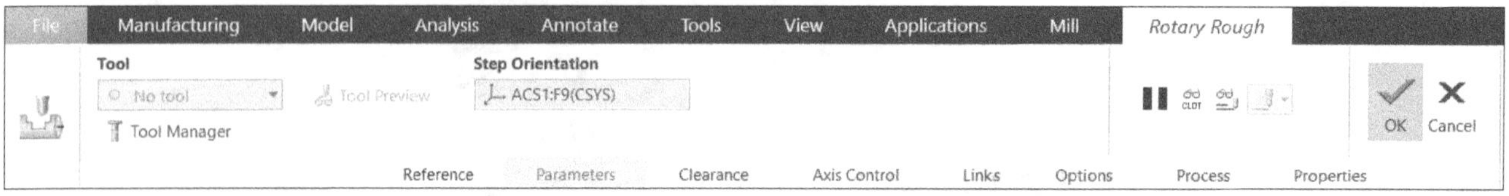

Figure-41. Rotary Rough contextual tab

- Select the cutting tool, coordinate system, and other settings as discussed earlier.
- Click on the **Reference** tab in **Ribbon** to define the reference parts and machining area. The options will be displayed as shown in Figure-42.

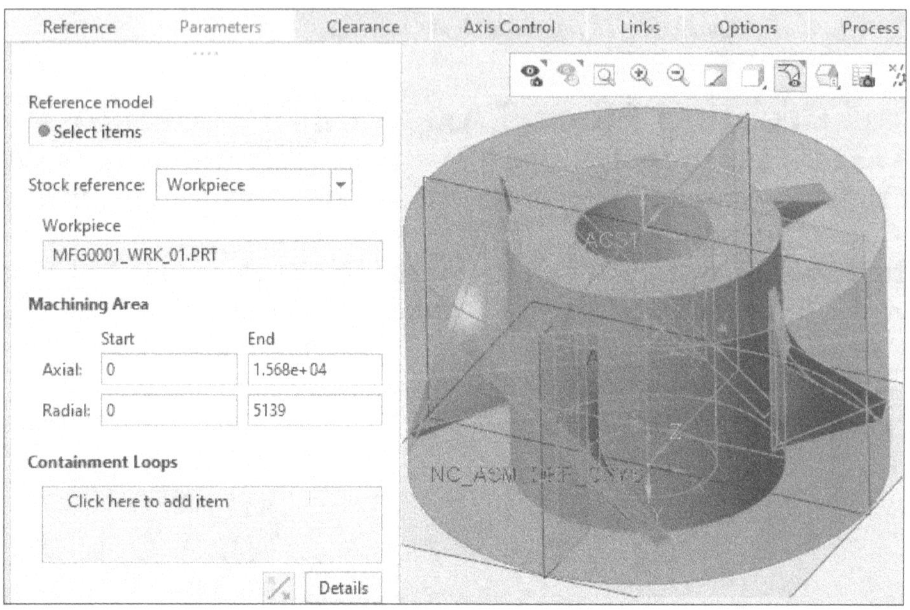

Figure-42. Reference tab

- Click in the **Reference part** selection field and select the model to be machined from graphics area if not selected by default.
- Select the **Workpiece** option from the **Stock reference** drop-down to use earlier created workpiece stock as current stock for toolpath. Select the **Bound cylinder** option from the drop-down to use a cylinder bounding the reference part as stock. Select the **Rough stock file** option to use an STL file for importing the stock. Select the **Stock model** option from the drop-down to select a stock model created earlier in the manufacturing setup after performing some operations.

- Specify desired values in the **Axial** and **Radial** edit boxes to define the limits within which 4-axis roughing operation will be performed. Values in **Axial** edit boxes define the start and end limits of machining zone along the length of cylindrical part. Values in **Radial** edit boxes define the machining limits along radius of part. You can also use the handles on the part to perform the same operation; refer to Figure-43.

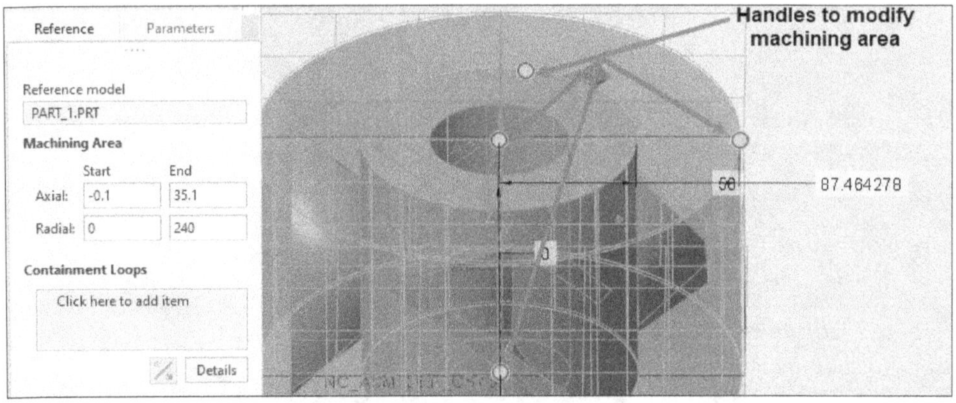

Figure-43. Handles for modifying machining area

- Click on the **Parameters** tab and specify cutting parameters as discussed earlier.
- Click on the **Preview Toolpath** button from the **Ribbon** to check preview of toolpath before creating it; refer to Figure-44. Click on the **OK** button to create the toolpath.

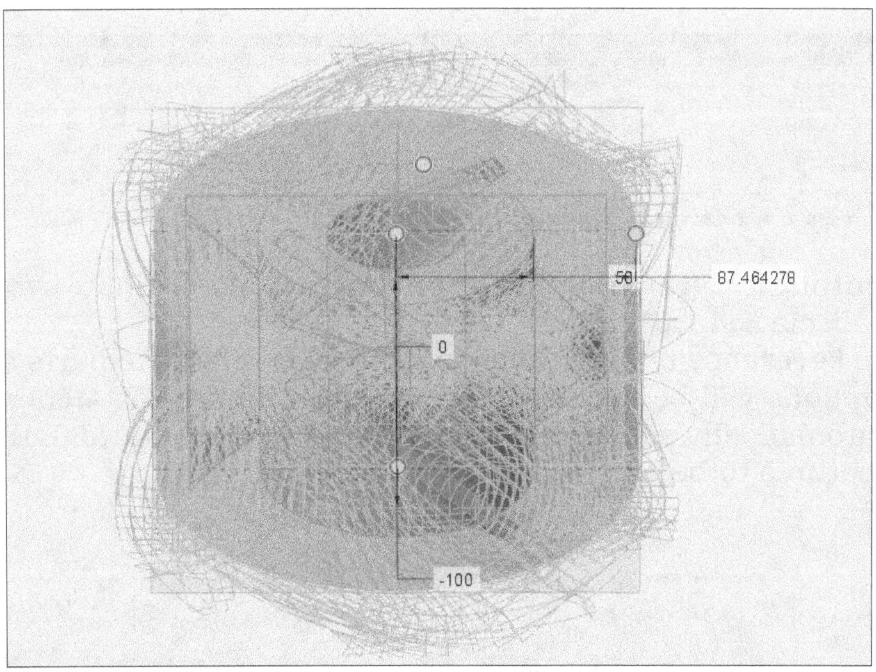

Figure-44. 4-axis rough toolpath created

Similarly, you can use the **HSM 4 Axis Rotary Finish** tool to create finishing toolpath for similar models; refer to Figure-45.

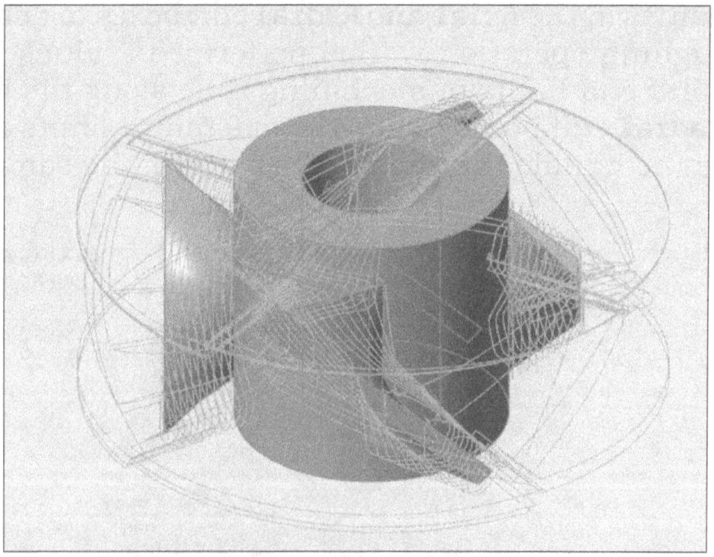

Figure-45. 4-axis rotary finish toolpath

HSM Undercut Machining

The **HSM Undercut Machining** tool is used to insert a 3-axis HSM undercut machining step. The procedure to use this tool is discussed next.

- Click on the **HSM Undercut Machining** tool from the **High Speed Milling** panel of **Mill** tab in the **Ribbon**. The **HSM Undercut Machining** contextual tab will be displayed in the **Ribbon**; refer to Figure-46.

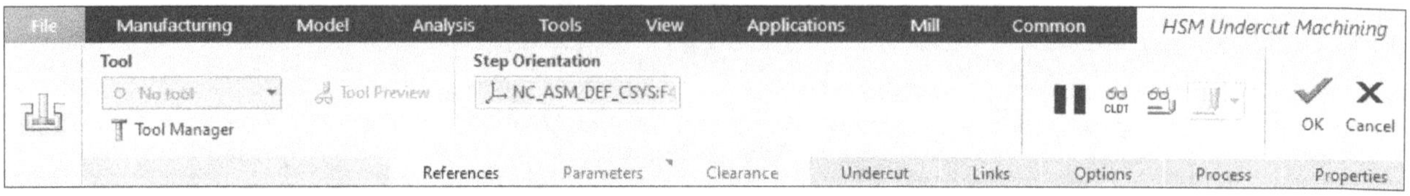

Figure-46. HSM undercut machining contextual tab

- Select the cutting tool (generally a side milling tool), co-ordinate system, and other settings as discussed earlier.
- Click on the **Reference** tab in **Ribbon** to define the reference parts and machining area. The options will be displayed as shown in Figure-47. Generally, reference model is automatically selected in this tab and this tool automatically identifies undercut features to be machined.

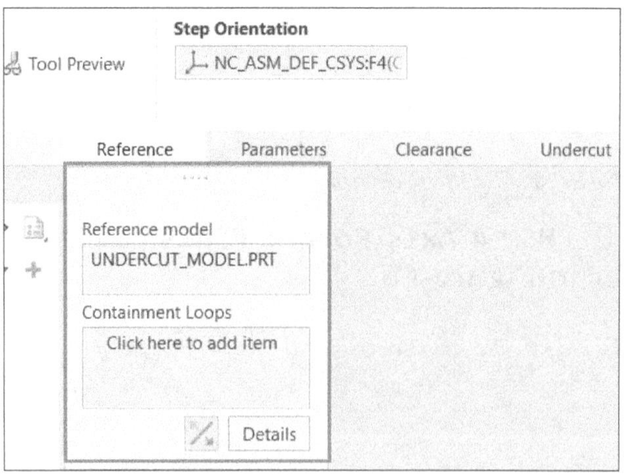

Figure-47. Reference tab

- Click on the **Undercut** tab in the **Ribbon**. The options will be displayed as shown in Figure-48.

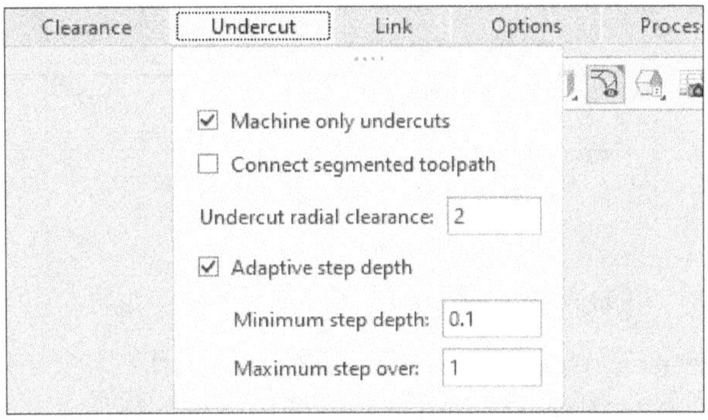

Figure-48. Undercut tab

- Select the **Clearance** tab from the **Ribbon** and define location of clearance plane at adequate distance from model to avoid collision when retracting/changing tool; refer to Figure-49.

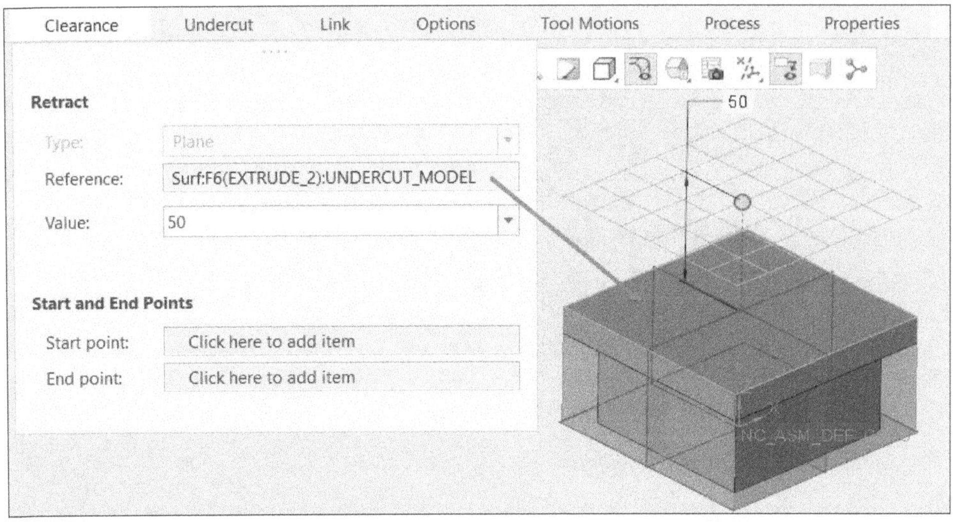

Figure-49. Clearance plane defined

- Select the **Machine only undercuts** check box to restrict machining to undercut areas only.
- Select the **Connect segmented toolpath** check box to join all segmented toolpath movements.
- Click in the **Undercut radial clearance** edit box and enter desired radial clearance value to ensure safe tool approach and retraction when machining undercut areas.
- Select **Adaptive step depth** check box to generate additional slices in shallow regions.
- Click in the **Minimum step depth** edit box and specify desired minimum distance between two consecutive passes along the machining direction.
- Click in the **Maximum step over** edit box and specify desired maximum step over value to define the spacing for additional slices in shallow areas.
- Click on the **Links** tab in the **Ribbon**. The options will be displayed as shown in Figure-50. Set desired parameters to define how two cutting passes will be linked and entry/exit path in the toolpath.

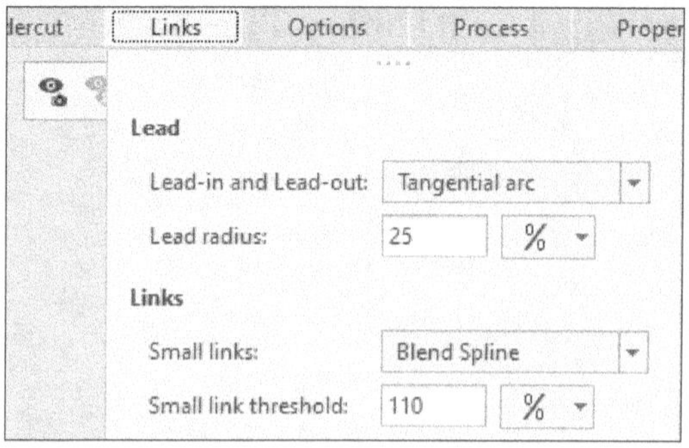

Figure-50. Link tab

- Specify other parameters as discussed earlier and click on the **OK** button from the **Ribbon** to generate the toolpath; refer to Figure-51.

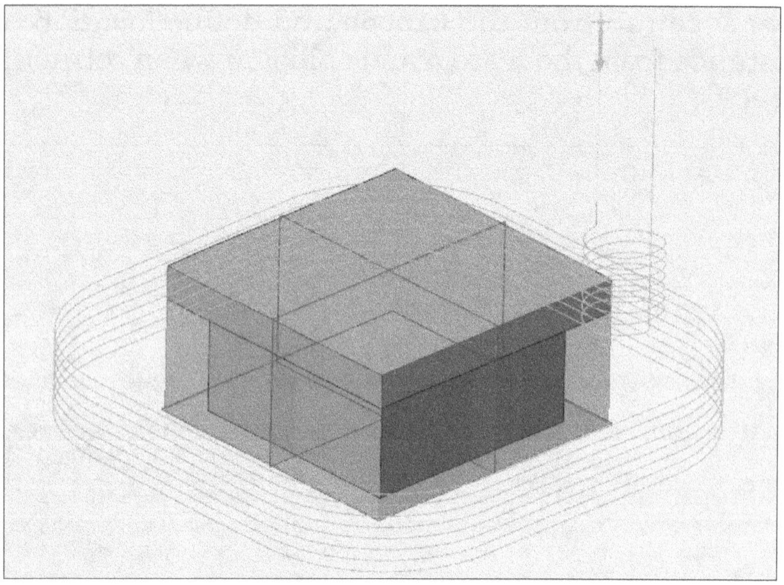

Figure-51. Undercut toolpath

PRACTICAL

Create toolpaths for machining the model show in Figure-52 using High Speed Toolpaths.

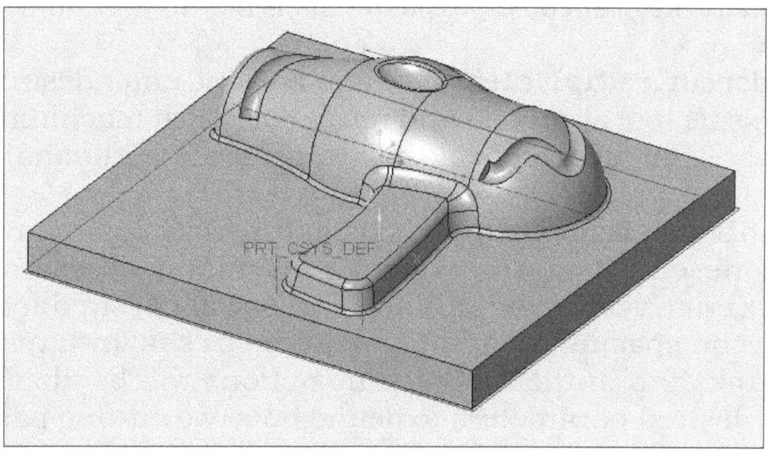

Figure-52. Model for High Speed Milling

Steps:

- Start a new manufacturing model file and insert the model as reference part.
- Generate the workpiece for the model.
- Set a 5 axis milling machine as current work center and create a new operation using appropriate coordinate system.
- Create a mill window to define boundaries of machining.
- Generate high speed roughing and rest roughing toolpaths.
- Generate the geodesic 5 axis finish toolpath.
- Check the material removal simulation.

Starting New Manufacturing File and Inserting Reference Part

- Start Creo Parametric and click on the **New** tool from **Quick Access Toolbar** at the top in the application window. The **New** dialog box will be displayed.
- Specify the name of file as **Practical**, clear the **Use default template** check box and click on the **OK** button. The **New File Options** dialog box will be displayed.
- Select **mmns mfg nc abs** template from the list and click on the **OK** button. The Creo Manufacturing environment will be displayed.
- Click on the **Assemble Reference Model** tool from the **Reference Model** drop-down in the **Components** tab of the **Ribbon**. The **Open** dialog box will be displayed.
- Select the **mold part.prt** file available in resources folder of this chapter and click on the **Open** button. Preview of part will be displayed with **Component Placement** contextual tab active in the **Ribbon**; refer to Figure-53.
- Select the **Default** option from the **Constraint Type** drop-down in the **Placement** tab of **Component Placement** contextual tab in the **Ribbon** and click on the **OK** button from the **Ribbon**.

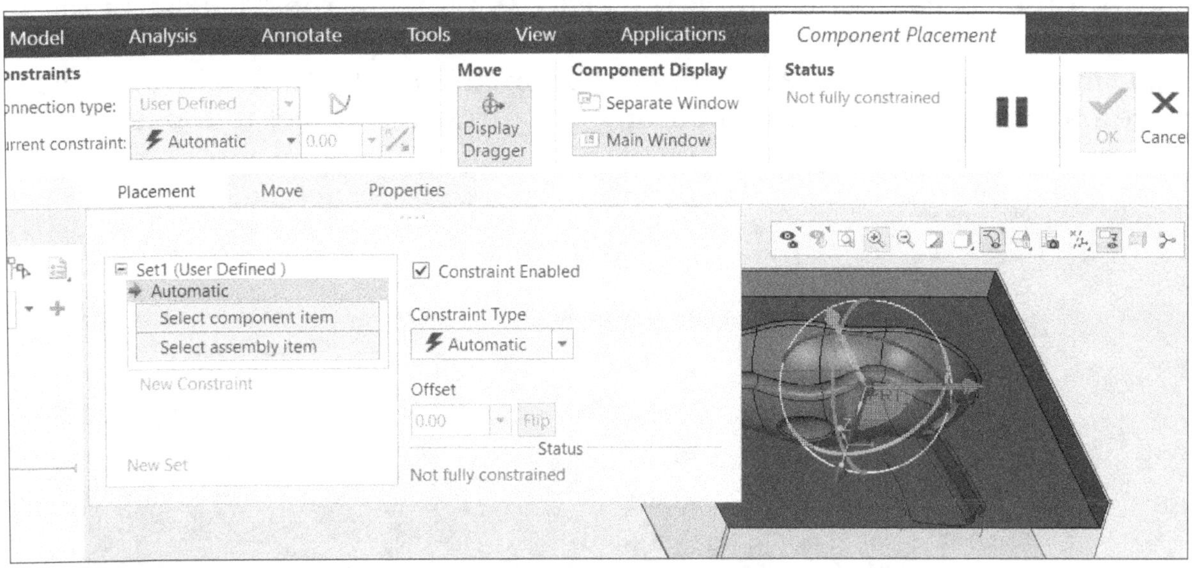

Figure-53. Preview of part

Creating Stock and Setting Machine

- Click on the **Automatic Workpiece** tool from the **Workpiece** drop-down in the **Manufacturing** tab of **Ribbon**. Preview of automatic workpiece creation will be displayed; refer to Figure-54.
- Make sure the **Rectangular** button is selected in the **Workpiece Type** section of **Ribbon** and click on the **OK** button to create the stock.

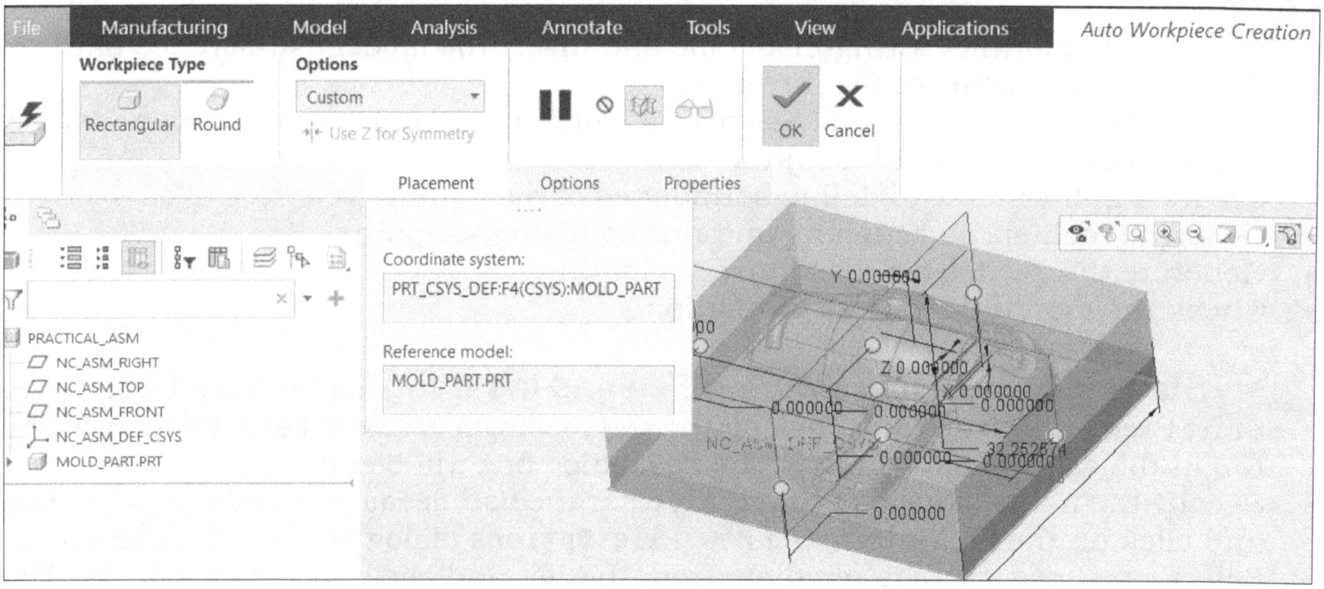

Figure-54. Automatic workpiece creation preview

- To set the milling machine for performing various operations, click on the **Mill** tool from the **Work Center** drop-down of **Machine Tool Setup** panel of **Manufacturing** tab in the **Ribbon**. The **Milling Work Center** dialog box will be displayed.
- Select the **5 Axis** option from the **Number of Axis** drop-down of **Output** tab in the **Milling Work Center** dialog box.
- Set the other parameters as discussed earlier and click on the **OK** button.

Creating Operation and Mill Window

- Click on the **Operation** tool from the **Process** panel in the **Manufacturing** tab of the **Ribbon**. The **Operation** contextual tab will be displayed.
- Click in the **Program Zero** selection box in the contextual tab and select the coordinate system with Z axis pointing upward with respect to top face of model; refer to Figure-55.

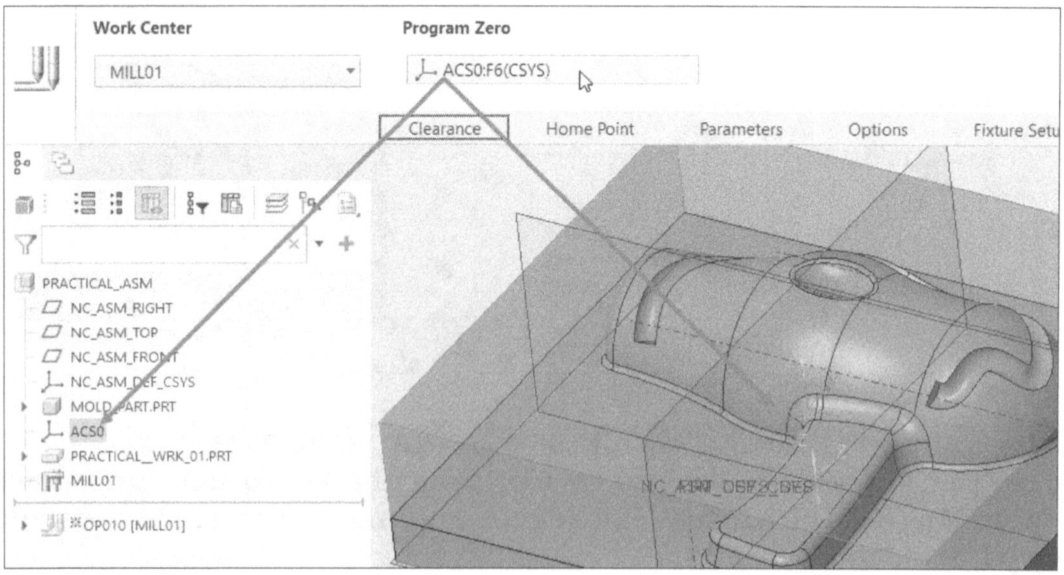

Figure-55. Program zero coordinate selected

- Select the **Plane** option from the **Type** drop-down in **Clearance** tab of the **Ribbon** and select top face of the stock; refer to Figure-56.

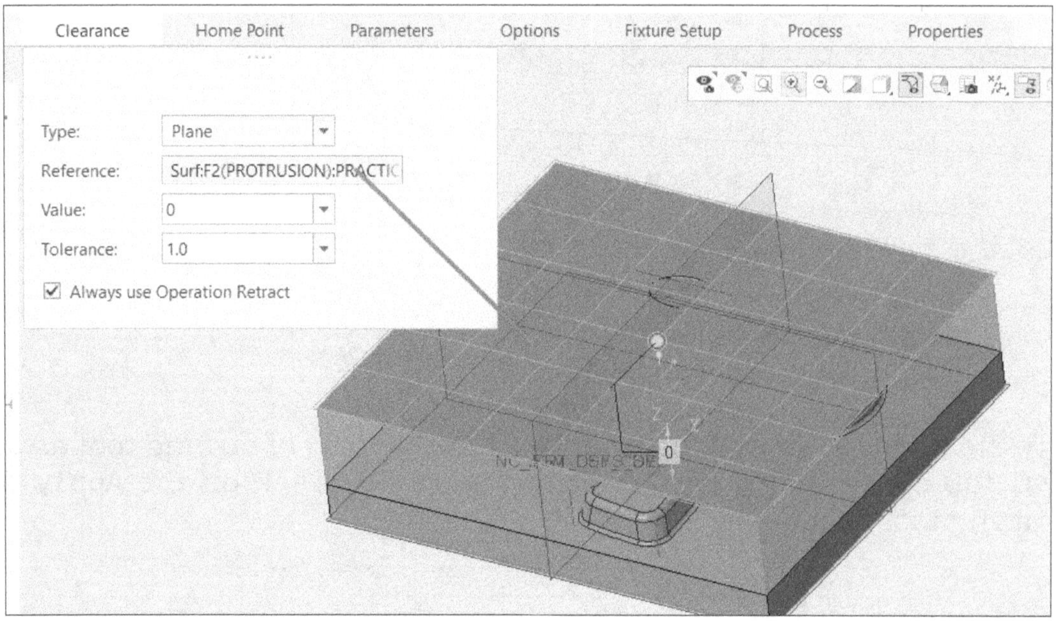

Figure-56. Face selected for clearance plane

- Specify desired distance value in the **Value** edit box to define distance of clearance plane from top face of stock. (We have specified it 5 in our case).
- Set the other parameters as discussed earlier and click on the **OK** button to create the operation.
- Click on the **Mill Window** tool from the **Manufacturing Geometry** panel in the **Manufacturing** tab of the **Ribbon**. The **Mill Window** contextual tab will be displayed.
- Select the top face of stock so that its boundaries can be used as mill window; refer to Figure-57.

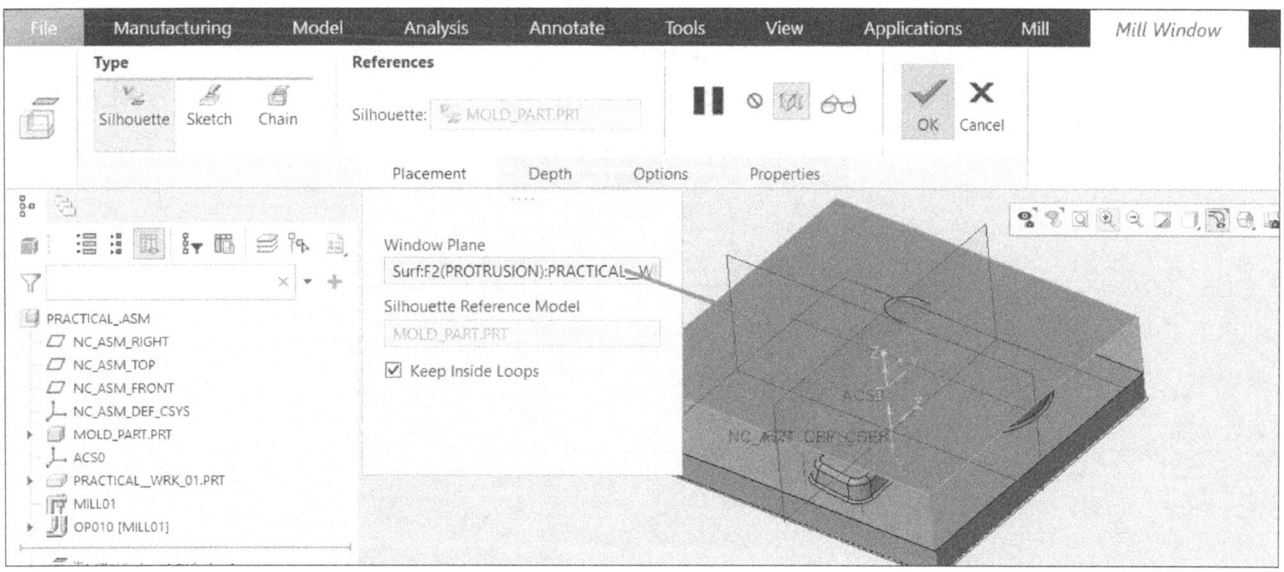

Figure-57. Face selected for mill window

- Click on the **OK** button from the **Ribbon** to create the mill window.

Creating Cutting Tool Setup

- Click on the **Cutting Tools** tool from the **Machine Tool Setup** panel of **Manufacturing** tab in the **Ribbon**. The **Tools Setup** dialog box will be displayed.
- Select the **END MILL** button from the **New** drop-down in the **Tools Setup** dialog box; refer to Figure-58.

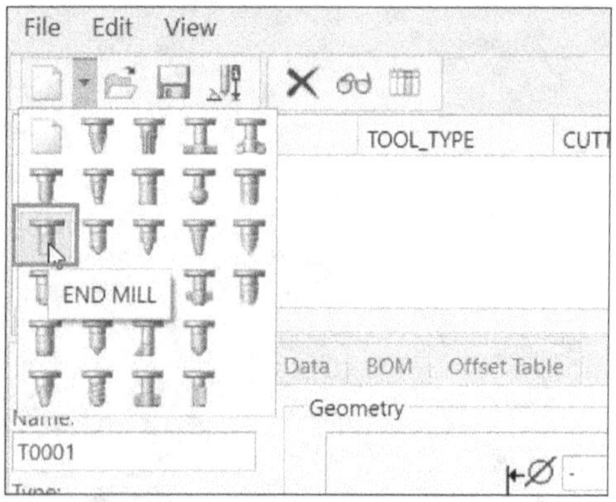

Figure-58. END MILL button

- Specify the diameter of end mill tool as **12** and length of cutting tool as **100** in the **General** tab of the dialog box; refer to Figure-59. Click on the **Apply** button to add cutting tool in the list.

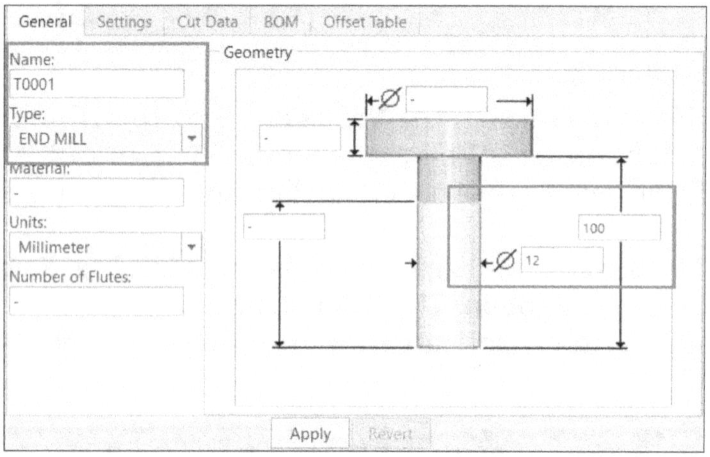

Figure-59. Specifying parameter of end mill tool

- Similarly, create a ball end mill of 6 MM and another ball end mill of 3 MM; refer to Figure-60.

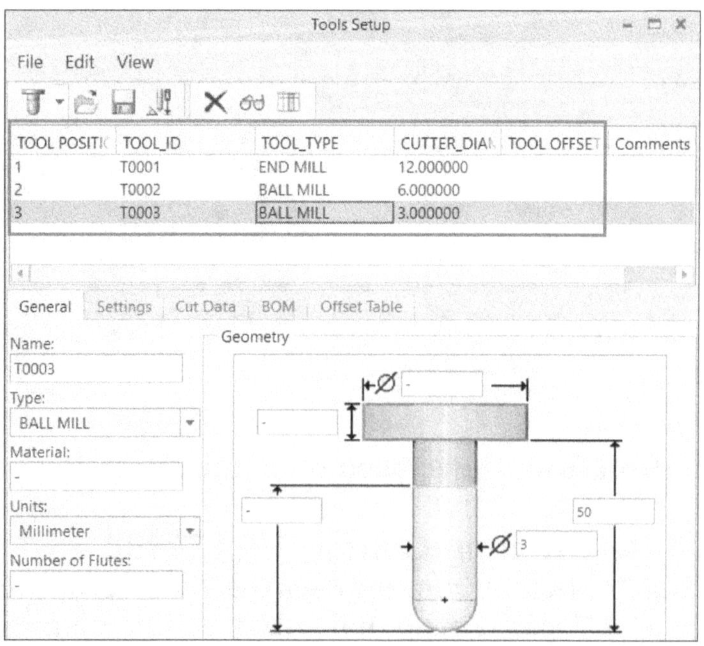

Figure-60. Cutting tools created

- After creating tools, click on the **OK** button from the dialog box.

Creating High Speed Roughing Toolpath

- Click on the **HSM Rough** tool from the **High Speed Milling** panel in the **Mill** tab of the **Ribbon**. The **HSM Rough** contextual tab will be displayed.
- Select the **T0001** cutting tool from the **Tool** drop-down at the top in the **Ribbon** and select the mill window earlier created; refer to Figure-61.

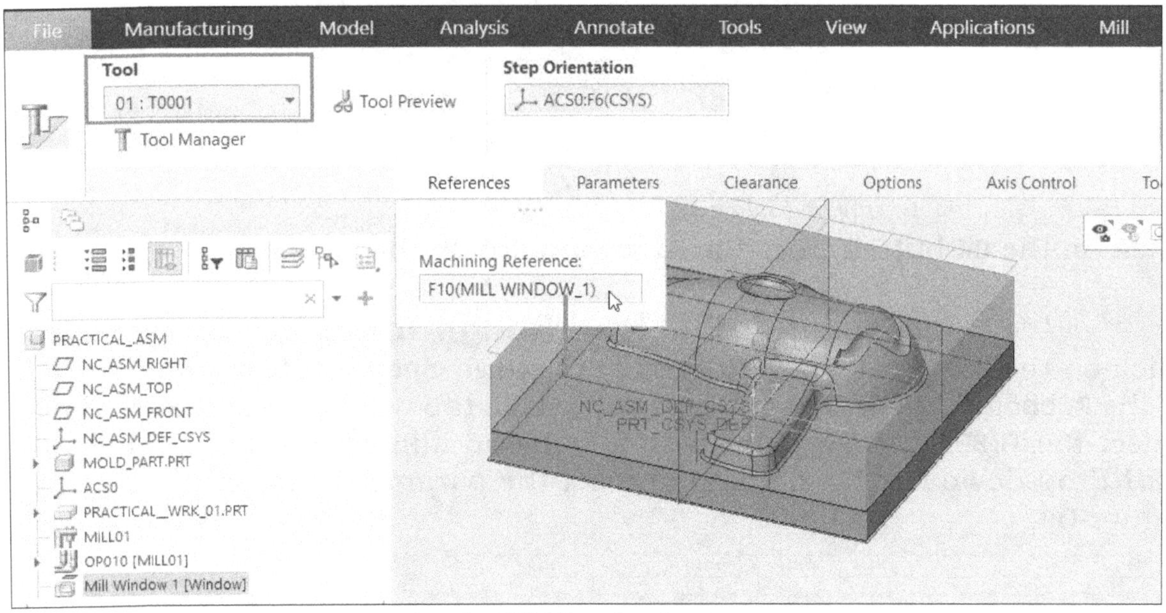

Figure-61. Selecting tool and mill window for HSM Rough toolpath

- Click on the **Parameters** tab and specify parameters as shown in Figure-62.

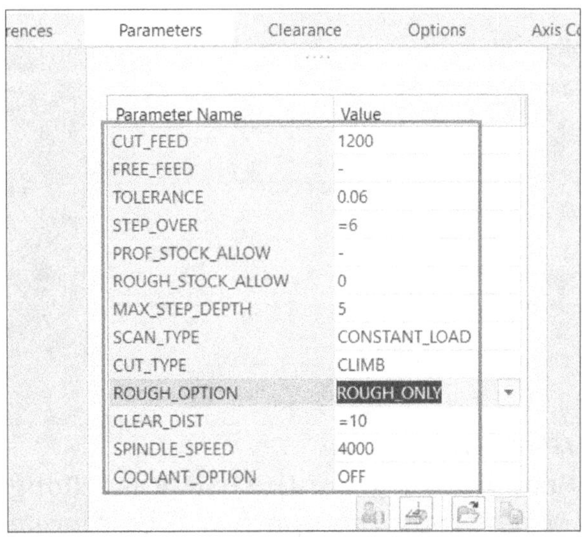

Figure-62. Specifying cutting parameters for HSM Rough

- Click on the **Preview Mode** button from the **Ribbon**. Preview of toolpath will be displayed; refer to Figure-63.

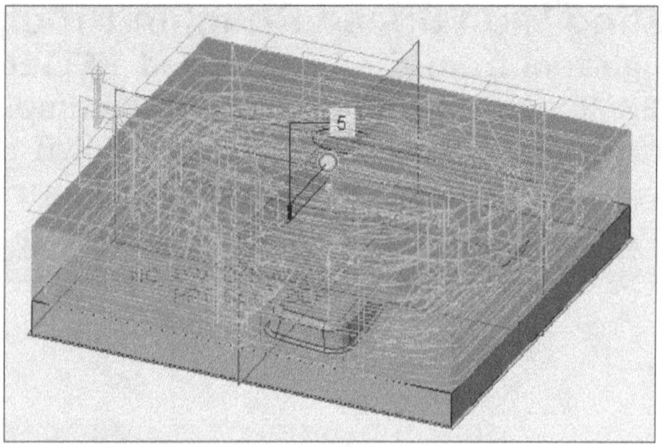

Figure-63. Preview of HSM rough toolpath

- Click on the **OK** button from the **Ribbon** to create the toolpath.

Creating HSM Rest Rough Toolpath

- Click on the **HSM Rest Rough** tool from the **High Speed Milling** panel of **Mill** tab in the **Ribbon**. The **HSM Rest Rough** contextual tab will be displayed in the **Ribbon**.
- Select the **T0002** cutting tool which is ball end mill with **6 MM** diameter from the **Tool** drop-down for the toolpath and set the parameters for cutting as shown in Figure-64.

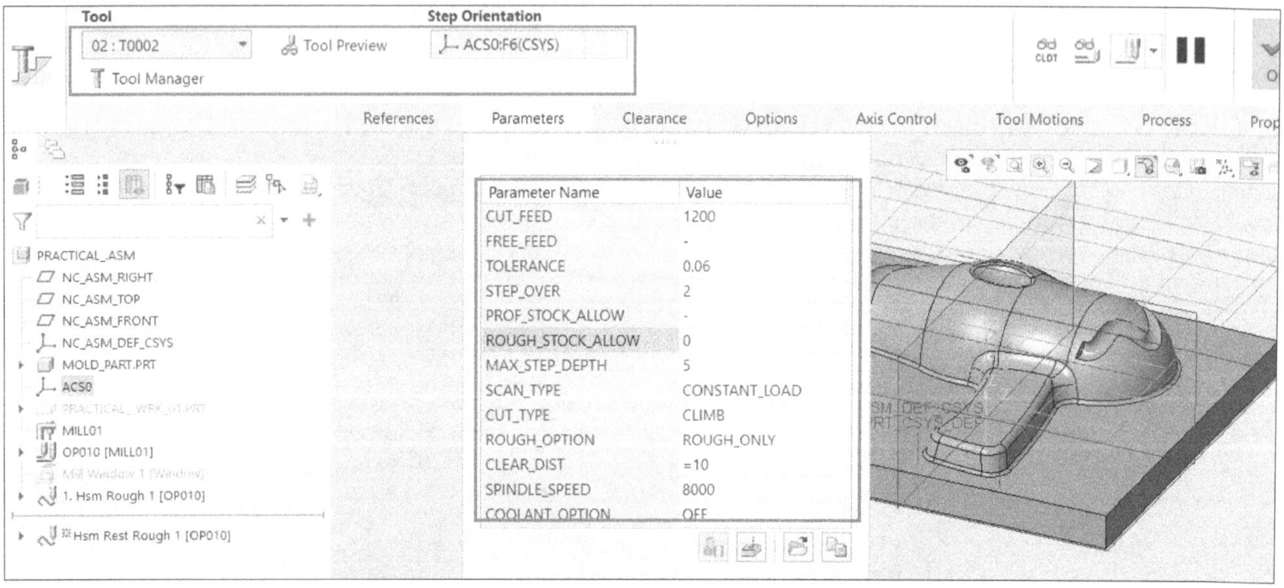

Figure-64. Parameters specified for HSM Rest Rough toolpath

- Click on the **Preview Mode** button from the **HSM Rest Rough** contextual tab in the **Ribbon**. Preview of HSM rest rough toolpath will be displayed; refer to Figure-65.

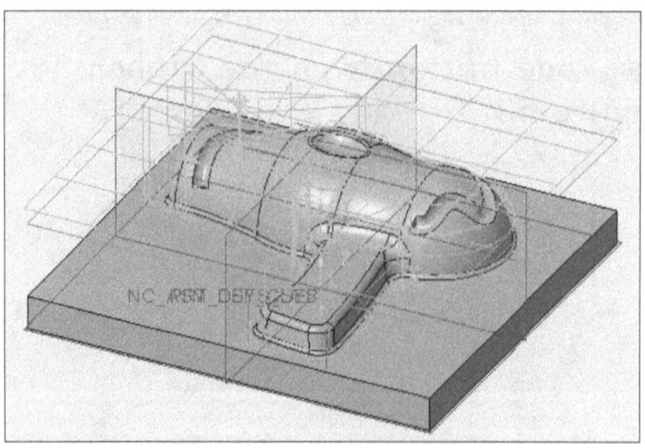

Figure-65. HSM rest rough toolpath preview

- Click on the **OK** button from the **Ribbon** to create the toolpath.

Creating Geodesic 5 Axis Finish Toolpath

- Click on the **Geodesic 5 Axis Finish** tool from the **High Speed Milling** panel of **Mill** tab in the **Ribbon**. The **Geodesic Finish** contextual tab will be displayed in the **Ribbon**.
- Select the **T0003** cutting tool which is 3 MM Ball end mill from the **Tool** drop-down in the **Ribbon**.
- Select the **Surface** option from the **Selection type** drop-down in the **Reference** tab and select the top faces of the model to be machined by finishing toolpath; refer to Figure-66.

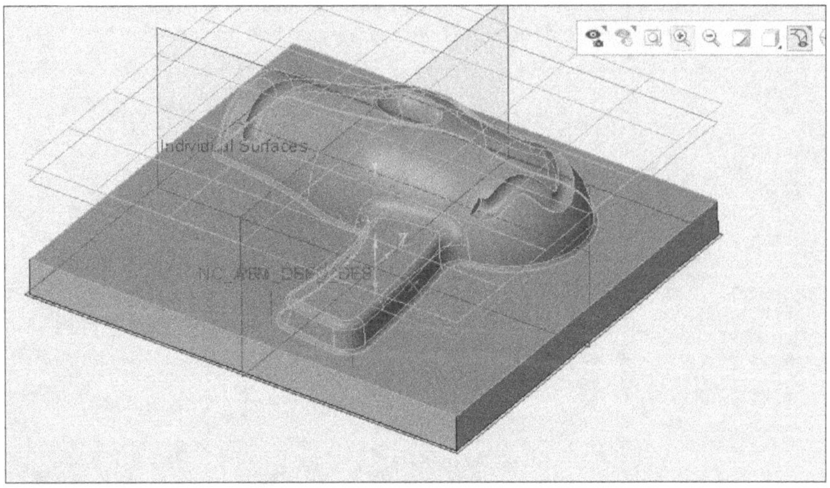

Figure-66. Faces selected for geodesic finish toolpath

- Set desired parameters in the **Parameters** tab and click on the **Preview Mode** button to check preview of the toolpath; refer to Figure-67.

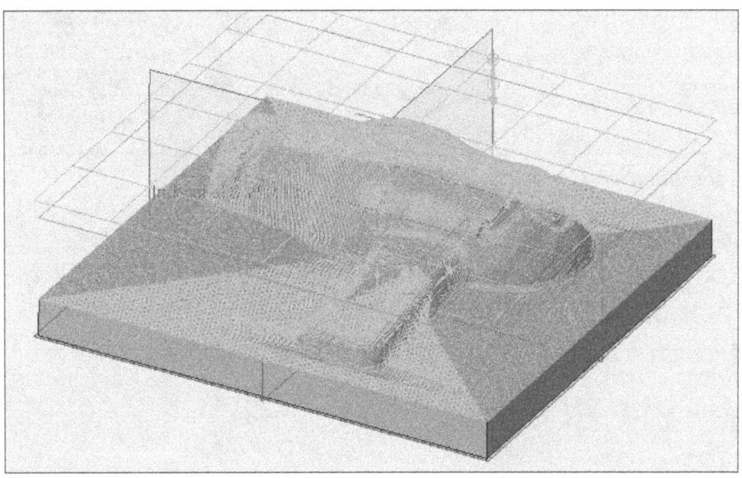

Figure-67. Preview of finish toolpath

- Click on the **OK** button from the **Ribbon** to create the toolpath.

To check the material removal simulation, right-click on the operation **OP010** from **Navigation Trees** and select the **Material Removal Simulation** option from the shortcut menu; refer to Figure-68. The environment to check simulation of material removal will be displayed. Play the simulation to check whether there are any issues in material removal by created toolpaths; refer to Figure-69.

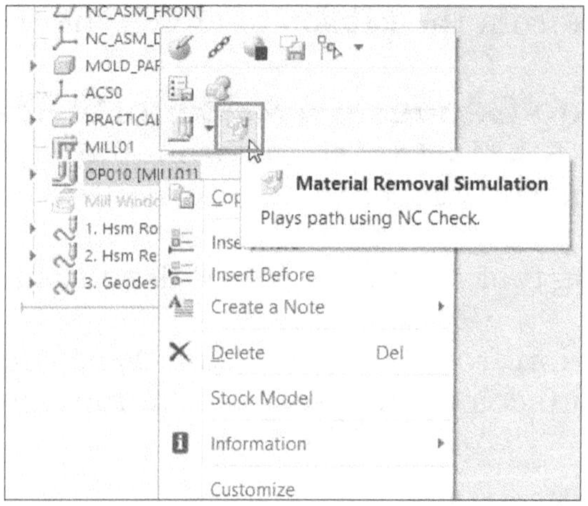

Figure-68. Material Removal Simulation option

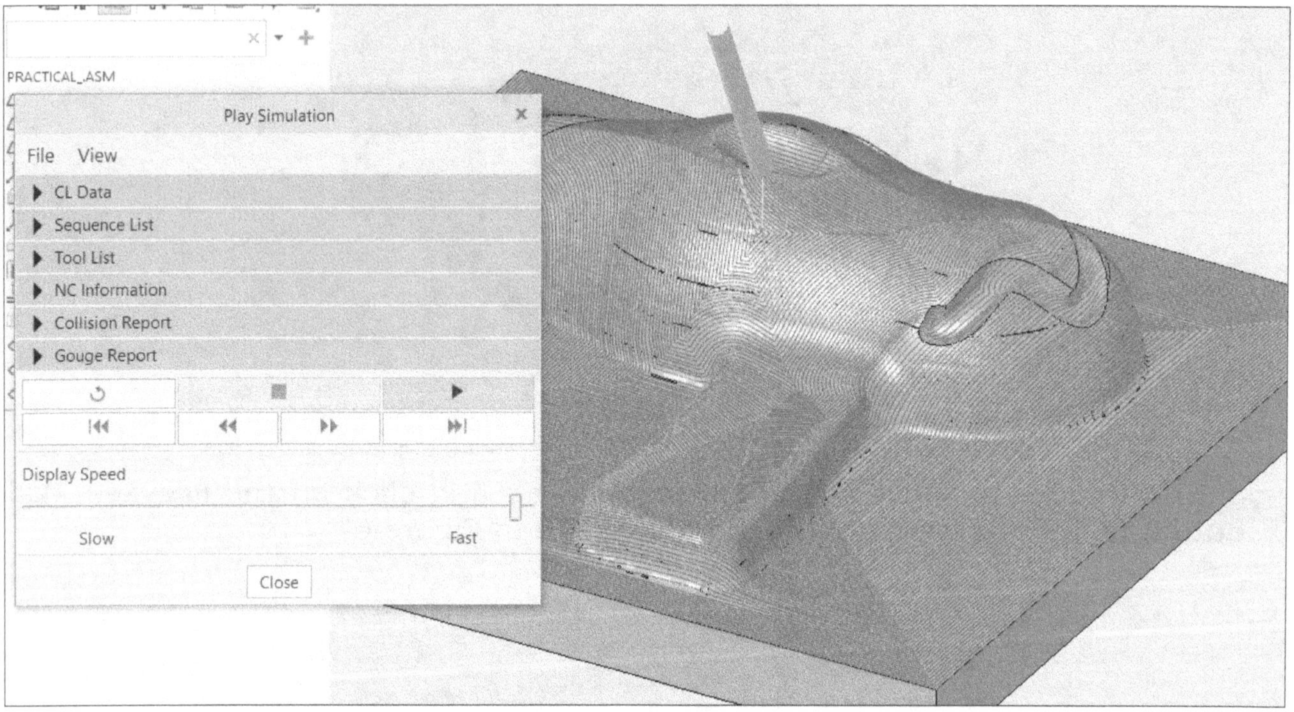

Figure-69. Material removal simulation of practical

PRACTICE 1

Create machining toolpath for the model shown in Figure-70. The stock for this model is a rectangular block of size 120x80x40.

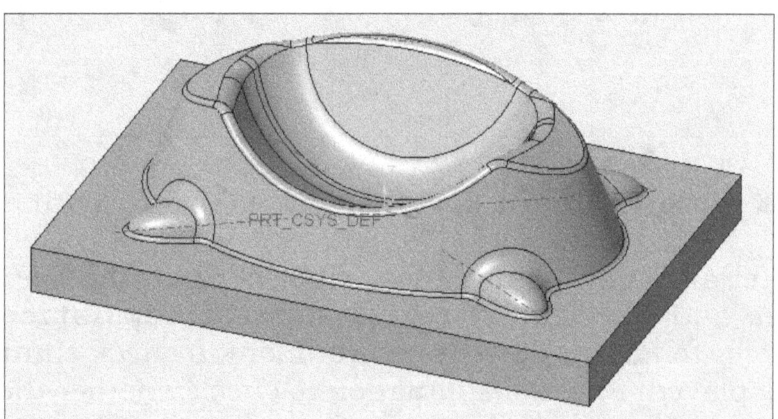

Figure-70. Practice model

SELF-ASSESSMENT

Q1. What is the main purpose of HSM Rough toolpaths?

A. To perform finishing with tight tolerances
B. To remove burr from sharp edges
C. To machine surface at low speed
D. To remove large portion of material at high speed

Q2. Which option ensures constant load on the cutting tool in HSM Rough Parameters tab?

A. SPIRAL
B. CONSTANT LOAD
C. TYPE 1
D. ROUGH ONLY

Q3. What does the 'ROUGH AND PROF' option do in the Parameters tab?

A. Performs profiling only
B. Performs roughing only
C. Performs both roughing and profiling
D. Performs simulation only

Q4. What is the function of the 'Search Angle Increment' option in 5-axis milling?
A. Defines clearance plane
B. Defines program zero
C. Increases/decreases tilt angle of tool
D. Adds new tool geometry

Q5. In which tab do you define the clearance plane for HSM Rough?

A. Parameters
B. Axis Control
C. Clearance
D. Reference

Q6. What is an in-process stock primarily used for?

A. Exporting drawings
B. Simulation and presentation
C. Editing toolpaths
D. Checking machine load

Q7. Which option is used to save the current stock in simulation?

A. Save Stock Status
B. Save Simulation
C. Save In-Process Stock
D. Export Toolpath

Q8. Which option allows you to load a previously saved stock in Material Removal Simulation?

A. Load Previous Setup
B. Open In-Process Stock
C. Insert Stock Model
D. Run Stock Simulation

Q9. What is required before generating a Rest Rough toolpath?

A. A profile toolpath
B. A saved stock model
C. A mill window
D. A clearance plane

Q10. What is the main difference between HSM Finish and HSM Rest Finish toolpaths?

A. Type of machine used
B. Tool diameter
C. Tighter tolerance in Rest Finish
D. Simulation requirement

Q11. What is the purpose of the Auto Deburring toolpath?

A. Smoothing internal pockets
B. Removing burrs from sharp edges
C. Adding chamfer
D. Creating 3D sketches

Q12. Which toolpath removes material using multi-axis movement?

A. HSM Rough
B. Auto Deburring
C. HSM 5 Axis Rough
D. HSM Rest Rough

Q13. Which strategy blends selected ceiling and floor faces when generating 5-axis toolpaths?

A. Offset from Floor Surface
B. Morph
C. Spiral
D. Constant Load

Q14. Which parameter controls maximum tilt angle for 5-axis cutting?

A. Free Feed
B. Search Angle Increment
C. Maximum Tool Tilt Angle
D. Feed Rate Ratio

Q15. What is the primary purpose of the Geodesic 5 Axis Finish tool in Creo?

A. To perform rough milling on 2D parts
B. To deburr sharp edges
C. To finish complex 3D surfaces using multi-axis tool motion
D. To drill holes automatically

Q16. In the Reference tab of the Geodesic tool, what does selecting the "Surface" option from the Selection type drop-down allow?

A. Use surface from previous operation
B. Select tool geometry
C. Use selected surface as machining reference
D. Define tool axis manually

Q17. Which pattern type generates toolpaths by offsetting multiple guide curves?

A. Morph between two curves
B. Parallel to multiple curves
C. Follow surface
D. Blend spline

Q18. What is the use of the "Create toolpath on holes" checkbox?

A. It lets you drill holes
B. It allows finishing on filled holes
C. It disables holes from machining
D. It creates new holes in model

Q19. Which tilting strategy uses the current cutting direction as a reference for tilt?

A. Fixed angle to axis
B. Tilt from origin
C. Relative to cutting direction
D. Freeform tilt

Q20. What does the "Automatic arc" option in the Link tab define?

A. Vertical arc for entry
B. Default plunge angle
C. Automatically selected arc at toolpath entry
D. Chamfer at exit

Q21. What does the "Lead Radius" parameter define?

A. Tool radius only
B. Radius of circular entry/exit arcs
C. Depth of cut
D. Axis of rotation

Q22. Which small gaps option allows tool to retract over the gap using clearance distance?

A. Direct
B. Blend Spline
C. Retract to clear distance
D. Follow Surface

Q23. What is defined in the "Check Surfaces" tab?

A. Areas for tool axis orientation
B. Surfaces to be ignored during machining
C. Tool diameter
D. Axis tilt angle

Q24. What does the "Add machining references" checkbox do?

A. Adds surfaces for roughing
B. Avoids machining fixtures, machine table, etc.
C. Optimizes cutting feed
D. Selects holes only

Q25. What does the Wall 5 Axis Finish tool primarily target?

A. Drill groups
B. Undercuts
C. Side walls of model
D. Floor surfaces

Q26. In Wall Finish toolpath, what defines the starting point on the tool profile?

A. Minimum lead angle
B. Preferred height
C. Surface curvature
D. Floor reference

Q27. Which toolpath is used to finish the base of a model?

A. Wall 5 Axis Finish
B. Floor 5 Axis Finish
C. Rotary Rough
D. Rest Rough

Q28. What is the HSM 4 Axis Rotary Rough tool typically used for?

A. Simple flat face milling
B. Pocket creation
C. Machining cylindrical parts like cam shafts
D. Hole drilling

Index

Ethics of an Engineer

- Engineers shall hold paramount the safety, health and welfare of the public and shall strive to comply with the principles of sustainable development in the performance of their professional duties.
- Engineers shall perform services only in areas of their competence.
- Engineers shall issue public statements only in an objective and truthful manner.
- Engineers shall act in professional manners for each employer or client as faithful agents or trustees, and shall avoid conflicts of interest.
- Engineers shall build their professional reputation on the merit of their services and shall not compete unfairly with others.
- Engineers shall act in such a manner as to uphold and enhance the honor, integrity, and dignity of the engineering profession and shall act with zero-tolerance for bribery, fraud, and corruption.
- Engineers shall continue their professional development throughout their careers, and shall provide opportunities for the professional development of those engineers under their supervision.

www.ingramcontent.com/pod-product-compliance
Lightning Source LLC
LaVergne TN
LVHW082027200926
848481LV00010B/2936